CHRISTIAN ETHICS AS WITNESS

Christian Ethics as Witness

Barth's Ethics for a World at Risk

DAVID HADDORFF

CASCADE Books • Eugene, Oregon

CHRISTIAN ETHICS AS WITNESS
Barth's Ethics for a World at Risk

Copyright © 2010 David Haddorff. All rights reserved. Except for brief quotations in critical publications or reviews, no part of this book may be reproduced in any manner without prior written permission from the publisher. Write: Permissions, Wipf and Stock Publishers, 199 W. 8th Ave., Suite 3, Eugene, OR 97401.

Cascade Books
An Imprint of Wipf and Stock Publishers
199 W. 8th Ave., Suite 3
Eugene, OR 97401

www.wipfandstock.com

ISBN 13: 978-1-60899-282-9

Cataloguing-in-Publication data:

Haddorff, David W. (David Wayne), 1958–

Christian ethics as witness : Barth's ethics for a world at risk / David Haddorff.

xii + 458 p.; 23 cm. Includes bibliographical references and index.

ISBN 13: 978-1-60899-282-9

1. Barth, Karl, 1886–1968. 2. Barth, Karl, 1886–1968—Kirchliche Dogmatik. English. 3. Christian ethics—Reformed authors. 4. Christian ethics—History—20th century. I. Title.

BX4827 .B3 H24 2010

Manufactured in the U.S.A.

For my mother

Contents

Acknowledgments | ix
Abbreviations | xi
Introduction | 1

PART ONE Ethics and Barth's Witness: *Theology and Practice*

CHAPTER ONE Theological Ethics in Transition | 23
CHAPTER TWO Barth's Early Ethics and the Trinitarian Other | 54
CHAPTER THREE Barth's Social Ethics: Witness in Tumultuous Times | 94

PART TWO Postmodernity and a World at Risk

CHAPTER FOUR Social Theory and Postmodernity | 127
CHAPTER FIVE From Modern to Postmodern Ethics | 163

PART THREE Witness and Barth's Ethics: *Toward Contemporary Understanding*

CHAPTER SIX Witness and the Word of God | 197
CHAPTER SEVEN Witness and Christian Moral Judgment | 229

CHAPTER EIGHT   Witness and the Powers | 268
CHAPTER NINE   Witness and Public Ethics: Options in Christian Ethics | 308

PART FOUR Christian Ethics as Witness: *Political, Economic, and Environmental*

CHAPTER TEN   Witness and Christian Responsibility | 343
CHAPTER ELEVEN   Political Witness: For Faith and Peace | 369
CHAPTER TWELVE   Economic Witness: For Love and Justice | 394
CHAPTER THIRTEEN   Environmental Witness: For Hope and Freedom | 415

Bibliography | 447
Index | 459

Acknowledgments

Writing a book is never an individual effort alone. I want to thank all the authors who've influenced my work, and whose names are scattered through this book. I want to thank the various individuals responsible for giving me opportunities to first test these ideas out in academic papers at various conferences over the past few years, in particular, the American Academy of Religion and the Society of Christian Ethics. Especially I want to thank Daniel Migliore for the invitation to give an address on "Barth and Democracy" at the 2008 conference on "Barth's Theological Ethics" held at Princeton Theological Seminary. I also want to thank Todd Cioffi for his fine response to my paper, and Cliff Anderson for assisting me with research at the Barth Center at Princeton.

I want to acknowledge the many friends and acquaintances with whom I've had fruitful conversations over time about this project such as John Burgess, Chris Roberts, Christophe Chalamet, Mike Dempsey, George Hunsinger, Todd Cioffi, Paul Molnar, Nick Healey, Gerald McKenny, Robert Song, Mark Kiley, Sally Kenel, Cliff Anderson, Daniel Migliore, Eric Gregory, Jesse Couenhoven, Travis Kroeker, Mark Nation, Victor Austin, Kimlyn Bender, John Webster, and Max Stackhouse. In particular, I acknowledge Gerald McKenny for reading and offering helpful suggestions for improving the book, all of which were incorporated into the final manuscript. Each of these people have taught me great deal about theology and ethics in their own writings and conversations, and have contributed in their own way in the completion of this book. I also want to acknowledge the encouraging support given by my department chair Rev. Michael Whalen, C.M., and other colleagues at St. John's University, especially Paul

Molnar and Nick Healy, from whom I've learned a good deal about Barth's theology. In all of their comments, written and oral, all of these mentioned have contributed to the development of my own thought in relation to this project.

I also want to thank others who have contributed their time in getting the manuscript ready for publication. I want to thank my graduate assistant Kathryn Hansen for her extensive work on the manuscript for the last two years, including preparing the entire manuscript for publication. Also I want to acknowledge the graduate assistant James Braile, who at the last minute was willing to proofread the entire manuscript, and my daughter Kelsey for her willingness to help with the bibliography. I want to thank Robin Parry, Kristen Bareman, and Matthew Stock at Cascade Press for their work editing, typesetting, and preparing the manuscript for publication.

I also want to acknowledge Fred Mueller, along with other ministers and seminary students of the Delaware-Raritan Classis, for their willingness to explore, in belief and practice, Christian witness in the local church. Along with my daughter Kelsey, I want to thank my wife Dana, my brothers Mike and Chris, and my stepfather Bud Klaus for their lasting support and encouragement. Lastly, for my mother, Betty Klaus, whose enduring faith and self-giving has demonstrated to me how a life of Christian witness can be lived in a world that *is* reconciled, but in the words of the *Barmen Declaration*, still "not yet redeemed." It is to her, I dedicate this book.

David Haddorff
Epiphany, 2010

Abbreviations

AS	Karl Barth. *Against the Stream: Shorter Post-War Writings 1946–52.* New York: Philosophical Library, 1954.
CD	Karl Barth. *Church Dogmatics.* 4 vols. Translated and edited by G. W. Bromiley and T. F. Torrance. Edinburgh: T. & T. Clark, 1936–77.
CL	Karl Barth. *The Christian Life.* Translated by Geoffrey W. Bromiley. Grand Rapids: Eerdmans, 1981.
CSC	Karl Barth. *Community, State, and Church: Three Essays.* With a New Introduction by David Haddorff. Eugene, OR: Wipf & Stock, 2005.
ET	Karl Barth. *Ethics.* Translated by Geoffrey W. Bromiley. New York: Seabury, 1981.
GA	Karl Barth. *God in Action.* Translated by E. G. Homrighausen and Karl J. Ernst. Manhasset: Round Table Press, 1963
GD	Karl Barth. *The Göttingen Dogmatics: Instruction in the Christian Religion. Volume I.* Edited by Hannelotte Reiffen. Translated by Geoffrey W. Bromiley. Grand Rapids: Eerdmans, 1991.
GHN	Karl Barth. *God Here and Now.* Translated By Paul M. Van Buren, with new introduction by George Hunsinger. London: Routledge, 2003.
HG	Karl Barth. *The Humanity of God.* Translated by J. N. Thomas. Richmond: John Knox, 1960.

TC   Karl Barth. *Theology and Church: Shorter Writings, 1920–28.* Introduction by T. F. Torrance. Translated by Louise Pettibone Smith. New York: Harper &Row, 1962.

RII Karl Barth. *The Epistle to the Romans.* 2nd ed. Oxford: Oxford University Press, 1933.

WG   Karl Barth. *The Word of God and the Word of Man.* New York: Harper & Row, 1957.

Introduction

This book brings together two long-standing interests of mine, namely Christian social ethics and social theory, and the theology and ethics of Karl Barth. Giving serious attention to both of these fields of inquiry is not an easy task, but requires a great deal of thinking about how the methodologies of these two fields fit together. On one hand, this really is not a problem for the social ethicist who occasionally refers to Barth's theology or ethics, by applying his thought to issues like church and state, war, or politics. On the other hand, it is a different matter when the ethicist takes Barth's theology seriously before discussing these or other issues in Christian ethics. Barth demands a great deal from his reader, especially the patience and perseverance to continue with his line of reasoning on various topics and how they interrelate with each other. Barth is a complex thinker and he requires more than a simple precursory reading. Furthermore, Barth demands that the reader critically examine his or her own presuppositions about the relationship between theology and ethics, which leads to a further investigation about the possible integration of faith and reason and the church and the academy. Is the Christian ethicist an academic professional, who stands outside theology, faith, and the church, when he or she address issues in society or the world? Or is the Christian ethicist also a theologian, who begins with the faith commitments of the church, and then seeks to give witness to that faith in society and the world? Of course, one might say that a good Christian ethicist splits the difference and takes a middle position, but even here, usually one side will invariably triumph over the other leading to a particular view of ethics, theology, church, world, and above all, God. Just as theologians have an ethics, so too, ethicists have a theology, whether it is recognized or unrecognized, hidden or public, or operative or dormant.

Barth is important for Christian social ethics because he not only takes theology and God seriously, but he also takes society seriously. Obviously, his place in the history of theology is secured by his monumental task of reformulating orthodox theology in his *Church Dogmatics*.[1] Still, this massive work was not written in an academic vacuum, but in the social and political context of the first sixty years of the tumultuous twentieth century, during a period of two World Wars, the Cold War, and the triumph of post-Christendom secularism. Regarding this, Timothy Gorringe writes: "To read Barth as first and foremost a person of ideas is to do him a profound injustice. The very structure of the *Dogmatics*, the integration of theology and ethics, the refusal to separate law and gospel, is sign of his determination not to allow so much as a knife blade between theory and praxis."[2] Although Barth sought to integrate theology and ethics, his ethics is less well-known and extensively studied than his theology, although this has changed in recent years with several publications.[3] Like these studies, my book seeks to describe Barth's ethics, but it also seeks to place Barth's ethics in the *context* of our current society and world. My fundamental claim is that Barth is important because he presents us with a theology and ethics of *witness*. I'm not claiming that witness is the *leitmotif* or master key of Barth's theology or ethics; rather, it serves as a particular entry point into the narrative of his theology and ethics. This description and interpretation of Barth's thought as witness, however, is not seen as an end in itself but as a *means* to critically engage contemporary social and cultural situation and contemporary Christian ethics. To reiterate, this book is more than a description of Barth's ethics. Rather, it engages Barth as the primary interlocutor in determining how Christian ethics *is* an ongoing task of Christian witness. Barth is chosen for this task because his thought remains centered

---

1. Barth, *Church Dogmatics*. Henceforth, all references to this book will be cited in the text in parenthesis and abbreviated as *CD*, followed by abbreviations of volumes and parts. Citations within the body of the text are made to the English, *CD* edition.

2. Gorringe, *Karl Barth*, 8.

3. In addition to Gorringe's book, some important works during the last two decades include: Biggar, *The Hastening That Waits*; Webster, *Ethics of Reconciliation*; Webster, *Moral Theology*; Clough, *Ethics in Crisis*; Nimmo, *Being in Action*; and most recently, McKenny, *Analogy of Grace*. Each of these books, in their own way, seeks to show how Barth integrated theology and ethics, that is, how his theology is ethical and his ethics is theological.

on God as an acting subject past, present, and future. For Barth both theology and ethics remain focused on the subject of God's action. In so doing, Barth develops a theological language for what a Christian ethics of witness looks like in theory and practice. Put differently, Barth's ethics is not an end in itself, but provides an *opening* for others to enter into this discussion about ethical responsibility in our secular age as a Christian witness to God's action. This makes Barth's voice about the Christian life relentlessly hopeful. "Nowhere does the overall hopeful character of Barth's theology come across more clearly than in this treatment of the task of witness."[4] In a postmodern age of global risk, it is the message of *hope* that our world desperately needs, that is, it needs to know that God has not abandoned the world but loves and cares for its future.

POSTMODERN WORLD AT RISK

What the world needs to hear is hope, but it remains difficult given the inherent ambiguities of our times. Our age promises the possibility of great hopes, but at the same time brings us uncertainties about our future. We continue to live our lives acting as if nothing has changed, and yet, we also know that a great deal has changed. We experience "cross-pressures," says Charles Taylor, which can either push us toward a more positive view of the future, or pull us away from hope in an increasingly secular world.[5] This leads to a kind of schizophrenic existence that remains hopeful yet skeptical, confident yet fearful, diligent yet apathetic, and optimistic yet pessimistic. Indeed, these "cross-pressures" are inherently self-contradictory, namely our materialism and naturalism is placed side-by-side with notions of the transcendental self arising above nature making ethics possible. So, on one hand, we live within "closed world structures (CWSs)" in which "nothing is demanded of us," or in which "we have no destiny we are called on to achieve."[6] On the other hand, persons also assume that "the colossal success of modern natural science and the associated technology can lead us to feel that it unlocks all mysteries, that it will ultimately explain everything."[7] Our core dilemma is that we feel apathetic, powerless, and pessimistic at the same time as we feel resourceful, powerful, and optimistic. "What pushes

4. Mangina, *Karl Barth*, 161.
5. Taylor, *Secular Age*, 594–616.
6. Ibid., 367.
7. Ibid., 548.

us one way or the other is what we might describe as our over-all take on human life," adds Taylor, "and its cosmic and (if any) spiritual surroundings. People's stance on the issue of belief in God, or of an open versus closed understanding of the immanent frame, usually emerge out of this general sense of things."[8] Whether we see the future as open or closed depends upon whether we think God remains sovereign over the future. Is God in control of time and our future or are we? How we answer this question has bearing on our view of the future as optimistic or pessimistic, open or closed.

Let's look further at these negative and positive, or closed and open, dimensions of our current circumstances. First, on negative side, we've lost the confidence of previous generations in knowing how to accomplish our hopes and goals. The future appears close-ended with little opportunity to shape our destiny. We become overwhelmed by the possibility of numerous dangers and risks that threaten human society, and indeed, life as we know it on earth. The overall pessimism comes not from human knowledge but from the human will. That is, we are aware of the problems that we confront, whether political, economic, or environmental, but we often remain paralyzed in knowing how to fix these problems. This is largely because these problems are no longer local or national but *global* problems. Human societies have always lived with threats and uncertainties, but today, we live in a world where "risks are lurking everywhere."[9] How can any one nation, or even groups of nations, address the problems of global violence and terrorism, global climate change, and the uncertainty of the global market? This ambiguity, even fear, of the future can lead to apathy, even despair, which takes away our initiative and hope for a better future. Second, on positive side, we still remain hopeful about the future because it appears to us as open-ended, and something that we can shape and influence in positive directions. Our optimism is not naïve but guarded and realistic. We question the past and seek to go beyond the core aspects of the modern way of life, which has led toward these global problems. We have learned from our mistakes. In the twenty-first century we are perhaps more aware that we've entered a time and space that seeks to alleviate the global risks posed by modern societies. We are more willing to talk about peace, justice, and environmental integrity, as a hope for the world, than previous decades

---

8. Ibid., 550.
9. Beck, *World at Risk*, 13.

of the last century. People do hope for a better world, and seriously believe that a better world is possible.

The ambiguity about the world's future, as open or closed, creates confusion about the nature of ethics itself, including how we think about moral agency and knowledge. Are we really free to change the world? Do we really know what is good? We know we must act for a better world, but we remain uncertain about the source of this moral knowledge and the moral imperatives that guide our actions. We generally distrust moral authorities, whether secular or religious, and remain unwilling or unable to provide legitimate reasons to believe in a common morality. These conflicts are at the heart of postmodernity or postmodern society. In Zygmunt Bauman's words, it is essentially a "discrepancy between demand and supply that has been recently described as the 'ethical crisis of postmodernity.'"[10] In postmodern society we are confronted by the ethical "demand" that we *must* believe and act in a pluralistic and technologically driven world; we cannot sit idle and do nothing. Yet, even though we are obviously aware of these problems, we remain confused about whether we can implement a positive course of action. Our ethical "supply," our sources of morality and wisdom, seems to be lacking. Although we have deep convictions about what is right and good, we cannot claim these convictions are true for all people; we are inherently skeptical of any objective moral claims. Bauman points to the fact that in postmodernity we know we must do something, but we don't know what to do or why we should do it. So, our knowledge and action, conscience and practice, truth and agency, remain paralyzed and rendered not useful in a world of risks that demands our action. Postmodernity is not only ambiguous about our future but also about the process of determining ethical actions which benefit humanity's future.

How does this postmodern ambiguity affect the strategy of Christian ethics? Can Christian ethics help with this postmodern discrepancy between moral knowledge and moral agency, that is, between our ability to know what is good and our ability to do it? What sources (or supply) does it draw from in answering such questions? Does it pull from specific theological sources, from the numerous nontheological sources of the social sciences, philosophy, and cultural studies, or does it combine these in some meaningful way? This raises the important issue of whether Christian ethics is simply another version of general strategy of ethics, or if it is something

10. Bauman, *Postmodern Ethics*, 17.

entirely distinct and unique offering an alternative understanding of the sources of ethical knowledge and agency. Like other ethical viewpoints, does it simply evaluate global risks and then seek to fix these problems, or does it offer an alternative vision, a greater hope, rooted in God's action and relationship to the world, for the world community? Is its strength its ability to work with other viewpoints providing a general account of global risks and prospects for a better world, or is its strength its unique theological and ethical vision of a world, which remains different from other viewpoints? Turning to such questions leads us to a fuller discussion of how theology is related to ethics, both in its historical and contemporary settings.

WHY BARTH?

For my response to these and other pertinent questions, I turn to the Swiss Reformed theologian Karl Barth. Barth's thought presents us with a unique challenge, in that not only did he write a great deal—as any Barth scholar surely knows—but the burgeoning supply of secondary literature on Barth continues to grow every day. This, coupled with the enormous amount of literature in the field of social ethics, social theory, and Christian ethics, obviously creates limits to the amount of material that can be cited and critically assessed.[11] Although I discuss numerous viewpoints, I often return to the central point that if Christian ethics wants to remain theological in our postmodern world-at-risk, it must be willing to consider or reconsider the theology and ethics of Barth. As Gerald Loughlin writes: "In so far as postmodernity is the weakening of univocal reason, the church is freed to recover its own self."[12] Indeed, as the church seeks to "recover its own self," it looks to its own beliefs and practices as the starting point for moral reflection and action. Yet, behind such beliefs and practices lies the firm conviction that God continues to act in the church and the world, and the church's mission and task to give witness to God's action in its proclamation and social action. In short, the church's ethics becomes an ethics of

---

11. With this in mind, my challenge was to limit my study to pertinent social scientific, ethical, and theological literature. Most references in this book will be to Barth's *Church Dogmatics*, however there will be references to Barth's other important works, especially in the areas of ethics and political thought, while the references to secondary material on Barth is kept at a minimum. In a similar way, my selection of materials in social ethics is also limited to important scholars in the field or to others who fit nicely with the perimeter of my project.

12. See Loughlin, "Doctrine," 51.

witness. By shifting the focus away from "univocal reason" and toward the church's witness, individual Christians can further rediscover their vocational identity as individual witnesses in their discipleship, while living out God's promise of faith, hope, and love in a world at risk.

This book takes the position that Christian ethics begins with a prior understanding of theological ethics, which is, at its core, an ethics of witness. Theology is not a creation of the theologian, but an intellectual discipline of the church reflecting about its witness to the gospel, as articulated in Scripture and the church's credo. It follows that a "theological ethics" cannot be anthropocentric but consistently relies upon God's grace as the source for human moral knowledge of the good. In turn, if a "Christian ethics" seeks to remain theological, it too rests upon God's grace for its deliberations and actions in choosing to do what is ethically right. Said differently, Christian ethics as witness is a theological *reminder* about what Christian ethics *ought* to be if it remains committed to the truth of the gospel. A Christian ethics of witness rises and falls with the truth of the gospel. Barth's thought, of course, is *not* the gospel as such, just as the theology of Augustine, Aquinas, Luther, Schleiermacher, or von Balthasar is not the gospel; in each case, the theologian seeks to articulate the gospel in language of *fides quaerens intellectum*. Like other great church theologians of the past, Barth understands God's gracious actions occurring prior to the human response of faith and action. Faith by its very nature is, of necessity, ordered toward the understanding of God, or put differently, with faith comes the *proper* understanding of God. In the opening pages of the *Church Dogmatics*, Barth writes that theology, as dogmatics, is "the scientific self-examination of the Christian church with respect to the content of its distinctive talk about God" (*CD* I/1:3). It is this "distinctive talk about God" that often presents unique challenges to those who see themselves as Christian *ethicists*. The language of witness, of course, is the language of the theology of the church in its *status confessionis*, and not the language of "ethics" in the secular academy. The academic study of ethics often incorporates all interested participants from religious studies, philosophy, the social sciences, and medical, business, or legal professionals. Christian ethics is a subcategory of the larger, and more inclusive, category of "ethics." This is perhaps why most Christian ethicists speak of their vocation as an "ethicist" rather than a "theologian." To be a Christian ethicist implies a certain willingness to push theology to the margins, while concentrating on a full-fledged ethical description and analysis at the human level of action and evaluation. Since there is clear separation between the disciplines of theology and ethics, theology inevitably becomes ancillary to ethics.

This separation of ethics from theology began long before Barth, and was one of the central features of the modern liberal theology that he rejected and sought to overcome. So, how did he see the relationship of ethics to theology? In one of his most interesting analogies regarding ethics, Barth equates the general category of ethics with the ancient people of Palestine, and theological ethics with the Israelites entering into and annexing the Promised Land.

> From the point of view of the general history of ethics, it means an annexation of the kind that took place on the entry of the children of Israel into Palestine. Other peoples for a long time maintained that they had a very old, if not the oldest, right of domicile in this country. But, according to Josh. 9:27, they could now at best exist only as hewers of wood and drawers of water. On no account had the Israelites to adopt or take part in their cultus and culture. Their liveliest resistance, therefore, could be expected, and their existence would necessarily be for the Israelites an almost invincible temptation. Ethics in the sense of that general conception is something entirely different from what alone the Christian doctrine of God can be as a doctrine of God's command. Whatever form the relationship between the two may take, there can be no question either of a positive recognition of Christian ethics by that conception or of an attachment of Christian ethics to it. Christian ethics cannot possibly be its continuation, development, and enrichment. (*CD* II/2: 518–19)

At first glance, Barth makes it sound as if Christian ethics has nothing in common with other ethical frameworks. Like the ancient Israelites, Christian ethics refuses to assimilate any methods or insights from general conceptions of ethics, but remains completely distinct from other accounts of ethics. As we shall see later, this interpretation is too simplistic. The point that Barth is making here is an important one, namely, does the foundation of Christian ethics lie in some general or unspecified account of "human ethics" where the principle actor is the human subject apart or isolated from divine-human encounter made visible in Jesus Christ? If so, this both denies God's freedom to act in such an encounter, but also creates a fictive account of the human subject in isolation from God. In plain language, how can Christian ethics remain "Christian" if it jettisons its most fundamental belief in the gospel that God is with us and for us in covenant-partnership, as revealed in Jesus Christ? For Barth the qualifying term "Christian" "goes all the way down" so to speak. Likewise, the Israelites did not simply take over the land, but annexed the land that originally "belonged to Yahweh" (*CD* II/2: 522). Just as the land originally belongs to God, the order and content of the good and ethics originally belongs to God. As the original possessor of land, God seeks to reclaim ownership over it through the annexation of the people of God. In the same way, Christian ethics seeks to reclaim ethics from the various anthropocentric methodologies that have sought to possess its structure and content. Yet, this annexation is primarily the work of God, not God's people. Thus, Christian ethics should not see itself as metadiscourse with the right to *usurp* other ethical discourses, but limits itself to the task of being a witness to the Canaanite inhabitants of the land, declaring to those inhabitants that Jesus Christ is Lord. What does this imply for Christian ethics? Although the tradition of Western ethics finds its roots in ancient philosophy, in the thought of Plato and Aristotle and others, this tradition is not the original owner or inhabitant of the land. Christian ethics simply acknowledges this fact and begins with the reality that God has acted and spoken. This is why there can be no assimilation or accommodation to alien ethical worldviews without the risk of being absorbed into this alien worldview and losing one's Christian identity. Saying this, however, does not imply that Christian ethics can completely isolate itself apart from its neighbors; it still exists in the land of Canaan. So, in the end, what this means is that with the "annexation" of other ethical worldviews, Christian ethics "puts an end to the discussion" to false dilemma or complete synthesis or diastasis or of assimilation or separation (*CD* II/2: 519). Cultural borrowings do take place, but only to such an extent they help clarify the original task and mission of Christian ethics.

What does the annexation of ethics look like in theory and practice? The detailed answer to this question, of course, will be developed in later chapters of the book. At this point, it is worth mentioning three sets of correspondences that arise from the analogy of the Israelite annexation. The first correspondence is between God and the land, the second is between God and the Israelites, and the third is between the Israelites and their neighbors. For our response we turn to two important essays that Barth wrote on the topic of ethics, namely the 1946 essay on "Christian Ethics," and the previously quoted essay "The Gift of Freedom," written in

1953.[13] Regarding the first point, as stated above God is the original owner of the land which implies God's ownership of the good and its embodiment in ethics. In this sense, what Barth calls "divine ethics" comes before "human ethics." Yet divine ethics is not composed of abstract ideas about the "good" apart from God's action in history—God *reveals* the good, and with it, the true nature of ethics. This revelation arises, not of necessity, but from God's free decision to act as Father, Son, and Spirit in gracious relationship toward God's human partner in creation, reconciliation, and redemption. "God's own freedom is trinitarian," says Barth, "embracing grace, thankfulness, and peace. It is the freedom of the living God. Only in this relational freedom is God's sovereign, almighty, the Lord of all." (*HG*: 72) Second, God's correspondence to the Israelites, as witnesses to God's ownership, implies a covenant-partnership that God freely chooses to have with the people of God, whom God has elected. Christian ethics gives witness to the fact that in Jesus Christ humanity is elected and brought into a covenant-partnership with God. In its annexation of ethics, Christian ethics articulates a general account of ethics as it objectively and really is, namely an ethics which emerges from the witness to God's free choice to be *for* us (*pro nobis*) as our covenant-partner. "God is free for *man*," says Barth, "free to coexist with man and, as the Lord of the covenant, to participate in his *history*. The concept of God without man is indeed as anomalous as wooden iron" (*HG*: 72). Lastly, just as the Israelites are free to dialogue with their neighbors, so too Christian ethics is free to dialogue with other ethical discourses. "Christian ethics does not rest, therefore, on a philosophy or *Weltanschauung* and it does not consist of the development of an idea or a principle or program" (*GHN*: 106). Christian ethics is free from all ethical methodologies that "lock" humanity in a "conversation with himself" (*GHN*: 106). Thus, Christian ethics is free from being assimilated or absorbed into other viewpoints, just as it is free from becoming sectarian and isolated from other viewpoints; it moves freely between the poles of synthesis and diastasis. In its critical engagement with other viewpoints, therefore, Christian ethics "tests everything and preserves the best, only the best, and that means those things by which from time to time God grace is best praised" (*GHN*: 110). All non-Christian viewpoints have the potential

---

13. Barth, "Christian Ethics," 105–14. Henceforth, all references to the book: Barth, *God Here and Now* will be cited in the text in parenthesis, and abbreviated as *GHN*. Also, Barth, "The Gift of Freedom," 69–96. Henceforth, all references to the book: Barth, *Humanity of God* will be cited in the text in parenthesis, and abbreviated as *HG*.

to be secular witnesses to God's grace, and the task of the Christian community is to listen to the witness of these other voices.

So, we've seen how in each set of correspondences there is a freedom between God and the good, God and God's human partner, and Christians and their neighbors. Saying this, let us explore further how this "gift of freedom" lies at the heart of Christian ethics. Ethics emerges from God's freedom to act making ethics itself a gift of freedom. "Ethics is reflection upon what man is required to do in and with the gift of freedom" (*HG*: 87). This "gift of freedom" is not grounded in the *imago Dei,* as many assume, but in God's trinitarian freedom to be Father, Son, and Spirit. Beginning with the human subject itself apart from this trinitarian relation leads to the fictive notion that human freedom is "self-assertion of one or many solitary individuals" rather than "coexisting" and "participating" with God in human history (*HG*: 71–72). God's freedom is the basis for human freedom in responsible witness and ethical action.

> This freedom of God as it is expressed in His being, word, and deed is the content of the Gospel. Receiving this good news from those who witness to it, the Christian *community* in the world is called to acknowledge it in faith, to respond to it in love, to set on it its hope and trust, and to proclaim it to the world which belongs to this free God. It is the privilege and mission of the Christian community to acknowledge and to confess the Gospel. By acknowledging and confessing Jesus Christ as the creation and revelation of God's freedom, this community is incorporated into the body of Christ and becomes the earthly and historical form of his existence. He is in its midst . . . Even in this central act God declines to be alone, without man. God insists on man's participation in His reconciling work. He wants man, not as a secondary God, to be sure, but as a truly free follower and co-worker, to repeat his divine "Yes" and "No." This is the meaning of God's covenant with man. This is the task man is called to fulfill when God enters into the covenant relationship with him. This is the freedom of discipleship bestowed upon him. (*HG*: 73–74, 81)

Christians are brought into fellowship with Jesus Christ in the context of the Christian community. The church's witness becomes the individual Christian's witness. In their witness, God calls Christians and the church to a task of saying No to the powers that oppress human freedom and Yes to God's reconciling love and grace, which brings us into fellowship with God and others in the surrounding community. God gives liberation and freedom to humanity who remains preoccupied with the ethical task. "God does not put man into the situation of Hercules at the crossroads. The opposite is true. God frees man from this false situation" (*HG*: 76). God brings freedom to choices and decision-making because God's freedom establishes human freedom. This freedom, of course, is discovered only in God's "gift" of grace concretely unveiled in the covenant-partnership between God and humanity made visible in Jesus Christ, as the divine and human representative. This is further manifested in the church, which is "incorporated into the body of Christ and becomes the earthly and historical form of his existence." In this way the church remains an important place from which Christians understand their witness to and *for* the world. In the essay on "Christian Ethics," Barth explores the more practical side by looking for correspondences in which "God does something and does it in such a way that man is thereby called to do something in turn" (*GHN*: 109). Just as God stands with and for others in Jesus Christ, so does Christian witness stand for human dignity and value. Just as God has forgiven sinners, so too, ethics demands the practice of forgiveness and reconciliation. Just as humanity is saved by grace alone, so too, ethics should neither be entirely optimistic, which denies human sin, or pessimistic, which denies God's grace; humanity is sinful but also reconciled and empowered to do the good. Just as God in Jesus Christ in his witness and actions, is responsible, so too, ethics demands that we act responsibly in our witness and actions. Just as God's covenant is inclusive of all persons, so too, ethics should be inclusive of differences within the human community. Just as Christ was a servant to others, so too, we should give of ourselves to others. Lastly, just as God has acted eschatologically, so too, we should act in such a way, privately and publicly, in prayer and work, in love and hope, knowing that God's decisive action is past, present, and future (*GHN*: 111–14). In each of these ways, human actions responsibly *correspond* to God's covenant-partnership with the world, and gives witness to the gracious trinitarian command that calls us forth to be children of God.

What these essays demonstrate is that Christian ethics as witness involves both knowledge and practice. Christian moral knowledge derives from the theological articulation of Christian witness. So, instead of beginning with ethical methodology or social scientific theory, this book argues that *theological* ethics provides the basis for Christian ethics. In turn, theology is understood within the process of *fides quaerens intellectum*, a reflective discipline, linked with the Christian community, which seeks to talk about

God from the standpoint of the biblical and church's witness to God's revelation, as principally unveiled in Jesus Christ. Theology must take seriously the church's confessional witness that the trinitarian God has acted in Jesus Christ and continues to act in the Holy Spirit. Put differently, Christian ethics depends on the witness of theological ethics, and theological ethics depends on the witness of God's revelation. Although theology and ethics can be distinguished they cannot be separated or driven apart because they are both rooted in the witness of God's revelation. Second, as practice, this book looks at the practical application of Christian *witness* within a deliberative framework that engages in dialectical and responsible analysis of contemporary issues in social ethics. It uses a dialectical form of moral reasoning that cannot be reduced to a deontological (rule-based), teleological (consequence-based) or areteological (virtue-based) ethical theory. Rather it envisions moral decision-making and action as a free *responsible* form of witness of individuals and the church. What this implies is a very close relationship between the living beliefs and practices of the church and Christian ethics. Saying this, however, does not imply that Christian ethics be reduced to the church's ethos, whether in beliefs, sacraments, or other practices. Christian ethics cannot begin with ecclesiology, but with the church's witness to God's trinitarian action. In the church's witness to Jesus Christ, Christians invoke and invite God's action, as veiled in mystery but also unveiled in the agency of Holy Spirit, which empowers the church to freely respond to this divine initiative in its practical judgments and actions. As Christians, in their vocation and discipleship, respond to God's action (or command of grace), they remain free to think and act in response to their unique circumstances. Christian ethics, then, is less a tightly controlled system of principles, rules, or even virtues, but more of a free and open-ended responsibility to God's gracious command to be with and for others, the church, and the world. It is an invitation to God's Yes to act in responsible freedom. "Human freedom is the *gift* of God in the free outpouring of His grace. To call man free is to recognize that God has *given* him freedom" (*HG*: 75).

STRUCTURE OF THE BOOK

The book is divided into four parts which basically moves from Barth's earliest to his latest writings. Yet, throughout these chapters is the continuing critical engagement with intellectual and social contexts, both past and present. In brief, the first 2 sections (chapters 1–5) demonstrates why *theological* ethics provides the basis for Christian ethics, and the last two sections (chapters 6–13) lays out the basic features of why and how Christian *witness* provides the framework for Christian ethics. The first several chapters describe how postmodernity has left us with a crisis of moral knowledge and practice, that is, of knowing and doing the good, and how Barth's theological ethics is helpful in addressing these problems. In part one (chapters 1–3), I sort through various theological and epistemological issues relevant to contemporary Christian theology and ethics. The first chapter, in particular, addresses the *Christian* (theological) context by looking at the general transition from modern to postmodern theological ethics. It begins with a general description of modernity ("methodological universalism") and how this is represented in the ethics of Immanuel Kant and Friedrich Schleiermacher. This legacy of "modern ethics" results in: 1) the separation of ethics from theology; and 2) the reduction of ethics to nontheological foundations. Modern theological ethics, with its emphasis on human agency, leaves little room for divine agency to act in the world. God becomes absent. Yet, we must ask, is the voice of God—as trinitarian *Other*—indeed silent?

In chapter 2, I discuss the transition to postmodern thought by looking at the early thought (1916–31) of Karl Barth. Barth's "postmodern turn" in theological ethics is evident in his departure from the ethics of Kant and Schleiermacher, while at the same time, opening himself to the divine Other, by developing a theological description of the moral life that begins with God's action. Reversing the anthropocentric structure of modern ethics, Barth asserts that human freedom depends upon God's freedom to act *in relatio*. This relational view of God—as "with" and "for" humanity—is principally revealed in the event of the Word of God. Beginning with the Word of God, therefore, Barth develops a theological ethics that includes a trinitarian command ethic and dialectical method. Chapter 3 continues the basic narrative of the previous chapter, in which Barth's ethics are situated within their historical and cultural context, namely the German struggle with Nazism in the 1930s. In this way, this chapter continues the narrative of chapter 2, while laying the groundwork for the theological discussion of chapter 6. In particular, I consider Barth's discussion of the issues of "natural law" and "law/gospel." After this, I look at Barth's social and political writings (1938–1950s) with particular focus on the 1946 essay: "The Christian Community and the Civil Community." This essay not only demonstrates how both the ecclesial and secular communities remain a witness to the

Word of God, but also a strategy for a dialectical social ethics within the context of post-Christendom. In the context of the ruins of 1946 Germany, Barth on several occasions gave this address, setting the stage for a post-Christendom Europe, one committed to constitutional democracy, human rights, and a social market or democratic socialist economy.

In part two (chapters 4–5), the subject shifts from theological to *social* and *ethical* analysis, within the postmodern situation. Here I look at both "deconstructionist" and "reflexive" (late-modern) thought regarding social theory (chapter 4) and ethical theory (chapter 5). The former includes individuals like Ulrich Beck, Zygmunt Bauman, and Alasdair MacIntrye, and the latter includes Jacques Derrida, Michel Foucault, and Richard Rorty. In chapter 4, I argue that although reflexive social theory fails to provide a strong argument for *how* we ought to live in the world, it remains a good conversation partner with Christian ethics, especially as it helps assess the "risks" of contemporary life. The fifth chapter discusses the same two theories, and concludes that a "reflexive" theory of moral realism, although better than the deconstructionist model, fails to account for a moral ontology of the good. Postmodernity has left us with a crisis of moral knowledge and practice, that is, of knowing and doing the good. Even if we know the good, we are often paralyzed from doing it. This is because there are not only "external risks" (or powers), like political, economic, and ideological absolutism, global violence, and environmental destruction that threaten persons and communities, but there are also "internal risks" (or powers), like the ideas of antirealism (relativism) and nihilism that correlate the "good" with "power" itself. If the good remains defined by power rather than the other way around, then there is no "good reason" to do what is right *apart* from power. If good truly exists then power itself must be good. It is *potestas*—the power to do good and not simply *potentia*—sheer authority or power to act. This logic leads us to consider God's agency and revelation, as the source of the good. This I argue makes sense in postmodernity only with *revelation* of the good by a good God. So, just as social theory needs ethics, a reflexive account of ethics needs a theological, rather than a philosophical or social scientific, account of moral realism. Although one task in these chapters is entirely descriptive, namely demonstrating the shift from modern to postmodern thought, another more important task relates theology to this discussion. Failure to do this leaves human moral knowledge and action remain paralyzed by the antirealist assumptions of deconstructionist postmodernism.

In part three (chapters 6–9), we return to Barth's theology and ethics considering now the entirety of his work, including the *Church Dogmatics*. Our task here is to discuss themes in Barth's ethics of witness in the context of contemporary Christian ethics. The focus here is more on the theoretical rather than the practical, thus, more on theological ethics. In chapter 6, we explore how Christian witness begins with theological ethics which begins with God's action in the Word of God. Mostly looking at *CD* II/2 and III/4, we look at Barth's theology of divine command and at the same time discuss how his critics misunderstand his theology. Barth's ethics is not a "divine command theory" as much as a trinitarian theology of divine action. This leads to the second point, which focuses on the centrality of how divine and human agencies are related. Unlike most Christian ethics, Barth rejects the basic presumption of the self-determinative moral agent, and instead, uses an Christological framework to redefine moral agency according to the human-divine action in Jesus Christ. This makes God's divine command a command of grace (not law), which practically speaking, makes it open-ended and dialectical. This dialectical approach implies saying Yes to responsible action of witness and No against the powers that threaten to undermine human freedom. These are the subjects of the following two chapters. Chapter 7 looks at how the *Yes* of moral judgment can be understood within a Christian ethics of witness. In this we look at the related ideas of vocation, discipleship, and witness, and their role in ethics. The chapter discusses why these concepts remain crucial for Christian ethics today. The next section focuses Barth's understanding of vocation, discipleship, and witness. Ethics as responsible witness leads to a vision of practical judgment which requires that the Christian freely test and judge his or her actions in response to God's trinitarian command of grace. The heterogeneity between God's Word and human word, between God's command of grace and the human law, is underwritten by a more fundamental covenant of grace, which provides the objective reality for freedom within responsibility. In the last section of the chapter, we explore further how Barth's thought relates to contemporary ethics by comparing Barth and Stanley Hauerwas on the subject of Christian witness.

In chapter 8 we discuss how Christian witness involves saying *No* against the powers. What are these powers? Barth singles out several, namely spiritual powers of leviathan, mammon, and ideology, or if one prefers, political, economic, and ideological absolutism, and the earthly chthonic powers of technology, entertainment, and fast-paced nature of modern life. It is

God not humanity that defeats the powers. Still, these powers remain a force that seeks to destroy human freedom because in their foolish attempt to "be like God," persons place themselves under their own power, which entraps and limits their own freedom. In resistance to the powers, Christian witness must affirm that they are defeated by Jesus Christ, and no longer control human destiny; only in Christ are we free from the powers. The Christian act of resistance against the powers is only possible because of *Christus Victor*.

Lastly in chapter 9 the subject shifts to the relation of Christian witness to public ethics. In many ways, this chapter serves as a summary of many of the ideas developed in previous chapters. Should Christian ethics begin with the particularity of Christian faith and practice or general human claims of moral truth, or in brief, should it be exclusivistic or inclusivistic? If, on the other hand, this is a false dilemma, and Christian ethics combines these two perspectives, then how is this accomplished? This chapter addresses this issue as it discusses Barth in conversation with three other important options in contemporary Christian ethics such as the "theocentric ethics" of James Gustafson, the "Christian realism" of Robin Lovin, and the "Radical Orthodoxy" of John Milbank. Gustafson and Lovin charge that Barth's ethics remains too exclusivistic both in theology and ethics; hence, he is unable to provide an adequate general theory of moral truth. Milbank, on the other hand, sees Barth as too "inclusive" of modern presumptions, and in particular, his acceptance of the "secular." Yet, in contrast to the others, Barth dialectically weaves his way between the twin poles of synthesis and diastasis avoiding the risks of secular reductionism and theological esotericism. The purpose for this comparison is to demonstrate how an ethics of witness is free to critically engage in public discourse in a way that remains beholden to God's gracious action to be with and for others.

The final section (chapters 10–13) moves from theory to practice in demonstrating how Christian witness becomes ethics in political, economic, and environmental practice. Chapter 10 looks at the subject of Christian responsibility. For Barth, Christian responsibility occurs in the context of three spheres of action, namely the interpersonal, the ecclesial, and the world (or social). Living under God's free grace, allows Christians the freedom to live out one's vocation of witness and discipleship in a responsible manner in the context of these three spheres, while avoiding the extreme polarities within each sphere. Without moving "back and forth," Christian ethics remains tied to one absolute perspective unable to encounter the freedom found in God's command of grace; in such cases both human and divine freedom are denied. Christians must responsibly act "for" the good and "against" evil, but they also must be cautious of absolutizing any particular moral strategy as Yes or No, because to do so fosters the risk of replacing one potential hegemony with another. Christian witness implies being responsible for others, the church, and the world. Following this, chapters 11–13 continue this analysis of Christian responsibility and witness, within the context of reconciliation, by examining the interface of Christology and ethics in *CD* IV/1–3, while bringing back into the discussion the powers discussed in chapter 8, and how responsible witness says both No and Yes. The basic argument here is that the Christian witness of faith, hope, and love provides an opening for the practice of various "goods" that contribute to greater peace, freedom, and justice.

In chapter 11 the central discussion focuses on political ethics. For this we turn the narrative in *CD* IV/1, where Christ as the Son of God and "high priest" exposes the human sin of pride and overcomes it with faith, thereby providing his disciples with the means for resisting witness of *faith*. In contrast to faith, then, stands the sin of pride which seeks to usurp God's kingdom with the lordless power of leviathan. The power of leviathan further drives nation-states and terrorist organizations to promote violence and war. Standing against leviathan, the church's witness of faith affirms the practice of *peace*, which leads to supporting constitutional democracy under law, peacemaking, and global cooperation. Christian faith leads to the practice of peace, which stands for humanity and the world and against pride and leviathan's preoccupation with powers and violence. Peace leads to cooperation, fellowship, and human freedom. Furthermore, in chapter 12, we shift toward economic ethics. To begin, we see in *CD* IV/2 how Christ as Son of Man, "royal man," and "exalted king" discloses the human sin of sloth while overcoming it with love, thereby providing his disciples with the means for resisting witness of *love*. In contrast to love, stands the sin of sloth which seeks to usurp God's kingdom with the lordless power of mammon. Against mammon stands love, moreover, which leads to the practice of *justice*. Witness affirms justice by supporting global "social market" economic reform and development, the practice of humane work, and global economic cooperation that moves between a total neoliberal free market and state-controlled communism. Since it is non-dialectical to either demonize or divinize the global market, this chapter presents a dialectical view of wealth and work that resists mammon, but not the market economy's role in social justice. Still, Christian love *resists* mammon by seeking the welfare of others in justice and work, which brings together Christian vocation with what Barth calls "counter-movements" that seek social justice.

Lastly, chapter 13 shifts toward environmental ethics. In *CD* IV/3, Barth explains how Christ as Prophet, the "true witness" who brings together into his one person divine and human agency as "high priest" and "royal man," discloses the sin of falsehood (or deception) and overcomes it with hope, thereby providing his disciples with the means for resisting witness of *hope*. It is the sin of falsehood which provides power to ideology, and it's the virtue of hope that resists its power. Ideology today has many faces, but no one more important than the common belief "there is no alternative" (TINA). This ideology gets at the heart of the crisis of postmodern apathy and despair. In the face of environment destruction and commoditization, the witness of hope says Yes to *freedom* by supporting global environmental stewardship, technological reform, and ecological sustainability. Yet, as Christian witness, this ethics of environmental reform can only be seen emerging from the freedom discovered in God's covenant-partnership with humanity and the world. More than political or economic ethics, Christian environmental ethics has often flirted with diverse cosmologies, whether pantheistic or panentheistic, to challenge the traditional Christian theocentric account of God-world relations. This chapter, then, looks at this theological debate by comparing Barth to other theologians, such as Sallie McFague. Christian hope and freedom for humanity, and humanity's relationship to nature, is not discovered in a new immanentist cosmology but in the witness of God's reconciliation in Jesus Christ.

PART ONE

Ethics and Barth's Witness
Theology and Practice

CHAPTER ONE

Theological Ethics in Transition

This chapter looks at the conversation between theology and ethics in its historical transition from modernity to postmodernity. The first part of the chapter discusses how the relationship of theology and ethics leads to an inherent tension within the strategies of theological and Christian ethics. The second part provides a general summary of the characteristics of modernity and its affect on modern theological ethics, with particular references to Rene Descartes, Immanuel Kant, and Friedrich Schleiermacher. Two of the most important characteristics of modern theology and ethics are the emphasis on *poesis* and *praxis*, which leads to two important ramifications, the displacement of the doctrine of the Trinity and the reduction of dogmatics to ethics. These trends carry over into postmodernity, where a problematic relationship between theology and ethics remains. The third section looks at how the "postmodern turn" in theological ethics leads to a search for the Divine *Other*. Postmodern thought, in many different forms, has sought to hear the voice of the *other*, usually the oppressed voice that has been drowned out by the hegemonic powers of modern life. Yet, in theology, this could also be applied to the otherness of God's Word. Has the voice of God been drowned out by these oppressive human powers? Has the voice of God been overshadowed by the power of the human subject itself in modern thought? If so, then a postmodern challenge is to hear God's voice afresh, thereby opening up or providing space for God's speech. Christian ethics is more than talking about moral principles and virtues and right courses of action. Rather, it must seek to be theological, for in doing so, it opens up space for God's Word to meet us in our particular circumstances.

THEOLOGICAL AND CHRISTIAN ETHICS

How should the relationship between Christian theology and Christian ethics be understood? Is Christian ethics a discipline that begins with dogmatic theology, including discussions about God, Christ, salvation, the church, and so on, or does it begin with general philosophical or scientific worldview about reality? Does it begin with Athens or Jerusalem? No doubt these two disciplines in the history of Christian thought, have remained strange bedfellows. On one side, there are those who see Christian ethics as entirely a separate discipline from doctrinal theology, and with the help of philosophy or the sciences, seek to establish a purely natural or *general* ethics based on human reason alone. On the other side, there are others who see Christian ethics as a related discipline of dogmatic (or systematic) theology, and seek to establish ethics through the *particular* interpretation of the moral life based on Christian convictions and practices. Whereas the former approach seeks to place the moral import of particular Christian beliefs, such as the covenant or incarnation, within a more general category of natural law or human experience, the latter approach interprets the generality of human morality through the lens of the particular Christian or biblical framework of established convictions or practices.

Recognizing the fact that Christian ethics should be both general and particular, how do these two frameworks relate to each other? Does one provide the foundation for the other, and if so, which one comes first? Let us begin with the generalist interdisciplinary perspective. As stated, there are many Christian ethicists who choose to begin their work with an interpretive foundation established by the general interplay of theology, philosophy, and the social sciences. Their strategy in doing so rests on the presumption that their work will appear to others in the academy as more objective, rational, and public. Although there is no agreement as to which sources establish such a generalist foundation, we may assume the balance of power, especially in *social* ethics, has shifted toward the social sciences. By relying on the apparent objectivity of sociological, anthropological, political, or economic descriptions and evaluations, Christian ethics becomes an entirely practical science related to the burgeoning field of professional ethics. What replaces the qualifier *Christian*, then, is the one's expertise in a particular field of study, whether it is social, medical, or business ethics. This implies that the relevance of Christian ethics occurs within the secular frameworks established by professional expertise, and theological discourse is used only, if at all, as a secondary resource of moral knowledge. Theology becomes pushed further into the margins and away from the central space within Christian ethics.[1]

Yet, for all of its apparent hegemony, this generalist interdisciplinary approach remains challenged by another group of Christian ethicists and theologians who seek to recover the use of theology in their work. This group seeks to frame the Christian moral life from within the particularity of ecclesial and doctrinal convictions and practices. The assumption here is that when Christian ethics relies too extensively on other secular perspectives it ends up reducing theological convictions to some other foundational moral language, whether philosophical, scientific, ideological, or experiential. In its worst form, it risks replacing the Christian gospel with some other gospel. Theologians John Milbank and Stanley Hauerwas, for example, have argued for some time that the errors of modern theology and ethics are rooted in its surrender to the logic and grammar of modern historical scholarship, philosophy, and the social sciences. Regarding this, Milbank writes:

> The pathos of modern theology is its false humility. For theology, this must be a fatal disease, because once theology surrenders its claim to be a metadiscourse, it cannot any longer articulate the word of the creator God, but is bound to turn into the oracular voice of some finite idol, such as historical scholarship, humanist psychology; or transcendental philosophy. If theology no longer seeks to position, qualify or criticize other discourses, then it is inevitable that these discourses will position theology: for the necessity of an ultimate organizing logic . . . cannot be wished away. A theology "positioned" by secular reason suffers two characteristic forms of confinement. Either it idolatrously connects knowledge of God with some particular immanent field of knowledge—"ultimate" cosmological causes, or

---

1. Stanley Hauerwas, for example, argues that "Christian ethics" is a modern invention that presumes a separation of ethics from theology. In order for Christian ethicists to make their thinking more applicable to a pluralistic and secular culture, they often marginalize theological commitments from their ethical analysis. This false dichotomy destroys the theological integrity of Christian ethics. See Hauerwas, "On Doctrine and Ethics," 21–40.

PART ONE: ETHICS AND BARTH'S WITNESS

"ultimate" psychological and subjective needs. Or else it is confined to intimations of sublimity beyond representation, so functioning to confirm negatively the questionable idea of an autonomous secular realm, completely transparent to rational understanding.[2]

Milbank reminds us that when theology becomes reduced to other voices, it invariably changes theology into some form of secular thought. This either reduces Christian convictions to some immanentist perspective, or removes them entirely from the discussion into some transcendental realm; either way these convictions become irrelevant. Instead, Milbank argues that convictions about God, and God's relation to the world, should be the basis for Christian thinking about particular issues of the moral life, which invariably means challenging or deconstructing modern secular thought. This implies that if Christian ethics seeks to move beyond secularism by embracing elements of the past that modernity has forgotten, then it moves in a postmodern, postliberal, or post-secular trajectory.[3] This shift in thought gives Christian ethics a fresh start by moving beyond the failures of modern liberal theology.

The key point here is that for Christian ethics to remain *Christian* it must first be theological, which challenges some secularizing trends in modern theology. This does not imply that such a theological starting point cannot engage in social or cultural analysis. Indeed, if Christian ethics is to be relevant for our contemporary context, it must explain the significant developments and shifts in thought that has taken place in society, culture, and in particular, theology and theological ethics. For this to occur, however, theology should remain part of the process of judgment from beginning to end, otherwise theology cannot be seen as a serious conversation partner. Regarding this point, Jeffrey Stout says: "Serious conversation with theology will be greatly limited if the voice of theology is not recognizably theological. Conversation partners must remain distinct enough to be identified, to be needed."[4] This conversation involves both critical and descriptive analysis. First, Christian ethics must use theology as *critical* discourse in challenging the idea that nontheological frameworks, like the

2. Milbank, *Theology and Social Theory*, 1.

3. For an introduction to these movements, see Vanhoozer, *Cambridge Companion to Postmodern Theology*; and Ward, *Blackwell Companion to Postmodern Theology*. The term "post-secular" is often equated with John Milbank and the Radical Orthodox movement. See Milbank, et al., *Radical Orthodoxy*; and Hemming, *Radical Orthodoxy?*

4. Stout, *Ethics after Babel*, 184.

social sciences, provide a foundation for Christian ethics. This challenges modernity's quest for a unitary method of ethical inquiry. Not only is the possibility of this unitary method difficult to support epistemologically, it also silences theology as conversation partner in Christian ethics. Second, Christian ethics uses theology as a *descriptive* discourse in determining what it believes about the objective world. When Christians say, for instance, that persons are created in the *imago Dei*, they are making a statement about the objective moral world. The particularities of Christian beliefs are not subjective but objective accounts of the moral structure of reality. Theological accounts of the world provide the basic framework for Christian ethics.

This book takes the position that Christian ethics begins with a prior understanding of theological ethics. This thesis has been defended by numerous theologians, including Karl Barth. Agreeing with Barth, this book presumes that theological ethics is not just a useful tool for Christian ethics, but remains the basic framework from which Christian ethics ought to be understood and articulated. Although this approach is essential for all historical periods, it is especially important for a postmodern context. Hence, basic to this chapter—and the entire book—is the distinction between theological and Christian ethics, and that the latter depends on the former for its own method, analysis, evaluation, and decision-making. In this book, the term *theological ethics* is used when discussing the theoretical and metaethical questions of ethical inquiry from the perspective of Christian convictions and doctrines about God and God's relationship to the world. According to Barth, for example, theological ethics, or "general ethics," emerges from "the claim, decision and judgment of God which in his Word become evident as the command confronting human action."[5] Theological ethics begins with God's covenantal relationship to humanity, as unveiled in Jesus Christ, which then opens up space for personal moral responsibility in response to God's gracious action. Barth writes: "Man does good in so far as he acts as one who is called by God to responsibility" (*CD* II/2: 546). Emerging from this theological framework, *Christian ethics* concentrates on the actual personal circumstances and actions, in which persons seek to act in responsible ways corresponding to overarching reality understood by theological ethics. In Barth's words, Christian ethics, or "special ethics," determines how the "specific, concrete, special, and even very special action of man can or cannot be called a good action, that is, an action that corresponds to the divine

---

5. Barth, *Christian Life*, 4. Henceforth, all references to this book will be cited in the text in parenthesis, and abbreviated as *CL*.

claim, agrees with the divine decision, and conforms to the divine judgment" (*CL*: 4). Just has human action corresponds to God's prior action, the task of Christian ethics corresponds to the task of theological ethics. "[M]an does good in so far as his action is Christian" (*CD* II/2: 547).

In this way, theological ethics provides the framework for Christian ethics. To understand how this distinction between Christian and theological ethics develops over time, we must turn to a brief description of modernity and its effect on theology and ethics. Entering into this field of historical study brings with it an obvious risk of oversimplification. Yet, some generalization is inevitable for us to point to the significant developments in ethics during the past several centuries. In the following section, we concentrate on the intellectual background behind the demise and recovery of theological ethics in the modern period. As modernity continued we see a general separating of theology (and theological ethics) from the strategy of Christian ethics, which pushes the ethical importance of Christian beliefs and practices further toward the margins. At the same time, in their desire to remain relevant to an increasingly secular world, Christian ethicists look to other nontheological frameworks, whether scientific or philosophical, for their own moral methodology, epistemology, and linguistic expression. Once theological ethics becomes separated from the task of Christian ethics, however, it becomes more difficult to explain *how* human and divine agency remains linked together in some meaningful way. God's agency remains separated from human agency which further isolates God from humanity and humanity from God. Christian ethics becomes entirely anthropocentric, thereby no different from any other secular version of ethics, except for occasional and obscure references to God or the Spirit's providential role in history. Christian ethics becomes just another version of secular ethics, one that is thoroughly immanent, naturalistic, and de-eschatologized. Without a theological account of divine agency as benevolently acting in the past, present, and future, the course of history and ethics becomes teleologically purposeless and directionless.

BEING MODERN

We begin with a general account of some of the basic characteristics of modern thought, and its effect on ethics. Scholars debate the European foundations of modernity, but most agree that modern life began during the seventeenth century. Although precursory movements, like the Renaissance and Reformation, radically altered late-Medieval society, it was the intellectual movement, in the next two centuries, known as the Enlightenment, which had significant impact on all areas of modern culture and society. The effects of modernity are still with us, as most persons assume that we remain *modern* people. What are the basic characteristics of modernity? At its most basic, modernity presumes an insatiable quest for "absolute certitude" in interpreting and understanding reality. Although important Enlightenment writings include Francis Bacon's *New Atlantis* (1627), John Locke's *Treatise on Two Governments*, and Adam Smith's *Wealth of Nations* (1776), perhaps the most important text is Rene Descartes' *Discourse on Method* (1637). Even though Descartes' book is not the most original or innovative of modern classics, it's influence rests more on its *method* for determining the certitude of absolute knowledge and truth. Behind modernity is a particular methodological way reality itself is understood.

Methodological Universalism

Albert Borgmann provides a useful scheme for understanding the *weltanschauung* of modernity, when he looks to Descartes' method the methodological pattern of modern thinking. This "methodological universalism" has four distinct characteristics, namely abstraction, dissection, reconstruction, and control.[6] These four factors provide a general summary of the "spirit" of modernity as well as the specific cognitive structure for all academic disciplines in the modern age, whether in the humanities, sciences, or in theology and ethics. Beginning in the seventeenth century there is a shift in thought which can be called modern, which continues until the present time. There is much debate regarding whether we live in a modern, late-modern, or postmodern world. Suffice it to say, modernity is both a comprehensive and dynamic reality. At its core, it represents one concrete or comprehensive worldview, but as we shall see, it also reveals a dynamic reality that further unveils two distinct worldviews. Modernity, in other words, is double-edged, so that on the surface it presents a worldview that is hopeful, optimistic, and utopian, but underneath it reveals a more nihilistic and pessimistic viewpoint. The character of modernity, says Anthony Giddens, consists of the tension of *"security versus danger and trust versus risk.* Modernity, as everyone living in the closing years of the twentieth

---

6. For his discussion of these four characteristics, see Borgmann, *Crossing the Postmodern Divide*, 34–37.

century can see, is a double-edged phenomenon."⁷ This ambiguity, as mentioned earlier, remains the core experience of the "immanent frame" of our secular age. When the latter underside of modernity dominates, we may say we have entered into a critical period of late-modernity or postmodernity.

With this being said, the first characteristic of modern thought is *abstraction*. Descartes presumes that to discover the truth about something, we must first critically disconnect ourselves as a "subject" from the "object" of our analysis. "Faced with a problem," says Borgmann, "one must first abstract from it—step back from stand regard it from a skeptical distance. One also needs to abstract the problem itself—sever it from the context and our tacit understandings."⁸ The process of abstraction occurs at two levels. At one level, when persons attempt to understand something, they begin by separating themselves from their object of study, which leads to a kind of ontological separateness. This disconnection results in the dichotomy between subject and object, self and the world, and the self and God. Modern thought presumes that human beings are ontologically independent from other persons, the community, nature, and God. At another level, to gain absolute certitude, one must isolate their object of study, thus removing it from other constitutive factors. This sets the agenda for the fragmentation in knowledge so typical of the modern period, where every subject matter, articulated by its specialists or experts, becomes reduced to its distinctive claims about knowledge and truth. The abstraction of theology, for example, led to its fragmentation into various unrelated disciplines such as biblical studies, and systemic, historical, moral (or ethical), and practical theology. This further means that Christian ethics, if it is to be consistent with the canons of modern ethical methodology, must separate itself from biblical studies or dogmatic and systematic discussions of God, salvation, and the church. As modernity continued, Christian ethics became more abstracted and separated from its theological grounding, which made the human subject, not God, the standard for human knowledge of the good. In modernity, says James Gustafson, "culturally, religiously, theologically, and ethically, man the human species, has become the measure of all things; all things have seen in the service of man."⁹

---

7. Giddens, *Consequence of Modernity*, 7.
8. Borgmann, *Crossing the Postmodern Divide*, 35.
9. Gustafson, *Ethics from a Theocentric Perspective*, 82.

The second task of methodological universalism involves the *dissection* of knowledge into its constitutive and simplest parts. Like the strategy of abstraction, dissection takes interrelated parts and isolates and reduces them to an independent status. In this way, human reason becomes reductionistic and mechanistic. This general pattern of reductionistic thinking not only comprises the natural and social sciences, but also the humanities, the arts, philosophy, and even theology. This way of thinking presumes that the individual parts comprising a whole are more determinative for the knowledge of the whole, than the whole itself. Modern medicine, for instance, fights disease not by assisting the body—as a healing organism—to heal itself, but by searching out and isolating the abnormal cells and destroying them; it begins not with the whole but with the various parts that comprise the whole. Likewise, the human person, scientifically understood, becomes reduced to her psychological, sociological, anthropological, physiological, or biological components. Another aspect of *dissection*, furthermore, is its mechanistic dimension. Relying on the Cartesian method, we perceive the world as a complex machine, operated by universal objective laws, which more often than not, are translated into mathematical or scientific formulas or facts. This contributes to our infatuation with scientific (as opposed to humanistic or religious) modes of reasoning and its application into new forms of technology. Although, for example, we still need architects to design a new building—if it is to be built—it must pass through the office of the engineer. Technology has replaced art as the most visible form of modern achievement.

These two factors of reductionism and functionalism, also apply to theology. Once theological knowledge is dissected into smaller and smaller pieces, it becomes reduced to other nontheological methods and analysis, particularly those disciplines that are most functional or practical. This means, in theory, that the core qualifier for theological ethics is no longer theology, as it was in premodern times, but ethics as seen through the interpretive lens of modern moral philosophy or the social sciences. It follows that the first-order languages of confession, worship, and preaching, and even the second-order language of doctrine, become increasingly unimportant in Christian moral reflection. In its final form, the abstraction and dissection of theology leads to the separation of Christian ethics from theology, and its reduction to a philosophically grounded universalist and functionalist discourse, such as a Kantianism or Utilitarianism. These two methods are simply one example of modernity's quest for "moral Esperanto," "an artificial moral language invented in the (unrealistic) hope that everyone will speak it."[10] Esperanto has forced Christian ethicists to assume that the "particular" study of theology is irrelevant to the more "general" study of ethics. By attempting to universalize Christian ethics, theologians have overlooked those particular claims unique to Christianity, thus making ethics inherently nontheological or even anti-theological.

The third characteristic of the Cartesian universal method reconstructs the epistemic foundations of human knowledge. Epistemological *foundationalism* assumes there are certain "clear and distinct" ideas that provide the foundation for other dependent ideas, concepts, and thought. In this way, modern thought tears downs buildings and intellectual edifices only to rebuild them in its own image. The modern search for truth, including moral truth, vigorously deconstructs cultural tradition, universal truth claims, and moral certainty only to recreate new structures of knowledge. Just as a building can be built or rebuilt only with a strong foundation, so too the critical, evaluative, and constructive nature of modern thought attempts to build on the "clear and distinct" ideas of universal reason. This new grounding of foundationalism corresponds to the fourth characteristic of the Cartesian method that points toward the power of *control*. In modernity, persons are in firm control of their own perception, evaluation, and implementation of their own knowledge. They not only have the God-given right to extend their power and domination over their own society and culture, but also over the external environment through applied science and technology. It was the economic, industrial, and technological revolutions, more than political revolutions that made industrial Western society a "world civilization." Regarding this point, Krishan Kumar writes: "For the world as a whole it became increasing obvious that to be a modern society was to be an industrial society. To modernize was to industrialize—that is, to become like the West."[11] This transformation is called *modernization*. Indeed, it is modernization that gives the Enlightenment project of methodological universalism its optimistic and utopian character, and its teleological paradigm of historical progress.

Not unlike other disciplines, theology is deeply shaped by the modern conceptions of these third and fourth aspects, namely epistemic foundationalism and progress. Regarding this Barth says, "it was possible to show that

10. Stout, *Ethics After Babel*, 294.
11. Kumar, *Post-Industrial to Post-Modern Society*, 83.

the old conceptions of Bible and dogma were contradictory and impossible in themselves, and by referring to them men could believe that they were entitled, indeed called, to go forward to the construction of a better edifice."[12] What this means for theology is the general departure from the "edifice" of God's special revelation as witnessed in Scripture or the creeds, and toward the new *foundation* based in human reason and experience and confidence in the historical-critical method. To be sure, this meant, at the very least, being critical of the tradition of pre-modern theology and the creeds.

> People now began to think that it was extremely significant that Athanasius and Augustine, Luther and Calvin, despite all their other admirable characteristics, were children of earlier, less enlightened times, still standing on the ground of the Ptolemaic system of the world and ignorant of the concept of natural law as now administered at the University of Göttingen and in other places of the true light. The whole of the Christian past was now fondly imagined as that of a rather credulous, naïve mythology which had fallen victim to a quite brutal authoritarian way of thinking, a blind literalism which ignored all intellectual difficulties. And as modern men, people felt themselves justified in making the necessary (necessary, of course, from other grounds) criticism of his legacy from the past—and armed to do so. And it was so easy to seize the requisite authority and weapons.[13]

Unsure of foundational doctrinal truths, modern theologians reconstructed Christian theology on the new foundations of human reason, experience, or ethics. With the use of natural and critical reason, it became "easy" to criticize the classical doctrines of the Trinity or Christology, or the biblical history and miracle stories. Yet, what replaced these traditions was the new "requisite authority" of human reason and "weapons" of human power and technological control. "The geocentric picture of the universe was replaced as a matter of course by the anthropocentric."[14] Consequently, modern theology and ethics becomes obsessively anthropocentric, and reflects, like moral philosophy, the turn to the autonomous and self-determinative moral subject as the standard for ethics. It is at this point, moreover, where this modern conception of *progress* becomes itself a new foundation. So, for example, Jesus' significance in modern theology became less the risen

12. Barth, *Protestant Theology in the Nineteenth Century*, 95
13. Ibid., 94.
14. Ibid., 24.

Christ, the second person of the Trinity, but the teacher of ethical maxims and principles, often summarized by his teaching about the kingdom of God. The liberal slogan the "Fatherhood of God and Brotherhood of man" summarized the liberal attempt to capture Jesus' eschatological message within the confines of various social progressive movements. Guarded with principles like love, freedom, and equality, Social Gospel liberals, for example, viewed the kingdom of God as the outworking of human history in economic, political, and social spheres.

Modernity's Ambiguity: Modernization or Modernism?

Obviously this modern utopian worldview became more difficult to defend with the emerging atrocities of the twentieth century. It is at this point, where modernity becomes double-edged, thereby the underside of modern progress begins to be reflexively understood and known. On the surface, modernity presents a solid, brilliant, and lucid picture of progress, but underneath it discloses a fragile, self-critical, and self-destructive side. The same can be said for modern theology, which for all of its glorious attempts to make the gospel credible to the modern world, it easily succumbs to the hegemony of nontheological and secular frameworks, which trivialize, even eviscerate, the Word from its privileged position in theological ethics. Nevertheless, once the "underside" of modernity is exposed we enter into postmodernity. The hidden self-destructiveness of modernity is evident in the fact that it has been at war with itself from its very beginning. Perhaps the best visual example of the ambiguous nature of modernity is found in modern art. Reflecting on the ambiguous nature of modernity, the nineteenth century French critic and poet Charles Baudelaire prophetically wrote: "Modernity is the transient, the fleeting, the contingent; it is one half of art, the other being the eternal and the immovable."[15] Unlike the art of earlier societies, Baudelaire maintains that modern art must continuously recreate itself, yet it does so by discarding the foundational realism of the eternal and the immovable. The modern quest for "absolute certainty" in art is undermined by its own deconstructive tendencies. This means that what modern art attempts to accomplish, in principle, is undercut by its own self-contradictory creative process. This example of modern art is simply one example of modernity's tendency to be inherently self-destructive.

---

15. Baudelaire, *Selected Writings on Art*, 403.

The two clashing ideological forces in modernity are: *modernization* and its application to society, and *modernism* and its application to culture. In short, these two ideologies represent the two poles of Baudelaire's description of modernity. As previously noted, modernization, as expressed in political, economic, and technological institutions, affirms the eternal *weltanshaung* of progress, which is grounded in the universal optimism of Enlightenment reason (i.e., the "eternal and immovable"). In contrast, modernism, as expressed in culture and the arts, expresses the transient flux of historical contingency, the preoccupation with the *avant garde*, and the *poiesis* of the creative artist (i.e., the "transient, fleeting, and contingent"). These two ideas stand in tension. On one side, modernization is the practical embodiment of the grand ideas of modernity including industrialization, capitalism, communism, liberal democracy, and technological innovation. It is thoroughly modern, in that, it affirms the confidence of human reason, the practical use of the scientific method, and social and cultural progress. On the other side, modernism—as a cultural movement—is subversive of the idea of modernization from the early nineteenth century period of Romanticism to the present time. It assumes that human autonomy is often held hostage by the apparent hegemonic social structures of modernization embodied in *lassiez-faire* capitalism, political totalitarianism, and techno-scientific rationality. Indeed, since modernism is inherently anti-traditional, it becomes equated with a particular tradition of the *avant garde*, antinomianism, and expressive individualism—as a kind of "new" tradition. By creating *avant garde* movements in the visual arts, music, architecture, and literature, cultural modernism challenges the canons of universal reason and tradition in the arts, while at the same time, preaches "modern" individual self-expression and self-realization.[16] Ironically, it is this combination of factors that lead to a "new" tradition, which strongly links it with other utopian ideologies of modernity, so with the ideology of modernization itself. Although committed to different tasks, these two movements, in the end, remain committed to the modern foundationalist ideas of creativity and progress.

---

16. This tradition includes the "romantic sensibility" of the poets Shelley, Keats, and Byron as well as the later poets and novelists Flaubert, Baudelaire, Rimbaud, Kafka, Joyce, Woolf, and Lawrence. Similar movements occur in the historical development of modernism in the visual arts (Romanticism to Dadaism, Surrealism, and Cubism) and music (Beethoven to Schoenberg and Cage).

The tension between the constructionist vision of modernization and deconstructionist vision of modernism reveals a deep-seated ambiguity that has become self-evident or *real* in postmodernity. As both theories seek to extend the ambiguous deconstructionist and reconstructionist tendencies of modernity into a "new" world, they also expose Baudelaire's fragile synthesis of the "eternal" and the "contingent." For all of its deconstruction of Enlightenment rationality, modernism could not depart from the presuppositions of methodological universalism. Despite the rejection of certain aspects of modern rationality, for example, cultural modernism uses its deconstructive method to disregard the "old" and embrace the "new" tradition as its *raison d'etre*. As a result, the progression becomes radically anthropocentric and egoistic, which undermines its own ability to critique the individualistic tendencies in modern life. Although there were communitarian, holistic, and traditional forms of Romantic thought, for example, as expressed in theology and philosophy, the general trend of modernism is toward the rejection of community in favor of expressive, and often hedonistic *individualism*. In short, both modernization and modernism remain anti-traditional, individualistic, anthropocentric, and celebrate the "new" over the "old," and the self over the community. When the "new" no longer remains attractive as an eternal ground for the contingent and fleeting, Baudelaire's synthesis begins to break apart. That is, when the "new" becomes boring, sullen, and meaningless, we are beginning to observe the transition from modernism to postmodernism, from modernity to postmodernity.

In summary, the epistemological underpinnings of modernity unavoidably lead toward a double-edged view of reality. The naïve hope for liberation from traditional political, economic, religious institutions collapses into the hopeless fate of being enslaved to ourselves. Progress itself becomes despair. When the negative *underside* of modernity becomes real and apparent, the underlying nihilism of this tradition begins to surface, which changes the modern sentiment of creativity and progress to one of self-destruction and pessimism. The utopianism of modernity changes into the dystopianism of postmodernity. How did this affect theology? On the positive side, modern theologians thought they could address the complexities of modern life with their excursions into religious experience, synthetic apologetics, and liberationist ethics. Yet, when the human person becomes the "measure of all things" this also raises the risk of failure, and with this failure, the loss of hope in humanity. The underside of modern theology eventually leads to a kind of internal skepticism and deconstruction of traditional Christian beliefs about God, Christ, and church and world, at the same time, a separation of divine and human agency, and a Promethean view of human power and ethical achievement.

MODERN THEOLOGY AND ETHICS

As mentioned above, modern theology remains generally tied to the project of modern thought, including aspects of methodological universalism. With this general background in mind, we examine two important modern figures that have shaped the discipline of theological ethics for over two hundred years, namely Immanuel Kant and Friedrich Schleiermacher. Kant's influence is crucial for understanding modern ethics (both philosophical and theological), while Schleiermacher's influence is more on doctrinal theology, but together both thinkers embody the characteristics of methodological universalism. Theological ethics, if it is to overcome the failures of the past, must begin, not with a new ethical theory or practice, but a new theology, that is, a theology that moves beyond Kant and Schleiermacher.

Kant and Schleiermacher

We begin with Immanuel Kant, who not only transformed modern moral philosophy, but deeply shaped modern theological and Christian ethics. In his 1784 essay, "What is Enlightenment?" Kant argued for the removal of all external constraints on autonomous reason whether found in institutional authority or philosophical or religious arguments.[17] The traditional intellectual authority of religion and metaphysics is irreversibly replaced with the individual exercise of "critical reason." Kant was convinced that sense perception couldn't tell us anything about faith or morality. Indeed, as he saw it, faith depended on revelation, while morality depended on the *a priori* and universal categories of rational thought. Human freedom allows the human subject to rise above the social and historical contingencies of nature becoming a "transcendental subject" to itself. For Kant, the task of "practical reason" must separate itself from theological or metaphysical grounds to function as an ethical practice or *praxis*. Nonetheless, at the heart of Kant's ethics is his understanding of the human will and the "categorical imperative." If persons are genuinely free, then they have an obligation to legislate their own actions. Moral actions are determined to be right or

---

17. Kant, *Metaphysics of Morals and What Is Enlightenment*, 85–92.

wrong, not by their ends or consequences, but by their adherence to self-legislated universal imperatives or maxims derived from human reason. As he put it, "the basis of obligation must not be sought in the nature of man, or in circumstances in the world in which he is placed, but *a priori* simply in the conceptions of pure reason."[18] This means the moral agent's "duty," or respect for the law, compels persons to obey universal moral principles as a universal moral law. Simply put, the fact that I *ought* to act in a certain way implies that I *can* act in this way. What is the universal moral law that applies to all persons? This law, or "categorical imperative," consists of two parts: 1) an action is good only if the moral agent wills its underlying principle as a universal law; and 2) that we should always treat others, not as a means, but as an end in themselves.[19] These two principles of Kantian ethics celebrates the agent's intention as the final arbiter of morality, and the principle of equal regard as the formal criterion of action. Such moral claims have led, in actual practice, to the legal support for human dignity, freedom, and rights, which has shaped modern liberal governments.

Kant's version of modern ethics was a positive step forward, but it also represents a departure from important theological positions. Modern ethics operates on the basis of universal moral rules, principles, and procedures, whose adherents must simply believe them to be true because they are "rational." It further presumes that because moral persons are rational, objective, and autonomous, they also have a "good will," which enables them to obey these universal moral maxims. In other words, if I *know* the good, I should simply be *able* to do it. In this way, modern ethics distanced itself from a theological account of ethics, which provided persons with a language that enabled them to: 1) seek to do the good; 2) accept responsibility for their evil actions; 3) when they fail, seek to be forgiven and reconciled to God and others. This pattern allows persons to first experience the bondage to sin and guilt, and second the freedom to act and be forgiven. Ignoring the language of sin/repentance and reconciliation/responsibility, the failure of modern secular reasoning promises a life free from sin and guilt, free from tradition bound social institutions, free to self-legislate a new foundation for ethics. Since theological claims about human sinfulness and God's grace were neither scientific nor objective, it was inevitable that these beliefs should be challenged by universal reason. As Zygmunt Bauman

18. Ibid., 5.
19. For a good discussion, see Donagan, "Common Morality," 53–72.

writes: "The modern project postulated the possibility of a human world free not only from sinners, but from sin itself; not just from people making wrong choices but from the very possibility of wrong choice."[20] Overall, Kant's approach had a secularizing influence on the tradition of Christian ethics. The hero of Enlightenment thought, in Charles Taylor's words, was the "disengaged human subject" who used "disengaged reason" to solve the world's problems. "The subject of disengagement and rational control has become a familiar modern figure."[21] Yet, when applied to Christian ethics, disengagement meant not only a movement from a theological account of ethics to a nontheological "rational" ethical foundation, but the movement from God, as divine *Other*, to the anthropocentric god of humanity. Indeed, the functions once attributed to God are not abolished, but shifted and relocated to persons, communities, and abstract universal laws. In modern ethics God is no longer needed to account for coherence and meaning. Indeed, as the critique of theology and ecclesiastical institutions heightened, it became more evident that not only was the Enlightenment a revolt for human freedom but a revolt against God.

In the midst of the growing secularization ushered in by the Enlightenment, our second important figure, Friedrich Schleiermacher combined Romanticism, Idealism, and the priority of religious experience to reconstruct the foundations of modern theology. Schleiermacher's thought greatly influenced later generations making him the quintessential "father" of modern *liberal* theology. In 1799, Schleiermacher published his famous *Speeches*, in which he argued that religion, at its core, is grounded in the human feeling (*Gefuhl*) or awareness of the divine. Later, in his most important theological work, *The Christian Faith*, he further argued that human knowledge of God emerges from our "awareness of absolute dependence," or, in other places "God-consciousness."[22] He took great liberties in reformulating the task of Christian dogmatics, thus began a long history of *poiesis*, or creative production, in modern theology. Although Schleiermacher's theology seeks to go beyond Enlightenment rationalism, its foundationalism relates the particularity of Christian doctrines, as expressions of Christian belief and practice, to the more general category of universal

20. Bauman, *Life in Fragments*, 4.
21. Taylor, *Sources of the Self*, 160.
22. Schleiermacher, *On Religion* and *Christian Faith*. For a good introduction to Schleiermacher's thought, see Mariña, *Cambridge Companion to Friedrich Schleiermacher*. Also see Welch, *Protestant Thought, Volume I*, 59–85.

religious experience. So, even though the general experience of "absolute dependence" and "God-consciousness" is universal, it is expressed in the church as the first-order language of prayer, preaching, worship, and ethics. In Christian theology, one can speak about the particular doctrines of God, salvation and sin, and the divinity of Christ, at the same time one can speak more generally about absolute dependence, our lack of and need for God-consciousness, and Christ's perfect embodiment of God-consciousness. Schleiermacher's understanding of Christianity was that it was the supreme example of religion.

The way the general and particular interact in theology is particularly evident in Schleiermacher's ethics. Although Schleiermacher never created a comprehensive system of ethics, he lectured and wrote extensively about philosophical ethics in several documents, including his 1812–13 *Ethics* lectures.[23] For Schleiermacher, "philosophical ethics" is the "science of the principles of history," thus, is more typical of what we would call today call a philosophy of culture (or cultural studies) or even sociology.[24] More specifically, what Schleiermacher means by ethics, then, is the process whereby these principles of nature and history become apparent to all persons through reason; it is reason that gives shape and form to nature. Grounded in his metaphysics, Schleiermacher's romantic sensibility led him to challenge the rationalism of Kantian moral philosophy. Thus, in his discussion of human freedom and nature, moral duty and virtue, and the highest good, Schleiermacher finds adequate space to reject Kantian themes like the autonomous self, the categorical imperative, and the false separation of ethics from religion. Frederick Beiser provides a good summary Schleiermacher's contribution to philosophical ethics: "Schleiermacher's comprehensive conception of ethics; his insistence that ethics broaden its horizons, that it investigate such important phenomena as love, free sociability, and friendship; his demand for the restoration for the highest good; his critique of the fact-norm distinction; and his insistence that our ethics ultimately depend upon our general metaphysical view of the world—all these remain a challenge to ethics today."[25]

Unlike Schleiermacher's philosophical ethics in which remains general in his discussion about God and religion, Schleiermacher's Christian ethics

---

23. Schleiermacher, *Lectures in Philosophical Ethics*. For a discussion of his philosophical ethics, see Mariña, *Cambridge Companion to Friedrich Schleiermacher*, 53–71.

24. Shelley, "Translator's Introduction," 22.

25. Beisner, "Schleiermacher's Ethics," 70.

relates the particularly of Christian faith to ethics. "The scientific form of the *Christian Ethics* is not due to its following the form of the philosophical ethics, but is given, rather, through the material: the expressions of faith regarding the incentives of faith."[26] Like his theology, Schleiermacher develops his Christian ethics from his conception of God-consciousness. Here he presents a similar understanding of the interdependent self, but through the language of dogmatic theology. Christian ethics is less about the specific principles or laws of morality, and more about the unique way it becomes embodied in action in the lives of Christians.

> Schleiermacher's entire philosophy of religion, and therefore his entire teaching of the nature of religion and Christianity, the things we first think of when his name is mentioned, was something secondary, auxiliary to the consolidation of this true concern of his, the ethical one. The fact that, in academic theory, he ranked theology below ethics, is but an expression of this state of affairs. With Schleiermacher is not a matter of doctrine, nor of his particular doctrine, or a matter of his particular doctrine only for the sake of the end to be achieved; with him it is a matter of life.[27]

For Schleiermacher the living power of God-consciousness, through the Holy Spirit, envelops, indeed infects, believers, within the context of the Christian community, enabling them to be pious and virtuous. Christian piety ushers in the realization of the kingdom of God, which entails the progress of humanity. Not unlike G. W. F. Hegel, Schleiermacher closely links the growth of reason (spirit) with the simultaneous development of culture, the arts, and civilization. It is no coincidence that H. Richard Niebuhr categorizes Schleiermacher's ethics as an example of the liberal "Christ of Culture" position. Niebuhr points out that "in his *Speeches on Religion*, as well as in his writings on ethics, he is a clear-cut representative of those who accommodate Christ to culture while selecting from culture what conforms most readily to Christ."[28]

The central point is that there is an inherent tension in Schleiermacher's thought between the general and the particular, his philosophical and Christian ethics. Indeed, his foundationalist philosophy is laid side by side with a more particular discussion of Christian ethics. Although

---

26. Herms, "Schleiermacher's Christian Ethics," 217.
27. Barth, *Protestant Theology in the Nineteenth Century*, 422.
28. Niebuhr, *Christ and Culture*, 94.

Schleiermacher does not see a contraction between these two methods, as they are "formally distinct," he never seeks to resolve the tension between the particularity of the Christian moral life and the generality of his philosophical ethics.[29] Indeed, most interpreters of Schleiermacher's ethics remain persuaded that he did not ultimately resolve this tension. So, at one level, he can discuss theoretical issues regarding moral duty, virtue, human nature, and the conscience, and on the other, he can discuss God, Christology, the church, sin, reconciliation, and communion with God. The general addresses the *condition humana* and the particular addresses the *Sittlenlehre*, the Christian way of living. This liberal method assumes that a moral general description of ethics needs a philosophical non-dogmatic language, while the more distinctive biblical and dogmatic language belongs to the church and Christians. In his refusal to resolve the tension the general and the particular, the world and the church, Schleiermacher remains a quintessentially modern thinker shaped by the ethos of methodological universalism.

Legacy of Liberal Theology

No doubt an overall assessment of modern theology ushers in mixed results. The great strength of theological liberalism, it can be argued, lies in its commitment to making religion, of which Christianity is the noblest expression, experientially intelligible to everyone, including its despises and admirers as well as the cultured and uncultured. By engaging modernity head-on, liberals have often responded with an articulate Christian voice within the emerging secular society. Nevertheless, this strength also reveals its most apparent weakness. To clarify the gospel in a skeptical world, theological liberalism, or what Karl Barth calls "neo-protestantism," typically chooses various nontheological categories, including philosophy and the sciences, to express the coherence of both theology and ethics. The more successful the theology and ethics, the more universally capable it is in communicating to the modern mind the core expressions of the Christian faith. Both Kant and Schleiermacher, for example, provide a similar *telos* in their thought, governed by themes of progress, control, and development, expressed by the notion of the civilizing power of the kingdom of God, or as Kant puts the "kingdom of ends." This progressive element is seen in liberal thought in Europe, Britain, and America during the nineteenth century and into the twentieth as well. In Germany, for example, this progressive

---

29. Herms, "Schleiermacher's Christian Ethics," 217.

strategy of modern theology continued to be formulated in new ways by Albrecht Ritschel, Adolph von Harnack, and Ernst Troelstsh. In America, the mid-nineteenth century theologian Horace Bushnell, often called the "Schleiermacher of America," shifted theology in a progressively liberal direction, despite his unwillingness to separate theology from Christian ethics.[30] Bushnell's optimism later influenced the progressive thought of liberal theology, including the Social Gospel movement and theologians such as Walter Rauschenbusch. This often led to a focus on the *praxis* of embodying of the kingdom of God in the world. The eschatological framework of modern theology moves in a utopian direction, in which it often mixes God's providence with Western ideological notions of social and cultural progress. In hindsight, we see how modern theology and ethics remains essentially tied to characteristics of methodological universalism, including modern progress.

With this in mind, the overall structure of modern theology begins with the commitment to both *poiesis* and *praxis*, or to theological creativity and ethics. Reinhard Hütter argues that modern theology has taken these two routes, both of which attempt to make theology universally understood as a rational and coherent system of belief. "Poiesis is generative activity whose criterion of quality resides in the work alone," says Hütter, "while praxis is an action whose criterion of quality resides both in the action itself and in the character of the agent."[31] First, the strategy of *poiesis* makes the theologian the creative subject, indeed the "creator" of theological construction. The assumption here is the truthfulness of Christian beliefs depends upon the creative re-articulation by the contemporary theologian. Second, the strategy of *praxis* reduces dogmatics to ethics with the hope that Christian beliefs will remain relevant for an enlarging secular world. This combination of *poiesis* and *praxis* makes the task of theology critical, apologetic, synthetic, and practical. First it remains critical of premodern authority, which allowed Protestant liberals and Catholic modernists to jettison traditional authorities, whether found in an infallible Scripture or an infallible ecclesial authority. Second, it is apologetic in that it feared that without the gospel's translation and assimilation, Christianity will no longer make sense in a secularized modern society. Third, the emphasis on

30. Haddorff, *Dependence and Freedom*, 3–6; 168–72. For a comparison of the theology of Schleiermacher and Bushnell, see my forthcoming essay, "Schleiermacher and Bushnell."

31. Hütter, *Suffering Divine Things*, 32.

synthesis consists in a never-ending search for new foundations, whether found in the universality of religious experience, modern scientific critical methods of inquiry, or an anthropocentrism grounded in a human moral agency. Lastly, this articulation of theology becomes operative in ethical practice. In each of these strategies, the constructive task of Christian theology reinterprets doctrine and applies it to moral action in one's social and cultural context. "The first task of the [liberal] theologian," says George Lindbeck, "is to identify the modern questions that must be addressed, and then to translate the gospel answers into a currently understandable conceptuality.[32] Yet, at this point, we must ask: With the continuing emphasis on translation and practice, is there a risk to replacing the Word of God with some other secular word? Is there a risk of replacing the Christian gospel with some other secular gospel? What does this say about God, humanity, and the world?

POSTMODERN THEOLOGY AND ETHICS

Charles Taylor argues in *A Secular Age* that modern thought, in its drive toward secularism, has led to a complete separation of God's transcendence from God's immanence, and the reduction of God to the "immanent frame" and the "closed world structures."[33] The "providential Deism" of the seventeenth and eighteenth centuries, which removes God from creation, lays the groundwork for atheism, anthropocentrism (or humanism), and materialism of the nineteenth and twentieth centuries. The secular rejection of transcendence is not entirely pervasive, as most people continue to hold onto ideas of meaning outside the immanentist and materialistic narratives, however, the dominant hegemonic subterranean background belief of our secular world is the "immanent frame" which perceives the world as reductive and flat. "It is the sense of an absence; it is the sense that all order, all meaning comes from us. We encounter no echo outside. In the world read this way, as so many of our contemporaries live it, the natural/supernatural distinction is no mere intellectual abstraction. A race of humans have arisen which has managed to experience its world entirely as immanent. In some respects we may judge this achievement a victory for darkness, but it is a remarkable achievement nonetheless."[34]

32. Lindbeck, *Nature of Doctrine*, 132.
33. Taylor, *Secular Age*, 542.
34. Ibid., 376.

Modern secularism has led the formation of worldviews from a collection of fragmented religious, secular, and humanistic beliefs. This affects the way we want to live our lives. "Some of us want to live it as open to something beyond; some live it as closed. It is something which permits closure, without demanding it."[35] This bricolage of beliefs, says Taylor, exists as a "remarkable achievement," although it remains internally inconsistent and cross-pressured. That is, on one hand, most persons assume they exist within a disenchanted, flat, and materialistic conception of space and time, but on the other hand, they also continue to desire and long for a comprehensive transcendent order, a cosmos, which provides structure, meaning, and purpose for our lives. In their background beliefs people remain "internally schizophrenic." Thus, secular humanity is not entirely satisfied existing only within the "immanent frame," but it is challenging to find a comprehensive language or framework, apart from religious belief, to bring the transcendence and immanence together. In sum, Taylor thinks that whilst our secular age is distressing and deeply ambiguous, it provides an opportunity for Christians to declare that there is a transcendental meaning and purpose to human existence and the world.

Immanence and the Other

How should theology respond to our current situation? Postmodern theology often responds by looking to the *other* side of modernity that has been rejected, silenced, and marginalized. In doing so, it seeks to move beyond the hegemony of methodological universalism and its effect on theology. Although there are many faces of postmodernity, David Tracy describes some of the common elements of postmodern thought.

> Postmodernity begins by trying to think the unthought of modernity. Beyond the early modern turn to the purely autonomous, self-grounding subject, beyond even the more recent turn to language (the first great contemporary challenge to modern subjectivism) lies the quintessential turn of postmodernity itself—the turn to the other. It is that turn, above all, that defines the intellectual as well as the ethical meaning of postmodernity. The other and the difference come forward now as central intellectual categories across all the major disciplines, including theology. The others and the different—both those from other cultures and those others not accounted for by the grand narrative of the dominate culture—return

35. Ibid., 543–44.

with the full force to unmask the social revolutionary narrative of modernity as ultimately an alibi-story, not a plausible reading of our human history together. Part of that return to otherness . . . is the return of biblical Judaism and Christianity to undo the complacencies of modernity, including modern theology.[36]

How should postmodern theology and ethics fully incorporate the voices of difference and otherness? Sharon Welch, in her book *A Feminist Ethic of Risk*, brings these two dimensions of difference and otherness together. Similar to postmodern theorists like Michel Foucault, she presumes a "qualified nihilism," in which power dominates ethics, while at the same time, she makes normative claims about values and structures that end oppression and transform society. Welch's perspective is neither an ethics of rights or care, but of solidarity and resistance—an ethic of "risk." Welch's immanentist theology of *praxis* asserts that liberation relies less on "ideal speech situations" and "universal consensus," but in the experience of universal and unlimited solidarity with other persons, especially the voices of oppressed groups. Using womanist narratives of resistance and risk, she uncovers the discourse of love, mutuality, and liberation, which "begin from a self created by love for nature and for other people."[37] Welch's ethics of risk doesn't disclose absolute moral claims, but dangerous memories of suffering and conflict that invariably leads to local practices of resistance and solidarity. This moral knowledge guides people to do what is fitting in particular circumstances and engage in reflexive and corrective behavior. Furthermore, this mode of reasoning extends to her later book *After Empire*, where her reflexive reasoning includes the voices of the other, as found in Native American and Buddhist thought (as well as Western sources), with the sole intention of addressing the contemporary risks of world violence and American hegemony. She finds commitments to a set of core values like compassion, laughter, resistance, creativity, and risk that provide a moral vision of peace that stands in contrast to militaristic domination. We respond to the social problems of our day, she says, by "seeing differences" and "learning from peoples who have different views of community, power, national identity, and global responsibility."[38]

36. Tracy, "Theology," 108.
37. Welch, *Feminist Ethic of Risk*, 165.
38. Welch, *After Empire*, xiv.

Welch's reflexive retrieval of the voices of the other, as immanent construals of moral vision, exemplifies one important trend in some versions of postmodern theology as developed in works by David Griffin and Gordon Kaufman.[39] Griffin, in particular, uses the framework of Process theology for developing a postmodern theology. In process thought, the creative power of the universe does not belong only to God but it "inherently belongs to the realm of finite existence as well as God." Indeed, "God is not an eternal being to whom the basic principles of existence do not apply, and who can, therefore, interrupt the causal process of the world at will. God is more the soul of the universe."[40] Similarly, Welch's theology of *poiesis* rejects traditional doctrines of God, and instead endorses a *praxis* theology that celebrates the relational power that unites communities of oppression and makes possible the experience of universal solidarity and accountability. Without God's immanent presence all solidarity remains local and disconnected from others. Through her analysis of womanist, Native American, and Buddhist narratives, Welch's approach is cognizant of philosophical and social scientific changes in postmodern thought. She unearths the hidden and silenced voices of oppression, while at the same time, offering a message of hope and care for a growing cynical world. Still, as I see it, although she adequately reveals the hidden voices of human oppression, she does not apply her same reflexive approach to disclosing the "hiddenness" of God. Her critique of classical theological conceptions of God has more to do with her attack upon classical modern misconceptions of God than traditional premodern ones.

To be sure the question still remains: how truly postmodern is this approach, when it cannot escape from the "immanent frame" and its "closed world structures"? If modern secularism results in the dominance of the "immanent frame," as Taylor suggests, then how do these immanentist versions of postmodern theology remain different from secularism? Are they not simply another example of modernity's "immanent frame"? Moreover, this question raises two additional points. First, these versions of liberal theology continue the task of *praxis* and *poiesis*, which directly links to the anti-traditional slant of modern liberal theology. Like the "a/theology" of Mark C. Taylor, who believes that postmodernity must begin with a sense

39. See Griffin, *God and Religion* and *Varieties*. See Kaufman, *Theological Imagination* and *In Face of Mystery*.

40. Griffin, "Postmodern Theology and A/Theology," 48.

of "irrecoverable loss" of the past, Welch presumes that both premodern and modern talk about God is really no longer useful for the task of social ethics.⁴¹ The goal is to find a kind of mystical or spiritual meaning in a nihilistic world. Second, this theology remains wedded to the novelty, the *poiesis*, of the "new," a quintessential *modern* idea. As social theorist Khrishan Kumar explains: "If modernism—including 'late-modernism'—is more likely to exhibit the 'shock of the new,' post-modernism is more likely to exhibit the 'shock of the old'"⁴² A truly *post*-modern theory is one that both criticizes and incorporates the past, and not one that simply rejects the past. As a double-coded phenomenon, postmodernity challenges modernity by becoming consciously aware and selectively critical of its Enlightenment history, while retrieving certain aspects of premodernity. In the same way, a postmodern theology is both synchronic and diachronic, in that it cannot simply reject the past (as did modernity), nor simply return to the past (premodern), but it can only critically reflect on the current situation by rediscovering the *old* in its continuous relationship to the *new*.

Regarding this, William Placher argues that modern theology got sidetracked when it attacked what it perceived to be the classical understanding of God. What it perceived to be the old classical position was really a modern secular (or new) position. That is, what process, feminist, liberationist, and postmodern theologians often label as the classical idea of God is really a composite picture of the God of the early modern seventeenth and eighteenth century, rather than the premodern God of Augustine, Aquinas, Luther, or Calvin. It follows that if contemporary theology seeks to go beyond the "immanent frame" of interpretation, it ought to consider the importance of premodern and classical thought. What is needed for contemporary theological ethics, then, is not a rejection of historical studies, but a "critical retrieval" of past theological and ethical reflection. This does not imply, however, simply returning to an uncritical premodern theology.

> We could not go back to that world if we wanted to, and we should not want to if we could. It was a world of terrible injustice and violence, and some aspects of its theology both reflected and even

41. Taylor, *Erring*, 6.

42. Kumar, *Post-Industrial to Post-Modern Society*, 111. Kumar further says, "Postmodernism neither repudiates nor imitates the past; it recovers and 'expands' the past to enrich the present . . . The culture of the avant-garde gives way to the culture of the post-avant-garde." Ibid., 111.

contributed to those horrors . . . If contemporary theology engages in critical retrievals of insights from premodern theology, then the retrievals must indeed always be critical, keeping in mind that what we retrieve was often embedded in contexts we can no longer accept. To engage in such critical retrievals while acknowledging our debts to modernity is to synthesize something new.[43]

Critically retrieving the old is also an important strategy in all movements, whether postmodern, postliberal, or post-secular, which refuse to pin their hopes on the modern apologetic correlation of theology with secular thought. Whether it is retrieving premodern theologians like Augustine, Aquinas, Calvin, Luther, or modern theologians like Barth, numerous theologians have sought to rethink the Christian tradition considering the past's continuity with the present. This is one of common features of the new sensibility of Radical Orthodoxy, inspired by John Milbank, Graham Ward, and others. Regarding this, Ward's description is helpful: "Employing the tools of critical reflexivity honed by continental thinking, taking on board the full implications of what has been termed the linguistic turn, Radical Orthodoxy reads the contemporary world through the Christian tradition, weaving it into the narrative of that tradition."[44] Ward reminds us that we cannot simply bypass modernity and retrieve premodern thought, without seriously looking at the postmodern turn in philosophy and theology. "Radical Orthodoxy," says John Milbank, "although it opposes the modern, also seeks to save it. It espouses, not the premodern, but an alternative version of modernity."[45] The task of Radical Orthodoxy is both synchronic and diachronic; it seeks to be unapologetic, not hegemonic, in its critical retrieval of the Christian narrative. The promise of a postmodern theology, then, lies not with a simple reclaiming of the old, but allowing the old to critically and creatively meet the new, or to put more directly, to *reframe* the new in light of the old.

Transcendence and Trinity

From our earlier discussion, we may recall that the modern strategy was to separate ethics *from* theology and develop an ethics based entirely upon anthropological and immanentist foundations. In the midst of the horror

43. Placher, *Domestication of Transcendence*, 2.
44. Ward, "Radical Orthodoxy and/as Cultural Politics," 106.
45. Milbank, "Programme of Radical Orthodoxy," 45.

of World War I, while still a pastor at Safenwil, Karl Barth warned about the dangers of idolatry when God is too closely identified with human experience, knowledge, and praxis.

> In the question, Is God righteous? our whole tower of Babel falls to pieces. In this now burning question, it becomes evident that we are looking for righteousness without God, that we are looking, in truth, for a god without God and against God—and that our quest is hopeless. It is clear that such a god is not God. He is not even righteous. He cannot prevent his worshippers, all the distinguished European and American apostles of civilization, welfare, and progress, all zealous citizens and pious Christians, from falling upon one another with fire and sword to the amazement and derision of the poor heathen in India and Africa. This god is really an unrighteous god, and it is high time for us to declare ourselves through-going doubters, skeptics, scoffers and atheists in regard to him. It is high time for us to confess freely and gladly: this god, to whom we have built the tower of Babel, is not God. He is an idol. He is dead.[46]

When God dies all that remains is humanity. Barth ironically says he would rather be an atheist if it meant rejecting the god that modern theology and Christendom had constructed. Modern theology had transformed theology into anthropology, divine righteousness into ethics, and Christendom into paganism. This is why it was necessary to turn to God's Word and to "God's Righteousness." God's "will is not a corrected continuation of our own. It approaches ours as a Wholly Other" (*WG*: 24). God's speech and acts are different from human speech and acts. This is why, for Barth, only by returning to the "strange new world within the Bible" was it possible to make sense out of the world in 1916 (*WG*: 28–50). Without God's Word as "Wholly Other," the nobility of civilization leads directly to the atrocities of human death with "fire and sword." By attempting to secure human freedom by separating itself from God, the source of freedom, Western Christendom lost its freedom in its own self-destruction in the Great War. With the death of God as "Wholly Other" all that remains is our ambivalent experiences of freedom and determinism, of fate and destiny. As Colin Gunton explains: "Otherness—the ontological distinction or infinite quality difference between God and which is not God—is important both for

---

46. Barth, "Righteousness of God," 22. Henceforth, all references the book *The Word of God and the Word of Man* will be cited in the text in parenthesis, and abbreviated as *WG*.

Theological Ethics in Transition 51

the contingency of the created order and for the freedom of the human persons. In a trinitarian understanding, because God has transcendental otherness—personal freedom and 'space'—with the dynamics of his being, he is able to grant to the world space to itself."[47] As Wholly Other, God is free to be trinitarian, and in so doing, gives freedom to the world and humanity to be itself, both in its distinction and relation to God.

Perhaps the most common way in modern thought to reject God's otherness is to marginalize the doctrine of the Trinity in favor of a more immanentist (or deistic) view of God. By using a contrastive model, which separated God's definable properties of transcendence from immanence, modern theology failed to provide a fully integrative model of God's trinitarian mystery. This inevitably lead to the bifurcation of theology into the two transcendentalist and immanentist camps, and with it the reduction of God's mystery to foundationalist rationalist principles. This polarization, in short, distorted the biblical vision of the mystery of God as present-as-radically-other, which removed the proper balance or relation between God's transcendence and immanence. So, on one side, extreme theologies of transcendence, like deism, removed God from human existence and the world, and with it, the possibility of revelation, providence, or eschatology. On the other hand, extreme theologies of immanence, like pantheism and panentheism, reject God's *Otherness*, and with it, the distinction between God and the world. At one extreme, deism sought to transcendentally remove divine agency from the world, in order to preserve human freedom and agency. At the other extreme, the immanentist philosophies of pantheism and panentheism found it necessary to synthesize these two agencies in the God-world relation, thereby making God the power of the human subject. Putting these two together, we are left, with two alternatives: 1) the Promethean option which gives humanity control and management over the world and cosmos; 2) the immanentist option (either pantheistic or panentheistic) which also gives humanity control over the world and cosmos, but does so, through as synthesis of human and divine agencies.[48] In either case, the only real agent left in the world is the person—as god, who replaces God (deism) or acts with God (immanentism).

When the god of humanity replaces the trinitarian God, the door opens toward postmodern nihilism. This argument is developed by thinkers

47. Gunton, *Promise of Trinitarian Theology*, 171.
48. See Quash, "Offering: Treasuring the Creation," 305–18

in the Radical Orthodox movement, who argue that the immanentist ontology of modernity—in contrast to a trinitarian participatory ontology—becomes self-destructive and incapable of proving a meaningful vision of reality. Because the world is no longer a place where the transcendent is experienced as *other*, it loses its freedom and becomes flattened, materialistic, monistic, and self-absorbed. What remains is nihilism. The "logic of nihilism," says Conor Cunningham, is "a sundering of the something, rendering it nothing, and then having the nothing be after all *as* something."[49] That is, the collapsing of the space between God's otherness and the world further collapses divine and human agency, which leads to the probability of nihilism. In other words, in a secular understanding, evident in both deism and liberal immanentist theology, the integrative God-world relationship is severed and is replaced with an anthropocentric worldview that no longer participates in the divine transcendent reality of God, which remains the source and structure of the good. Human knowledge of the good becomes detached from its moral ontology—the moral structure of reality—which creates the opportunity to define the good however we choose to do, including our own power relations. The good becomes power and power becomes the good. This removes any hope to be free from the oppressive power relations that shape many unjust forms of human relationships. The possibility of ethics itself becomes problematic, as persons seem to lose the power and capability to both know and do the good.

As we shall see in later chapters, this anthropocentric logic becomes a serious problem for developing a postmodern ethics, apart from a theological perspective. Although it attempts to speak ethically, it cannot offer an adequate theory of social justice or community because it cannot escape its moral epistemology of autonomy and its ontological atomism. By rejecting the basic premise that humanity "was created for communion," postmodernity cannot allow either the divine or human *other* to speak in ethical discourse and deliberation.[50] Not only do we—as persons—remain alone, removed from the divine *Other*, but since persons remain ontologically separate from others, we remain isolated and removed even from the human *other*. This leads to ontological separateness, violence, and nihilism. Alternatively, if theological ethics is to truly challenge the "immanent frame" and the "closed world structures" it must begin with the mysterious

---

49. Cunningham, *Geneology of Nihilism*, xiii.
50. Cavanaugh, "The City," 182.

revelation or unveiling of God as the trinitarian *Other*. Moreover, as a *postmodern* theological ethics it can incorporate critical retrievals of premodern (and modern) theology in its task of integrating theology and ethics into the strategies of theological (general) and Christian (special) ethics. These are strategies which Karl Barth attempted to employ in theology and ethics. Even in his early writings, Barth found it necessary to develop a trinitarian conception of theological and Christian ethics grounded in God's speech—the Word of God. In the Word of God, God refuses to be *silent* as mysterious transcendent *Other*. The Word of God speaks in the revelation of the Trinity. Yet, as Trinity, God freely speaks the dialectical word of No and Yes, that is, God says No to human sinfulness and the evil powers of oppression but Yes to the victory over sin and the powers through reconciliation and redemption.

CHAPTER TWO

Barth's Early Ethics and the Trinitarian Other

This chapter looks at the early development of the theological ethics of Karl Barth. Because of his significant wrestling with the problems of modern theology and ethics in the early twentieth century, the early years of Barth's thinking (1916–31) provides an important point of departure for our study. Barth rejects the anthropocentric "immanent frame" of liberal theology, by shifting theology away from personal religious consciousness toward a genuine search for the divine trinitarian *Other*; his method is deconstructive and critical before it becomes constructive and positivist. With this in mind, two important points must be stated about Barth's early thought. First, there is a fundamental diastasis between God and humanity, which relativizes any human attempt to reach God through reason or experience. God is the divine *Other*, and God's otherness remains a mystery beyond human abstract thinking about God. Once applied to ethics, God's negative judgment stands against all forms of identification of God's Word with any particular ethical theory and practice. There is heterogeneity between God's Word and the modern autonomous moral subject. This leads Barth to reject the basic modern view of the self, as a reflexive moral subject who, through reflection and deliberation, confidently claims to determine right from wrong.

Second, in response to the fundamental negative diastasis (No), in the context of God's revelation, we discover God's gracious and positive action toward humanity and the world (Yes). In these early writings, Barth is always seeking a firmer grasp of God's Yes, while retaining a commitment to God's otherness. Barth's theological ethics, for example, moves back and forth between the No and the Yes. So, for example, the diastasis between the human and divine, between God's command and the human law, is underwritten by a more fundamental *covenant* of grace, which provides the objective reality for freedom within responsibility. Barth's dialectical ethics of No and Yes reverses the general trend of modern ethics by claiming that human freedom emerges, not against God's sovereignty, but *in relatio* with God's freedom. This relational view of God is principally revealed in the event of the Word of God, as understood within God's trinitarian action as creator, reconciler, and redeemer. So, unlike modern ethics' preoccupation with moral principles and law and autonomous moral reasoning, Barth's ethics is grounded in one's relationship toward God and others, and the various demands that saliently arise from these relations. In short, it presents an ethics of responsibility to God as the divine *Other* as the basis for responsibility to the human *other*.

REASSESSING BARTH

The last chapter focused on the transition from modern to postmodern theological ethics. Considering this postmodern turn, there is perhaps no more important figure than the Swiss Reformed theologian, Karl Barth. For years, Barth was known as the quintessential neo-orthodox theologian who challenged liberal theology, and instead developed a magnificent corpus of dogmatic theology, expressed primarily in his *Church Dogmatics*. For many of his liberal critics, Barth was seen as a kind premodern traditionalist theologian, whose massive tomes appeared rather irrelevant to the complex theory and issues in contemporary theology and ethics. Barth was seen by these modernists as a kind of conservative reactionary, and radically out of step with modernity. Yet, as time went on, these modern types of theology began to ironically appear out of step with the shift toward the late-modern or postmodern. With this passage of time, Barth became seen less as a premodern thinker and more of anti-modern thinker. Yet, seeing Barth as anti-modern implies that he remain always in reaction to modernity. It is true that Barth's early writings display an obvious reaction to the liberal ethos that dominated Continental theology, and yet this negative portrait is only part of the story. Rather than seeing the early Barth as reactionary, it is better to see him as constructive in both critical and dialectical ways. That is, he *critically* goes beyond modern and premodern discourse, and *dialectically* engages the best of these discourses; he embraces both the old and the new. The inability to nicely place Barth into premodern, modern, or anti-modern paradigms, has led some recent scholars to see him as principally a postmodern figure. As Nigel Biggar writes: "Barth's orthodoxy might be described as 'postmodern' in that he makes no attempt to justify his dogmatic assumptions in terms of logical possibility, common experience, or historical evidence."[1] If the postmodern embraces both the *old* as well as the *new*, then Barth's interest in developing a "new" theology grounded in biblical and traditional theological "old" discourse perhaps makes him more postmodern than either pre-modern or anti-modern. So, our question is: is Barth a postmodern theologian?

Postmodern Barth

During the 1990s there was a surplus of books that placed Barth in the context of postmodern thought, or claim that he is a postmodern theologian.[2] William Stacey Johnson, for example, demonstrates how Barth's postmodern trinitarian theology shifts ethical knowledge away from rational foundationalist principles toward the ongoing task of invoking and responding to God's Word in relation to concrete others.[3] This postmodern ethical inquiry is perpetually an "open-ended ethics of otherness," thus, never resting upon foundations that are fixed in human experience, but emerging with the claim of being with and for the *other*.[4] Although in agreement with Johnson's proposal that Barth's theology has a postmodern and open-ended trajectory, it remains a risky proposition to draw direct parallels between Barth and nonfoundationalist and deconstructionist thinkers, such as Jacques Derrida. In agreement with Bruce McCormack, if nonfoundationalism and deconstructionism is what is meant by postmodern then Barth is not postmodernist but a modernist.[5] If Barth is understood as postmodern

1. Biggar, "Barth's Trinitarian Ethic," 223.
2. Some important works include: Lowe, *Theology and Difference*; Webb, *Refiguring Theology*; Roberts, *Theology on Its Way;* Ward, *Barth, Derrida and the Language of Theology*; Andrews, *Deconstructing Barth*; Johnson, *Mystery of God*; and Thompson and Mostert, *Karl Barth*.
3. Johnson, *Mystery of God*, 153–83.
4. Ibid., 153–75.
5. McCormack, *Orthodox and Modern*, 109–66.

figure, therefore, it is not his similarity to thinkers like Derrida and Michel Foucault, but rather his departure from the anthropocentric foundations of modern theology that makes him such. As Graham Ward puts it, Barth provides a "critique of modernity by repudiating the secular and the metaphysics of nihilism intrinsic to secularism."[6] In later chapters it will become clear that underlying Barth's work is the motif of theological realism, which stands in direct *conflict* with much secular postmodern thought. Although the *otherness* of God's reality precedes all human thought and language about God, it is the language of revelation, the Word of God, which reveals the truth about God and humanity. It is Barth's critical stance against specific anthropocentric assumptions of modern theology and ethics that makes him especially relevant for contemporary reassessment of modernity and postmodernity. Yet, in saying this, it is also remains problematic to refer to Barth as a "postmodern theologian." Rather, it is better to see him as a modern theologian who wrestles with the ambiguities—or double-edged nature—of modern thought, thus, opening up an alternative way to think about theology and ethics that resonates well with our current postmodern situation (or postmodernity). This is why Barth's thought remains current and relevant to our circumstances today.

Therefore, it is reductionistic to equate Barth with the intellectual currents of postmodernism. It is true that Barth's trajectory departs from many of the modernist presuppositions that lay behind the liberal theology of his day, but he also challenges the deconstructivist claims of postmodern*ism* in our day. Barth's thought remains critical of both modern epistemological foundationalism and postmodern nonfoundationalism. To assume otherwise undermines Barth's own *realist* conceptions of the self-positing Word. Put differently, not only does Barth reject the anthropocentric foundations of modern epistemological realism, but he would also reject the postmodern denial of realism (i.e., antirealism) as found in nihilism and deconstructionism. The task of theological ethics must, in his words, "continually begin again at the beginning" with the Word of God (*CD* I/2: 868). The Word of God is the only foundation for theological ethics. If Barth's theological ethics moves in a general postmodern trajectory, then we must also see him has an emphatic postmodern *realist*.[7] Indeed, what makes his ethics both postmodern and realist is his same commitment to the centrality of the Word of God.

6. Ward, "Barth, Modernity, and Postmodernity," 291.
7. Haddorff, "Postmodern Realism," 269–86.

Why Dogmatics Matters

In his important book, *Barth's Ethics of Reconciliation*, John Webster points out that what makes Barth's ethics "radically anti-modern" are two central convictions.[8] First, Barth rejects the modern separation of Christian ethics from theology, and instead insists that "Christian ethics is properly to be located within dogmatics."[9] This implies that the content of Christian ethics depends upon a broader framework of theological ethics, which further depends on dogmatic theology. Second, Barth rejects the modern anthropological myth of the autonomous and free moral agent, and instead offers a view of the human subject as related to God in Jesus Christ. That is, Barth's Christological understanding of moral anthropology, says Webster, is "essentialist" and "ecstatic."[10] It is essentialist, in that persons discover *who* they truly are only by placing themselves within the "ordered reality which is governed by God's dealings with creation in Jesus Christ." Moreover, it is ecstatic, in that, true humanness can only be discovered "in relation to Jesus Christ" which further implies being a "participant in his history."[11] So, what makes Barth's thought "anti-modern," says Webster, is the presumption that only by subjecting oneself to the Christologically-construed divine reality outside oneself, which depends on dogmatic language for its articulation, can the self fully understand its own identity and moral agency. Generally agreeing with Webster, I claim that Barth's criticism of modern theology further leads to an re-articulation of theological ethics that attempts to go beyond modern anthropocentrism. It is Barth's Word-centered positive construal of ethics that drives us toward an alternative starting point than modern human consciousness. Barth's ethics is relevant for postmodernity because it drives us beyond the primacy of the modern moral subject in search of the *other* who engages us here and now.

Still, Barth's relevance for postmodernity does not necessarily lead to the assumption that he is the quintessential "postmodern theologian" or that his thought offers a "theology of postmodern-*ism*." Again, Webster is useful in this regard. In a later essay relating Barth to postmodernism, Webster claims that before making any direct analogies to postmodernism, one must "step back" and ascertain the general framework from which

---

8. Webster, *Barth's Ethics of Reconciliation*, 216.
9. Ibid., 216.
10. Ibid., 223–30.
11. Ibid., 224–25.

Barth is working, which implies two basic rules of engagement: 1) Barth uses theology as a way "map our situation" theologically, 2) that theology is articulated through the language of dogmatics.[12] By allowing theology to "map our situation," Webster says that Barth teaches us to calmly and confidently remain committed to the theological task, without falling into the temptation of reducing it to the various intellectual and social realities that apparently define one's age, whether National Socialism in Barth's time, or postmodernity in our own. So, how does Barth's theology help us "map the situation" of postmodernity? If we do indeed live in a postmodern society, how should the task of dogmatics continue in this context? Moreover, what is the task of theological and Christian ethics in the context of postmodernity? In answering these questions, we concentrate on Barth's writings, and in particular, his early writings because it is there where we first see him critically engage and depart from modern liberal thought. So, my way of "mapping the situation" is to begin with the beginning, so to speak, that is with Barth's early thought. In this discussion, we see how he eventually departs from of the methodological universalism of modern theology and ethics, shifting them in new direction that begins with the speech of the divine *Other*—the Word of God. More particularly, Barth shifts ethics, including discussions of moral knowledge and agency, away from the human subject and toward the divine subject, and in so doing, develops an alternative version of theological and Christian ethics.

THE DIVINE OTHER SPEAKS: 1916–26

Although known principally as a dogmatic (or systematic) theologian, Barth wrote extensively about ethics from his earliest writings and throughout the *Church Dogmatics*. Indeed, much of Barth's early writings focused on the relation of theology to ethics, which opened up avenues for his later work in dogmatic theology. So our task in this section is to focus on some of these early writings before 1932, namely the essays in *The Word of God and the Word of Man* and his *Ethics* lectures. In these writings, we see Barth's turn away from the liberal theology of his teachers, which began during his pastorate at Safenwil, Switzerland, to which he was first called in 1911. It was the tragic events of 1914, including Christian support for the political war aims of Kaiser Willhem II, which created the first turning point in the young Reformed pastor's life. Dissatisfied with the theology

12. Webster, "Barth, Modernity, and Postmodernity," 13–28.

behind the movements of religious socialism and theological liberalism, which supported Germany's entrance into the war, Barth sought for an alternative transcendental starting point to theology, one that would take God seriously and to open himself to the otherness and mystery of God.

God's Righteousness and Tambach

As mentioned in the last chapter, this new departure can be seen in his 1916 essay "The Righteousness of God," where he uses the phrase "Wholly Other" to refer to the difference between *who* God is, in God's righteousness and action, and *who* humanity is, in political, moral, and religious, and even Christian practice. "There is a fundamentally different way to come into relation with the righteousness of God. This *other* way we enter not by speech nor reflection nor reason, but being still, by listening to and not silencing the conscience when we have hardly begin to hear its voice" (*WG*: 23). This turn toward what Bruce McCormack calls "critical realism" begins with the premise that to take human moral action seriously we must first take *God* seriously, but the problem was that liberal theology had turned this basic principle around.[13] Barth's message is clear: God *is* God and we are not! God's otherness reveals a *diastasis* that exists between human moral knowledge and actions and God's righteousness. In a similar way, in the same year, he delivered the speech "The Strange New World Within the Bible," in which Barth argues that "God's morality" is revealed in the strange *other* world of the Bible which at the same time, stands in contrast to human conceptions of morality. For example, in this biblical world, "the true hero is the lost son, who is absolutely lost and feeding swine—and not his moral elder brother" (*WG*: 40)! If we are to be true to God's otherness as revealed in the strangeness of the Bible, we must go beyond allowing it to provide *answers* but also allowing it to provide the *questions* we seek to ask. What are these answers? Who is this God that revealed in the Bible? Interestingly, Barth moves from the "Wholly Other" language of the earlier 1916 essay to the language of the Trinity. The search for the otherness of God in the "strange new world" of the Bible, leads to the conclusion that

---

13. Bruce McCormack argues that Barth's theology is "critical," in that it is generally accepts Kant's critique of metaphysics, which posits that there "is no epistemological way that leads from the empirical world to the divine source." It is also "realist," in that God is the "reality which is complete and whole in itself apart from and prior to the knowing activity of human individuals." McCormack, *Karl Barth's Critically Realistic*, 129–30.

God's otherness *is* trinitarian, thereby revealing a relational God who is with and for persons, communities, and the world.

> Who is this God? The heavenly Father! But the heavenly Father even upon *earth*, and upon earth really the *heavenly* Father. He will not allow life to be split into "here" and "beyond." He will not leave to death the task of freeing us from sin and sorrow. He will bless us, not with the power of the church but with the power of life and resurrection. In Christ he caused his word to be made flesh . . . Who is God? The Son who has become "the mediator of my soul." But more than that: He has become the mediator for the whole world, the redeeming Word, was in the beginning of all things and is earnestly expected by all things. He is the redeemer of my brothers and sisters. He is the redeemer of a humanity gone astray and ruled by evil spirits and powers. He is the redeemer of the groaning creation about us . . . Who is God? The Spirit in his believers . . . The Holy Spirit makes a new heaven and new earth and, therefore, new men, new families, new relationships, new politics. It has no respect for old traditions simply because they are traditions, for old solemnities simply because they are solemn, for old powers simply because they are powerful. The *Holy* Spirit has respect only for truth, for itself. (*WG*: 49–50)

Without a doubt, Barth's most important work during the wartime period is his *Epistle to the Romans* (*Der Römerbrief*) in 1919. Although, I will focus more extensively on the second edition published three years later, in this earlier edition, like other writings of the time, Barth develops a dialectical theology of No and Yes, of God's negative judgment against idolatry but positive judgment of grace and freedom. Barth's *Römerbrief* is not so much an exegetical commentary on the text, or a work in biblical scholarship, as much as a work of theology in which the text provides the background for an ongoing theological argument. In this way, he uses the Pauline text to argue against idealistic conceptions of ethics, which posits the knowledge of the "good" apart from any appropriation of the theology of human sinfulness and God's righteousness. Moreover, this critical approach is used to attack religious individualism found in liberalism (and Pietism), capitalism, militarism, political nationalism and patriotism, religious socialism, and established forms of religion (i.e., Christendom), all themes that Barth had been struggling with since 1913.[14] This vertical

---

14. McCormack, *Karl Barth's Critically Realistic*, 135–83. Also, Chung, *Karl Barth*, 114–61.

diastasis between God and the world, says Paul Chung, "is structured in a dialectical and organic way rather than remaining dualistic. According to Barth, the power of God erupts from above, cutting through the world longitudinally or perpendicularity."[15] Unlike the second edition, Barth develops an *organicist* view of God's kingdom, begun by Jesus Christ, which continues to grow and develop dialectically and analogously in a way that both challenges and affirms the social order. Unlike liberal theology, however, Barth insists that it is wrongheaded to equate "God's revolution" or God's kingdom with any particular social movement, ideology, or ethical theory. "The cause of divine renewal may not be mixed up with the cause of human progress. The divine may not be politicized and the human not divinized not even for the sake of democracy and social democracy."[16] Yet, once this diastasis is affirmed, Christians can dialectically affirm that God's action is a "counter-movement for freedom."[17] Such a freedom is not antinomian because Paul admonishes Christians toward moral exhortation, which means practicing love and justice toward others, while if need be, resisting legitimate authority. Barth admits there are "confused situations," like the "dirty businesses" of politics, where one is often powerless to do the good, or left with any options except sinful ones.[18] Yet, even in this confusion, Christians may continue to work toward a better world through political and social organizations that seek to improve the common good of society. In so doing, they must not be idealistic, utopian, or ideological, but responsive to God's action in history, begun with Jesus Christ. In the revolutionary years of 1918, Barth is calling Christians to remain committed to God's kingdom, which cannot be ushered in through political or social movements, but only by divine action, of which Christian may respond with their own human actions of peace and justice.

These themes continue in Barth's 1919 lecture "The Christian's Place in Society," which serves as an important bridge between the two editions

---

15. Chung, *Karl Barth*, 116.

16. As quoted in Ibid., 40. Chung writes: "Barth's political position can be summarized as a countermovement to the existing society and its institutions; Christians act and join in solidarity with those who prepare the way for a new society which will be positively and affirmatively consider in light of the Revolution of God." Ibid., 139.

17. As quoted in Ibid., 142.

18. Barth writes: "*all* politics as the struggle for power, as the devilish art of winning elections, is *fundamentally* dirty." This citation from *Romans I*, is quoted in Jehle, *Ever Against the Stream*, 41.

of *Der Römerbrief*. Given in Tambach, Germany at a conference of religious socialists, this "Tambach lecture" remains a mysterious work, and no doubt, would have seemed rather confusing during its first hearing. This apparent ambiguity largely emerges from the fact that Barth is engaging in essentially a dialectical and analogical argument. Not unlike the *Römerbrief*, Barth first draws a negative distinction or *diastasis* between human and divine action, thereby claiming that God is "over us, behind us and beyond us" (*WG*: 274). This implies that Christians should never assume, says Barth, that through their "criticizing, protesting, reforming, organizing, democratizing, socializing, and revolutionizing—*however fundamental and thoroughgoing these may be*—we satisfy the ideal of the kingdom of God" (*WG*: 320). Political and social *praxis*, no matter how good, cannot usher in the fulfillment of God's kingdom. This diastasis, however, unveils the hidden Yes of God's gracious action. The purpose for redirecting his socialist audience away from the preoccupation with the *praxis*, is to positively direct them towards Christ, who is and remains the source of both the Christian's "affirmation" and "criticism," both the Yes and No, of the social order. It follows that Christian social ethics, at its core, is eschatological; it must seek to be aware of, responding to, and wait for God's eschatological action. By beginning with divine agency, the positive dialectic affirms that Christian identity and ethics is not so much a position or "standpoint" as much as it is a "way of life" that remains attentive to the God's "movement in history." As Barth writes: "[For] our position is really an instant in a *movement*," he adds, "and any view of it is comparable to the momentary view of a bird in flight" (*WG*: 282). What Barth is saying is that the human position, the position of being a faithful actor in the world, remains unstable by itself without God's prior action. It is God's movement or God's agency "from a third dimension" that remains the grounding for all human action, including the praxis of religious socialism. It is God's movement, he further states, "which transcends and yet penetrates all these other movements and give them their inner meaning and motive" (*WG*: 283). Christian social action cannot be strictly identified with God's action, but neither can it be completely separated from it, making it irrelevant to God's purposes in history.

The question still remains: what does Christian moral responsibility mean considering "God's movement" in history? How can human action be *related* to divine action? In the Tambach lecture, as in other early writings, Barth dialectical reasoning consistently returns to the No as a way to reveal the hidden Yes. Christian responsibility cannot begin with an "abstract" conception of the good, as defined by Enlightenment "perfect criticism," that is, Christians cannot assume that they really *know* the good—as revealed in God's movement. Both our moral knowledge and action stand under God's judgment. Saying this however, should not lead to a passive acceptance of the status quo with "perfect naiveté" (*WG*: 320). Christians should not be in despair or remain frozen in their social action. Rather, Christians should dialectically engage society, which means neither seeking to control or "clericalize society" or abandoned society and give it up to be "ruled by its own logos" and "its own hypostases and powers" (*WG*: 280). Once Christians reject these extreme positions of domination and abandonment, they can begin to look for God's revealed Yes as "an *affirmation* of the world as it is" (*WG*: 298). In this context he develops an *analogy* between divine and human action, namely that the human is a *parable* of the divine. Consequently Christian social action remains only *parabolic* of its "heavenly analogue" and in no way can be strictly identified with God's action in history. The purpose here is not to diminish human action, but only to place human action within the context of divine action, or put differently, he seeks to resituate human agency and freedom within God's agency and freedom. God's action remains a mystery, an otherness, to which we may point and wait, but also the ground on which we choose to act. "The *other*," he declares, "which we try to represent by parable in our thought, speech and action, the *other*, for whose actual appearing we yearn, being tired of mere parables, is not simply some other thing, but is the wholly other kingdom which is *God's*" (*WG*: 320). So, although God's No relativizes a strict identification of human with divine action, God's Yes, affirms human *parabolic* action, which provides for a basis for Christian social action and witness. The Christian view of society should neither be entirely "culture-affirming" nor "culture-denying" but mixture of both and seen in light of God's Yes and No.

Dialectical Movement and Romans II

In looking at these various early writings, we continue to see a dialectical pattern of criticism (or deconstruction) and affirmation, or simply put, the No and Yes. This gets us at the heart of Barth's "back and forth" theological logic of reasoning, which at this point, must be discussed in more detail, given the fact that Barth himself began thinking about theological method at this point in his development. To begin, let us distinguish between two kinds of dialectical thinking, with one being vertical and the other horizontal; one being the relationship of human and divine and the other relating to human thought more generally. For Barth, the horizontal dialectic depends entirely upon the vertical. Both kinds are developed in his 1922 lecture "The Word of God and the Task of Ministry." Here Barth argues that the task of theology remains a difficult yet *necessary* task of the church. Theologians can only speak about God with caution and embarrassment, yet because God has spoken through God's Word, they must give an account of this revelation. "We must recognize both, our obligation and our inability, and thereby give God the glory" (*WG*: 186). Like Calvin, Barth argues there is a diastasis between God and humanity that cannot be bridged by human reason, but only by God's revelation, which, through grace, is accommodated to sinful human reason.[19] As Bruce McCormack puts it: "Barth's dogmatic method presupposes an initial dialectical movement of negation in which God's judgment is invited to fall on all previous efforts (including our own)."[20] Still, because God has spoken in the Word of God, the synthesis of the divine and human, the No of human sin, is also addressed by God's Yes of reconciliation. Unlike Hegel's dialectical method, in which conflict is resolved in a higher synthesis, Barth insists that his dialectical approach seeks to "correlate every position and negation one against the other, to clarify "Yes" by "no" and "No" by "yes" with persisting longer than a movement in a rigid Yes or No" (*WG*: 172). In brief, it is the Word of God that makes the task of theology and ethics (as well as other sciences) possible but not infallible.

Barth uses this dialectical method to articulate theology and ethics on different grounds than modern liberal theology, which sought to establish a broader conception of human knowledge or experience of the autonomous moral subject. Barth argues that such a conception of moral knowledge and agency can neither be strictly identified or completely isolated (or separated) from the moral reality discovered in God's *freedom* to act in Jesus Christ, particularly in the resurrection. To neglect this is to reject the way

---

19. Barth learned much from the writing of his Calvin lectures delivered that same year, in which Calvin's argumentation includes the vertical dialectical movement from point to counterpoint, from human inability to know God to God's revelation. Calvin's theology discloses a mystery of God that can never be systemized or synthesized into neat formulas. It was this background that helped his discussion of theology as a "dialectical science." See Barth, *Theology of John Calvin*.

20. McCormack, *Karl Barth's Critically Realistic*, 345.

the world actually is *objectively* constituted and understood to be real; it rejects the way things really are. To be sure, Barth concentrated more on the No than on the Yes in his early writings. Indeed, in his introduction to the *Word of God and Word of Man* in 1924, Barth would comment that these early writings were often "one-sided" and made the "No louder than the Yes" (*WG*: 8). Yet, this negative dialectic simply confirms Barth's rejection of the many principles of modern theology and ethics, and his attempt, however undeveloped, to go beyond them with a positive ethics. For this positive dialectic, it was necessary to understand Christian ethics within the framework of dogmatic theology. This strategy would eventually culminate in his 1928–31 *Ethics* lectures at Münster and Bonn. Before we discuss these, however, we must look as some important developments in early mid 1920s.

Shortly after *Romans* was published, Barth began reevaluating and rewriting this book, which led to the publication of the second edition in 1922. In this later edition of the *Römerbrief*, there is a more intense dialectical movement between the No and Yes, thereby making both more prominent than in the first edition. By too closely identifying God with human righteousness and ethics, social progress, Western culture, the nation-state, and even Christianity, Christian theology and ethics had marginalized God's freedom to act in grace by turning God into the "No-God" of humanity. The result was a great crisis. "The reality to which life bears witness must be disclosed in the deep things of all observable phenomena, in their whole context—and in their KRISIS" (*R II*: 425). The *Krisis* disrupts and overturns the notion that human flourishing is possible without divine grace. The central theological problem in *Romans* II, says Bruce McCormack was "how can God make Himself known to human beings without ceasing—at any point in the process of Self-communication—to be the Subject of revelation?"[21] This problem Barth solved by developing more futurist-orientated "consistent eschatology" in contrast to the more liberal past/present-orientated (more organicist and immanentist) "process eschatology" of *Romans I*.[22] This shift in eschatology leads Barth to unleash a more vibrant vertical diastasis between God's Word and human culture and society, yet at the same time, a stronger ethic of responsibility. Reflecting on Paul's argument in *Romans*, Barth insists that "good conscience" is impos-

21. Ibid., 207.
22. Ibid., 209–40.

sible without the "great disturbance" of God's action of grace. Christian ethics is principally about *what* God has done in Christ and not with the human content of ethical knowledge or action. "God is God: this is the pre-supposition of ethics" (*R II*: 439). Only after one sees that "Christ, the mercy of God, provides the answer" is it possible to talk about the possibility for moral responsibility in ethics (*R II*: 427). Yet, when human agency is seen in light of divine agency, it is possible to talk about Christian ethics as a real possibility in a world that denies the *Krisis,* the divine interruption, of God's grace. The No opens the door for the Yes.

Let us first look at the negative side of the dialectic, where Barth sees the contemporary situation as an "ethics in crisis."[23] The modern age has led to a crisis of human knowledge of God, and consequently the good. The real God, the Wholly Other, stands in contrast to all human-centered approaches to theology and ethics, whether grounded in reason or experience. The world and its inhabitants have become a "formless and tumultuous chaos, a chaos of the forces of nature and of the human soul; their life is illusion."[24] In a nihilistic world without God there is no ground for moral knowledge or action. "There is no positive position of men which is sufficient to provide a foundation for human solidarity; for every positive position—religious temperament, moral consciousness, humanitarianism—already contains within itself the seed of the disruption of society" (*R II*: 100). Even Christians are guilty of "arrogance" when they demand that God "accommodate" and "adjust Himself" to what we think is in our best interest.

> Our well-regulated, pleasurable life longs for some hours of devotion, some prolongation into infinity. And so, when we set God upon the throne of the world, we mean by God ourselves. In "believing" on Him, we justify, enjoy, and adore ourselves. Our devotion consists in a solemn affirmation of ourselves and of the world and in a pious setting aside of the contradiction. Under the banners of humanity and emotion we rise in rebellion against God. We confound time with eternity. That is our *unrighteousness.*—Such is our relation to God apart from and without Christ, on this side resurrection, and before we are called to order. God Himself is not

23. This phrase is taken from Clough, *Ethics in Crisis.* Clough particularly concentrates on the ethical sections of the Romans commentaries. Central to Clough's analysis are the important themes of "crisis" and "dialectic," two themes that also feature in this book.

24. Barth, *Epistle to the Romans,* 37. Henceforth, all references to this book will be cited in the text in parenthesis, and abbreviated as *R II*.

acknowledged as God and what is called "God" is in fact Man. By living to ourselves, we serve the "No-God." (*R II*: 44)

In transforming God into ourselves, we reject the possibility that ethics begins with God's revelation and God's action, thereby rejecting that God is the "pre-supposition of ethics" (*R II*: 439). It is in God's *gracious* judgment, not human moral judgment, where the possibility of ethics remains. This means in practical terms that there can be no strict identification, or even correlation, of God's command with any particular political, economic, or social-cultural cause or aspiration. Just as there is a diastasis between humanity and God, so too, there is a diastasis between humanity and the good. In both cases, this gap cannot be bridged by the anthropocentric schemes of reason, experience, or good (or virtuous) works, where God is turned into "No-God." God's judgment of grace lies behind a good conscience, or as he succinctly puts it, "[G]race is the axe laid at the root of the good conscience" (*R II*: 430). What this means is that the No of God's judgment against human righteousness is answered by God's Yes of grace, thereby transforming ethics into a form of "witness" to God's gracious action. Human moral acts, says Barth, "in spite of their relativity, are pregnant with parabolic significance, powerful in bearing witness, capable of concentrating attention upon the 'Beyond'" (*R II*: 461). As McCormack says, "[W]hat emerges is an 'ethic of witness'—witness to the divine command contained in God's Self-revelation in Jesus Christ."[25] This ethics of witness reverses the modern paradigm of *praxis*, which privileges ethics over theology, and instead views ethics within the structure of dogmatic theology. "The problem of 'ethics' is, therefore, identical with the problem of 'dogmatics': *Soli Deo Gloria*" (*R II*: 431). It is divine grace alone, not virtue or intellect, which answers the problem of ethics and dogmatics. Not only does this heal the rift between ethics and dogmatics, but also rift between human and divine agency. Barth links a discussion of human-divine agency with ethics, by discussing the significance of "primary" and "secondary" ethical action. Primary action is one's response to God in worship, which

---

25. McCormack, *Karl Barth's Critically Realistic*, 275. Prior to this quote, McCormack writes: "In the first edition he [Barth] had worked with two not entirely compatible ethical programs: a realistically conceived 'divine command' ethic (in the realm of interpersonal relationships) and an idealistic ethic (in the realm of politics). In *Romans* II that inconsistency was overcome. Barth everywhere provides a critical correction to idealistic ethics and that he makes the unintuitable Christ the standard by which human activity is to be judged and measured, rather than Kant's universal law of reason." Ibid, 275.

"represents love toward God; it represents the existential action of men which is directed towards the unsearchable majesty of God." It is worship and prayer as "primary" ethical activities of witness that that provide the basis for other human "secondary" actions. "As the love of men towards men, Agape is the answer of the man who under grace is directed towards the unsearchable God" (*R II*: 452). The love of God, then, is "extended, or rather translated, into the secondary action of love." In this way, this human act of love is a "parable of love toward God" (*R II*: 452). Christian worship, as a "primary activity" of witness, provides the basis for other human "secondary" actions of the love of our neighbor.

It follows that the human action of love corresponds as *parable* or analogy of God's actions of love. Given this, Barth is able to theologically conceive of human ethical action as parabolic of divine action, thereby leading to "an unconditional, genuine preference for the good of the other" (*R II*: 455). The ethics of love (*agape*), however, "can never be the simple, direct, unmistakable thing which sentimentalists yearn after—because it is indissolubly linked with agape which is directed toward God" (*R II*: 454). Human love cannot be grounded in any goodness of human relationality or mutuality, but only in one's relation to God's love, the objective source of love and the good. This presupposes a moral self that as deeply *related* to God and consequently related to his or her neighbor. Although there is a diastasis between humanity and God, it doesn't lead to decentering or "loss of the self" but to a transformed self, embodying an ethics of mutual correction, grounded in divine justification and forgiveness. This is how positive Christian ethics of *agape*, grounded in the divine-human relation, is extended to the human other. Saying this, however, Barth is not content to allow the analogy to work only one way. That is, it is also possible that the *otherness* of the other remains a parable of the otherness of God. Regarding this, Barth says, "[D]o we in the unknowable neighbor apprehend the Unknown God?" That is, in the "otherness of the other" we discover the "riddle of existence," namely our need for hope, reconciliation, and redemption (*R II*: 494). In both ways, the analogy reveals the human dependence on God's grace for the possibility of ethics. There remains a fundamental correspondence between the vertical and horizontal dimensions, namely between us and God and us and others, with the priority always with the vertical. Just as love heals the relationship between us and God, so too, love heals the broken relations with the human other, who demands our attention. "The discovery of the One in the other can occur only as each single individual is confronted by the particular concrete others" (*R II*: 476). This theme, of responsibility for the *other*, is more fully developed later in his *Ethics* lectures, where concrete *other* appears before us, as a disclosure of the otherness of God. Before we discuss this important work, however, we must look at some other important writings in the mid-1920s.

Writings in the mid-1920s

While Barth was revising *Romans II* in 1921, he accepted his first academic position at the German university at Göttingen, where he remained until 1925. It was during this period that Barth immersed himself in his new task, lecturing on numerous topics in Reformed theology. It was also during this period when he began to more critically engage the ethics of Kant and Schleiermacher. In 1922, he gave an important lecture on ethics, entitled "The Problem with Ethics Today" (*WG*: 136–217). This lecture continued his critical stance against the Christian ethics of his day, insisting that the "old ethics" is "gone forever" (*WG*: 149). Both Christianity and culture are in a "crisis" because they have identified social initiatives in politics, economics, and culture with the *good* of God's kingdom, thus failing to harken to God's judgment. So, what went wrong in modern ethics? For Barth the central problem with modern Christian ethics is that it presupposes an autonomous moral subject that mistakenly begins, in his words, "from the viewpoint of spectators," which sacralizes human freedom and knowledge, while it denigrates God's freedom and knowledge (*WG*: 137). Autonomy and independence led to a "naïve belief" that human nature and society not only *knew* the good but was generally capable of *doing* it. The only remaining quandary for Christian ethics then was whether to follow "Kant or Schleiermacher," because "it was obvious that what to do was to further this infinitely imperfect but infinitely perfectible culture" (*WG*: 145). What Barth argues is that Christian ethics must move beyond Kant or Schleiermacher, by challenging the starting point, from which both depend, namely the priority of the autonomous moral subject. In this context he devotes several pages to a critique of Kant's ethics. Like postmodern criticisms of Kant, Barth argues that that Kant's moral subject is a "fiction," since "it is difficult to connect him [moral subject] logically with the actual world where he must answer his question and live his *life*." No "real person" has "pure and autonomous and good will," nor is "there no such thing in time or space as a human will determined by pure practical reason" (*WG*:

154). Because Kant's idealistic subject is removed from human existence, reasons Barth, "all that we can conceive of the categorical imperative is its inconceivability" (*WG*: 155). In short, the possibility of ethics becomes an "impossibility." This too has made true Christianity "impossible as an ethic" because Christian ethics has been strictly identified with various forms of cultural-Christianity (*WG*: 147). Only when these presuppositions of modern ethics, particularly the autonomous moral subject, are seen as bankrupt, then it is possible to bridge the gap between the Christian and her culture providing a positive way to talk about Christian ethics.

So, only by realizing the modern "problem of ethics" or the "impossibility of ethics" are we ready to listen to God. As stated before, Barth's ethics remains dialectically linked with God's No and Yes, with judgment and gracious forgiveness. God's forgiveness makes ethics possible because it shines its light on the "shadowy realm of our ethics" and "makes it certain that our ordinary work will go on" (*WG*: 172). Saying Yes to responsible "service" and "witness" toward God and our neighbor, implies that Christians can act responsibility in the "tasks of industry, science, art, politics and even religion" (*WG*: 173). Saying this, however, Barth is quick to remind Christians not to identify ethical action with God's revelation, because to do so repeatedly commits the error of identifying the Christian *with* Christ.

> Jesus Christ is *not* the crowning keystone in the arch of *our* thinking. Jesus Christ is *not* a supernatural miracle that we may or may not consider true. Jesus Christ is *not* the goal which we hope to reach after conversion, at the end of the history of our heart and conscience. Jesus Christ is *not* a figure of our history to which we may "relate" ourselves. And Jesus Christ is *least of all* an object of religious and mystical experience. So far as he is this to us, he is not Jesus Christ. (*WG*: 181)

By the time Barth wrote "The Problem of Ethics," he was in the process of working out a more Christologically-centered dialectical theology and integrating it into his dogmatics and ethics. It is this concentration on Christology that serves as the basic link between the early and later periods of Barth's thought, between *Romans II* and the *Church Dogmatics*. Barth's new Christology enabled him to speak about the eternal Word as both veiled and unveiled, both hidden and revealed, in the humanity of Jesus Christ. As we shall see in later chapters, this focus on Christology also helped him more fully develop Christian ethics as a form of Christian witness. Nevertheless, this shift in thought also lead to a more positive appreciation of culture—even secular culture—than is found in his earlier writings. Rather than focusing primarily on crisis, Barth's new dialectical construal consists of both crisis *and* hope, which remained principally grounded in the divine-human nature of Jesus Christ. This enabled him to move beyond his earlier *diastasis* of Christ and culture (crisis), which he used to evaluate liberal theology.

This shift is further evident in his important 1926 essay "Church and Culture."[26] Here, Barth rejects Schleiermacher's optimistic theology of culture, which emerges with the union between God's Spirit and human religious consciousness. Instead, Barth argues that the "work of culture takes its place among the earthly signs by which the Church must make God's goodness, his friendship for men, visible to itself and the world" (*TC*: 344). Barth goes on to say: "There can be no thought of a general sanctifying of cultural achievement, such as Schleiermacher accomplished with his idealism, but there is even less place for a basic blindness to the possibility that culture may be revelatory, that it can be filled with the promise. . . . The Church will not see the coming of the kingdom of God in any human cultural achievement, but it will be alert for the signs which, perhaps in many cultural achievements, announce that the kingdom approaches" (*TC*: 344). God's revelation cannot be found in culture *itself*, but in the Word, which provides the basis for the church's witness to the divine "signs" of culture. Just as the Word is inseparably linked with humanity in Jesus Christ, so too by *analogy*, the church and culture are linked through this same Word.[27] Thus, unlike his earlier writings, where culture stands in the *crisis* of judgment by the Word, Barth's new emphasis on Christology enables him to explain how culture is *liberated* by the same Word. Just as "in Christ the separation between God and man is not a final reality," so too, "[C]ulture *can* be a witness to the promise which was given man in the beginning." "In Christ, it *is*" (*TC*: 343). Only "in Christ" does human culture—not

26. Barth, "Church and Culture," 334–54. Henceforth, all references to the book: Barth, *Theology and Church* will be cited in the text in parenthesis, and abbreviated as *TC*.

27. On this point, Paul Metzger writes: "The question is not *whether* a synthesis between Word and world is to be ventured, but rather *how*. As in Christology proper, so too, here, it is crucial to engage the world of culture not from below, but from above, proceeding downward. As the divine Word takes to himself a potential human nature in incarnation, so too, Barth's theology of the Word becomes a theology for the world, and its own way, a worldly theology." Metzger, *Word of Christ*, 81.

unlike the church—find its true meaning and purpose. In a dialectical and analogical fashion, the church neither stands absolutely and uncritically against or for culture, but *with* culture, as it is understood "in Christ." Because the Word has come to us in the humanity of Christ, both the church and culture stand with Christ by being "in Christ." Yet, there can be no strict identification of Christ with the church or culture, as Christ also stands above the church and culture as its head and judge. There will always remain a vertical diastasis between the Word of God and the church and culture, but this "crisis," this No, is also radically altered by God's Yes through divine reconciliation.

Christian ethics must remain eschatological if it is to remain "Christian." In Barth's view, the Kingdom of God is both already and not yet, thus, the already of divine reconciliation waits for the not yet of redemption. So, says Barth, for our "redemption in its true, strict sense we *wait*" (*TC*: 348). Eschatological "waiting" does not lead to passivity, however, as the church can act today in "eschatological anticipation" of its final redemption. In "Church and Culture," Barth applies this ecclesiological and eschatological discussion to the nature of culture itself. Just as the church exists between the already and the not yet, between reconciliation and redemption, so too, by *analogy* human culture, must reject the twin temptations of "deification" and demonization. The first assumes that the church and culture is completely good or holy because it is *already* fully redeemed, and the second presumes that the church and culture is so evil that it is unredeemable. Both the church and culture are neither demonic or divine, but reconciled, and *partially* redeemed, by the Word and the Spirit. So, it follows that the church neither "undervalues" or "deifies" (overvalues) human culture, but gives *witness* to the "promise" and "boundless hope" of future redemption (*TC*: 349). The church should reject both extreme positions of diastasis and synthesis, of strict separation and identification, in its relation to culture. Rather, in a dialectical relation, the church seeks to distinguish—and then relate—itself to culture by analogy. This dialectical pattern will become a more important device by which Barth approaches many subjects in theology and theological ethics.

Moreover, Barth's dialectical view of culture leads to similar understanding of how nontheological sources ought to be used in theology and ethics. What does it mean when Barth claims that culture itself *can* be a witness to the God's promise of redemption? In the *Göttingen Dogmatics* (1924–25), the most important dogmatic work at the time, he asks the important question: are there "nonbiblical witnesses to revelation" of the Word?[28] Following the same dialectical pattern, he refuses to stand absolutely against or for the "noble pagan's" witness to revelation. On one side, Barth agrees with Calvin and Luther's rejection of Zwingli's apparent inclusiveness of "a whole series of noble pagans, including Hercules and Theseus," but on the other, it would be wrong to "shout 'Impossible'" as a "sign of culpable obduracy." That is to say, dialectically, "[W]e need to treat this idea with caution on both sides" (*GD*: 150). On this point, he further says:

> We have properly no reason to maintain the absoluteness of Christianity. It is revelation that is absolute. Who is to say that it could not come as well to those whose voices we do not hear in the canon? The canon, the witness to revelation, cannot be thought of as closed in principle. Nevertheless, before we extend it even hypothetically, we must remember what we must find in such nonbiblical witnesses to revelation—if they are indeed genuine witnesses to *revelation*—the one revelation at all events, that is, indirect communication of the hidden God who is as such the revealed God, God's encounter with us, and hence the cross and the resurrection, offence and faith. This is the issue in the canon, in the OT and the NT. This is what the witness to revelation, to the incarnation, to Christ, is all about. (*GD*: 150)

In this passage Barth remains cautious about extreme positions of exclusion and inclusion. "It makes no sense to shut the gates of the castle" and exclude all voices, nor does it make sense to "tear down the gates" and open them to all voices (*GD*: 150). Rejecting these extremes, the theologian must begin with the "indirect communication" of revelation of God in history, namely the incarnation in Jesus Christ. This remains the only absolute. Nevertheless, once this is said, the theologian can then dialectically determine which sources give witness to this reality. "All reflection on how God *can* reveal himself is in truth only 'thinking after' of the fact that God *has* revealed himself" (*GD*: 151). In Barth's judgment, the Bible, as well as legitimate nonbiblical sources, can only *point* to the objective revelation in the Word—it cannot *claim* to be that revelation. In this way, the Scriptural, or even non-Scriptural, witness can only seek to demonstrate how "the full paradox of God's encounter with us is seen and expressed and not in some way concealed, expunged, softened, or eliminated" (*GD*: 150). The

---

28. Barth, *Göttingen Dogmatics*, 150. Henceforth, all references to this book will be cited in the text in parenthesis, and abbreviated as *GD*.

particularity of the revelation in the Christ event, doesn't give us general ideas about "God," but remains the only standard by which biblical and nonbiblical sources are evaluated. No doubt this criteria makes the witnessing task more difficult for nonbiblical sources than for biblical sources, and even Old Testament sources than New Testament ones. Barth does not rule out in *principle* any source of knowledge that may give witness to the particularity of revelation in the Word of God. As we shall see, in the *Church Dogmatics*, he develops a more positive account about how secular voices of others ought to be incorporated.

ETHICS LECTURES: 1928–31

After spending four years at Göttingen, Barth took positions at Münster in 1925 and Bonn in 1930. The Swiss theologian remained in Germany until 1935, when he was barred from teaching in the university because of his resistance to the Nazi regime. Afterwards he returned to Switzerland, where he became professor at Basel until his retirement in 1962. Nevertheless, returning to our narrative, we've seen that in mid-1920s there were some important developments in Barth's theology and ethics. It is these developments that lay the foundation for his 1928–31 "Ethics" lectures at Münster and Bonn, which bring to completion the development of his early thought in theological and Christian ethics.[29] Similar to the role the *Göttingen Dogmatics* plays in Barth's dogmatics, it is his *Ethics* that becomes the basis for his mature ethical thought in the *Church Dogmatics* and other social and political writings. In these lectures he sets in motion the basic themes that would occupy him throughout his career, including the revelation of the Word of God, its threefold embodiment in God's trinitarian actions of creation, reconciliation, and redemption, and the divine command that emerges within these relational spheres. This work is divided into four chapters, with the first hundred pages devoted to the theoretical issues involved in theological ethics (introduction), and the other chapters each devoted to an ethics of creation (two), reconciliation (three), and redemption (four). My discussion of the text will focus mostly on the "Introduction," as this lays the groundwork for his theological ethics as a whole. After that, I discuss his trinitarian ethics of creation, reconciliation, and redemption.

---

29. Barth, *Ethics*. Henceforth, all references to this book will be cited in the text in parenthesis, and abbreviated as *ET*.

The Way of Theological Ethics

Christian ethicists cannot underestimate the importance of Barth's *Ethics*, not only in his entire theological corpus, but in the entire history of theological ethics. This work is important because it attempts to completely restructure the task of ethics from the standpoint of the revelation of divine *Other* as creator, reconciler, and redeemer. The entire work presents a new theological grounding, says John Webster, which makes Barth's *Ethics* a "strikingly anti-modern text." "In its own way," adds Webster, "it is as subversive of some of the axioms of modernity as is the work of Heidegger and Wittgenstein."[30] Webster further writes:

> Barth's quarrel with modernity (whether in philosophical or Christian dress) is that it falsely considers the transcendent freedom of God's will to be essentially alien to the cause of humanity, and thereby commits itself to develop an anthropology in which the only safe haven against the insistent requirements of God is undermined moral inwardness, Barth's understanding of God as Word—communication presence evoking moral response—and of human agency as truly itself when exercised in the "the direction corresponding to [God's] own order," are not the least part of his legacy to Christian theology of moral knowledge, will and freedom.[31]

In *Ethics* Barth intends to develop a "theological way" to do Christian ethics, thereby challenging any notion of ethics that defines the good apart from God's revelation in the Word of God. "If theological ethics speaks about man," he says, "it does not have in view man as he understands himself but man as he knows that he is understood, as he finds himself addressed by the Word of God that has come to him" (*ET*: 461). Barth's concern here is not just with carving out a space for theological convictions within the sphere of ethics, but undermining the modernist epistemological foundations of ethics, while at the same time, demonstrating an entirely new pathway for theological ethics. It presents both a No and a Yes. On one side, like earlier writings, he begins with a No, a formal criticizing of the Enlightenment view of the autonomous self and moral agency, or as Webster puts it, the "primacy

---

30. Webster, *Barth's Moral Theology*, 42. Webster further writes: "Like those philosophical figures, Barth does not make interiority fundamental to what it means to be human. One of the most important themes of the *Ethics* lectures is Barth's persistent refusal to allow that moral consciousness is basic." Ibid., 42.

31. Ibid., 64.

of inwardness."[32] A strictly "theological" ethics shatters the "egocentricity" of a "human ethics" that presumes an autonomous moral agent who claims that "self-reflection, self-understanding, and self-responsibility want to tell him what is good" (*ET*: 43). On the other side, unlike his earlier writings that concentrated on the No of "crisis," his *Ethics* develops a comprehensive ethics of the Yes beginning with God's action in the Word of God. Such a positive account of ethics enables him to establish a trinitarian account of God's command and a responsive account of human moral agency that encounters this command. Barth writes: "The goodness of human conduct can be sought only in the goodness of the Word addressed to man" (*ET*: 15).

With these general observations in mind, Barth begins his *Ethics* with methodological discussion of the relations between ethics and dogmatic theology and theological and philosophical ethics. At first he admits that ethics is an odd discipline, in that it often can be understood from and within many different viewpoints, including the social sciences, philosophy, law, and religion. In all these disciplines, however, there is a tension between descriptive and normative ethics, that is, between the "is" and the "ought." It is true that all these disciplines, at various times, engage in descriptive ethics where they are not attempting to make declarative normative ethical statements but simply to describe human moral behavior. The "ethical problem," says Barth, emerges when these disciplines do more than make descriptive statements about the good, thereby claiming to make normative judgments about what is good or right for all persons. When this occurs the "ethical question" of the "morality of goodness and rightness" is understood as the basis for practical moral action (*ET*: 5). Yet, by making normative judgments, we still return to the "ethical question" regarding the epistemological origin of our knowledge of the good. What is the good, how do we know the good, and where do we get this knowledge? Barth admits that philosophical and scientific sources are helpful in the "investigation" of the "ethical question" of the good, but these sources also "become a problem and call for all ethical knowledge. The ethical problem cannot begin where the natural, historical, and legal constancy of human action has not become a problem" (*ET*: 5). The "ethical question," raised by descriptive disciplines becomes an "ethical problem" of knowledge, since it cannot rise above custom and law and appeals to a more normative "transcendent factor" toward which all ethics points and seeks (*ET*: 5). The appeal to "metaphysics" in

---

32. Ibid., 42.

philosophy positively attempts to address this "transcendent reality," but it can only do so from a disengaged "attitude of a spectator" and not as one who is "heard," "claimed," and "grasped" by the "reality of the Word of God" and thus "made responsible" by this divine Other (*ET*: 17). Ethics must make a choice: either it must begin with God's revelation or with human reflection in determining the nature of the good. Theological ethics, if it is to remain theological, must begin with God's revelation.

Beginning with the Word of God, rather than human reason or culture, makes theological ethics unique, but not "isolated" from other versions of ethics. Unlike other approaches, the "way of theological ethics" is distinct in that it begins with God's speech. It "cannot act as though God had not spoken," nor can it find its "root in anything but thinking this object (as object)!"(*ET*: 40). Yet, saying this also implies that theological ethics should remain in conversation with other disciplines, particularly philosophical ethics. Barth's explanation of the "way of theological ethics" is distinguished from three other approaches: 1) one extreme is the "synthesis" or "apologetic" type, which translates Christian ethics into a generalist or common language like philosophy; 2) the other extreme is the "diastasis" or "isolationist" approach, which contrasts Christian norms from outside ones, thus, limiting Christian ethics to confines of the church; and 3) is the mediating Thomistic theory of Roman Catholic moral theology, which allows the particularity of the theological to build upon the generality of natural law.

With this in mind, let us turn to each of these theories in more depth. The first method, which Barth calls the "apologetics" or the "synthesis" approach, attempts "to establish and justify theological thinking in the context of philosophical, or, more generally and precisely, nontheological thinking" (*ET*: 21). In this approach, theological convictions remain epistemologically grounded in various foundationalist forms of underlying philosophical or scientific rationality. Distinctive theological claims about moral knowledge and action, of human agency and deliberation, are synthesized or absorbed into a larger "general" nontheological or secular worldview. The "apologetic" intention here is that Christian particularity will appear more rational or coherent to others outside the Christian community, particularly to other intellectuals in the academy. It intends to incorporate the particular into the general. In contrast, at the opposite extreme, is the second method Barth calls the "method of isolation" or the "diastasis" approach (*ET*: 24). Here ethics relies only on its special sources and remains essential *ecclesial* in content and applicability as "what Christian morality requires is only binding for Christians" (*ET*: 27). Christian moral knowledge is grounded in "secrets which philosophy, to be serious philosophy, neither knows nor ought to know" (*ET*: 27). It follows that the particularly of Christian morality is either seen as the only moral truth or placed side-by-side with other versions of ethics. Either way, the focus remains set firmly on the particular and not the general. Lastly, the mediating position of Catholic moral theology seeks to relate moral philosophy and theology, the general and the particular, with the latter surpassing or perfecting the former. Grace builds on nature, faith builds on reason, and theological virtue builds on the cardinal virtues. Specific theological claims about God, humanity, sin, grace, justification, sanctification builds on natural conceptions of law, virtue, and conscience. This theory is grounded in "the fundamental Roman Catholic conception of the harmony, rooted in the concept of being, between nature and supernature, nature and grace, reason and revelation, man and God" (*ET*: 30). Although this theory is preferable to the other two by seeking to mediate between the general and the particular, its weakness lies in the fact that it invariably collapses into another version of the "apologetics" model. "Is not metaphysics viewed as a basic discipline superior to both philosophy and theology, a relapse into apologetics," which in turn, ends up losing its "true origin and subject matter" (*ET*: 31). The God of grace, as being and act, which is revealed in the Word of God, is replaced with another God, of law or virtue, that humanity can "master" and control through rational deliberation and understanding. God's free command is lost. Not only does this theory drift toward the "synthesis" approach, but it also, at other times, drifts toward the "isolationist" approach when specific theological directives are applied only to the church, or Christians within the church. So, for example, a special ethical demand, like "love of enemies," can be seen as a particular council of perfection applying only saints, while a general directive regarding justice applies to everyone. Love and justice are separated. So, inasmuch as moral theology seeks to mediate, it tends to fall to one side or the other of the dialectic between synthesis and diastasis, or the general and the particular.

A theological ethics rooted in God's trinitarian action rejects all these theories. Barth writes, "we cannot approve either the methodological subordination of Christian morals to morals in general, the independence of morals in general alongside and over against Christian morals, or the assumed superiority of a theological moral teaching that draws from a special source" (*ET*: 46). Barth's dialectical logic stands against these three approaches for two basic reasons. The first reason has to do with how dogmatic *theology* stands in relation to other viewpoints. How is theology understood in these moral theories? If the "apologetics" extreme drifts toward secular *reductionism* in which the Christian voice is lost, then the latter "isolationist" view drifts toward theological *esotericism* in which the voice of the other is lost. If the first leads to the inferiority and undervaluing of theology, the second leads to the superiority and overvaluing of theology in dialogue with other sciences. "Theology does not really need to safeguard its own rank among the other sciences by a frenzied posture of absoluteness or by allotting to the others roles which it regards as less valuable in relation to its own" (*ET*: 41).[33] The mediating position of Thomistic moral theology also errors by drifting from one side of the dialectic to the other, depending on whether the subject is general ethics or Christian ethics. Most often the mediating approach becomes another version of the reductionism, in which theology becomes incorporated into philosophy. The second reason for rejecting these three methods has to do with the moral *epistemology* of ethics and practice. If the synthesis approach positively affirms a general conception of moral truth or moral ontology for all persons it does so with the loss of distinctiveness of Christian belief and practice. It assumes that in order to explain an objectivist understanding of moral knowledge it must begin with some nontheological account of general moral knowledge, as found in philosophy or the sciences. This assumes, therefore, that particular theological claims about truth are not objective. In contrast, if the diastasis viewpoint positively holds onto this distinctiveness, it does so with an apparent loss of a general conception of moral truth or moral ontology, which pushes it toward ethical particularism. Christian truths remain true for Christians, but it is debatable whether they ought to be true for other people. In either case, something is gained but also something is lost. The mediating position of moral theology attempts to reconcile by holding the general in balance with the particular, but this cannot be done without lessening the overall influence of each side. That is, when the general is

33. Barth further writes: "A self-aware theology which bears strongly in mind its objective and scientific nature will be the very last to set itself its own task in such a way as to deny all other sciences, to view them as impossible, or even to discredit them as less valuable, and to condemn them from its own standpoint to a mere appearance of existence under the suspicion of pagan ungodliness . . . A theology that is set on its own feet can unreservedly acknowledge the justification and even equal justification of other sciences. Human thought is necessarily shown its limits by the particular object of theology, by the Word of God" (*ET*: 41).

emphasized the particular is lost, and when the particular is affirmed, the general is lost.

Aware of the problem with each of these theories, Barth attempts to avoid the risks of reductionism, esotericism, and mediation by placing *both* theological and nontheological sources, both general and particular convictions of moral truth, under the revealed authority of the Word of God. The "true diastasis," he says, "is not between theology and philosophy but between them and their genuine subject," namely, the Word of God (*ET*: 28). There is heterogeneity between all human conceptions of the good, whether philosophical, scientific, or religious, and the freedom of Word of God. All "human thought," whether "general or particular," is "necessarily shown its limits by the particular object of theology, by the Word of God" (*ET*: 41). Putting this another way is that all these three theories err by beginning with ethical *method* itself, that is, they begin placing together in conversation theology, philosophy, and the sciences or revealed and natural truth claims. This human conversation is useful but only after God speaks. For Barth, theological ethics remains distinct from the other approaches because it is grounded in God's triune agency, which remains critical of methodology and is dialectical in movement. A trinitarian conception of ethics remains more open ended and inclusive because it rests ultimately on divine, not human, freedom. If there is to be a legitimate form of theological ethics, then it must begin with God's act as creator, reconciler, and redeemer.

The Trinitarian Commander and Moral Judgment

Theological ethics begins with the question: Who is God and how does this God speak? Who and what is the Word of God? Anticipating themes that would later be fully expressed in *CD* II/2, Barth explain how the Word of God is the "event" of "divine commanding" that is "specific" to our particular circumstances (*ET*: 50). "The Word of God is the Word of God only in act. The Word of God is *decision*. God *acts*" (*ET*: 45). What does this mean to say that God acts, and what does this divine action say about ethics? It simply means that God acts in freedom, unveiling the good, so that we may know it and obediently act in response to its claim. This "command" is revealed in three ways corresponding to God's trinitarian action as creator, reconciler, and redeemer. To neglect one or more of these divine events, is to radically misunderstand both the reality of God and the good that is revealed. For example, it would be wrong to begin *only* with an ethics of creation or "orders of creation" theology or "natural law" as is found in many versions of Protestant and Catholic theology. This theologically overlooks the fact that God makes it possible for Christians to be justified, sanctified, and eschatologically perfected; it denies that God has spoken in the Word of God—as reconciler and redeemer. Likewise, and ethics of reconciliation or redemption might become too perfectionist, too otherworldly, or even too docetic, denying that Christians remain creatures on earth, linked to other non-human creatures and the worldly environment. This version of ethics neglects creation by overemphasizing reconciliation or redemption.

Furthermore, God's trinitarian command remains a free and "unconditioned" command in which we encounter God's *judgment* of our knowledge and action. This "unconditioned" command is *specific,* namely it is not based on our generalized interpretation of principles, laws, or virtues. The content of God's command is not some general information from which we may, through deliberation and reflection, determine proper courses of action. Otherwise, God's command would be "conditional" upon our own perceptions, reflections, and deliberations. "The truth of God is not a general and theoretical and consequently conditioned truth. It reveals itself in the concrete event of our own conduct as our decision for or against the command of the good that is given to us" (*ET*: 63). Barth is careful here to not equate the divine command with abstract propositions but with a gracious action that confronts our ill-conceived autonomy by calling us to forgiveness and moral responsibility. The command to be responsible is not impersonal and abstract but is personal and concrete. "Thus the good arises out of responsibility and therefore out of the divine speaking to which man responds with his acts." In brief, he says, "[M]an does good acts when he is led by God to responsibility" (*ET*: 49). That is, in the promise of redemption, the Christian in hope, guided by his conscience, lives out in gratitude, freedom, and responsibility. In response to God's command as redeemer, "my conduct at this moment is a step forward, i.e. a step toward the future which is promised me by God's Word, the future of the Lord and lordship over all people and things" (*ET*: 487). As a "child of God," the redeemed person can step forward in freedom and responsibility. The divine command is not a heteronomous command that bears down upon us as much as a declaration and *permission* to step out in freedom and confidence and openly respond to our circumstances in ways that seem fitting to God's gracious claim upon us.

It is very important to understand that Barth's account of theological ethics cannot be equated or linked with any particular moral theory. God's command is not an "object of theory" but the trinitarian *action* of the living God in the command of "life" (creation), "law" (reconciliation), and "promise" (redemption) (*ET*: 77). Consequently, Barth neither endorses a divine command theory, nor any deontological moral philosophy, such as Kant's "categorical imperative." Unlike these theories, God's command is not an abstract principle or rule, as much as an invitation to act in responsible freedom to God's prior action upon us and the world. All ethical theory, Barth argues, involves "synergism" between the good (or God) and the human moral agent. This synergism "pretends to be idealistic," but remains an "ethics of conditioned truth, and therefore an ethics of empty concepts" (*ET*: 80). All theories, in the end, are conditioned upon our claims and interpretations, which rules out in principle, the free act of divine agency. No doubt God commands the good, but this command is not an *abstract* formal principle or rule. "A general, formal, and abstract command is obviously no command but an object of theory like any other" (*ET*: 77). Furthermore, this is why Christian ethics ought to be cautious about equating God's command with abstract principles of biblical imperatives and/or religious experiences. The imperatives of Scripture, he says, are "relatively concrete" commands addressed to specific communities and people. "Their concreteness is *relative*" (*ET*: 81). Even important texts such as the Decalogue and the Sermon on the Mount are "general summaries" of commands, which cannot be directly or absolutely applied to concrete situations. Christians must resist a strict "biblicism which thinks it sees the direct command to us in the relatively concrete imperatives, whether individually or collectively" (*ET*: 81). This "philosophical" reading of Scripture translates these relative commands into absolute real commands for all time, including our own. This hermeneutical method relies on the methods of moral casuistry that promote deliberative techniques that apply general commands (or principles) to specific circumstances and moral acts as right and wrong. This method must be rejected as an imposition on God's free command, both to the writers of the Bible and to the Christian community today.

Additionally all deliberative methods put the human moral agent, not God, at the center of ethical inquiry. In so doing, it assumes the individual "possesses a standard of goodness" and thus becomes "Hercules at the crossroads" deciding between good and evil (*ET*: 74). This assumption rests on the "illusion" that ethics is nothing but the use of "free choice" to fill the "empty concepts" of the good with our own deliberations and actions. "For what fills the empty concepts, the source of concreteness, and consequently the criterion of good and evil, is the freedom of human choice, or, in other words, man himself" (*ET*: 79). In saying this, we must be clear that Barth does not reject the process of ethical reflection and deliberation in principle, but only when it usurps the capacity to encounter God's command as creator, reconciler, and redeemer. So, we might ask: How should we understand the process of ethical reflection and judgment? Regarding this, he writes:

> The point of ethical reflection, then, cannot be to try to find the truth of the good but to give an account of what it means that we *are* found by it, it gives an account of the character of responsibility that our conduct will always have in face of it. The moment of reflection can be filled only by preparation for the moment of action that immediately follows. It has no independent worth—a point overlooked in all ethics oriented to a supposed being of the good. Its worth, the worth of all ethical theory, can lie only in its relation to practice. It is there that the revelation and knowledge of the good take place. It is there that the good is real as the crisis of our willing and doing, whether good or evil [cf. 2 Cor. 5:10]. It is there in our decision that the good finds us and is then also found by us as one finds a judge. Knowledge of the good is knowledge of the judge who, as we decide, declares salvation or perdition to be our eternal destiny." (*ET*: 74)

The task of ethical reflection, thus, is not about the *process* of moral deliberation and action, but about being able to hear and respond to the Word of God, as it confronts us in our particularity. In God's command we hear the Word that proclaims *who* God is in relation to humanity. In the midst of our reflection and action, therefore, we are "grasped" by who God is in God's *judgment* toward us as sinners saved by grace. We become aware of our sinfulness and God's graciousness, which leads us forward in our *responsive acts* of obedience to God. At every point along the continuum, we invite God's judgment upon our reflection and action. As quoted above: "The moment of reflection can be filled only by preparation for the moment of action that immediately follows" (*ET*: 74). Hence, rather than beginning, as casuistry does, with a hypothetical or abstract circumstance or situation and then reasons toward appropriate moral action, the one who hears God's command can only reflect and listen, deliberate and listen, and act and listen. Once we act we further invite God's judgment upon our actions, opening our reflection to God's command, which further guides us toward future responsible actions. God's judgment, or God's prior decision and action toward us, lays the groundwork for our response to God through our responsible action. "To be mature is to act with awareness of the responsibility of our acts" (*ET*: 89). Barth's ethics, theoretically speaking, is an open-ended ethics of responsibility and not an ethics of law or virtue, of decision or character.

In the final introductory section of *Ethics*, Barth further develops themes that will resurface in *CD* II/2, such as how "God's command as judgment" relates to the doctrine of election and ethics, the law to the gospel, and his dialectical anthropology of *simul iustis et peccator*—all themes that will be discussed in later chapters. Suffice it say that affirming God's "command as judgment" means having our lives *open* before God and standing within a moment of "crisis" that is, we stand as sinners saved by grace and redeemed by the Holy Spirit. Awareness of our sinful actions and God's forgiveness leads directly to responsible action. God is the judge, but his judgments are not based on the law but on grace, and not on damnation but election. "That God *judges* us means above all that he *loves* us" (*ET*: 91). He further says:

> It is not at all true that God's mercy comes to us as *we* convert *ourselves*. The Word and Spirit of God guarantee the existence of the relation between the divine Yes and the human Yes. They are the guarantee as they themselves are in relation. The existence of the relation is not guaranteed directly but *indirectly*—indirectly inasmuch as we must always go back to God's own gracious will and take refuge in *prayer* to find it guaranteed. . . . Instead of being content to seek the reality of sanctification in the eternally hidden action of divine election, many have thought, and still think, that they should seek it and can find it in some supposedly real saintliness of man which can be perceived and guaranteed directly apart from prayer and the answering of prayer." (*ET*: 113)

In the gospel, God has *elected* us to be a responsible witness to the truth that is revealed in the Word of God. Our response is our Yes toward God's prior act of Yes "This Yes is to God's grace, as it is itself grace" (*ET*: 108). Those who realize that God's *judgment* is one of grace and forgiveness, realize they are created, reconciled, and in the process of being redeemed; they are justified and are being sanctified by "the internal testimony of the Holy Spirit" (*ET*: 99). In our sanctification, we inevitably return to our sinfulness and God's graciousness. This means being more than "penitent," but implies *metanoia* to a new way of life of responsibility before God's judgment. This is why Barth places so much emphasis on *prayer* as form of Christian moral action. Prayer invites and invokes God's presence and judgment upon us; it requests and seeks to place the person under the authority of the "divine court" determining how one ought to live as sinner saved by grace. Put differently, the Christian moral life belongs to the pilgrimage of the Christian life of discipleship. Therefore, we might summarize this section by presenting two possible scenarios for Christian ethics. On one side, we have the many versions of ethics, whether secular or Christian, which envision the moral agent as a self-reflective, autonomous, and deliberative self, who like "Hercules at the crossroads" freely chooses between good and evil (*ET*: 74). On the other side, we see the moral agent who places herself under a "superior court" of God's *judgment*, who, while reflecting and deliberating, also "watches and prays" and steps forward in confidence and freedom into *responsible* action, further inviting God's judgment upon her action. Most versions of Christian ethics take the former position, and Barth is encouraging his readers to take the latter. One of the principle purposes of Barth's introductory lectures is rhetorical, namely it forces the hearer to answer the question: Which path will you follow?

Ethics of Creation, Reconciliation, and Redemption

The principle command of God the creator is a "command of life." God's Yes is for "life itself," which affirms the human needs for food, love, sleep, health, happiness, and respect for human life. "Because only as life together with man can our life be genuine life *together*, because only as such can it place us primarily before the command of respect for life" (*ET*: 143). Christians learn to *know* God's command through various "callings" in which persons are situated, including sexuality, friendship, kinship, age, guidance (cultural context), endowment and finitude (*ET*: 173–208). The content of the command is discovered in the various social roles and communal contexts or "orders" including, work, marriage, family, nationality, and friendship (*ET*: 208–46). Barth would later, in *CD* III/4, replace "order" with "freedom" as the central motif in his ethics of creation. Yet, even in these early lectures, he still places "orders" within a framework of "callings," which give them a certain openness and dynamism missing from traditional Protestant accounts of the "order of creation" theology. These "callings" challenge the modern secular assumption of the transcendent "fictive" moral subject who can rise above their own particular circumstances and become a moral subject from nowhere. Christian moral consciousness, within the sphere of creation, cannot be reduced to the historical embeddings of these "callings" within an ethics of creation. God's command is *fulfilled* in the virtue and life of "faith," which "bridges the distance between creature and Creator without removing it" (*ET*: 250). Unlike his later theology, where God's covenant-partnership with humanity remains the "inner basis" of creation, Barth's theology of the covenant is not well developed in his *Ethics* lectures.

Although Barth's ethics of creation remains similar to Catholic "natural law" and Protestant "orders of creation" ethics, where he significantly departs from these approaches is his ethics of reconciliation and redemption, or if one prefers, an ethics of the Son and the Spirit. Humanity is not only a creature situated within creation, but is also a reconciled and redeemed sinner, whose life has been altered by God gracious judgment of election. Overall, the doctrine of reconciliation plays a central role in *Ethics* just as it does in his later *Church Dogmatics*. Hence, the command of God the Reconciler serves in this work, a kind of "entry point," into his theological ethics as a whole, which begins with the reconciling divine action in God's Word. As stated previously, God's judgment is a judgment of grace and election, which makes the law the "concrete form and voice of the gospel" (*ET*: 91). God's reconciling "command of law," therefore, is *known* in "authority," whose *content* is expressed in "humility," and *fulfilled* in "love." It is the gospel of forgiveness and reconciliation that give shape to the moral law. Lastly, this alters how individuals "ought" to act in relation to others. Just as God the reconciler forgives and reconciles the sinner, so too, Christians should seek to forgive and be reconciled to their neighbor; this command is for the good of the *other*. The *other* is not some generic neighbor but "my neighbor"; a definite other "who is set over against us by Christ, representing Christ" (*ET*: 350). We have not chosen this *other*, but he or she has been chosen "for us" by God, thereby giving this *other* has authority over us, just as Christ has "authority" over us. The otherness of the person confronts us as a judgment of God's reconciliation to be "with" and "for" the good of the *other*, that is, to be a "Christ to the other" (*ET*: 430). Through the "authority" of the *other*, I am morally educated and guided, corrected by civil law, and influenced by culture. It is through our respect for the *other*, to seek our neighbor's welfare, that we respect the institutions of education, civil law, social custom, the church, and state. Although Barth would develop his "ethics of reconciliation" along different lines years later, at this point he radically departs from a "natural law" or "orders of creation" perspective by placing the state and civil society within the relationship of the reconciling covenant of God and within the commitment of responsibility for the *other*. This responsibility is captured in "concrete tasks of love," or as he puts it, "love is in the most literal sense responsibility" (*ET*: 456). Moral actions of love become "possible and real" only in the context of God's love "for us" (*pro nobis*) and our responsive love of God. There cannot be an "anthropological definition of love without closing the circle and defining love theologically" (*ET*: 458). Barth reminds us in his *Ethics* lectures that most discussions of Christian morality end at this point, with an ethics of love and justice, of love of God and neighbor.

However, God is also the redeemer, who gives the eschatological promise of grace through the Holy Spirit to be God's children. Like the other spheres, the "command of promise" involves knowledge, content, and fulfillment: we know the command through our "conscience"; the content of which is character of "gratitude"; it is fulfilled in the virtue of "hope"; these three together make it possible to have an ethics of "openness to the promise under which we are placed as hearers of the Word" (*ET*: 512). The most important section in the ethics of redemption is his discussion of *conscience*. This section is important because this is one of few accounts of the conscience found in his writings as a whole, and it clearly distinguishes him from other moral theologians. In this section, Barth clearly rejects the subjective language, whether philosophical or theological, that defines the conscience as a faculty of human reason or experience. The main struggle, therefore, is not between theological and philosophical accounts of the conscience, but between an anthropocentric ethics prioritizes the moral subject and a theological ethics of God's command. In the introduction, he writes: "Philosophy is not ancillary to theology. With philosophy, theology can only want to be ancillary to the church and to Christ" (*ET*: 45). What this means is that theological ethics is not superior or more privileged than other moral discourses, like philosophy, to explain the conscience's knowledge of the good because this knowledge cannot be identified with some posited human value or standard of excellence. God's Word stands in judgment of all human ethical speech, whether philosophical or theological, but it also "opens up" the opportunity to know the good in our conscience, through the *relationship* between God and God's children. If the Holy Spirit stands in judgment of the conscience, then it cannot be a natural, self-evident, and autonomous faculty of human reason, which like a "bird in flight" objectively evaluates one's circumstances. This anthropocentric approach is dependent upon "*the* great anthropological myth, the myth of apostasy and revolt, *the* great lie, because deity that is taken up into our will is no longer deity, no longer the Creator" (*ET*: 210). When finite humanity, like the infinite God, confidently proclaims that it has the capacity to *know* good and evil, it also proclaims "there is no God because we ourselves are God" (*ET*: 210). For Barth, such a scenario is unthinkable because it says too much about humanity and too little about God's grace. That is, it says too much about the human capacity to know and act on the good apart from God's grace, and too little about the freedom of God's grace to command the good in specific circumstances. Persons continually sin by reenacting the fall and claiming sovereignty over the good—something that belongs to God alone.

What is the Christian view of the conscience? In Barth's view, the conscience begins not with a faculty or disposition of human character, but with God's character as expressed *in relatio* to humanity in the Word of God. The conscience is a result of the redemptive promise of *being* a child of God. The conscience can only be understood eschatologically. Related to this point, he writes:

> Conscience is *the* freedom of man to the extent that in its pronouncement he makes an unconditional decision about himself. He does this in virtue of his being as a child of God, as which alone he has a conscience that establishes his freedom and does not destroy it. As a captive to the Word of God, he *is* free. As authority and freedom do not compete in God but are one and the same, so the freedom of conscience finds no competitor in the authority of God but is freedom in virtue of this authority. As the freedom of the *children* of God, is no other than God's *own* freedom which is in itself authority too. When we call man free, we have in mind his pure future in his present. His pure future is his redemption. Redemption means liberation, liberation from the limits within which we belong to God here and now as his creatures and as sinners saved by grace. (*ET*: 482)

Christians understand the *freedom* of the conscience only in their awareness of redemption as an eschatological reality. Christian ethics is eschatological, in that it is framed by the teleological process of redemption. Persons, at their core, are constituted by an ongoing relationship and history with God, and not by their isolated faculties and states of being human apart from God. Barth says "to have a conscience is no more and no less than to have the Holy Spirit. For 'no one knows what is in God except the Spirit of God'" (1 Cor 2:11) (*ET*: 477). True moral knowledge emerges with the "co-knowledge" of God's Word, which defines conscience within the "concrete fellowship with God the Redeemer" (*ET*: 477). Barth argues that human moral character and virtue is not something we possess or develop through practice, but is best understood as an "event" in the dynamic *relationship* of the person with God. Christian ethics does not begin with the "unrolling of a psychological schema or the variation of a table of Christian duties and virtues" (*ET*: 52). Rather, moral character and virtue, like the conscience, is embodied in God's relational action toward us, namely what God has done (creation), what God is doing (reconciliation), and what God will do in us (redemption). The task and theory of theological ethics, including discussions of conscience and action, must first begin with, and rely upon, *God's* action, and only then, a human response.

The eschatological nature of theological ethics is further understood in how we meet with and respond to God's agency or prior action. Hence, for Barth, harkening one's conscience doesn't mean passively listening to God's voice to tell us what to do, but actively "waiting" upon God's divine action and responsibly "hastening" toward the fulfillment of God's kingdom. This is where Barth's "consistent eschatology," as first developed in *Romans II*, becomes most operative in his ethics. Just as the future impinges on the present, so too, "waiting" and listening to the Word also implies "hastening" and embracing the Word, leading to action in the world. Barth writes:

> Hastening means that we are summoned. It means that we are summoned in the present but for our future: to surrender, but to surrender to the living God; to rest, but to rest in the unrest of the *act* of life. The surrender and rest have to be taken seriously if our hastening is really to be obedience to the command of conscience. The same conscience does indeed say with great urgency: "Wait." But also says: "Hasten." We have time, but we have it for eternity. We cannot be content with merely inward exertion and activity. A purely preparatory and inactive readiness and openness cannot be what is required of us, but an open and ready action. (*ET*: 490)

The freedom of conscience and responsible action, therefore, depend upon our willingness to harken and actively respond to the Word of God. In contrast, we dramatically *loose* our freedom of agency and action when we think *we* have power over our conscience, character, and virtue to control our present and future actions. The horizontal substance of God's command, in our relations to others, depends on its vertical substance. The divine command—as a command of *freedom*—pulls us away from our preoccupation with our own moral consciousness and behavior, and draws us toward *hearing* and then *responding* to God's Word. God brings *freedom* to the conscience and the moral life in and through our obedience and responsibility to the Word. Barth thinks that Christian ethics is not about the human subject and her moral consciousness, but rather about being attentive and aware of God's action, through the command of grace, upon our lives and respond appropriately and responsibly to that command.

This makes Christian ethics, most basically, an ethics of *witness* to God's trinitarian command as unveiled in the Word of God. We may recall how Barth understands the love command in the context of our obligation to the *other*, as a representative of Christ. There is an analogy between God's turning toward us in love, and our turning toward the other in love. In this way, Christians are both the object and subject of witness to Jesus Christ in the world. In both cases, God is the divine actor of reconciliation who acts upon humanity in Jesus Christ. First, God acts through Christ toward us through the witness of the *other*—who objectively needs our love and justice, and second, God acts through Christ toward the *other* in and through our subjective witness to Christ through our responsible actions. Responsible moral action, at its core, is a responsive action of *witness* to God's prior gracious (and good) action upon us and upon the other whom we come across in our daily living. He writes:

> Reconciling is the work of God's goodness. But we are commanded to be witnesses of the divine goodness to our neighbors, as we have previously heard that we must welcome and accept them as witness of it. The power of this witness cannot have its source in us. Witnessing needs a commission and authority which is not at our disposal and which we cannot acquire. The preacher does not control the Word of God to which he testifies. God himself must speak if man is to speak aright. Yet the witness of the preacher is required and commanded, and so, too, is that of the Christian life in general. (*ET*: 343)

Christian witness emerges within the context of "the reality of God's commanding, of God's Word so far as it claims us men and finds our faith and obedience" (*ET*: 35). Christians bear "witness" to the revelation of the Word of God through God's actions of creation, reconciliation, and redemption, where God's declarative Yes of the divine command emerges within these relational spheres. Christians are in "no position" to "waive this threefold movement of our Christian knowledge or to state this thrice-determined Christian truth in a single word. The one Word is God's own Word which we cannot speak but can only hear spoken to us. And what we hear is threefold" (*ET*: 53). In God's trinitarian action, God is primary actor, and we are the listener and responder. This interaction creates a dynamic ethics of responsibility and not an ethical system based on abstract laws, principles, or even virtues. If ethics "were a system, we should have to be able to trace it back to *one* word" (*ET*: 53). A systematic ethics wrongly assumes that the "real situation of man, and concepts like conscience, sin, and grace, although they may have psychological and historical importance, can only hamper and confuse the question of ethics, the question of the true law, value, or good, the question of the quality of human conduct to be deduced from these criteria" (*ET*: 20). Because Barth's ethics begins with the speech and acts of the trinitarian divine Other's gracious action upon us and the world, he presents a theological challenge to all "systems" of ethics beginning with the "egocentricity" of human "self-reflection, self-understanding, and self-responsibility" (*ET*: 43). In this way, Barth's trinitarian ethics presents a "challenge to modernity," says William Stacey Johnson, which makes Barth's thought "not merely 'anti-modern,' and even less is it naively 'premodern,' but it points to a possibility that may designated genuinely 'postmodern.'" Barth's attack on modern autonomous ethics, continues Johnson, seeks not "negate it but to sublate it, to give it its proper orientation. True freedom is the freedom for obedience, and true obedience is freedom for the 'other.'"[34]

CONCLUSION

In summary, in Barth's early writings we see the maturing of a theological ethics that gives witness to the self-revealing divine trinitarian *Other*,

---

34. Johnson, *The Mystery of God*, 154–55. Johnson adds: "It is not that he wishes to turn back the hands of time to an age that had yet to strive for the Enlightenment ideals of freedom and tolerance. It is, rather, that he wished to reorient modernity according to a theological enriched understanding of its own high-minded goals. Modernity, for the most part, has repudiated the ethics of divine command in favor of moral theories that exalt human autonomy and our own definitions of the good life . . . Barth's validation of theology through the prism of ethics contributes to a shift away from the ontology-based approach of premodernity, and from the epistemology-based approach of modernity, and toward an ethically-based openness that is postmodern." Ibid., 155.

who remains free from human ideology, synthesis, and idolatrous reconceptualization. This enables him to reject the methodological universalism of modern ethics, as he encountered it through neo-Kantian and Schleiermacherian liberal Protestant theology of Ritschl, Harnack, and Troelstsch. Following Kant, these theologians transformed theology into ethics, and the teaching of Jesus into a universal rational moral code of *praxis*. Following Schleiermacher, Christianity is the noblest form of religion, and is most practically expressed through its ethics, which transforms culture, arts, and society. The task of the Christian moral life is to creatively transform belief into action, and make Christian belief apologetically relevant and practical to a modern audience. Modern theology's anthropocentrism places the autonomous and disengaged moral subject at the center of the moral universe, who with absolute certainty can objectively and rationally discern moral knowledge, and with the help of deductive methods of casuistry, clearly discern a strategy for human action in any given moral situation or circumstance. It was these presumptions of liberal theology and ethics, which at their core presumed the separation of ethics from theology, Barth rejected throughout his life, both in his numerous writings and his work as a pastor then professor at various institutions. There is a dialectical consistency of thought from Barth's earliest writings to the *Ethics*. His theological ethics remains open to culture and nontheological sources (or "parables"), while rejecting the apologetical or correlationalist method of liberal theology. He is careful to reject both the extremes of synthesis and diastasis, of apologetics and isolation, of secular reductionism and theological esotericism. What he rejects is that such viewpoints work as a foundationalist discourse for theological ethics. In this way, his ethics remains anthropologically—not theologically—nonfoundational, in that it objectively begins with God's divine action in the Word of God. We saw how this culminated in his *Ethics* lectures, where he formulates a trinitarian command ethics, which presumes an ongoing covenantal history between God and the moral subject, structured by the spheres of divine action in the creation, reconciliation, and redemption of humanity.

CHAPTER THREE

Barth's Social Ethics: Witness in Tumultuous Times

In the last chapter, we saw how Barth, in his early writings, responded theologically and practically to the events around him during 1910s and 1920s. Reversing the dominant structure of modern ethics, which attempts to secure human freedom by separating humanity from God, Barth saw clearly that human freedom depends upon God's freedom to act *in relatio*. Thus, his task, in these early writings, was not to simply contrast God's action and our action as the way to preserve human autonomy, but instead attempts to demonstrate how divine agency establishes, rather than negates, human agency. This theme more fully emerges from the period of the *Römerbrief* to his *Ethics* lectures, were we saw how the events of World War I and its aftermath influenced Barth's early theological and ethical writings. One important lesson we drew from this study is that if Christian ethics is to give witness to God's action in a particular time and place, it is necessary to understand social and cultural context of that time and place. This chapter continues the historical narrative of the last chapter by looking at Barth's theological and practical engagement of the tumultuous historical period in Europe beginning in the early 1930s until his retirement in the early 1960s. Our task in this chapter is not to delve into the theology and ethics of the *Church Dogmatics*, but to focus on Barth's life and thought, as responsible *witness*, within its historical context. We do this by looking at several shorter, important theological and ethical writings. These occasional lectures and essays develop specific themes that will be more fully explored in the *Church Dogmatics*, which will discuss in later chapters. As we saw in the last chapter, it is important to remember that Barth both wrote and lived his ethics. While writing and speaking, he experienced the rise of Nazism in Germany, World War II, the rebuilding of Europe, and the Cold War. In short, these events provide the historical setting for Barth's writing and speaking about ethics as Christian witness.

BARTH'S ETHICS IN TRANSITION: 1930s

Before we look at the important events of the 1930s, it is important to discuss the transition of Barth's thought from the period of his *Ethics* lectures to his writing of the *Church Dogmatics*. Barth's first discussion of ethics in the *Church Dogmatics* is found in *CD* I/2 (1938), which was written seven years after his revised *Ethics* lectures. In this section, he devotes a brief section explaining the link between ethics and theology (or dogmatics). Although much of this material was first used in *Ethics,* he extends the argument why ethics remains inseparably linked to dogmatics and further warns about the risks of separating them into "independent disciplines." Once ethics departs from Christian revelation and proclamation, it becomes "absorbed" by other frameworks or "foundations" like "Platonic, Aristotelian, Stoic, or Romantic anthropology or ontology into order to maintain its autonomy in face of dogmatics" (*CD* I/2: 791–92). In *CD* I/2, Barth chose not extend the underlying theological framework that would be needed for a comprehensive account of ethics. This he would do in *CD* II/2 (1942), where devotes an entire chapter (270 pages) to the "Command of God" (*CD* II/2: 509–781). Here he links the doctrines of God and election to ethics through the divine command which provides the theological framework for his theological ethics. Although the basic content of Barth's theological ethics finds its genesis in the *Ethics* lectures, it is the in-depth theological material that is later added, which sets the framework for his fully developed trinitarian divine command ethics.

Overall, we can say that Barth's *Ethics* serves as a midway point from the *Römerbrief* to his mature ethics, as developed in the *Church Dogmatics*. We may summarize the argument in *Ethics* as follows: 1) one must be aware of the "superior court" of God's gracious trinitarian judgment; 2) one must move forward in confidence and freedom into responsible action; and 3) in one's action, one must further seek God's gracious judgment upon one's action, inviting a divine response. These three themes continue into his mature writings, including the inseparable relations between dogmatics and ethics, the basic trinitarian structure of the divine command, and corresponding ethics of witness and responsibility. Of these, the least formally developed theme in *Ethics* is the last, namely an ethics of witness and responsibility. Barth would work out in much more detail later how this witness-responsibility correspondence ought to be understood. For this to occur, two important issues would need to be addressed: 1) the relationship between human and divine agency and witness; and 2) the moral responsibility of the moral agent. Although these themes will be discussed later, at this point, some general comments about how *Ethics* is a transitional document can be made.

From Ethics to the Church Dogmatics

In his early writings, Barth is consistently trying to find adequate space for human action, even while, remaining committed to the priority of divine action. Yet, it is not until his theology becomes more Christologically-focused in the 1920s and 30s, that Barth's theological ethics moves in the direction of fully relating human and divine action and agency. Yet, in *Ethics* this Christological center has not yet been integrated into the structure of his ethics as a whole. In this way his *Ethics* lectures stand halfway between the *Romans* period, which stress the diastasis or contrastive tension between the agencies of God and humanity, and the *Church Dogmatics*, where he fully relates the two agencies into his Chalcedonian Christology and analogously into human action. By the time Barth published his first volume of the *CD* I/1 in 1932, he firmly states that "to understand God from man is either impossibility or something one can do only in the form of Christology and not anthropology (not even a Christology translated into anthropology). There is a way from Christology to anthropology, but there is no way from anthropology to Christology" (*CD* I/1: 131). This Christological shift in thought changes the way Barth understands how both the divine command and human responsibility are understood. Although Barth's notion of command is essentially a *relational* command, not a deontological one, in *Ethics* it often appears superficially like a deontological imperative. The divine command is often dialectically contrasted with the human *choice* between the paths of obedience and responsibility or disobedience and irresponsibility. In simple terms, God acts and humanity responds with obedience or disobedience. So, he writes: "We may live responsibly or irresponsibly. To be mature is to act with awareness of the responsibility of our acts" (*ET*: 89). This either/or language often seems to shift his ethics more toward a vertically based deontological ethics, and away from a *relational* ethics of witness and responsibility, which remains an underlying theme thorough these lectures. Unlike his later writings, his *Ethics* lectures don't fully explore the covenant-partnership and correspondence of the divine and human relationship, and its relationship to the revelation of the Word of God (including Christology). These themes, of course, will be more fully developed in late volumes of the *Church Dogmatics,* something explored later in this chapter.

Following his *Ethics* lectures, there are other important writings, written in the early 1930s, that serve as a transition toward the *Church Dogmatics*. In *CD* I/1 Barth lays out structure for his dogmatics, as science, unveiled by the Word of God in its threefold form of the church's preaching, Scripture, and revelation in God's speech, decision, and action principally in Jesus Christ. Standing against a theology of God's Word is an anthropocentric theology of religious consciousness and experience, or what he calls "Christian Cartesianism." In this closed-ended framework the Christian is bound by his "personal experience of faith as such, in his 'word-bound ego,' among the contents of his consciousness" (*CD* I/1: 215). The religious "I" becomes a closed self trapped by her own consciousness and experience. In the threefold form of the Word of God, Christian knowledge and experience is opened-up in its hearing of the divine *Other*, the Word of God. "When God's Word is heard and proclaimed, something takes place that for all our hermeneutical skill cannot be brought about by hermeneutical skill" (*CD* I/1: 148). With the Word of God comes a new interpretive scheme, made visible in worship and proclamation, which makes faith and ethics possible.

Although Barth did not formally discuss ethics until *CD* I/2 (1938), he engaged in theoretical and practical debates about important ethical issues. For it was in these years that he saw the rise of Adolph Hitler and the Nazis, the German Christian movement, and the Confessing church movement. Indeed, during these years two additional pieces of the theological puzzle would be added to Barth's ethics by vigorous debates about "natural theology" and "law and gospel." These intense theological debates were not just diminutive academic debates in some theological ivory tower removed from human experience. Rather, these theological debates took place within the context of the rise of Hitler and the Nazis and the growing Nazification of the church and society. Theological ideas matter because they invariably shape personal beliefs and practices. This is why debates over natural theology and law and gospel were not only important in 1930s Germany, but remain so even for today. Not unlike the tumultuous years of the 1930s, we too face numerous social risks that threaten to destroy human freedom. It is important to look back at these lessons of history, and be reminded that theology matters, especially in troubled times. Again, what is important about this development is how Barth's social and political thought, developed alongside his theology of Christian witness and debates over law and gospel and natural theology. They are intertwined. Only by doing theology and "only theology" as a Christian witness is it possible to fully engage in social witness—this is the legacy of Barth's thought in the 1930s.

The German Struggle and Natural Theology

Beginning in the tumultuous years of the early 1930s, Barth's life seems to accelerate in constant movement. Not only was Barth conducting his normal duties of teaching and writing, but he also began actively organizing and consolidating the Christian response to the emerging church conflict over the rise of Hitler and National Socialism in Germany and the German Christian Movement. When the Nazi sympathizer (and "German Christian" leader) Ludwig Muller became Reich bishop of the German Evangelical Church in 1934 this signaled a growing political battle within the church in its relation to the state.[1] Alternatively, Martin Niemoller, a friend of Barth, formed the "Pastor's Emergency League," which later became the basis for the Confessing Church Movement. Although largely conservative and patriotic (many supported Hitler's regime), this group of pastors and some academics, stood against the emerging Nazification of the church through the state's infringement upon the church. Barth's uncompromising *No* to Hitler and his supporters, like the German Christians,

---

1. Barth's worst fears were realized when Hitler became Chancellor in January 1933 and began dismantling the Weimar Republic and religious freedom in Germany. Moreover, at the same time, the nationalist ideology of the German Christians began to spread into the Evangelical (Lutheran and Reformed) churches. In spring 1933, an ecclesiastical constitution was established that created a united German Evangelical Church, with a strong hierarchical polity including the new office of "Reich bishop" which reported directly to the Führer. By 1934, Hitler's government had sufficiently corrupted internal church administration by replacing church and state representatives, and controlling local synods and consistories.

made him a target for both admiration and disparagement.[2] Regardless, Barth became the principal theological voice of the Confessing Church principally through his contacts and the publication of a new pamphlet series, *Theologishe Existenz heute*, which was first published in 1933. In these pamphlets Barth is calling for the church to remain faithful in its witness by remaining theological. "The decisive thing which I seek to bring to these problems today, is to carry on theology, and only theology, now as previously, and as if nothing had happened."[3] Barth's commitment to do "only theology" "as if nothing had happened" was not a call to passivity, but call for directly challenging the theology behind the ideology of the German Christians and the Nazi regime. A false theology of race, nation, blood, and soil can only be exposed by a theology of the Word that stands independent of ideology. It is only the Word that can stand in judgment of all ideology, regardless of time or place. So, doing "only theology" "as if nothing had happened" frees theology, rooted in the gospel, to be *political*. For Barth, the critical engagement of politics is possible only from the standpoint of a theology committed to the primacy of God's Word and the gospel.

One year later, in 1934, Barth, almost single-handedly, wrote the *Barmen Declaration*, the Confessing Church's public commitment and confession to the exclusiveness of Jesus Christ, as Lord of the church and state.[4] At its core, this confessional document stands against the takeover of the church by the German Christians and their strict identification of church and state, of theology and politics, and law and gospel. This synthesis corrupted the church internally through the theological heresy of the German Christians, and externally by absolutizing the power of the state thus providing an apology for the Nazification of the church and state. Barmen includes six succinct paragraphs: 1) the church must hear and obey the one Word of God (Jesus Christ) and no other voice, person, events, powers, or sources of truth as God's revelation; 2) Jesus Christ claims our *whole* life, and rejects the idea that other "lords" rule over other areas of our lives; 3) the church, too, must not be forced to have its message altered by prevailing social ideologies or political convictions; 4) the church does have a proper form of

2. Although Barth had many theological critics who shared his politics, like Rudolph Bultmann, Paul Tillich, and Emil Brunner, he also had many who appreciated his theology but disagreed with his politics, including many supporters of the "two kingdoms" theology within the Confessing Church.

3. Ibid., p. 147.

4. This new translation of the Barmen Declaration (1984) can be found in Jüngel, *Christ, Justice, and Peace*, xxi–xxix.

government, but rejects the notion that there are special leaders (*Führer*) of authority over and within the church; 5) draws for a separation of duties of church and state, and rejects the state becoming the church and the church becoming the state; and 6) the church's task and mission should not be corrupted by its pride and desire for power and prestige. This confession argues that the church's task is not to withdrawal from politics, but must draw attention or *remind* the state that God's kingdom stands above both the church and state. "Scripture tells us that by divine appointment the State, in this still unredeemed world in which also the Church is situated, has the task of maintaining justice and peace, so far as human discernment and human ability makes this possible, by means of threat and use of force."[5] That is, through its witness to the gospel, the church reminds the state of its proper task to be a responsible agent of peace and justice in the world. The state, in turn, must give the church its freedom to stand apart from the state, enabling the church to freely give witness to the kingdom. Nevertheless, both church and state remain committed to peace and justice, in a world that is "not yet redeemed." This is because the agencies of the church and state are not fully separated but only distinguished in such a way that both can become a *witness* to Christ's Lordship.

This document was written in the context of a growing debate between the Confessing Church and the German Christians over the relationship of the law and the gospel. The German Christians used the Lutheran two kingdoms theory, to completely separate church and state into the two functions of law and gospel, which allowed them to legitimize the Nazi regime. The gospel applied the church, whereas the law applied to the state. The gospel, therefore, cannot be political. In contrast, through Barth's influence, the Barmen Declaration sought more directly to apply the gospel to politics. This would be problematic for those theologians who sought to support the Nazi regime. An academic conference was held at Anbasch a few weeks later, in which academics like Paul Althaus and Werner Elert affirmed that "God's word speaks to us as law and gospel." As Confessionalist Lutheran theologians, Althaus and Elert used the separation of law and gospel to defend the "two kingdoms" theory, which neatly separated church and state into two separate realms. "The law," they pointed out, "binds us to the natural orders to which we are subject, such as family, folk, and race (i.e. blood relationship)."[6] Indeed, regarding natural theology, Elert later

5. Ibid., p. xxviii.
6. Cochrane, *Church's Confession*, 191.

wrote: "The proposition that apart from Christ no truth is to be acknowledged as God's revelation is a rejection of the divine authority of the divine law *beside* that of the gospel"[7] Since Barmen did not address the longstanding debate between Lutherans and Reformed about the relationship of the law and the gospel, what worried Elert and Althaus is that Barth was implicitly placing the gospel *before* the law, by placing them both *under* the Word of God. From their perspective, Barmen reflected a kind of "anarchist theology," that undermined the authority of social institutions established in God's ordered creation. Yet, Barth was no anarchist but a democratic constitutionalist who realized that the traditional law-gospel pattern was incapable of challenging the ideology of the German Christians. Barth rightly surmised that this law-gospel pattern, once blended with a liberal naiveté, was the basis for the natural theology of the German Christians. A year later, in his essay "Gospel and Law," he eventually worked out his position more clearly as we shall see, but before that he was forced to write his famous *Nein* to natural theology against Emil Brunner. These various debates, which remained intertwined, are important for discussing the impact of ideology on theology, and how Barth attempts to set theology *free* from ideologies of German nationalism, totalitarianism, anti-Semitism.

This debate over natural theology peaked when Barth's friend, and fellow Swiss Reformed theologian, Emil Brunner published his pamphlet *Nature and Grace*, in which he attacked Barth's apparent unbending rejection of natural theology.[8] Brunner and Barth had been debating the theological implications for the dialectic of law and gospel for several years, and what was the proper Reformed position. On one side, Brunner insisted the law, as a "point of contact," prepared the way for the gospel by revealing both an incipient knowledge of sin and God's righteousness and judgment. On the other side, Barth claimed that such a point of contact effectively removed the priority of the gospel, which simply repeated the mistake found in the two kingdoms theology of the German Christians, and before that, theological liberalism. For Barth, Brunner's theology undermined the first paragraph of the Barmen Declaration, namely that "Jesus Christ is the one voice" in revelation.[9] This is why Barth so keenly focused on theological

---

7. Ibid., p. 191.
8. For a good discussion of this debate, see Hart, *Regarding Karl Barth*, 139–72.
9. The reason why Barth so vehemently responded in his essay "Nein!," was the fact that Brunner's essay had won the praise of German Christian theologians like Hirsch and other mainstream confessionalists like Althaus and Elert. The fact that Brunner was Swiss

arguments that would lead to an alternative or second source of revelation. Although Barth's *Nein* was written in 1934, his final discussion of the issue is found in *CD* II/1, which was written in 1939 (*CD* II/1: 84ff.). In his summary, there are three principle errors of natural theology. First, it presumes that humans ought to seek autonomy and self-sufficiency, *apart* from God's gracious action. In short, it is anthropocentric, while it denies God's freedom to act. Second, it pieces together ideas "about God" into an abstraction that is far different from the relational and covenantal God of biblical revelation. Because it is anthropocentric it creates, if you will, its own *image* of God. Third, it always takes the shape of the beliefs and values of a particular culture and class of people that develop its implications for doctrine, ethics, and preaching. It domesticates the gospel, which results in particular kind of secular reductionism and cultural Christianity. This last issue, in Barth's mind, demonstrates in a practical way how natural theology was linked to ideology of Nazism and its support by the German Christians.

In summary, the central error of natural theology is that it places humanity at the center of the universe, and claims to know God, apart from God's own self-revelation. It denies God's freedom to act in God's self-revelation. To argue that God speaks in history, nature, culture, or society apart from what God has spoken in Jesus Christ is to deny the *true* revelation of the Word of God. It rejects the knowledge of God in revelation and God's freedom to act in that revelation. In short, it corrupts the content of theological ethics. This is why Barth surmised that when Christians formulate a political theology from the doctrine of creation or natural law, they begin at the wrong place, and endanger themselves to inevitable borrowings of nontheological viewpoints. This risks an ideological takeover of theology, and the replacing of the Word of God with some "other word." Further, not only theology and ethics but political thought as well can be corrupted by reliance upon natural theology. There are only a few small steps from natural theology to the German Christians, and the German Christians to the Nazis. Barth feared that this pattern toward theological, ecclesial, and political corruption could happen in places like Western Europe and the United States where a commitment to natural theology (and liberal theology) were dominant.

Reformed and an outspoken critic of the German Christians, made it more poignant, because being "closer to the truth" he was "much more dangerous." Barth had seen others like his longtime friend Fredrich Gogarten become swayed by the ideology of the German Christians, which led to the demise of their journal *Zwischen den Zeiten*, and no doubt feared that many others in the Confessing Church would be swayed by Brunner's argument in *Nature and Grace*.

Christian as Witness

In August 1934 Barth gave an important lecture at a student international summer conference at La Châtaigneraie, Switzerland entitled "The Christian as a Witness." Although the theme of witness was something that Barth previously addressed, this speech is important because he directly focuses on this topic during the tumultuous summer of 1934 in the aftermath of the Barmen Declaration. In this address, Barth remains committed to doing "only theology" in the context growing totalitarianism; this led to various sorts of criticism from the audience afterward. Before we look at this criticism and Barth's response, however, let us turn to the speech itself. What is Christian witness? Whatever the Christian thinks about witness, Barth says it must pattern itself after the biblical witnesses, including prophets and apostles. In using the biblical witnesses as a paradigm for Christian witness, he says succinctly that the "Christian as a witness is a disciple of the biblical witnesses."[10] As a disciple of the biblical witness, the Christian responds to God's action with both words and deeds that gives testimony to God's action. The Christian witness "is the *task* of this human word to *remind other men of God's reign, grace, and judgment*" (*GA*: 95). Wherever there is a witness there is "intelligent speech" that reminds others of God's action in grace and judgment. As a legal concept, a "witness" is someone who gives a truthful testimony about something that has actually happened. The particular testimony of the witness, then, is authoritative in its declaration about a particular objective event that has happened. As the community of witness, therefore, the church *reminds* the world that God has objectively acted in gracious judgment and that "God's right must be vindicated" (*GA*: 95). The church cannot vindicate God but only give witness to God's vindication by the actions of God alone. Consequently, Christian witness must be seen as the outgrowth of God's freedom to act as a self-witness. "The original and real witness is God Himself and He alone." God "must speak for God, and God alone is adequate as God's witness" (*GA*: 99). Without God's action, in short, there can be no community of witnesses, and without witnesses, there is no church.

God has chosen to act in such a way that there are witnesses. God graciously invites others into God's own self-witness empowering them to further give witness to God's gracious covenant (*GA*: 97). As both the object

---

10. Barth, *God in Action*, 113. Henceforth, all references to this book will be cited in the text in parenthesis, and abbreviated as *GA*.

and subject of witness, God "lets the miracle happen" that the Christian is "placed in the position of being permitted to be a witness of His own testimony" (*GA*: 101). "Where *this* dynamic word of *the* testimony is spoken and heard, there is 'the Church'" (*GA*: 97). Christians, in "gratitude" and "reverence," respond to God's prior action in their calling to be witnesses by declaring to others what they have in fact received as witnesses. "The large question which every true witness in the beginning of his way is just this: have you been told something before you go and say something to others" (*GA*: 105)? In their "thankfulness" for what they have received, Christians "reverently" subordinate their own testimony to that of God's own witness. A Christian witness is someone "whose autonomy has been attacked. He can no longer be his own master; he is constrained to obey" (*GA*: 106). Christian obedience follows from God's invitation to respond to God's gracious calling to be a disciple of Jesus Christ.

> The Church is not in the world to present a message about certain ideas and directions concerning the condition of the world. At bottom, the Church is in the world only with a book in its hands. We have no other possibility to bear witness except to explain this book. And if we are asked, what have you to say? We can only answer, here something has been said and what is said we want to hear. Whenever we make our own ideas our theme and subject, our testimony is no longer pure. . . . Certainly, even the witness will have ideas and convictions of his own. He occupies a place in human life; he lives in the midst of definite historical situations. But in and beyond these incidental factors of his existence, everything depends on whether he subordinates himself as he says the words, He is the Lord, and I am His servant. Whatever testimony is spoken in the realization of this subordination will be genuine testimony. We shall not be able to prevent giving voice to our ideas and convictions also; but we must be on guard against being a second master besides Him who alone is Primary Lord. Subordination means this very concrete discipleship. (*GA*: 107–9)

Christians remain a witness, not by their "religious and moral virtues" but by God's grace alone which enables them to have hope and confidence that God has acted and will continue act in the future. A real witness knows that he has been *made* a witness and the he is *called* to be a witness. He knows that God's testimony has already been given to him and to the world" (*GA*: 102). Being a witness takes place in the ongoing movement from "baptism" to the "Lord's Supper." "We do not live our Christian life between birth and death, but between the two sacraments of baptism and the Lord's Supper" (*GA*: 111). In baptism, Christians "become" a witness, in that they discover the "word which overcomes the world, because in our baptism we are reminded of the word which has already overcome us" (*GA*: 105). In "the sacrament of the Lord's Supper," Christians "remain" witnesses in their affirmation that the sacrament "proclaims, and continues to proclaim, the presence of Jesus Christ in our behalf" (*GA*: 111). In *becoming* and *remaining* a witness, Christians are empowered in their encounter with the living Christ, through the Spirit, in the gathered community of Word and Sacrament to be witnesses to the world. In the sacraments of baptism and the Eucharist, Christians are reminded of God's action to incorporate us into Christ's body, the living historical community of God's witness in the world. In this discovery, the Christian cannot remain immobile or static in their movement. In witness, the Christian chooses "flight" from one's own "wisdom and folly" and toward God's wisdom revealed in the Word of God. Witness is "flight" from our own self-witness as morally virtuous people to God's witness. In short, witness is "flight" "from here to there" (*GA*: 118)!

As mentioned above, following this address several students and professors asked Barth poignant questions about what they perceived to problematic areas of his address. Most of the comments were concerned that Barth had not sufficiently discussed how witness leads to ethical action in the world. Many saw Barth as too "one-sided" or "narrow" in his discussion of the Christian as witness. They feared Barth was advocating the Christian's withdrawal from society, while neglecting, even discrediting, Christian social ethics. They thought that Barth appeared excessively preoccupied with the church and not with the world, which is why they insisted his idea of witness needed to be "supplemented and integrated in respect to life" (*GA*: 132). In response to this litany of misunderstanding, Barth responded by saying: "[I]n looking at the situation, in which I'm facing you, I feel like a man who is making a vain attempt to swim against a torrent" (*GA*: 132). With this opportunity of "swimming against the torrent," Barth then responded to his audience by telling them why he came to his conclusion. He then tells the story of his struggles with preaching the gospel while a pastor at Safenwil, in light to the historical events happening around him, including the growing influences of "secularism." He saw the problem inherent in the fact that the church saw secularism as something that existed outside the church alone, rather than something that threatens the church from the inside. In all of its piety, "sincerity," "fervent zeal," and "devotion to deeds of charity," the church identified itself too closely with the noble virtues of Western civilization. So, when the church was able to be a "real witness" to secular society, it failed because it replaced God's action with human action. The church became preoccupied with maintaining, or possibly changing, the world through its teaching and activism, and in so doing, forgot its witness to God's action and became a "godless Church."

> And they proceeded to fit their actions to their ideas with the evangelization and works of charity, with social activity, and, in our own day, with a remarkable fusion of Christianity and nationalism. All along the line, it was the Church which was no longer Church, and did not care to remain any longer the Church of God. It was, and meant to be, the Church of the pious man, the Church of the good man, the Church of the moral man, but, at any rate, the Church of *man*. And now I maintain that this modern Church is a near relative of the Godless modern world. It is the reverse side of this world. What the world did when it tore itself loose from God, the Church, and modern Christianity did and still does . . . My dear friends from England and America, I am from Germany. And there we have reached the end of the road at whose beginning you are standing. If you begin to take the pious *man* serious, if you do not care to be one-sided, you will reach the same end before which the official German Church stands today. From what we have experienced in Germany during his later years—this remarkable apostasy of the Church to nationalism, and I'm sure that every one of you is horrified and says in his heart: I think the God that I am not a German Christian! I assure you it will be the end of your road, too. It has its beginning with "Christian life" and ends in paganism. (*GA*: 134–35; 137)

Gospel and Law

Barth's comments to the audience at the summer conference in 1934 remain consistent with his theological engagement of natural law and, as we shall see, the relationship of gospel and law. In each case, Barth is calling for the church to be a real *witness* to God's gracious action, which empowers Christians and the church to say No to the powers and Yes to God's reconciling grace. If Christian ethics is to be grounded in Christian witness, then it must begin with God's gracious action in the revelation of God's witness of the gospel and not in Christian virtue, human law, or natural theology. Nevertheless, after the summer of 1934, Barth continued to give speeches, but his works were eventually banned, and when he refused, as a professor, to give public allegiance to Hitler's rule, he was expelled from Germany one year later in July, 1935. Later that autumn pastor Karl Immer of Barmen asked Barth to come there to give his lecture "*Evangelium und Gesetz*" ("Gospel and Law"), as a farewell address to confessing Christians in Germany.[11] Although Barth attempted to return to Germany, he was stopped by the Gestapo and was forced to return to Switzerland. Instead of Barth, Immer himself publicly read the address to the overflowing church at Barmen, with the Gestapo present. In this important document it appears on the surface that Barth was doing theology and "only theology," yet this theology was also invariably political in its overtones. It was a theological criticism of the German Christian falsifications of the law, and their justification for the Nazi's ideology of family, folk, and race.

As previously said, the dialectic of law and gospel was a core issue of debate between the Lutheran and Reformed traditions. Yet, in important ways, Barth goes beyond these old debates by placing the gospel *before* the law. That is, he gives primacy to the Word of God in both gospel and law. He writes: "If the Law is also *God's Word*, if it is further *grace* that God's Word is spoken aloud and become audible, and if grace means nothing else than *Jesus Christ*, then it is not only uncertain and dangerous but perverse to want to understand the Law of God on the basis of any other thing, of any other event different from the event in which the will of God, tearing in two the veil of our theories and interpretations, is visible as grace in both and content" (*CSC*: 77). By placing the gospel before the law, Barth reverses the usual understanding of how they are related. In traditional Protestant dogmatics, the law (what God wills *from* us) in a sense prepares the heart for the gospel by declaring our sinfulness and need for God's grace, or in short, prepares us for salvation. In contrast, the gospel (what God wills *for* us), responds to the law's preparation by releasing the repentant from sin's bondage. By placing the gospel before the law, Barth argues: "[F]rom what God does *for* us, we infer what he wants *with* us and *from* us" (*CSC*: 78). The gospel is God's work, which includes both content and form; it includes both the indicative and the imperative. Although "the content of the Gospel also has a form," says Barth, this is not saying that the law is "simply one of God's works, but is precisely the work of God which makes room for the Gospel in our human sphere and room for us men in the sphere of the Gospel" (*CSC*: 81). The law is not simply a list of God's moral commands

---

11. Barth, *Community, State, and Church*, 71–100. Henceforth, all references to this book will be cited in the text in parenthesis, and abbreviated as *CSC*.

or principles that demand our obedience. Rather, the law itself is a form of grace, which is demonstrated in the gospel. The law has a gracious, not legalistic, content. This leads him to criticize any other law other than the one that remains the "form" of the gospel whose "content" is grace. In this way the law cannot be completely separated from the gospel, for to do so, replaces the gospel-infused law with another human law, ideology, or secular framework, and consequently another gospel.

A Christian ethics of freedom and responsibility is only possible when the gospel remains the content of the moral law. So what does it mean for the church to be responsible in its freedom? Barth says that the "Church would not be the Church," if it would not become "visible and apprehensible also for the world, for state and society," and if it failed to obey the law, in "its commands, its questions, its admonitions, and its accusations" (*CSC*: 79). Indeed, he adds: "The Church would not be the Church if these aspects of the Law would not, as such, become the prophetic witness *for* the will of God *against* all of men's sinful presumption, *against* all their lawlessness and unrighteous. Thus, we can certainly make the general and comprehensive statement that the Law is nothing else than the *necessary form of the Gospel*, whose content is grace" (*CSC*: 79–80). As the form and content of the Word of God, law and gospel are distinguished but not separated into "more and less, better and worse," or "between divine and human or good and evil!" (*CSC*: 81) The gospel takes "priority over the law" because it declares firmly what God has done *for* us in Jesus Christ; this is the content of the gospel. In contrast, the law as form of the gospel tells us what we must do *for* God, but only after considering the content of the gospel, of God's reconciliation of the sinner. Prayer, repentance, and forgiveness become the foundation of Christian moral action; Christian *witness* to the gospel leads to a free obedience of God's commands as found in the Decalogue, for example. "Thus there can never be claims and demands which would have legal validity from another source or in themselves: there can only be *witnesses*" (*CSC*: 83). Christian witnesses are primarily concerned, not with the law, but with "the grace of God, which has accomplished everything for us and whose end must be this accomplishment" (*CSC*: 83). In contrast, once God's law is *separated* from its gracious content, its perverted sense of witness collapses into blind obedience to civil law, social custom, and ideologies like Nazism. The law cannot simply stand on its own, but has to be interpreted, or filled with a "particular content," which conceivably take on many social, cultural, or historical ideological forms. Thus, the

German Christians sought to contextualize God's law into the form of the "'*Volksnomoi*' (people's laws)" of nation, race, and people. In Barth's judgment, this "deformation and distortion of the Law" led to the ideologies of German nationalism and anti-Semitism (*CSC*: 91). Both law and gospel are transformed into some form of ideology.

Inasmuch as Barth is doing "only theology," he is also providing a critical argument against natural law and ideology. As we've seen, the false separation of ethics from theology, human action from divine action, and human law from God's law, all derive from the *separation* of law and gospel in modern theology and ethics. This separation, says Eberhard Busch, has led to an "emancipation of ethics from the gospel of grace."[12] Once Christian ethics is "emancipated" from grace, it remains formed by other non-Christian or nontheological moral frameworks that replace the gospel of grace with some other gospel as the content of the law. This inevitable fact alters the political significance of the gospel and the theological significance of the natural law. To be sure, this fundamental error has wide-ranging implications for political witness and its criticism of natural law and ideology. It is the judgment of the gospel that challenges us to see that our values, beliefs, and practices are often illusions rooted in destructive ideologies. This is why natural law cannot be the basis for Christian ethics. In a 1941 public letter to British church leaders, for example, Barth chastised them for relying too heavily upon natural law in their political moral judgments. He writes: "[A]ll arguments based on Natural Law are Janus-headed. They do not lead to the light of clear decisions, but to the misty twilight in which cats become grey. They lead to Munich."[13] Barth often cites the failure of the 1938 Munich Agreement as evidence of the pernicious effect of natural law reasoning in political decisions. He is often critical of how Western democracies, driven by their own distorted views of natural or positive law, became corrupted in their own lies and deception. Indeed, at one point, he says by failing to "honor democracy" and defend the norms of "freedom, justice, and responsibility," Western democracies provided an opening for the triumph of the Nazi regime to emerge and flourish.[14] Natural law reasoning, by itself, was unable to distinguish, says Barth, "between a legitimate state and robber state, between democracy

---

12. Busch, *Great Passion*, 154.
13. Barth, *Letter to Great Britain*, 17.
14. Barth, *Church and the Political Problem*, 70.

and absolute dictatorship."¹⁵ Any society that ignores the political witness of the gospel fails to distinguish truth from lies, which provides openings for false ideologies to govern society. There is a direct link, then, between natural law and ideology, one that cannot be internally challenged by the law itself, which has been separated from its true content of the gospel. The gospel directly challenges the ideologically laden forms of natural law.

In summary, Barth's refinement of the law/gospel distinction, and its implications for natural theology and natural law, follow the same trajectory as his theological ethics a decade earlier. We saw that in his *Ethics* lectures Barth provided a complete overhaul of theological ethics by developing a trinitarian command ethics. This led him to be critical of the common use of orders of creation and natural law in Christian ethics. Ethics cannot begin with the human subject as separate from God's action in the gospel. A superficial reading of Barth's ethics will focus only on Barth's No, particularly his rejection of natural theology and natural law. Regarding this misinterpretation, John Webster writes: "Barth's ethics sometimes gets derailed over overlooking the fact that he uses this (apparently) purely imperative word in a way which embraces both indicative and imperative."¹⁶ What is important here is how the indicative (moral nature of reality) provides the framework for the imperative (responsible actions). We are reminded that postmodernity has led to a crisis of moral knowledge and responsible action. Moral realism is problematic in postmodernity because it cannot provide a coherent moral ontology. For Barth, this discussion cannot be adequately answered without addressing *both* human and divine agency. There can be no moral ontology without accounting for divine *and* human moral knowledge, moral agency, moral identity, and responsible action. So, theological ethics begins God's revelation and trinitarian agency as creator, reconciler, and redeemer before it discusses human responsible moral action. The gospel comes *before* the law!

CHRISTIAN WITNESS AFTER CHRISTENDOM

Church and State as War Approaches

We have seen how Barth often responded to the important social and political events from World War I to the rise of Nazism, including how his commitment to do "only theology" led his challenges against Nazism and

15. Barth, *Church and the War*, 5.
16. Webster, *Barth's Ethics of Reconciliation*, 154–55.

the German Christians and the writing of the Barmen Declaration. In this section, we continue this descriptive narrative by looking at developments after the Barmen Declaration, including later developments during World War II and the later Cold War. To begin, Barth's first significant political writing after Barmen was the 1938 article, *Rechtfertigung und Recht*.[17] It is here where Barth first develops a Christologically-centered notion of the state, by theologically relating God's divine action of justification and human action of civil justice. This is a practical outgrowth of his view of the relation and correspondence of divine and human agency. Before one can *relate* justification and justice, however, it is necessary to reject the two extremes of separation into two agencies and identification (and reduction) of two agencies into human agency. The first leads to the "pietistic sterility on one hand," and the second leads to "the sterility of the Enlightenment on the other" (*CSC*: 105). The pietistic error separates justification and human justice (diastasis) into a pure church and demonic state, while the enlightenment error collapses justification into human justice (synthesis) into a secular church and divine state. The first neglects the gospel's demand for human justice, and the second neglects God's act of justification or the gospel itself. Instead, an analogy is drawn between God's gracious relationship to the sinner and the church *and* God's relationship to the "powers" of the state. Just as God's reconciling covenant of grace extends to sinners, so too, it extends to the "powers" of the state because even they belong "originally and ultimately to Jesus Christ" (*CSC*: 118). Barth admits that the state can deny that its "true substance, dignity, function, and purpose" belongs under God's redemption, and instead become an idolatrous state, claiming for itself its own divine myth and demanding worship (*CSC*: 118). Yet, in saying this, even if the state, such as the Nazi regime, seeks to become totalitarian and hegemonic, there are "no circumstances in which the demonic state can finally achieve what it desires" in its desire to become the "Beast out of the abyss" (*CSC*: 118–19).

Church and state remain related under God's divine act of justification, and in this relation, Christians in human justice seek to serve both church and state. Both church and the state belong to the "Christological sphere" (*CSC*: 120). So, unlike Augustine, Barth's Christological perspective insists that there can be no identification of the *civitas terrena* with the

---

17. The literal translation of this essay is: "Justification and Justice." However, when it was translated from German, it was given title: "Church and State." Hereafter, I will refer to this essay as either "Rechtfertigung und Recht," or more simply as the "1938 essay."

civitas Cain (*CSC*: 125), nor can there be a complete opposition or separation of the *civitas Dei* from the *civitas terrena*. This means that church and state are distinguished and related, and not strictly separated or identified. The church and state are related in their representative roles, namely the church as witness and intercessor, and the state as guardian of the law and protector of the common good. The state's duty means giving the church its freedom to be the church, which in turn gives the state its freedom and identity, for without the *witness* of the church, the state remains ignorant of its true mission. In so doing, the church's role is not just an independent bystander but a positive intercessor and witness to state. The church serves a priestly function providing intercession for good of the state. It does this by simply *being* the church, which invariably "expects the best" from the state (*CSC*: 140). As a witness to the Kingdom, the church enlightens the state that it belongs "originally and ultimately to Jesus Christ," and thus is freed, under Christ's reconciliation, to be a community of peace and justice (*CSC*: 118). Being responsible to the state implies that Christians intercede on the state's behalf as well as actively respond in moral judgment and action *to* the actions of their state without seeking to *be* the state.

Nonetheless, the church's witness to the kingdom forces it to not be naïve about the power of the state. "[T]hus there is clearly no cause for the Church to act as though it lived, in relation to the State, in a night in which all cats are grey" (*CSC*: 119). The fact remains there are "just" and "unjust" states, and Christians must act responsibly in each of these situations. For Christians, says Barth, the "fulfillment of political duty means rather responsible choices of authority, responsible decision about the validity of laws, responsible care for their maintenance, in a word, political action, which may also mean political struggle" (*CSC*: 144) Accordingly, as World War II approached, Barth continued to engage in political struggle. In the same year, 1938, he wrote the essay "The Political Problem of Our Day," in which he posits an "unbridgeable gulf" between the "Church and National Socialism," which cannot be bridged by "reforming" or "praying" for the German State. Prayer leads to action *against* the Nazi State, and the "restoration" of both the state and church within Germany. "It is a choice where I would rather say 'No' with the crudest democratically-minded fellow citizen than 'Yes' or 'Yes and No' with most pious fellow-Christian!"[18] In saying No to National Socialism, the church is saying Yes to what God has done

---

18. Barth, *Church and the Political Problem*, 58.

(justification) and what persons can do (justice). Although the state may say No to the Christian, the Christian cannot say No and "refuse the state his service." "A fundamental Christian No cannot be given here, because it would in fact be a fundamental No to the earthly State as such, which is impossible from the Christian point of view" (*CSC*: 142–43). As a result, Christian witness responds to God's action in establishing the kingdom of God, by declaring that the state is neither "imaginary" nor "ideal" but a "real State" that is grounded in God's rule and not various forms of Christian patriotism or nationalism (*CSC*: 121). In its witness to the state, the church has the *freedom* to say No to destructive power and Yes to democratic freedom, justice, and peace. On this basis, Barth argues that the "democratic conception of the State" is a "justifiable expansion of the thought of the New Testament" (*CSC*: 145). In the church's witness to the kingdom of God, it declares to the state that it can indeed be a free and just society, capable of practicing democracy and peacemaking. It is divine justification that establishes a "true order" which as a "concrete law of freedom," enables the state to embody a "true order of human affairs—the justice, wisdom and peace, equity and care for human welfare" (*CSC*: 147–48).

During this time, Barth's ethics demonstrates, in practice, how Christian witness involves both a No to the powers and a Yes to positive responsible action for the good of others, the church, and the world. So, just as Barth's ethics challenged the ideologies of totalitarianism, nationalism, and militarism, it also positively sought to develop a positive Christian witness of justice, freedom, and peace. Through the 1930s, Barth continued to write and give speeches supporting the struggling Confessing Church in Germany. After the outbreak of the war, Barth wrote and spoke clearly supporting the Allied cause and the church's support for war against Germany and its allies. Barth's wartime writings are adamant about the possible injustice of war, but of the greater injustice of allowing National Socialism to spread across Europe. Furthermore, he became increasingly critical of Swiss neutrality, and how Swiss collaboration with Germany restricted certain freedoms and liberties within Switzerland. Indeed, by 1941 the Swiss government censured his speeches, and eventually banned him from giving public speeches altogether, and even tapped his phones. In Barth's mind, it was more responsible to be true to the convictions of justice and freedom, and allow refugees a place to live, and accept the possibility of hardship and war than to lose your freedom and dignity as a nation. Barth's critical stance against the Swiss government led to ongoing tense relationship between Barth and state authorities throughout the postwar years, and even until his death in 1968.

Postwar Cooperation: Two Communities of Witness

After the end of the war, Barth changed his political message from one of resistance to the Nazi regime to one of forgiveness and reconciliation with Germany. Political responsibility should lead toward the fostering of civil community where the "concepts of order, freedom, community, power and responsibility are balanced in equal proportions, where none of these elements is made an absolute dominating all the others."[19] Although Barth generally preferred the constitutional democracies of the West, his non-ideological perspective led him to take a position "between West and East," namely between a Christian anti-communism and a Christian pro-communism. This position was controversial, to say the least. He was severely criticized for not speaking out against Soviet aggression, like he had done against Nazi Germany. Nevertheless, it was in the ashes and destruction of various German cities that Barth delivered arguably his most important essay in theological politics in 1946, entitled *Christengemeinde und Burgergemeinde* or "The Christian Community and the Civil Community" (*CSC*: 149–89). In this 1946 essay Barth describes the kingdom of God as the center of two concentric circles, of which the Christian community is the "inner circle" and the civil community is the "outer circle." The "inner circle" by way of witness and reminder reveals to the "outer circle" that it too is centered in Jesus Christ. He writes: "the existence of the State [is] an allegory, an analogue to the Kingdom of God which the Church preaches and believes in" (*CSC*: 169). In this way, the Christian community serves as a "model and prototype" of the civil community (*CSC*: 186).

> However much human error and human tyranny may be involved in it, the State is not a product of sin but one of the constants of the divine Providence and government of the world in its action against human sin: it is there an instrument of divine grace. The civil community shares both a common origin and a common center with the Christian community . . . Its existence is not separate from the Kingdom of Jesus Christ; its foundations and its influence are not autonomous. It is outside the Church but not outside the range of Christ's domination—it is an exponent of His kingdom. . . . [This]

19. Barth, *Against the Stream*, 95. Henceforth, all references to this book will be cited in the text in parenthesis, and abbreviated as *AS*.

makes one thing quite impossible, however: a Christian decision to be indifferent; a non-political Christianity. The Church can in no case be indifferent or neutral towards this manifestation of an order so clearly related to its own mission. Such indifference would be equivalent to the opposition of which it is said in Romans 13:2 that it is a rebellion against the ordinance of God—and rebels secure their own condemnation. (*CSC*: 156–57)

Whereas he uses the language of "intercession" in the 1938 essay, here, in the 1946 essay, he reverts back to Barmen's language of *reminder*. The church *reminds* the state of its true purpose, which is to bring honor to God. Although Barth continues the line of thinking established earlier calling for the "priestly role" of the church, he places a greater activist responsibly upon the church in calling the state to a particular political direction. The church continues to *be* the church through its intercessory role of being a witness to the gospel, praying and working for the good of the state, making distinctions between just and unjust governments, and declaring firmly that the state falls under God's rule. More than earlier essays, Barth makes a stronger argument for the relation of the civil and Christian communities, so that both give *witness* to Christ's rule. However, by "reminding" the state of its function, purpose, and hope, the church becomes more aware of its own political task. Through its own moral deliberation, the church "will choose and desire whichever seems to be the better political system in any particular situation, and in accordance with this choice and desire it will offer its support here and its resistance there." "It is in the making of such distinctions, judgments, and choices from its own centre, and in the practical decision which necessarily flow from that centre," Barth continues, "that the Christian community expresses its 'subordination' to the civil community and fulfills its share of political responsibility" (*CSC*: 162–63). As members of the inner circle, Christians "are also automatically members of the wider circle. They cannot halt at the boundary where the inner and outer circles meet, though the work of faith, love and hope which they are under orders to perform will assume different forms on either side of the boundary" (*CSC*: 158–59). In other words, it is not possible for the church to be indifferent to the political order because the state's power is explicitly intertwined to the mission of the church. In this way, the church always remains part of the order of creation just as the state remains part of the order of redemption.

Moreover, another obvious difference from earlier accounts is that the categories of church (*Kirke*) and state (*Stadt*) have changed to Christian community (*Christengemeinde*) and civil community (*Bürgergemeinde*). The *Christengemeinde*, the *ecclesia*, becomes most apparent in the gathered community, of Christians "in one place, region, or country" through the Holy Sprit and who seek to hear and obey the Word of God. The *Bürgergemeinde*, in contrast, is the "commonality of all the people in one place, region, or country in so far as they belong together under a constitutional system of government that is equally valid for and binding on them all, and which is defended and maintained by force" (*CSC*: 150). Instead of beginning with "institutions and offices," Barth begins with communities of persons gathered "together in corporate bodies in the service of common tasks" (*CSC*: 150). John Howard Yoder rightly claims that this document stands as one of earliest testaments to how the church and state ought to interact in a post-Christendom and post-Constantinian world. "Barth is not post-Constantinian," says Yoder because of the lessons of how Nazism manipulated the church in Germany, but "because a shrewd reading of history enables him to be pre-Constantinian, not in a privatistic way but in an historically realistic and accountable way. . . . By definition the faith community is epistemology prior to the wider world."[20] Christ's reconciliation of the civil community allows it to remain genuinely secular and distinct from the church, yet *related* to the church's mission. By choosing to grant the church its freedom to be a witness, the civil community envisions its own freedom and identity, for without the witness of the church, the civil community remains in self-deception and ignorance because of its reliance on natural law. "All it can do is grope around and experiment with the convictions which it derives from natural law, never certain whether it may not in the end be an illusion to rely on it as the final authority and therefore always making vigorous use, openly or secretly, of a more a less refined positivism" (*CSC*: 164). There is a differentiated hierarchy within the relation of the two communities in their proximity to revelation of the Word of God.

Because of the Christian community's witness to the civil community, the latter becomes not only a guardian but also a *witness* to the kingdom of God. By way of "reminder," the church gives parabolic witness to a clear "direction and a line" of political thinking that "on the whole toward the form of State, which, if is not actually realized in the so-called 'democracies,' is at any rate more or less honestly clearly intended and desired" (*CSC*:

---

20. Yoder, *Karl Barth and the Problem of War*, 185.

182). Democracy becomes an important analogical practice linking the two communities. This linkage can be seen in perhaps the most important part of the 1946 essay, where Barth discusses twelve analogies beginning with the church and moving outward to the civil community (*CSC*: 169–82). These analogies include: 1) just as the incarnation displays that God stands with humanity, so too the civil community should defend the dignity and rights of humanity before serving any cause that apparently serves humanity; 2) just as church gives witness to God's gracious justification, so too, the civil community, along with the church, will support governments, most clearly embodied in constitutional democracies, of impartial justice; 3) just as Christ came to the poor and lost, so too, the church should support civil governments that seek to address the needs of the poor; 4) just as God gives freedom to the church and state through God's gracious covenant, so too, the church should reject totalitarian and authoritarian governments; 5) just as the church is primarily a responsible community of individuals, so too, the church should reject radical political individualism and collectivism; 6) just as the equality of Christians is established in baptism, so too, it provides the basis for a political doctrine of equality of all its citizens; 7) just as the multiplicity of spiritual gifts within the church provide the basis for diversity, so too, it provides for an understanding separation of powers in government; 8) just as the Word of God is not secret but publicly proclaimed, so too, the state should also forbid secrecy that undermines the freedom of its citizens; 9) just as this Word is unbounded and free, so too, the state should insure the freedom of speech; 10) just as the church, as a collective body, serves individuals within the church, so too, the civil community, as a collective body, serves its citizens; 11) just as the church is diverse yet one, so too, the civil community should relativize its boundaries and be inclusive of difference; and 12) just as God is both a God of judgment and mercy, so too, the church reminds the state that it may, as an act of last resort, engage in violence as the way to maximize peace—which remains the final word; only the state, not the church, may use force to bring about peace and justice.

In the previous list of analogies, Barth clearly prefers a constitutional and liberal democratic state to other forms, whether of the far political right or left. In each case, he says No to the extreme ideological causes including totalitarian and anarchist governments, individualism and collectivism, and the unjust practices of political deception, secrecy, and coercion. On the other side, he defends constitutional democracies, impartial justice, separation of governmental powers, equality and freedom of all citizens, cultural plurality and religious diversity, and freedom of speech and of the press. Taken together, these analogies justify the promotion of civil laws protecting social and economic justice, basic human rights, self-determination, political equality, equal protection, and the freedom to engage the institutional life of society through the family, education, art, science, religion, and culture. To preserve order and security, the civil community seeks to rid the society of disorder, violence, and injustice through balancing the power of individual rights and responsibilities with community rights and responsibilities. Yet, we must recall that these political ideas, emerge first from the faith community, and by analogy, move outward into secular polity. The political life of the Christian community provides a particular *ethos*, in which, the civil community can envision the practices of power, authority, responsibility, participation, and plurality.

Freedom against Ideology

In Barth's political writings he is careful to present a *dialectical* view that remains dialectical in movement in its criticism of injustice and affirmation of freedom, justice, and peace within the civil community. Before and during World War II, the tone is generally more negative against German aggression and Swiss collaboration. After the war, however, the tone has shifted toward a more positive relation between the civil and Christian communities, and the building of a more favorably democratic, just, and peaceful society. Besides the 1946 essay, this view is apparent in a series of short postwar political writings collected in *Against the Stream*. It was in this postwar setting that Barth became severely criticized for not attacking Soviet aggression, like he had done against Nazi Germany. For the Swiss theologian there was a difference. In 1949 he wrote: "Ten years ago we said that the Church is, and remains, the Church, and must not therefore keep an un-Christian silence. Today we say that the Church is, and remains, the Church, and must not therefore speak an un-Christian word" (*AG*: 137). In the emerging world of the Cold War and the threat of nuclear weapons, Barth's position "between West and East" became the logical outgrowth of his commitment to an ideologically free politics that strove for freedom, justice, and peace. What Barth's Western critics failed to see at the time was that he was consistent in thought from the 1930s onward to the 1950s. Throughout this twenty year period, he was opposed to the intimate linking of Christian ethics with nationalism and other forms of ideology.

So, for example, in 1934, he said: "From what we have experienced in Germany during these latter days—this remarkable apostasy of the Church to nationalism, and I'm sure that every one of you is horrified and says in his heart: I thank thee God that I am not a German Christian!" (*GA*: 137). Years later, in 1958, he wrote: "[T]he present-day Western power has at least this one point in common with the Eastern, that it too, in its own way, seeks to dissuade the Christian Church from being the church."[21] In both circumstances, when church becomes absorbed into the "paganism" of nationalism or political ideology, it ceases being a witness to Jesus Christ. This was the case both in Nazi Germany and during the Cold War. In both cases, Barth said No to the church's unwillingness to resist and challenge the dominant ideology of the time, and Yes to the church's witness against the ideological powers. The church can only be free to be a witness to freedom, justice, and peace when it is free from all ideology. Only then can the church give witness to God's kingdom as "supreme and victorious over all economic, political, ideological, cultural, and also religious realms of life."[22] There is a continuous line in his political writings, thus, that presents both a No and a Yes, that is, a dialectic of resistance against the power of ideology, and the affirmation and support for a non-ideological politics, one that was truly committed to human freedom, justice, and peace.

In 1951, Barth published his "ethics of creation" (*CD* III/4), which was his most extensive work on Christian ethics. This important work departed significantly from his earlier discussion in *Ethics*. As pointed out earlier, Barth's ethics underwent significant development in the 1930s, when confronted by the threats of natural theology and the German Christians. In particular, he moved away from a simple equation of an ethics of law grounded within an "orders of creation," as found in his earlier *Ethics* lectures, to an ethics shaped by a gospel of responsible "freedom." We recall that his *Ethics* lectures were given at various locations from 1928 to 1933. However, it was almost two decades later, in 1951, that Barth published his revised "ethics of creation" in *CD* III/4. Here he completely reworked the structure of his creation-ethics according to the gospel and the covenant of grace. In the last section of this volume, Barth sums up nicely his task when he contrasts his own ethics of freedom to that of "order" and "law." "Instead of 'freedom' would it not be much more simply and realistic to say 'law'? Yet we have placed the whole doctrine of the 'command' of God the Creator under the term

21. Barth and Hamel, *How to Serve God*, 51.
22. Ibid., 52.

'freedom': 'freedom before God' first; then 'freedom for fellowship'; then 'freedom for life'; and finally 'freedom in limitation.' The question whether it would not have been better to speak of 'law' instead of 'freedom' thus applies to this whole tract of ethics" (*CD* III/4: 648). As mentioned above, in *CD* III/4, Barth uses the main category of freedom as the basis for the four following sections including, freedom before God, freedom for fellowship, freedom for life, and freedom in limitation. In each case Barth reworks the basic structure of his *Ethics* lectures with rewritten and expanding material. In the section "freedom for fellowship," for example, he not only discusses marriage and family, but goes into greater detail about human sexuality and parent-child relations. In addition, he further discusses how fellowship extends beyond the family to one's community, nation, and world, and in so doing, discusses various topics such as immigration, nationalism, and internationalism. Moreover, in the "freedom for life" section, he not only discusses the subject of work, calling, and vocation, but elaborates on many other controversial ethical issues dealing with the "respect and protection of life," such as capital punishment, euthanasia, suicide, war, health, and a discussion of non-human life and the environment. Furthermore, he departs fundamentally from his earlier lectures in including other sections including the first section "freedom before God" and the last section "freedom in limitation." In the first section, for example, he places his entire ethics of creation within the framework of the Sabbath commandment, worship, prayer, and confession. Christian ethics is not about the rational process of deliberating and acting as an independent moral subject, as much as being dependent upon God by listening and responding to God's prior gracious action. Human freedom is a gift that emerges through encountering God's freedom to command our responsible action.

In the last section of *CD* III/4, Barth develops a section not included in his earlier lectures in which he discusses how freedom remains circumscribed or limited by human finitude and societal structures. Recognition of the power of fate, finitude, and limitedness can easily lead to the loss of joy, hope, and meaning. This can lead to one's rejection of God's promise and hopeless disregard for oneself and others. This in turn leads to sin against another's dignity and intrinsic worth.

> In one form or another we are all guilty of sinning against ourselves and one another in this sense. But the *condititio sine qua non* of this sin consists in the fact that the honor which every man has as such is from God and therefore constant. Man can be godless. But

> God—and this is the decisive point—does not become "man-less."
> He is always the Creator and Lord of man. And because he is not
> "man-less," the godless of man can be only a human notion, however frightful in itself and serious in its consequences. There is no
> ontological godlessness. Even the most rabid atheist cannot achieve
> this either theoretically or practically. (*CD* III/4: 652)

Even if persons deny or reject God, God does not deny or reject persons. At its core, human dignity, value, and "honor," are grounded in God's affirmation of humanity through God's gracious covenant, which serves as the "inner basis" or inner meaning and structure to creation. Barth's ethics of creation remains shaped by not only God's action as creator, but also as reconciler and redeemer. A creation-based ethics that is grounded in natural structures, laws, principles, norms, or values cannot ultimately become an ethics of responsible freedom. Rather, it can only be an ethics of law and order, in which, the order of creation is preserved and affirmed. Freedom becomes only the freedom to obey the principle, rule, or norm. Barth's vision of Christian ethics can be open-ended because he begins and ends with God's freedom to act and human freedom to respond to God's prior gracious action. Both divine and human freedom come together and meet in the dual agency of Jesus Christ, who together unites God's gracious action and the human obedient response. A creation-based ethics that ignores the centrality of God's reconciling action in Jesus Christ fails to do justice to either God's freedom or corresponding human freedom. Indeed, without freedom, ethics becomes only a tyranny of ethical ideas, principles, or norms, all of which can become potentially hegemonic and a threat to human freedom itself. Without genuine freedom the power of the good is in danger of being reduced to power itself or the "powers" that attempt to eradicate human freedom, faith, hope, and love.

In the midst of the emerging Cold War, Barth remained a free thinker, who practiced what he preached. Barth's unwillingness to say No to communism and the Soviet Union, as he did Nazi Germany, is rooted his theological (and non-ideological) position, which is first developed in earliest writings on politics. From the beginning, Barth is advocating a non-ideological form of politics that is governed by what was most *practically* beneficial to persons within their communities. As Frank Jehle puts it, Barth remains committed to a "non-ideological politics, strictly orientated toward political issues themselves."[23] During the emerging Cold War,

23. Jehle, *Ever Against the Stream*, 44.

Barth chose to stand "between" the ideologies of the West and East. For Barth the main difference between the Nazis and the Soviet Communists, is that the latter was blatantly atheist and secular and did not attempt to cloak itself as a form of nationalist Christianity, like the former. It was the integrity of the church and its gospel that was primarily at stake. Moreover, because the state is neither divine or demonic it is not necessary, at every instance, to blatantly eulogize or condemn every historical manifestation of the state; sometimes the church must simply be silent and wait, while continuing to bear witness to Christ's rule. Barth saw it as unnecessary to jump on the anti-Communist bandwagon because he had doubts that this inflammatory rhetoric would really succeed in the long run, and indeed, may eventually lead to violent conflict, possibly even nuclear war. After the horror of World War II, Barth was concerned, above all, with peace in Europe. Meanwhile, during the 1950s and 60s, he was pressing his Christian humanist concern that the church—and the state—as the "inner and outer circles" of the kingdom stand in solidarity with *all* humanity. Barth's Christian humanism led him to defend human rights and the democratic and peacemaking functions of the state. As Stalinist atrocities became better known, he often publicly denounced the tyranny of Stalin, as he had Hitler. Moreover, in 1958, Barth, as a participant in the *Kirchliche Bruderschaften* (Church Brotherhoods), took further action through the writing of a petition (*Anfrage*) addressed to the Synod of the Evangelical Church in Germany. This document remained critical of West Germany's rearmament (as a member of NATO) and more important, the continuing proliferation of nuclear weapons. "The prospect of a future war to be waged with the use of modern means of annihilation has created a new situation, in the face which the Church *cannot* remain *neutral*."[24] Barth's stance against the preparation, development, and deployment of nuclear weapons remained perhaps his last great cause; a cause in which the church could rightly declare a *status confessionis*.

Christian Witness after Secularism

In the beginning of pages of *CD* IV/3, published in 1959, Barth writes an interesting section on the church's witness to Jesus Christ as prophet in the context of the growing secularism of modern society. With the breakdown of Christendom and the emergence of secular society, Barth sees the freeing

---

24. Quoted in Yoder, *Karl Barth and the Problem of War*, 102.

of both secular society, from the church, and the church from "Christian" society. The church is neither fully separated from society (diastasis), nor strictly identified with secular society (synthesis), but stands in dialectically free relationship to society and the larger world. It follows that the world can learn from the church and the church can learn from the world. So, even though the secularism and "inner paganism" of modern Western society is on the increase, this does not rule out a similar emerging conversation and awareness of the importance of humanistic concerns. There is a false belief that assumes the breakdown of Christendom directly leads *only* toward the inevitability of Nietzschian nihilism and disregard for human rights. Indeed, the worldwide interest in human rights (and humanism) and political democracy, after World War II, represents a "new turning" in ethical insight against the risks and powers established in various forms of racial, ethnic, and sexual discrimination, provincialism and militant nationalism that dominated much of modern history. This "new turning was not primarily and spontaneously Christian in its origins, but has only become such" (*CD* IV/3: 30). The task, therefore, is for Christians and the church to work with others for the good of world, by seeking greater peace, justice, and political freedom, and in so doing, give witness to God's reconciliation of the world

In this age after Christendom, Barth's theological and practical engagement in politics is critical and dialectical. It is critical, in that he discriminated among positions and unmasked the hidden ideological commitments that stand contrary to the Word of God, and dialectical, in that he often maneuvered between two uncompromising poles of thought, that is, between an absolute Yes and No. Yet in this movement, there was a lifelong persuasion toward a socialist-democratic conception of constitutional liberal democracy. Again, a "proper state" or "just state" is a community where "order, freedom, community, power and responsibility are balanced in equal proportions" (*AS*: 96). Barth's concern, above all, was with human freedom and responsibility before God. Christians should never equate particular human actions for justice with God's action, but neither do they refuse to believe that God does intervene in the world. This implies rejecting any ideologies that replace God's divine action with human action, while at the same time, practically working with the "aim of helping people" (*CL*: 266). So, how should responsible Christian social witness proceed? Barth responds by saying that such a view "neither identifies its own human strategies with the kingdom of God nor over 'against' it but 'along side' it, and in so doing, human righteous action will be "kingdom-like" (*CL*: 266). Realizing this important point, leads to a greater understanding of human freedom. He says:

> They are absolved from wasting time and energy over the impassable limits of their sphere of action and thus missing the opportunities that present themselves in this sphere. They may and can and should rise up and accept responsibility of the utmost of their power for the doing of a little righteousness. The only concern would be their awareness of how far they fall short, in this sphere of what is not only commanded but also possible for them. (*CL*: 265)

Barth's seeming un-heroic claim for humanity to do a "little righteous," and to do what is only "possible" seems out of step with the often heroic claims of some contemporary versions of Christian social ethics that seeks to accomplish the impossible. These rather Promethean visions of ethics may have forgotten one important lesson, namely that there really is no theological basis to address social realities that does not involve the answer revealed in God's covenant of grace. Yet, because it is a command of grace, it drives the church and Christians to stand with and for others, the church, and the world. Moreover, since the civil community, which remains under Christ's authority, is both the *guardian* of the common good and a *witness* to the kingdom of God, it too, with support by Christians, must engage in responsible political action that brings freedom to humanity and the world. In 1960, he writes, "[T]he true community of Jesus Christ is the society in which it is given to men to see and understand the world as it is, to accept solidarity with it, and to be pledged and committed to it." Indeed, he adds, "the Church as the true community exists essentially for the world and may thereby be known as the true Church" (*CD* IV/3: 780). The world does not know that it has been reconciled to God, which is the power and source of all peace, justice, and freedom. This is why the civil community *needs* the church, as the true witnessing community. Still, the church must be true to its witness, which does not offer a political program or strategy as much as a set of beliefs and practices that give witness to God's kingdom. Practically speaking, this frees the church to be a witness as a confessing community of faith in the world. It also frees the civil community to be a secular community reconciled by God in Jesus Christ to be an indirect witness to God's kingdom through its efforts to establish a more just, free, and peaceful society.

PART TWO

Postmodernity and a World at Risk

CHAPTER FOUR

Social Theory and Postmodernity

The last two chapters have demonstrated the fact that the church, as a witnessing community, cannot rise above and live outside its surrounding society and culture. In his 1924 essay "Church and Culture," for example, Barth writes that the church cannot give witness without conversing with the "actual political and economic standards of its own age. Throughout its own course, the Church swims along in the stream of culture" (*TC*: 351). This does not imply, of course, that the church ought to accommodate itself to its surrounding culture, only that the church cannot "free itself even partially" from society and culture (*TC*: 350). Christian witness arises within its particular social and historical context. Since Christian witness remains linked to particular settings, it remains a priority for Christian ethics to fully understand that particular social and historical setting. In the next two chapters, therefore, our task is to describe and evaluate the "signs of our times" in contemporary social and ethical thought, so that we may more critically relate it to our task in Christian ethics as witness. Here we delve further into our understanding of postmodernity by building on what was previously said in the first chapter, namely that it is linked with the ambiguous and double-edged character of modernity. This chapter looks at contemporary social theory in the context of postmodernity. For this we look at social theories about postmodernity, risk society, and globalization. Before we begin our social analysis, however, it is important to link this chapter with the two previous ones. In short, what is the relationship between theological ethics and social analysis?

SOCIETY AND SECULAR PARABLES

Many of Barth's critics, both during his lifetime and after, have often assumed that his intense commitment to dogmatic theology and "only theology" makes his approach irrelevant for social and political ethics. It is misguided, however, to think that Barth rejects the use of all nontheological sources in theological and Christian ethics because he did not actively use them in his own dogmatic theology. Barth's approach, says Nigel Biggar, does not prohibit the Christian ethicist from seeking to integrate a vigorous use of the nontheological sciences into their "theologically derived ethical framework."[1] Indeed, in relation to the secular world, says Barth in the late 1930s, Christians should be "absolutely open to all that one can learn from general human ethical inquiry and reply. It can be absolutely open because it has absolutely nothing to fear from this quarter" (*CD* II/2: 524). Later, in the 1950s, in *CD* IV/3, he wrote: "We can and must be prepared to encounter 'parables of the kingdom' in the full biblical sense, not merely in the witness of the Bible and the various arrangements, works and words of the Christian Church, but also in the secular sphere, i.e. in the strange interruption of the secularism of life in the world. In the narrow corner in which we have our place and task we cannot but eavesdrop in the world at large" (*CD* IV/3: 117). Barth's ethics encourages us to listen to the *other*, because in doing so, we also encounter the Word of God as gracious judgment. Being open to the outsider implies more than listening to them, but inviting their words to contribute to a fuller understanding of Christian social witness. By "eavesdropping" on other viewpoints, Christians "may learn to listen to others." "We may hear what is said by the whole history of religion, poetry, mythology and philosophy" (*CD* IV/3: 108). So, even though Barth himself remained committed to the dogmatic task, the *openness* of his method provides a strong argument for how critical engagement with nontheological sources in ethics may proceed. This extends to openness toward nontheological sources of truth as "parables." Outside the church, Barth says, there are "secular parables of the kingdom" that bear witness to the truth, and "illumine, accentuate, or explain the biblical witness in a particular time and situation" (*CD* IV/3: 115). Obviously, in

1. Biggar, *Hastening that Waits*, 160–61.

critically conversing with current social theory, our task is not to establish a new foundationalism for ethics, but to clarify the *boundaries* of the world which Christians inhabit. As Kathryn Tanner reminds us, "the distinctiveness of a Christian way of life is not so much formed *by* the boundary as *at* it: Christian distinctiveness is something that emerges in the very cultural processes occurring at the boundary, processes that construct a distinctive identity for Christian social practices through the distinctive use of cultural materials shared with others."[2] Although Christians have their own specific set of convictions and practices that shape their personal and communal lives, they also live in diverse cultures and societies, which today—at least in the West—are generally pluralistic societies. This shared existence implies that Christian social ethics, like theology, ought to strongly listen to non-Christian conceptual frameworks. Taking its cue from Barth and Tanner, this chapter assumes an "eavesdropping" strategy that remains open to hearing "parables of the kingdom" wherever we may find them in our postmodern secular world.

This strategy of "eavesdropping" involves not only listening but making judgments of Yes and No. This Yes and No involves more than just deciding which secular theory "fits" with Christian ethics. Both the Yes and the No are not, at their core, anthropological. Rather, they invite us to encounter God's action as God's judgment of No against all anthropocentric approaches to ethics, and at the same time, God's judgment of Yes for Christian responsible witness in correspondence to God's gracious command. Theological ethics must remain cautious about all ethical methodologies, whether apologetic or isolationist, which do not begin with God's trinitarian action. Not unlike some postmodern theorists like Jacques Derrida, who will be discussed shortly, Barth's theological approach inevitably deconstructs the epistemological foundations of modern ethical theory, and formulates a practical ethics that addresses the contingent needs of the *other* in her concrete particularity. For both thinkers, this strategy recognizes a basic heterogeneity between two orders. For Derrida the variance is between Enlightenment conceptions of moral knowledge and the demand for responsibility to the *other*, whereas for Barth it is between this modern moral epistemology and the event of the Word of God. For Barth any ethics that fails to consider the importance of this event, between God and us, fails to fully grasp the objective truth reveled in God's trinitarian

2. Tanner, *Theories of Culture*, 115.

freedom for decision and act in the Word of God as creator, reconciler, and redeemer. Simply put, "good and evil action is simply being obedient or disobedient to the knowledge of ours about God and ourselves" (*GHN*: 110). Consequently, in our analysis of contemporary social and ethical theory, we must be willing to both listen to and critically dialogue with the "secular parables" that come our way.

SOCIAL THEORY AND POSTMODERNITY

To begin, in this section, we seek to provide a brief summary *weltanschauung* of postmodernity by looking at contemporary social theory. What is the origin of the idea of postmodernity? The term "post-modern" was first used in the 1930s in a way similar to "modernism," namely to refer to the current *avant garde* cultural developments. Arnold Toynbee, in *A Study of History* (1954) later claimed that with the disintegration, irrationality, and anarchy of the twentieth century, Western society had entered a "Post-Modern Age." Although this age is inherently self-destructive, Toynbee hoped that a new consensus for a "World State" could be based on a synthesis of the "higher religions."[3] Later, in the 1970s, sociologist Daniel Bell, equated post-modernism with the fruition of antinomianism, anti-intellectualism, and unrestrained hedonism, which characterized the mass anti-modern and countercultural movements of the twentieth century, especially the pop and aquarian movements of the 1960s.[4] Bell writes: "The effort to find excitement and meaning in literature and art as a substitute for religion led to modernism as a culture mode. Yet modernism is exhausted and the various kinds of post-modernism (in the psychedelic effort to explain consciousness without boundaries) are simply the decomposition of the self in an effort to erase individual ego."[5] As Bell sees it, postmodernism saw its mission to replace political, economic, social, and religious authority, caused by modernization, with social anarchy, fragmentation, and hedonistic self-indulgence. In short, before the 1980s, "postmodern culture" was seen as the logical extension of the social fragmentation and subjectivism of the cultural modernism of the late twentieth century.

---

3. Toynbee, *Study of History*, vol. 9, 182–89.
4. See Bell, *Cultural Contradictions*, 51–54; 120–45.
5. Ibid., 29.

What Is Postmodernity?

Since the 1980s, however, the unhyphenated term postmodern has enlarged beyond simply another stage of cultural modernism to include many other cultural, social, and intellectual factors. This leads to distinctions between the various "posts," such as postmodern, postmodernism, and postmodernity. Consider Graham Ward's description: "Postmodernism enables us to distinguish certain elements in our contemporary world which are other than postmodern and yet, all too often, can belong together as characteristics of postmodernity."[6] How do these three terms relate to each other? My entrance into this discussion is primarily through social—not cultural—analysis. Hence, in social thought there is a shift from the culturally infused term postmodernism to the socially infused term postmodernity. Therefore, as I'm using these terms, postmodernism remains essentially aesthetic and cultural, while postmodernity incorporates social factors, including the political and economic. In this way, postmodernity remains a more descriptive and inclusive category, since it can also be stretched to include the culture of postmodernism. It follows that postmodernity remains an important descriptive category of the contemporary social and cultural setting of philosophical and theological inquiry as well. There is, says Best and Kellner, "a shared discourse of the postmodern, common perspectives, and defining features that coalesce into an emergent postmodern paradigm."[7]

Postmodernity is the logical extension of modernity, but it also reacts against it, seeking to move beyond it, and critically reflecting back on modernity's failures. Earlier, we described how the optimistic side of "methodological universalism," of modernity's progress was matched by its self-destructive "other" consisting of the fragmentation, reductionism, mechanism, and deconstruction. Essentially, in modernity the positive side wins out, whereas in postmodernity the negative side wins out. So what is postmodernity? Postmodernity remains linked with modernity. This is why both terms "postmodern" and "late-modern" give us insight into our contemporary setting. Simply put, postmodernity is the extension of the double-edged nature of modernity to its critical or "late" stage. Postmodernity is modernity that has become aware of its own inherent risks and side effects, that is, it is aware of its own self-contradictions, ambiguities, and self-destructiveness. This awareness of risk and danger leads

6. Ward, "Introduction," xxii.
7. Best and Kellner, *Postmodern Turn*, xi.

to a preoccupation with fear and discontentment. Postmodernity is an age of fear, uncertainty, and discontentment. Yet, in other ways, postmodernity is the intensification or hyperextension of the critical side of modernity. In this way postmodernity also seeks to go beyond modernity and turn toward a new perspective, not governed by the metanarratives of modernity.

Nevertheless, this positive side of postmodernity can also lead to a diversity of interpretations. Kevin Vanhoozer succinctly describes the "conflict of descriptions" in his comprehensive summary of several themes of the "postmodern condition."[8] First, postmodernity presumes a "new Copernican revolution" in experience and consciousness, in which time and space have become flattened and compressed, and reason has become radically particularized and historicized within specific social, culture, and historical settings. This *nomadic* consciousness and experience, as stated earlier, accepts that the world is "fleeting and temporal" without the illusions of the modern "eternal and absolute"; this creates a kind of human freedom not available in modernity. A second theme is a "protest against the 'natural,'" and seeks to replace this with the historical and political. There is no objective "natural" world, but only a world shaped by power, manipulation, and force that has now been uncovered and emancipated. There is a freedom from the dominance of the natural and the scientific as ways of viewing reality. The third takes this critical stance further by preaching an "iconoclastic purge" of all modern ideologies and metanarratives. Postmodernity exists after all the idols of modernity have been demolished. "The result: a postmodern critique of *impure* reason."[9] The fourth theme shifts the focus toward the integrity of the other, in the "return of the repressed," which brings to our attention the voices of the oppressed others of modernity. Respecting the difference of the other becomes the basis for a more positive response to demise of all totalizing systems of oppression. The fifth theme is the "recovery of 'messianic' religion," which was silenced by the oppression of modern secularism. The prophetic and mystical voices of religion and their search for meaning beyond modern paradigms of secular and scientific thought become an important feature for postmodern spirituality. This generally does not, however, lead to a recovery of pre-modern religious orthodoxy, but a search for a non-institutional and most likely, an individualist spirituality.

8. Vanhoozer, *Cambridge Companion to Postmodern Theology*, 13–20.
9. Ibid., 16.

In considering these more "positive" themes of postmodernity, we must be careful not to present a unified description of postmodern society. There are various "postmodern turns" including the arts and humanities, culture and society, and the intellectual (theoretical, philosophical, and theological). These various "turns" leads to a multiplicity of descriptions. Postmodernity, at its core, remains ambiguous and self-contradictory, thus, remains the logical extension of the double-edged nature of modernity. Consider John Milbank's definition:

> Above all, it [postmodernity] means the obliteration of boundaries, the confusion of categories. In the postmodern times in which we live, there is no longer any easy distinction to be made between nature and culture, private interior and public exterior, hierarchical summit and material depth; nor between idea and thing, message and means, production and exchange, product and delivery, the state and the market, humans and animals, humans and machines, image and reality—nor beginning, middle, and end. Everything is made to run into everything else; everything gets blended, undone, and then reblended. There are no longer any clear centers of control, and this means that new weight is given to plurality and the proliferation of difference. However, none of these differences ever assumed the status of the distinct essence: rather they are temporal events, destined to vanish and be displaced.[10]

Milbank's presents a view of postmodernity as a self-contradictory condition that seems to defy description. Given its complexity, I don't presume to provide a complete description of contemporary postmodern society. Rather my task is to simplify this description and focus on two basic strands of critical social theory, so that we may better understand ourselves and our world as it relates to Christian ethics and theology. Basically there are two positions in contemporary critical theory, namely deconstructionist (postmodern) and reflexive (late-modern) thought. Even though both theories do have an ethical concern, as the next chapter makes clear, the deconstructionist position presents a more synchronic, fragmented, and non-utopian (even dystopian) view of society, while the second views society as more diachronic, unified, and cautiously optimistic. The first group sees the present (postmodern) as radically breaking with the logic of the modern past, while the second sees the present (late-modern) as a transformation within the process of modernity. Put differently, the first offers a "strong" response

10. Milbank, "Gospel of Affinity," 1.

to modernity with the emphasis on *post*-modernity, while the second, offers a "weak" response to postmodernity with the emphasis on late-*modernity*. The first, like modernism, presumes that Baudelaire's "transient and fleeting" side has won out, whereas the second, like modernization, presumes at least some vestiges of the "objective and universal" remain. Yet both theories are obviously aware of the ambiguity of the present age, but they choose to emphasize one side more than the other. Overall Christian ethicists prefer the "weak" reflexive view over the "strong" deconstructionist view because it remains less relativistic and more concerned with the strategy of social ethics. Although I largely agree with this premise, my task is not to definitively prove that one social theory is better, or more true, than the other, for this would replace the centrality of the Word of God with the word of social theory as the foundation for theological ethics. Once this caveat is stated, however, the theologian can listen to these social theories, determining if there are ways in which these theories help elucidate the God's command of grace in our time.

Deconstructionist Postmodernism

The strong, or deconstructionist, view of postmodernity remains the mainstream view of postmodern*ism*. Self-proclaimed postmodernists attack modernity's preoccupation with Enlightenment "absolute certainty" and its practical embodiment in modern social structures. Clearly this vision follows in the footsteps of the German philosopher Friedrich Nietzsche, who is perhaps the first great critic of modernity. Nietzsche attacked the reliability of the Cartesian method itself by undercutting its foundation. In his *Notebooks*, published in 1873, he writes: "What is truth? A mobile army of metaphors, metonyms and anthropomorphisms." Indeed, he adds: "Truths are illusions which we have forgotten are illusions."[11] In contrast to modern certainty, Nietzsche argued that all factual truths are illusions as they are grounded in particular interpretations of those who have power to establish them as "true." Nietzsche aims to discredit objective truth and knowledge because of its underlying relationship to power. Since all that really exists is *power*, mainstream postmodernists, following Nietzsche, often disclose the hidden or masked power relations that lead to the loss of realism, society, and the self. Following Nietzsche, postmodern theory is essentially deconstructive and suspicious of the various power games used by persons and structures in society.

11. Nietzsche, "On Truth and Lie," 46.

This is evident in the fact that postmodernists often celebrate the collapse of all progressive "grand narratives" or metanarratives of modernity. Jean-Francois Lyotard argues, for example, that all-embracing theories—such as political liberalism, capitalism, communism, industrialism, and scientism—presuppose the emancipation of human reason and will from various social structures, which is no longer tenable in the "postmodern condition."[12] Hence, there is no metanarrative, metalanguage, or metatheory through which all things can be represented, understood, connected, or symbolized. Postmodernists have lost faith in the assurances of modern attempts to create a better world through social planning, political or economic strategies, religion, or techno-scientific innovations and progress. In short, they reject the ideology of modernization. Moreover, they further reject modern attempts to realize social justice, since these efforts are clouded by oppressive power structures. For all of its lip service to the ideals of justice, love, and brotherhood, modernity only disguises its real commitment to power, domination, and manipulation of innocent persons and communities. In modernity, says Gianni Vattimo, "all thought that pretends to discern truth is but an expression of the will-to-power—even to domination—of those making the truth-claims over those who are being addressed by them."[13] Hence, mainstream postmodernists, like Lyotard, Michel Foucault, and Jacques Derrida are suspicious of universal and absolute truth-claims whether scientific, philosophical, or religious, bureaucratic social organizations, comprehensive ideologies like capitalism or communism, or any other totalistic discourse.[14] Subjective interpolations of cultural rhetoric replace totalistic social discourse. All discourse is antifoundationalist and rhetorical.

Since postmodernity is the *other* of modernity, it reveals, celebrates, and liberates the oppressed and repressed underside of modernity. Lyotard argues, for example, that postmodernity is not so much a new age as an age that was previously repressed, hidden, and unacknowledged.[15] The new age of postmodernity, once it rejects the hegemony of power filtered through the particular oppressive understandings of class, race, sex, sexual preference, and civilization, seeks to celebrate the recognition of the *other*,

12. Lyotard, *Postmodern Condition*.
13. Vattimo, *End of Modernity*, xii.
14. In addition to Lyotard, see Derrida, *Margins of Philosophy*; Foucault, *Power/Knowledge*; Foucault, *Politics, Philosophy, Culture*.
15. Lyotard, *Postmodern Condition*, xxv.

in all its plurality and difference. Moral responsibility in postmodernity cannot be linked to the grand schemes of utopia but only to the other; it is a responsibility to "otherness." By abandoning modern conceptions of the self, history, and truth, therefore, we encounter the otherness of these perspectives, which frees the subject from these modern misconceptions. Yet, postmodernists are cautious about the celebration of otherness as ushering in a new progressive future. With its focus on the responsibility to otherness, deconstructionist thought is often skeptical of social or political movements that may veil hidden power relations. Because their task is primarily to unmask hidden power agendas, not to shape political action, postmodernists are often labeled nonpolitical or apolitical. The loss of the political invariably leads to the rejection of the *meaning* of history itself, as a comprehensive pattern that places the variety of human events into some narrative whole. History is the disintegration of events into fragmentary parts. As John Webster puts it, "postmodernism characteristically rejects an idea that human existence and time constitutes an ordered whole; history is dispersed into a non-sequential, non-developmental, non-utopian, non-eschatological scatter of elements."[16] With fragmentation as the governing paradigm, postmodernity presumes chaos, flimsiness, and instability as our common experience of *reality* itself. Ihab Hassan, for instance, claims the most significant qualifier for postmodernity is the term "indeterminacy" or "indetermanence," which refers to a combination of pluralism, eclecticism, randomness, discontinuity, and difference.[17] Thus, echoing Baudelaire's negative side of modernity, postmodernists embrace the pole of contingency, particularity, and historicism, while rejecting the other pole of absolute and eternal reason. Postmodernity radically breaks from modernity, revealing its ambiguous *other*.

The radical discontinuity between modernity and postmodernity, is perhaps most evident in the cultural reflections about aesthetics in contemporary culture. The solid foundations of modernity melt into the air of postmodern virtual reality. David Harvey writes: "The general implication is that through the experience of everything from food, to culinary habits, music, television, entertainment, and cinema, it is now possible to experi-

---

16. Webster, *Word and Church*, 269.

17. Hassan, "Culture of Postmodernism," 119–31. Hassan claims that modernism included characteristics such as purpose, hierarchy, centering, semantics, paradigm, determinacy, transcendence, metaphysics, and God the Father, while postmodernism includes features such as play, anarchy, dispersal, rhetoric, syntagm, indeterminacy, immense, irony, and the Holy Ghost. Ibid., 123–24.

ence the world's geography vicariously, as a simulacrum. The interweaving of simulacra in daily life brings together worlds (of commodities) in the same space and time. This happens in such a way as to conceal almost perfectly a trace of origin, of the labour processes that produced them, or the social relations implicated in their production."[18] Postmodernists claim that the solid reality of objective realism celebrated by modernity, is replaced with a "simulacrum" and the "aestheticization of reality." This correlates with theory of commodity fetishism, first envisioned by Karl Marx, but given new importance by postmodernists. In postmodernity, "signifier" (image or symbol) and the "referent" (real object) have inevitably exchanged places, so that the "signifier" becomes the real object and the "referent" becomes the image. The image becomes everything.[19] Since reality is transformed into images, it further becomes fragmented, unstable, and flattened-out, which alters the way persons describe objects, establish commitments, and gain knowledge about the world, others, and themselves. Moreover, once this aesthetic idea is combined with global capitalism, the combination becomes lethal for society and culture. Not only are products and labor transformed into monetary commodities, as Karl Marx thought, but *culture* itself becomes a commodity that is exchanged and marketed. Furthermore, if commodity production shifts from the creation of real objects to signs, images, and packages, then competition and success among firms is often construed as a conflict of images and marketing strategies. The economic "regime of accumulation" is becoming increasingly the "regime of signification."[20] Hence, commodities and cultural artifacts are increasingly being understood by their sign-value not their use-value. This means that when culture is perceived only as a signifier (image), it separates persons and communities from their culture; it forces persons to question the meaning of their own culture. To counteract this growing *anomie*, people use advertizing to manipulate taste and opinion and style through increased number of signifiers and sign-value of new products, which further leads to an increasingly shallow and flattened-out existence. This nihilistic and dytopic trend perpetuates a downward spiral of meaningless consumption, which leads to crises in meaning and "sulleness" for persons and cultures.[21]

18. Harvey, *Condition of Postmodernity*, 300.
19. Baudrillard, *Selected Writings*.
20. Lash, *Sociology of Postmodernism*, 40–44.
21. Borgmann, *Crossing the Postmodern Divide*, 110–16.

Inasmuch as postmodern thought seeks to resist hegemonic forces in the world, principally global capitalism, it remains unable to overcome the apparent reality of a fragmented and *dystopian* social order. This is where the nihilism of postmodernism "spills over" into the discourse of globalization. Global societies are becoming more violent, meaningless, and fragmented. Global capitalism may be creating a new wealthy class, but it has also rapidly decentered the economic base from both urban and rural communities. The irony is that with intensified and unrestricted capital flows from country to country, corporation to corporation, and financial trader to financial trader, there emerges a real threat of collapse of the real economy in which common citizens work and live. This demonstrates the tension between the financial economy and the real economy, which became apparent in the financial collapse of late 2008. When communities suffer the loss of capital and wealth within the real economy, they may become breeding grounds for alienation and sullen resentment. This encourages a revival of various ideologies that promote nationalism, neo-tribalism, ethnocentrism, and various forms of international terrorism that seems bent on mass violence and destruction. It is ironic that with globalization has also come a return to locality, particularity, cultural isolation, and militant religious fundamentalism. It is also ironic that since the terrorist attacks in 2001, and the intensified efforts in national security, there has also grown a lingering sense of insecurity of being a victim of terrorist violence. All this leads to a more heightened sense of hostility and resentment, which further leads to increased distrust, intolerance, and more violence. Moving through the first decade of the twenty-first century we still remain committed to the ideas of justice, peace, equality, and freedom, but we are fearful that these once heralded ideas of modern society may become only fading lights of the past.

Moreover, postmodernity has made it very difficult to talk about ethics. With the death of modern certainty, it remains more problematic to provide any prescriptive or normative moral judgments or ethical statements. Ethics remains in a continuous "holding pattern." Chaos and moral uncertainty have arrived in full force. For many postmodernists this reality should not necessarily lead to despair, but with the death of all metanarratives there is no grounding for hope for society as a whole, except those resistant intellectuals who challenge all totalistic discourse. This "implosion of secularism," as Graham Ward says, makes "no appeal possible to any authority outside the system itself—no principal, no shared ontology, no grounding epistemology, no transcendental meditation. And so we move beyond the death of God which modernity announced, to a final forgetting of the transcendental altogether, to a state of godlessness so profound that nothing can be conceived behind the exchange of signs and the creation of symbolic structures."[22] There are no remaining metanarratives of liberation because all of these presume some form of hidden power discourse of oppression of the marginalized *other*. The struggle is to find hope, meaning, and purpose in a world that has lost its belief in the utopian dreams of modern society. Yet this strategy can only be achieved through the deconstruction of the values and beliefs that gave modernity its optimism. Postmodern deconstructionism has really nothing in itself to offer as a positive alternative to modernity. Ironically, inasmuch as it tries to distance itself from modernity, it remains within some of the main traditions of modern thought, including its hidden commitments to the individualistic, relativistic, and secularistic ideas of modernity.

Reflexive Late-Modernity

Of course, not all assessments of postmodernity lead to the dour conclusions of the deconstructionist model. Other social theorists stress a *reflexive* attitude toward contemporary society, which insists on more continuous linkage to modernity. In reflexive thought, modernity is not completely dead, but it has simply shifted into a new self-critical (reflexive) phase of late-modernity. This is the "weak" view of postmodernity. This view splits the difference between modernist and deconstructionist schemes of thought by claiming we are living in an ambiguous or contradictory stage of late-modernity. Its difference from the deconstructionist theories lie in its understanding of reflexivity, namely its presumption that society itself can be self-critical, moral, and above all, transformational, without succumbing to certain modernist metanarratives of emancipation. Although reflexivity can be understood to be either institutional or personal, its central characteristic is the "freeing of agency" of the self, which invariably leads individuals and society itself to be self-confrontational. Sociologist Scott Lash, provides a good definition: "First there is structural reflexivity in which agency, set free from the constraints of social structure, then reflects on the 'rules' and 'resources' of such structure; reflects on agency's social conditions of existence. Second there is self-reflexivity in which agency reflects on itself. In self-reflexivity previous

---

22. Ward, "Introduction," xix.

heteronomous monitoring of agents is displaced by self-monitoring."[23] Both structural and self-reflexivity confronts the hegemonic structures or agents that curtail individual and social freedom. Reflexive thought is critical of both modern subject-centered reason and postmodern deconstructionist and post-structuralist thought. Jürgen Habermas, for example, argues that modernity, from the beginning, has fostered a "counterdiscourse" of "communicative reason."[24] This counter-discourse presumes that persons are intersubjectively constituted by society, history, and language, and thus seek consensual agreement through communicative interaction and the democratic process. Although the implication of Enlightenment thought has colonized the "lifeworld" of persons and their life-sustaining communities, persons do have the reflexive capacity to interact with the world and each other through communicative reason and the "ideal-speech situation." Such a starting point to human interaction presumes that acceptance of difference and openness to the other, which fosters an equal commitment toward other persons. Through the intersubjective process of communication, diverse persons within a pluralistic society can forge common ethical norms and work together for common purposes. Not unlike Habermas, German sociologist Ulrich Beck claims that persons are no longer naïve about the hidden dangers and threats of modernity, nor are they powerless to change society. Rejecting Habermas' social theory as idealistic and unworkable, however, Beck finds a universal solidarity in the experience of *risk*. Beck's theory of social risk provides a helpful corrective to Habermas' social theory because it takes more seriously the contemporary risks that society faces in our contemporary world. It takes more seriously some of the more sober social realities of postmodernity, without jettisoning the reflexive capacity to address these risks.

Reflexive theorists like Beck and Anthony Giddens argue that the experience of risk is both threatening and hopeful. This experience involves a tension between two ambiguous or contradictory realities: 1) the threatening experience of risk; 2) the reflexive capacity to assess and evaluate these risks with the hope of reversing their potential side effects. On one hand, the experience of risk is ubiquitous. From morning wakefulness to evening sleep, we experience the endless amounts of information that shape our perception of the world, as a world at *risk*. Unlike previous generations, we are more aware of the disastrous side effects of pollution, nuclear energy, global

23. Lash, "Reflexivity and its Doubles," 115–16.
24. Habermas, *Philosophical Discourse of Modernity*, 1–34; 161–216.

climate change, and ozone depletion, all of which contribute to global climate change. In addition, further risks include political risks of terrorism and violent conflicts, the economic risks of global market meltdown, and the social risks of divorce, unwed childbearing, and alcohol and drug addiction. The daily occurrences of fear, anxiety, distress, ambivalence, and shock all characterize the experience of postmodern risk. Rather than the world "being more and more under our control," says Giddens, "it seems out of our control—a runaway world."[25] On the other hand, even with greater fragmentation, rootlessness, and despair, our world has the knowledge, experience, and ability to overcome these risks that underlie the patterns of daily living. Although we live, says Giddens, in a world of "radical doubt" which fuels anxiety and uncertainty, we can also "discern clear prospects for a renewal of political engagement, albeit along different lines from those hitherto dominant."[26] Modernity was blind to its own risks, whereas we see them clearly; this makes our age both more uncertain but also more hopefully realistic. Late-modern political engagement is rooted in our evaluation of the power structures that hide or mask global risks. Global society is no longer naïve about the hidden dangers and threats of modernity, nor are they powerless to confront and evaluate these risks.

At its core, reflexive social theory is not a critical theory of society but a theory of *critical society*. Reflexive thinkers challenge Max Weber's understanding of modernization which leads to the triumph of instrumental rationality, bureaucratically controlled social structures, or the triumph of the "iron cage." In *Reflexive Modernization*, for example, Beck writes: "If simple (or orthodox) modernization means, at bottom, first the disembedding and second re-embedding of traditional social forms by industrial social forms, then reflexive modernization means first the disembedding and second the re-embedding of industrial society by another modernity."[27] The Weberian notion of "simple modernization," presumes that persons are increasing being subjugated to heteronomous social structures and instrumental rationality. In contrast to Weber's distressing notion of modernization, Beck offers a different, more positive, reading of what he calls "reflexive modernization." This involves the process of empowering and freeing of persons and communities from powerful political, economic, and other institutional structures. Modernization does not automatically lead to greater atomization,

25. Giddens, *Runaway World*, 20.
26. Giddens, "Living in a Post-Traditional Society," 107.
27. Beck, "Reinvention of Politics," 2.

isolation, or the loss of the self, but to the re-embedding or restructuring of relationships, groups, communities, and traditions.[28] Although this theory causes individuals to reflect critically on those traditional institutions to which they belong, it is not anti-traditional or antisocial.[29] Indeed, with greater reflexivity, persons become more interdependent with others, both locally and globally, in their freely chosen community or tradition and in global relations that transcend local boundaries. The process of globalization brings the possibility of the freeing of moral agency throughout the world, thereby contributing to a reengagement of a truly democratic way of life. Hence, reflexive social thought attempts to overcome the ambiguous tension between determinism and freedom, which remains the core experience of postmodern (or late-modern) society. For all of its guarded optimism, however, it cannot guarantee that persons will respond and act appropriately to such risks. The future is undetermined by the social and cultural structures of contemporary life, which enhances both our experience of human *freedom* and our greater awareness of *risk*. This means, in short, there is a hidden ambiguity in the theory of reflexive social thought; there is hope for a better world, but a better world is not an automatic outcome. The future of the world depends on human freedom to act and change the world.

To summarize, how shall we compare these two theories of contemporary life? As stated earlier, neither theory is *objectively* true, in that neither provides a foundation for a theological assessment of Christian social ethics. Inasmuch as the reflexive (or weak) view of postmodernity is more transformational and less deconstructive, it appears to be more applicable to the task of Christian social ethics. In contrast to the more dystopian view of postmodernity, which sees persons as victims of hegemonic structures, a reflexive theory, insofar as it presumes these structures, also claims persons have the capacity to critically reflect upon and challenge their power. It remains cautiously optimistic. Even though it acknowledges our age as ambiguous and filled with radical doubt, its quest for absolute certainty, as developed in the theory of "reflexive modernization" assumes that people are more capable today, than in the past, of ushering in a better world. Accordingly, it remains tied too closely to modern utopianism, which underestimates the self-destructive *other* side of modernity. As John Milbank

28. These themes are developed in Giddens, *Consequence of Modernity* and *Modernity and Self-Identity*.

29. Giddens, "Living in a Post-Traditional Society," 56–109.

earlier reminded us, postmodernity's lack of confidence in the universal and objective has led to the "obliteration of boundaries" and the "confusion of categories." Society is *messier* than reflexive social theory would have it!

This radical break is more evident in cultural studies than in sociology. No doubt the present age is continuous with the past, but it also has broken from the past in many ways. Anthropologist Renato Rosaldo, for example, demonstrates how ethnography, during the last century, has undergone a three-stage development from a modernist Western imperialist perspective to a postmodernist respect of individual cultures.[30] The ethnographer is increasingly less an "objective," detached observer and more of an active participant. Rosaldo, for instance, argues that cultural analysis must be "processual" or historical in that it demonstrates "how ideas, events and institutions interact and change through time."[31] So, contemporary society is ambiguous, in that it is synchronic and diachronic, homogeneous and heterogeneous, and pessimistic and optimistic. In postmodernity social and cultural analysis requires, in the words of Clifford Geertz, a "thick description," namely a description about how the meaning, thought, beliefs, and practices of people are "intelligently understood" within the context of a particular culture.[32] A "thick description" presumes that society, culture, and tradition are interactive, interdependent, and overlap each other. What this means is that both social theories, or "strong" and "weak" views, describe the same world in different ways. There is no *one* theory that can fully describe the multiple variants that comprise postmodern society; therefore, we must broaden our description, so that we may include other ways to view society, including globalization and risk. Both globalization and risk are two important factors of postmodernity. Indeed, these two concepts of globalization and risk help overlap deconstructionist and reflexive thought

---

30. Rosaldo, *Culture and Truth*. Rosaldo claims the first "heroic" imperialistic method viewed primitive cultures in light of Western Civilization, and the second, or the "classic" sociological period, viewed cultures as internally coherent systems that could be compared to other similar cultures by an overarching essential theory of "culture." In contrast, the third period discards the universalistic pretensions of an overarching "scientific" theory of culture, and instead examines particular cultures as on-going traditions that often interact with other various cultures. This development parallels the movement from modern to postmodern society; indeed, the first two theories are thoroughly modern while the third is postmodern. For another important work detailing the history of ethnography, see Clifford, *Predicament of Culture*.

31. Rosaldo, *Culture and Truth*, 92.

32. Geertz, *Interpretation of Cultures*.

in ways that help reframe the debate, giving us a "thick description" of postmodernity. We first look at globalization and then risk society.

GLOBALIZATION AND RISK SOCIETY

During the last ten years there has been an explosion of academic writing on the effect of cultural and social developments of globalization in the world. During this time, the social sciences have loaded this term with increasingly more descriptions, making it methodologically into a kind of new all-embracing metanarrative. Such inclusively invariably brings caution, especially in postmodernity. "Globalization is on everybody's lips;" says Zygmunt Bauman, "a fad word fast turning into a shibboleth, a magic incantation, a pass-key meant to unlock the gates to all present and future mysteries."[33] Like other "vogue words," globalization shares a "similar fate," adds Bauman, namely "the more experiences they pretend to make transparent, the more they become opaque."[34] Bauman's comments remind us of the risks of engaging in the descriptive labeling of our times, and the hidden ideological presuppositions about economic, political, and cultural matters in such descriptions.

Many Globalizations

In *Global Transformations*, David Held and the other social scientists argue there are three trends in the globalization debate.[35] First, the "hyperglobalists," believe the economic changes in the world directly affect the political and cultural changes. This group tends to be rather utopian and argue that global society is becoming more interdependent, democratic, and peaceful. They include either free market advocates or residual socialist thinkers influenced by Marx or other nuanced versions of socialism. The debate remains essentially economic. Second, the "skeptics" argue that culture and political regionalization, in response to global capitalism, is the most important trend in the world. This leads to a resurgence of nationalism, tribalism and terrorism, and persecution of ethnic and religious minorities, which may lead not only regional but also international violence. The world is becoming less interdependent and more polarized and violent. Third, the "transformationalists" argue that both global and local, both economic and

33. Bauman, *Globalization*, 1.
34. Ibid., 1.
35. Held et al., *Global Transformations*, 2–10.

social/cultural, forces are rapidly transforming all societies of the world in different ways, some for good and some for the worse. It is the changing shape of economic, political, and cultural *power* that determines how particular societies change. Although the typology of *Global Transformations* is extremely helpful, we seek to relate globalization to our earlier discussion of postmodernity. Like the two kinds of postmodern discourse, we can draw a similar twofold distinction between "narrow" and "broad" types of globalization rhetoric. The first "narrow" perspective focuses almost exclusively on the economic effect of global capitalism on the world. This position, most definitely corresponds to the "hyperglobalists," but also draws on the apocalyptic sentiment of the "skeptics." In contrast, the second "broad" perspective speaks about other globalizing trends, namely political, social, cultural, and even intellectual changes, which fits rather nicely with the cautious optimism of the "transformationalists." Since the "narrow" view is tied to the growth of global capitalism it is more likely to argue that globalization is a more recent phenomena, whereas the "broad" view links globalization to trends that even predate modernity; the first is synchronic and the second is diachronic.

This leads us to a more direct comparison of two viewpoints of globalization and postmodernity. First, there is a similarity between "strong" view of postmodernity (deconstructionists) and the "narrow" view of (economic) globalization. In this view, postmodernism *is* the culture of global capitalism or late-capitalism. Likewise, many who defend the "weak" view (reflexivists) presume that a "broad" view of globalization remains the most inclusive terminology used in the late-modern world. Furthermore, just as postmodern discourse is divided over its analysis of global capitalism, so too is globalization discourse. On one side, the narrow view often becomes polarized into two contrasting positions on globalization, as either *entirely* good or bad, while, on the other, the broad view generally makes an important distinction between globalization (the globalizing trends of society and culture), and neoliberal globalism (the spread of global capitalism). Both globalization and globalism have positive and negative features, although the former leans toward the positive, and the latter toward the negative.

The reduction of globalization to the economic, in the narrow view, implies that one must logically stand either for *or* against global capitalism. Its proponents, what we might call the pro-globalists includes those free market economic, political and business leaders that believe that with the spread of free markets, democracy, and global information through the Internet, the world has the potential to develop an international civil society, a new cosmopolitan culture, modeled after the free and democratic societies of the world. The developing world will be transformed into the developed world, which will lead to an international cosmopolitan culture that remains democratic, capitalist, prosperous, and free. In contrast to the pro-globalists are the anti-globalists. These argue that neoliberal globalism signifies the triumph of an Americanized version of *laissez faire* capitalism or cowboy capitalism into the global arena, namely a kind of Americanized global capitalism. This homogeneous power threatens to usurp the local economic—as well as political and cultural—communities and identities through monetary commodities and signs, leading to a growing separation of the rich and poor and destruction of the environment. The diversity of the global societies, in all their cultural richness, is at risk of collapsing into MacWorld.[36] The commodity fetishism of capitalism is altering human understanding of human and environmental justice.

In my judgment, this debate between the pro-globalists and anti-globalists remains too much controlled by an economic ideological perspective about the complexity of globalization. Globalization, a broad social reality, must be seen as more multidimensional and diverse than simply a struggle between neoliberal economic (*laissez faire*) economic philosophy and its various socialist, communistic, eco-political alternatives. A better analysis is found in the book *Many Globalizations*, edited by Samuel Huntington and Peter Berger, who argue for a broader analysis of two comprehensive cultures, namely the "Davos culture" and the "faculty club culture."[37] The "Davos culture" is named after the World Economic Summit Meeting (or World Economic Forum, WEF) held in the Swiss city of Davos, and typifies the international groups of entrepreneurs, government officials, economists, and others who regularly meet at international or regional gatherings or summits and propose new agendas about international free trade, world financial agreements, and expanded markets. The goal of this international business community, of course, is to support the spread of free markets through political liberalization and international cooperation. Throughout the last decade, there was an ongoing battle with the anti-globalization "faculty club" culture about the pros and cons of globalization. With the worldwide economic downturn of Fall 2008 and the significant infusion of capital from Western governments into their financial and domestic economies,

36. Barber, *Jihad vs. McWorld*.
37. Berger and Huntington, *Many Globalizations*, 3ff.

it remains more uncertain how the neoliberal global free market policies remain real options for the future economy. Still, the era of international cooperation is not dead. Indeed, whatever hope there is for revived global economy must rely on international cooperation, including free trade agreements. There is still a future for the Davos culture, though perhaps one that is less ideologically neoliberal, in resisting the drive toward economic nationalism or protectionism.

In contrast, is the "faculty club" culture, which obviously is best represented by intelligentsia, including academics in various disciplines, found primarily in Western universities. This position also includes those academics involved in various foundations, nonprofit organizations, social action groups, and "non-governmental organizations" (NGOs), like Amnesty International and the Sierra Club, and global policy networks. Two of the most important groups linked with this movement are the World Social Forum (WSF), which has met annually since the 2001 meeting at Porto Alegre, Brazil, and the International Forum on Globalization (IGF). There is no doubt that the faculty club consists of a variety of persons and viewpoints about possible alternatives to economic globalization. Yet, it is often difficult to know exactly what they are really prescribing as real economic alternative. Some in this culture presume a hidden Marxist or neo-Marxist ideology, which colors their negative view of globalism, while others presume some kind of democratic socialism or social market capitalism. Some are radicals and others are reformers; some seek a radical alternative to neoliberalism and others seek to reform the current system toward a more human social market. Overall, they seek to empower political authority to foster economic justice, human rights, environmental reform, and multiculturalism. They seek to change the hearts and minds of the masses, media, and government leaders. Still, the faculty club does not present a unified view of what the real alternative to capitalism is, nor how this alternative would actually work in the current global economy. It appears with the recent worldwide economic crisis that the faculty club culture has perhaps won one important battle against the liberalizing policies of the Davos culture. They too call for global cooperation, but perhaps one directed more to Main Street than Wall Street. With the emphasis on governmental neo-Keynesian stimulation of the economy in the United States, including providing investment and incentives for a more green economy, we see the continuing importance for the voice of the faculty club culture. Yet, one hidden danger for this group is to neglect the responsibility for the global economy and global cooperation. The anti-globalization and local utopian rhetoric of the faculty club has always stood in contrast to its humane commitment to international sustainable development. If the faculty club is to provide a helpful voice for current and future economic crises, it must also seek to find ways to encourage economic growth and development along with its commitment to global justice and ecological sustainability.

The more dangerous, and less helpful, side of the faculty club is the rhetorically guided strongly anti-globalization faction of the movement, which has often argued against the hegemonic capitalist era that has dominated the world since World War II. Capitalism is the engine that drives postmodern culture. This view, of course, is not new, but is grounded in varieties of Marxist thought that has been critical of *laissez faire* capitalism for the last one hundred fifty years. The materialist presumption here is that the economic sphere drives the social and cultural spheres. For instance, Francois Lyotard claims the postmodern condition is a "condition of knowledge" that begins with the formation of the "post-industrial age."[38] Likewise, Frederic Jameson, in his magisterial description of "postmodern culture" says that it is simply "the cultural logic of late capitalism."[39] So, just as modernism reacted to the monopolistic capitalism of the late-nineteenth century, so too, postmodernism reacts to the hegemony of corporate, neo-liberal, or global capitalism of today's world. Ironically, with more diversity and pluralism in postmodernity also comes more homogeneity—a "McDonaldization" of reality—that enforces similarity, standardization, and hegemonic control by economic power. Whatever changes occur in society, they do so within the social structure dominated by the hegemonic power of a global capitalism and the demise of the nation-state. Indeed, the social fragmentation of postmodern culture is directly caused by the alienation created by global capitalism. The result, as stated earlier, is a dystopian future governed by the simulacrum of virtual reality, or more regionalization, fragmentation, and tribalism.

Critically speaking, we must be critical of any form of social analysis that ideologically tends to become crypto-fascist or totalitarian. What are the ideological presuppositions that lie behind such descriptions, analyses, and evaluations? As stated, is it not true that many these postmodernists also presume a hidden Marxist analysis of society and culture? Are they

---

38. Lyotard, *Postmodern Condition*. Lyotard depends on Daniel Bell's description of the post-industrial economy in Bell, *Coming of Post-Industrial Society*.

39. Jameson, *Postmodernism*, 46.

not also driven by a particular ideology? Much anti-globalism reduces the debate over globalization and postmodernism to its economic base. On this form of reductionism, Krishan Kumar writes: "Capitalism is being made to do too much work. The world is indeed still capitalist, and post-modernity exists in that world. But how far should the post-modern condition be explained by the mechanics of capitalist development? If 'post-modern capitalism' is different from early forms of capitalism should not the emphasis lie on the first term as much as the second? How much autonomy exists in the social and cultural spheres? There lurks here, as of old, the scent of an excessive degree of determinism and reductionism."[40] Limiting postmodernism to the cultural sphere ironically reinforces the reductionist and deterministic features of Enlightenment reason, especially through the hidden ideology of the political left and Marxism. The superstructure of postmodern culture cannot simply be carried by the base socioeconomic system of global capitalism. Many postmodernists overlook the convergence, inclusiveness, and complementariness of culture and society by reducing everything to an economic foundation. All social risks can be explained away once they are linked to the hegemony of global capitalism. What is needed, therefore, is a way to move beyond these ideologically driven categories. As stated above, both the Davos and faculty club cultures must become less ideological and more committed to the problems and risks of the global economy. There must be a renewed emphasizes on global cooperation both in creating wealth and capital and an equal distribution of that wealth, particularly in societies with extensive poverty and significant gaps between the rich and poor. Neither the neoliberalism of the Davos or the Marxist-laden theories of faculty club will solve the problems linked with the global economy. Rather it is the moderates in each group who can listen to each other, and forge policies that strengthen global cooperation, free trade, economic justice, and sustainable development that will help address the risks of potential short-term and long-term economic catastrophe. In this age of "many globalizations" people should seek to build on the practices of cooperation to foster a better world.

Postmodernity and Globalization

What is the relationship between postmodernity and globalization? By themselves both terms are prone toward oversimplification and generaliza-

---

40. Kumar, *Post-Industrial to Post-Modern Society*, 193.

tion, which invites ideological reductionism. Given our definition of modern thought as inherently isolationist (or separatist) and reductionistic, which separates various elements of society, it ought to be posited that an authentic *post*-modern thought, at least in theory, should seek to *integrate* these various concepts. That is, if modern thought seeks to separate the cultural from the social, the aesthetic from the theoretical and scientific, the sacred from secular, and scientific from religious, it ought to be the synthetic goal of *post*modern thought to dedifferentiate these categories so that they remain interdependent with each other, or at the very least, lose their autonomy. Indeed, as Christian philosopher Nancy Murphy writes: a true *post*-modern perspective is one that recognizes "a complex mutual conditioning between part and whole." Indeed she goes on to say, "this represents a significant enough departure from the predominant modes of modern thought to mark the beginning of a new, postmodern era."[41] Just as postmodernity is inclusive of the past and tradition, so too its reasoning moves toward holism and integration of culture and society. Ironically, many postmodernists, like Lyotard and Jameson, are not *post*-modern enough.

Overall, the broad view of globalization presents a more helpful view of contemporary life that intentionally avoids being reduced to the economic categories, whether in neoliberal or Marxist language. Instead, globalization can be seen as a complex set of often ambiguous, even contradictory features. Anthony Giddens writes: "Globalisation thus is a complex set of processes, not a single one. And these operate in a contradictory oppositional fashion. Most people think of globalization as simply 'pulling away' power or in the loans from local communities and nations into the global arena. And indeed this is one of its consequences. Nations do lose some of the economic power they once had. Yet it also has an opposite effect. The globalization not only pulls up words, but also pushes downwards, creating pressures from local economy."[42] Globalization has broken down barriers and boundaries that separated nations, cultures, and societies. With the global spread of various technologies, information, economic capital, political, and cultural beliefs and practices, we also see that individuals and societies are becoming more transnational, multidimensional, and pluralistic. Yet, with greater interconnectedness and interdependence also comes a greater awareness of one's own cultural uniqueness, traditions, and dissimilarity to a "global culture" dominated by Western (especially American) capitalism.

41. Murphy, *Anglo-American Postmodernity*, 34–35.
42. Giddens, *Runaway World*, 30–31.

Roland Robertson calls this trend "glocalization," in which the universal (global) and the particular (local) are linked in correlative interaction.[43] In this view, globalization does not seek to obliterate traditional culture but to accelerate and promote its development. This broad view blends the *old* and *new* together forging a view of society as homogeneous and heterogeneous, similar and different, historically constituted and future seeking.

It follows that the globalizing trends in society and culture cannot be reduced simply to the growth of the global capitalist economy. There are "many globalizations." To reiterate, many scholars like Beck and Robertson, contrast "globalization" with "globalism."[44] Globalization or "globality," as Beck puts it, is a process whereby the social and cultural boundaries of the world are shrinking and the world is becoming a global society.[45] In contrast, globalism is the proliferation of the *ideology* of neoliberal global capitalism and the spread of the world free market. The trends of globalization (globality) are irreversible, but the trends of globalism (neoliberalism) are not; globalization does not necessarily presume the spread of free market capitalism, for to do so, reduces the political, social, and cultural spheres to the economic sphere. In this way, one can be for globalization but against globalism. Those against globalism refuse to believe the economy drives social, cultural, and political development, therefore, the reflexive nature of society "fights back" against the potentially hegemonic risks associated not only with the global capitalism but also political tribalism and terrorism, and ecological devastation. There is a correlation, therefore, between the broad view of globalization and reflexive postmodernity. Both perspectives of contemporary life reject the "hyperglobalist" scenario of the future, either in its capitalist or Marxist versions, and instead offer a view of the future as neither non-utopian nor non-dystopian; rather it is double-edged, ambiguous, and open-ended. As Robertson puts it, "[C]ultural clashes and tensions are an inevitable feature of globalization. What should be called the dark side of globalization involves the militancy and, indeed, violence that not infrequently accompanies these clashes."[46] Dialogue and debate among the various heterogeneous communities of the world can lead to a deepening reflexivity about the risks that confront global society, which

43. Robertson, "Globalization and the Future," 56. Also see Robertson, "Globalization: Times-Space," 25–44.
44. Beck, *What Is Globalization?*
45. Ibid., 10ff.
46. Robertson, "Globalization and the Future," 61.

draws together opposing forces in combined efforts to challenge such risks. In other words, cultural difference and otherness does not necessarily lead to conflict, but to greater interdependence in light of the global risks that diverse cultures share with each other. The experience of global risk, therefore, leads to recognition of the value of otherness and difference, which remains one of the central features of postmodernity. Yet it is just this emphasis on otherness and difference that makes postmodernity a more inclusive category for social/cultural analysis than globalization. David Tracy explains:

> "Postmodern" represents an insistence that modern rationality did enact a strategy of containment toward all who were other and different, who did not fit the modern foundational project of rationality. This same narrowness is often present implicitly in some contemporary theories of globalization, which reflect far too little on global technology's monological force and thereby upon its ignoring of cultural difference and otherness . . . However, postmodernity is also a multifaceted social-scientific notion that helps to interpret many major social and cultural changes occurring at the end of the 20th century: especially the globalization of all social systems from the economy through culture and politics and religion, and the extraordinary pace of technological change, especially in communications.[47]

Globalization becomes stretched in too many directions when it incorporates economic, political, and cultural developments without addressing its link to the theoretical issues raised in the debate over modernity/postmodernity. Stated differently, globalization can be stretched to include social and cultural elements, but it must inevitably return to the epistemological and moral issues governing human moral knowledge and action. To encapsulate all the trends of postmodernity into the theory of globalization, either in its narrow or broad forms, is reductionistic and fails to explain how our current society has altered the way we think about ethics. The globalization metanarratives are easily deconstructed as just the latest versions of a modern "totalistic" discourse. There is no one social scientific term that encapsulates the complexity of our society, and to reduce these complexities to the pattern of globalization is to do injustice to the totality of human experience.

---

47. Tracy, "Public Theology, Hope, and the Mass Media," 240–41.

What Is Risk Society?

Throughout this chapter it has become clear that postmodernity is an age of both promise and threat, of uncertainty and risk. One common feature of all the theories mentioned above is the concept of *risk*. Risk points to the real and fabricated dangers and threats to our hope for a better future. Like all forms of social analysis, including globalization, the language of risk remains potentially ideology and reductionistic. Yet the human experience of risk is one important way we encounter, in biblical language, the "principalities and powers" in our lives. Indeed, in chapter 8, I argue that risk is a secular parable of the theological language of powers. The language of risk, therefore, can be an important dialectical feature of Christian social ethics. As mentioned above, two of its leading proponents are sociologists Anthony Giddens and Ulrich Beck. They argue that unlike traditional cultures, we ambiguously see ourselves as having power over risk whilst at the same time we remain powerless in our ability to alleviate its effect on our lives. So, on one side, humanity is more optimistic about alleviating risk than traditional cultures, and on the other, we are more aware of its power over us causing catastrophic consequences. We are more hopeful *and* more pessimistic at the same time. Anthony Giddens writes:

> Risk was supposed to be a way of regulating the future, of normalizing it and bringing it under our dominion. Things haven't turned out that way. Our very attempts to control the future tend to rebound upon us, forcing us to look for different ways of relating to uncertainty. The best way to explain what is going on is to make a distinction between two types of risk. One I shall call external risk. External risk is risk experienced as coming from the outside, from the fixities of traditional nature. I want to distinguish this from manufactured risk, by which I mean risk created by the very impact of our developing knowledge upon the world. Manufactured risk refers to risk situations which we have very little historical experience of confronting. Most environmental risks, such as those connected with global warming, fall into this category.[48]

Giddens rightly points out that in premodern and modern society risks were principally caused by the "external risks" of nature, such as earthquakes, floods, pestilence, famine, and drought, (excluding wars and other human evils), whereas in postmodernity we also experience an escalating number of "manufactured risks" that we have created through our own actions, wheth-

---

48. Giddens, *Runaway World*, 43–44.

er through the misguided use of technology or environmental exploitation. We no longer accept modern progress, without awareness of its risks or side effects. Beginning in the late twentieth century, therefore, global society is in the process of shifting—or has shifted—from the modern industrial paradigm to the postmodern *risk* paradigm. Whereas modern society fostered wealth production, postmodern society manufactures risk production. We are becoming risk-conscious. For some, like some postmodernists, this reality leads to a greater sense of hopelessness, powerlessness, and sullen resentment, while for others it leads to greater reflexivity and resistance; these two responses are consistent with the two types of critical social theory discussed in this chapter. The difference between these theories emerges in their confidence in human knowledge to resist the risk-generating hegemonic powers. Does the power of manufactured risk so overwhelm us that we become complacent and unable to act, or do we become risk-takers ourselves by resisting the power of risk over our lives? Is the future open or closed?

Before persons and communities are able to resist manufactured risks, we must first understand *what* they are. Although there are numerous risks that threaten human survival, perhaps the most obvious ones are linked with the ecological crises. In *Risk Society*, Ulrich Beck writes:

> *The latency phase of risk threats is coming to an end.* The invisible hazards are becoming *visible*. Damage to and destruction of nature no longer occur outside our personal experience in the sphere of chemical physical or biological chains of effects; instead they strike more and more clearly our eyes, ears, and noses. To list only the most conspicuous phenomena: the rapid transformation of forests into skeletons, inland waterways and seas crowned with foam, animal bodies smeared with oil, erosion of buildings and artistic monuments by pollution, the chain of toxic accidents, scandals and catastrophes, and the reporting about these things in the media. The lists of toxins and pollutants in foodstuffs and articles of daily use grow longer and longer.[49]

Postmodernity is aware of the ecological risks that were hidden from previous generations, namely those that were ushered in by the false hopes of modern technological and industrial development or modernization. Although ecological risks are numerous, they include, at the very least, the threats associated with the sole reliance on nonrenewable energy sources and increasing waste production (fossil fuels and nuclear) and its impact on

49. Beck, *Risk Society*, 55.

deforestation, global warming, global climate change, and increased greenhouse gases, which leads to toxic levels of air, water, and land pollution and their impact on non-human habitats, agriculture, and human health. Clearly, these risks are global and cross all boundaries affecting all cultures, persons, and living things, thus, reveal one important aspect of globalization's "dark side." The ecological crisis puts all living things at risk, which makes them all potential "risk losers." There are, of course, "risk winners" and "risk losers" in all societies, but whereas earlier industrial risks primarily affected the poor, working class, and industrialized communities, the nature of contemporary and future ecological risks are democratic and universal. Rather than the rich and powerful, therefore, the true risk winners are those persons and communities who have the internal social, moral, and technological *resources* to challenge the power of risk production. Clearly, risk winners make it possible for all living things to have a sustainable future. If these persons and communities fail to act responsibly, however, all living things become risk losers.

In addition, there are other technological, economic, and political risks that threaten the world. First, there are risks associated with technological development and techno-scientific public discourse. The power of misguided technology threatens all life through nuclear holocaust, weapons of mass destruction, and ecological devastation. Technology becomes an instrument to control various aspects of our lives, including how we interpret reality. With the triumph of techno-scientific public discourse, power lies in the hands of experts who speak an esoteric language that is disconnected from most persons and their communities. This makes it difficult for most persons and communities to challenge the power of risk production. Second, there are risks created by economic structures. These risks are most evident in arguments against the global market by anti-globalists and postmodernists. With globalization come the risks associated with de-centering of local economies, stressing the financial over the real economy, proliferation of transnational corporations, and the market's negative effect on the activities of work, leisure, commodity fetishism, and excessive consumption. There is a fear that the power of the global market will expand into all areas of human life, making the market *ethos* a hegemonic power, and allowing the morality of the market to govern the moral practices of civil society and morality. Yet, the risks of the financial crisis of 2008 have led to a new revival of economic protectionism and reliance on the state for economic infusion of capital and investment. "Faced with this danger," says Beck, "hardcore neoliberals have converted from faith in the market to faith in the state."[50] The tenuous prospect of the world economy "is without a doubt a central source of risk in the world risk society."[51]

Besides ecological, technological, and economic spheres, the last area of risk is the political. With the increasing power of rouge political institutions, mixed with a revival of various forms of nationalism, comes the threat of greater totalitarianism, tribalism and regionalization, terrorism and more intra-national and international conflict. Before 9/11 the risks focused on the tribal violence and "ethnic cleansing" associated with Kosovo and Africa. The fear was that these regional conflicts would spill over into other neighboring countries, and create a new revival of the politics of genocide. Nevertheless, the awareness of risk has dramatically increased since 9/11. "The end of the World Trade Center gave the Americans an idea of what it means to awaken suddenly in the strange new world risk society."[52] The horrendous events of 9/11 have fostered the fear of the greater risks of terrorist violence both in America and around the world. The events of 9/11 have shifted Western nations, particular the United States, to not just employ troops in "peacekeeping" roles but to actively engage in full-fledged "war on terrorism" in Afghanistan and Iraq. The fear of terrorism has led to an escalation of world violence, which remains a continuing political risk in world risk society. "To put it pointedly," continues Beck, "the beliefs in 'global terrorism' springs from an unintended self-endangerment of modern Western society."[53] Not only is there a risk of global terrorism, but the use of nuclear weapons remains a possibility in our dangerous world. There is a concern that states such North Korea or Iran could use nuclear weapons on their neighboring enemies such as South Korea or Israel. Indeed, the threat also remains that other terrorist organizations could manage to find and detonate nuclear devices or "dirty bombs" in populated areas causing significant devastation of property and human life. These are not unrealistic risks. The last two decades have demonstrated that with more war, terrorism, genocide, "ethnic cleansing," and emerging forms of political nationalism comes the growing risks of increased tribalization and worldwide violence.

---

50. Beck, *World at Risk*, 201.
51. Ibid., 203.
52. Ibid., 68.
53. Ibid., 203.

The dangers of political, economic, and environmental catastrophes lurk on the horizon breeding fear in our world at risk.

Religion and God

This rather pessimistic outlook, however, is only one half of the picture of world risk society. Inasmuch as these numerous risks appear on the horizon, reflexive thinkers like Beck and Giddens, argue there is also the "freeing of agency" that occurs simply by experiencing risk itself. Awareness of risk leads to ethical resistance against the potential threats, dangers, and even catastrophes these risks pose to humanity and the world. So, unlike modernity, the issue is not so much who controls the power of production of wealth and goods of society—although these are still important—but who controls the power to produce and assess the "risks" and "bads" of society. More simply put, who has *power* to define and evaluate the risks of society? Which institutions control the knowledge, moral discourse, and social practices of persons and communities? The legacy of modernity has taught us to accept the truth of experts. Contemporary societies generally accept the fact that scientific experts are the most capable of evaluating global manufactured risks through their "expert languages" of medical science, techno-scientific jargon, or economic, legal, or political discourse. Yet, since the visible side-effects of these risks are becoming self-evident, there is no one scientific language or rationality that governs human understanding and analysis of these risks; with the "freeing of agency" expert knowledge is becoming *democratic*. That is, since all persons experience the risks of society, *all* persons are learning how to see themselves as the experts. This "freeing of agency," which allows common people to become aware of the risks that confront society is central to the understanding of reflexive late-modernity or reflexive modernization.

It follows that when people become aware that "expert language" itself is hegemonic and often devalues individuals, communities, and the environment, they strive for a new language to articulate this risk and new forms of community that can resist this power of risk. For a pluralistic society, therefore, to be reflexive and a "risk winner," it needs to have its various moral voices heard in the process of risk assessment and evaluation. Expert language loses its coherence among persons and communities because it hides or masks the severity of risks that common persons experience daily in their lives. In contrast, the "lay languages" of the common people, which emerge from particular cultural and religious traditions, becomes a democratic way to confront or resist the risks of society.[54] This becomes the promise of new political action or the transformative power of democratic politics. As risks become more universal, therefore, various lay and public languages will become necessary for a comprehensive risk assessment and strategic democratic politics. In theory, religion and religious ethics becomes one important lay voice in this democratic strategy.

The problem, however, is that reflexive social theory (and globalization theory) either avoids religion altogether or misconstrues its effect on the world. Generally speaking, religion takes a back seat to the more important discussions of familial, economic, political, and techno-scientific institutions. Religious institutions and individuals can help contribute to a better world, but they don't offer anything *new* to the "round-table discussion" of democratic dialogue. Furthermore, when religion does have something to contribute to this dialogue, it is the more progressive, not traditionalist, voice of religion that is more persuasive. This religious voice can be heard in alternative groups within the religious institutions themselves that evaluate their own structures and outside social risks. These movements, such as the feminist or ecological movements, not only challenge the religion's traditional views, but also contribute to "round table" discussions. So, if religion is to flourish it will be among these reflexive liberal groups. In contrast, the negative impact of religion occurs through those conservative and fundamentalist groups that become intolerant of other views. Fundamentalism misuses tradition for its own purposes, and usually uses its beliefs to demonize rather than dialogue with others. Fundamentalism contributes little to the kind of dialogic life politics, and cosmopolitan global culture, which needs to effectively build *trust* in risk society. It is exclusively uncommunicative. Saying this, however, there is little or no distinction between traditional or (orthodox) religion and fundamentalism in much social scientific literature. It is often presumed that all conservative religion is fundamentalist. The positive form of religion remains a progressive and pluralistic one; one that is inclusivistic and addresses the important issues of risk and trust in society without reverting to fundamentalism. This reasoning seems to rule out a specifically *Christian* form of social witness that challenges both conservative and liberal ideology, or in other words, it seems to rule out the possibility of a theologically informed social ethics.

54. Wynne, "May the Sheep Safely Graze," 44–83.

Another criticism of the theory of "critical society" or global reflexivity has to do with ethical judgment. All social theory must appeal to *ethical* discourse if it is to be able to explain *why* persons are capable of making moral judgments. Risk assessment and analysis always leads to *ethical* assessment and analysis, yet in social theory there is very little discussion of ethics and ethical theory. Anthony Giddens presumes, for example, that the disembedding character of modernity forces persons to reconstitute themselves into trusting and meaningful relationships, associations, and other groups, which revitalizes institutions and gives them the reflexive capacity to evaluate the risks of society. Ulrich Beck, in a slightly different view, presumes that the risks of modernity force persons, as a kind of existential reflex, to fight for survival and attack those structures and institutions that produce the risks. It follows that Beck's optimism is grounded in the sub-politics of feminist and ecological groups that challenge the status quo, whereas Giddens' hope rests in the capacity for persons to find meaningful intimate relationships, in what he calls "pure relationships," and their extension into other social groupings in society. Both social theories work toward some form of international cooperation or "cosmopolitan moment" in which people from diverse backgrounds can work together for a better world.

Nevertheless, the question still remains: where is the source of this practical knowledge or the origin of the *good* in this social reflex? Where does our conception of the good come from? Obviously, these questions pertain more to ethical theory than to social theory, but nonetheless, it ought to be explained in any theory that pertains to human moral knowledge and agency. Social theory wrongly presumes that a theory of moral reflexivity can be articulated without appealing to some moral framework for ethics. For this one needs to engage philosophical and theological conceptual frameworks and language. Once we inevitably move from social *theory* to social *ethics*, therefore, it is difficult to imagine how religion, theology, and ethics cannot be central issues of discussion. In much social theory, these three are all discourses that pertain more to "cultural studies" than to the gritty business of democratic politics that practically shapes a better world. Social theory presumes that the risks of society can only be alleviated through changes in politics. The ethical boundaries between various social institutions are strategically demarcated and defined by the social sciences, and invariably religion, theology, and ethics remain in the background.

In response to this secularist viewpoint, there is a growing amount of literature on the role of religion and ethics in contemporary global society. The most ambitious project is the four-volume work *God and Globalization*, edited by Max Stackhouse.[55] Besides bringing religion and ethics back to the center stage in the discussion, Stackhouse has organized the work around the specific theological themes of "powers" or "moral and spiritual energies," which are found in all religions, that shape social, cultural, and personal life. He writes:

> But what makes life interesting is the intellectual and conventional structures that interact with these mechanical and organic factors, that transcend them in distinctive ways, that give them an ethical orientation, that alter them by intentionally intervening in their ordinary patterns, and see in them possibilities that these factors themselves do not naturally contain or generate. The transcendence that allows humans to analyze the material and organic factors and their causation, the intentions that reach beyond what is, to imagine what might be, and the meanings or relationships to which people dedicate their lives, suggest that "moral and spiritual energies" are more than myth and are critical to personally and social life.[56]

Stackhouse argues that religion—the power that identifies the divine or sacred, the center of being, meaning, purpose, and morality of a community—further clarifies, in ways that social theory cannot, the "powers" that shape a community's existence. Stackhouse seeks to frame ethical analysis within the theological—not social scientific—understanding of social and cultural reality. If Christian social ethics is to remain *Christian* it must define the "social" in light of the "theological" and not the other way around. As Stackhouse rightly says in another place, the core problem for Christian social ethics today is not that Christian churches have neglected social issues, but rather that they have "neglected key theological motifs and turned to secular, neo-pagan, and anti-Christian monisms to define the problems we face."[57] Although the series *God and Globalization* seeks to elevate theology as an important conversation partner, it doesn't present a unified

---

55. These four volumes are entitled, *God and Globalization*, volumes 1–4. The subtitles of these volumes are: Stackhouse and Paris, *Religion and the Powers of the Common Life*; Stackhouse and Browning, *Spirit and the Modern Authorities*; Stackhouse and Obenchain, *Christ and the Dominions of Civilization*; and Stackhouse, *Globalization and Grace*.

56. Stackhouse, "General Introduction," 34.

57. Stackhouse, "Christian Social Ethics in a Global Era," 12.

theological viewpoint. The various authors of the essays, in volumes 1–3, represent different expertise in areas of Christian social ethics, but lack a common theological perspective that unites them together. This situation improves in the last volume, written solely by Stackhouse, in which he directly engages the correlation of theology with social ethics. Of the four volumes, *Globalization and Grace* attempts to present a unified view of God's providential action in relation to the age of globalization. Nevertheless, as a whole, this series does not fully explain how theological ethics serves as a basis for Christian ethics. There is, for example, too little discussion about how action of the trinitarian God, as creator, reconciler, and redeemer, relates to social scientific analysis of religion and globalization. Because divine and human agency, and theology and the social sciences, are not sufficiently distinguished, the danger is that divine agency collapses into human agency, and theology collapses into a social-scientific framework. As stated in the last chapter, this is a problem with the apologetic strategy, in which theology attempts to correlate and synthesize its own voice with the voices of others. So, for all of its appeal to a theological paradigm, this series fails to allow theology to shape its social analysis. Rather, once the social analysis begins the social scientific method takes over and theology recedes into the background.

There are serious problems when Christian ethicists begin their analysis with social theory rather than theology, as it privileges one theoretical and moral framework over another. As John Webster warns, "it is important that 'postmodernity' should not be allowed to become itself an eschatological term, as if the advent of postmodernity were the new age, such that the church and its theology now find themselves in an entirely altered situation, which requires them to rethink the fabric of Christian culture."[58] Social theory, whether postmodern or reflexive, relies principally on a materialistic, organic, or "immanentist" form of causation, usually mediated through the power of social and cultural institutions or agencies. So, when Christian ethics begins and ends with a secular social analysis, it also risks its own deconstruction. By relying upon the *reductionistic* categories of social theory, Christian social ethics risks becoming just another secular metanarrative. However, if theology is to govern our analysis of social theory, we need to allow its categories to shape our understanding of the social world, which implies beginning with a theological ethics that

58. Webster, *Word and Church*, 266.

fully integrates dogmatic theology. This shift toward theological ethics, as stated in last chapter, was a central feature in Barth's early writings. Before we return to a further discussion of Barth's ethics, however, we continue the same line of reasoning begun in this chapter by relating social theory more specifically to the modern/postmodern developments in secular ethics. For that we turn to the next chapter.

CHAPTER FIVE

From Modern to Postmodern Ethics

This chapter shifts our focus from social theory to ethical philosophy, showing how it too has been shaped by the transition from modernity to postmodernity. In chapters 1–2, we introduced this theological transition by looking at the shift from Kant and Schleiermacher to Barth. In the last chapter, we discussed characteristics of postmodernity as understood within current social theory, and concluded that social theory, by itself, cannot provide an answer to the problem of moral epistemology in social ethics. Although social theory makes positive contributions to our understanding of the social world we inhabit, it fails to provide a strong argument for *how* we ought to live in the world. With this in mind, this chapter follows the same dialectical method of reasoning as found in the last chapter by looking at ethical theory. Again, the strategy is not to establish a new hermeneutical foundation for Christian social ethics. Rather, it uses the Barthian strategy of "eavesdropping" on other viewpoints, thereby determining their similarity and dissimilarity from a theologically conceived ethical framework. Neither philosophy nor theology, says Barth, "can demonstrate the Word of God" but rather "can only bear witness, and the power of their witness is the power of the free God." "Philosophy is *not* ancillary to theology. With philosophy, theology can only want to be ancillary to the church and to Christ" (*ET*: 44–45). In its witness to the Word of God, theological ethics remains critically open to the various nontheological viewpoints that it meets along the way.

WHAT IS POSTMODERN ETHICS?

Similar to the last chapter we can say there are two general streams of postmodern ethical thought, namely deconstructionist (and pragmatist) and reflexive ethical theory. Although the latter is preferable to the former, I argue that reflexive ethics, by itself, fails to answer *how* persons gain the moral knowledge needed to evaluate social risks. Indeed, the question remains: is it possible to talk about the good and the right, without an explicit discussion of God as the divine *Other*? Hence, this chapter describes deconstructionist and reflexive moral thought in the context of several points of discussion relating to the subject of *ethics*, including: 1) the nature of the moral subject (person); 2) the relationship of the person to social structures and institutions; 3) the explanation and justification of moral truth; 4) the strategy of normative ethics; and 5) metaethics and power. Each of these issues raises certain problems or risks that make it increasingly difficult, without theological ethics, to talk at all about content of moral knowledge in postmodern society.

The Postmodern Turn

Before we discuss the differences between deconstructionist and reflexive ethics, it is important to remember that both are shaped by the general transition from modernity to postmodernity. All ethical theory, to a greater or lesser extent, has been shaped by this "postmodern turn." Unlike the modern obsession with the general, the universal, the theoretical, and the timeless, postmodernity emphasizes the singular, particular, practical, and the timely. Martha Nussbaum provides a good summary of this transition in ethical theory.

> Anglo-American moral philosophy is turning from an ethics based on enlightenment ideals of universality to an ethics based on tradition and particularity; from an ethics based on principles to an ethics based on virtue; from an ethics dedicated to the elaboration of systematic theoretical justifications to an ethics suspicious of theory and respectful of local wisdom; from an ethics based on the isolated individual to an ethics based on affiliation and care; from an ahistorical detached ethics to an ethics rooted in concreteness and history.[1]

---

1. Nussbaum, "Virtue Revived," 9.

Recalling our earlier discussion of Kant and Schleiermacher, modern ethics, in both moral philosophy and theology, presume certain elements of methodological universalism that are rejected in the postmodern turn.[2] What are these characteristics of modern ethics? First, its anthropocentrism implies a homogeneous definition of the self, which celebrates the rational, disengaged, and transcendental subject, separated from history and society. Second, it follows that social and historical particularities are overlooked in favor of universalist and ahistorical accounts of the transcendental human subject. Practically speaking, this means the subject is free to shape social structures according to the human will. Third, just as scientific laws are universal, modernists assume there are universal or natural moral laws, which are comprehended by all persons regardless of culture, religion, or individual preference. Since moral truth is self-evident and understood through human reason and the conscience, it follows that its justification rests on a universalist understanding of objective rationality that transcends local communities and traditions; its objectivity is essentially tradition-less. Fourth, since theology cannot be objectively true, the beliefs and values that derive from religious convictions remain forever attached to one's subjective beliefs or opinions. The objective reason used in ethical discourse remains separated from the subjective reason used in theological discourse. The fifth, and last, feature is the notion of a free moral agency of persons which allows persons to both *know* the good, through universalist moral principles, and *do* the good, by the sheer ability of the human will. In brief, because a person *knows* the good they are also able to do the good. So, comprehensively understood, modern ethics values the disengaged, autonomous, and rational person, who rises above his or her personal and communal particularity, and espouses a universal ethic that applies to all persons. At its core, modern ethics attempts to transcend the particularity of a specific culture's morality and discover a scientifically based universal human ethics.

In contrast, postmodern ethics discloses the hidden *otherness* of this modern viewpoint. First, unlike the (mythical) disengaged self of modernity, the postmodern self is thoroughly situated or embedded in history, language, and culture with all their specificity. Since the self is thoroughly contingent upon finite existence, Kant's transcendental subject serves as a fictional account of the human subject. Second, unlike the modernist emphasis on the infallible nature of human reason and the goodness of the will, postmodern thought stresses the fallibility of human reason and the

2. MacIntyre, *Whose Justice*, 209–348.

ambiguous nature of the human will and action. Third, unlike the modernist stress on universal and absolute moral truth, emerging from some kind of moral realism, postmodern antirealism presumes that moral truth is entirely perspectivist or relativist and relies on local wisdom. Fourth, unlike the modern preoccupation with universal schemes of normative ethics, the postmodern situation celebrates local and customary accounts of relative morality. Our learning about morality is more likely to come from the cultural anthropologist, who studies the *ethos* of a particular community, rather than from a moral philosopher who rises above all particular differences and articulates a "position from nowhere." Absolute certainty is simply another metanarrative that is deconstructed in particularistic turn of postmodernity.

Particularism and Moral Epistemology

Now that we've looked at the basic diverges between modern and postmodern ethics, we can further clarify two problems within postmodernity. These are: 1) different perspectives on the impact of cultural particularism; and 2) different viewpoints on the moral epistemology of the moral subject. The first problem explores what is meant by the *particularistic* turn of postmodern ethics. According to Gene Outka, this shift has parented two responses, namely "tradition-dependency" and "cultural contingency."[3] The former view claims that persons are embedded in the historicity of their moral language, which shapes individual and communal beliefs and practices. This *diachronic* view, exemplified by Alasdair MacIntyre, can be called "tradition-dependent" or "community-dependent" ethics.[4] It values social differences but seeks to continue the discussion about the possibility of moral truth, normative ethics, and a common morality. It accepts ethical plurality without endorsing a view of ethical pluralism. In contrast, the latter view of socio-cultural contingency presumes that persons are completely acculturated into all their moral beliefs and practices. This *synchronic* view of contingency is exemplified by Richard Rorty, who claims "there is nothing 'beneath' socialization or prior to history which is definetory of the human."[5] If, as Rorty claims, "sociality goes all the way down," then even traditions or communities cannot transcend their own socialization. In short, traditions

---

3. Outka, "Particularist Turn," 93–118.
4. Ibid., 95.
5. Rorty, *Contingency, Irony, and Solidarity*, xiii.

and communities are *not* reflexive. "A culture does not 'decide' to accept certain idioms and discard others, as an act of will or the conclusion of argument."[6] Once we consider both theories, we may conclude there are more grave risks associated with the latter view, in that it appears to lack a self-critical perspective. Without the reflexive capacity to evaluate one's own sociality, ethical thinking collapses into moral tribalism and ethical pluralism. This point will be clarified later, when I discuss the thought of Rorty and MacIntyre accompanying the two main traditions of postmodern ethics. Before that, however, we discuss the second problem, of moral knowledge, as relating to the debate between moral realism and antirealism.

The second significant problem is how moral epistemology is understood in postmodernity. The debate about moral truth in postmodernity is rooted in the distinction between moral realism and antirealism. At its most basic level, this question asks whether persons and cultures discover the moral truth that is already present in human existence, or whether they create or invent moral truth for themselves? The *realist* asserts that moral truth, like scientific truth, is not simply true because some persons, groups, or communities choose to make them "true" or "good" for either personal or social reasons. Indeed, moral realism rejects moral theories that ground ethical judgment in personal or social preferences, convention (law), pleasure, or utility. Moral truth is grounded in the *reality* of things, or the "way things really are" in the world. As Jeffrey Stout points out the ancient Greeks believed, in error, that the Sun revolved around the Earth and slavery was ethical, and today we no longer accept these accounts of reality as "true."[7] Moral realism claims that discovering moral truth, like scientific truth, takes longer for some communities than for others. Once we discover this truth, however, we must have our lives and worldviews shaped by its *reality*. Using Stout's example, we've discovered that geocentric view of the solar system and slavery no longer conform to reality as we know it.

The tradition of Western theological and philosophical ethics has always claimed some type of realist perspective, whether grounded in various versions of natural law, divine command theory, or a creation-constituted universal rationality. For Christians, moral realism is affirmed because it is grounded in the conviction that God created a moral universe with moral truths that, once discovered, becomes the basis for our individual lives and

---

6. Outka, "Particularist Turn," 102.
7. Stout, *Ethics After Babel*, 21–32.

communities. In postmodernity, a philosophically grounded moral realism can only be possible from the standpoint of a reflexive moral theory, yet as we shall see, this theory too has problems without a view of *theological realism*. Nevertheless, unlike the strategy of moral realists, antirealists claim that moral truth does not have any ontological existence apart from our ability to create and invent its application to our lives.[8] Moral values, virtues, principles are not universal or objective, nor can they be "discovered" in and through God's revelation, human reason and experience, or in the natural world. This perspective, typical of much postmodern thought, presumes that morality cannot give us real knowledge about how things really *are* in the world because no such actual knowledge really exists. Although, in theory, there are many types of antirealism, for our purposes we can discuss the two views of ethical relativism and ethical perspectivism. Alasdair MacIntyre explains the difference between these two viewpoints:

> The relativist challenge rests upon a denial that rational debate between and rational choice among rival traditions is possible; the perspectivist challenge puts in question the possibility of making truth claims from within any one tradition. For if there is a multiplicity of rival traditions, each with its own characteristic modes of rational justification internal to it, then that very fact entails that no one tradition can offer those outside it good reasons for excluding the theses of its rival. Yet if this is so, no one tradition is entitled to arrogate to itself an exclusive title; no one tradition can deny legitimacy to its rivals.[9]

We discuss these two theories in more detail by beginning with ethical relativism. In its crudest form this position simply says that because we have no absolute *certainty* about moral truth claims, this makes the notion of "moral truth" itself vacuous. It is fruitless to have a dialogue or debate about moral truth because it cannot be *proved* to be true. This view, also called "hard relativism," is oddly the postmodern other to the Enlightenment's absolute certainty in moral judgment.[10] Because absolute certainty no longer exists, relativism moves to the other pole on the spectrum by claiming there is *no* truth. It has long been pointed out, the great irony of this position is that it denies what it affirms, thereby making absolute non-certainty an absolute

8. Blackburn, "How to be an Ethical Antirealist," 361–76.
9. MacIntyre, *Whose Justice*, 352.
10. William Schweiker makes the distinction between "hard" and "soft" relativism. See Schweiker, *Responsibility in Christian Ethics*, 22–24.

judgment. It is self-contradictory. Unlike this theory, the second theory of *perspectivism* or "soft relativism" argues that cultural morality serves a functional purpose for a particular culture. "In this form of relativism," says William Schweiker, "there are distinctive moral factors (i.e., moral values and norms not reducible to other facets of life, but these are interrelated with other factors in culture, like beliefs about family structure, political power, or human finitude."[11] This means that moral claims are invented to be normative within the context of linguistic, historical, and socio-cultural contingencies, but since all moral codes are particular, no person or community can judge outside moral codes as right or wrong. This view leads to ethical pluralism. Since moralities are like incommensurable self-referential languages they cannot be removed from their particular context, nor can they be translated into other languages without losing their meaning. This makes it simply impossible for cross-cultural shared meanings to develop about the good from diverse cultures or moral traditions. A common understanding of the good becomes not only problematic to justify but also difficult to implement into practice.

POSTMODERN ETHICS: DECONSTRUCTIONIST AND PRAGMATIST

We have seen how there are divergences of thought within postmodern ethics. With these distinctions in mind, we now turn to a discussion of the two central approaches to ethics that correspond to the two approaches in the previous chapter. Although both the deconstruction and reflexive viewpoints challenge the absolute certainty of modernist ethics, they differ on the degree of enculturation and on the claims of moral realism/antirealism. Deconstruction theorists, driven by their commitments to socio-cultural contingency and antirealism, become paralyzed in making normative moral judgments for social improvement. In their rejection of modern utopian metanarratives, they implicitly accept a dystopian view of society as cynical, fragmented, and nihilistic. In contrast, reflexive thought believes that with the self-criticism of modernity comes a freeing of agency, a self-reflective capacity, to challenge not only the utopian risks of modernity but the dystopian ones of postmodern skepticism and pessimism. In the next section, I discuss deconstructionist ethics as it relates to the six issues mentioned in the beginning of the chapter. I begin with

11. Ibid., 22.

European post-structuralism and deconstructionism and end with the American pragmatism of Richard Rorty.

Post-Structuralism

Two good examples of deconstructionist ethics are Jacques Derrida and Jean Francois-Lyotard. For post-structuralists like Derrida, all language remains contextual and relative to the act of interpreting by persons in continual flux. Saying this, however, does not imply that Derrida is a moral relativist. Deconstruction is principally not about the truth of moral claims as much as it is about the character of language and texts. Texts are not fixed entities but are in continual flux and change, and can be violently altered and changed by later interpreters. Since no text has a final meaning, any particular meaning from a text remains contextual, local, and limited. Any attempt to find the true, correct, or right meaning of a text must be endlessly postponed or deferred. This is what Derrida implies by his concept of *différance*, which combines the meaning of "difference" between objects in texts and objects in one's life with the "deferral" of all true meaning of the text. So, for example, whatever similarities may appear between the narrative of the Bible and one's personal history is overshadowed by a more fundamental *différance*, which presumes dissimilarity, suspicion, incompleteness, and intertextuality. Texts are not integrated totalities but diffused collections of other texts, which, held together, lead to more interpretations and more texts, never to reach a state of finality or completeness. Unlike modernity's confidence in the certainty of human knowledge, Derrida implies that all human knowledge remains provisional, contextual, and unfinished. Moreover, the deconstructive view of texts and language spills over into how the human subject is understood. That is, just as texts don't have authors with purposive intentions, so too, language does not have persons with stable, coherent identities. Derrida proposes a radical *decentering* of the subject, which invariably leads to the death of the modern subject. This does not imply that there is no such thing as a personal identity of the subject. Rather, it makes the claim that just as texts are constantly changing, a particular human identity remains in a never-ending process of flux, change, and movement. In short, there is no *continuous* entity called the self. Rather, the self, like the text, is continually remade within new relative and indeterminate situations. The modern subject, the "I am" of Descartes, in postmodernity, becomes deconstructed, fragmented, and thrown into a multiplicity of meanings, purposes, and interpretations. The self remains in a constant heterogeneous state of becoming.

Likewise, since ethical knowledge is also deconstructed and remains in constant flux, there are no objective grounds for making normative moral judgments. Although there is a strong ethical concern about human injustice in Derrida's writings, it remains problematic to offer reasons why we "ought" to be concerned. Given his Marxist sympathies, Derrida remains hopeful for justice and democracy, but these ideas remain "indeterminate" and not tied to any practical social embodiment in contemporary practice.[12] Indeed, although Derrida is generally critical of institutional religion and its message of "determinate messianism," he is willing to hold out for the "messianic without messianism," and the idea of justice and democracy.[13] Derrida is not a pessimist, but he fails to find any determinacy or permanence for his hope, which makes his theory rather unworkable for a social ethics that seeks to find objective reasons for having hope in our world. Derrida's eschatology is eschatology without hope.

In a similar way, Lyotard's deconstructionist method wages "war on totality" as found in any universal metanarratives. Yet, at the same time, Lyotard opens the door to a social ethics of embodiment by discussing the importance of "little narratives" in ethics and politics.[14] These "little narratives" do not depend on external objective validation, but are the internal language and practices of the communities that authorize and legitimate them; they are self-legitimating. Hence, since discourse about truth and morality can only be understood within the confines of some local determinism, some interpretative community, its purported meanings and anticipated effects are bound to break down when taken out of these isolated domains. Hence, individuals must learn to depend on "local narratives" for the way they perceive the world. These narratives enable persons to *create* or *invent* their ethics without the use of metanarratives. In the end, however, like Derrida, there is no way to claim they are true because to do so would imply a "totalistic" account of morality, which is no longer possible in the postmodern condition.

Perhaps the best example of this type of postmodern ethics is Michel Foucault. In *History of Sexuality* (1978), *The Use of Pleasure* (1985), and

12. Derrida, *Specters of Marx*.
13. Ibid., 59.
14. Lyotard, *Differend* and *Political Writings*.

Care of the Self (1986), Foucault traces the "genealogy" of the modern subject. He demonstrates how the characteristics of the Cartesian self, namely agency, autonomy, and transcendence are products of modern society and historical creation. Given the "death of modern man," what remains of human subjectivity? He writes: "From the idea that the self is not given to us I think there is only one possible consequence: we have to create ourselves as a work of art."[15] Like Derrida, Foucault claims there is no core essential, authentic, or potential self to be realized. Rather, the postmodern self must create *who* it is at any particular moment by piecing together cultural discourses, as tools, into a collective identity. Regarding this, Foucault writes: "[T]o all those who still wish to talk about man, about his reign or his liberation, to all those who still ask themselves questions about what man is in his essence, to all those who wish to take him as their starting-point in their attempts to reach the truth . . . to all these warped and twisted forms of reflection we can answer only with a philosophical laugh."[16] Like Lyotard, Foucault rejects the totalistic languages of freedom or liberation but affirms the use of local languages to enable persons to resist the various forms of power that destroy the self and community. "It is through the re-appearance of this knowledge, of these local popular knowledges, these disqualified knowledges, that criticism performs its work."[17] Power produces domination but also *resistance* to domination.

Since repression is always local and particular, Foucault argues the resistance should always be local and particular. His concept of "local resistance" implies that persons can resist at the sight of repression. The social practices and games of power in society "give one's self the rules of law, the techniques of management, and also the ethics, the ethos, the practice of self which would allow these games of power to be played with a minimum of domination."[18] Still, even though persons may engage in local resistance, it remains problematic for any person or community to judge right or wrong outside their own moral codes or cultures. In this way, Foucault's understanding of ethics relies heavily on the thought of philosopher Friedrich Nietzsche. Indeed, Nietzsche stands behind much deconstructionist thought. In *The Will to Power* Nietzsche writes: "Knowledge works

---

15. Quoted in Dreyfus and Rabinow, *Michel Foucault*, 287.
16. Foucault, *Order of Things*, 342–43.
17 17. Foucault, *Power/Knowledge*, 82.
18. Foucault, "Ethic of the Care," 18.

as an *instrument* of power."[19] Moral truth, if it can be found, does not exist in Kantian universal imperatives, but as the instrumental means by which persons and communities struggle for their own existence and by so doing "struggle for power."[20] So, what Foucault learns from Nietzsche is that it is "impossible for knowledge not to engender power."[21] This means the "side effects" of modern knowledge and truth disclose a masked form of "power." Thus, even the most noble and benevolent intentions and consequences mask the hidden hegemonic power relations that forcibly marginalize, devalue, and homogenize the *other*. Since the *other* (marginalized person) is always pushed aside for some utopian or idealistic purpose, persons, who care for themselves, can also learn to appreciate the other as a victim of larger social forces. Being in the presence of the other evokes awe, reverence, respect, caring, and friendship. Therefore, being and acting morally responsible means being open to the *otherness* of the other or practicing a responsibility to otherness.

With his dual commitment to deconstruct modern knowledge, including ethics, and his personal resistance to oppressive power relations, Foucault's thought is at the very least paradoxical, if not contradictory. Without explicitly acknowledging it, he presumes that some power configurations are bad, while other power structures are clearly better than others. How can this be? Charles Taylor puts it well: "Foucault's analysis seems to bring evils to light; and yet he wants to distance himself from the suggestion which would seem inescapably to follow, that the negation or overcoming of these evils promotes a good."[22] Like Derrida or Lyotard, his understanding of the death of the modern self undermines the possibility of a resistance ethic, which he so desperately wants for individuals and communities. To be sure he calls for self-creative acts of local resistance, but this implies a self that knows which power relations to resist, why resistance itself is *good*, and what power relations are *evil*. The self cannot know with absolute certainty that particular kinds of moral knowledge are true and good because that would affirm some form of moral realism presupposed by the modern subject.

As a result, deconstructionist ethics remains a problematic risk because it fails to provide any normative criteria, in a pluralistic society and

19. Nietzsche, *Will to Power*, 11.
20. Nietzsche, *Twilight of Idols*, 71.
21. Foucault, *Power/Knowledge*, 52.
22. Taylor, "Foucault on Freedom and Truth," 69.

culture, for assessing which ideologies, structures, or institutional patterns and processes are better than others. All one can do is *track* the differences among discourses and disclose the hidden power relations and effects. Making moral judgments is in a continuous holding pattern. To make prescriptive moral judgments means committing to some position that may ultimately be deconstructed and unmasked. Persons can, if they choose to, speak out in rather *ad hoc* and local fashion against violence, prejudice, and other kinds of injustice, but they cannot claim they are doing it because it is good or right in any normative or objective sense. Although these theorists implicitly endorse *hidden* normative criteria of responsibility toward the good of otherness, they cannot provide a fundamentally *good* reason for practicing responsible ethics. If all normative ethical statements are really masked forms of power and manipulation, then why should I risk my own self-interest and act responsibly toward the *other*? The other may be my enemy who seeks to have power over me. Once morality is reduced to power, then ethics becomes reduced to the Nietzschian "will-to-power" and "might makes right." The most basic threat to persons in postmodernity, then, is that the language of power dominates our language of ethics.

Pragmatism

Another stream of mainstream postmodern thought emerges from the pragmatism of philosopher Richard Rorty. Unlike European postmodernists, Rorty's Deweyan pragmatism does feel the compulsion to deconstruct the modern subject because it already begins from the standpoint of socio-cultural contingency. Rorty agrees with the others that there are no abstract, universalist, or utopian narratives of emancipation that actually exists in contemporary society; even political discourse in democracy is the result of concrete, local, and ambiguous moral discourses. Still, distancing himself from the others, he is more outspoken about the goods of liberal democracy. "Deweyan pragmatists urge us to think of ourselves as part of a pageant of historical progress which will gradually encompass all of the human race, and are willing to argue that the vocabulary which twentieth-century social democrats use is the best vocabulary the race has come up with so far. . . . But pragmatists are quite sure that their own vocabulary will be superseded—and, from their point of view, the sooner the better."[23] For Rorty, the self-assertive nature of modernity has created worthy examples

23. Rorty, "Cosmopolitanism," 62–68.

of reformist politics such as the free press, universal education, republican government, and the rest of the apparatus of liberal democracy. These developments are good because they *work* better than other alternatives, and not because "these institutions are truer to human nature, or more rational, or in better accord with the universal moral law, than feudalism or totalitarianism."[24] Through the democratic process of conversation and dialogue, persons can learn to live with complicated differences, and forge new paths forward into an uncertain future. Since Rorty is a pragmatist and perspectivist, he is simply not satisfied with allowing differences to remain differences, however. Rather, inventing a practical ethic to live by becomes the most important function of a liberal, democratic society. Rorty is more willing than Derrida to base his hope in justice within a pragmatically ordered and educated democratic society. "Our children need to learn, early on, to see the inequalities between their own fortunes and those of other children as neither the Will of God nor the necessary price for economic efficiency, but as an inevitable tragedy."[25] Although persons, theoretically speaking, are socially and culturally contingent, Rorty remains hopeful because of the witness of history and of those who have sought the inspiration to live in a more just and humane world.

In his book *Contigency, Irony, and Solidarity*, considered by many to be his most important book, Rorty's hero is the "liberal ironist." A "liberal" is someone who thinks cruelty to persons is immoral, and an "ironist" is a person who faces the contingency of his beliefs. So, a "liberal ironist" is a person who can simultaneously claim his moral beliefs are socially and culturally conditioned, yet still be willing to defend them to his last breath. Like other deconstructionists, he rejects traditional religious, philosophical, or scientific claims about an essential and fixed human nature, which are grounded in a divinized world that proposes "the world as a divine creation."[26] Instead, we must accept the fact that the world is "de-divinized," which presumes "that we try to get to the point where we no longer worship *anything*, where we treat *nothing* as a quasi-divinity, where we treat *everything*—our language, our conscience, our community—as a product of time and chance."[27] Although Rorty denies moral realism, he argues that personal

---

24. Rorty, "Habermas and Lyotard," 170.
25. Rorty, *Philosophy and Social Hope*, 204.
26. Rorty, *Contigency, Irony, and Solidarity*, 21.
27. Ibid., 22.

and social moral behavior will not necessarily degenerate and ultimately disappear into relativism or nihilism. Even the ironist understands this point, and is willing to affirm the pragmatic truth of his "final vocabulary."[28] It is this personal commitment to one's truth that leads to moral action. Rorty's philosophy asks persons to commit themselves to beliefs and practices that remain relative and contingent and could theoretically change at any time. Indeed, why are the beliefs and actions of a liberal ironist any better than any other person? Inasmuch as Rorty attempts to offer a pragmatic answer to this question, his antirealist presumptions present a similar contradictory view that rejects any normative language of right/wrong or good/bad for ethics. So, even though his liberal social philosophy attempts to explain why persons ought to care for society and others, there is no normative or objective reasons for doing so. Ethically speaking, there is no normative moral claim that prohibits someone from being a narcissist or a nihilist.

For all of their celebration of difference and particularity, deconstructionists and pragmatists do prefer one set moral beliefs over others. They do prefer political freedom over tyranny, personal liberty over slavery, and social inclusion over exclusion. Still, they cannot appeal to some ethical norm or objective good in their justification for why some ideas and practices are "better" than others. At its core, there is, in Anthony Thiselton's words, a "forked rhetoric" that dominates postmodern ethical thought. He further explains: "On one side it has de-centered the self, de-centered ethics, and de-centered society; on the other side it claims simply to leave everything as it is. But how can it be "emancipatory" if it leaves everything as it is? It rightly unmasks instances of manipulative power which disguise themselves as claims to truth. But does this lost innocence entail the universal doctrinal cynicism that all truth-claims are bids for power? Does it invoke contextual pragmatism which views all truth-claims as relative only to the internal norm of given communities?"[29] Most deconstructionists personally prefer justice to injustice, peace to violence, and freedom to slavery, which inspires persons to resist hegemonic power relations. Yet, given their commitment to an antirealist conception of moral truth, there is no reason why other persons *ought* to choose this language or final vocabulary. Why should we choose democracy over facisim, or freedom over terrorism? Despite their commitment to perspectivism, their theories, in a world dominated by

28. Ibid., 73.
29. Thiselton, *Interpreting God*, 135.

power, easily collapse into relativism, which makes it impossible to talk at all about normative ethics. Once ethics becomes reduced to power, there is no *good* reason why persons should prefer injustice to justice, violence to peace, and slavery to freedom, if it is not in their self-interest to do so? If there is no good or right reason to act morally, then *why* should one be moral in the first place? Deconstructionist thinkers, in theory, present persons who are unable to move beyond their socio-cultural contingency to *reflect* about themselves, others, society, moral truth, or normative ethics. That is, without moral reflexivity, they become paralyzed in making normative moral judgments for social improvement. Although they hope for a better world, they cannot account for why this is more ethical than the current world in which we live.

REFLEXIVE ETHICS: SELF TO SOCIETY

In contrast to deconstructionist ethics, reflexive moral thought affirms that with the self-criticism of modernity comes a "freeing of agency," a self-reflective capacity, to challenge not only the utopian risks of modernity but the dystopian ones of postmodern skepticism and pessimism. Hence, although reflexive realist epistemology departs from premodern theological accounts of moral realism, as found in natural law (or naturalism) or the divine command, it nonetheless attempts to establish some kind of correlation between an objective moral order and subjective consciousness. In *Sources of the Self*, Charles Taylor argues that the modern self, in contrast to ancient or medieval self, rejects an external universal objective moral order, but seek to ground a similar moral order in our own powers of construction or our own activity of willing. Taylor says: "We are now in an age in which the publicly accessible cosmic order of meanings is an impossibility. The only way we can explore the order in which we are set with an aim to defining moral sources is through . . . personal resonance."[30] This "process of internalization" transfers outside objective sources of moral knowledge to the subject's consciousness. As moral sources are channeled through "personal resonance," these sources can lead to greater reflexivity, creativity, and personal and social transformation. Although this realist conception of moral truth is challenged by deconstructionists, it has continued into postmodernity as viewed through the relationship with some external *other*.

30. Taylor, *Sources of the Self*, 512.

Although numerous theorists could be mentioned as examples of reflexive moral thought, I have selected *four* particular representatives. These four have been selected because they represent an *expansive* reflexive movement moving outward in concentric circles from the moral self, to identifiable groups, to diachronic moral traditions, and finally to society. The purpose is to show the variety of reflexive thought, while demonstrating how each theory remains committed to some form of moral realism. So, the first is the hermeneutical theory of Zygmunt Bauman, who engages personal other as the source of moral truth; the second is a feminist "ethic of care," represented by Carol Gilligan, who grounds moral knowledge in the interdependent nature of the person and gender-human experience; the third view, represented by Alasdair MacIntyre, grounds moral knowledge in a diachronic tradition-constituted rationality; and lastly, is the social theory of Ulrich Beck, whom we discussed in the last chapter. All four views presume the particularistic turn of postmodernity, but also describe how the self and society are reflexive, which moves the argument toward more normative and responsible moral action.

Self to Other

A direct alternative to deconstructionist thought is the "postmodern ethics" of Zygmunt Bauman. Like other postmodernists, Bauman attacks the modernist attempt to reduce persons, in all their particularity, to a kind of general anthropocentrism or universal humanity, which inevitably reduces morality to power. Unlike them, however, Bauman discovers a common moral condition from the personal encounter of the self and the other, which suggests not just a "responsibility to otherness," but a theory of "responsibility *for the Other*."[31] At its core, Bauman's ethic of postmodern responsibility relies heavily upon the thought of Emmanual Levinas. Like Levinas, Bauman prioritizes the "moral self" over the "social self." That is, the practice of being moral ("being-for-the-other") precedes the act of self-constitution ("being-for-oneself") and socialization ("being-with-the-other"). This establishes the basis for persons to evaluate unjust power structures and relations of society, once considering the moral obligations and responsibility they have for others. Moral responsibility, then, emerges through the moral subject's *encounter* with the claim of the other "face to face," which provides the moral knowledge necessary to act responsibly "for

31. Bauman, *Postmodern Ethics*, 14.

the other."[32] So, encountering the moral claims of the other makes it possible for the "moral self" to understand, practice, and embody the *reality* of the moral life. Bauman's apparent account of moral realism rests on the moral claims that the other presents *to* the self. With the demise of moral absolutes and norms in postmodernity, he writes, this "has made the responsibilities of the actor more profound, and, indeed, more consequential, then ever before."[33] To be sure, Bauman admits embodying the moral life into actual practice is deeply "contradictory" and "ambiguous." A postmodern ethic refuses to transcend the "messiness" of the human condition and society. Hence, unlike modern theory, which claims the "not-yet-resolved" is "in-principle-resolvable," postmodern ethics is incurably *aporetic*, which implies that even good intentions may lead to negative consequences. Indeed, says Bauman, "virtually every moral impulse, if acted upon in full, leads to immoral consequences (most characteristically, the impulse to care for the Other, when taken to its extreme, leads to the annihilation of the autonomy of the Other, to domination and oppression)."[34] Given this point, moral responsibility for the other always demands more than we are capable of acting upon, or put differently, the process of being moral will never be complete or satisfied with the standards that it creates for itself. At its core, Bauman's theory is concerned more with the freedom and the demands of *love* for the other, than with abstract principles of justice, which is often intertwined with other forms of hegemonic social control.

Although Bauman grounds moral reflexivity in the self/other encounter, he appears to present community and tradition itself as hegemonic. Although better than a world of "privatized individuals," Bauman argues community cannot cultivate moral selves either because it "replaces the torments of moral responsibility with the certainty of discipline and submission."[35] Bauman is rightly deeply suspicious about how alignments of power mitigate moral responsibility, but are *all* groups, communities, and traditions heteronomous and hegemonic? Cannot the moral self be shaped by a socially constitutive narrative or worldview that transcends the self/other interaction? It is true that community uses its own prejudices and power to manipulate persons, but are there not at least some groups, communities, and traditions that foster moral responsibility *for* the other?

32. Ibid., 85–92.
33. Bauman, *Life in Fragments*, 6.
34. Bauman, *Postmodern Ethics*, 11.
35. Bauman, *Life in Fragments*, 278.

Can the moral self, as interdependent self, be understood *without* formative groups, communities, and traditions? This presumption becomes problematic when applied to social ethics, where judgments are made about persons we don't meet "face to face." And yet, Bauman is correct to point out the hidden dangers of communities that seek to form strong identities. Communities often form themselves to the exclusion of the other. What communities and traditions call their "distinctiveness" is really a "division into 'us' and 'them.'"[36] The power of group homogeneity is by its very nature exclusionary of the other, whereas in a "bizarre yet perverse way" the stranger's "presence is comforting, even reassuring."[37]

The second example of a reflexive theorist is psychologist Carol Gilligan. Since her seminal publication of *In a Different Voice* (1982), she has influenced a generation of diverse voices in feminist ethics. Like Bauman, Gilligan seeks to move beyond the standpoint of the "generalized other" to the standpoint of the "concrete other." Her notion of the relational self presents an alternative to the modern disengaged self or the postmodern decentered self, while her notion of autonomy implies that one's self-determination and moral responsibility occurs only in relationship with and for others.[38] This understanding of the relational self serves as the basic structure for her feminist "ethic of care," which emerges from the tension between male/female and justice/care polarities. Modern moral theory leaps from experience of male rationality to human rationality without even considering women's experience or rationality. Hence, Gilligan's feminist analysis demonstrates how modern moral theories of development, from Sigmund Freud to Lawrence Kolhberg, have failed to fit the "truth of women's experience" into their empirical and methodological studies, which elevates as a model the independent and autonomous self instead of the interdependent and relational self.[39] "The notion of the relational self," says Frazier and Lacey, "in contrast to both atomistic and inter-subjective selves, nicely captures our empirical and logical interdependence and the certainty to our identity of our relations with others and with the practices and institutions, whilst retaining an ideal of human uniqueness and discreteness as central to our sense of ourselves."[40]

36. Bauman, *Community*, 2.
37. Ibid., 145.
38. Benhabib, *Situating the Self*, 148–77.
39. Gilligan, *In a Different Voice*, 62.
40. Frazer and Lacey, *Politics of Community*, 178. Indeed, the relational self "entails

Gilligan's theory makes two central claims. On one hand, she repeatedly contrasts the "woman's voice" of care with the "male voice" of justice; these views are viewed as gender-specific ideals comprising the differences between female and male experiences, rationality, and morality. Male reasoning abstracts universal ethical principles from concrete situations, whereas woman's reasoning, more experientially, begins and ends with the concrete situation of human relationships. In contrast to the abstract voice of justice, which presumes human separateness, and the priority of individual equality, the voice of care is more concrete and contextual, presumes human connectedness, and the priority of maintaining human relationships. On the other hand, she also emphatically states that both theories are inclusive of all persons, regardless of gender, and through isolating these "voices" or perspectives, she yields a "more encompassing view of the lives of both of the sexes."[41] So, she is attempting to provide a comprehensive account of how moral judgments are related to emotional experiences. Hence, Gilligan's intention is to see an ethics of justice complimented by an ethics of care; these voices remain complimentary not oppositional. She is not interested only in developing a human ethics based on women's experience, but a human ethic based on human experience. Nevertheless, although Gilligan's care ethic presents a *realist* account of reflexive postmodern feminist thinking, she remains controversial in feminist thought. Some critics argue that she presents a "conservative voice" that simply revives traditional middle-class conceptions of femininity, namely associating women with care, concreteness, and relationships.[42] Others criticize Gilligan's insistence on the equality of the two voices, by arguing for the *superiority* of the feminine over the masculine justice voice, and that the voices of justice and care are incommensurable.[43] The deconstructionist Iris Young, for example, criticizes Gilligan's "relational self" as simply too modern, which continues the fundamental belief that subjects can truly understand and communicate with other selves, which implies a unified center of desire. More like Foucault and Derrida, Young celebrates heterogeneity, opacity and difference.[44]

---

the collapse of any self/other or individual/community dichotomy without abandoning the idea of genuine agency and subjectivity." Ibid., 178.
41. Gilligan, *In a Different Voice*, 4.
42. Card, *Feminist Ethics*, 17.
43 For example, see: Ruddick, *Maternal Thinking* and Noddings, *Caring*.
44. Young, *Throwing Like a Girl*.

Gilligan's feminist theory presents an alternative reading of moral realism and the human person considering the particularistic turn in postmodernity. As Susan Heckman puts it: "Gilligan cannot claim that her interpretation is truer and more objective because she has defined truth as a function of theoretical perspective. The 'truth' that Gilligan claims for her perspective is thus a truth that is *internal* to the theoretical perspective itself, just as the 'truth' of the dominate conception is *internal* to that perspective."[45] In brief, Gilligan's approach presents an example of internal realism. "Internal realism," as Hilary Putnam reminds us, "is, at bottom, just the insistence that realism is not incompatible with conceptual relativity."[46] This means that one's understanding of the moral life always emerges from a particular system of beliefs and set of internally constituted rules, but aims one's perspective at a larger reality it attempts to explain; it begins from a particular perspective but moves toward a comprehensive picture of reality. In Gilligan's case, she begins from the standpoint of women's rationality and experience in order to *discover* something *real* about human morality. Indeed, even more than Bauman, she includes the reflexive capacity of groups and community into her method. Saying this, however, she also shows little appreciation of how diachronic communities, tradition, and pluralistic society can nurture reflexivity. For that we turn to further examples.

Tradition to Society

In contrast to Bauman and Gilligan, MacIntyre places at the center of his theory the importance of tradition and community, thereby having an impact on Christian ethics. In his various works, he argues that morality is a tradition-guided inquiry that consists of an institutionally embodied set of shared convictions, commitments, and practices. In *After Virtue* (1984), MacIntyre concludes that with the demise of the "Enlightenment project," the justification of moral truth occurs within its own "narrative" context or what he calls a "tradition of moral enquiry." His moral theory presumes that communal virtues and practices determine the course of the moral life more than modernist quest for "clear and distinct" moral ideas, which provide foundations for universal moral principles. This conclusion sets the agenda for his later works *Whose Justice? Which Rationality?* (1988) and *Three Rival*

---

45. Heckman, *Moral Voices*, 5.
46. Putnam, *Many Faces of Realism*, 111.

Traditions of Moral Enquiry (1989), in which he develops further his understanding of tradition-constituted rationality, which implies that persons are, at their core, interdependent upon communities and traditions for their identity, and both persons and traditions are *reflexive*, in that it is the tradition that nurtures participants to engage in an ongoing self-reflective description, analysis, and critique of their own behavior in light of their own and other traditions. "To be outside all traditions," says MacIntyre, "is to be a stranger to enquiry; it is to be in a state of intellectual and moral destitution."[47] Not unlike scientific traditions, therefore, moral traditions attempt to explain something *real* about the world, and will inevitably come across situations where the traditions must be altered, transformed, or self-corrected due to contemporary circumstances. It is at this point where truth is *discovered* and dialogue with "rival traditions" becomes useful. MacIntyre uses the term, "epistemological crises" to signify when a tradition is unable to effectively answer these problems through the use of its own resources, as found in its own beliefs, institutions, and practices. At this point, it may seek to borrow or dialogue with other traditions, or generate a new imaginative response to the new situation. In either case, the reference point is how well these new resources correspond to reality itself.

MacIntyre's *correspondence* theory of truth presumes that we correspond our particular moral perspectives with the world of real objects, and in so doing, discover truth. "So correspondence or the lack of it becomes a feature of the developing complex conception of truth."[48] MacIntyre's "correspondence theory" splits the difference between universalist and antirealist epistemologies, thus advances a reflexive account of how moral traditions justify their moral claims. There are two kinds of justification for truth claims in MacIntyre's thought: 1) what we may call "diachronic justification" demonstrates how one's own tradition has solved problems its predecessor could not, and to explain why its predecessor could not solve them; and 2) what may call "synchronic justification" explains why one's tradition is better equipped than its rivals to address internal and external problems, or said differently, why some traditions are better than others.[49] Diachronic justification occurs when a tradition is capable, given its own resources or the resources of rival traditions, to reconstitute itself

---

47. MacIntyre, *Whose Justice*, 367.
48. Ibid., 357.
49. Murphy, *Anglo-American Postmodernity*, 57–58, 124–25.

in the midst of an intellectual crises. More crucial for conversation among traditions is synchronic justification, which allows traditions the reflexive capacity to demonstrate that they have better answers to the internal problems of other rival traditions. The failure or success of traditions is based on whether they can surmount their own epistemological crises while still yet remaining linked with its own authoritative texts, beliefs, and practices, as well as provide answers to the internal crises of other rival traditions. Hence, traditions can learn how to use a second language, so that dialogue with a rival tradition is possible. Although critics have argued that MacIntyre's tradition-constituted rationality remains too close to perspectivism, he would argue that through the dialogue among traditions, one tradition can understand its own defects from a rival tradition. So, even though MacIntyre argues that ethics is only intelligible from within the particular language and practices of a moral tradition, he further says that rational arguments can take place among traditions, which in the end, appeals to whole of reality. Not unlike Gilligan, MacIntyre presents a theory of "internal realism" that begins with the particular and moves outward toward the general; that is, from a particular moral tradition and moves outward toward a human morality.

We've learned that dialogue and conversation are important for any reflexive moral theory, whether it is between the self and the other, men and women, or among communities and traditions, but what about society itself? Can a pluralistic society, composed of various conflictive traditions and power structures, become morally reflexive of itself so that it can speak with one *common* voice and act as one community? As mentioned in the last chapter, the theory of reflexive modernization provides such a reflexive theory of *critical society*. Representatives of this view, like Ulrich Beck and Anthony Giddens, argue that the postmodern self is not simply emptied-out and flattened-out by the power of economic and political structures, but can be deepened and enhanced through human relationships and communities. The formation of life-sustaining communities is possible in postmodern society. Our practical struggle with the risks of contemporary life, forces us to *restructure* meaningful relationships, new social groups, and revitalized institutions. For society to accomplish this, however, it must rely on *all* voices of society, especially those moral and ethical perspectives that challenge the power of those structures responsible for risk production. As the risks increase, so does the *reflexivity* to access, analyze, and evaluate these risks.

Nevertheless, as mentioned earlier, the core problem in postmodernity is both knowing the various risks of our age, and finding the means, in a fragmented society, to interpret and alter their negative side effects. Indeed, there is both the problem of having the *awareness* of the contemporary risks we face as a society, and the moral and political *ability* to alleviate disastrous side effects. Beck's answers to these two problems are grounded in how "critical society" can effectively use lay public languages for risk assessment. Regarding this, Beck argues that "more urgently than ever, we need ideas and theories that will allow us to conceive the new which is rolling over us in a new way, and allow us to live and act within it. At the same time we must retain good relations with the treasures of tradition, without a misconceived and sorrowful turn to the new, which always remains old anyway."[50] For Beck, reflexivity is more of a "reflex," against the power structures and "monopolies of truth" that comprise simple modernity. Reflexivity has less to do with abstract ethical or scientific knowledge than with a Kantian-like practical knowledge society has by opening its eyes and ears and experiencing the sights and sounds that surround it; this reflex emerges within the multiple lay voices, communities, and traditions of society. In *Risk Society*, Beck writes: "Determinations of risks are the form in which ethics, and with it also philosophy, culture, and politics, is resurrected inside the centers of modernization—in business, the natural sciences, and the technical disciplines."[51] The battles that rage between expert and lay moral languages will, in the end, work together in addressing the experience of risk. In that way, these groups will provide a comprehensive knowledge of the threat or risk, and the steps necessary to alleviate its negative side effects.

Moreover, given the fact there is a plurality and diversity of societies, religions, politics, the communities of the world cannot learn to cooperate without forming a "cosmopolitan moment." "The 'cosmopolitan moment' of world risk society means," says Beck, "first the *conditio humana* of the irreversible non-excludability of those who are culturally different."[52] This can lead to the awareness that all persons and communities must depend on and cooperate with each other if our world is to survive. World risk society forces humanity into a position to choose apathy or action, noninvolvement or involvement, indeterminate cynicism and pessimism, or determination

---

50. Beck, *Risk Society*, 12.
51. Ibid., 28.
52. Beck, *World at Risk*, 233.

and transformation. We need global cooperation. "National isolationism is an illusion, a fiction, a relic—it is counterproductive and condemned to failure."[53] This is why one of the real enemies of world risk society is variant forms of social and cultural nationalism. "National sovereignty does not make cooperation possible; rather, it is transnational cooperation that makes national sovereignty possible."[54] Although this goal of global cooperation is arguably the right course of action, there are numerous other people and communities committed to the alternative, a strident nationalist and individualist ideology. Again, this simply points to the apparently irresolvable ethical problems of moral knowledge and agency underlying all social theory. Social theory, as stated in the last chapter, simply assumes that people *have* knowledge of the good, which enables them to evaluate the conditions of power in society and the world. Just as there are social risks there are moral epistemological risks. The determination of the good remains an overarching problem in postmodernity for all moral theory, regardless whether it's a reflexive or deconstructionist.

POSTMODERN ETHICS AND MORAL ONTOLOGY

In our consideration of the previous section, we may conclude that the positive contribution of reflexive theories is that they split the difference between a modernist and deconstructionist account of ethics. That is, it shifts anthropological discussions away from the terse debate between two notions of the moral self, namely the modern disengaged self and the postmodern decentered self. Instead of these two views, it offers and integrated vision of the *relational* self. Clearly, this reflexive model, grounded in the relational self, attempts to alleviate the risks of both approaches, yet still provides a way for individuals and communities to be self-critical, moral, and above all, transformational, without succumbing to naïve modern utopian metanarratives. Yet, we must ask: is the notion of the relational self truly supportable without any notion of theological ethics, and behind this, an understanding of divine action and agency. Is it possible to talk about the relational self and a theory of moral realism without a Creator, who has created the relational self and its capacity to know the good? Is reflexive ethics incomplete without God?

53. Ibid., 233.
54. Ibid.

Why Ethics Needs Theology

To reiterate, as we've seen, reflexive theory attaches a *realist* content of ethics to particular relationships. This form of moral realism depends on the linguistic, cultural, and socio-historical meanings discovered in the interaction between self/other, woman/humanity, self/tradition, and self/society. In so doing, it affirms that persons experience the reality of the *good* in their lives through an encounter with others (or the Other), moral traditions, and society. This discovery of moral truth, at its core, is rooted in a reflexive theory of the "relational self." As Paul Ricoeur puts it: "the selfhood of oneself implies otherness to such an intimate degree that one cannot be thought of without the other."[55] At this point, we may observe some basic convergences between postmodern ethics to Barth's early theological ethics, as described in chapter two. That is, just as Barth begins with the encounter with the divine *Other* in the Word of God, so too, a postmodern reflexive ethics begins with an encounter with the human *other*. It is through the other that we become aware of the ethical self. Yet, given the differences about how the "other" and the "good" is understood, making such a comparison invariably raises serious problems about the usefulness of reflexive theory for Christian ethics. With this, the question still remains: although reflexive theories seek to overcome the *risks* of the antirealist and dystopian trends in postmodernity, do they in fact do so? In their various attempts to free moral agency from the contingencies of society and culture through reflexive knowledge have they provided an adequate argument for the objective *goodness* of that knowledge? Have they provided an argument for why reality itself is good? In postmodern society, the power of techno-scientific languages and institutions not only prevents persons from taking genuine ethical action, but creates ambiguity regarding the ontological goodness of moral knowledge. Since all forms of absolute and universal truth, including moral knowledge, have been deconstructed, the postmodern self is deeply suspicious, cynical, and critical of hidden forms of manipulation and power.

In postmodernity what *really* exists is power. If the modern self was innocently optimistic about human achievements, the postmodern self is inherently pessimistic and sullen about such achievements because they disguise hidden power-claims and manipulative means to control persons through bureaucratic organizations, mass advertising, information technol-

---

55. Ricouer, *Oneself as Another*, 3.

ogy, and various social institutions. The risk is that life-enhancing moral languages are replaced with rhetoric that attempts *only* to unmask the hidden power-claims of others. Driven by the distrust of others, persons become preoccupied with self-protection, self-interest, control, and power. "The postmodern self is thus predisposed to assume a stance of readiness of conflict."[56] If exclusion, conflict, and the "will-to-power" have become the norm in postmodern society, then the question arises: *why* I should care about others at all! If the language of morality is, at its core, a language of power, there seems little reason to care for anything or anyone except oneself. With this in mind, a reflexive ethics must not only address the nature of persons and their communities, the basis for moral knowledge, and a strategy for normative ethics, but the relationship of ethics to power. This gets us to the underlying moral ontology or metaethical reality behind such a relationship. What is the moral nature of reality? How is this reality related to an understanding of God-as-power? If, on one hand, power, instead of moral value, defines the boundaries and substance of ethical action, then all realist attempts to explain *why* there should be a normative human ethics no longer becomes possible. If power is used to create or invent ethics, then a realist conception of morality collapses into the view of moral relativism or perspectivism. Is power inherently good or evil? Without a realist conception of moral truth we will never know for sure. If, on the other hand, moral value (goodness, rightness, etc,) defines the proper use of power, then power can be turned toward good, rather than evil. This view, however, implies that good or right transcends our socio-cultural perspectives, or what Charles Taylor calls the "immanent frame" and the "closed world structures" of our secular age.[57] By grounding moral realism in the immanence of the self/other constitution, gender-human experience, and even a tradition of moral inquiry, reflexive moral theory avoids this interaction between power and value, which opens them up to the deconstructionist critique.

Indeed, of the three reflexive theories presented here, only MacIntyre presupposes any discussion about metaethics through the lens of the Aristotelian-Thomist metaphysical tradition. Yet even MacIntyre's philosophical account does not fully explain, in theological language, why value and goodness are greater than power, or in other words, why *reality* itself is good, and why it has the force to shape power for the good instead of

56. Thiselton, *Interpreting God*, 131.
57. Taylor, *Secular Age*, 551.

evil. As John Milbank writes: "A tension arises here, between MacIntyre's 'philosophic' perspective upon Christianity on the one hand, which concedes the rhetorical, persuasive character of its fundamental texts, practices and creedal beliefs, but even treats these only from the point of view of testing their validity by a universal method (dialectics), and, on the other hand, a theological perspective (whether that of Augustine or Aquinas or Barth) which speaks in modes beyond the point where dialectics leaves off, namely, in terms of the imaginative explication of texts, practices, and beliefs."[58] Milbank remains critical of MacIntyre because he cloaks his discussions of theological figures like Augustine and Aquinas in the guise of philosophical dialectics. No doubt, the tension between Milbank and MacIntyre is symptomatic of the tension between philosophy and theology more generally, and indeed, within the various traditions of theology itself. Given our earlier discussions on Milbank and Radical Orthodoxy is it no surprise why he would be critical of MacIntyre's retrieval of Aristotle's virtue ethics, for this moral tradition, like all non-Christian moral traditions, presumes an "ontology of violence." Putting this aside, however, the main point is that Milbank reminds us that we cannot ground a Christian moral theory in any "heretical" immanentist and secularist narrative or *mythos*. If a Christian account of the good is to remain radically orthodox, it must begin with a strictly theological account of reality, and not with a reflexive ethics grounded in the relational self. As Milbank succinctly puts it, "only theology can overcome metaphysics."[59]

Inasmuch as reflexive moral theory seeks to go beyond the modern/postmodern divide, it remains thoroughly modern in its approach to theological ethics, which as we've seen, leads to a separation of ethics from theology. Being unable to account for, as Barth puts it, the "whence and whither," of the good, reflexive theorists remain paralyzed and unable to provide for what Charles Taylor calls a "moral ontology." The term "moral ontology" refers to the intellectual framework or *weltanschauung* that stands behind particular construals of moral epistemology and agency. A "moral ontology," says Taylor, is "the 'background picture' lying behind our moral and spiritual intuitions."[60] Such a background picture provides the basic link between one's moral identity and one's moral orientation.

58. Milbank, *Theology and Social Theory*, 328.
59. Milbank, *Word Made Strange*, 36–52.
60. Taylor, *Sources of the Self*, 8.

"To know who you are is to be oriented in moral space, a space in which questions arise about what is good or bad, what is worth doing and what is not, what has meaning and importance for you and what is trivial and secondary."[61] A moral ontology, therefore, is a comprehensive scheme that is both general and particular. First, it describes *general* moral reality that encompasses the beliefs, practices, and values of human life. Second, it describes the *particular* characteristics of human moral identity such as moral self-understanding, moral agency, and interpersonal interaction. A moral ontology provides moral framework for one's personal and communal life, and the general and specific components of her moral existence, which, in theory, enables her to understand and articulate what is good.

The central problem is that the epistemological framework in postmodernity has made it increasingly difficult to understand and articulate a coherent moral ontology. Without a moral ontology, persons and communities, being disconnected from each other, invariably lose their capacity for certainty regarding their moral knowledge and action. Ethics itself becomes problematic, because it becomes increasingly difficult to understand of why *reality* itself is good. This eventually leads to the separation of the ethical question of "What ought I to do?" from the deeper question "What is the moral reality?" Without a moral ontology there is no basic coherence between one's moral identity and one's orientation, or between one's moral knowledge and one's moral action. Without such a linkage, the meaning of the good and good action becomes difficult to define and practice. As Taylor later writes in *A Secular Age*, "[T]here is certainly a widespread sense of loss here, if not always of God, then at least of meaning."[62] Without the *meaning* of the good, ethics invariably becomes reduced to power. The awareness of this loss of meaning remains one important defining characteristic of postmodernity. Reflexive moral theories try to overcome this loss of meaning by speaking of an interdependent self's relation to others, communities, and social risks. Yet, these theories still cannot by themselves account for why reality itself is good; they cannot provide a coherent argument for a moral ontology of goodness. In postmodernity, the lack of a moral ontology has led to the affirmation, at least in principle, that all of reality, including human identity, is shaped more by *power* than the good. With their incongruity toward God-talk they find it more difficult to ex-

---

61. Ibid., 28.
62. Taylor, *Secular Age*, 552.

plain why reality itself is good. Even though these theories attempt to wage war on modern anthropocentrism, they fail to attack the false *separation* of ethics from theology, which Barth so clearly recognized as the "anthropocentric myth" of modern thought. For Barth, "*the* great anthropological myth, the myth of apostasy and revolt, *the* great lie, because deity that is taken up into our will is no longer deity, no longer the Creator" (*ET*: 210). While modern ethics made it possible to talk about ethics without talking about God, postmodern or late-modern ethics undermines its own ability to discover the good, while ignoring the question of God. In either case, "there is no God because we ourselves are God" (*ET*: 210). Once we become "God," all that remains is our power.

Goodness or Power?

Before we end this chapter, it is important to raise one more question: is it possible to affirm moral realism and a moral ontology without confessing God's existence? That is, is there an alternative way to speak about the goodness of reality without God? For this issue we turn to the philosopher Iris Murdoch, who presents a philosophy of moral realism without God. In *Metaphysics as a Guide to Morals*, Murdoch believes that modern ethics has failed because it lost its "metaphysical" base for ethical inquiry. In short, it was a major mistake to separate metaphysics from ethics. As a moral realist, she affirms that we discover rather than invent morality. Moral values are real in the sense that they exist apart from our social construction or even interpretation of them, and by discovering them we get a clearer picture about reality itself. "Life is a spiritual pilgrimage inspired by the disturbing magnetism of truth, involving *ipso facto* a purification of energy and desire in the light of a vision of what is good."[63] Through our understanding of the contingent and imperfect, Murdoch argues persons get a glimpse of the unconditioned and perfect, the good. Since the unconditioned nature of the Good is *both* moral and religious, she no longer sees the existence of God as important for developing a coherent ethics. Instead, inspired by Platonic philosophy, she insists that we need to replace our metaphysical understanding of God with the Good as the most basic part of an ethical system. In the end, we "need a theology which can continue without

---

63. Murdoch, *Metaphysics as a Guide to Morals*, 14.

God."[64] Murdoch attempts to explain how a metaphysically grounded realist ethics exists without God, but is this possible?

> Murdoch insists that the Good is that in which the "light of truth is seen; it reveals the world, hitherto invisible, and is also a source of life." But it is absolutely important to note that as the source of life the Good does not bind its power to finite, created life. The Good does not recognize or respond to what is other than itself. In other words, the Good does not symbolize the transformation of value creating power so that power respects and enhances finite life. And this is why, I believe, it is difficult for Murdoch to specify the ground for the value of the individual. In grasping this point we have isolated the inner limits of the Good as a symbol of the real.[65]

William Schweiker claims that Murdoch is forced to separate the content of the Good from the power that shapes finite reality, which makes her metaphysical account of the Good deeply problematic. Although Murdoch speaks about a transcendent Good, this reality does not have the *power* to care, respect, and enhance finite life. To be sure, Murdoch's philosophy affirms a moral ontology of the good, but it cannot explain why existence or creation itself is good. Existence itself risks becoming meaningless and empty if one cannot link the Good to a benevolent God who defines mundane life as good.[66] Murdoch presumes that the Good simply is, and has no goal or *telos* beyond itself. But, we might ask, why is *reality* ultimately good rather than evil? If the will to power is hegemonic then how can we trust reality by calling it Good? Indeed, why does our knowledge of the Good compel us to be responsible for anything except ourselves, indeed even ourselves? Without a good God, we have no objective basis to believe that reality *is* "Good." For us to actually know that reality is good is to know there is an objective or unconditioned reality that truly exists outside the self that is not dependent on human knowledge or imagination. Put differently, a moral ontology of the Good is only possible if its own reality is created by the *Goodness* of God. Again, this is why ethics needs theology.[67]

---

64. Ibid., 511.

65. Schweiker, "Sovereignty of God's Goodness," 229–30. Schweiker quotes from Murdoch, *Fire and the Sun*, 4.

66. Hauerwas, "Mudochian Muddles," 190–208.

67. This is an important theme in Long's, *Goodness of God*. He writes: "Theology is necessary to make sense of the moral life precisely because it allows for a mysterious and enchanting good that calls to itself rather than to some good that we achieve, define,

CONCLUSION

Our descriptive analysis of various types nontheological ethics thus far serves the descriptive purpose of, as Barth says, "eavesdropping on the world" (*CD* IV/3: 117). Yet, it moves us, as it did in chapters 1–2, toward the normative claim for the necessity of a *theological* ethics. Even though a reflexive ethical theory provides a better argument for explaining how persons can learn and practice moral responsibility, it also presumes that theology makes no difference to the discussion of ethics. Rather, it continues the modern Cartesian search for reflexive moral foundations, whether found in rational or experiential, whether philosophical or scientific discourse. Yet, it is just this anthropocentric "foundation" that remains problematic for postmodernity. In postmodernity, we need a way that not only discovers the Good in the nature of reality, but more importantly, a way to discover moral knowledge that is addressed by the *Goodness* of that reality. This is why a philosophical or social scientific theory of human reflexivity lacks the ability to explain why reality compels persons to use power in the service of the Good rather than for self-interest. If the Good remains defined by power, then there is no *good* reason to do what is right apart from power. When the Good cannot be distinguished from power then we have a *crisis* of moral knowledge that cannot be overcome with a new social or ethical theory. How can we know for sure that what we presume to be good is not some masked form of power that seeks to oppress ourselves or others? This problem drives us to the question: can we even talk about such Goodness without God's revelation? It appears that just as social theory needs ethics, so too does reflexive and metaphysical accounts of ethics need a theological account of ethics. What we need, therefore, is a moral ontology that is defined by the act of a benevolent creator and not a "metaphysics without God."

Saying this, however, does not imply that theology provides the *answer* to the problem of a moral ontology in postmodernity. The answer to this problem is not discovered in a new theological method or argument, but in the actions of a free God who chooses to act with and for others in a covenantal-partnership. The only "answer," in short, is God's *Word* of grace. Only God's gracious Word—as the Good—overcomes the problem of human power and postmodern nihilism. In *CD* II/2, Barth writes: "The grace of God protests against all man-made ethics as such. But it protests

---

create, or explain through our volitional activities alone. Christian theology calls this good, God." Ibid., 26.

positively. It does not only say No to man. It also says Yes" (*CD* II/2: 517). By retraining to the priority of God's gracious action, we have engaged in a kind of "ad hoc apologetics" that simply uses reason and logic to further understand the significance of the theological, as it relates to contemporary secular thought.[68] This "ad hoc" approach, however, stands in contrast to the "apologetical" method that Barth repeatedly rejects, namely a method that attempts to ground theological ethics in some other kind of *general* human ethics, as discerned through philosophy or the sciences. "Apologetics in this case would be the attempt to establish and justify the theologico-ethical inquiry within the framework and on the foundation of the presuppositions and methods of non-theological, of wholly human thinking and language" (*CD* II/2: 520). In contrast, a positive "ad hoc" apologetical argument begins with "sincere conviction that theological ethics must be measured against a general ethics" (*CD* II/2: 521). Only a theological ethics that begins with God's gracious *action* can provide a coherent argument for why reality itself is good, especially in postmodernity where a moral ontology of the good is largely shaped by immanent frameworks of power. In short, it is not "theology" as such, but the "grace of God" that "*is* the answer to the ethical problem" (*CD* II/2: 516).

---

68. Werpehowski, "Ad Hoc Apologetics," 282–301.

PART THREE

Witness and Barth's Ethics
Toward Contemporary Understanding

CHAPTER SIX

Witness and the Word of God

In the last two chapters, we have examined two central responses to the postmodern situation, and concluded that neither theory, as such, can tell us with certainty what the *good* is and how we ought to practice it in the world. The crisis of postmodernity affects both the "supply" and "demand" of ethics, that is of moral knowledge and action, of truth and agency, and embodying and doing the good. Without a coherent moral ontology there is no coherent understanding of moral realism; we cannot have a coherent view of the good because we cannot account for the moral structure of the good. This chapter returns to a discussion of theology and ethics in Barth's thought, while keeping in mind the social and intellectual context described in the previous two chapters. In chapters 2–3, we discussed various developments in Barth's ethics, looking at both his early and later writings. This chapter returns to Barth's theology extending our analysis into other later writings, including the *Church Dogmatics*. Nevertheless, we continue the same line of reasoning developed in chapters 4–5 regarding the possibility of ethics within postmodernity. In a sense, therefore, we have returned full circle to the question raised in chapter one: how can we understand the task of theological and Christian ethics in postmodernity? In postmodernity, there remains a *crisis* of moral knowledge and action. This was not unlike Barth's experience of *crisis* in the aftermath of the World War I, in which the existing methodological types of Christian ethics proved inadequate in addressing this crisis. For Barth, the answer to this crisis was dependent on God's action, which required a theological, rather than philosophical or scientific description and evaluation. We've seen how a nontheological account of moral realism by itself remains inherently ambiguous, since it cannot escape the immanent circularity of a "hermeneutics of suspicion" that challenges any claim of moral certainty and truth. Should Christian ethics begin with the Cartesian search for reflexive foundations of the good, as found in human reason or experience? If so, is this quest not problematic given the crisis of moral epistemology in postmodernity?

So far we've examined Barth's ethics in the context of the various historical events of the early mid-twentieth century. Our historical narrative led to a discussion how the debates over law and gospel and natural theology clarified the noetic or epistemological criteria for theological ethics. The principle discussion focused on the reality of the good as revealed in God's commanding action in the gospel. We further discussed Barth's theoretical and practical ethics, particularly the relationship of church and state, at various stages of his thought from the 1930s to 1950s. Rather than despairing about the prospects of the church in largely post-Christendom society, Barth welcomed the opportunity for the church to be an authentic witness to the civil community. In later chapters, we will return to an in-depth practical discussion of Barth's social ethics, something discussed in part in chapters 2–3. As stated above, however, now it is time to shift our focus to a more detailed study of the theoretical side of Barth's ethics. For this, we depart from the historical narrative and look at all of Barth's writings, particularly the *Church Dogmatics*. Barth planned to write ethical sections in each of five-part structure of the *CD*, including volumes on theological prolegomena, God, creation, reconciliation, and redemption. In the end, he completed the brief prolegomena section in *CD* I/2 (1938), the section on God and the divine command in *CD* II/2 (1942), and the ethics of creation in *CD* III/4 (1951), while he partially completed the ethics of reconciliation in *CD* IV/4 and *The Christian Life* (1958–61). Saying this, of course, does not imply that Barth's ethics must be restricted to these particular ethical sections of the *CD*. Anyone who has read Barth extensively knows that ethical themes flow throughout his theological writings as a whole, including his occasional theological, social, and political writings, some of which were discussed in chapter 3. Although it is important to examine all of Barth's mature ethical writings, the theological argument of the *CD* epistemologically drives us toward the doctrine of reconciliation in

CD IV/1–4. Barth's ethics of reconciliation serves as the "entry point" into his theological ethics as a whole. The ethical sections of *CD* II/2 and *CD* III/4, thus, need to be understood within the corpus of his later writings in *CD* IV/1–4. In addressing Barth's ethics, many Christian ethicists, unfamiliar with the complexity of Barth's theology, often begin their analysis with *CD* II/2 on the topic of God's command or *CD* III/4 on the doctrine of creation and ethics. In doing so, they fail to consider how these discussion belong to his theology as a whole, particularly the doctrine of reconciliation, which is the epistemological starting point for his ethics as a whole.

THEOLOGICAL ETHICS: REALISM, COMMAND, AND AGENCY

In the following section, we return to the discussion of Barth's theological ethics. Since we already discussed the basic structure of his trinitarian command ethics, as worked out in his *Ethics* lectures, there is no need discuss this further. However, if we are going to understand how Christian ethics *is* Christian witness, we must discuss the various related topics in theological ethics that pertain to a comprehensive account of divine and human action. We must also relate Barth's thought to various other contemporary viewpoints, including his critics, so that we can see the various issues at stake in developing an ethics of witness. As mentioned earlier, Barth's first significant trajectory into ethics in the *Church Dogmatics* is the last part of the doctrine of God after he discusses at length the doctrine of election (*CD* II/2: 509–781). Here Barth develops, in much greater detail, the basic arguments in *Ethics*, particularly as it relates to God's gracious command as *claim* of God's election, as *decision* of God's sovereignty over the good, and God's *judgment*, which is always a judgment of grace. We are not going to discuss this large section in detail, but focus on particular issues that pertain to our study. Suffice it say, Barth reminds us that when Christian ethics engages in God-talk and its relation to ethics, it engages in theological ethics. One important topic in theological ethics is the moral framework or moral ontology that provides the structure for how we understand the knowledge of the good and moral agency. Who is God and how does God act in relation to the moral structure (moral ontology) of existence? Without God there is no good reason to affirm that reality itself is good. As we have seen in previous chapters, the problem with moral ontology in postmodernity is that there is no significant reason to claim reality itself as *good*, apart from a good *God*.

Theological Realism and Analogia fidei

All versions of theological and Christian ethics affirm some kind of moral ontology although this is understood differently in various approaches. Moral ontology is uniquely shaped by the distinct traditions of natural law, orders of creation, or divine command theory. In each theory, moral epistemology and divine and human relations are singularly understood and interpreted. Specifically, in each moral framework, there is an interaction of divine and human agency. First it must determine how God reveals the knowledge of good, and second how humans appropriate this knowledge and respond with appropriate action. Does God's agency work through an intermediately structure like "nature" or "creation" or does God directly command what is good? Does humanity use conscience and deliberation to ascertain the good, or does it simply adhere to what God has commanded in Scripture? These differences led to divergent viewpoints in theological ethics. As mentioned earlier, because of the various pitfalls that each of these options present, Barth finds reasons to reject all of them and instead begin with God's trinitarian action in the Word of God. The overarching problem with any moral theory that denies God's action is the empty *space* that is posited between God's revelation, either in nature, creation, or commands, and the self-deliberative moral agent, which is then *filled* by human reflection and action. Inasmuch as various moral theories give lip-service to God, they speak more about human reflection and deliberation than about God's commanding action. The method moves theological ethics from a theocentric to an anthropocentric position, thus, from theology to psychology and sociology. Barth rightly presumes that God cannot be a *free* trinitarian subject if God is limited to the act of creation and is not also the reconciler and redeemer, that is, the Son and the Spirit. Seeing the deistic potential of such a hyper-transcendent theology, Barth shifts the focus away from humanity's deliberation and action and toward God's revelation in the Word of God as trinitarian *Other*. Only in this revelatory event do we discover the *reality* of the good as reconciling and redemptive *grace*.

Without this starting point in the Word of God, theological ethics builds itself upon some *fictional* account of human moral agency and moral knowledge. Obviously Barth presumes that all forms and methods of ethics are obviously aware of the problem of good knowledge and action, but he says they are incapable of supplying a real and objective *answer* to this problem. Theological ethics cannot be placed side by side with other versions of ethics because it alone gives *witness* to the answer of the ethical problem raised by all versions of ethics. There is only one Word of God which supplies the answer to the ethical problem. If Christian ethics is to be both theological and realist, it must "continually begin again at the beginning," that is, with the Word of God (*CD* I/2: 868). Regarding this point, he writes:

> Comprehensively, ethics is an attempt to answer theoretically the question of what may be called *good* human action. Theological ethics such as it is attempted here finds both this question and its answer in God's Word. It thus finds it where theological dogmatics as the critical science of true church proclamation finds all its answers and questions. Theological ethics can be understood only as an integral element of dogmatics. The Word of God, with which dogmatics (and consequently theological ethics) is concerned at every point as the basis, object, content, and norm of true church proclamation, is, however, Jesus Christ in the divine-human unity of his being and work. Precisely for this reason, ethics cannot be understood and ventured as an independent discipline working on its own presuppositions and according to its own methods, but only as an integral element in dogmatics. (*CL*: 3–4)

Theological ethics cannot begin with some objectively neutral investigation into the "nature" of the good apart from the revelation of the Word of God. It remains problematic to equate God's command with some broader human ethic based on reason or experience, as this denies the *objective* reality of the good, which is established in and through the human-divine encounter *in* Jesus Christ. For Barth, as John Webster clearly says, "good human action is action which is most in accord with the way the world is constituted in Jesus Christ."[1] Christian ethics must refuse the temptation to see itself as a subcategory of a generic discipline called "ethics." Rather, its sees itself as a witness to divine action, which shapes not only the nature of good moral action, but more importantly, the origin and reality of the good in human life. Accordingly, a moral theory of human flourishing *apart* from the revelation of the Word of God is grounded in some fictive account of the moral person. Rather, it is the particular way humans are *related* to the trinitarian God, which establishes and nurtures our moral knowledge and moral agency. This human-divine relation begins with Jesus Christ. This is why there can be no objectivity or independence of ethical terms such as

---

1. Webster, *Barth's Ethics of Reconciliation*, 219.

the moral subject, conscience, and command, apart from this revelation in the Word. To begin in another place invariably *reduces* these terms to some other viewpoint that disregards the Word of God—the revelation of the good. Only in the Word of God do we really and objectively discover who "God," and "humanity" truly are, and what the "good" really is. We cannot talk about any of these terms without also referring to Jesus Christ.

It is the theological realism unveiled in God's revelation in the Word of God that provides the basis for the understanding of moral ontology and moral realism. Christians assume that God has acted in some objective way, thereby establishing the moral structure of things (moral ontology) and the content of the good (moral realism). Just as moral realism refers to those statements of moral truth that remain objectively true independent of our apprehending them as "true," so too, theological realism refers to those statements about God that remain objectively true regardless of our subjective truth claims about them. As Webster further writes: "This highly objectivist account of knowledge is clearly an entailment of a prior conviction that God's act of self-manifestation is noetically fundamental and has priority over the functioning or malfunctioning of human cognition and consciousness."[2] The objectivity of Christian moral realism is grounded in the theological realism of God's gracious action, which subsequently establishes the moral ontology for Christian ethics. When ethicists, Christian or otherwise, seek to talk about a moral ontology deriving from the anthropocentric search for the good, they misrepresent the true and objective *good* reality of God and humanity in covenant-partnership. We saw earlier how difficult it is in postmodernity, where power defines the good, to establish some kind of moral realism and moral ontology based on reflexive knowledge. Without grace all that remains is power. So, we might ask: how can ethics be possible if it has false information about the goodness of reality? How is it possible if it misrepresents, from the Christian view, *who* God and humanity really are? How can Christian ethics be "Christian" without talking about Jesus Christ? It is this logic that leads Barth to say that "correct ethics can only be Christian ethics," and that a systematic or "scientific" account of Christian ethics cannot be "differentiated from theological ethics." "In the last analysis," he adds, "there is only one ethics, theological ethics" (*CD* II/2: 542). And the "aim of theological ethics" is "Christian doctrine of God, or, more exactly, the knowledge of the electing grace of God in

---

2. Ibid., 193.

Jesus Christ" (*CD* II/2: 543). All other forms of ethics, whether philosophical or religious, secular or confessional, general or particular, cannot be the foundation for Christian ethics because they deny the fundamental witness to this claim about God's reconciling action in Jesus Christ.

In recalling Barth's analogy of the Israelites' annexation of Canaan as a description about the relation of Christian ethics to other versions of ethics, let us think about what this says about faith and ethics. One important aspect of this analogy is that the Israelites were a people of *faith* who believed that God had given them the gift of the covenant. This covenant-partnership, of course, extends to all humanity in the electing grace of God in Jesus Christ. In this divine-human act God elects "man to be His creature and His partner. Even more, He wants him to be His *child*" (*HG*: 82). As children of God we are given the gift of freedom and faith. "Human freedom is the God-given freedom to obey. *Faith* is the obedience of the *pilgrim* who has his vision and his trust set upon God's free act of reconciliation" (*HG*: 82). Having faith is not an innate capacity that persons can nurture through good works, but comes only with the knowledge of our covenant-partnership with God. "Faith is not one of the various capacities of man, whether native or acquired" (*CD* I/1: 238). Yet, as a gift of grace, faith opens up our capacity to understand the good as revealed in God's Word. This knowledge is *noetic* but it is also *ontic,* namely it is knowledge that shapes and transforms one's *being* in relation to God, others, and the world. In *CD* I/1, he writes:

> In believing he can think of himself as grounded, not in self but only in this object, as existing indeed only this object. He has not created his own faith; the Word has created it. He has not come to faith; faith has come to him. He has not adopted faith; faith has been granted to him through the Word. As a believer he cannot see himself as the acting subject of the work done here. It is his experience and act. He is not at all a block or stone in faith but a self-determining man. . . . In his freedom, in the full use of his freedom as a man, he must see himself as another man that he had no power to become, that he still has no power to become, that he is not free to become or to be (though he is free as he becomes and is), in short, that he can be only by being this man. Man acts as he believes, but the fact he believes as he acts is God's act. Man is the subject of faith. Man believes, not God. (*CD* I/1: 244–45)

It is in this section in *CD* I/1, where Barth's makes his famous distinction between the "analogy of being" (*analogia entis*) and the "analogy of faith" (*analogia fidei*). The first approach, the *analogia entis*, mistakenly assumes that because humans share in God's being through their created nature as *imago Dei*, then it becomes possible to have knowledge of God (or the good) from that standpoint of our creaturely faculties including reason and experience. Regarding moral knowledge, this presumes that persons can objectively discover the human good through natural reason or experience or through some "moral order" established through God's creation (order of creation). In short, the *analogia entis* claims to know God or the good apart from God's own self-revelation in the Word of God. In contrast, the approach that Barth prefers is what he calls the *analogia fidei*, which posits the analogy, not between divine and human being, but between divine and human *action*. By God's action of grace and the corresponding human action of faith, the believing person is shaped noetically and ontically by God's grace. This means that humanity can have knowledge of the good and the power to act upon this knowledge in freedom. Ethics is now truly possible, not just as a theory or standard of human behavior, but as a real possibility of knowing and doing the good. "Christian ethics has to do with man, who is wholly lost, wholly rescued and therefore is claimed as the whole man" (*GHN*: 114). All this is possible because of God's grace, which establishes the true structure or moral ontology for ethics. As Stanley Hauerwas writes: "Barth's development of the *anlogia fidei* was not an attempt to develop a theory or method of analogy based on prior metaphysical claims but an attempt to display the metaphysical claims intrinsic to theological speech."[3] Therefore, in contrast to the *analogia entis*, which begins with human experience and reason and then correlates the inner world of faith to that objective world, Barth begins with the objective world of faith *analogia fidei* and then integrates the outer world of human experience and reason. We discover moral knowledge and action in our encounter with the Word of God. In God's trinitarian action we are given the freedom to respond in faith to this objective world of God's gracious command.

Although natural law cannot be the basis for our human moral knowledge of the good or guide for moral action, the Word of God reveals what is morally true for all persons. The simple error of any form of Christian naturalism is to begin with the *analogia entis* instead of the *analogia fidei*.

---

3. Hauerwas, *With the Grain*, 189.

As Paul Molnar writes: "what Barth was trying to avoid in his rejection of the *analogia entis* was any attempt to understand God which bypassed Jesus Christ as the only possible starting point."[4] Rejecting the priority of the Word of God implies rejecting theological realism, and with it, the conjoining of God's revelatory truth with God's freedom to declare the origin and reality of the good in the acts of creation, reconciliation, and redemption. Unlike Schleiermacher, for instance, who correlates a "general" (or universalist) philosophical ethics with more singular language of Christian ethics, Barth begins with the particular language of Christian theology and describes how other languages relate to the Word of God. Hence, the *analogia fidei* establishes a reconceived *analogia entis* that is grounded in God's action, or better yet, God's trinitarian being-in-act. This allows Barth to broadly accept a parabolic notion of "general revelation" while specifically rejecting the methods of natural theology and natural law. The way to the general is through the particular. Again, using Barth's analogy, we are reminded that the faithful Israelites continued to live with their Canaan neighbors even though they chose not to believe in their gods. Only with the eyes of faith is it possible to see the world and read human experience properly. So the moral knowledge that persons learn through their reason and experience must not be isolated as an independent source of the good, but must be understood and interpreted through the lens of the Word of God, the true source of the good. The Word of God establishes a general knowledge of ethics, which makes both Christian ethics *and* human ethics possible. Theological realism provides the basis for moral realism.

Barth's Command Ethics and Its Critics

Now that we've looked at Barth's approach, we need to consider how other Christian ethicists criticize his view of theological ethics. Barth remains a polarizing figure in theology, but even more so in ethics. This is nowhere more evident than in Barth's command ethics, where he is often misunderstood as a strange sort of divine command theorist. William Schweiker, for example, argues that Barth's ambiguous "divine command theory" is both helpful and problematic. Schweiker admires Barth's theological ethics for the postmodern context because instead of assuming the "good is power" he defines "power as good," or the "power of the good." Yet, he also writes: "By doing so Barth provided a theological axiology and a principle of moral

---

4. Molnar, *Divine Freedom*, 58.

rightness but at the expense of necessarily transforming ethics into divine ethics."[5] In Schweiker's judgment, Barth simply goes too far by forcing us to make the hard choice between God and humanity, which invariably results in the separation of divine and human ethics. Barth's divine command ethics remains incomplete and problematic to the task of Christian ethics today because it denies, or at the very least, limits the very *human* process of hermeneutical moral reasoning. Barth's Word-centered theology concentrates so intensely on divine knowledge and action that it neglects human moral knowledge and action. This criticism builds on the earlier criticisms of Robin Lovin and James Gustafson, who presume that Barth's "divine command theory" is insufficient for theological ethics.[6] More will be said about these theologians in a later chapter, yet here we can say that much of the criticism on Barth's ethics focuses on process of moral judgment and deliberation. Often Barth's divine command ethics is viewed as a philosophical version of "act-deontology."[7] This theory implies that the moral agent hears and obeys God's particular command in the context of a particular situation, and not like Kant, following a general moral rule or principle. The command of God appears to be an occasionalistic, episodic, or *situational* theological categorical imperative demanding obedience. This theory rules out human experience and reflection about the human good in response to God's command, and instead simply requires *obedience* to God's specific charge. Generally, these critics argue that Barth's ethics precludes the systematic, predictable, and deliberative tasks that we normally associate with the strategy of practical reasoning and moral agency in Christian ethics.

What of these criticisms? We begin first with Barth's understanding of divine command, and its bearing on moral theory and theology. Succinctly put, these critics are right to claim that a "divine command theory" or "act-deontology" ethic is inadequate by itself, but they are wrong to apply this objection to Barth. The primary problem is the categorizing of Barth's ethics as an ethical *theory* that is governed by the language and logic of ethical methodology, instead of an ethics governed by the trinitarian logic of revealed Word of God. This, analogically speaking, is like using the ethical language of the Canaanites to describe, criticize, and evaluate the covenantal language of the Israelites. On what basis can such a criticism be made except by some

---

5. Schweiker, *Power, Value, and Conviction*, 129.

6. See Lovin, *Christian Faith and Public Choices*, 18–43; and Gustafson, *Ethics from a Theocentric Perspective*, vol. 2, 33.

7. Lovin, *Christian Faith and Public Choices*, 27.

nontheological worldview? This dependence on ethical methodology is why critics of Barth's view of command often unknowingly embrace various confusions and misunderstandings. They refuse to enter into the domain of dogmatic theology, which makes their criticism insufficiently theological. The simple fact is that Barth is simply not doing Christian ethics in the same way that most Christian ethicists do. For Barth, ethical theory and methodology itself is explicitly rejected as a foundation for theological ethics. "Christian ethics does not rest," says Barth, "on a philosophy or *Weltanschauung* and it does not consist of the development of an idea or a principle or program. Man answers the question about the good with these sorts of answers when he is locked in a conversation with himself" (*GHN*: 106). Human conversation about the divine command is the not the same thing as God's action which disrupts all human attempts to categorize or control ethical concepts and methods. The divine command is not an ethical idea but God's act of grace. When one reads Barth philosophically or through the lens of ethical theory instead of dogmatics, therefore, one not only grossly misunderstands Barth but begins—as well as ends—in a dramatically different place. Indeed, this strategy imposes an *alien* moral ontology (informed by ethical methodology) upon Barth's work, which leads to further misunderstandings and misrepresentations of his thought. Approaching Barth's ethics rightly implies questioning the notion that all "divine command" theories are the same. Indeed, Barth is simply *not* a divine command theorist in the traditional Occamist or voluntarist sense. Rather the language of command is used to explain how the Christian engages in responsible witness in *relation* to God's action through God's gracious covenant.

At this point, we must elaborate further about the divine command as *act*, including looking at four important interrelated points. The first point is that Barth's notion of divine command *prioritizes* divine action and agency. The command begins with God's act and not the human act of reflexive or deliberative thought. Beginning with divine action serves as a critical challenge to any anthropocentric approach to ethics. Looking at Barth's context, this stress on God's action was not uncommon or entirely unique, as others in his generation were also developing Christian ethics along similar lines. Like his contemporaries Emil Brunner and Dietrich Bonhoeffer, Barth's attraction to the language of command rests in the priority of God's agency to human agency.[8] This was a critical device to pull

---

8. See Brunner, *Divine Imperative*, 111–21; and Bonhoeffer, *Ethics*, 277–85. Suffice it say, Barth's theology of divine command differs from Brunner and Bonhoeffer, in that

theological ethics away from its preoccupation with anthropocentric conceptions of the human subject's relation to God. These theologians insisted that if Christian ethics is to remain theological, then it is wrongheaded to concentrate exclusively on the issues of moral consciousness, deliberative casuistry, and self-determinative action, while ignoring the prior reality and action of the Word of God. The methodological task of Christian ethics is not just rationally and logically applying God's moral law to one's circumstances. It is not casuistic. It has to be more than gathering information and sources, applying this information to one's present circumstances, deliberating on possible courses of action, and then making the prudent decisions. There is nothing distinctly Christian or theological about this entire process of this type of reasoning and action. Indeed, God's agency and freedom is *removed* from this entire process, which makes God—as an acting reality in the world—an irrelevant factor in ethical deliberation. With this in mind, the language of command became an attractive way for these theologians to speak about a living God's engagement with persons, society, and the world. This was especially pertinent during a time in which the Nazification of the church and society were justified by the language and moral laws of this casuistic method of Christian ethics.

The second point is that Barth understands the command as a *relational* series of actions or correspondence between God and humanity, rather than a set of propositional or hermeneutical commands understood by human reason. As Barth succinctly states: "we never at any point know the divine command in itself and as such, but only in its relations" (*CD* II/2: 550). What we learn in God's command is a relational knowledge that provokes us to embrace the world as it *ought* to be in relation to God as creator, reconciler, and redeemer. In distinguishing Barth from his critics, it is helpful to compare his relational command ethics to Kant's more autocratic "categorical imperative." Similar to Kant, Barth sees the command as an authoritative imperative that summons our responsible action, and insofar as we disobey this command, it judges our actions. Yet, Kant further proposed that the good, derived from autonomous moral reasoning, claims persons to do good for no other reason than respect for the moral law. When the law is understood as a deontological principle, separated

---

the latter pair attempt to establish moral principles from the "orders" and "mandates" of creation. In Barth's view this embodies a kind of natural theology. Furthermore, the principle locus of Barth's command theory occurs under the doctrine of reconciliation and not creation, as with Brunner and Bonhoeffer.

from the gospel's content, it takes upon itself another legal form derived from human reflection or experience. It no longer is God's law but human law. God's command, says Barth, is not "the timeless truth of a general principle, or a collection of such truths, but the specific content of what is always a special event between God and man in its historical reality" (*CL*: 4). God's command is not a formal principle or moral imperative that is imposed on us by God. Rather, it is gracious gift of freedom to have permission to analyze, investigate, and test moral knowledge and action. The imperative is rooted in the indicative of the gospel. "Christian ethics is the fruit of Christian faith, Christian law is the form of the Christian gospel, and Christian ethics is the imperative of the indicative of Christian dogmatics" (*GHN*: 114). God's command cannot be understood as a moral theory such as rationalism or intuitionism. Rather, when one talks about the command, one begins first with the "special event" of the encounter between God and humanity, which emerges from their covenant relationship made visible in Jesus Christ.

The third point is that the divine command as act is thoroughly a *gracious* command—a command of grace understood in the context of God's gracious actions. "As the doctrine of God's command, ethics interprets the law as the form of the gospel, i.e. as the sanctification which comes to man through the electing God" (*CD* II/2: 509). Only through God's gracious work of justification and sanctification does the human agent have the freedom to listen and respond to God's command. The primary interpretive task of theological ethics is being aware of, and responding to, the grace of the trinitarian God, who creates, reconciles, and redeems his creatures in covenant relationship. "God's own freedom is trinitarian, embracing grace, thankfulness, and peace" (*WG*: 72). We saw in chapter 2 how Barth early on rejected the false separation of ethics from theology, of human action from divine action, and of the human law from God's law. This separation presumes a "Pelegian-like" theological anthropology that eradicates the need for the divine agency of *grace* in ethical judgment. Once the human moral law, instead of divine grace, becomes the foundation for ethics, this closes off (or separates) God's agency from human agency, which invariably further separates God's freedom from human freedom. This further leads to the false notion that human freedom is possible only apart from, or in contrast to, divine freedom, which presumes that humanity can know and do the good without God's grace. In contrast, Barth argued that moral action emerges within the context of an encounter or "event" in which the divine trinitarian *Other* embraces, challenges, and empowers us to live according to God's desired covenantal relationship. "The command of God orders us to be free" (*CD* II/2: 588). To reiterate, the "indicative" comes before the "imperative," which is to say that it is not the moral law that matters as much as the moral law giver. By beginning with divine gracious action, it remains necessary to see the divine law as the "form of the gospel" whose "content is grace," which permits persons the freedom and responsibility to act within this gracious covenant relationship.

The last point is that the divine command is an act of the *trinitarian* God. "God's freedom is the freedom of the Father and the Son in the unity of the Spirit" (*GHN*: 71). Only in the Word of God—as Trinity—is the "command of grace" heard and encountered. This is why theological (and Christian) ethics must be trinitarian. It is misguided, for example, to assume that the content of Christian ethics is discovered *only* in the agency of God the creator or the nature that God creates. This separates, indeed eliminates, God's agency in the gospel, as revealed in God's actions as reconciler and redeemer. So, God's command expresses the content of *who* God is in these three relational spheres, which is circumscribed by the divine-human action in God's gracious decision to be *pro nobis* in Jesus Christ.

> Human freedom is not realized in the solitary detachment of an individual in isolation from his fellow men. God is *a se* (for himself), but He is *pro nobis* (for us). For us! It is true that He who gave man freedom because He is man's friend, is also *pro me* (for me). But I am not Man, I am only *a man*, and I am a man only in relation to my fellow men. Only in encounter and in communion with them may I receive the gift of freedom. God is *pro me* because he is *pro nobis*. . . . Human freedom is not to be understood as a freedom to assert, to preserve, to justify and save oneself. God is primarily free *for*; the Father is free for the Son, the Son for the Father in the unity of the Spirit." (*HG*: 77–78)

We only know the good because God had demonstrated it to us in God's *freedom* to be with and for humanity in Jesus Christ, which in the end, serves the human good. This "christological qualification," Nigel Biggar argues, determines the divine command not as autocratic or heteronomous but basically *eudaemonist*.[9] "[W]e should obey God's command," says Biggar, "not out of spineless deference to the capricious wishes of an almighty despot, but out of regard for our own best good, which this gracious God alone

---

9. Biggar, "Barth's Trinitarian Ethic," 215.

truly understands and which he intends with all his heart."[10] On one hand, viewing Barth's ethics as eudaemonistic seems inconsistent with his claim that theological ethics begins solely with God's Word, and not with any philosophical or theological ethical theory of "human flourishing," such as found in Aristotelian or Thomistic ethics. On the other hand, the idea of eudaemonism, broadly conceived, refers to any ethical theory that simply claims that the good or right is consistent with the *good* of humanity. Once applied to Barth, this could imply that it is *only* through the divine command that persons even know the human good. This is how Barth himself uses the word eudemonism, when he says that since God's command is "desirable and pleasant and true and good and beautiful. In the face of it, the justifiable concern of eudemonism need not be displaced" (*CD* II/2: 652). The key point here is that God's command is not void of content, but filled with the content of the good as revealed in and through God's trinitarian goodness. Since God *is* good, what God commands is also good as an expression of God's freedom. Only in God's freedom to be the Trinity can we find the source of human freedom. Freedom, of course, is relational and derives from what we are in our actual nature—relational beings capable of acting the good of ourselves and others. The command is a relational command filled with grace. God's command is not a legal imperative, says Barth, but "consists in the fact that it is *permission*—the *granting* of a very definite *freedom*" (*CD* II/2: 585). With the command of grace comes the freedom to act as a responsible witness within the covenant-partnership with the trinitarian God.

God Who Acts: Divine and Human Agency

One of the central features of Barth's theology and ethics, as a whole, is the relationship of divine and human action. By beginning and returning to Christology, Barth develops a pattern of dialectical reasoning that flows through much of his writing on various other doctrinal and ethical topics. This "Chalcedonian pattern," as George Hunsinger aptly calls it, emerges from Barth's emphasis on Chalcedonian "two natures and one person" Christology and its application to many other areas of his theology and ethics. Hunsinger writes:

> The Chalceadonian pattern is used to specify counter positions that would be doctrinally incoherent (and also incoherent with Scrip-

10. Ibid., 215.

ture). "Without separation or division" means that no independent human autonomy can be posited in relation to God. "Without confusion or change" means that no divine determinism or monism can be posited in relation to humanity. Finally, "complete in deity and complete in humanity" means the no symmetrical relationship can be posited between divine and human actions (or better, none that is not asymmetrical).[11]

Barth's ethics, like his theology, is an elaborate development of making distinctions, and then finding how these distinctions are further related in such a way that they can explain a larger, more comprehensive, or coherent picture of Christian truth. That is, he develops the dialectical logic of distinguishing and then relating without falling into the temptations of separation and identification. This is particularly the case in how the relation of human and divine agency is placed within the particular agency of Jesus Christ, as "two natures and one person." This "Chalcedonian pattern" provides the language for how the distinctions and relations of divine and human agency are understood in theory and practice. Again, we recall there is no way from anthropology to Christology, but only Christology to anthropology. This means we must begin with divine and human agency in relation rather than in separation. Beginning with anthropology, for instance, often results in the separation of divine from human agency. God's actions are not human actions, nor are human actions the same as God's actions. There is God, on one side, acting as creator and redeemer apart from humanity, and there is humanity, on the other side, responding in faith to God's gracious action. Yet, in this discussion, the particular agency of Jesus Christ is often not considered important in relating these two agencies.

Jesus Christ, as fully God and fully human, becomes the entry point into our discussion of divine and human agency. Rather than separating divine from human agency, Barth seeks to first distinguish divine from human agency (i.e., "two natures"), but then relate them within the unity of Christ's "one person." On this theme, Barth writes:

> We have to steer a course between that Scylla and this Charybdis. Neither the free commanding of God nor the action of freely responsible man can be shut up in a general law we control. The event between them cannot be understood and presented in a series of applications of such a law. God and man are not for us unwritten

11. Hunsinger, *How to Read Karl Barth*, 204. For an excellent summary of Barth's Chalcedonian Christology, see Hunsinger, "Karl Barth's Christology," 127–42.

pages or unknown quantities. The particular facticity of the event between them is not the only thing we can know and say about it. Who the commanding God is and who responsible man is—God in the mystery of his commanding and man in the mystery of his obedience or disobedience—is not hidden from us but is revealed and may be known in the one Jesus Christ: God *and* man, if not in their essence, at least in their work and there in their manner; God *and* man, accessible to human apprehension, if not expressible in human worlds, at least describable and attestable. (*CL*: 5)

In his discussion of the "Chalcedonian pattern," Hunsinger further discusses how this pattern affects Barth's discussion of divine and human agency, or more definitively, Barth's theology of "double agency."[12] This pattern of "double agency" implies that both human *and* divine action emerges from the human-divine event made objectively real in Jesus Christ, as fully God and fully man. "The miracle and mystery of double agency is thus understood to be patterned after the great miracle and mystery of the incarnation," says Hunsinger, "which the former finds it basis, limit, and final hope."[13] Although this incarnational event in Jesus Christ is extended by *analogy* to persons, it is never duplicated in human agency; otherwise, we would literally *be* Christ. The miracle and mystery of the incarnation is analogously extended to humanity through God's election. Most basically, says Barth, we cannot talk about some notion of generic humanity "outside the humanity of Jesus Christ (*CD* II/2: 541). Only in Jesus Christ is human agency restored, healed, and allowed to live in free response to God's gracious command. It is this gracious beginning of the gospel that provides an entry point into a full-fledged ethics of responsibility and witness.

To be sure, this "Chalcedonian pattern" is further seen in Barth's theological account of the *election* of human beings in Jesus Christ. In fact, it is in the doctrine of election that Barth's theory of double agency becomes concretely manifested. Just as double agency conceives of a space and freedom for persons to respond to God's action, while further inviting God's further action, so too, Barth's view of election further explains how divine and human action (or agency) is related in Jesus Christ. In the incarnation when the "Word became flesh" (John 1:14), we discover the character and election of both God *and* humanity in Jesus Christ as fully God and fully human. This divine-human encounter becomes our basis for the self-identity

12. Hunsinger, *How to Read Karl Barth*, 218–24.
13. Ibid., 223.

of God and humanity, the responsible moral life, and human freedom and agency. God acts in and through the covenant of grace made visible in Jesus Christ as both the divine elector and the human elected, which makes it possible for our corresponding agency to be altered by Christ's own obedient and faithful actions. This inseparable relation Barth would, in the late 1950s, call "the-anthropology," which combines "theology" and "anthropology" together implying that the human subject cannot stand in isolation from God, but only in relation to God. He writes: "'Theology,' in the literal sense, means the science and doctrine of God. A very precise definition of the Christian endeavor in this respect would really require the more complex term 'The-anthropology.' For an abstract doctrine of God has no place in the Christian realm, only a 'doctrine of God and of man,' a doctrine of the commerce and communion between God and man" (*HG*: 11). In Jesus Christ, God performs a kind of double-action. First, God comes to us in human flesh, but second, Jesus as the "new man," as the representative of humanity, approaches God as a free human subject. As the electing God, God fulfills the divine side of the covenant by being our God, but also as the elected human, God, in the humanity of Christ, fulfills the human side of the covenant in choosing to be God's people. All human history is grounded in this one man's history, and all of humanity's relationship to God is grounded in this one man's relationship with God. "As the true God is the God who is and acts and reveals himself in Jesus Christ, so true man is the man who is bound to him and set over against him in Jesus Christ" (*CL*: 20). In the Word of God we encounter God and humanity, and divine and human action. Being cannot be separated from action, but rather, is being-in-action.[14] This obviously has implications for Christian ethics. On this point, Paul Molnar writes: [H]ere Jesus Christ is seen as the solution to the problem of Christian ethics because he himself is the one who not only acts for us as God in the incarnation and resurrection but because he acts obediently for us as the only man who truly and completely obeyed God's will."[15] It follows that when God acts *pro nobis* in

---

14. This is an important theme in Paul Nimmo's recent book on Barth's theological ethics. Nimmo argues that Barth develops an "*actualistic ontology*, in which, within the covenant of grace, the ethical agent as a being in action is called to correspond to the Being in action of God. In other words, for Barth, there was a specific formal and material understanding of the context for all ethical action and of the human person who engaged in it." Nimmo, *Being in Action*, 1.

15. Molnar, *Incarnation and Resurrection*, 42.

Jesus Christ, God is taking responsibility *pro nobis* and for our well-being upon himself, which makes human responsibility possible.

We now are in a better situation to understand how Barth's view of the divine command is the *other* side of the doctrine of election. It is no coincidence that his extensive discussion of the divine command in *CD* II/2 takes place immediately following his discussion of election. This makes the divine command the practical embodiment of the doctrine of election. How these two doctrines are related corresponds to his theology of gospel and law. As pointed out earlier, when Barth placed the gospel before the law, he privileged God's gracious action of election prior to the divine command. In this way, the gospel and law (as well as election and command) can be distinguished with priority beginning with election and the gospel before the command and moral law. The central claim that I am making here is that just as the gospel is the content of the law so is election the content of the divine command, and just as the law is the form of the gospel so is the command the form of election. Since God has elected humanity, in the gospel, as a covenant-partner through the humanity of Jesus Christ, it makes it possible for Christians to act in responsible freedom. If Christ is our representative, then we are made one in Christ through the power of Holy Spirit. "The grace of God is the liberation of these specific people for free, spontaneous, and responsible cooperation in this history." That is, in God's "free grace" the people of the covenant are "given the status of subjects" and should not be seen as "marionettes who move only at his will" (*CL*: 102). Christians are invited and enabled to participate in God's freedom but also summoned to cooperate with God's freedom for the good of others. Christian ethics is being responsible to God and to others in bearing witness to the truth of this covenant relationship.

For most Christian ethicists, these various detours into Christology and election may seem to unnecessarily complicate the basic idea of human agency and ethical action. In fact, most would simply see these theological issues as irrelevant for any discussion of human agency. Where God's agency is included in most ethical schemes, it is usually incorporated in some general way as creator of the natural law or universal moral principles. This, in itself, is not entirely misguided but just incomplete because it fails to be trinitarian in its theology. More difficult questions would come from Christian theologians and ethicists who know enough about Barth's theology to be critical of his Christocentric view of moral agency. One important question from this quarter might be the following: if persons are elected in Jesus Christ, who represents both human and divine purposes, then how can we think of human action (apart from Christ) as free and responsible? To some readers, Barth gets very close to saying that God's grace simply overwhelms the human agent depriving her of her own moral agency and freedom. If God's command emerges from the covenant of grace established in Jesus Christ as both the elect and the elected, then how can humanity hear it, and respond with a free will? Does Barth argue that God's grace is everything and human freedom is nothing? Does he simply erode human agency by overemphasizing divine agency? The simple answer to these questions, as we shall see, is that Barth does not deny human free will or eradicate human deliberation and agency. Yet, more critically, we may say that such critical questions inherently presume that human freedom is truly possible only in its separation from divine agency, something that Barth would rightly deny. This error drives humanity and God apart into two ontologically separate entities and agencies, without attempting to relate the two agencies together in one covenant relation. Without Jesus Christ we have humanity and God acting as independent subjects, governed by a misguided view of autonomous freedom *from* the other, not with and for the other.

If Christian ethics is to be an ethics of witness and responsibility in relation to God's command, then it must reject any notion of human agency that limits, neglects, or rejects the interrelated importance of divine agency. In so doing, it challenges any approach to moral agency that refuses to acknowledge the language of Chalcedon, namely "without separation or division" "without confusion or change," and "complete in deity and complete in humanity." In short, it must reject any notion of human agency that either separates or identifies itself with divine action. First, Barth rejects any account of moral agency that solely begins with the human subject, and completely separates itself from divine agency, which leaves God outside the realm of human action. The human agent is not isolated from God; she does not "live in a vacuum" by her own "self-will." When persons deny their relation to God as covenant-partner, they isolate themselves from the form and content of the good; this leads to a crisis of both knowing and doing the good. Postmodern criticism has rightly attacked the notion of the modern autonomous moral agent as a fiction or illusion, but by rejecting divine agency, it fails to establish a moral ontology that subordinates power to the good. Without God all that remains is human power, which is easily corrupted by the spiritual and earthly powers that people create as parody of God's sovereignty. Second, Barth further rejects any notion that God's action is strictly identified *with* human action, so that human action strictly embodies God's action in the world. The human agent is not a puppet of the divine will. This misconception alters both an understanding of God and humanity, by removing the covenant-partnership, and replacing it with capricious God or divinized humanity. Either God is seen as a tyrant or humanity is seen as a God or having god-like powers or aspirations. In either the case the two subjects of God and humanity are confused (or identified) and reduced to the agency of one or the other. When either God is everything or humanity is everything, this rules out the possibility of two agents acting in relation to each other, and with it, a covenant-partnership. In both these extremes of separation and identification of divine and human agency, it is the human subject that becomes the central agent of deliberation and action.

Although many Christian ethicists assume the moral subject may act in relation to others and her environment, they also assume that, as a moral self, she is an independent and free moral agent of deliberation and action. This presumes a theological commitment to the notion that persons are given power by God to be co-creators of God's world, carrying out God's purposes for the world. We recall that only in relation to God's freedom, in Jesus Christ, is the human person free. "This does not mean that he [man] becomes a co-creator, co-savior, or co-regent in God's activity. It does not mean the he becomes a kind of co-God. It simply means that in its place and within its limits his creaturely activity can take the form of correspondence to the divine activity. Man neither is nor can be a second Jesus Christ, so that in his place and within his limits he with his action is the witness of Jesus Christ and therefore of God's will and work" (*CD* III/4: 482).

By stressing human co-creative power apart from Jesus Christ, many Christian ethicists, invariably reject God's covenantal relationship of grace made *real* in Jesus Christ. This leads to a different understanding of the source of our moral knowledge, being, and action. Put differently, in many versions of Christian ethics the noetic basis for ethics (knowledge of the good) is grounded in the ontological (or ontic) structure of human nature, namely the interpersonal, hermeneutical, and reflexive activity of the human subject. They assume the general ideas discussed in the previous chapter about the reflexive moral self. Yet once the noetic and ontic are strictly defined by the perimeters of human nature and agency, there is no reason *why* God's agency, as most fully revealed in the incarnation, remains important for Christian ethics. This raises the fundamental question: if one's theory of moral agency fails to incorporate the reality of divine agency, then can it really be called a Christian theory? How can a theory of moral agency be Christian if it fails to account for God's covenant-partnership with humanity? Barth continuously reminds us that we must first begin with God's agency before we attempt to explain how human agency is "related" to God's action. Furthermore, we cannot really speak about the history of this relation unless we also talk about the revelation and history of Jesus Christ, who reveals both the *ontic* and *noetic* framework for our understanding of God and humanity. It follows that a Christian understanding of moral agency must begin with Jesus Christ, where human and divine agency are neither separated nor identified, but related in the unity of Christ's person. Otherwise, as Barth says, we become a "second Jesus" carrying out God's purposes as "co-creator, co-savior, or co-regent in God's activity" (*CD* III/4: 482). Any Christian account of moral agency, in short, must begin with the Christological question: who is Christ, and how is his personal agency determinative of human agency in general?

The Christian gospel proclaims that in Jesus Christ God acts in freedom for the good of humanity, so that when humanity acts, it too can act in responsible *correspondence* to this prior gracious action. Since God is the primary actor and humanity is the responder, and that human action corresponds to divine action, human freedom cannot be separated from this covenant relationship, which is itself a freely chosen covenant. When persons invoke God's action, God acts "according to His own good pleasure and purpose, to His own glory, and therefore in their [persons] own best interest too" (*CL*: 106). Since God has already acted to be with us and for us in Jesus Christ, we are empowered by the Holy Spirit to act in responsible freedom. God's agency is not heteronomous, in that it does not control or completely overwhelm the person's self-determining response or her personal freedom. To deny human freedom would be to deny the covenant of freedom, as covenant-partnership, which God has already established in Jesus Christ. So, when God acts, God acts for the *good* of humanity, and when reconciled humanity acts, it corresponds to this divine good action in acts of responsible freedom. Hence, God's grace both limits and liberates human freedom. It is only in our limited or situated freedom, as discovered within the gracious covenant with God, that can we encounter our true freedom and responsibility. Humanity cannot be truly free apart from this covenant-partnership made real in Jesus Christ. Indeed, it is the freedom and responsibility of Jesus Christ that makes it possible for humanity to be free and responsible. Barth writes: "It is as He makes Himself responsible for man that God makes man, too, responsible" (*CD* II/2: 511). In Jesus Christ, God gives persons the freedom to be responsible witnesses. Grace liberates us so that we may hear God's command and act in responsible ways consistent with that command of grace, which serves humanity's good. Barth writes:

> We live in responsibility, which means that our being and willing, what we do and what we do not do, is a continuous answer to the Word of God spoken to us as a command. . . . Man does not belong to himself. He does not exist in a vacuum. He is not given over to the caprice of an alien power, nor to his own self-will. He may or may not know and will it, but because Jesus Christ as very God and very man is the beginning of all the ways and works of God, man is inseparably linked with God and confronted by Him. He is subjected to the divine will Word and command, and called to realize the true purpose of his existence as a covenant-partner with God. As a man, he is objectively tested by this determination and objectively questioned as to its fulfillment. This is the essence of his responsibility. (*CD* II/2: 641)

CORRESPONDENCE AND RESPONSIBLE WITNESS

Christian Witness

Christian ethics is an ethics of responsible witness of the Christian community to God's prior, present, and future action. Barth argues that impersonal moral principles, rules, or platitudes tell us little about God's activities and relationship to the church and world. By pointing to God's action and to the church's witness to that action, Barth challenges the basic methodology and criteria for how most methods of ethics are understood. Although we can discover an ethics of witness emerging in his early writings, it is not until the later *CD* IV/1–3, where this theme is fully developed in relation to his Christological account of divine and human agency. As early as *CD* I/1 (1932), however, Barth first explores the meaning of witness, where he says being a witness means "pointing in a specific direction beyond the self and on to another." "What makes a man a witness is solely and exclusively that other, the thing attested" (*CD* I/1: 111–12). The Word of God is the source for an ethics of witness. This witness consists of both God's action and the human response, which makes it an integrative twofold process. Perhaps his clearest statement about this twofold framework appears many years later in *CD* IV/3, where he describes witness as consisting of a correspondence of God and human action. The Christian, says Barth, is

> in fact a witness in the twofold sense that he as seen and heard the acts of God, or in the New Testament His one consummating and conclusive act, which is also as such God's Word directed to and received by him, and that he is called to the work of declaration, faithfully, if without any claim, addressing, imparting and proclaiming to others that which he has seen as God's act and heard as His Word. . . . He, the witness, may and can and will live by it, and do so joyfully for all his incompatibility, defiance and conflict with the pious and less pious world, and above all with himself. As and to the extent that he exists as a witness, even in his weakness and corruption he stands on solid, eternal ground and need not fear nor hate anyone, even himself, since he has God on his side. (*CD* IV/3: 593)

In the covenant relationship, made real in Jesus Christ, Christians become free to respond in witnessing action to God's reconciling work. This involves an event of correspondence between God and humanity; an event that elicits human permission and responsibility in responding to God's prior action. In this twofold movement, God acts first making it possible for people to be God's witnesses. God has accomplished this task in Jesus Christ by drawing persons into a covenant-relationship with the trinitarian God making it possible to be "on God's side." The Pauline language of being "in Christ" implies that "Christ should live in the Christian by the Holy Spirit in the purpose of his vocation." Being "in Christ" implies the corresponding "self-giving of Christ to the Christian and the Christian to Christ," which "is the goal of vocation, the true being of the Christian" (*CD* IV/3: 594). This relationship between Christ and the Christian makes it possible for Christians to be a vocational witness to God's work in the world, as well as, human corresponding actions in God's name. "The essence of their vocation is that God makes them His witnesses" (*CD* IV/3: 575). This Christ-Christian relationship, in other words, creates a "community of action" in which "Christ is engaged in a work in perfect fellowship" with the Christian, who also acts "in perfect fellowship with the working of Christ" (*CD* IV/3: 597). Of course, this is a "differentiated fellowship of action" in which Christ is the initiator and superior, and the disciple is the responder and subordinate. Nevertheless, in this differentiated fellowship, the disciple remains a free subject giving responsible witness in voice and action to God's gracious command of obedience. This makes it possible, therefore, for the Christian: "[I]n all circumstances and with his whole existence he is a responsible witness to the Word of God" (*CD* IV/3: 609). In this way Christians, both individually and within the church, act as "responsible witnesses" to God's initiative by "declaring," "addressing, imparting, and proclaiming" that which God seeks for human existence. Responsible Christian witness becomes the basis for Christian ethics.

Many versions of Christian ethics cannot be an ethics of witness because they begin and end with the human subject's moral deliberation and action. Ethics remains in a closed circle of immanence in which God cannot act as a free *other* engaging humanity or the world. Instead of beginning with God's freedom to act in covenant-partnership, most versions of Christian ethics usually begin with priority of the reflective and deliberative moral subject. In a rather deistic fashion, God's agency collapses into a deistic-like creator of the moral law or natural law. Such a view proposes that God's role in ethics is limited to that of the *creator* of the moral order (moral ontology) established by "creation" or "nature." In contrast, Barth begins with the trinitarian God's past, present, and future objective actions of *grace* as the content of the moral law. God is a free subject who chooses to graciously act in covenant-partnership with humanity as Father, Son, and Spirit, or as creator, reconciler, and redeemer. Grace, not law, takes the priority in ethics. This becomes important, as we shall see, in explaining how grace and law (or gospel and law) are related in Christian ethics. In Barth's judgment, grace comes before law, which makes the moral law dependent on God's gracious acts. God's mystery remains clearly undefined until we discover God's gracious actions in the Word of God, unveiled in the gospel of Jesus Christ. Theological (and Christian) ethics needs no noetic justification apart from that which emerges from the divine self-manifestation of God in Jesus Christ. "Barth's ethics is not best interpreted as reflection upon an immanent world of moral *meaning*," says Webster, "but as reflection upon a transcendent order of *being* and *value* organized around the grace of God in the gospel of Jesus Christ."[16] Thus, to begin in any other place but the Word of God is to reject the nature of reality itself, or the way things objectively

---

16. Webster, *Barth's Ethics of Reconciliation*, 219.

are in Jesus Christ. "It is He," says Barth, "He who is the reality. He is not I. He is not we" (*CD* I/2: 368).

Saying this, however, we still need to examine further how human freedom corresponds to divine action in Christian witness. Since Christ is our representative, does that imply that Christ is everything and we are nothing? Is Barth guilty of christomonism, as some critics allege? The clue to unpacking the answer to this question is by looking more closely at the *correspondence* of human and divine action as witness. Barth's various discussions of human-divine correspondence developed in the 1930s and afterwards, much like his thought on law and gospel. Unlike *Ethics,* for example, where correspondence and covenant remain unexplored themes, in *CD* II/2, they fully emerge out of his discussion of the doctrine of God and election. These two words are important entry points into the particular way he understands the agency and responsibility of the moral agent. Here he relates themes of Christian *witness* and responsibility to the *correspondence* between God's action and human action as fully revealed in the covenant of grace.

> It is the grace of God which is attested to us by the claim of God. The grace of God wills and creates the covenant between God and man. It therefore determines man to existence in the covenant. It determines him to be a partner of God. It therefore determines his action to correspondence, conformity, and uniformity with God's action. How can God will and create this covenant, or man exist in this covenant, or God be gracious to man, without this determination of man? . . . God's action is that He sent Jesus, that He offered Him up for us, that, again for us, He exalted and glorified Him, and that in and with Him He also elected and created His people, that He elected and created Israel and the Church to be the place of faith in Jesus and a witness to Him. It is to this, therefore, that the required uniformity of our action with God's action must always be related. The determination of man is always to reflect this. The covenant of grace alone constitutes the real relationship between God and man. Man is determined only to be the partner of the gracious God. What other claim can be considered in relation to this partner, indeed what other claim can be known by man at all, except that he must be one to whom God is gracious, and think and speak and act as such? God's action is that He is gracious, and man in his action is committed to correspondence to this action. . . . What are we to do? We are to do what corresponds to this grace. We are to respond to the existence of Jesus Christ and His people. With

our action we are to render an account to this grace. By it and by it alone we are challenged. To it and to it alone we are responsible. (*CD* II/2: 575–76)

It is especially worth noting, in this passage, how the words elected, witness, correspondence, and covenant relate to God's command. In Jesus Christ, God has *elected* and "determined" humanity to be God's "covenant-partner." In this relationship, humanity is liberated by God's grace to freely respond in active *witness* to God's prior initiative as gracious covenant-partner. When God "determines" humanity to be a covenant-partner, thus, God is choosing to act, not against, but with and for human freedom established in Jesus Christ. In Jesus Christ humanity is set free! This is why Christian ethics must begin with the gospel, not the principles or norms of the law. Still, as we've seen, because the law remains the "form" of the gospel, it also shapes moral responsibility. So, what does it mean to act responsibly as witness? In above passage, Barth says that to act as a responsible witness is acting in "correspondence, conformity, and uniformity with God's action." First, Barth does not imply that God acts through human persons to accomplish his will, for that would imply the "deification of man" and the emergence of a "second Christ" (*CD* II/2: 577). As covenant-partners, persons and God do not become identical, but remain distinct agents. Only in the one person of Jesus Christ does God and humanity act in "uniformity," without ceasing to be God and humanity in themselves. By placing our faith in Jesus Christ, therefore, we are acting in "uniformity" with God's purposes in Christ. Second, what Barth understands as acting in "conformity" to God's action means once again, being conformed to God's action in the human-divine encounter in Jesus Christ. For Barth, says Paul Nimmo, there is a movement from the "decentering of the ethical agent from herself to a recentering of her ethical activity and ethical reflection on and in Jesus Christ, to whose salvific action she is called to witness."[17] Only in this encounter, are persons made covenant-partners, in their justification, with God, in grace and freedom. That is, by looking to Jesus Christ, not as moral example or model, but as mediator, Savior, and the Lord who establishes our covenant-relationship with God, we are free to embrace the relational and responsible character of God's gracious command.

---

17. Nimmo, *Being in Action*, 188. For further discussion of conformity and participation in Christ as the "*telos* of ethical action," see ibid., 171–85.

Correspondence and Invocation

Still, we must probe deeper into what it means for the individual Christian to act as responsible witness in correspondence to God's gracious command. Suffice it to say, that Barth makes it clear that God seeks to *cooperate* with humanity in fulfilling the divine will and purpose. In God's covenant-partnership with humanity, God has acted, acts, and will act in such a way that human cooperation is desired, permitted, and commanded. In the context of the doctrine of providence in *CD* III/3, he writes, "[W]e do not rightly describe even Christian faith and Christian obedience if we do not think of them as a human co-operation in doing of the will of God" (*CD* III/3: 286). Although this cooperation is under God's lordship, "nonetheless it is a real co-operation" (*CD* III/3: 286). That is, when God cooperates with humanity, God's "own activity precedes, accompanies and follows that activity, and nothing can be done except the will of God" (*CD* III/3: 113). In expressing this point, Barth discusses at length the doctrine of *concursus Dei*, which simply affirms that "God 'concurs' with the creature, but the creature does not 'concur' with God" (*CD* III/3: 113). The doctrine of *concursus Dei* does not deny human free will, but only that humanity does not have the power to alter God's will. "That is," says Barth, "the activity of the creature does not impose any conditions on the activity of God" (*CD* III/3: 113). Saying this, however, does not imply that human action cannot make a real difference in the world. In God's divine ruling over the world, God "cooperates" in such a way that the "rights and honor and dignity and freedom of the creature are not suppressed and extinguished but vindicated and revealed" (*CD* III/3: 145). Put differently, although human action is circumscribed by God's divine action as covenant-partner, it is still permitted to flourish benefiting ourselves and others within this covenant-partnership. Indeed, we are commanded to act in responsible ways that give witness to God's covenant relationship with the world.

One good example of the significance of human action, as correspondence to divine action, is Barth's doctrine of baptism. In the practice of water baptism, we do not see "merely" a human action, says Barth, but a "pre-eminent human action." "It is human action which simply responds to divine action" (*CD* IV/4: 143). In baptism, persons

> are not engulfed and covered as by a divine landslide or swept away as by a divine flood. They are taken seriously as God's partners.... Matters are not decided over their heads. They are not just objects

who are discussed, moved and pushed around. Precisely in the covenant of grace, the house of the Father, the kingdom of Jesus Christ and the Holy Ghost, there can be no talk of divine omnicausality. One is attacking this house and kingdom at the very foundations if one fails to see that, even if in total subjection to the rule of Him who alone can rule here, there is given to men, to all the men concerned, not merely a place of their own and freedom of movement, but also the freedom of decision, with commission to exercise it." (*CD* IV/4: 143)

Barth's doctrine of believer's baptism is placed within the unfinished *CD* IV/4, or his "ethics of reconciliation," and it is here, where he more fully elaborates *human* side of this divine-human correspondence. Baptism is not something that happens "above our heads" but something that we actually do, as part our covenant-partnership with God. Baptism is a quintessential "act of obedience made in free responsibility"; it is essentially an act of Christian ethics (*CD* IV/4: 153). When one is baptized one affirms one's reconciliation by choosing to freely act as a witness to God's prior action of grace through the baptism of the Holy Spirit. "This is the pledge which the Christian has made in baptism in God's pledge to him." God's Yes to humanity now corresponds to humanity's Yes toward God. Yet, Barth asks: "[H]ow can their Yes, spoken to God's Yes, be an idle Yes? They set to work energetically to respond to this Yes" (*CD* IV/4: 161). In this way, baptism is more than one act of obedience, but is a continuous response to God's command to act in the "obedience of free responsibility." In this act of obedience, the baptized is also acting in hope. It is the "hope of these men in *Him*" which serves as the basis for "their own *action* in this hope." "The meaning of baptism consists," continues Barth, "in the fact that the community and its candidates let Jesus Christ be the future of their action, that they act in hope in him" (*CD* IV/4: 207). Baptism is an ethical act of responsibility and witness that corresponds to God's past, present, and future actions as creator, reconciler, and redeemer. In this way, baptism serves as a prototype of all ethical actions as active responses to God's prior command of grace.

Earlier in the *CD* IV/4 fragments (*The Christian Life*), Barth seeks for the word that will best describe the reconciled human agent's action in relation to God's gracious action in the covenant. After discussing several alternatives like freedom, conversion, decision, repentance, thanksgiving, and faithfulness, he settles upon the notion of "invocation," because this word most clearly provides an opening for genuine "human action" affecting the entirety of the Christian life as it corresponds to God's action (*CL*: 42). As a form of petitionary prayer, "invocation" remains a genuine human act of a reconciled and "humble and resolute" sinner who fully acknowledges God's goodness in "gratitude, praise, and above all petition" (*CL*: 43). The language, like in baptism, here stresses the human free and active obedience as corresponding to God's divine action, and not simply a "passive" obedience or compliance with divine power and will. Thus, invocation is a "normal action corresponding to the fulfillment of the covenant in Jesus Christ" (*CL*: 43). In a true covenant-partnership, God acts and the persons respond, but we also see how persons act and God responds. With invocation, says Barth, "man in his whole humanity takes his proper place over against God" (*CL*: 43). By saying that the human agent can be placed "over against God," Barth not simply finding a limited space for human agency within encompassing view of divine agency, but he is affirming a genuine human agency, a genuine human freedom that based, like in the act of baptism, on a "wholly free, conscious and voluntary decision" (*CD* IV/4: 163).

Likewise, the human act of prayer plays an important factor in Barth's entire set of ethical and dogmatic writings. Like baptism, prayer is a genuine human ethical act because it affirms, in words and action, the good as revealed by God. As a particular kind of prayer, invocation emerges from the human side of the covenant-partnership. Accordingly, Barth uses the *Lord's Prayer* as an example of the correspondence between human and divine actions in his ethics of reconciliation. When the Christian invokes God's action, and prays "thy will be done," she is also liberated to give witness to God's gracious covenant "on earth as it is in heaven." What God wills for God's "children" is to "actualize the partnership in this history. They have to express in word and deed his fatherhood and their sonship" (*CL*: 85). That is, in response to God's command, persons act in such a way that they further invite God to respond to their own actions, renewing their covenant-partnership. "Invocation," says Barth, "aims at the renewal, or rather the dynamic actualization, of what has become a static, stagnant, and frozen relationship with him" (*CL*: 85). From God's side, of course, the covenant-partnership is anything but "static" or "frozen," but from the human side, it is possible to reject God as covenant-partner in favor of human autonomy and self-determination. Once this occurs, God is understood no longer as the "Father" of the covenant, but "a God seated on a distant throne, an alien and sinister God" (*CL*: 86). By rejecting the covenant, persons corrupt the noetic and ontic view of themselves and God. In contrast, in affirming the covenant-partnership, persons affirm that witness and responsibility are legitimate human responses, in word and deed, to their living and vibrant relationship to their "Father" in heaven. As "children of God," then, persons are "freed for responsible decision and action" (*CL*: 86). "We cannot speak of human action—and this is what gives it its force and dignity—without immediately thinking of its continuation of the other side, on God's side" (*CL*: 102). In God's partnership with humanity, made real in Jesus Christ, God has chosen to act in a cooperative way with rather than against humanity. The language shifts from correspondence to cooperation. When Christians call upon God in invocation they are not only inviting God to act here and now, but they are also actively having a "part in the history in which God is their partner and they are his partners" (*CL*: 104).

In closing, we have seen how correspondence sets the framework for moral agency. How this applies to actual responsible ethical human actions, we will explore in later chapters. Suffice it say that in our covenant-partnership with God, persons are given permission to act in freedom and responsibility, but they may act in error, in commission or omission, and misuse of this freedom. Still, Christian ethics is an ethics of freedom that invites one to act, reflect, and act again. Because Christian witness begins with God's gracious action in the Word of God and not with ethical methods or reflexive analysis, it remains free from excessive deliberation or analysis about specific courses of action. "The command of God protests against what man permits himself, or knows how to create or find elsewhere by way of permission" (*CD* II/2: 594). So, what does mean to act in permission? What does it mean to act in freedom? Are there any guidelines to this freedom? These questions push us toward the practical side of Christian ethics, or what Barth calls "special ethics." We begin our discussion of special ethics in the next two chapters, where we see that responsible witness can take the form of either actions *for* the good or resistance *against* evil; they take the form of either a Yes or a No. In chapter 8, we explore the No side of this dialectic, namely how God's command calls persons to protest against is the "lordless powers" that are human-created realities that deprive humanity of its freedom, peace, hope, and moral responsibly toward God, others, and the world. Just as God has acted decisively in Jesus Christ to defeat the powers, the Christians correspond to this divine action by resisting and "unmasking" the true evil of these powers. The human No against the powers corresponds to the divine No against the powers. Before that, however, we must first explore the Yes of responsible witness, leading to a conception of moral judgment as open-ended and dialectical. The reason for this ordering is simply that the Yes of moral judgment comes before the No of resistance, or put differently, we can only discern the No against the powers through the Yes of responsible moral judgment. Regardless of their ordering, both the Yes and the No cannot be conceived apart from God's gracious initiative to include us into a covenant-partnership.

> It is enough to say that God's "Yes" and "No," spoken in His active reconciliation, is not proclaimed apart from man. Even in this central act God declines to be alone, without man. God insists on man's participation in His reconciling work. He wants man, not as a secondary God, to be sure, but as a truly free follower and coworker, to repeat his divine "Yes" and "No." This is the meaning of God's covenant with man. This is the task man is called to fulfill when God enters into the covenant relationship with him. This is the freedom of discipleship bestowed upon him. (*HG*: 81)

CHAPTER SEVEN

Witness and Christian Moral Judgment

Ethics as Christian witness begins with God's action to be "with us" and "for us" in Jesus Christ. In this event, God has given Christians the *freedom* to respond, as witnesses, to this objective reality both individually and collectively within the church. This leads to a particular dialectical understanding of ethical judgment and action. That is, Christians give witness by both standing against the various powers that oppress humanity and standing with and for others, the church, and the world. In chapter two, we saw how Barth's dialectical thought during the *Römerbrief* period often began with the No of transcendent judgment, which opened up the triumphant Yes of divine grace and the possibility for witness; the vertical diastasis of the No leads to the Yes of responsible ethical action. With the *Ethics* lectures, however, this pattern of No-Yes is reversed, in that the Yes of the trinitarian commander sets the stage for his theological and Christian ethics of witness. We further saw how this Yes-No pattern of gospel *before* law set the agenda for his theological criticism of the German Christians and Nazism. To be sure, this Yes-No pattern, rooted in God's reconciliation, continues into the *Church Dogmatics*, including the ethical sections found in *CD* I/2, II/2, III/4, and IV/4, as well as other occasional social and political writings. "God says 'Yes.' Only once this 'Yes' is said, He also says 'No'" (*HG*: 78). Therefore, the dialectical Yes-No pattern becomes a predominant pattern in Barth's mature writings as a whole. This pattern will, therefore, be the basic organizational motif for the next two chapters, as this chapter looks at the Yes of responsible moral judgment and action and the next chapter looks at the No of resistance against the lordless powers. Just as the law can only be understood in light of the gospel, so too, the No of resistance against the powers can only be understood in light of the Yes of the liberating freedom of Christian vocation, witness, and discipleship.

WITNESS AND LIBERATION

We begin by looking at themes of witness and liberation, as developed primarily in *CD* IV/2–3, and in particular, how *liberation* provides a framework for Christian responsibility and witness. Afterward, the chapter focuses on the dialectical process of moral judgment, in which we explore how the process of moral deliberation talks place within an ethics of responsible witness. This discussion incorporates all of Barth's mature ethical writings from the 1930s to around 1960, or in particular, from *CD* II/2 to *CD* IV/4 fragments (*The Christian Life*). Lastly, this chapter explores Barth's ethics in comparison to contemporary Christian ethics, by comparing him to the important theologian and ethicist Stanley Hauerwas. Although both theologians understand Christian ethics as witness, they do differ on how witness is understood and its relation to ecclesiology, moral agency, and ethical methodology. This comparison is helpful in further understanding the various issues behind an ethics of witness in our contemporary world.

Discipleship after Christendom

As mentioned in the last chapter, the Christian *vocation*, the Christians way of life and identity, is rooted in the relationship between persons and Jesus Christ their Savior and Lord. This relationship becomes the basis for Christian witness, that is, what one professes and proclaims to the world through their words and actions. Further, this relationship becomes the basis for how the Christian lives in response to Christ's call to "follow him," namely *discipleship*. These three aspects of the Christian life are interrelated and emerge from the particular context in which Christians live their lives. The way the Christian lives out her discipleship, vocation, and witness corresponds to God's free and gracious command, here and now in this unique time and place. The "place of responsibility" is the "unique opportunity" that a person finds herself in time in the context of our knowledge of "becoming" and "perishing" (*CD* III/4: 607). Christian witness therefore, remains particular to our own time, one in which, the church is no longer the dominant power in society. This is why Barth discusses these particular terms of discipleship, vocation, and witness in the context of living *after* Christendom. Yet, ironically this period after *corpus christianum* creates the possibility for clearer constitution of Christian identity. Certain aspects of Christendom remain; however, the simple argument that one is born a Christian because one is born and baptized within a Christian culture no longer applies to modern pluralistic society.

> The idea of a Christianity which is automatically given and received with the rest of our inheritance has now become historically impossible, no matter how tenaciously it may linger on and even renew itself in various attempts at restoration by the Church and the world. . . . Hence a man can no longer be brought up as a member of it. His Christianity can no longer derive from the fact that he is member of it. Whether he likes it or not, therefore, he is asked today whether or not this Christianity of his has some other basis than the scrap of tradition which may still remain as an anachronistic relic. It may thus be argued that today even from the historical standpoint there can be no escaping the startling recognition that a man's being as a Christian is either grounded in his vocation or it is simply an illusion which seems beautiful perhaps in the after-glow of a time vanished beyond recall. (*CD* IV/3: 525)

The secularity that dominates our era of post-Christendom has ironically given the church its *freedom* to discover the true nature of the Christian way of life and identity—as vocation. As we shall see later in more detail this means more than simply belonging to the "Christian ethos" with its set of beliefs, practices, and values. Although beliefs and practices are important they are not ends in themselves. Christianity or the "Christian ethos" should not "allow itself to be understood as an end in itself" (*CD* IV/3: 560). So, instead of beginning with the church's culture as the source for Christian identity, we begin with God's freedom to establish a covenant-partnership unveiled in God's trinitarian action. The freedom of the church to be itself is possible only because God is free to be God in covenant-partnership. What does it mean to exist in covenant-partnership with God? It means being aware or "awakened" to the objective and constitutive reality that God has claimed you, as a person, to be in fellowship with God, and that you no longer remain isolated and alone but belong to God. Through the power of the Holy Spirit, the individual's will and action is conformed to Christ's will and action, which makes it possible to live a life of Christian witness and discipleship. This is Christian liberation, and what the Pauline witness implies by being "in" Christ. A liberated person is a person that is decentered from the power of solitariness, isolation, and autonomy, or put differently, the person's life becomes "an 'eccentric' life, i.e., one which has its centre outside itself" (*CD* IV/2: 788). Just as Christ chooses to not just live "concentrically" for himself but "eccentrically" for others, so too, the Christian, as a witness and disciple, chooses to live not only for oneself but "eccentrically" for Christ.

> That Christ is in the Christian means, then, that as the Mediator between God and man He does not exist merely for Himself and to that extent concentrically, but that in His prophetic work, in the calling of His disciples and Christians, with no self-surrender but in supreme expression of Himself, He also exists eccentrically, i.e. in and with the realisation of the existence of these men, as the ruling principle of the history lived by them in their own freedom. . . . That the Christian is in Christ means *mutatis mutandis* for him, too, that as one who is called by the one Mediator between God and man in the exercise of His prophetic office he cannot exist for himself and to that extent concentrically, but that, without detriment to his humanity, awakened rather to genuine humanity, he also exists eccentrically, in and with the realisation of his own existence, being received and adopted as an integral element in the life and history of Christ. (*CD* IV/3: 548)

Just as human agency and freedom, as genuine expressions of humanity, are fulfilled in Jesus Christ, so too, as the disciple participates in Christ through the power of the Holy Spirit, he or she participates in divine agency and freedom. "The fact that His call is the call to this discipleship, and therefore to fellowship with Him, thus shows us particularly clear that vocation is not merely *vocatio unica* but also *vocatio continua*" (*CD* IV/3: 536). Henceforth, one cannot be either a Christian or a "genuine free person" without being joined to Christ, through the agency of Holy Spirit. "That Christ should live in the Christian by the Holy Spirit is the purpose of his vocation" (*CD* IV/3: 594). Knowledge of one's identity and mission is possible only by discovering one's relation to the identity and mission of Jesus Christ. As the disciple lives "eccentrically" for Christ, she further discovers that she no longer lives "concentrically" for herself, but "eccentrically" for others. "In vocation, then, it is a matter of God on one side and the world on the other" (*CD* IV/3: 576). Although the goal of the Christian life is fellowship with Jesus Christ, the purpose of the *unio cum Christo* is not a spiritual, mystical union, but a practical engagement in Christ's "prophetic work" for the world. "The Word of the work which God does in and on them is to be sounded out and heard in the world" (*CD* IV/3: 576). The *raison d'être* of Christian vocation is practically embodied in Christian witness and discipleship. He writes:

> We will again begin by stating that the call to *discipleship* is the particular form of the summons by which Jesus discloses and reveals Himself to a man in order to claim and sanctify him as His own, and as His *witness* in the world. It means the coming of grace, for what is disclosed and revealed in Jesus is the *reconciliation* of the world with God as his reconciliation and therefore the fullness of salvation. . . . Discipleship very properly describes the *relationship* between Him and His followers as a history which in this way is proper to Him and Him alone. Jesus goes, and the disciple *accompanies* Him on the same way. It is Jesus who chooses the common way, and treads it first. The Christian follows Him on the way which He has chosen, treading in His steps (1 Pet 2:21). (*CD* IV/2: 534–35)

Without reconciliation between God and humanity there is no *real* human freedom. Put differently, Christian witness and discipleship are possible *only* because of God's reconciling covenant which establishes human freedom (liberation). Human freedom depends upon our liberation from our distorted autonomous notions of *potentia* even, as we perceive it, in service of the right and the good (*potestas*). Rather, our freedom can only be realized in God's divine *potestas* to create a covenant-partnership with us in communal fellowship. True human freedom discovers itself only in relation or "correspondence" to God's freedom. Yet, how reconciliation is understood has a strong bearing on how Christian ethics is understood. Personal freedom, then, is not, says Barth, a choice "between two possibilities, but between his one and only possibility and his own impossibility, and thus between his being and his nonbeing, between the reality and the unreality of his freedom" (*CD* III/2: 196–97). Freedom is not something a person does in free actions of the will, but the state of being (or becoming) in which a person finds herself in covenant-partnership with God. This awareness of one's reality in freedom is possible only because of God's action of reconciliation in Jesus Christ. For Barth, reconciliation is an *objective* reality accomplished by God once through the covenant of grace, but it is further encountered in the lives of Christians who, by faith, become aware of how God has acted determinatively in the concrete history of Jesus Christ. What Christians do with this salvific knowledge is important! This is where the knowledge and task of Christian witness begins its journey. It is not enough to simply acknowledge one's witness, but to understand how this witness leads directly to one's ethical actions. Christian witness is always a "responsible witness of the Word of God" serving both "God and men" (*CD* IV/3: 609). So, what actually happens in the witness of this covenant? Is salvation primarily an individual or communal event? We must investigate further how soteriology shapes our understanding of ethics as responsible witness, and whether witness is expressed individually or communally? How we answer these questions inevitably affects how we understand the ethical actions of "responsible witness?"

Witness: Individual or Communal?

In the subsection "The Christian as Witness" in *CD* IV/3, Barth describes in detail what he calls the "classic" view of Christian existence, namely one in which the "Christian ethos" takes a predominant role. Rather than looking to God or Christology, Christians look to the church—as culture—for their understanding of Christian meaning and identity. It is in the context of this "Christian ethos" in which Christian beliefs, values, and ethical actions are understood and practiced. Inasmuch as the church remains important for Christian existence, Barth asks, should the "Christian ethos" be the "common denominator that we seek" and thus be seen as an "end in itself" (*CD* IV/3: 560–61)?

> Christians, we are told, are those who are the recipients of grace. They are illumined and awakened by the work of the Word and Spirit of the Lord. They are born again and converted. They have peace with God. For them the reconciliation of the world to God in Jesus Christ, and the justification fulfilled in sanctification established in Him, have not taken place in vain as for all the rest. They have their own personal share in the fruit of this divine action—the share which is effective in their lives and experienced by them. As they repent and believe, and continue to do so, they have the forgiveness of their sins and are also introduced to and empowered for life corresponding to this liberation. They are the beloved of God who may love Him in return. They have the freedom as his children to converse with Him as their Father. On the basis of the resurrection of Jesus Christ they have the sure and open prospect of their own resurrection, and are already granted a foretaste of the eternal life of which they now know themselves to be the heirs. (*CD* IV/3: 562)

On the surface this "classic" account of Christian existence appears to present a clear and acceptable account of the meaning and content of the gospel. Yet, as one digs beneath the surface there emerges some internal problems with this rather ecclesially-centered view that identifies Christian existence by the perimeters of the beliefs and practices of the "Christian ethos." Here the church sees the *beneficia Christi* as the means by which Christians distinguish between themselves as believers, saved by grace, and other nonbelievers, who remain cut off from the gracious benefits of Christ's reconciliation. Barth admits that one's personal assurance of God's salvation is not an unimportant aspect of the Christian life. "But can his salvation as known by him be the principle which dominates his Christian existence," asks Barth, "the nail on which everything is hung?" (*CD* IV/3: 566). The soteriological error of this "classic" view is that it begins with subjective experience of salvation *pro me* (for me) as the basic framework for how the Christian views his life in the church and society. This logic has led individuals and churches to take the divine message of liberation—the gospel—and use it to separate themselves from others within and outside their own congregations. This fosters the destructive attitude of "pious egocentricity" that constantly distinguishes between the pious and irreverent, the saint and sinner, the insider and the outsider, the saved and the unregenerate, and the Christian and the non-Christian (*CD* IV/3: 568). The separation between "us" and "them" dramatically affects how Christians, both collectively and individually, understand themselves in relation to outsiders. This collectively leads to a perverted notion of witness focused on a preoccupation with the church as an end in itself, that is, a form of ecclesial introspection where the church loses its mission to be a public witness. It remains quite willing to allow secular society to remain a godless place separated from the *beneficia Christi* found in the church. Ironically this leads to a passive acceptance, even accommodation, to the various patterns of secular society. The church no longer sees itself as related to the world outside the church, which makes the church itself "egocentric." "Is not every form of egocentricity excused and even confirmed and sanctified, if egocentricity in this sacred form is the divinely willed meaning of Christian existence and the Christian song of praise consists finally only in a many-tongued but monotonous *pro me, pro me*, and similar possessive expressions" (*CD* IV/3: 567)?

The egocentric containment of grace within the Christian ethos must be challenged by the gospel of reconciliation that affirms that Jesus Christ is the Savior and Lord of the entire *world*. Barth reverses the "classic" view and claims that reconciliation is an objective event that reconciles God with the world *pro nobis* (for all), and secondarily—or derivatively—it is an event encountered *pro me*. The "provisional character" of the church "points beyond itself to the fellowship of all men in the fact of which it is a witness and herald" (*CD* II/2: 196). Christians are simply aware of something that others don't see or experience. This is why the Christian is a "model of supreme objectivity" (*CD* IV/3: 653). The "objective reality" of the event of reconciliation is that God in Christ has defeated the powers and liberated humanity. Christian witness proclaims and demonstrates in practice that God has acted, is acting, and will act *pro nobis*. Rather than egocentrically looking to church as ethos, the Christian looks outward to the world discovering her "task" of giving witness to God's action in the world. Instead of standing only within the walls of the church, Christians look through these walls to world, and in so doing, stand within the "environment of the man Jesus." "Its particularity consists in the fact that by its existence it has to witness to Him in fact of the whole world, to summon the whole world to faith in Him" (*CD* II/2: 196). In this way, the Christian life, the church, or even fellowship and union with Christ are not ends in themselves, but an invitation to participate in Christ's ongoing prophetic work in the world. The Christian is a "witness of the living Jesus Christ as the Word of God and therefore a witness to the whole world and to all men of the divine act of grace which has taken place in all men" (*CD* IV/3: 652). Indeed, just as Jesus Christ is "God's gracious act of salvation effected for the whole world, so He is the Word which calls certain men to the attestation of this act" (*CD* IV/3: 650).

Christian witness affirms that God's divine action in the world is not contingent upon Christian witness and discipleship. Christians, says Barth, "must accept the fact that success of his witness is not in his own hands but in the hands of the One whom he has to serve it" (*CD* IV/3: 657). God's truth and love remains objectively true even though there are no witnesses, or Christians fail in their discipleship. The fact that there are specific disciples who are called to attest and give witness to Christ's liberation of humanity relies upon God's patience and mercy to allow both the church and world the time to give and receive this truth of reconciliation. "If the message is to be given, the world must see and hear at least an indication, or sign, of what has taken place. The break made by God in Jesus must become history. This is why Jesus calls his disciples" (*CD* IV/3: 544). That is, God "makes them witnesses of His being in His past, present and future action in the world and in history, of His being in His actions among and upon with men" (*CD* IV/3: 575). Saying this, however, does not deny that Christians cannot have a significant effect on the world by their actions. Again, Barth never denies the free will, or even human self-determination, but simply argues that from the Christian viewpoint definitions of human freedom cannot be seen apart from God's freedom to act "for" humanity's benefit. A theological view of human freedom and witness begins *with* the divine-human encounter made visible in Jesus Christ, but is extended by *analogy* to all persons. God first acts in and through the covenant of grace, which provides the framework for human beings to respond by invoking God's presence into the realm of human freedom. "It is as He makes Himself responsible for man that God makes man, too, responsible" (*CD* II/2: 511). It is Christ's responsibility to be with and for humanity, and this enables Christians to engage in witness and discipleship, and to seek to embody moral responsibility in their actions toward others, the church, and the world. Indeed, when this divine-human covenant is rejected in favor of an anthropocentric conception of moral agency, human beings ironically fall under the potentially hegemonic influences of the powers, thus, endangering human freedom and hope for a better world.

Christian Liberation

We now look at how "Christian liberation" affects the process of moral judgment and decision-making through God's reconciling grace. For this we must look more intently at the important subsection "The Liberation of the Christian" in *CD* IV/3. Unlike his "ethics of creation" (*CD* III/4) where he uses the controlling principle of "freedom," in his ethics of reconciliation he uses the stronger word "liberation." Although recognizing the similarity of the two words, Barth prefers the more "dynamic term 'liberation' to the more static 'freedom,'" when considering the corresponding call to be a "witness of Jesus Christ" (*CD* IV/3: 663). More particularly, liberation "does not signify merely a release from some authority or power which illegitimately binds man and dominates him to his own destruction, but also redemption to responsibility to a very different court which demands his attention and obedience and which as a genuine, valid and saving claim upon him" (*CD* IV/3: 663). So what does it mean, practically speaking, for the Christian to be *liberated* in his or her witness and discipleship, and how does this differ from the person not aware of this liberation?

> What ought man to do, what can he do, when God and his fellow-man are absent for him, when his existence has no horizon because of his unlimited freedom of will, when he is set under the dominion of things and has to serve them, when he thinks he has to live by the leave and under the compulsion of desire and demand? Under these fatal and mutually interwoven presuppositions, what is he to grasp as the first or most essential or best or even the right thing joyously to decide on and confidently to accomplish? Who is to advise him in this regard? How can he advise himself? Instead of indecision we might speak of confusion, because the man who is unadvised or ill-advised can never refrain from doing something, and by reason of the variety of his undertakings his experimentation necessarily betrays him into hopeless confusion. But the Christian as a witness of Jesus Christ leaves the presuppositions behind, and with them he also leaves the indecision and confusion which they inevitably produce . . . Delivered from indecision, the Christian is led at once beyond all theory to practice, to action. By his Lord, and as His servant, he is not called or engaged to, nor empowered for, either theorising or experimenting, but rather obedience. (*CD* IV/3: 669)

In this important passage, Barth demonstrates what the Christian disciple is liberated *from* and what he or she is liberated to *do*. First, the person is liberated from solitude and isolation so that they can enter into fellowship and community. Unlike the various ideologies of personal autonomy that promise individual freedom and liberty from others, Barth claims that true liberty is the freedom to be with and for others. He is critical of worldviews that stress human autonomy, individualism, and solitariness because they separate persons from God and other persons. In so doing, they create the justification for injustice and violence. "The solitary man is the potential, and in a more refined or blatant way the actual, enemy of all others" (*CD*: IV/2: 421). Radical individualism will always be strong temptation for persons who deny their covenant-partnership with God. When people withdrawal from God and others, they fall into the "cavern of fatherless and brotherless isolation" instead of entering into the "open country of fellowship" with "God as his Father" and his "neighbor as his brother" (*CD* IV/3: 664). When this happens persons inevitably distort the true nature of human freedom, claiming to stand independent of God and others, like "Hercules at the crossroads" (*CD*: IV/1: 746). The isolation from others, moreover, leads to the further consequence of binding oneself to other things with the hope that they will bring personal meaning and freedom. These things may include obsessive attachments to social and cultural elements and institutions, material goods, and "machines and gadgets" (*CD* IV/3: 666). The point here, of course, is not to devalue the importance of these various attachments of human life, but simply to argue that these things must not be sought as ends in themselves. Otherwise, they are given too much power and serve as idols or symbols of human hope and freedom. In short, they become powers that stand against—not for—human freedom. It is for the "sake of men and not of things that the Christian, himself a man among men, is called to be a witness and exists as such" (*CD* IV/3: 666).

A second feature of Christian liberation includes being freed from the burden of autonomous decision-making. Liberation involves being freed from the necessity of free choice and "unlimited possibilities," to the true freedom discovered in "one possibility" (*CD* IV/3: 665). Moral agency itself is freed to choose and act in responsible witness by being aware of one's situated freedom that remains definite and purposive. Moral agency, without reconciliation and liberation, presumes an underlying worldview of human existence without "horizon, contour or shape," which further leads to a nightmarish scenario of uncertainty and anxiety (*CD* IV/3: 665). That is, by affirming an "unlimited freedom of the will" we risk turning our freedom in the necessity of fate and falling victim to the oppressive regime of the powers. It becomes more difficult to do and know what the right or good is in particular circumstances. This leads to moral relativism and endless confusion about what is right or good. In postmodern society, as discussed earlier, the power of moral relativism itself becomes a social and cultural problem that needs to be addressed. In contrast to these dire circumstances, the liberation of the Christian leads to a purposive and forward-guided life that actually opens up new possibilities within a particular development of God's eschatological purpose of reconciliation and redemption. In this movement, the "element of chance" and the "burden of anxiety and embarrassment" are removed so that the Christian is free to respond, in freedom, to the call to be a disciple and witness (*CD* IV/3: 665). Responding to the call of Jesus means "seizing of a new opportunity that was not present yesterday but is now given in and with the call of Jesus" (*CD* IV/2: 538). The call to discipleship overrides the many possible choices that one might have in a given situation. Discipleship limits choices, in that, it rules out other "psychological, historical, economic, or political" factors that might interfere with a specific course of action in a given situation. In short, the call of discipleship itself "creates the situation" in which we act. "In obedience we are not about to leap. We are already leaping" (*CD* IV/2: 542).

A third feature of liberation includes being freed from power of the appetites of desire and compulsion. As stated earlier, moral decision-making can remain captive to the various attachments that people infuse with personal meaning. Personal moral judgment becomes arduous when one places oneself "under the dominion of things and has to serve them," that is, under the power of one's "compulsion of desire and demand" (*CD* IV/3: 669). Without God's gracious covenant, persons are driven by their compulsions, desires, pressures, and the demands placed on them by themselves and others. They fall under the power of outside influences that seek to take away their own personal freedom and dignity. With liberation, however, comes the power to reject these false or "illusionary" desires and wants, and the security in "active waiting" upon God gracious action. There is freedom in knowing that God has acted, is acting, and will act in the future. Acknowledging this liberates the Christian from his or her "wishful-thinking, self-justification, and demanding which do not further this but rather poison and impede it" (*CD* IV/3: 667). This, furthermore, leads to the fourth feature of liberation, which implies the freedom of the human will from indecision and the freedom for action. We've discussed earlier the problems with a nontheological ethics that relies on the decision-making of the autonomous moral agent. Barth thinks that without an awareness of grace the moral agent remains both compelled and unable to make moral decisions that benefit oneself, others, and the world. This confusion, no doubt, is inflated because persons really think they act on the good, as they understand in their conscience, but in this apparent freedom they become slaves of their own attachments and desires. With the liberation of grace, however, comes the freedom to move from this state of confusion, of constant deliberation about action, to concrete action—to the task of being a witness. In the call of discipleship, the Christian turns away from their misguided self-generated theorizing, and turns toward others in responsible witness. True self-denial implies taking the step of faith "into the open, into the freedom of a definite decision and act" (*CD* IV/2: 539). In obedience to Christ, the Christian is encouraged not to "feel, or think, or consider, or mediate! Not turn it over in your heart and mind! But *do* something brave" (*CD* IV/2: 540).

The fifth feature of liberation is the freeing of the conscience from excessive moralism and legalism and toward the freedom of decision-making.

In this section, Barth compares a "false dialectic" of the "moral and the immoral" to a "real dialectic" of "forgiveness and gratitude" (*CD* IV/3: 670). What this simply means is that for Christians the most basic moral decision is not between good and evil, as society understands it, but between choosing to respond or not respond to God's command to be or not be a disciple of Jesus. To be sure, if ethics is only about autonomously choosing between good and evil, then there would be no reason to talk about reconciliation, discipleship, or witness. Without a covenant of grace, ethical judgment and action is reduced to making a decision "between two possibilities" like "Hercules at the crossroads," which leads to an "overestimation" of oneself, like "Atlas bearing and holding together the great building of the universe" (*CD* IV/1: 746, 450). This makes humanity, not God, the great sovereign power in the world, which leads ironically to the loss of human freedom and enslavement to human power. In contrast, true human freedom "means being in a spontaneous and therefore willing agreement with the sovereign freedom of God" (*CD* IV/1: 449). The conscience is liberated, thus, when it becomes free to respond in obedience and responsibility to the Word of God. As he writes in another place: "What is the meaning of the 'conscience' in Christian ethics? Very simply it means that we may know what God has done for us. And we may therefore also know about ourselves, and know about ourselves as God knows about us, in order that we might then, on the basis of this knowledge, so choose and determine ourselves and our acts as God has chosen and determine us. Good and evil action is simply being obedient or disobedient to the knowledge of ours about God and ourselves" (*GHN*: 110).

We recall that Barth rejected early on the notion that the conscience ought to be defined simply as a faculty of human reason or experience. Such an account neglects the drama of creation, sin, reconciliation, forgiveness, gratitude, redemption, and so on. In particular, it fails to consider how the conscience is understood eschatologically. "It is not," says Barth, "the function of conscience to interpret and apply, as though the command in itself were empty and needed concrete filling. In conscience then, we are not made judges, but witnesses to the judgment to which we are subjected" (*CD* II/2: 668). People, at their core, are relational beings, who are created, reconciled, and redeemed by gracious *judgment* of the trinitarian God. Since persons find their true freedom in this covenant-relationship with God, the conscience discovers its liberation as much in prayer as in responsible action. Without a relationship to God, nurtured by faith and obedience, life becomes anxious and uncertain. Obviously the many people who suffer from anxiety are aware of its power, but even many others who remain convinced that they are free from its power, are also affected by its influence. "It may be more grievously felt by some, more lightly by others; more sincerely admitted by some, anxiously or defiantly silenced and stifled by others." Regardless of how people perceive its power over their lives, it "arises and operates in all men" (*CD* IV/3: 672). In contrast, in the Christian vocation of discipleship and witness, the believer realizes that he or she cannot be sustained without prayer, since it is prayer, which frees persons from the anxiety that surrounds their lives. "As the Christian prays, he actually anticipates his own liberation from anxiety even when engulfed by it." Indeed, in prayer, the Christian "comes to himself again in the face of anxiety, finding the solid ground and appointed path of his vocation" (*CD* IV/3: 673). The liberation of the conscience moves us from anxiety to prayer.

As liberation frees the self for witness, discipleship, and vocation, it also frees the self from excessive forms of Christian perfectionism. Thus, in describing these various aspects of Christian liberation, Barth presents an important set of caveats, shaped by the eschatological reality of "waiting" for the "not yet." These include: 1) the provisionality of liberation, in that it is a developmental process and "not in any sense complete" for the individual; 2) that its "exemplary significance" today is an "anticipation" of what will be in a future time for all people; 3) that liberation cannot be isolated from the vocation of witness and discipleship, and that whatever satisfaction one gains from this, comes from God's grace in Jesus Christ; and 4) liberation cannot be isolated, separated, or applied to any "project" or program apart from God's purpose of reconciliation (*CD* IV/3: 673–80). On this latter point, he says, [T]here are no legitimate expectations, projects or attempts which can have as their theme the abstract and personal liberation of the Christian" (*CD* IV/3: 678). Taken together, these strategies for liberation of the individual or a community cannot be imagined, planned, or transformed into actions isolated from God's prior action. The Christian should not identify liberation with any "alternation" of his personal life, including his lifestyle, ethical behavior, or achievement, nor with any social political movement or strategy to transform society toward some utopian vision of God's kingdom. Personal and communal liberation is governed solely by God's divine initiative to defeat the powers bring reconciliation and redemption to the world. "Again," Barth says, "discipleship is not the recognition and adoption of a programme, ideal or law, or the attempt to fulfill it. It is not the execution of a path of individual or social construction imparted and commended by Jesus" (*CD* IV/2: 536).

CHRISTIAN MORAL JUDGMENT

We are now able to discuss more fully the task of moral judgment. As said above, liberation frees the person's conscience, will, and agency *for* moral action. Still, we must discuss further how this applies to the process of moral judgment itself. How does liberation affect the process of moral judgment? Broadly speaking, Christian witness, including discipleship and vocation, seeks to avoid the extreme positions of complete separation or identification. When Christians separate from the world they reject the world as godless and demonic, or alternatively, when they identify with the world they accommodate themselves to the powers and forces of the world. In contrast, Christian witness and discipleship is possible because Christ liberates persons from the tyranny of the powers, at the same time, liberates persons to serve God, neighbor, and the world. Without God's grace, persons are not free to resist the self-destructive powers that enslave us and others, whereas with grace, humans are empowered to be truly human in the humanity of Jesus Christ. This being said, we can now look further into the subject of moral judgment itself as a positive process of deliberation. That is, one that avoids autonomous choosing between two alternatives, like "Hercules at the crossroads" (*CD* IV/1: 746). Rather, the Christian is "liberated but also summoned to manifest, indicate and attest what is said to him and received by him as a Word of reconciliation directed not to him alone but to the whole world and all men." Just as God has graciously acted *pro nobis*, Christians are liberated in their corresponding freedom and "responsible witness of the Word of God" to serve both "God and men" (*CD* IV/3: 609).

What Shall We Do?

The question remains: how is Christian witness linked to the process of practical moral judgment? Although Barth is extremely cautious about decisionist ethical methodologies that jettison the priority of divine action in human reflection and action, he does not rule out strategies for a more *dialectical* form of moral judgment. In one of the most important sections of *CD* II/2 called "The Sovereignty of the Divine Decision," Barth expands upon material found in *Ethics*, in answering the perennial question: "what shall we do?" In this section, he summarizes the movement from theory to practice, from moral knowledge to moral action. In approaching the question of the "what," for example, our posture should not consist anxiously searching for the right or good answer as much as being "open" and "preparing ourselves for fuller openness to truth" (*CD* II/2: 647).

> Our one concern must be with truth itself, and not with rights and wrongs of either anxiety. The truth itself demands complete openness. From the standpoint of the truth itself thoroughgoing conservatives are as useless as thoroughgoing modernists. The old will persist and the new will come if they are worthy to do so. And the old will pass and the new be excluded if they are not. The question: *What* ought we to do? cannot be the question of our anxiety, but only the retention or discovery of what is intrinsically valuable. And what is intrinsically valuable truth is the command of God which always surpasses what we consider worthy either to be retained or to come, which always transcends our hypotheses and convictions of yesterday, today, and tomorrow." (*CD* II/2: 648)

Before we decide what we must do, we must prayerfully seek to be *open* to God's prior command, which opens ourselves to work of the Holy Spirit in the church and our individual lives. With "complete openness" to the situation, we must invite or invoke God's gracious command within the present time. "The truth itself demands complete openness" (*CD* II/2: 648). What does this mean for ethics? First, it implies the process of "bracketing" our conceptions of what we consider good or right action, whether found in past decisions, moral rules or principles, or qualities of moral character. We need to put aside "what" we presume to be right or good and remain open to the possibility that such moral knowledge may be misguided. Moral answers of yesterday may not apply to today's situation, nor may today's answers apply to future issues. With each particular situation comes a unique set of characteristics that require a "fitting" response. That is to say we must be willing to question any humanly conceived or socially derived moral framework, whether new or old, liberal or conservative, or radical or traditionalist. If we refuse to do this we invite the possibility of allowing ideology to govern Christian moral judgment. Besides "bracketing," the second task of openness implies seeking or invoking God's command in the space between our reflecting and responsible action so that we may discover what is "intrinsically valuable." The space that exists between our reflecting and our action does not remain neutral or passive, but actively invokes God's command through our prayer and active listening. We must recall that God's command is not a principle or norm that imposes its will upon us; it is not a deontological but relational command. In plain language, it is not a voice in our head (or heart) that tells us what to do—this, as we've seen, is the wrong conception of the command. Rather, it is being "actively open" to the discovery of what is "intrinsically valuable" (*CD* II/2: 648). Since the command is gracious it can never be anything other than "intrinsically valuable." Since God does not command evil, we discover the content or "what" of the good when we discover what is "intrinsically valuable."

So where does this "discovery" of the good come from? Barth is clear this discovery of what it is intrinsically valuable does not come to us through secretly revealed principles, intuition, or spiritual experiences. Rather, it comes from "previous ethical reflection and testing." He writes: "[T]he more truly it derives from previous ethical reflection and testing, the less will this process be injurious to it, the more surely will it again prove its value" (*CD* II/2: 648). In our accumulated wisdom from past decisions, actions, and testing through our openness to God's gracious judgment, we begin to discern what is "intrinsically valuable." The "what" of ethical action, thus, relies on God's command, but this is less an immediate action-reaction response, then a careful reliance on our conscience, our understanding how the Christian community has reflected on ethical matters over time, and how past "testing" has led to reflective judgments about God's will. Again, we must recall the importance of the correspondence between human and divine agency. God acts and we respond in our "testing," but in our responsive action we also actively wait and listen for God's corresponding response to our action. This is how we remain open to God's gracious judgment. This correspondence happens individually and within the church community. We learn from our mistakes and past actions. Although we learn a great deal from the tradition of Christian ethics, this "preparation" can never tell us with absolute certainty what we must do in a *particular* situation. Knowing the "what" means actively engaging in reflection and deliberation, but doing so, remaining *open* to God's active agency, through the Spirit, in our lives for the benefit of us, others, and the world.

Casuistry and Moral Judgment

Nevertheless, the question still remains: what is "ethical reflection" and how does it affect responsible moral action? How do we determine what is intrinsically valuable and good? We've seen how it involves learning, reflection, and testing. These ideas are repeated in the 1953 lecture entitled "The Gift of Freedom." Here Barth says the following. "Ethics is reflection upon what man is required to do in and with the gift of freedom" (*HG*: 87). The Christian ethicist should not attempt too much or too little, but rather "realize his calling and talents" in responding to the gracious command of the trinitarian God. Moreover, when the Christian ethicist engages in "ethical reflection," she must dialectically recognize the "two spheres of freedom," namely "the free God is the free man's Lord, Creator, Reconciler, and Redeemer, and that free man is God's creature, partner, and child" (*HG*: 87). This covenant-partnership serves as the basis for further "ethical reflection," based on our active reflection on Scripture, church tradition, and contemporary church discernment. "It must do this in order to be admonished, nourished, enriched, perhaps also stirred and warned, by the use which the fathers and brethren made and are still are making of Christian freedom" (*HG*: 87). Christian ethics remains open to a conversational engagement with God and Christian community. Ethical reflection begins with these dialectical encounters. So, for us to go further into the process of ethical reflection, we must discuss further how *dialectic* works in Barth's ethics. This, we might say, is the practical side of the command. In chapter two, we saw how Barth's dialectical theological logic shapes the interplay between the church and society (and culture) and the use of theological and nontheological sources in theological ethics. At this point, we must discuss further how dialectic is used in practical moral judgment.

Today is widely accepted that the dialectical motif remains operative in all of Barth's writings, not just the period of the *Römerbrief* and its aftermath. In contrast to the earlier scholarship of Hans Urs von Balthasar, which insisted on a radical shift in Barth's thinking from his "dialectical" stage of the 1920s to "analogical" stage of the 1930s and beyond, today there is much consensus that both dialectical and analogical themes existed throughout his work.[1] There is both a Yes and No, a back and forth movement, not only in the *Ethics* and the *Church Dogmatics* but also his earlier works, including his lectures on the *Reformed Confessions, John Calvin*, and *Göttingen Dogmatics*, all given while in Germany prior to 1931, and now

---

1. The important earlier work here is the 1951 book on Barth, written by Hans Urs von Balthasar. See von Balthasar, *The Theology of Karl Barth*. The latter view is developed in McCormack's, *Karl Barth's Critically Realistic Dialectical Theology*.

published in English.[2] These works show a continuity of thought between the *Romans II* period and the *Church Dogmatics*, a decade later. This link between the early and later periods of Barth's thought is grounded in Barth's newly developed Christology in the mid-1920s, which enabled him to speak about the eternal Word is both veiled and unveiled, both hidden and revealed, in the humanity of Jesus Christ.[3] There is no doubt Barth's theology changed over time, but it does not consist of radical disruptions in method or thought as was previously supposed. Rather, it remains theologically open-ended, while at the same time, centered on the Word of God, which remains the core of his dialectical movement. Indeed, just as the "postmodern" elements of Barth's thought cannot be limited to his early writings, so too, the dialectical nature of his thought remain important until his last unfinished section of the *The Christian Life*. This will become clearer in later chapters.

With this being said, we have seen how Barth gives us hints about how ethical decisions are made, even without a formal moral theory of casuistry. There is no doubt that Barth vehemently rejects casuistry from his early writings onward, and gives his most sustained critical analysis in the beginning of *CD* III/4. Here he gives three related arguments against "casuistical ethics," which he identifies with various forms of rationalistic reductionism. This casuistic reductionistic method is used to interpret divine commands, biblical texts, ethical norms or laws, or ethical methods that attempt to apply general principles to specific human actions. Barth gives three basic reasons for why casuistry cannot be accepted in Christian ethics. First, it begins with the human subject, as "lord, king, and judge" of good and evil, and in so doing, denies God's sovereignty and freedom. Second, casuistry "makes the objectively untenable assumption that the command of God is a universal rule, an empty form, or rather a tissue of such rules and forms"

---

2. In addition to his lectures on *Ethics*, as previously noted, other early works include: his 1922 lectures on Calvin, Barth, *Theology of John Calvin*; his 1923 lectures on the Reformed confessions, Barth, *Theology of the Reformed Confessions*; and his 1924 lectures on dogmatics, Barth, *Göttingen Dogmatics*.

3. After 1924, as Bruce McCormack strongly argues, Barth's theology became more Christologically-grounded, when he discovered the Reformed doctrines of *anhypostasis* and *enhypostasis*. "The anhypostatic-enhypostatic model was well suited for clarifying what was at stake in speaking of revelation as revelation in concealment, as indirect communication. For the Subject of this revelation is the Person of the Logos who is veiled Himself in human flesh." McCormack, *Karl Barth's Critically Realistic*, 362.

(*CD* III/4: 11). God's command, in the form of general principles or rules, cannot stand on its own but needs to be creatively applied to particular cases by the ethicist. Third, casuistry replaces the free covenant-partnership with God, with abstract methodology or ethical set of norms that the Christian must obey or practice. "It openly interposes something other and alien between the command of God and the man who is called to obey Him" (*CD* III/4: 13). Once casuistry takes over, Christian ethics is no longer a responsible ethics of witness but legalistic set of commands established by the church or deduced from the Scriptural narrative. Christian ethics, he says later, "cannot be a legalistic and casuistic ethic, nor can it be an obscure ethics of the *kairos* in general. Its task is to expound *this kairos*—that of the event between God and man" (*CL*: 5). Nevertheless, in his rejection of casuistry, as we've seen, Barth does not reject the actual *process* of moral deliberation as it relates to moral action. Even in *CD* III/4 he admits that he supports a "casuistry of the prophetic ethos" in which God addresses us and we respond in active responsible actions (*CD* III/4: 9). Indeed, we've seen how this dialectical "back and forth" movement works within the corresponding movements within the human-divine covenant-partnership.

Inasmuch as Barth rejects casuistry the question still remains: does he not engage in some casuistic-like form of practical moral reasoning? Addressing this problem, Nigel Biggar claims that Barth "concedes much more in practice to casuistry than his theory allows."[4] That is, in theory Barth rejects casuistry as the "epitome of the closed, rationalistic ethical system," but in practice he develops a sort of open-ended way of casuistic method of reasoning.[5] "What Barth has in mind here is that the application of a rule to a particular case might not determine that only one course of action is permissible, but that two or more are equally so."[6] So, says Biggar, Barth uses an open-ended form of casuistry, even though he denies, in theory, that he is using such a method. As a result, Biggar concludes that Barth's ethical method is incomplete and contradictory as its stands, and would be greatly improved and more coherent if he could have recognized and used this unique form of open-ended casuistry in both theory and practice. Is Barth's ethics rooted in some form of contradiction regarding casuistry? Biggar is right to point out a tension between Barth's theory and practice. Still this dialectical tension only becomes a "contradiction" when one posits

4. Biggar, "Barth's Trinitarian Ethic," 222.
5. Biggar, *Hastening that Waits*, 163.
6. Biggar, "Barth's Trinitarian Ethic," 222.

a prior commitment to the determinative structure of ethical methodology. This not only places ethical methodology before dogmatics and Christian ethics before theological ethics, but most importantly, the ethical agent's freedom before God's freedom. The problem with Biggar's analysis is that he separates the task of the Christian ethicist from the Christian's witness to God's determination to be our covenant-partner. Biggar privileges an ethics of casuistry over an ethics of witness, which limits or even negates God's freedom to act.[7] Indeed, he presupposes a separation of human from divine agency, or put differently, the prioritizing of human agency *over* divine agency. This stands in direct contradiction to the entire tenor of Barth's understanding of theology and ethics as witness. As Trevor Hart puts it, Barth "does not insist, does not deride, exclude or belittle moral reflection as such (any more than reason in general), but only independent moral reflection—that is, moral reflection which there is at the time only the activity of the human subject to be taken into account."[8]

The tension that does exist between Barth's theory and practice is rooted in the dialectical tension emerging from the vertical relationship between God and humanity in covenantal-partnership. This is a tension between context and content. Although the particular circumstances of one's ethical decisions and actions remain the context of ethics as a form of responsible witness, the content of ethical judgment and action remains the prerogative of God alone. The context is analogous to the law and the content is analogous to grace; the context is the form of the content which is rooted in God's grace. Hence, the content is always God's gracious judgment and not our methodological reasoning about our situational context. Rather than practicing a rationalist open-ended form of casuistry, as Biggar claims, Barth's dialectical ethics remains in constant movement "back and forth" between God's free command and our responsible human action, as guided by ethical reflection. For the individual, moral discernment takes

---

7. In summarizing Barth's "ethical method," Biggar writes: "Barth's ethical method, then, is to proceed from the Bible through its notion of salvation history to incarnational Christology, out into a systematic trinitarian theology and then on to ethics; and only at this last point does the Bible specifically ethical material come into play." Ibid., 224. Biggar's definition is saturated with his own commitment to the priority of method itself. Barth's ethics does not proceed from a method of moving from the principles of the Bible to dogmatics to ethics to practice, but from God's gracious act of freedom to empower us to be responsible witnesses in covenant-partnership.

8. Hart, *Regarding Karl Barth,* 87. Along the lines developed here, Hart also provides a good description and critique of Biggar's position in ibid., 82–88.

place when one encounters God's command, but this discernment, at its core, is relational and responsive—not rationalistic or deductive. In our ethical deliberations, we will inevitably reflect upon our prior experiences and actions, while also inviting and listening to God's judgment on our past actions. We bring to our decisions all that we know and aspire to be in our calling to follow Christ. This is why, in Barth's "ethics of creation" (*CD* III/4), he argues that "special ethics" or practical ethics, serves primarily a pedagogical, or instructional, purpose, rather than a casuistic method for determining right courses of action. Barth writes:

> Special ethics may thus serve as an instructional preparation for the ethical event. And as such instruction it will be plainly distinguished not only from all casuistry but also from an ethics which is satisfied with a formless reference to the God who claims, decides and judges in the ethical event, to the Holy Spirit, or the "command of the hour" and such like. But everything depends on whether anything can be known about the horizontal, the permanence, continuity and constancy of the divine command and human action. On this basis special ethics can become a formed reference to the ethical event and therefore perform its service as instructional preparation. (*CD* III/4: 18)

The instructional or pedagogical task of "special ethics" (Christian ethics) provides the background for the task of Christian moral judgment. Yet once the process of moral deliberation and judgment begins, the process remains neither rigidly closed nor completely open-ended. It is not inherently rationalistic but relational and responsive to God's gracious command. Yet, as mentioned earlier, this command is not an occasionalistic or situational moral imperative (or moral law) that we hear in our head or in our heart. Rather it is a gracious *permission* to act in responsible freedom, in any particular circumstance, according to our understanding of Christian ethics. Put differently, God's command, which always remains a command of grace, does not so much give us knowledge or content about one specific course of action, but the freedom to act, test, and judge one's actions in response to God's judgment of grace.[9] Being open to God's command

9. See McKenny, "Heterogeneity and Ethical Deliberation," 205–24. In his critique of Biggar, McKenny interestingly argues that Barth's ethical deliberation "involves an irreducible heterogeneity between the weighing of reasons or values that count for or against a possible course of action, on the one hand, and the act of testing these possible courses of action in encounter with the decision of God concerning them, on the other hand." Ibid., 205.

implies hearing God's judgment of our actions, as right or wrong, after we have already acted, which prepares us for future actions that we may encounter. There is a place for ethical reflection based on one's encounter with Scripture, church tradition, and the contemporary Christian community as well as a place for one's own personal reflection on one's past actions. Yet, none of these sources point us toward a method of casuistry, even the type of "open-ended" form of casuistry that Bigger recommends. There is, in other words, a "constancy" and "concreteness" of the command, which implies that it is the sustaining freedom (constancy) in our relationship with God that gives the freedom to address each situation afresh (concreteness).[10] The parameters of this relationship make the task of ethical reasoning neither completely definite nor completely indefinite; it is neither rigidly closed nor completely open-ended. The pedagogical task of Christian ethics provides the narrative framework, which forms the limits of moral judgment and possible courses of moral action. Christian ethics cannot logically tell us prior to our moral situations how to act, but neither is it irrelevant for the tasks of moral deliberation and action. Regardless of how much we know about Christian ethics, we must still decide, choose, and act. Yet, the more we know, the more we are conversant with a tradition that has addressed moral issues of the past, which inevitably helps us with our present circumstances.

In all of our deliberations and actions, we remain *free* to respond in ways fitting with God's gracious command. Yet, in our choosing and acting, we can never be absolutely certain that we fully understand God's command within our present situations. As Gerald McKenny argues, there is always, in Barth's mind, a diastasis or "heterogeneity" between our ethical deliberations and actions *and* God's command; an "ineliminable heterogeneity in deliberation between analysis and testing."[11] Yet, such a claim "does not deny that in any situation of choice," adds McKenny, there is "a positive relation between at least one of our possibilities of action and the command of God."[12] In our obedience to God's command, we are invited to participate, learn, reflect and act, while placing before God our ethical prescriptions and actions, seeking God's gracious response. The heteroge-

---

10. For the most concise argument on this theme, see *CL*: 4–7. For longer discussions of this theme, see *CD* II/2: 661ff. and *CD* III/4: 6–31. In each of these sections, Barth consistently is at pains to distinguish his position from a deliberative method of casuistry.

11. McKenny, "Heterogeneity and Ethical Deliberation," 221.

12. Ibid., 219.

neity between God's Word and human word, between God's command of grace and the human law, therefore, is underwritten by a more fundamental covenant of *grace*, which provides the objective reality for freedom within responsibility. In McKenny's recent book *The Analogy of Grace*, he develops further the structure of Barth's "moral theology" by distinguishing between "ethical instruction" and "ethical reflection."[13] The former prepares one for the encounter with God's gracious command by gaining as much moral knowledge as possible, whereas the latter rationally *tests* specific courses of action in one's particular situation. So, in ethical instruction we learn about possible courses of action, whereas in ethical reflection we step forward testing these courses of action knowing that it is always God who freely decides which course of action corresponds to God's command. This command, which always occurs within our covenant relationship with others, further instructs us about the rightness or wrongness of our choices and acts, while inviting us toward future moral actions. When one is "subjected to the divine will, Word, and command," says Barth, one is "called to realize the true purpose of his existence as a covenant-partner with God. As a man, he is objectively tested by this determination and objectively questioned as to its fulfillment. This is the essence of his responsibility" (*CD* II/2: 641).

Ethics as Christian witness, therefore, begins with the freedom to learn and test our actions, and the same time, to listen and act again, knowing that God's grace will sustain one's actions and efforts in being a responsible witness to God's gracious command. Put differently, Christian ethics, we might say, is a kind of adventure or journey discovering the implications of God's gracious command in the concreteness our lives and decisions. Yet, as we undertake this adventurous journey we are not solitary, map-less vagabonds moving from place to place, but pilgrims, within a community, seeking to be guided by our map and destination, even though our map remains blurred and partially veiled. Even though we see in a glass darkly, we are given permission and remain free to continue forward seeking God's gracious judgment upon our deliberations and actions. We are not alone. In our covenant-partnership with God we have been given the gift of freedom through the gospel, which further invites and encourages us to moral decisions and actions. "Receiving this good news from those who witness to it," says Barth, "the Christian *community* in the world is called to acknowledge it in faith, to respond to it in love, to set on it its hope and trust, and to proclaim it to the world which belongs to this free God" (*HG*: 73).

13. See McKenny, *Analogy of Grace*, 225–87.

Witness and Christian Moral Judgment 253

Dialectical Moral Judgment

We must now return to the question of Christian moral judgment. The question still remains: even though Barth formally rejects casuistry, does his theological elaboration of special ethics take on any particular logical form that might be helpful in the task of Christian ethics? To be sure, Barth does use a dialectical form of reasoning that moves back and forth between extreme options, that is, between the absolute Yes and No. This dialectical movement is consistent with seeing Christian ethics as a "gift" of freedom. Christian ethics is an adventure and a journey. As stated above, the "adventure" of Christian ethics involves the task of "instructional preparation," including an open-ended discussion and evaluation of specific issues that confront our lives. This form of reasoning is worked out, more practically, in Barth's numerous social and political writings, as well as his discussion of practical ethics in the *CD* and *The Christian Life*, where he uses a dialectical logic of reasoning. Central to the strategy of interpreting the circumstances of the ethical event is the pedagogy of developing broad ethical guidelines, while ruling out possible extremes of absolute Yes or No. This dialectical "back and forth" reasoning, in theory, is perhaps more apparent in his "ethics of reconciliation" (*CD* IV/4) than in his "ethics of creation" (*CD* III/4). In *The Christian Life*, he writes:

> Certainly in relation to man—perhaps temporarily or more permanently, perhaps joyfully or anxiously—they will have to say Yes or No, and say it resolutely, to current ideas and life-forms. Certainly in relation to him they will not be afraid of taking sides for and against. But in so doing they will think and speak in terms of theses and not principles. In this field there can be no absolute Yes or No carrying an absolute commitment. One reason for this is that an absolute guarantee of human right and work cannot be expected from the rule of any idea or the power of any life-form. From one standpoint or another, every idea or life–form will sooner or later prove a threat to man. Hence Christians looking always to the only problem that seriously and finally interests them, must allow themselves the liberty in certain circumstances of saying only a partial Yes or No where a total one is expected, or of saying Yes today where they said No yesterday, and visa versa. Their totally definitive decision is for man and not for any cause. They will never let themselves be addressed as prisoners of their own decisions or slaves of any sacrosanct consistency. (*CL*: 268)

Christian ethics, as a pedagogical strategy, remains free to analyze and evaluate any contemporary circumstance or situation, or any "idea" or "life-form," but it must be reluctant to make *absolute* Yes or No judgments. Making absolute Yes or No judgments presumes that our deliberations and actions are absolute embodiments of God's command, and no longer need any further guidance from God's gracious evaluative response. Simply put, these absolutist judgments remain too overconfident of our moral knowledge and practice. Rather, the Christian ethicist is better persuaded to make "partial" or "relative" judgments of Yes or No. In other words, in our moral judgments we may drift toward one side or the other of the polarity, while at the same time, knowing that we may, in other circumstances, drift back the other way. This dialectical strategy of "back and forth," once applied to contemporary issues in ethics, becomes an important way to think about complex issues without oversimplifying these events or claiming overconfidence in one's moral judgments. So, in making partial or relative judgments, Christians should remain both confident and cautious of their social witness. Christians are confident that God's command remains a gracious permission to proceed toward responsible judgment and action, but Christians must also remain cautious about seeking to make *absolute* or timeless judgments or actions of Yes or No. Such absolute judgments and actions ignore the difference between our moral knowledge, evaluations, and actions, and the objective moral reality, in God's command, fully revealed in God's Word—Jesus Christ.

Hence, Barth is not against the process of ethical deliberation *per se*, but attacks any form of reasoning that conceives of God's command of the good *in abstraco* from the human-divine event in Jesus Christ. There is a consistent theme in Barth's theology that the vertical relationship of the covenant defines the horizontal implications and actions of the covenant. Unlike many versions of Christian ethics which place humanity at the center of the axis of these two covenants, Barth places the Word of God, which is unveiled and veiled in Jesus Christ. Thus, the vertical heterogeneity or diastasis that exists between divine and human agency cannot be bridged by good human actions, but only in the divine-human unity of action in Jesus Christ. Since Christians are not Jesus Christ, they are incapable of fully and completely embodying God's command in any particular *practice* of human action. It would appear, therefore, that the strategy of Christian ethics is littered with ambiguity and uncertainty. Yet, as we've said, the No is answered by the Yes. "The grace of God protests against all man-made ethics as such. But it protests positively. It does not only say No to man. It also says Yes" (*CD* II/2: 517). In Jesus Christ, persons are given *freedom* and *responsibility* to act upon God's divine claim and command of grace. Barth rejects all forms of casuistry-laden "man-made" ethics because this denies true moral responsibility in relation to God who demands something from us. "God cannot draw him [a person] to Himself without involving him in responsibility" (*CD* II/2: 511). Christian ethics, at its root, is not about autonomous moral deliberation and action, but about being able to hear and respond, in the midst of deliberations and actions, to the Word of God.

Lastly, the task of Christian ethics is not about the individual Christian acting alone as a moral agent, nor even as part of a community of moral agents, but rather of acting in such a way that he or she is included in God's purposes. As George Hunsinger reminds us, although human and divine agency can be distinguished they cannot be fully separated because of the "double agency" of Jesus Christ. Once this Christological ground in ethics is removed and replaced with human moral agency, then God's agency is removed from the task of ethics. This separation, moreover, reduces God's free and gracious command to abstract principles or rules, whether derived from Scripture, natural law, or human experience. God's free command of grace becomes reduced to a static moral law, and human freedom becomes reduced to slavish obedience. That is to say, independent human moral reflection becomes sacralized apart from God's reconciling action in Jesus Christ, thus misrepresenting humanity's need for grace, while at the same time, denying God's freedom. We must recall that not only God's command but also human and divine freedom are only found *in concreto* in the event of the Word of God. All other frameworks of Christian ethics, whether teleological or deontological, whether grounded in moral laws or virtues, remain deficient because they lose this careful balance of human and divine freedom. The Christian moral life is not about obeying moral rules or laws or embodying virtues, but listening, testing, and acting, thus opening up space for more listening, testing, and acting. This is why, Barth says, the question "what ought we to do?" presupposes "the testing of our conduct our responsibility" (*CD* II/2: 659). Reflection and testing of one's moral actions invites corresponding human and divine moral judgment, which opens up the space or distance between God and us. This space is filled by God's gracious command of freedom and responsibility. Indeed, this also applies to any ethical method of casuistry that deliberate from general principles toward individual moral acts. This process cannot determine, by itself, right moral action because it closes off the space between God and humanity, thus closes off God's judgment from our actions. The practice of ethics, then, emerges within the context of one's witness and responsibility to God's command of grace, which is grounded in God's election of humanity in Jesus Christ. Again, ethics is not about acting alone, but acting in such a way that we are included in God's purposes. God, says Barth, "wills to take him into His service, to commission him for a share of His own work. He wills to make him a witness of Jesus Christ and therefore a witness to His own glory" (*CD* II/2: 510).

HAUERWAS AND BARTH ON AGENCY AND WITNESS

It is useful, at this point, to compare Barth to developments in contemporary Christian ethics as it pertains to our discussion of witness and moral judgment. One of the most important contemporary writers to have addressed these topics of witness, judgment, and agency is the theologian and ethicist Stanley Hauerwas. In this generation, perhaps more than any other figure, Hauerwas has reminded Christian ethicists that their work ought to remain, at its core, theological, and that Christian ethics *is* Christian witness. Hauerwas remains an interesting conversation partner with Barth because they offer similar, yet distinct, approaches to Christian ethics. So, our purpose in comparing Hauerwas and Barth is to dig deeper into our discussion of Christian witness as pertains to related issues like methodology and moral agency. These topics of witness, methodology, and agency are of central importance for any type of Christian ethics that also claims to be theological ethics. In so doing, we must further clarify vital issues at stake in developing a contemporary ethics of Christian witness.

Hauerwas' Barthian Turn

In one of his earliest books, Hauerwas criticizes Barth's command ethics as unable to address how Christ and the church influence the development of moral character.[14] Along with Alasdair MacIntyre, Hauerwas, in his early writings, rejects modern decisionist methods (i.e., "quandary ethics"), whether deontological or utilitarian, and instead develops a community-based character ethics that incorporates both the ethics of virtue and narrative. In his 1983 book, *The Peaceable Kingdom*, which provides a good summation

---

14. See Hauerwas, *Character and the Christian Life.*

of his early thought, Hauerwas took this emphasis on ethical methodology and demonstrated how the Christian narrative ("story of Jesus") invariably shapes the character of those who seek to follow Jesus, further embodying virtues needed to sustain the church over time.[15] Drawing from John Howard Yoder, Hauerwas claims that it is the pacifist witness of the church, along with other virtues and practices, which enables the church to remain faithful to its mission and proclaim to the world the *truth* of Christian witness. So, if the church becomes the moral community that sustains the Christian moral life, then without the church there can be essentially *no* Christian ethics. Since the 1980s, Hauerwas has repeatedly returned to this theme throughout his various excursions into different areas of ethics and theology.[16] In all of these diverse writings, Hauerwas draws the reader back into the living reality of the worshipping, sacramental, and character-forming community of church, as the center from which Christian ethics emerges as a form of witness to the living God and the world.

In recent years, Hauerwas admittedly shows more satisfaction and appreciation of Barth's theology and ethics, even to the point of occasionally calling himself a "Barthian."[17] Hauerwas strongly defends Barth on numerous occasions, especially his Gifford Lectures, *With the Grain of the Universe*, where he devotes several chapters to Barth's theology and ethics. In these lectures, Hauerwas praises Barth for delivering a "frontal attack on some of the most cherished conceits of modernity, not the least being the conceit that humans are the measure of all that is." Indeed, says Hauerwas, "Barth shows us the way that theology must be done if the subject of theology, that is, the God of Jesus Christ, is to be more than just another piece of the metaphysical furniture in the universe."[18] Like Barth, Hauerwas remains committed to a few central theses, while exploring a wide horizon of interrelated ideas and subjects that comprise his main concern, namely discipleship and the Christian life. Nevertheless, for all of their similarity,

---

15. Hauerwas, *Peaceable Kingdom*.

16. The sheer volume of Hauerwas' writings is too numerous to list here. Thankfully, his more important writings are available in the general reader, Berkman and Cartwright, *Hauerwas Reader*.

17. In a recent book he writes: "Good Barthian (and Yoderian) that I am, I had to resist those who thought that justice qua justice was more important than the justice God has shown us in the cross and resurrection of Jesus." Hauerwas, *Performing the Faith*, 230. Of course, Hauerwas' greatest debt to Barth is demonstrated in his 2000–2001 Gifford Lectures, *With the Grain*.

18. Ibid., 145–46.

258   PART THREE: WITNESS AND BARTH'S ETHICS

there are two crucial issues of difference regarding how moral agency works in the moral theories of Hauerwas and Barth, which once articulated, will further clarify our understanding of ethics as witness. That is, in our discussion of the two issues of ethical methodology and witness, we open up the related issue of whether divine *or* human action should be prioritized in one's theory of moral agency. So, what is the difference between Hauerwas and Barth? Simply put, I argue that Barth begins with *divine* action and finds space for human action, whereas Hauerwas begins with *human* action and finds space for divine action. This may overstate the difference between them, but their respective theories of moral agency bears this distinction out in concrete ways, particularly in their discussions of ethical methodology and Christian witness.

Ethical Methodology and Agency

The first issue looks at the question of the priority of divine and human agency to the interplay between theological and ethical methodology. No doubt Hauerwas is a very creative, nuanced, and eclectic writer, who has inspired a generation of Christian thinkers to begin their ethical reasoning with theology and the church, yet he is also significant for his development of an ethical methodology that includes the language of narrative, character, and virtue. In a 1996 article tracing his thought on moral agency—or in his more colorful language, why "I quit worrying about agency and learned to love stories"—Hauerwas claims that the moral self is "more properly constituted by retrospective rather than prospective judgments."[19] He goes on to say that the "telling of the story entailed no agency more determinative than the skills the story itself makes possible."[20] What does this mean? What exactly is the constitutive interplay between the skills and the story, and is there an ethical methodology that holds the two together? Although

19. Hauerwas, "Agency," 185.

20. Ibid., 187. Prior to this sentence, he adds: "What MacIntyre helped me see is that we don't need an account of agency in itself to understand our ability to acquire character. Rather character is the source of our agency, that is, our ability to act with integrity. Interestingly enough, this puts me closer to my other conversation partners in *Character and the Christian Life*, that is, Aristotle and Aquinas. We often forget that they had no account of agency or the self as such. Rather they discussed the kind of issues we associate with the language of agency in terms of the voluntary and the involuntary. They needed no account of agency or the self to insure our ability to act in a manner in which the virtues can be acquired. I began to understand that if the significance of habituations appreciated, then questions of agency become secondary." Ibid.

Hauerwas consistently argues for the theological or "narrative" grounding of Christian ethics, he has often returned to the language of ethical methodology, of character and virtue—of MacIntyre and Aristotle—to explain his understanding of moral agency. This is not to say that Hauerwas' method is philosophical or nontheological, as he also draws from Christian accounts of virtue such as Thomas Aquinas. Yet, compared to Barth's insistence on beginning ethics with God's action, as demonstrated in his trinitarian command ethic, Hauerwas' entry into the discussion of moral agency begins with a discussion of the self, in the context of community, narrative, and tradition. Although Hauerwas writes about the importance of doctrine, including the Trinity, in ethics, he devotes little attention how these doctrines make any difference to moral agency. So, although Hauerwas is guided by theology, his theological ethics remains, in Michael's Banner's words, "insufficiently dogmatic."[21] The point here is not that Hauerwas needs to write another *Church Dogmatics*, but that it is unclear, apart from his ecclesiology, how Christian theology infuses his version of Christian ethics. This becomes an important issue in explaining how ethical methodology ought to be related to theological ethics.

Inasmuch as Hauerwas grounds his ethical theory within the scriptural/doctrinal narrative (theology), he repeatedly returns to the language of ethical methodology to explain his theological ethics. Indeed, one may go so far as to say that Hauerwas never completely separates himself from the legacy of liberal (apologetic) theology, which relies extensively upon nontheological frameworks in explaining theological ethics. In contrast, as we have seen, Barth refuses to place moral agency, and theological ethics more generally, within a framework of ethical theory or methodology. By placing ethics within dogmatics, Barth simply refuses to articulate his ethics through the language of ethical methodology, including divine command theory. The issue here is the following: Should theological ethics begin with God's agency or human agency, God's command of grace or our ethical methods, or perhaps most simply, the ethics of grace or law? By privileging the language of virtue and character, Hauerwas shifts the focus toward the community's character, practices, and skills, rather than God's trinitarian agency, which defines the correspondence between divine and human action, and the particular role of Jesus Christ in this interaction. One important consequence of this methodological turn is that it

---

21. On this point, see Banner, *Christian Ethics*, 20.

further *limits* how theological language may be used by Christians to speak about ethics by channeling Christian performance through a virtue moral theory. The danger of Hauerwas' position is that it potentially allows a singular virtue-based theory to provide the hermeneutical framework for the scriptural narrative and its witness to the Word of God. On this point, Hauerwas stands in contrast to his interlocutor John Howard Yoder, who admittedly relies more on Barth on this particular point of contention.[22] Like Hauerwas and Barth, Yoder also looks to the church as the place in which Christian ethics emerges as a way of life in the world. Yet, more like Barth than Hauerwas, Yoder adds one important caveat, when he says: "the life of the community is prior to all possible methodological distinctions."[23] Elaborating on this point, Yoder further states:

> Instead of making the case for the priority of one style, what I have argued is thus that all of them are needed, precisely because none of them may be dominant. . . . Instead of seeking to settle on the right idiom, the greater value will inhere in the skills of mixing and matching according to the shape of a particular debate. The exercise of that skill, within the complementarily of the various components of adequate moral discourse, might be called a virtue; but it will also be a duty, and it will also be useful. . . . Precisely because of my commitment to a community which in turn is committed to canonical accountability, I saw no way to squeeze accountability into such a strait jacket.[24]

Both Hauerwas and Yoder look to the church's witness as the context for Christian ethics, yet they take different positions on how this witness relates to ethical methodology. Yoder's more critical attitude toward methodology, like Barth, raises important questions about the potential hegemony of methodological frameworks in Christian ethics. More particularly, Yoder blatantly rejects the priority of what he calls "methodologism" in Christian ethics, and it's privileging of particular ethical concepts like virtue, duty, rights, or utility and imposing them on the freedom of Christian moral judgment. Rather, the church has the freedom to engage in various forms

---

22. Of course, perhaps no theologian has had more influence on Hauerwas than Yoder. Yet on this crucial point of ethical methodology, Hauerwas' ethics is more deeply shaped, not unlike MacIntyre, by the Aristotlian-Thomist tradition. For the most thorough account of his virtue ethics, see Hauerwas and Pinches, *Christians Among the Virtues*.

23. Yoder, "Walk and Word," 82.

24. Ibid., 86–87.

of communal "practical moral reasoning" that foster a variety of such methods. Thus, Yoder contends, there is nothing in *theory* that forbids the isolation of moral concepts, whether they are virtues, practices, rules, or principles from a narrative construal of communal convictions, and their application to particular moral issues. Indeed, this *ad hoc* pattern of matching resources with issues is consistent with how New Testament communities used ethical resources available to them in confronting particular issues; the biblical narrative itself allows for such a flexible use of moral theory.[25] In a similar trajectory, in Barth's view, a Word-centered ethics can *commandeer* any "method" for ethical analysis as long as it doesn't become the primary language of interpreting God's ethical and gracious command. The privileging of one particular methodology, however, endangers the freedom of the Word to address the Christian community's witness. As pointed out earlier, Barth uses the language of command, conscience, and moral judgment, but at the same time, refuses to articulate these terms within the framework of ethical methodology. Like Yoder, Barth is no "methodologist," which is to say that he refuses to develop his theological ethics from the standpoint of any particular ethical theory. Instead, his ethical discourse, as articulated in the various moral languages of command, principles, and virtues, become pedagogical tools for better understanding how the action of the trinitarian God is "related" to the vocational action of Christian witness. Indeed, there is no reason in *theory* to reject any particular language or idiom of ethical discourse as long as it does not seek to unseat the Word of God from its privileged position. Once a particular ethical methodology becomes the primary way of interpreting the Christian moral life, it risks replacing the Word of God with the word of ethical methodology.

Christian Witness and Agency

The second difference between Hauerwas and Barth pertains to how divine and human agency relates to Christian witness. In the *Blackwell Companion to Christian Ethics*, edited by Hauerwas and Samuel Wells, they write the following:

> God gives many gifts to the Church to form, shape, and maintain its life. Some of these gifts are practices, regular patterns of action that embody the goods that God conveys. Others are powers or charisms, faculties that enable the Church to carry out the sometimes demand-

25. For example, see Meeks, *Moral World of the First Christians*.

ing practices God has given it. . . . Much of the rest of the regular practice of the Church may be taken together under the single designation of "witness." For witness names the Christian hope that every action—whether for peace, for justice, for stability, for alleviating distress, for empowering the young our weak, for comforting the lonely, for showing mercy to the outcast, for offering hospitality, for making friends, or for earning a living—points to God, and invites an inquiry into the joy that inspires such actions.[26]

The understanding of witness here moves unilaterally from worship practices to ethical actions, so that witness is primarily understood as something Christians *perform* or *do*. Christian worship empowers Christians to give witness, say Hauerwas and Wells, as they learn how to "discern and embody Christ's life in the world."[27] Accordingly, for Hauerwas and Wells, the beliefs and practices (including sacraments) that constitute the church declare, in specific practical actions, the presence of the Spirit in the world. The truth of Christianity is linked with faithful Christian witness, which becomes embodied in specific practices and actions that bear witness to the truth of the gospel. So, with this in mind, we can now begin to see why Hauerwas criticizes Barth's view of witness. Although Hauerwas praises Barth's emphasis on the "truth" of Christian witness, Barth inevitably fails to move from this truth to the "practice" of that witness. In Hauerwas' words, it "remains an open question whether or not Barth's ecclesiology is sufficient to sustain the witness that he thought was intrinsic to Christianity."[28] In no way, continues Hauerwas, does Barth "deny that the church is constituted by the proclamation of gospel. What he cannot acknowledge is that the community called the church is constitutive of the gospel proclamation."[29] Furthermore, although Barth has a strong doctrine of sanctification, Hauerwas maintains that Barth "never quite brings himself to explain how our human agency is involved in the Spirit's work. As a result, Barth's understanding of our faith in Jesus Christ made possible by the Spirit falls short."[30]

Let us further unpack these comments. In Hauerwas' judgment, the problem is not with Barth's Christology and the "truth" of witness, but with his ecclesiology, which keeps him from talking about the "practice" of

26. Hauerwas and Wells, *Blackwell Companion to Christian Ethics*, 19.
27. Ibid., 51.
28. Hauerwas, *With the Grain*, 39.
29. Ibid., 145.
30. Ibid.

Christian witness. Hauerwas' problem with Barth's ecclesiology is rooted in *how* the divine action of the Spirit interacts with the human action of Christian witness. In Hauerwas' mind, Barth lacks a sufficient doctrine of the sanctified visible church, as the body of Christ, which unites Christians with their Lord in their faithful witness through the sacraments and practices of the church.[31] For Hauerwas the beliefs and practices (including sacraments) that constitute the church declare, in specific practical actions, the presence of the Spirit in the world. The church, as the body of Christ, is the *visible* embodiment of Jesus Christ in the world. So, it appears that Hauerwas' main problem with Barth's account of moral agency is that he fails to explain how divine action actually shapes human action (including character and virtues) through the Spirit-infused practices or sacraments of the church, which leads to particular concrete actions (or actual performance) of Christian witness as demonstrated particularly in actions of nonviolence. In short, Barth fails to take the final step in linking his ecclesiology with Christian witness, which fails to provide a specific performative account of Christian witness.[32]

So what are we to think about these criticisms? To be sure Hauerwas raises an interesting point about the possible insufficiency of Barth's ethics. However, this criticism is pregnant with Hauerwas' own assumptions about the *performance* of Christian witness. This shifts the focus away from divine agency to human agency or said differently from Jesus Christ to the church. The main problem with Hauerwas' criticism of Barth, therefore, is that it presumes their underlying differences are rooted in their respective accounts of the work of the Holy Spirit (divine action) in lives of Christians

---

31. Hauerwas' criticism of Barth's ecclesiology is similar to others who question Barth's pneumatology in its relation to the human action of Christian witness. For a list of contributors to this debate, and an excellent response from Barth's ecclesiology, see Webster, *Confessing God*, 153–93; and Healy, "Karl Barth's Ecclesiology Reconsidered," 287–99.

32. Hauerwas further writes: "Barth's *Dogmatics* is a performance, a witness, through which we learn the skills to go on in a way no doubt different from Barth. For there is no way to be faithful to Barth without being different from Barth. That is why Dietrich Bonhoeffer, exactly because he followed Barth in his own way, witnesses to the power of Barth's performance." Hauerwas, *Performing the Faith*, 25. According to Hauerwas, however, Barth's performance of Christian witness was to write the *Church Dogmatics*, and not to provide a reliable account of practical ethics. Moreover, his theology was "not sufficiently catholic" in his sacraments (i.e., he was Zwinglian), because was unable to explain why the practices of the church, as the body of Christ, makes any difference to the task of Christian witness. On these various points, see Hauerwas, *With the Grain*, 145, 192,199, 215.

and the church. This makes it appear that the issue of disagreement is over the theology of divine agency not human agency, but this remains a misplaced argument. In plain language, Hauerwas is correct to differentiate his own view of witness from Barth's, but he situates the fundamental genesis of this difference in the wrong place. As stated above, the crucial difference between the two thinkers is that Barth (not Hauerwas) begins with the divine action of the Word (and Spirit) instead of human agency and action. These different starting points dramatically affect their views of Christian witness. Hauerwas follows Barth in insisting the primary task of the church in the world is to *be* the church, that is, to bear witness to the reality of Jesus Christ. Yet, in Barth's judgment, Christian witness is "twofold," in that it begins with God's gracious action, which shifts our attention away from *our* practices and actions and toward the "true witness" of Jesus Christ. "It is He, He who is the reality. He is not I. He is not we" (*CD* I/2: 368).

In Barth's view the church's witness begins with *God's* action, whereas for Hauerwas divine agency principally emerges through the *human* practice of the Christian community. Since Christian witness *is* performance, says Hauerwas, the "truth of Christian convictions depend upon the faithfulness of the church."[33] No doubt Hauerwas rejects the idea that the gospel is contingent upon faithful performance for that would imply that unfaithfulness could disprove the gospel's truth. Still, he explicitly writes: "Christianity is unintelligible without witnesses, that is, without people whose practices exhibit their committed assent to a particular way of structuring the whole."[34] Regardless of Hauerwas' intentions, Barth would draw a firmer distinction between Christianity's intelligibility, which rests in the objective revelation in God's Word, and the task of Christian witness, which remains the "declaration, explication and application of the Gospel" as revealed in that Word (*CD* IV/3: 843). For Barth, divine agency cannot be strictly identified with ecclesial practices or human acts of Christian witness, which would risk making God's action contingent upon human action. Barth would reject what Hauerwas appears to claim, namely that Christianity's intelligibility is strongly linked with faithful Christian witness. If so, the burden of "true witness" rests primary with the *faithfulness* of the church, embodied in the practical actions of Christian character, practices, and virtue. Can Christian truth be reduced to ecclesial practice? If so, where is the uniqueness of the

---

33. Hauerwas, *Performing the Faith*, 231.
34. Hauerwas, *With the Grain*, 214.

"true witness" of Jesus Christ? Accordingly, it is not so much the performance of the church that matters as God's performance in Jesus Christ and the Spirit. And even though Christians give witness to God's performance in proclamation and practice, it cannot determine the "truth" or intelligibility of ecclesial proclamation. For Hauerwas the performance of the Word and the Spirit appear to remain contingent upon human performance in the church, which invariably reduces divine agency to human agency.

Although Hauerwas draws upon Barth's theology, his ecclesial-centered approach remains, in many ways, distinct from Barth's approach. Following Barth, Hauerwas detests liberal theology, but unlike Barth, he implicitly continues its lasting legacy, not only in terms of the primacy of ethical methodology over dogmatics, but also on the emphasis on the *praxis* or performance of the gospel. For Barth the church's witness always begins with *God's* determinative gracious action, whereas for Hauerwas witness occurs with the human action of the Christian community "pointing to God." For Barth only in the "double agency" of the divine-human encounter made real in Jesus Christ as "true witness" is human agency set free to cooperate with God's agency in fulfilling the divine will and purpose.[35] Since there is no generic humanity "outside the humanity of Jesus Christ," then Christology takes precedence over ecclesiology in Christian ethics (*CD* II/2, 541). It is only *in* Christ's "true witness" as the reconciling prophet, priest, and king that Christian witness as ethics is understood. Christian witness for Christians, then, becomes less a performance of prescribed ecclesial practices and ethical actions, than an open-ended corresponding response to God's reconciling action in Jesus Christ. In short, whereas Hauerwas moves toward a church-centered theology, Barth moves toward a Word-centered one. Such an ecclesially-centered theology potentially undervalues the importance of how divine agency in the command of grace, stands in judgment of the church (as well as the world), something so evident in Barth's writings. Christian witness proclaims to the world what has *in fact* already taken place in this divine-human covenant of reconciliation. In this sense, the burden falls upon God's action, not human action. God's decision to have witnesses is grounded in God's love for humanity and the world in and through the covenant of grace. This covenant of grace is not dependent on the faithful witness or performance of the church, but on the actions of the trinitarian God. God's action in the world does not

---

35. See Hunsinger, *How to Read Karl Bart*h, 185–224.

leave persons powerless or passive but *active* in response to what God has done. Christian ethics is an ethics of correspondence between divine and human action, but that correspondence in grounded in God's covenantal-partnership with humanity. The Yes comes before the No, and the No is always answered by the Yes.

CONCLUSION

This chapter argues that Christian ethics, as a form of witness, must be critical of using ethical methods of casuistic reasoning in determining absolute courses of moral action. Christian ethics is not closed system of rational reasoning from general principles to specific cases but a "gift of freedom" that links our unique circumstances in which we find ourselves and God's command of grace. "Man becomes free and is free by choosing, deciding, and determining himself in accordance with the freedom of God" (*HG*: 76–77). God's command is an "event" of grace and freedom in which, the Christian is called to "witness" in correspondence to God's command in "freedom" toward "responsible" action. These three themes of responsibility, witness, and freedom become important threads through the *Church Dogmatics*. Of these, the theme of "freedom" becomes the salient theme in the first volume-length treatment of special ethics in *CD* III/4, but continues into his ethics of reconciliation. Although "responsibility" and "witness" remain important themes in all volumes, they become especially important in the volume and parts on the doctrine of reconciliation (*CD* IV/1–4). In any case, this is why Barth is against systematic theories of ethics that presume an autonomous moral agent because it denies this human-divine encounter in covenant-partnership. Our understanding of rightness or wrongness cannot be comprehended without God's command of grace, nor can we act without God's command of freedom. We've seen how the Yes of God's command gives freedom or "liberation" to moral judgment, particularly how this leads to a dialectical movement of testing and acting, of listening and responding, to God's gracious command for responsible witness. This presumes a freedom in decision-making not evident in casuistic methods of ethics. The freedom, however, rests not in the moral subject's relation to the command, but in God's reconciling action in Jesus Christ *pro nobis*, which makes the person a covenant-partner with God's action in the world. The focal point here remains Christology not ecclesiology. When ecclesiology becomes a map from which we speak about Christian witness, then there is a danger of "pious egocentricity" and the "Christian ethos" becoming an "end in itself" (*CD* IV/3: 560). This leads to a view of salvation *pro me* rather than *pro nobis*, which can lead to the church's isolation from the world. This undermines the church's mission and witness which is to serve the world, that is, to be with and for the world. This becomes a potential danger in any ecclesially-centered theology that concentrates on the church's ethos as the basis for Christian ethics. The Yes of Christian witness primarily rests in God's gracious action in Jesus Christ *for* the world, and not in the church's practice or sacramental performance. The truth of the gospel is not found in our faithfulness but in God's faithfulness, not in our character but in God's character, and not in our performance but in God's performance.

CHAPTER EIGHT

Witness and the Powers

This chapter explores further Barth's ethics of reconciliation as a "responsible witness of the Word of God" serving both "God and men" (*CD* IV/3: 609). The Yes of responsible moral judgment corresponds, in this chapter, to the No of resistance against the powers. This chapter begins with a theological discussion of the powers and its relation to ethics as it pertains to the subjects of evil, eschatology, and reconciliation. Central to this is a discussion of Christ's victory over the powers, the triumph of *Christus victor*. Following this general discussion is a specific analysis of Barth's discussion of the "spiritual powers" of leviathan, mammon, and ideology, and the "chthonic powers" such as technology, fashion, entertainment. Afterward, our discussion broadens to consider the language of risk as a "secular parable" of the powers, enabling us to further define and characterize the various forces in today's world. The analogy between the theologically informed powers to the socially informed parable of risk and hegemony demonstrates how secular words may be integrated into the task of Christian witness. These secular concepts may be useful for Christian ethics but only after they have been commandeered by the Word of God. In doing so, however, we must remain cautious about the dominant synthesis (apologetic) approach that seeks to replace a theological understanding of moral agency with a secular one. This occurs when Christian ethicists simply adopt secular frameworks of moral and political agency without questioning the particular secular worldview that lies behind social scientific premises. With this in mind, this chapter returns to a discussion of globalization and how various Christian ethicists approach the topic of human agency from within a framework of globalization's potential hegemony. To reiterate, Christian ethics must avoid the apologetic error of synthesis which leads to a form of secular reductionism and a silencing of the Word of God. The chapter closes by returning again to *Christus victor* or the "strange battle" of Jesus Christ, and how this opens up the way for the liberation of moral judgment. Thus, this chapter loops back or circles back to the themes of the last chapter. The Yes of liberation comes before the No of resistance, but the No of resistance further corresponds to the Yes of liberation. This is a reoccurring Yes-No-Yes pattern, which implies that the Word of God is the beginning and the end and the alpha and omega. In the prophetic witness of *Christus victor* the No against the powers is answered by the Yes of responsible witness. The last word—just like the first word—is never No but always Yes.

CHRIST AND THE POWERS

In recent years, there has been a renewed interest in developing a theological account of the "principalities and powers" by various biblical scholars and theologians.[1] There is no doubt this interest goes hand in hand with the tragic events of the late twentieth and early twenty-first centuries. This past century, perhaps more than most, has brought to the surface the insatiable human quest and use of hegemonic power, whether political, economic, ideological, or socio-cultural. This is but another example of the transition from modern to postmodern society, in which the increasing power of *risk* emerges from its shadow to become a real force in the world. Scattered throughout Barth's writings are various references to the "powers" that interfere in human life. Barth was well aware of the social forces, created by human sin, that deprive humanity of its freedom to live in peace, justice, and hope. Indeed, no one was more aware of the multiple faces of *power* than Barth, who struggled to provide a theological account of reality in the midst of the growing imperialism of World War I, Fascism in World War II, and the East-West ideological conflict of the Cold War. Guided by his theology of gospel and law, and sin and grace, he dialectically talked about

---

1. See Yoder *Politics of Jesus*, 134–61. Walter Wink has written several books on this subject, including the latest his latest: *When the Powers Fall*.

both the limitations and realities of human freedom. This is why Clifford Green, on one side, calls Barth a "theologian of freedom," and, on the other side, Timothy Gorringe calls him a theologian "against hegemony."[2] The Christian life is both a revolt *against* the powers and activism *for* human freedom, justice, and peace. Real liberation from the powers is possible only because God's victory over the powers in the reconciliation of God and humanity through Jesus Christ. In Jesus Christ, Christians "are made responsible within the world of unrighteousness and disorder and therefore in the sphere of the domination of these powers and forces." With "freedom and joy as their theme," he adds, "Christians fight the fight for human righteousness against human unrighteousness" (*CL*: 267).

Powers, Evil, and Nothingness

Beginning in the *Romans* period, Barth refers to the "principalities and powers" as destructive features of human life. He associates these powers with destructive and relatively hegemonic "isms," like nationalism, idealism, socialism (and communism), capitalism, theological liberalism (or neo-protestantism), and so on. The church stands against these powers, as a witness to "God's revolution" of divine judgment and grace, which intervenes into human life. God's freedom calls the church to reject all the ideologies and powers that seek to destroy the church's freedom. Theology, by itself, is political, in the sense that it must reject all forms of ideology that corrupt or interfere with the freedom of God's Word to address us and demand responsible action in the world. In the 1930s, he practically shifts his focus to the political situation in Germany. In his 1938 address *Rechtfertigung und Recht*, Barth discusses the powers in relation to church and state. Rejecting the claim that the state is a demonic power, he seeks to find a "vital" and "positive" connection between the "two realms" or "powers" of the church and the state by placing them both within the "Christological sphere" (*CSC*: 120). Both the church and state belong to Christ's kingdom. God's gracious relationship to the sinner and the church is no different than God's relationship to the "powers" of the state. All powers, even though seen by some as demonic, nonetheless, belong "originally and ultimately to Jesus Christ" (*CSC*: 118).

---

2. Regarding these themes, see Green, *Karl Barth*; and Gorringe, *Karl Barth*.

One year later, Barth writes his first extensive discussion of the "powers" in his discussion the "perfections of God's freedom" in *CD* II/1. He writes:

> Created powers, and above all the powers of opposition and therefore of powerlessness, are always distinct from God's power. He gives them a place, and this applies not only to the powers created through His work but also to the powers of opposition and powerlessness, to the possibility of the impossible, of that which has been excluded by His own act. Yet this does not mean that He abandons even part of His lordship over them, He is even partially powerless over against them, or that they have even partially an independent position and function in relation to Him. On the contrary, it is by His power that He creates or at any rate tolerates other powers. In this His power is always power in and over them, and He is always first and last the only one who is full of power. He is not at any point limited or determined by them, but at every point He limits and determines them. He is the "King of Kings" and as their true Creator and Preserver or as the righteous Judge. Thus none of them can escape Him but only serve him and will definitely serve Him in one way or another. (*CD* II/I: 538)

In the omnipotence of God's grace, God has defeated the evil powers, and their real power, over human life and death. Whatever power these powers have is circumscribed by his God's power of grace, which is evident in God's actions in creation, reconciliation, and redemption. Yet, the evil powers continue to seek to deprive persons of freedom and keep them from acknowledging the objective reality that God has defeated and destroyed their true power. From the human standpoint, these powers continue to apparently have power over human freedom, yet from God's standpoint, the true reality is that God has decisively acted and destroyed the "regime of evil." Because of God's covenant of grace, humanity is really set free from the powers that seek human destruction; all that is left is realizing this fact—and praising God for it! In saying this, however, Barth is not naïve about the evil powers that wreak havoc in the world. Nevertheless, as the passage above indicates, Barth's view of the powers is ultimately shaped by Christ's reconciling victory as "King of Kings" and "righteous Judge" rather than God as "Creator and Preserver." Yet before we discuss how the doctrine of reconciliation shapes Barth's view of the powers, we must turn briefly to how God's providence, which is also shaped by reconciliation, pertains to Barth's understanding of evil and sin as "nothingness."

In a controversial section in *CD* III/2 entitled "God and Nothingness," Barth discusses the problem of evil in the context of the doctrines of creation and providence. Here Barth uses the word "nothingness" (*das Nichtige*) to discuss the power that "opposes and resists" God's gracious care, which is discovered only in God's Yes of reconciliation in Jesus Christ (*CD* III/3: 305). In using this word, Barth is not saying sin, evil, and the powers exist as "nothing," like illusion or fantasy, but they are indeed "real." The word "nothingness" does not mean that it is harmless or powerless, says Eberhard Busch, but in a "twofold sense that it has an annihilating force for the creature, and that the Creator has the power to reduce it to nothing."[3] From our human standpoint, evil, sin, death, and eternal punishment as "nothingness" really do exist as a real possibility, the "shadowy side" of creation, which threatens to annihilate, destroy, and deprive us of our own happiness and flourishing (*CD* III/3: 299). Yet, from the standpoint of God's revelation, we learn that God's gracious power is the "real" power which ultimately is the only power that can destroy the annihilating force of nothingness. What is "evil by nature" or "intrinsically evil" cannot be linked essentially to the attributes of either God or humanity, but must be seen as a third thing that exists "only as their frontier" (*CD* III/3: 360). We get true insight into the power of nothingness only in the death and resurrection of Jesus Christ, in which God takes up the human cause against evil and confronts it directly in the cruelty, suffering, and death on the cross. Thus, "true nothingness is that which brought Jesus Christ to the cross, and that which he defeated there" (*CD* III/3: 305). Only with the cross do we see the "true reality" of nothingness as an evil power that stands *against* God's gracious goodness and justice by seeking to destroy humanity's freedom from becoming liberated as a covenant-partner with God.

In this discussion in *CD* III/3 Barth does not explicitly link the structural power of the "powers" with nothingness. Yet, we may assume that the nothingness is the force or power behind the powers. Jesus Christ did confront the powers of his day in his teaching and actions. Nevertheless, Jesus is more than a revolutionary or resistor against "empire."[4] Rather,

3. Busch, *Great Passion*, 189.

4. The topic of "Jesus and Empire" is a reoccurring theme in recent biblical ethics and historical Jesus research. This has carried over into the study of Christology and Christian ethics. For a good example, see Rieger, *Christ and Empire*. This book follows in the tradition of liberation theology, but does so by integrating recent work on empire, theology, and ethics. Still, Rieger is more interested in how we interpret Christology than with discussing what he thinks Christology actually is in itself. The book's central point is that we

as God the reconciler, Jesus Christ acted *pro nobis* making possible what humanity itself could never do, namely overcome the annihilating force of nothingness. Once this central point is rejected, not only is nothingness misunderstood, but so is the real nature of God and humanity. "There are a few heresies so pernicious as that of a God who faces nothingness more or less unaffected and unconcerned, and the parallel doctrine of man as one who must engage in independent conflict against it. We know well enough what it means to be alien and adverse to grace and therefore without it. A graceless God would be a null and evil God, and a self-sufficient, self-reliant creaturely subject is a null and evil creature" (*CD* III/3: 360). The first heresy claims that God is not affected by God's battle with evil, suffering, and death. Nothingness is real because God really has confronted, is confronting, and will confront its power over humanity. Although the victory is won, the battle continues in the "prophetic witness" of Jesus Christ in the world, in the Holy Spirit, and through the church's struggle on earth as witness to God's reconciling victory. By denying that God reconciled the world in Jesus Christ, we deny that nothingness is our real enemy, something that only God can defeat. This means that there is a direct line between, on one hand, denying Jesus Christ's victory over the powers, and on the other, our denying its real destructive power over us. The first heresy about God leads directly to the second heresy about humanity. Rather than accepting God as our covenant-partner, we stand in "self-reliance" denying our need for God's grace. This culminates in the worldview that nothingness is "ultimately innocuous" and something that can be "overlooked, forgotten, unnoticed, unexpected and disregarded" (*CD* III/3: 300). Nothingness no longer is a real threat to our existence, but something over which we have control to define, shape, and transform. This leads to an underestimating or undervaluing of the power of nothingness, the power of sin and evil, and the various structures or "powers" that arise from its influence. People mistakenly believe, in their affliction, they can actually have power over its negative side effects. Ironically, this delusion of power to control nothingness often leads to the realization that we cannot control its power over us; in our attempt to control nothingness, it controls us.

---

need to deconstruct Christologies, in order that we might find the resources or "surplus" so that we will be able to properly resist the empire. Consequently, Rieger is more interested in determining how Christology might help us find ways to resist the empire of our time than with explaining how Jesus Christ himself brings victory over the powers.

Nevertheless, the underlying power of nothingness as a threat does not go away simply because we see it as threat to our existence. This is where the power of nothingness becomes a power that we cooperate with and support through our actions. Eventually we realize that we cannot overcome nothingness on our own, but rather than turn to God's grace we remain "self-reliant." In turn, we become too willing to accept the "reality" of evil and the powers as an "ontic peculiarity" as simply part of our existence, something we must resist and struggle against and hopefully overcome. "Real evil can then be interpreted as transitory, and not intolerable imperfection, and real death as 'rest in God'" (*CD* III/3: 300). Yet, the real problem of nothingness, as a real power, remains both in our individual and collective sinful actions. In recognizing its power over us, people often become complacent, fatalistic, cynical, or even nihilistic. In this way, people become too willing to directly "cooperate with what is attempted against them" as part of our natural existence (*CD* III/3: 300). When people accept nothingness as a normal part of life, they inevitably find ways to *cooperate* with political and economic injustice, violence, and human oppression. They cooperate with the powers, and when things turn out bad, they curse God for allowing evil to exist. We then justify our faithlessness by further rejecting God's gracious promise to be our covenant-partner. In rejecting God's grace we strengthen the powers making them potentially hegemonic. Still, in the midst of human confusion, God's self-determination remains constant, says Barth, as God "would rather be unblest with His creature than be the blessed God of an unblest creature." God "would rather let himself be injured and humiliated in making the assault and repulse of nothingness His own concern than leave His creature alone in this affliction" (*CD* III/3: 358). It is grace, not the threat of nothingness that ultimately triumphs.

Reconciliation and the Powers

We are now able to discuss how Jesus Christ's "twofold witness," both as God's initiative and corresponding human response brings victory (*Christus victor*) over the powers. In later chapters, we will discuss more fully the Christology of *CD* IV/1–3. First, in *CD* IV/1 Barth's Christology focuses on the Son of God, the great "high priest," who acts *pro nobis* as our savior, mediator, and judge. God becomes the *servant* standing with and for humanity bringing renewal and restoration to the covenant-partnership. In God's act of justification God makes it possible for humanity to be reconciled with God, so that it can proclaim to the world that God's victory over the powers is a *fait accompli*. Second, in *CD* IV/2 Barth's Christology focuses on Christ as Son of Man, the man of Nazareth, who acts *pro nobis*, as our representative, in faithful obedience toward God. Jesus Christ unveils the divine act of sanctification as the Holy Spirit "up-builds" or empowers the church to be a visible witness of love in its proclamation, mission, and politics (*CD* IV/2). This witness here is that God desires that humanity seek what is good, to seek peace, justice, and freedom. Lastly, in *CD* IV/3 Barth's Christology shifts toward Jesus Christ as Prophet, the "One" who brings together into unity Christ's offices of priest and king, bring together God's "deity and humanity, of God's humiliation and man's exaltation, of the justification and sanctification of man, of faith and love" (*CD* IV/3: 4). As prophet, Jesus Christ acts *pro nobis* as "true witness" and *Christus victor*, and empowers the visible church's mission and witness through the Holy Spirit. This threefold event of God's reconciliation reveals Jesus Christ as prophet, priest, and king, as the one who has victory over nothingness and the powers. Without this victory, people remain controlled by the threat of nothingness and potential hegemonic force of the powers.

As we have seen, God's victory over the powers in Jesus Christ remains an important theme in various portions of the *Church Dogmatics*. About the same time, in 1953, the Dutch Reformed theologian Hendrik Berkof wrote an important book entitled *Christ and the Powers*, which no doubt could have caused Barth to look further into the Pauline and Deutero-Pauline accounts of the "principalities and powers," which he did in his ethics of reconciliation—*The Christian Life*.[5] It is here where he more fully discusses the "lordless powers" in the context of his discussion of the Lord's Prayer, and particularly between the petitions, "Hallowed be Thy Name" and "Thy Kingdom Come" (*CL*: 213–33). Giving honor to God's name and acknowledging that God's kingdom has come leads us to the greater awareness that the fullness of the kingdom has not yet been fully realized. With awareness of reconciliation comes the awareness of sin. In the midst of God's order there is the human disorder that seeks to dishonor God and disregard that God's kingdom indeed has come with Jesus Christ. In this context, Barth makes it clear that these powers are not simply occasional hindrances to an otherwise undisturbed existence. Rather they really cause disruption in society. They are the "motors of society" that inhabit "man's great and small conventions, customs, habits, traditions, and institutions" (*CL*: 216). In his words, these powers are:

5. Berkhof, *Christ and the Powers*.

> the hidden wirepullers in man's great and small enterprises, movements, achievements, and revolutions. They are not just potencies but the real factors and agents of human progress, regress, and stagnation in politics, economics, scholarship, technology, and art, and also of the evolutions and retardations in all the personal life of the individual. It is not really people who do things, whether leaders or the masses. Through mankind's fault, things are invisibly done without and above man, even above the human individual in all his uniqueness, by the host of absolutisms, of powers that seek to be lordless and that make an impressive enough attempt to exhibit and present themselves as such. (*CL*: 216)

Barth's understanding of the powers is principally based upon his reading of various passages of the New Testament, particularly the Pauline corpus. He refused to simply dismiss these passages as mythological and outdated first century explanations of reality. Thus he argues that the New Testament writers were "less hindered than we are by the world picture of their contemporaries" because unlike them, we do not take "freely into account the strange reality and efficacy" of the evil powers that exert influence on human affairs (*CL*: 217). This means simply that the task of biblical interpretation does not begin by demythologizing the text, making it more relevant to a modern audience, but instead using the biblical narrative to demythologize the various powers that repress human freedom. The Bible is allowed to speak and challenge our view of things. Instead of modern methods shaping our use of the Bible to fit our world, the Bible, as a witness to God's Word, addresses and challenges us in the context of our world.

What does the Bible say about the powers? Beginning with the narrative of the fall in Genesis 3, the temptation will always be the same: "'You will be like God' (Gen 3:5), you will be your own lord and masters" (*CL*: 214). In their foolish attempt to "be like God" humans have placed themselves under their own *power*, which entraps them, and becomes a power over them. By rejecting God's covenant of grace, people seek to live under their own disordered power of revolt against God's "objective" benevolent order. Indeed, this leads to a further denial that God is "with" and "for" us in Jesus Christ. In so doing they reject their *true* humanity, as reconciled, and rather revert to a "false" or "illusionary" belief and practice that they alone have power and lordship. "It may be presupposed that man's fall and alienation from God is the root of all evil and therefore of this evil too. This is the final and true basis of the disorder" (*CL*: 213). In separating themselves from God and each other, humans have brought *disorder* into the world. This disorder of sin, Barth says, "both inwardly and outwardly controls and penetrates and poisons and disrupts all human relations and interconnections" (*CL*: 211). The history of human society, therefore, remains not only a history of rejection of God, but also, a history of rejection *and* subjection of people through power. "World history is the confirmation and repetition of this twofold history. Where all are against God, the hand of each can only be against that of others" (*CL*: 212). The irony, of course, is that the more that the creature insists on its own freedom, sovereignty, and power *apart* from God's gracious covenant, the more it lives by the "myth and illusion" that it indeed is free and powerful. This irony, of course, exists in many forms including our misconception of nothingness. Barth writes:

> To be sure, he thinks he can take them in hand, control them, and direct them as he pleases, for they are undoubtedly the forces of his own possibilities and capacities, of his own ability. In reality, however, they escape from him, they have already escaped from him. They are entities with their own right and dignity. They are long since alienated from him. They act at their own pleasure, as absolutes, without him, behind him, over him, and against him, according to the law by which they arose, in exact correspondence to the law by which man himself thought that he should flee from God. As he did to God, so the different forms of his own capacity now do to him. In reality, he does not control them but they him. They do not serve him be he must serve them. (*CL*: 214–15)

The powers are not part of the objective reality of God's reign, but remain "pseudo-objective" forces that threaten to be determinative of humanity's future. They are not intrinsically hegemonic, but act *as if* they are because humanity, corrupted by its estrangement from God, infuses them with hegemonic power. In reality they only have a "limited and relative power" because they have been defeated by Jesus Christ (*CL*: 215). *Christus victor* triumphs over the powers. The powers are fallen and the world has been "de-demonized" but humanity is unaware of these realities (*CL*: 218). Instead, human communities continue to live in a "kingdom of disorder" where the powers wreak havoc both personally and socially. "As the powers tear apart the individual, so—because there are so many of them and in such competition—they tear apart society also. Giving rights to no one, they make it impossible for any to grant mutual rights (*CL*: 233). Their great lie is that they promise "liberation, strength, ease, simplification, and enrichment," but they cannot do this because "they are inhuman" (*CL*: 232–33). These powers appear, at first, to be under humanity's control, but "they now confront him as robots which he himself has to serve, and not without being forced to fear their possible pranks" (*CL*: 228). Their goal is to seek to disrupt and ruin society as well as the individual, and "destroy," "oppress," "afflict," and "harass" people (*CL*: 233). "They would inevitably destroy him if they were allowed to work without restriction, if a limit were not imposed on them" (*CL*: 233). The powers corrupt social institutions that give order and meaning to people's lives and create instead communities of disorder and chaos. It is the *ignorance* of the powers, both in their existence and falleness, which serves as its greatest potential threat to humanity.

Powers and Eschatology

So, what are Christians to do in response to the powers? Christians cannot assume that we have the power to control their influence over our lives. We cannot have victory over the powers by ourselves. We may recall from the last chapter that human correspondence to God's gracious command begins with our Yes to God's grace, but it further leads to our No against the powers. Only with our acknowledgment that God has acted, is acting, and will act in the future do we have the promise that divine agency establishes and situates human agency. Ethics is eschatological, as it must be framed by God's reconciliation and redemption. Responsible ethical action, says Barth, "will not be unlike God's act but also like it, running parallel to it on our level, a modest but clear analogue to the extent that it is directed against the abomination that has already been defeated and removed in God's complete act in Jesus Christ and which will be visibly shown before the eyes of all to be a shattered power in the manifestation of Jesus Christ as the goal of our path" (*CL*: 175). In their correspondence to Christ's victory over the powers, Christians are called to give resistance to the powers, but only because they first recognize that God has acted decisively against them. Hence, Christian resistance primarily emerges from commitment to the Word and God and a corresponding *analogue* of God's gracious action, and not from a hatred of the powers, which potentially may be directed at people instead of the powers.[6]

6. Barth's most condensed writing on the "call to discipleship" is found in *CD* IV/2: 533–53. This text was made more accessible, when it was published in the Facet series by Fortress Press. See Barth, *Call to Discipleship*.

> Obviously Christian action in this sphere will have the nature of a movement of resistance: not to other people of the world with whom the Christian finds and knows himself to be in solidarity, not against their interests as such, since these affect him too, but against the desecration of the name of God which pollutes this sphere and which is brought about by the mixture of light and darkness that rules it, against the system of the ambivalence of the knowledge and ignorance of the one true and living God . . . When Christians pray for the hallowing of God's name by God himself, they are praying concretely that he will put an end to this abominable vacillation. For the holy name of God which is desecrated in the world is unequivocally the name of him who is not without or against man but *for* man, the God who liberates and thus rules man, the God who loves him. If, then, the Christian's action follows this petition, necessarily it will be action not only in the presupposed coexistence with God but also in the coexistence with man that results directly from it. (*CL*: 202–3)

In their praying Christians affirm the objective reality of God's eschatological victory over the "regime of evil." It is God's judgment against the powers that ultimately matters, and Christian *witness* simply corresponds to this fact by proclaiming God's past, present, and future gracious actions. "As the message of God's freeing of man from this bondage it constantly proclaims to all what God has done for them, and will do, in Jesus Christ" (*CL*: 218). When Christians give witness to God's victory, they are also empowered to embody "resistance" against the powers. Yet, in their corresponding acts of resistance, they must also remain cautious about making absolute value judgments about right principles or courses of action. That is, Christian moral judgment must always remain tentative and cautious about practical courses of action, while at the same time it remains purposeful and resolute in bearing witness to the reality of *Christus victor*. Christian witness to God's grace in the world implies being perceptive about God's victory over the powers, but also about their deceptive influence—indeed control—over the human imagination. When persons make ultimate judgments about what is good and bad or Yes and No they risk replacing one destructive power with another. "From one standpoint or another," says Barth, "every idea or life-form will sooner or later prove a threat to man" (*CL*: 268). By falling under the spell of the powers, persons eventually imposed on themselves some form of personal, social, or cultural hegemony. Yet, even when the powers are acknowledged and *named* as potential risks within the scientific-technological world, this does not necessarily provide individuals with the means to be free from their power. Only realizing the objective reality of God's kingdom, and its victory over the powers, is it possible to reject the "reality and efficacy" of the powers (*CL*: 215).

NAMING THE POWERS

Can these powers be *named* or do they remain a mystery? As mentioned above, Barth sees these powers surfacing in human conventions, customs, habits, traditions, and institutions. More particularly, they often emerge in the areas of "politics, economics, scholarship, technology, and art, and also of the evolutions and retardations in all the personal life of the individual" (*CL*: 216). Since they are not hegemonic, but act *as if* they are by asserting their influence over individual and social life, they inevitably become a kind of "absolutism" that seeks to control human life. What are the "lordless powers"? Barth divides the powers into two groups, namely the "spiritual forces" of political, economic, and ideological absolutism, and the "chthonic powers" or "spirits of the earth" as found in technology, sport, pleasure seeking, and transportation (addiction to speed) (*CL*: 221–33). Of these, he devotes more space to the former "spiritual forces," amongst which he specifically names the powers of "leviathan," "mammon," and "ideology." We first discuss these three powers, and then move on to a brief discussion of the "chthonic powers."

Leviathan

The first power Barth mentions is "leviathan" or political absolutism. Not all political states become the power of leviathan, but only those that seek to usurp God's freedom and destroy human freedom. Leviathan rejects its true identity as civil community and seeks to destroy human freedom, hope, and peace. New Testament writers themselves were not naïve about the "political absolutisms" that "work behind and above the attitudes and acts of the great and little potentates, the highly diversified governments of the day." Like them, Barth argues that theology of politics should not be preoccupied with political theory as such, but the "question of the demonic which is visibly at work in all politics" (*CL*: 219). The "demonic" surfaces or becomes visible in politics when the state uses power to stand against what is best for humanity and the world. He writes:

> Now if power breaks loose from law, if the one who should be active in the service of the divine order chooses to value and love as such his sovereignty and dominion, his power and force over others, if he undertakes to establish and exercise these things for their own sake, as the man does who emancipates himself from God, then inasmuch as they too emancipate themselves from him and become his master, the demonism in politics arises. Law or right is no longer the order that helps man, which safeguards his life, which gives him freedom and peace. It is the establishment and strengthening of the power which is seized and exercised by some in the subjugation of the others. Power no longer protects the right, nor finds in it its determination and limit. It subjects the right to itself and makes triumphant use of it. The state no longer serves man; man, both ruled and ruling, has to serve the state. The demonism of politics consists in the idea of "empire," which is always inhuman as such. This can be a monarchical, aristocratic, democratic, nationalistic, or socialistic, idea. (*CL*: 219–20)

As examples of leviathan, Barth specifically mentions the various types of totalitarianism found in the Facisims of Germany and Italy and Stalinist Russia, and the earlier "monarchical despotism of Louis XIV" and the "revolutionary despotism of the French Revolution" (*CL*: 220). Besides these obvious examples, Barth argues that any political ideology, once united with the state's power, can destroy the good in human politics. Using the deception that the state stands "for" its people, as their "guardian," leviathan uses any means necessary to "fascinate" and attract its followers, while it "demonizes" its enemies. Leviathan rejects its true identity as the "just state" that has been "dedemonized already in Jesus Christ," and in so doing, seeks to separate itself and humanity from God's rule and to further wreak havoc in the world. As an "empire," leviathan seeks to change the "normal" or "just" state into the "marginal" or "unjust" state. Instead of serving humanity and the world, the state forces humanity (and the world) to serve its own disastrous ends. Political authority, if it is to be just and right (*Recht*), must integrate power and the moral law, which ultimately depends upon God's revelation of grace in Jesus Christ. Thus, when persons reject God's authority and say No to God's established "objective" order of redemption and place themselves as masters of the political realm, the "demonic" in politics emerges within human society (*CL*: 219). There is a fine line between the dialectical polarity between the "demonic" state that denies God's sovereignty over the state, and the "divine" state that places itself above God sovereignty. Both are driven by the "myth of the state" as an "earthly God," as found in the "mythical language" of the "Beast from the abyss" in Rev 13:1–8 (*CL*: 220).

Moreover, Barth sees leviathan's message of Yes and No, of attraction and oppression, as emerging from its particular ideology and "program and structure." Thus, the power of leviathan is not principally located in an evil tyrant or group of tyrants, but a totalitarian *system* or program, in which all dissenting or alternative voices are eliminated. It is a form of systematic evil that promises freedom to its adherents and cruelty to its enemies. This is how the state becomes totalitarian, namely, the "total" or "end" of society. Any nation, with the power available, is susceptible to the temptation to replace the "might of right" with the "right of might" (*CL*: 221). Barth admits the temptation of leviathan, the love of power and empire, remains a temptation for any society, at any time, under any system of government. Indeed, Barth warns that any state, including the democratic states of Western Europe and the United States, are not "immune to the tendency to become at least a little Leviathan" (*CL*: 221). Regardless, Christian social witness stands "against" leviathan and "for" human freedom, hope, and peace. Christian political witness implies both unmasking the power of leviathan, while working for the good of the state and the civil community.

Mammon

Similar to leviathan, the second power "mammon" is not simply equated with economic resources and wealth, but *only when* they become an idol and a power over and against human freedom. Economic resources can be considered "neutral" or "even good in themselves" and as "part of man's nature," but, as a "demonic power," they no longer serve the human need to "guarantee and secure a livelihood" but become an end in itself. Mammon is a luring power, and "idol" that invites people to seek "emancipation from God" by seeking their own comfort and security in their material resources and possessions. As a "promise" to gain human salvation, apart from God, the love of mammon forces people to accumulate more and more, as a way to "consolidate the guarantee and security it seems to offer" (*CL*: 222). This need for security and comfort creates the need for more accumulation of possessions, which inevitably leads to more "anxiety" and fear of losing these material things that one possesses. Ironically, people's greatest fear is losing their possessions so they remain committed to accumulate more possessions as a way to satisfy this fear, which is to say that what people strive to own eventually owns them. Barth writes:

> If his resources are to be faithful to him, to serve him and give him comfort, does he not have to be faithful to them and serve them? When he perceives this and asks accordingly, then in a very harmless form here or in greater measure there they acquire power over him. Mammon, the close relative of Leviathan, is born. It mounts its throne. The worship of it begins, whether wittingly or unwittingly, openly or discreetly, cheerfully or sighingly. Along with the many other things that it is, powerful not in one or other evil alone but in and over all people, the spirit of this world is also the spirit of Mammon, the spirit of our resources or possessions attempting self-absolutization." (*CL*: 222)

The basis of Barth's critical evaluation of the power of mammon is Jesus' important imperative: "You cannot love God and mammon" (Matt 6:24; Luke 16:13). These texts present mammon as an alternative *Christos* to Jesus Christ. God and mammon are two competing objects of love and devotion. The power and false lordship of mammon, therefore, is all-embracing, perhaps even more so than leviathan, as it seeks to have control over all people's intentions and actions in their personal and communal lives. Since the kingdom of God remains present but not yet fully realized, Barth claims that even in our attempts to "pray for liberation" from its power, "we people are not free in relation to mammon" (*CL*: 223). Yet we must distinguish and discern the claims of both God and mammon over our lives, and not presume that through our resolute will and actions we can be freed from its power. Barth is realistic about the monetary grip that mammon has over people's lives, including Christians. In a money-driven economy, mammon usurps other areas of human life, drawing people away from God's covenantal promise. It convinces people that they can find their freedom and security through economic resources and possessions, which left unchecked, will continue to spiral out of control.

Furthermore, unlike the world of Scripture, where mammon is indirectly linked with money, in today's world we cannot escape the reality of the power of money, as mammon. "Even as a material good, money had and has only symbolic value. So, even though a comprehensive meaning of mammon (e.g., "riches" or "wealth") extends beyond money, the power of money best captures the "symbolic value" and power of mammon in today's world (*CL*: 224).

> Money is a flexible but powerful instrument, which supposedly handled by man, in reality follows its own law. In a thousand ways it can establish some opinions and even convictions and suppress others. It can create brutal facts. It can cause the market to rise and then to fall again. It can arrest this crisis and cause another. It can serve peace yet pursue cold war even in the midst of peace. It can make ready for a bloody war and finally bring it about. It can bring provisionally paradise here and the corresponding provisional hell there. It does not have to do all these things, but it can. It can and does: not money as such, but the money that man thinks he possesses, although in truth it possess him, and it does so because he wants to have it without God and thus create a vacuum in which this intrinsically harmless but useful fiction becomes an absolutist demon, and man himself can only be its football and slave. Mammon, then is no reality, and yet it is one—and what a reality!—not to mention what happens when Mammon meets and joins and comes to terms with that other demon Leviathan, political absolutism. (*CL*: 224)

Barth remains aware of the potential "takeover" of various spheres of life by the enlarging power of money in the world. Unlike gold and silver coins, which, as raw materials, hold more than symbolic value, paper money's real power is symbolic, namely as an instrument to acquire commodities. "In all its inner worthlessness," says Barth, "revealed in the glorious discovery of paper money and especially in purely book transactions, money is, if not *the*, at least *a* capital epitome and standard not merely of economic values, but of all human values, for what can one not buy for money"(*CL*: 224)? Money becomes a demonic "power" that defines, alters, and orients human behavior. The falsification of money's power is grounded in the "conventional fiction" that having money appears as a person's "real achievement," a "symbol of his ability," and his "measurable economic capacity." Money itself has no value, but it is the "classic representation of real values" including the values of human dignity and worth. "Economically speaking he is worth what money he either has, or earns through his work, or has prospects of (e.g., by inheritance). In short, he *is* to the degree that he can pay, that he is credit-worthy" (*CL*: 223). Indeed, personal dignity is measured by its "monetary sale value." Mammon corrupts persons to assume that economic power, either in actual possessions or credit, becomes the means to gain personal security and freedom. Yet this remains a lie and deception that keeps humanity from discovering true human security and freedom in and through the covenant of grace.

Ideology

The third power mentioned in *The Christian Life* is "ideology." This remains the most inclusive of all the powers since it can incorporate various political and economic frameworks into its larger ideological structure. Barth discusses ideology as power that "seizes power" of human thinking and becomes a "fiction," "illusion," as well as "lying spirit" (*CL*: 233). In the beginning, ideologies serve people and society by helping people determine what course of action to take that best serves society. However, this original "wonderful ability" of the human spirit is corrupted when persons seek to separate from God, and become "independent of the living Spirit of God." What was once linked to the freedom of human spirit and imagination is now characterized by "a distinctive numbness, hardening, and rigidity." Now these "remarkable ideas," no longer remain "provisional and transitory" or "relative," but acquire a state of "permanent normatively" or "absoluteness" (*CL*: 225). What were originally considered as "hypotheses" that could be questioned, discussed, expanded, or altered now becomes absolute and rigid "theses." "His ideal becomes an idol" (*CL*: 225). With the transition from relative to absolute, from hypothesis to thesis, and from freedom to bondage, these sets of ideas become an ideology. It is at this dangerous stage when ideologies persuade persons to stand against others, and justify their own existence *apart* from God.

Although ideologies bind people together into a kind of pseudo-community, it also drives them away from others who disagree or have alternative viewpoints. An ideologically driven person naturally seeks to convert others to her viewpoint, which further seeks to eliminate the "other's" personal freedom and individuality. Ideologies create "enemies," says Barth, because they are enlarged to be a "solution not only to the personal problems of his own life but to each and all of the problems of the world" (*CL*: 225). They are inherently conflictive, utopian, and potentially violent. Still, for all of their power, Barth consistently reminds us that ideologies generally do not become absolutely hegemonic. As fallen powers, they are not "omnipotent intellectual forces" but "very potent ones" that contribute to historical development and change (*CL*: 226). Even though ideologies seem to gain victory for a period of time, their power often remains short-lived over constructive force of the human imagination. "Man does not live only as he thinks" (*CL*: 225). It is a blessing that persons continue to alter or develop new ideologies, based on beliefs and social practices, as society itself changes. Whether persons acknowledge it or not, they are in "transition from one ideology to another," as they move from "old ideas to new" (*CL*: 225). Thankfully, persons and communities get bored with only one viewpoint so they often move from one ideology to another thus limiting the power of one particular ideology.

The substance of ideologies is often recognizable in human speech slogans, and propaganda. When words describing some aspect of human existence are universalized, absolutized, and systemized as a thesis or theory, these words becomes an ideology. Wherever, Barth says, "we find an '*ism*' there lurks an ideology," and with it, the potential demise of human freedom. So, ideas become "idealism," history becomes "historicism," and freedom becomes "liberalism." "In every field '*ism*' shows that one view, one concept, one figure in the field of human life, one possibility of human outlook and action, has assumed the role of regulator and dictator in relation to all the rest, and that round this principle a system has developed in face of which man is more or less on the point of losing his freedom or has already lost it" (*CL*: 226).[7] The Christian must be cautious of every "ism" as a potential ideology, and every "ian" as a disciple of an ideology that seeks to convert one to an ideological cause. Moreover, ideologies can be found in "slogans or catchwords." Slogans are "not designed to teach, instruct, or convince the hearer or the reader." Rather, they limit reflection and deliberation and instead require strict obedience. "Slogans are simply vents with whose help ideologies surface and in the form of loud whistles call for general applause and acknowledgment" (*CL*: 226). Many slogans are tied to a particular "ism" like nationalism, communism, or liberalism, or to some form of solidarity movement like "Germany, wake up," "Workers of the world unite," or "Equal rights for all" (*CL*: 226). Slogans combine words in such a way that they shape an entire way of perception and practice, such as "the American way of life," "the free world," or "historical-critical method." Slogans, on the surface, seem innocent enough, but underneath they have the power to shape people's attitudes, beliefs, and values, especially in ways the divide them from others and the larger community.

Lastly, Barth mentions perhaps the most deceptive and damaging form of ideology, namely "propaganda." Like slogans, propaganda is gener-

---

7. In this section, Barth further mentions numerous political, economic, religious, and philosophical ideologies, including socialism, communism, capitalism, conservativism, radicalism, Marxism, Stalinism, biblicism, confessionalism, pietism, christocentrism, monotheism, pantheism, atheism, and numerous other "isms" (*CL*: 226).

Witness and the Powers 287

ated so that it may convert others to a particular point of view, however, it far more deceptive in its influence and power over human beliefs and practices. He writes:

> One should note that the truth needs no propaganda and does not engage in it. As the truth, it simply speaks for itself and opposes falsehood. Propaganda is a sure sign that what is at issue is not the truth but an ideology which needs it, to whose nature it corresponds, and which is not ashamed to make use of that, as we see today and the propaganda of furtive anti-Semitism, of communism and anticommunism, and also of moral rearmament, which expressly boasts that it champions and proclaims an ideology and will cause it to triumph. If only we could say of the church that it does not engage in propaganda! To the extent that it does it makes itself unworthy of the truth to which it must bear witness by obviously confusing it with an ideology and thinking it can handle it as such. It would be as well for all of us to realize that as we are daily washed around by so much open and hidden propaganda, we too are undoubtedly caught in the series of more than one of these destructive powers the spirit. (*CL*: 227)

Behind this passage is no doubt Barth's own experiences with the rise of Nazism in Germany in the 1930s, and how the "special ministry of propaganda" led by Joseph Goebbels, shaped German popular opinion through the radio, press, cinema, and theater. Through the power of advertising, propaganda seeks to integrate the masses into one *weltanschauung* through its use of apologetics and polemics. It uses tools of persuasion to present a world that is "black and white" rather than grey, and in so doing, states clearly who the insiders are and who the outsiders are. It is a tool of separation and oppression. "Propaganda can be direct or indirect, the crude work of the village smith or the refined work of the skilled mechanic, totally ingenious and well-meaning but also poisoned and bitter, skillful on one hand and unskillful on the other" (*CL*: 227). For Barth, propaganda will always exist as long as people have the means to communicate ideas to others. Propaganda will always find new innovative means by which it can spread its power around the globe, whether in print or in visual images.

Whether ideologies are macro or micro, that is whether they are grand metanarratives like liberalism or socialism, or the micro ideologies of slogans or propaganda, they all promise freedom and solidarity through absolute loyalty in thought and practice. In our sinfulness, persons use ideology as a power *against* others who disregard its power. Ideologies become tyrannical and restrict its followers to become unreflective "disciples" and "functionaries" (*CL*: 226). Like many postmodernists, Barth discredits modern foundationalist ideologies by stripping them of their metanarrative status and their power to oppress innocent victims. Yet, unlike them, he evaluates ideology theologically through the language of sin, forgiveness, and reconciliation, and not by class consciousness or cultural hegemony. Christian social witness cannot commit itself to any ideological cause as "good," but only to the Word of God, which shatters all human ideological proposals. Barth rightly rejects any absolutist claims of ideology that usurps the Word of God of its legitimate authority over the Christian life; Christians stand against ideologies that stand *between* them and God. Being free from ideology allows Christians to remain "nonconformists" and strategically independent from all views, which positively allows them to serve others in the world. Christians, he says, may "speak very conservatively today and very progressively or even revolutionarily tomorrow—or vice versa"(*AS*: 92). "Christian politics are always bound to seem strange," he adds, "incalculable and surprising in the eyes of the world—otherwise they would not be Christian" (*AS*: 92). Christian politics is neither ideologically liberal nor conservative, but stands as an *alternative* to all ideological positions. In the same way, the church rejects all cultural religion, which remains shaped by particular social and cultural ideologies. Only by standing as an *alternative* to all ideological positions, the church can be true to its confession as a "confessing church."

So where does that leave us with ideology and the other powers? Barth has no illusions that the power of ideology will be eradicated by better ideas or worldviews, just as he thinks that mammon and leviathan can be replaced with a new economic social order or a better government. There is no utopian fix for humanity's problems. This is why it is unrealistic to place one's hope in anything other than God's action as the means to annihilate the powers. These ideological, political, and economic powers existed long before the modern symbols of propaganda, totalitarianism, and paper money. Again, only by God's action to be with and for us in Jesus Christ, thus establishing the covenant of reconciliation, is it possible for us, in our actions, to seek to respond responsibly within this covenant relationship. Christians must understand that God has chosen us to be *free* from the powers and seek to live in responsible freedom and witness. Being a witness to God's gracious action is the Christians' primary responsibility. Yet, this witness is active not passive, and it is social not individual. How does the Christian engage in active social witness? First, social witness seeks to distinguish between the freedom of God's command and the enslaving force of the powers which seeks to annihilate human freedom. This involves resistance against the powers. Still, Christian confidence rests not in our ability to fight off the powers, but in Christ's victory over them. This leads to the second task of witness, namely to take small steps toward objectively making a difference in world. This leads to specific actions in the world toward freedom, justice, and peace. Christians are empowered to make a difference only because we are empowered to be witnesses to the fact that Christ has defeated the powers.

Chthonic Powers

In contrast to the spiritual powers of leviathan, mammon, and ideology, the chthonic powers emerge from the context of the "physical sphere of the created cosmos," including the interaction of persons, communities, societies, and nations within the world (*CL*: 227). Unlike the earlier set of powers, which are rooted in ideas or theories, these are rooted in human work, activities, and experiences. The origin of these powers emerges from human creativity and freedom itself, yet over time, these various human creations ironically seek to gain control over their creator. That is, originally people have the power to set free the chthonic powers to serve humanity's needs and desires, but in the end, it is these human needs and desires that serves the powers. It is the creative person, says Barth, that

> is the one who discovers them and sees how useful they can be in his service. It is his spirit that triumphs in their exploitation. It is he who is at the helm, who pulls the levers, who presses the knobs. Nevertheless they automatically and autonomously rumble and work and roll and roar and clatter outside him, without him, past him and over him. He finds that he himself is subject to their laws, which he has foreseen, to their power, which he as released. . . . In simplifying and easing his life, they also complicate it and make it more difficult. They take away his little anxieties but create new and bigger ones. They seem to promise courage and a greater zest for life, but increased worry about life is the fulfillment of their promise. Like the spiritual forces, but in a way this is felt more directly, the chthonic powers, which for a change draw downward instead of up, serve in and of themselves to bind the man who has broken free from God, to put him under obligation to tyrannize him, to lead him where he does not want to go [cf. John 21:18], to rob him

of his freedom under the pretext and appearance of granting every kind of freedom. Their lordship is certainly not an unconditional one. It has only a limited sphere. But like the sphere of Leviathan and Mammon and the ideologies, this sphere is as big as the sphere of life of fallen man as such. (*CL*: 228–29)

The most obvious example of chthonic powers, says Barth, is technology. In *The Christian Life*, Barth chooses to discuss other examples of the powers by referring to fashion, sports, entertainment (and pleasure), and transportation (speed). Although he doesn't discuss technology in this section, he does refer to it in other writings, including in *CD* III/4, where he discusses its particular affect on war and violence. It is the development of "modern technology" that has altered how we ought to think about war. That is, its "methods, instruments, and machines" has blurred the distinction between combatants and noncombantants; with massive bombing war will now extend "conflict to the civilian population" (*CD* III/4: 453). What this means is that technology, as an end in itself, has altered our understanding of human needs and morality. "The technical mastery which goes beyond what is vitally necessary," explains Barth, "which at bottom has its meaning and purpose in itself, and which, in order to exist and augment itself, must always evoke new and doubtful needs, inevitably becomes the monster which in many ways we now see it to be, so that finally and ridiculously it is little more than a technique and destruction, of war and annihilation" (*CD* III/4: 395). Technology is a power that has control over human freedom. It has, furthermore, greatly contributed to the dehumanization and mechanization of labor and the "spiritual impoverishment of the artisan." As a power technology seeks to reduce human work to a "form of demonic power" which "devours" people forcing them to be "condemned to purely mechanical employment" (*CD* III/4: 547). For all of its negativity, technology, as simply a product of human creativity and power, is not "soulless" but can be used as an instrument to benefit humanity and the world. As an instrument for good or evil, technology remains simply a power that persons can use for their desired ends.

Another power is cultural fashion and taste. Great art, music, sculpture, and poetry can withstand the test of time, but fashion and cultural tastes often change without any standard or norm of excellence. Barth admits that fashion and taste appears as a rather "trivial" power, yet it is the underlying mysterious phenomena why fashion and taste seem to have such influence in shaping the day-to-day existence of personal and social life. "Who inspires and directs these processes, which are not a matter of indifference to the feeling for life and all that it implies" (*CL*: 229). Who are these people that set the cultural trends for people within society to follow? Why this particular trend and not another? Why should "this industry be so lucrative"? Persons are not entirely free if they cannot remain indifferent to the various cultural trends that shape personal appearance, clothing, lifestyle, hairstyles, and so on. Rejecting this power elicits the possibility of being ostracized or rejected by others in society. As another practical embodiment of mammon, it risks turning persons into commodities by making them an extension of the popular "labels" that they choose to wear or not wear. We become the clothes we wear; we change our identity with new suit, dress, or hairstyle. Moreover, another related power is the influence of sports on society. Like cultural fashion it has the power to shape modern personal and social identity. "What is behind the enthusiasm of millions of sporting fans who watch the players with such passionate and often frenzied excitement? What has made the industrializing and commercializing of sport so clearly remunerative" (*CL*: 229)? Barth uses the example of the football World Cup to explain how the mood of an entire nation can be either elevated to ecstasy or fall to depths of despair when their national team wins or loses. "Is there a measure representation here"? What is the true human need behind the desirers to make "heroes" and celebrities of athletes? Is it a "primitive need" for success, achievement, or power that draws us toward the sports icon? Why is it necessary that the Olympic Games, an international sporting event, be displayed as a "regular cultic form of worship, praise, laud, and thanksgiving? So many facts, questions, and riddles" (*CL*: 230)! In this aggrandizement of sports, we have a "special form of derangement," in which "man has lost and continually loses his true majesty" (*CL*: 230). People inevitably support, encourage, and promote the powers of fashion, taste, and sports, yet behind their backs, these influences seek to have power over them, and with it, their own human dignity, as most fully reveled in Jesus Christ.

Another chthonic power involves how human pleasure and entertainment, sought as an end in itself, deprives humanity of the freedom to enjoy these activities as they truly are, that is, as expressions of human joy. Everyone enjoys human pleasure and entertainment, whether found in "companionship," or in "sport," "jazz," "cinema," "television," "reading," "alcohol," or "sex." "The real point," says Barth, "is that in order to have the enjoyment sought in them, people have to be joyous" (*CL*: 230). This explains the fact that when persons attempt to find joy in the pleasure itself, they often afterwards feel "uneasy, tense, and hectic" and have a "sour or bitter taste left on the palate." The "thirst for desire" for more pleasure can never be quenched. There is nothing inherently evil in human pleasure, entertainment, sports, fashion, or technology in themselves, but only when they become independent of God's moral law as the form of the gospel. These "forces" are human creations to serve the integrity and dignity of the human person and community, but when these "forces" become "powers" they "possess" and "oppress" human freedom. Moreover, the same pattern exists in the "field of transportation." Modern technology has made it possible for there to be faster means for travel and movement, whether by ship, train, car, or airliner. It appears on the surface that technological development in travel, unlike war, has as whole benefited humanity. Yet, the deeper question is: "What do they propose to do with the time and energy saved?" "How far is the enhance speed of our movements to and fro really necessary or rewarding?" (*CL*: 231). How has it affected the value of personal relations to others, one's community, or one's environment?

> Do not modern travelers rush undeviatingly past a hundred noteworthy things, blind where their forefathers could see, and perhaps flying over them altogether in the void? Has life really become easier and not harder through our happily achieved accelerations? Meanwhile, we suppress the common complaint of the pedestrian of what is to become of him (initially because he lets himself be given a ride so gladly). We note with concern how so many homeless motorcars are choking our overcrowded roads and streets. We have noted the evening lines of traffic moving slowly enough on the roads leading into and out of our cities. We ask ourselves timidly where the increasing traffic, making a mock of highway planning and its many devices, will not finally prove to be the biggest obstacle to efficient transportation, and whether in the new future the same problem might not arise in the air as well. And how can we fail to note the daily lists of traffic accidents and their victims, who total numbers (in 1960, 65,000 in Europe) have already reached and even surpassed the number lost in war? We regard it as very dubious comfort that their growth is not so bad in relation to the increase in the number of vehicles now on the roads. We also note the devastation of the countryside as freeways cut ruthlessly through arable land, pastures, and whole villages. We ask whether the speed that motorized man is allowed is not bought too dearly in view of its obvious hostility to life. (*CL*: 231–32)

This hectic pace of modern life is a "wheel" from which we cannot escape. The questions remain: where is it this frantic life going, and why can we not slow down? More than perhaps any other chthonic power, this addiction to speed has become our fate. It has led to "[T]he bondage of the will!" Since Barth's time persons have become more reliant on technology as it applies to transportation, but even more so, regarding information and communication. As technology has shifted toward the development of personal computers, and the further development of the Internet and cell phones, we now have instant communication with others. Still, we might ask, what has this technology done for us? Have these new forms of technology, Barth asks, "given us a more open, profound, fruitful, beautiful, and kindly view of the cosmos around us, a more vital one than that of Goethe?" Again, like the other powers, rather than rejecting all technology as evil, Barth assumes that we need to readjust the hectic pace of our lives, so that we remain faithful in our discipleship and witness. God is sovereign regardless of how fast we move or communicate from place to place; Christ still remains Lord whether we travel by "car or on foot" (*CL*: 232). Again, we must recall, that the powers only remain a tyrannical force if one fails to note that Christ indeed has won the victory over the powers, and it remains the task of Christians and the church to bear witness to their falleness.

HEGEMONY AND THE POWERS

Christian social ethics is obviously aware of the various powers that promote destruction on persons and communities, including the one's Barth mentions. Yet, for many ethicists Barth's theological discussion of the powers detracts from the social-scientific driven descriptive task, and the practical and transformative task of social action. The direct line of reasoning from the descriptive to the practical task can all be accomplished without any, or very little, discussion of God's agency or action. The overall assumption in much contemporary Christian ethics is that the human subject is a free and independent moral subject, who remains the primary moral agent and *power* in the world. Thus, if there is evil in the world, it is our task as persons to resist and eradicate it; it is our task to *transform* the world. This assumption runs very deep in Christian ethics largely because of the underlying modernist beliefs in human power and progress. It is true that much discussion about social transformation in Christian thought is also rooted in the Spirit's agency in the world. There is an intermingling of human and divine agency to such an extent that it is not clear whether it is actually people or the Spirit who is the "transformative agent" in the world. In these accounts of Christian ethics there really is no theology of correspondence or relation of divine and human agency. It is Christologically vacuous. It relies more on the modernist assumptions of human power and progress, rather than the incarnation for its radical accounts of Christian social ethics.

Power and Agency

In postmodernity, we are more confident in our knowledge of the potential risks that affect us, than with the means or ability to eradicate their potential hegemony. As mentioned earlier, in Zygmunt Bauman's words, it is essentially a "discrepancy between demand and supply that has been recently described as the 'ethical crisis of postmodernity.'"[8] So, we are aware of the powers that endanger human freedom, but we also seem powerless to do anything about them. In short, in postmodernity there is a crisis of human agency. Are persons free to resist the powers, or are they captive to their potential hegemony? The problem of moral (and political) agency is one of the central issues in current social theory. With this in mind, there is important overlap between the theological view of the powers and contemporary social theory. Yet, many Christian ethicists rely more on the social sciences, rather than theology, as the vehicle by which to explain the destructive force of the powers in contemporary life. In doing so, they absorb or incorporate much of the ideological baggage that remains inseparably linked with these social descriptions and evaluations.

How do these secular descriptions and evaluations affect the strategy of Christian ethics? In answering this question, we turn again to the topic of globalization, as an illustration of how Christian ethics can become ideological by presupposing social scientific descriptions and evaluations. For this, we must look at the development of ideology within the discourse of globalization. It is perhaps ironic that in the early 1960s, when Barth calls ideology one the spiritual powers, social scientists were beginning to talk about the "end of ideology." In 1960, sociologist Daniel Bell, in *The End of Ideology*, argued that the old tired extremist ideologies, like Marxism and unregulated capitalism, were succumbing to a moral, rational, and less divisive "third way" that practiced democratic politics, a mixed economy,

---

8. Bauman, *Postmodern Ethics*, 17.

and the welfare state.[9] Yet, with a sudden upsurge of ideological politics in the later 1960s and 1970s, Bell's thesis became less tenable. Not only did the ideologies of the Cold War generate conflicts like the Vietnam War, but also the various protest movements during and after the war, such as the Civil Rights movement, the antiwar movement, the feminist movement, and later the environmental movement. All these ideological movements point to the fact that the tired old ideologies, particularly of the political left, remained alive and well a century later. However, with the collapse of Communism in the Soviet Union and Eastern Europe in the late 1980s and early 1990s, new momentum emerged again for Bell's thesis, this time in Francis Fukuyama's 1992 book *The End of History and the Last of Man*.[10] Like Bell, Fukuyama postulated the emergence of a "deideologized world," but unlike Bell, Fukuyama argued that the end of ideology means not the convergence of socialism and liberal capitalism, but the unabashed victory of economic and political liberalism. Fukuyama predicted the spread of the free market, consumerist culture, new information technology, and political democracy as the "final form" of human government. Later, Fukuyama pointed to the growing trend of globalization as the confirmation of his earlier thesis; indeed, with the United States as the sole superpower it makes it inevitable that the power of Americanization will accompany globalization.[11] The fact that Fukuyama has insisted that globalization has ushered in the "end of ideology" has fueled a return of ideological analysis of the economic globalism or global capitalism, which has led many social scientists to proclaim that economic globalization ("globalism" or "neoliberalism") is often seen as the dominant ideology or hegemony of our time.

As we saw earlier in chapter 4, globalization, in theory, can include discussions of not only the economic, but also the political, cultural, and social. It can become an all-embracing, even totalitarian, framework for social ethics, if it remains linked only with one particular ideological framework. This is why it is important, as discussed earlier, to draw a distinction between its "broad" and "narrow" categories, and be cautious of reducing globalization discourse to the ideological battles between the pro-globalists and the anti-globalists. The former "Davos culture" remains in favor of the spread of free markets around the globe, and the latter "faculty club culture"

---

9. Bell, *End of Ideology*.
10. Fukuyama, *End of History*.
11. Fukuyama, "Second Thoughts," 16–44.

remains vehemently against this global capitalist ideology. The pro-globalists claim that economic neoliberalization bring greater opportunity, freedom, cooperation, benefit, and democratic government. In contrast, the anti-globalists present global capitalism as the most dominant hegemonic power and of our age. This critique is governed by two basic problems created by the global free market. The first we may call the problem of *power*, which assumes that market and corporate hegemony enshrines greed, deprives communities and nation-states of power, and destroys political, social, and cultural freedom. In so doing, it destroys political agency and possibility for true political democracy. The second is the problem of *justice*. This demonstrates how global capitalism creates economic inequality, trade imbalances, insecurity, and financial injustices, while lowering real wages and labor standards, causing a global race to the bottom while endangering life itself through environmental destruction. In both cases anti-globalists challenge powerful international agencies like the WTO and the IMF, multinational corporations, and political forces like the Washington consensus. Still, since the economic crisis of 2008, the world has dramatically changed, which reframes the debate along different lines. Just as 9/11 changed the way people thought about the threat of violence, the global economic financial crisis of 2008 led to a restructuring analysis of the threat of economic collapse. As stated in chapter 4, what is needed is movement beyond the ideologically laden theories of the pro-globalists and anti-globalists toward true global economic cooperation, which concentrates on the creation of wealth, economic justice, and sustainable development.

The most common approach to the study of neoliberal globalism is the legacy of liberation theology, which seeks to use theological descriptions as subversive beliefs and practices that challenge power. The subversive power of resistance has long been a theme in liberation and feminist theology. It is evident, for example, in two recent works in feminist Christian ethics on globalization. Drawing from the social sciences, these books approach the tension between hegemony and moral agency largely from the standpoint of the social sciences. So, Cynthia Moe-Lobeda argues that the globalization "disables moral agency by disabling democracy," while Rebecca Todd Peters argues that a "democratized understanding of power ought to serve as the context for exercising moral agency."[12] Central to both books, therefore, is

---

12. Moe-Lobeda, *Healing a Broken World*, 4; and Peters, *In Search of the Good Life*, 23. Nevertheless, there are some differences in these books. Peters rarely speaks about God's agency at all other than calling the church and society to act toward a more just society.

the assumption that globalization is more than potentially hegemonic, as it thoroughly corrupts moral and political agency, which makes the search for the common good extremely difficult. The way out of this morass is through using the power of subversive and resistant political agency, which makes it possible for individuals and society to be transformed from within its own structures. Similar arguments have been developed by many other authors including Ulrich Duchrow, who has insisted for some time for the church to declare its *status confessionis* against globalization. Not unlike the issues of National Socialism and Apartheid, the church must be a "confessing church" against the tyranny of evil. Duchrow and others have influenced collective bodies like the World Council of Churches (WCC) to write documents on the negative impact of globalization and to call for resistance and change through empowering democratic politics. In these various writings, it is assumed that "radical" changes are needed in the political process for persons and communities to live in ways that are ecologically sustainable. Regarding this, in their recent book *Property for People, Not for Profit*, Duchrow and Franz Hinkelammert write:

> So this is the difference between now and the ages of National Socialism and apartheid: it was intentional, visible and audible acts which caused exclusiveness and murder, separation and discrimination, while in the global market it is the indirect effects of an intentional system that promises wealth, while admitting to be absolute and without alternative, which destroy life and are causing the deaths of people and nature. . . . Consequently, it is not enough to attack the present disaster in purely moral terms and attribute it primarily to the intentional evil actions of the actors. Instead we must realize that making private property an absolute necessity leads to the destruction of human and nature life—especially if coupled with the capital mechanisms for money accumulation in the absolute market, leading to the systematic reduction of political oversight regulating the economy according to the criterion of the common good.[13]

In contrast, Moe-Lobeda presents a stronger theological argument by recovering Martin Luther's notion of the Holy Spirit's immanent dwelling presence. The power of the Spirit's indwelling presence, then, becomes the basis for the church a "subversive" account of moral agency that can eventually lead to changes in political agency and democratic politics.

13. Duchrow and Hinkelammert, *Property for People*, 210–11. Also see Duchrow, *Global Economy*.

Obviously, not all Christian ethicists would accept these authors' radical proposal regarding the neo-Marxist elimination of private property. We must be cautious about the underlying commitment to ideological ideas that permeate books that synthesize theological claims with neo-Marxist ideology or any ideology for that matter. Many books on globalization, including those mentioned here, often address social and economic problems through the lens of social analysis, without fully distinguishing this from a theological viewpoint committed to resisting ideology—as a *power*. Christian witness means seeking a non-ideological perspective that, in fact, challenges all ideological perspectives, whether left or right, liberal or conservative, or pro-globalist or anti-globalist. It remains very difficult for Christian social ethics to remain non-ideological, for to do so would imply committing itself to certain Christological assumptions about the relation of human and divine agency. For example, to argue that capitalism's hegemony can be alleviated through establishing moral agency through a revitalized democracy, simply ignores a theological account of moral agency that relates divine and human action together in Jesus Christ, but is extended by analogy to human action more generally. God first acts in and through the covenant of grace, which provides the framework for human beings to respond by invoking God's presence into the realm of human freedom. The error of anti-globalism is that it too easily denies the mediating divine-human agency in Jesus Christ, and separates these two-forms of agency, which makes humans the central actors in the world. Consequently, what is often missing in the strategy of Christian social ethics is any discussion of divine agency by itself, or how it is related or corresponds to human agency. Sadly many Christian ethicists today fail to perceive of God as a *living* God that actively engages persons and the world; their sole concentration on human agency leaves little room for any theological account of divine agency. These works generally draw from the social sciences for their account of agency and hegemony, which presumes that hegemonies are destroyed through human political freedom and radical political action. These works continue to present the modern theological dichotomy that God is either "absent" from the world and that we must go about changing the world by ourselves, or that God is an "immanent" power that is guiding local communities of resistance, liberation, and change. God cannot accomplish anything directly but only through human beings who are empowered by God's Spirit to instigate political change. In other words, God's agency remains contingent upon human agency, thus, the only real power in the world is human beings—not God.

The fallacy in these sociological or political accounts of moral agency is that they reject any form of divine agency in the world to which human agency can correspond in ethical witness and responsible action. This fallacy, of course, is most deeply Christological, in that it falsely assumes that we discover the real "humanity" by looking at sinful humanity in *isolation* from the humanity of Jesus Christ. Once this anthropocentric framework is carried over into Christian ethics, it eventually *separates* divine and human agency, or ironically, it *identifies* divine agency with human agency. Following Barth's dialectical reasoning, we say that the first error places God outside the realm of human action, and limits God's agency to that of the creator of nature and the moral law. This *Deistic* error could be found in various versions of the analogy of being, natural law, and natural theology. The opposite error is when God's action is strictly identified *with* human action, so that human action strictly embodies God's immanent action in the world, usually through the agency of the Spirit. In Barth's judgment, this error was rooted the liberal theology of Schleiermacher, which became embodied not only in utopian social movements like Religious Socialism and Communism but also in the German nationalism before and after World War I, and later in the German Christian movement. In both these extremes of separation and identification of divine and human agency, it is the human subject that becomes the central agent of deliberation and action in the world.

Secular Words and the Word of God

We have seen how social theory ought to be distinguished and related to our understanding of theological ethics. Once we have clearly distinguished secular social theory from the theological, we may then move to relate them together. At this point, therefore, we must explore further how these theories can be seen, not as foundational arguments, but as "secular parables" of truth. Not all ideas derived from social theory are antithetical to our theological viewpoint. In our earlier discussion of social and ethical theory, we came across ideas that may elucidate and contribute to our understanding of Christian ethics as witness. Two concepts in particular are risk society and hegemony. What is risk society? To reiterate, the side effects of modernity, once hidden from critical view, are now becoming real and self-evident to expert and non-expert alike. A risk is simply what persons seek to *objectify* and *personify* as threats to human life. Sociologist Anthony Giddens reminds us that our principle challenges today are the human-created risks rather than the external risks outside human control. These risks, says Ulrich Beck, often remain hidden by the powerful institutions and expert languages, which remain hegemonic. For human societies to engage in adequate risk assessment and evaluation, and the "freeing of moral agency" they must rely on various lay languages of the common people, which emerges from particular cultural and religious traditions. "An initial insight is key:" says Beck, "when it comes to hazards, no one is expert—especially not the experts."[14] As risks become more apparent, say Giddens and Beck, specific languages, like religion, are crucial for the comprehensive analysis of risk and for common courses of action in addressing their threatening power. Once the risks are *named* people can begin working together politically to resist and overcome these risks. This reflexive awareness or knowledge of risks gives humanity a reason to be hopeful and optimistic that they can accomplish positive political outcomes. An ethics of responsibility, to our knowledge of risks, then provides the foundation for *political* agency, which in turn, becomes the positive power for changing society. This more positive account of reflexive moral agency, however, is always in tension with the potential hegemony of the threats and risks against human freedom. There is no guarantee that humanity can ever change its current situation.

The tension between power and agency further leads to the concept of "hegemony." The idea of "cultural hegemony" is first developed in the early twentieth century by the neo-Marxist Antonio Gramsci.[15] In many ways, Gramsci sought to develop a concept of ideology that split the difference between Karl Marx and Karl Mannheim. Suffice it to say, Marx and Mannheim reflect the two central divergent intellectual traditions of ideology.[16] The first *epistemological* tradition is ultimately rooted in *The*

---

14. Beck, *World at Risk*, 35. For a more extensive argument along these lines, see Wynne, "May the Sheep Safely Graze," 44–83.

15. Gramsci, *Selections from Prison Notebooks*. This discussion of Gramsci is also dependent on the descriptions found in Eagleton, *Ideology*, 112–23.

16. See Marx and Engels, *German Ideology* and Mannheim, *Ideology and Utopia*. Regarding these two traditions, Terry Eagleton writes: "Roughly speaking, one central lineage, from Hegel to Marx to Georg Lukács and some later Marxist thinkers, has been much preoccupied with ideas of true and false cognition, with ideology as illusion, but a couple of distortion and mystification; whereas the alternative tradition of thought has been less epistemological than sociological, concerned more with a function of ideas

Germany Ideology, by Karl Marx and Friedrich Engels. Marx and Engels redefined "ideology" as the particular philosophy of the bourgeois that refuses to challenge the injustices of the real world, but masks and sublimates these problems by offering an *illusionary* view of the world. This tradition rests upon a "hermeneutics of suspicion," which presumes that ideology is a *false* set of ideas that claim to present a general universal truth but instead remain a device for the economically and politically powerful (bourgeois) to oppress the powerless (proletariat). These ideologies, including religion, further alienate persons from themselves until the unjust power relations are altered through radical change. Therefore, this negative and oppressive ideology has to be unmasked and replaced with a philosophy that brings liberation—the revolution of the proletariat and the formation of the classless society. In contrast, the *sociological* view is developed in Karl Mannheim's book *Ideology and Utopia*. Unlike Marx and Engels, Mannheim offers an all-encompassing account of ideology as a *weltanschauung*, a world-view including conscious or unconscious beliefs, habits, and social practices, which all societies naturally develop through their own ongoing development. Hence, ideologies differ from culture to culture and even within cultures; conflict over ideologies is common in pluralistic societies. They are less illusionary and false than simply myopic and shortsighted; yet, for all of their apparent benignity, they can also be extremely dangerous, especially when they attempt to violently establish a set of power relations in a society that oppresses the powerless and eviscerates personal and communal freedom. So, although ideologies are generally *neutral* they can become oppressive, and it here when societies seek to be transformed by new more humanistic ideology, generated by the social desire for "utopia." It is utopia, then, that drives society to form new ideologies.

With this in mind, Gramsci is similar to Marx in saying that cultural power is hegemonic because it is then used to establish or reinforce a set of ideological beliefs and practices. Yet, Gramsci is also similar to Mannheim in saying that power is cultural because it emerges from the cultural beliefs and practices of a given society. Splitting this difference, Gramsci argues that hegemony in society is not just political, nor does it exist as an alien and oppressive ideology of the bourgeois, but it exists as a cultural power that emerges from social beliefs and practices. Gramsci's account presumes that conflict between ideologies is inevitable, and that the cultural hege-

within social life than with their reality or unreality." Eagleton, *Ideology*, 3. For further discussion, see ibid., 70–91; 107–10.

mony established by the false, wrong, and ill-conceived ideologies must be replaced with a new cultural pattern of beliefs and practices. What makes cultural hegemony particularly difficult to unmask, is that it seemingly works *with* (not against) the "consent" of the proletariat. Hegemony occurs within the beliefs and social practices of society, which in turn, reinforce its ideological power over people's lives. Cultural hegemony is a two-way not a one-way street. This makes it possible to argue, for example, that the social practices of capitalism, like consumption, inevitably shape people's convictions (or lack thereof) about economic justice. This makes ideology a power that determines the *way* people live their lives and *what* they believe. What people need in order to resist this cultural hegemony is the reflexive capacity and political will to live and believe differently than what is propagated through the hegemonic power. Not unlike the social theory of risk, the freeing of moral agency comes through recognition of destructive power, and the alleviation of these risks or hegemonies comes through political agency—the power of democratic politics.

Before we simply accept these social theories as a correct interpretation of our current circumstances, we must again *relate* them to a theological framework. Should secular concepts like risk and hegemony be used in concert with a theological conception of the powers? In previous chapters, we have made distinctions between the two extreme approaches of synthesis and diastasis, while also using the *dialectical* logic of distinguishing and relating. This means that these concepts must be distinguished before they are either identified or separated. How can they be distinguished? Although risk and hegemony attempt to name the powers that threaten humanity, they fail to properly account for the underlying ambiguities caused by human alienation from God. In brief, these theories lack a doctrine of sin, which explains how humanity is estranged from its objective self-knowledge, including its own purpose and meaning. These secular ideas do nothing to challenge the anthropocentric assumption that we are our own "lords and masters" (*CL*: 214). This apparent freedom *from* God creates the illusion that humanity can create for itself its own "reflexive" powers, abilities, agencies, and possibilities separate from the divine source of all power. When any secular ideas attempt to unseat the Word from its primary seat of authority and claim too much, the result leads to synthesis and secular reductionism. That is, by claiming to be comprehensive, they are asserting their authority over human descriptions, experiences, and reasoning.

Nevertheless, this does not mean these theories should be rejected out of hand. These secular viewpoints can be related to a theological view that gives "precedence to the Word." One of the central themes of this book is that Christians have an obligation to seriously listen to the voices of others; we must "eavesdrop in the world at large" (*CD* IV/3: 117). "In principle," says Nigel Biggar, "Barth's theological ethics is inclusive of the data of human 'experience,' although it retains the right to challenge what that is assumed to be."[17] Avoiding the risk of esotericism, Christian moral discourse must determine whether human words, intentionally or not, give *witness* to the Word of God. This is possible because the Word of God *commanders* these secular words and gives them their true meaning. Said differently, it is the Word of God that brings together both the *divine* reality, to which Scripture bears witness, and the *human* reality of culture, including secular words that attempt to explain that reality. There are secular "parables of kingdom," Barth says, that are analogical to the witness of Scripture. Yet, they must be:

> in material agreement with it, illumine, accentuate or explain the biblical witness in a particular time in situation, thus confirming it in the deepest sense by helping to make it sure and concretely evident and certain. They can only be words which will lead the community more truly and profoundly than ever before to Scripture. . . . We refer, then, to the words in which the community, when it hears them, can find itself lightened, gladdened and encouraged in the execution of its own task. The community is not Atlas bearing the burden of the whole world on the shoulders. For all its dedication to the cause which it represents in the world, the cause is not its own, nor does the triumph of this cause depend upon it. But the One who has particularly entrusted His cause to it will see to it that it is not left to its own resources in championing it. Even within the world which opposes it, He will ensure that, as there are always acts of His rule in general, so, too, there will be raised up witnesses to its cause, which is really His. (*CD* IV/3: 115)

As long as secular words do not tempt the Christian community from straying from its task of bearing *witness* to the Word of God, they may be utilized for living according to that task. Secular words serve God's purposes and cause because God is their ruler. "All the powers and forces of the whole cosmos are subjected to Him as He was and is and will be this One who

---

17. Biggar, *Hastening that Waits*, 156.

accomplishes reconciliation and makes peace between God and man" (*CD* IV/3: 116). Secular languages, like risk and hegemony, create opportunities for Christian ethics to evaluate the ideological structure of the powers. Christian ethics has no choice but to define and resist the powers that endanger human life. Nevertheless, inasmuch as these words remain helpful, we must also recall that Barth said that "every idea or life-form will sooner or later prove a threat to man" (*CL*: 268). Only with God's eschatological action in Jesus Christ, including his victory over the powers, is it possible to be free from the power of ideology. Ideology seeks to be absolutely sacrosanct, demanding loyalty, while further demanding its adherents convert others to its viewpoint, while rejecting them if they disagree. Ideology always remains a temptation for theology, especially apologetic theology that seems intently interesting in translating the gospel into other languages.

Christus Victor and the Powers

We live in a world where the "lordless powers" continue to flourish, creating unnecessary political, economic, and ideological risks for humanity. The power of leviathan becomes visible in the risks of heightened nationalism, worldwide terrorism, and escalation of global violence. The power of mammon becomes visible in the risks of hegemonic neoliberalism, global economic crises, injustice, and poverty. Finally, the power of ideology becomes visible in the risks of global environmental crisis and climate change. These problems of global violence, economic collapse, and environmental climate change, in Ulrich Beck's words, are visible manifestations of a "world at risk." "Incalculable risks and manufactured insecurities resulting from the triumph of modernity mark the *conditio humana* at the beginning of the twenty-first century."[18] Since global risks make the challenge more difficult for any one particular nation or society, it is absolutely necessary for there to be movement toward global cooperation and humane cosmopolitanism. "When risk is perceived as omnipresent," says Beck, "three reactions are possible: *denial, apathy, or transformation.*"[19] If a "world at risk" is going to survive, it must choose transformation over denial, apathy, or nihilism. That is, the world must reject utopian ideologies of social or cultural emancipation, or alternatively dystopian worldviews of determinism and hopelessness, and instead look to the objectively real *risks* that threaten humanity such

18. Beck, *World at Risk*, 191.
19. Ibid., 48.

as worldwide violence, economic collapse, and environmental catastrophe. Nevertheless, our current postmodern (or late-modern), circumstances remain deeply ambiguous, double-edged, and even schizophrenic. Our social ethics hopes for a better future, but we also remain unsure about how we will be able to manage this transformation. The inherent problem is not with human ignorance of the risks, but with human agency, power, and will to actually change our destructive practices. We know what the risks are but seem paralyzed by our inability to change them. Like a squirrel in a cage, we appear trapped by our own deterministic choices and actions, and the naturalistic forces that surround and embody our lives as individuals within a "world at risk."

Without God's providential and reconciling purposes, without *Christus victor*, the only hope for humanity is that humanity itself, its beliefs and actions will be transformed into a progressive power for good. Christian witness rejects the modern doctrines of self-authenticating human freedom, and the deterministic doctrine that denies human freedom. Christian witness is against both the absolutizing of human freedom and human determinism. We might say that both of these are risks that endanger true human freedom. These risks commit the same fallacy, namely they conceive of moral agency in anthropocentric terms, defining human freedom apart from God's relationship with humanity. This anthropocentric error continues in postmodernity. We are more cautious, cynical, and even pessimistic about humanity's benevolence and power to correct the problems that it has created. If God is absent then all that remains is human political action. In much social theory the tension between human freedom and the hegemonic powers must be broken through the power of *political* agency—through democratic politics. This means that if Christians and the church are to make any difference in the world, it can only do so as a political agent. Christians become the transformative power in the world when they work through political agencies to bring about a world of peace and justice. This entire scheme of social change can be developed without any discussion of God's agency or the correspondence between human and divine agency, nor any conversation about Christian *witness*. Christians and the church no longer act as witness to God's action for the world in *Christus victor*, but become the principle actors of social change. In such a view, the line between Christian social ethics and Christian social witness is broken. Once this occurs, God's gracious action for the world is no longer needed in a world that is dominated by human ethical descriptions and actions. All that is needed is for us to adequately describe the problem, whatever it is, and then to empower ourselves and others to fix the problem. In such descriptions, God is not ultimately in control of the past, present, and future, but we are!

In such a scheme there is no *Christus victor* acting *pro nobis*, just humanity as *humana victor* acting *pro nobis*. One of the most interesting sections of *CD* IV/3 is Barth's discussion of Jesus Christ's prophetic witness as "victor" or *Christus victor*. The prophetic witness of Jesus Christ displays a past, present, and future victory in the "strange battle" of Jesus Christ over the powers of darkness (*CD* IV/3: 362). In correspondence to Jesus' "war" against the powers, Christians should not perceive the future as an open neutral space of nothingness waiting to be filled by human action, nor as puppets living out a predetermined drama. Rather, *Christus victor* has brought an end to humanity's future through the covenant of grace.

> This is the attack of Jesus with which the struggle of light and against darkness is opened. It is not merely a declaration of war. It is at the same time His decisive stroke in the war. It is a remarkable stroke in a strange and remarkable war. For the attack is that of the love of the Father and the Son. It is the attack of the grace of God. . . . Now that the grace of God is manifested in the world, the great divine Yes has been spoken, salvation and life have taken place and are revealed in the midst and this change has been accomplished, things cannot, must not, and will not go on as before in the world and in human life, in its relationships and orders, in the interconnections of men and their inner and outer existence. . . . The faithfulness of the Creator has not failed. In this transition from the old aeon to the new literally nothing in His creation will be broken or extinguished or destroyed. His faithfulness will triumph in the fact that in form it must and will undergo a total and radical and universal transformation. (*CD* IV/3: 240–41)

Christian liberation from the powers through *Christus victor* has given humanity provisional or penultimate time, a "free space of becoming," so to speak, to move forward toward the absolute future of the consummation. In denying Christ's victory, both Christians and non-Christians can adopt what Barth calls the "anxious view" in which they begin to lose hope in the meaning of existence and become pessimistic, cynical, or at worst nihilistic. In this "anxious view" people lose faith in what is "intrinsically right and beautiful and good" and passively accept the "hostile and autarchic world" (*CD* IV/3: 238). Rather than being challenged by the light of Jesus' victory, they would rather live in a dark world of immanent catastrophe.

Still, Christ has not left humanity alone but has acted as *victor* decisively *pro nobis,* and in the Holy Spirit, has liberated us to be "contemporaries of Jesus Christ," which empowers us to be Christ's witnesses of faith, hope, and love. Because of Christ's work, humanity is "liberated and summoned, as to faith and love, so also to hope" (*CD* IV/3: 918). This makes Christian ethics as the form of witness possible, which gives faith, hope, and love to the world, something that we will discuss in the last section of this book. "The Christian community dares to hope in Jesus Christ and therefore it dares to hope for the world" (*CD* IV/3: 720). *Christus victor* makes it possible to hope.

CHAPTER NINE

Witness and Public Ethics: Options in Christian Ethics

This chapter concludes this section exploring themes in Barth's theological ethics in the context of contemporary Christian ethics. We have mostly been concerned with theoretical rather than practical issues, thereby looking at issues like moral knowledge, agency, and judgment. These various theoretical issues that Barth began struggling with in the early twentieth century still remain with us a century later. After a period of great liberal optimism and growing internationalism came the crisis of World War I. This horrific event challenged Barth and others of his generation to rethink strategies of Christian ethics, both in method and in practice. Central to this debate was the issue of how dogmatic theology and ethics are related to each other. Do they remain separate or related disciplines? If separate, what differentiates their methods, sources, and strategies? If related, how should they be integrated into one comprehensive theory? One important issue arising from this interaction is how the particular moral claims of Christian faith relate to the more general claims of an inclusive human ethics. The complications of relating the particular to the general are intensified in postmodernity. We have seen how trends in modern ethics led to the general, inclusive, and the universal, whereas postmodern ethics has turned to the local, exclusive, and the particular. What this means for Christian ethics is perhaps a closer or tighter relationship

Witness and Public Ethics: Options in Christian Ethics 309

between theology and ethics, which supports a stronger emphasis on the ethical content of Christian faith claims. This is a positive development because it has revived interest in the importance of theology—particularly ecclesiology—for Christian ethics. Still, this "ecclesial turn" in Christian ethics has also raised additional questions about the fundamental relationship between the church and secular society. Critics of this viewpoint often claim that it is sectarian and incapable of offering a "public" perspective on important issues because it cannot escape the confines of theological or ecclesial language. This view of ethics, say its critics, risks becoming esoteric and isolated from the world. Christian theologians and ethicists remain divided regarding these and other issues.

In chapter 2, we discussed how in *Ethics*, Barth distinguishes the "way" of theological ethics from the synthesis (apologetics), diastasis (isolationist), and mediating (Catholic moral theology) approaches. In *CD* II/2, Barth develops this same typology, but develops a stronger argument against the "neo-Protestant" "apologetics" approach, while also, expanding his discussion of the Catholic mediation of moral philosophy and theology (*CD* II/2: 520–35).[1] The problem with all these theories essentially is that they begin with ethical *methodology* itself rather than with God's free and gracious action as the triune God. "The grace of God protests against all man-made ethics as such. But it protests positively. It does not only say No to man. It also says Yes" (*CD* II/2: 517). Barth is against rule-based or principle-based theories as much as virtue-based theories because they place a methodology between us and God, which hinders our ability to listen, respond, and act in response to God's gracious command. With this in mind, this chapter looks at the two most common options in contemporary Christian ethics, which use two distinct methods of relating theology to ethics, namely the synthesis (apologetics) and the diastasis (isolationist) methods. Barth, of course, rejects these approaches and calls for the alternative "way of theological ethics" or the dialectical approach of Yes and No in relation to God's gracious command. Before this, however, we must first set the stage by looking the problem of relating the general and the particular in contemporary Christian ethics.

---

1. Of these three positions, it is obvious that Barth prefers that Catholic "mediating" approach for its attempt to take the general and the particular seriously. Still, the strategy of combining and coordinating "the Christian and the human" ends up "emptying out" the distinctively "Christian content" (*CD* II/2: 534). In a sense all three theories lack the presupposition that ethics begins with God's gracious action as trinitarian commander.

GENERAL AND PARTICULAR

How should we see the task of Christian ethics today? Should Christian ethics provide a common morality or general ethics for all persons, or does it speak to those within the church in particular? Should Christian ethics begin with a particular "special method" and "special sources," or should it borrow other non-Christian methods and sources? Should it stand exclusively upon its own beliefs, values, and practices, or should it find correspondences between its beliefs and practices and other religious and intellectual traditions? Should Christian ethics be exclusive or inclusive of other viewpoints? Should it start with the general and move to the particular, or begin with particular and move to the general? Can Christian ethics be inclusive without losing its distinctiveness, and can it be exclusive without becoming esoteric? Answers to these questions address some of the most important challenges and risks of our time, and no doubt, create much diversity, if not division, among Christian theologians and ethicists. Just as there is greater need to communicate in a pluralistic society and world, so is there a need to understand one's own identity, history, and tradition. This tension is but another example of the ambiguity of globalization and postmodernity, in which there is a revived interest in locality and globality at the same time. How is it possible for Christian ethics to insist on the uniquely Christian or theological viewpoint, at the same time offering a framework for a common morality for all people in a pluralistic society and world? If so, how should it be understood?

Regarding this important debate in contemporary Christian ethics, it is useful to compare two introductory "companions" of Christian ethics. The first book is *The Cambridge Companion to Christian Ethics*, edited by Robin Gill.[2] This book represents the most common approach to contemporary Christian ethics, which integrates various sources of moral reflection, ethical methods, and descriptions and evaluations of important contemporary ethical problems. This book is divided into three sections, including the "grounds," "approaches," and "issues" of Christian ethics. The first section looks at biblical ethics as the primarily source or "ground" for moral decisions. The second examines the common "approaches" or methodological strategies used by ethicists in approaching ethical problems. These methodological approaches included chapters on natural law, virtue, feminist and liberation theology, and world religions. The last part looks at numerous

---

2. Gill, *Cambridge Companion to Christian Ethics*.

issues in social and medical ethics, including war, the arms trade, social justice, ecology, business and economics, world family trends, and genetics. Regarding these issues, the common approach consists of incorporating information from the sciences, along with Scripture and ethical methods, in its descriptive and evaluative analysis of each of these issues. The contributors of these essays do not seek to be too prescriptive in their evaluations of specific issues, but rather to expose the reader to the variety of ways Christians have thought about such issues. In contrast, the second book is *The Blackwell Companion to Christian Ethics*, edited by Stanley Hauerwas and Samuel Wells.[3] This book rejects the first approach and organizes its many articles along the lines of liturgical practice of Christian worship, including "meeting one another," "re-encountering the story," "being embodied," "re-enacting the story" and "being commissioned." Like the first book, this volume addresses many contemporary ethical issues, but besides using Scripture as the primary source for Christian ethics, it further situates these discussions in the language of the church and dogmatic theology. This latter approach takes more seriously Christian doctrine and practice within the Christian community as the starting point for Christian ethical reflection and action. Whereas the first volume begins with a generalist and broad methodological framework, guided by Scripture, reason, and the sciences, the second volume begins with the particularistic and confessional approach of the Christian community. Like the first volume, the Blackwell contributors are not overly prescriptive; however, they offer a sharper criticism of secular culture as well as a determinative path for Christian reflection and action by linking Christian practices or "skills" with particular virtues. Indeed, this latter book is less interested in offering a variety of perspectives, and more interested in finding one form of prescriptive practice that emerges from Christian witness. Therefore, the Cambridge volume seeks to move rather quickly to a more general account of Christian ethics emerging from the interplay of sources and methods, whereas the Blackwell volume seeks to remain rooted within the particular beliefs and practices of the Christian community. The former approach remains tied more to a modern generalist approach of separating ethics from theology, while the latter approach fits more with postmodern particularistic approach to integrate ethics and theology.

---

3. Hauerwas and Wells, *Blackwell Companion to Christian Ethics*.

Although both books refer to Barth in numerous places, it would appear on the surface that he would be more sympathetic with the methodology of the *Blackwell Companion*. Like Barth, the essays in this volume remain critical of the separation of ethics from theology, thus removing academic Christian ethics further from the church's witness. In one of his best essays on Christian ethics, Barth writes: "This is why it is imperative to recognize the essence of theology as lying in the liturgical action of adoration, thanksgiving, and petition. The old saying, *Lex orandi lex credendi*, far from being a pious statement, is one of the most profound descriptions the theological method" (*HG*: 90). Barth insists "prayer is the law of faith," which implies that theology and ethics emerge from within the context of the worship of the Christian community. Christian ethics cannot be Christian without the church's witness. Still, overall, I think it would be more accurate to say that Barth would probably not completely agree with either approach. Barth would no doubt be critical of the paucity of theology present in the pluralistic framework of the Cambridge volume, which makes it theologically incoherent, and worse, incapable of being an ethics of witness. Many of the essays in this book reflect the apologetic or synthesis approach of liberal theology, the most common approach among Protestant and Catholic ethicists today. Nevertheless, Barth would be theologically troubled by the ecclesially-centered approach that runs through the essays of the Blackwell volume. Although theologically coherent and substantive, this approach concentrates too much on ecclesiology, while neglecting other doctrines like revelation, God (Trinity), and reconciliation, which epistemologically set the stage for ecclesiology. Although it is not directly intended, many of the essays move from church practices or sacraments to moral action, without first establishing the priority of divine agency. The danger here is that Christian ethics becomes too much the ethics of the Christian ethos; the church as moral culture becomes an end in itself. This approach moves too close to the isolationist approach of Christian ethics, which Barth encountered in the various versions of conservative (and pietistic) forms of Christianity. To be sure the main point here is not to critically analyze these two textbooks, but to use them as a departure point into our discussion of how Christian ethics engages secular society. In the remainder of the chapter, we will look at two basic approaches to this question that correspond to these two books, including looking at the thought of James Gustafson, Robin Lovin, and John Milbank, among others.

BARTH AND HIS LIBERAL CRITICS: EXCLUSIVISM OR SYNTHESIS?

Perhaps the most common criticism of Barth's ethics is that it is excessively controlled by the method of dogmatic theology, and more particularly, by his own Christocentric theology. It is Barth's apparent unwillingness to alter his Christological (and trinitarian) approach to theological ethics that leads his critics to say that his theology and ethics are too *exclusivistic*. Barth's critics allege that he concentrates so much on the particularity of Christian faith and confession that he fails to account for a more general conception of ethics. Barth remains so fixed on distinguishing his position from the liberal apologetics approach that he cannot account for a general ethics or common morality. If so, how can Barth's ethics really be useful in a diverse, pluralistic, postmodern society, such as ours today? It appears that Barth's approach may offer an occasional insight about the human condition, but as a whole, his method is unworkable as a strategy of contemporary Christian ethics. Barth's doctrinal emphasis cannot provide a coherent ethical method for understanding the context of a pluralistic and diverse world, and ethical action in that context.

Barth's Critics: Gustafson and Lovin

One important critic of Barth's apparent exclusivism is the fellow Reformed theologian-ethicist, James Gustafson. One of the most influential Christian ethicists of his generation, Gustafson, like Barth, committed himself to the basic premise that Christian ethics emerges within the framework of theological ethics. Gustafson's inclusive method, furthermore, of relating theological sources, ethical methods, and practical issues is consistent with the approach of the *Cambridge Companion*. This being said, Gustafson admires Barth because Barth places his ethics within a theological framework, rejects anthropocentrism, and emphasizes the priority of God's action. Gustafson further agrees with Barth that Christian ethics begin with a "theocentric" theology and "biblical vision of life" that offers a particular view of Christian stewardship, vocation, calling, and moral responsibility. Similar to Barth, Gustafson writes: "The first task of a theological ethician is to develop a coherent interpretation of God."[4] Yet, in saying this, he also remains critical of Barth's latent exclusivism that apparently emerges from

---

4. Gustafson, *Ethics from a Theocentric Perspective*, Vol. 2, 27.

his "singular Christological interpretation." Gustafson's criticism is primarily of Barth's theology of divine action rather than his divine command ethics. Rejecting Barth's trinitarian command ethics, Gustafson develops a more generalized "theocentric" interpretation of God's governance.[5] In this way, "ethics is shaped by the account one renders of God and God's relation to the world. How God is construed, and how the world is construed in light of one's convictions about the ultimate power and the powers that bring life into being, sustain it, and bear down upon it is the most critical choice made in theological ethics."[6] It is therefore Barth's doctrine of God, namely his "personalist" doctrines of revelation and the "anthromorphic" accounts of the Trinity that Gustafson finds problematic. Accordingly, it follows that the central difference between Barth and Gustafson is how "God" is understood, and how this affects their respective accounts of theological ethics. Unlike Barth, Gustafson excludes distinctive Christian claims about the incarnation, the work of the Holy Spirit, and the Trinity from his account of theocentric ethics. Gustafson admits that his "preference for the Reformed tradition" relies more specifically on the thought of Schleiermacher than Barth, and the anthropocentric question of human *knowledge* of God rather than the revelation of the *identity* of the trinitarian God. Regarding this point, Gustafson writes: "Knowledge or at least indications of the ordering of the ultimate power and powers, comes through experience and our perceptions and interpretations of the requisites for life together in the world—not only with other individuals, but in institutions and communities."[7] By emphasizing the knowledge gleaned from the human experience of this theocentric reality, Gustafson shifts from divine to human agency, from God's revelation, as a source of the good, to the hermeneutical strategy of reason and experience in determining the good. In all these ways, Gustafson embodies many of the characteristics of liberal modern theology and ethics as discussed in earlier chapters, particularly chapter 1. We recall that modern theology marginalized trinitarian theology, thereby reducing talk about God to a kind of monism and stressed either God's transcendence or immanence. Moreover, with the rise of the historical-critical method in biblical studies, the gap increased between the Bible and the contemporary reader, which fosters a general skepticism

5. Ibid., 26–42.
6. Ibid., 27.
7. Ibid., 39–40.

toward the reliability of "what God reveals" in the biblical text. Hence, the doctrines of revelation and Trinity often became the usual casualties of the modern epistemological crises.

With this in mind, we may distinguish Barth from Gustafson in the following ways. First, unlike Barth's trinitarian theocentrism, Gustafson's grounds his theological realism in the human experience of the rather monistic "powers that bear down upon us." In this way, Gustafson's theocentrism ironically becomes anthropocentric, since who this God is can only be known by human experience. Unlike Gustafson, Barth says that God cannot be captured or colonized by human experience or thought. The diastasis between human knowledge and God's revelation can only be bridged by God's free action of grace, which communicates God's self-identity. Second, unlike Barth's particularism, Gustafson interprets divine knowledge through the generalist modern epistemological categories of religious experience, reason, and nature. Inasmuch as he attempts to begin with particular theological claims about God, his ethics becomes shaped by the reflexive moral subject's experience of the "powers bearing down upon us." In contrast, Barth's particularistic understanding of doctrine regards epistemological questions and answers as secondary to—and emerging from—relational ones. God's revelation is not so much *what* is revealed but *who* is revealed. Lastly, unlike Barth's dialectical method, Gustafson, like Schleiermacher, too easily accommodates himself to apologetic (or synthetic) frameworks of nontheological ways of interpreting experience, reason, and nature apart from God's revelation. Regarding this point, Stanley Hauerwas offers the insight that Gustafson jettisons Christian theological claims about God, in order to adopt an "ahistorical" viewpoint grounded in human rationality and experience.[8] "Gustafson does not seek to show how the particular has universal significance," says Hauerwas, "as he seeks 'to overcome' that particularity." Hauerwas suspects the reason that Gustafson seeks to "overcome" Christian particularity is "it fails to do justice to the kind of theocentrism he is willing to defend."[9] Unlike Barth's trinitarian theology, therefore, Gustafson fits his Christian ethics into a rather monistic philosophical theism. Indeed, although he appeals to John Calvin, Jonathan Edwards, and H. Richard Niebuhr and others in the Reformed tradition, he also significantly departs from their descriptions

8. Hauerwas, *Wilderness Wanderings*, 62–81.
9. Ibid., 78.

of God's governance. As Douglas Ottati points out "there is no equivalent in Gustafson's position to Calvin's benevolent parent, Barth's humanity of God, or Niebuhr's christologically founded assurance that God destroys only to reestablish and renew."[10] Barth's theological ethics is thus more consistent with Reformed theologians like Calvin and Edwards, as well as with the broader incarnational theology of Catholic Christianity.

Similar to Gustafson's critique, perhaps the most common complaint against Barth's ethics is that his Word-centered approach prohibits the development of a general ethics and the pluralistic search for a common morality. It is thus assumed that Barth cannot provide an adequate theory of moral realism, and with it, an adequate theory of Christian ethics. Again, because of this theological exclusivism, he cannot offer a public ethics for a diverse and pluralistic society. Robin Lovin, for example, offers a typical example of this criticism. Following Reinhold Niebuhr, Lovin claims a comprehensive "Christian Realism" involves the three-part structure of theological, moral, and political realism.[11] In his 2000 Presidential Address to the *Society of Christian Ethics*, Lovin says the following:

> One could, for example, develop Christian ethics so dependent on theological realism as to preclude a shared search for the human good. Mistrust of the surrounding culture and theological confusions that human nature is fallen and confused about its own destiny may drive one to the conclusion that revelation alone provides a reliable starting point for ethics, ruling out the moral realisms found in Catholic natural law theory, the Social Gospel's investigation of social dynamics, and the Niebuhrian realists' study of human nature. We find this sort of strong theological realism in Barth's ethics, and it is echoed in the new movement that calls itself "Radical Orthodoxy."[12]

---

10. Ottati, "The Reformed Tradition," 56. Prior to this statement, Ottati further writes: "Within the frame of Reformed theological ethics, Gustafson's position becomes most controversial at this point. Gustafson maintains the otherness or independence of God from human needs, wants, and desires by insisting that God's purposes do not guarantee the human good. Like Calvin and others, he also associates God with interdependent process of nature and history that sustain human beings and that continue to create new possibilities. So understood, the divine governance furnishes us with grounds for appropriately measure confidence in the dependability of things as well as for senses of gratitude, possibilities, and direction." Ibid., 56.

11. Lovin, "Christian Realism," 3–18. For a more detailed account of Niebuhr's thought and Christian Realism, see Lovin, *Reinhold Niebuhr and Christian Realism*.

12. Lovin, "Christian Realism," 8.

It is interesting to see that Lovin places Barth and Radical Orthodoxy together as examples of Christian ethics that overstress theological realism to the neglect of moral realism. As we shall see later in this chapter, there are important differences between Barth and Radical Orthodoxy. Nevertheless, the issue here is the relation between theological and moral realism, or in other language, between Christian truth-claims about God's revelation and truth-claims about the human knowledge of the good. Lovin argues that theological realism is essential for moral realism, in that it provides a grounding for moral knowledge that relates to the general and specific "conditions of human flourishing." Because a "Christian realist," Lovin says, "believes that what God is doing in creation and human history is thus embedded in the conditions of life, this realist also believes that what God is doing and what God wills for us to do can be known, at least in part, by the observations of those conditions."[13] In a pluralistic world, the truth of moral knowledge emerges through the process of conversation through a shared commitment to research and discussion. It is both "cognitivist and fallibalist," says Lovin, in that it presumes that real moral knowledge is possible, yet dependent upon our own investigations and discussions. Indeed, it further presumes that moral truth has developed over time through epistemological discussion and correction. Contrasting Barth with Niebuhr, Lovin, more recently writes: "The Christian realist's critical attitude thus rejects moral absolutes drawn from human experience, but it also differs from Barth's theological ethics, which declares common experience theologically irrelevant and relies solely on the command of God as the starting point for ethics."[14] Lovin faults Barth for simply dismissing out hand other sources of moral knowledge like natural law and social analysis as formative for Christian social ethics. In contrast, Barth's Word-based theological realism, says Lovin, precludes such a generalized investigative task because it does not permit the possibility of a *shared* understanding of the human good.

Is it a legitimate criticism to say that Barth seems to rule out the possibility of a more general moral realism? We've already seen how Barth deals with the relationship between theological ethics and a more general ethics. In particular, we saw how Barth is not only open to the use of non-theological viewpoints, but positively *invites* them into the task of theological ethics. By interpreting the world theologically, Christian identity and

13. Ibid., 4.
14. Lovin, *Christian Realism and the New Realities*, 94.

practice in the world begins with being witnesses to God's Word, but it also implies listening to the *other*. As mentioned before, Barth claims there are "secular parables of the kingdom" that bear witness to the truth, and "illumine, accentuate, or explain the biblical witness in a particular time and situation" (*CD* IV/3: 115). Since, Christians are called to encounter the Word wherever it addresses them in all their particularity, they to have a duty to seriously listen to the voices of others. Regarding this, in one of his more quotable phrases, he says, "God may speak to us through Russian Communism, a flute concerto, a blossoming shurb, or a dead dog" (*CD* I/1: 55). The point here is that because the Word comes to us in its otherness, so too, we must be attentive to the Word in the *other*. Christian ethics, therefore, is open to the outside perspectives, but remains cautious only when these viewpoints usurp their place within the conversation and become a second source of revelation apart from the Word of God. On this theme, Barth says:

> Curiosity is a power motive in the pursuit of knowledge. And even human conduct can itself be a legitimate object of high-minded curiosity. Practice can be the object of theory. Our *inter-esse* can be the object of our "interest." We again remind ourselves of the task, or, at any rate, the initial task, of history and psychology, which in the broader sense of the term, include studies like statistics and sociology. The curiosity is misguided only when it refuses to recognize any limits to its investigation. i.e. to admit the independent existence of the ethical question beyond the sphere of its researches, or—which is far worse—when it tries to identify its own enquiries with ethical questions, to pretend that it is itself ethics. Ethics, too, is theory. (*CD* II/2: 657–58)

Christian ethics should use a variety of intellectual sources, like the social sciences, when it promotes a theologically richer analysis of the circumstances of human society and culture. It should reject these sources only when they leap from their descriptive analysis toward the area of *normative* ethics. Secular sources of social and ethical analysis remain useful for Christian ethics in their descriptive forms, but begin to become problematic only once they seek to establish another *word*, that is, another ethical epistemology and moral ontology. For to accept the *word* of the natural law reasoning or the social sciences would be to ignore or disregard the Word of God, which as a living Word, engages us in God's command of grace. We've learned that Barth's emphatic *Nein* against natural theology is rooted in the broader attack against the correlationalist strategy of "apologetics," which he equates with Schleiermacher and liberal theology. In Barth's mind, liberal theology as well as natural law and orders of creation theology all provided the foundation for the development of heretical beliefs of the German Christians, and Nazism. What these various movements have in common is the correlative or synthetic principle, as articulated by the conjunction "and," which places on equal footing the Word with other human words, ideas, or ideologies; the Word of God *and* nature, creation, culture, nation, state, and so on. The danger of "apologetics" is this seeks "to establish and justify the theologico-ethical inquiry within the framework and on the foundation of the presumptions and methods of nontheological, of wholly human thinking and language" (*CD* II/2: 520).

In contrast, Barth establishes a theological, rather than a philosophical or scientific, account of moral realism, which is grounded in God's divine speech-act, the Word of God. The search for moral knowledge, orientation, and identity is discovered, not through the *reflexive*—thus anthropocentric—search for the human good in the human other, community, or tradition, but through encountering the speech and acts of the divine *Other*. It is Barth's theological commitments, as derived from dogmatics, which establishes his account of theological and moral realism and human agency. So, in summary, the crucial difference between the methods of Gustafson and Lovin on one side, and Barth on the other, is their different conceptions of the relation between ethics and theology, and how moral realism itself is understood within that relational framework. Once the task of "public ethics" begins many Christian ethicists (including Gustafson and Lovin) implicitly presupposes a moral ontology that separates ethics from dogmatic theology into two separate disciplines, which makes Christian ethics simply another version of a larger, more comprehensive, version of general ethics. By avoiding the particularity of Christian proclamation—that the Word has come to us in the flesh (John 1:14)—many Christian ethicists ground their ethics in the veracity of in the shared authorities of the social sciences or philosophy, which form their theory of moral realism. This is a risky move. Although this method avoids the risk of theological escoterism, it cannot avoid the risk of secular reductionism. That is, by beginning with inclusiveness and plurality as definitive for a *shared* understanding of moral realism, it invites the *synthesis* of the Word with other frameworks and viewpoints. This synthetic metanarrative remains an easy target for postmodern deconstruction, which eviscerates the *realism* of Christian theology and ethics altogether. In doing so, it ironically invites the risk of antirealism, which denies an objective moral reality grounded in God's covenantal relationship with humanity and the world. The problem of the "whence" and "whither" of the good remains a problem for all reflexive theories of ethics, including the various versions of Christian ethics that begin with nature or human experience. All versions of ethics, if they are to be coherent, must provide for a moral ontology that provides an argument for why *reality* itself is good. The theological answer to this question implies more than an impersonal "Creator" of moral laws, but a gracious and loving God who stands with us and for us in Jesus Christ in the covenant of grace. "The grace of God protests against all man-made ethics as such. But it protests positively. It does not only say No to man. It also says Yes" (*CD* II/2: 517).

Word of God and Public Ethics

Often Barth's critics don't criticize his public ethics *per se,* for example, as echoed in *Barmen Declaration,* but the theological basis on which his public ethics is grounded. As stated earlier, these critics often fault Barth for *not* having a general ethics based on naturalistic sources or a creation-based ethics. Unlike Emil Brunner and Dietrich Bonheoffer, argues Robin Lovin, "Barth's position is impossible for public ethics. If we are to choose our actions by reason and defend them publicly by argument, we must either limit the freedom of God or abandon the metaethics that bases all moral meaning on God's will."[15] The assumption here is that Barth's theology prevents him from developing a public ethics that is open to analysis, debate, and criticism. Similarly, William Schweiker applauds Barth's ethics of responsibility, but criticizes him for not providing a realistic account of the goodness of finite existence or what Schweiker calls the "integrity of life." Not only is God good, says Schweiker, but also that which is "other than God," like the created order and human life, which implies that the "integrity of life" itself provides moral ontology of responsibility within a pluralistic society. That is, if Christians are to have a public ethic within pluralistic society, they must be able to talk about the *good* of creation by itself without appeal to Christological or ecclesiological premises. Schweiker understands theological ethics, then, as a "kind of hermeneutical phenomenology," or a "way of analyzing and articulating the lived structure of reality in order to

---

15. Lovin, *Christian Faith and Public Choices,* 42.

provide orientation and guidance for life."[16] This moral ontology, grounded in life's integrity including human dignity, provides an account of human togetherness, moral responsibility, and political responsibility. From this standpoint, Barth's ethics apparently cannot account for the very *human* process and power of hermeneutical moral reasoning, moral analysis, and deliberation as the basis for responsible moral action in a pluralistic society. In addressing these criticisms, we look first at some general comments of relating Barth and his critics, and then second more particularly at how this leads to a public ethics of witness.

It is odd that Barth's critics claim he has no creation-based ethics, since it is in his doctrine of creation that he works out such a rich account of human relatedness for ethics. Yet, as we have seen, creation cannot stand apart from God's reconciling action in Jesus Christ. In Barth's view, the knowledge of God is always mediated through a sign or sacrament, which represents, indeed, embodies God's truth. The principle sign or sacrament of God is the *humanity* of Jesus Christ. When theological ethics begins with "nature," "creation," or "life" instead of the Word made flesh, it rejects the moral reality of the good revealed in history, and with it God's freedom to act. Consequently, when ethics grounds its knowledge of the good in relation to creation, natural law, or life itself, it begins with an *abstraction* of the human apart from God, which inevitably leads to *normative* borrowings of other viewpoints. In so doing it becomes a philosophy or a theology that may be inclusive of other nontheological viewpoints, but ironically not the Word of God. Jesus Christ becomes marginalized, or even worse, expendable. This invariably *separates* theological realism from moral realism, as it inadvertently separates divine from human agency, the gospel from the law, and the knowledge of grace from knowledge of the moral law. The assumption here is that humanity can confidently claim to know what is truly good, apart from God's own self-revelation in Jesus Christ. This fundamentally neglects God's trinitarian freedom to act as creator, reconciler, and redeemer. In doing this, it rejects God's freedom to declare the *origin* and *reality* of the good in the acts of creation, reconciliation, and redemption.

When Christian ethicists separate moral realism from theological realism they mistakenly isolate, thus "abstract," God's action in creation from God's action in reconciliation and redemption. This theological error invariably rejects the creedal confessions and scriptural affirmation that

---

16. Schweiker, *Theological Ethics*, xxi.

the "Word was in the beginning" and "all things were made through him" (John 1:2–3). It rejects the notion that creation is part of the history of grace that God accomplishes through Jesus Christ, and with it, the covenantal understanding of creation. For Barth, the creation is the "external basis" of covenant and the covenant is the "internal basis" of creation, which allows him to emphatically proclaim "creation sets the stage for the story of grace" (*CD* III/1: 43). The history of covenant, then, is a history of a relationship between God and humanity, and to isolate (or separate) God's action in creation from reconciliation and redemption is to tear asunder the relationship that God seeks to establish with humanity. To reiterate, it is the *covenant*, not nature, that establishes Barth's theology and "ethics of creation" as developed in *CD* III/4. God's concrete and objective actions in the covenant are always prior to the human subjective experience and understanding of created reality or nature. It is God's decisive covenantal act to be *with* and *for* humanity in Jesus Christ. Furthermore, without this covenant-partnership, creation also is misunderstood "as it is" because its eschatological destiny—what it will be in its ultimate transformation—is denied. Only through God's actions in the covenant is creation united with eschatology, for without this "inner basis" to creation, the created order simply becomes the same thing as "nature." As a result when one talks about nature or even creation without talking about God's covenant, one inevitably moves toward the idea of a "God-less world" and a "world-less God." When God as covenant-partner and creation are driven apart into separate ontological realms, we are led to errors about who God is and what nature (or creation) is: God becomes an abstraction, and creation is reduced to a materialistic closed system of natural contingency. "Where the covenant is no longer seen in creation or creation in the covenant, the affirmation that creation is benefit cannot be sustained" (*CD* III/1: 334). Nature is no longer seen as purposive or as a "benefit" to humanity, but a threat to its existence. When "creation and benefit are mutually exclusive ideas," then "creation is not beneficent but maleficent. Creation as such is the origin of sheer darkness and horror, of falsehood, shame and evil" (*CD* III/4: 334). When theological ethics fails to see creation in light of a covenantal eschatology, then the purpose of creation itself becomes problematic, which makes it more difficult to have hope for creation. God's past creative and salvific activity is separated from God's present and future activity.

Does the commitment to the primacy of the Word of God keep Christian ethics from being inclusive of other viewpoints in a pluralistic society? Most critics of Barth think his exclusivism rules out any notion of a general ethics of inclusivity. Yet, the line of reasoning here is that Barth's theological realism *establishes* his moral realism, which drives his ethics toward a general and inclusive approach of moral knowledge. If Christian ethics is to adequately be general and inclusive, it must begin with God's freedom to act in this particular and exclusive way. Barth's basic scheme of ethics is objective and inclusive even though it is expressed in the particular and exclusive language of *Christian* theology. John Webster explains:

> Barth is not claiming that God in Christ is "the reality" in an exclusive sense, in a way which amounts to an ontological disenfranchisement of all other "realities." The reality of Jesus Christ as the self-positing of God includes within itself all other realities, and it is in him and from him that they have their inalienable substance. Barth's apparent ontological exclusivism is in fact an inclusivism: *solus Christus* embraces and does not suspend or absorb the world of creatures and actions. Barth's *Dogmatics,* then, is to be read as in its entirety a singly extended realist claim that God in his self-manifestation has both epistemological and ontological priority, and that it is to that self-establishing reality that faith and theology *refer.*[17]

Barth does not preclude a pluralistic search for the human good, but he simply refuses to jettison theological commitments once the task of public ethics begins. Barth's moral realism is not inherently exclusive but *inclusive* of other viewpoints. Interestingly, Webster goes on to say there are strong resemblances between Barth's command ethics and natural law. No doubt Barth opposed natural law theory because of the assumption that moral truth can be known by nature, which is "independent of God's particular acts of self-communication. But he did not reject the ontological vision which the natural law tradition articulates, in which the good at real are inseparable."[18] Indeed, as stated earlier, what Barth rejects is not the *relation* of theological realism and moral realism, the good and the real, but their isolation and separation into two isolated realities. By integrating the good and the real, Barth argues for a theologically grounded moral realism that is inclusive of other viewpoints. In this way, Barth's account of moral realism is post-liberal and dialectical, in that it rejects the synthesist option of liberal theology moving from the particular to the general, while at the same time, it moves back and forth between synthesis and diastasis, or between secular

17. Webster, *Barth's Ethics of Reconciliation,* 29.
18. Webster, *Barth,* 156.

reductionism and theological esotericism. Not unlike the term *post*-modern, the term *post*-liberal critically "looks back," as if in a rear view mirror, upon the failures of liberalism, and in so doing, it also "looks beyond" these same failures. Because it is both diachronic and synchronic, it both incorporates the old and the new. It does not propose a particular method, but deconstructs modern or liberal presumptions in the context of a theology of the Word. Without God's address to humanity through the Word, which is the source of the good, humanity is left groping for an understanding of the good that transcends the "will to power." Any realist form of ethics, grounded in the reflexive subject is potentially erroneous because its basic moral understanding of the self and the good are abstracted, and viewed in isolation from the basic objective conditions of human existence including the human person as sinner but redeemed and reconciled to God *by God*.

Witness and Public Ethics

As we saw in chapter 7 Barth's ethics does incorporate a dialectical form of moral judgment in Christian witness that maybe used in public ethics. Hence, there is no need to rehearse the argument from that chapter. Barth does provide an argument for moral judgment that is not rationalistic or casuistic but relational, dialectical, and open-ended. Criticisms of Barth's ethical "method" are usually superficial and repetitive, as they fail to peruse all of Barth's writings—of which there are many—and neglect to consider Barth's own criticism of the position they represent. The more important question for Christian ethics, therefore, is not whether Barth's method works, but whether synthetic (or apologetic) theories at their core, are actually theories of Christian witness. If not, what prohibits these theories from becoming another secular version of humanistic or naturalistic ethics?

Aware of this problem, in his recent book, Robin Lovin calls for an "unapologetic principle" for Christian faith claims in the public sphere, thereby allowing Christian ethics to remain Christian within a pluralistic society.[19] There is no need to translate Christian claims into some form of "public reason" to speak about the common goods for human flourishing. This "unapologetic principle" can be used for all moral traditions, whether religious or secular, including the church and the secular university. "Faith influences the shape of social life by bringing to the public forum of each social context a comprehensive idea of the human good, centered in the

---

19. Robin Lovin, *Christian Realism and the New Realities*, 129.

person as the image of God in whom these diverse goods are united."[20] So, the question is: can we really talk about this human *good* apart from a good God who has created the world good? Furthermore, how can we talk about this good God *apart* from the revelation in Jesus Christ, the Word of God? For many Christian ethicists making such an Christological claim about the incarnation (or Trinity) is too Christian and cannot be held up to the scrutiny of a more generalist ethics in a pluralistic society. Instead, what is needed is another "master concept" or "superior point" that links human existence and experience with some notion of God as creator or providential preserver, between *confusio hominum* and *providentia Dei* (*CD* IV/3: 707). The most common "master concept" that bridges this gap between the divine and human realms is the claim that humanity is created *imago Dei*. This "master concept" establishes a ground for human dignity, created in God's image and likeness, within a large world of dignity, value, and meaning. Barth too places human dignity at the center of his public ethics, but would add that such a belief cannot be sustained by simply affirming the "integrity of life" or even the *imago Dei*. The main problem is that both of these concepts are free-floating abstractions isolated from God's revelation of grace in history. For Barth, human dignity is not something gained through "self-reflection," but visibly manifested in the incarnation, where God chooses to be "with" us and "for" us in Jesus Christ (*CD* III/4: 327). Both God and humanity are unveiled in Jesus Christ. "There is no time when God was not the covenant-partner of man" (*CD* III/2: 218). So, if Christian ethics is to remain a form of witness, it needs to begin with how God has chosen to address humanity, and not, with general abstractions about human dignity framed by appeals to religious language. This is why "life" or "creation" itself can never be our "ethical lord, teacher, and master." "In theological ethics the concept of life cannot be given this tyrannical, totalitarian function" (*CD* III/4: 326).

Christian public ethics is not just another worldview about human dignity and life's integrity within a pluralistic society of many worldviews. Rather, it is witness to God's being and action in our world that establishes human dignity and life's integrity. These concepts are not just ideas or abstractions but are embodied in the actions of a gracious God establishing a covenant-partnership. "The beginning of our knowledge of God—of this God—is not a beginning which we can make with Him. It can only the

20. Ibid., 220.

beginning which He has made with us" (*CD* II/1: 190). This knowledge of God gives testimony to God's decision to be our covenant-partner. Only in Jesus Christ do we discover that there is no "godlessness" in the human as well as no "humanlessness" in God. Apart from the incarnation, the *imago Dei* cannot tell us with certainty whose image and likeness humanity is created to be. Just as there is no abstract God without the human, so there can be no abstract humanity without God. It follows that whatever dignity and value human nature intrinsically has, it cannot be isolated from who God is, but only dynamically interrelated with God's being and action. In this way, Barth's *actualism* and *relationalism* (or personalism) says that being and action cannot be understood apart from the history of Jesus Christ, who reveals the *personal* being and gracious action of God, as Trinity, and humanity as covenant-partner with God.

> Man generally, the man with fellow-man has indeed a part in the divine likeness of the man Jesus, the man for the fellow-man. As man generally is modeled on the man Jesus and His being for others, and as the man Jesus is modeled on God, it has to be said of man generally that he is created in the image of God. . . . It is inevitable that we should recall the triune being of God at this point. God exists in relationship and fellowship. As the Father of the Son and the Son of the Father He is Himself I and Thou, confronting Himself and yet always on and the same in the Holy Ghost. God created man in His own image, in correspondence with His own being and essence. He created Him in the image which emerges even in His work as the Creator and Lord of the covenant. (*CD* III/2: 323–24)

A generic public ethics of the human good presumes that humanity can rise above the ambiguity of *confusio hominum* and both know and do the good apart from God's grace. Even if we establish the idea of a "common grace" given to all humanity through God's agency as creator or *providentia Dei* we still cannot overcome the problem of *confusio hominum* and the reality of human sin, or in Barth's language, "nothingness." The reality is that the powers do exist to deprive humanity of its freedom. A public ethics without a soteriological doctrine of God's Yes of reconciliation cannot account for the ultimate victory over the potentially hegemonic forces of No and the inevitable oppression of the powers. If Christian ethics is to give witness to God's action in public life, it cannot remain silent but proclaim God's Yes against the No of the powers and *confusio hominum*. A pluralistic and secular society cannot do this on its own but must rely on the witness of the church to proclaim that the real source of the human good, as "real man" or "true human," and the victor over the powers and human sin, as *Christus victor*, is the same Jesus Christ. It is Jesus Christ who is the real source of human dignity and life's relational integrity, and who establishes an *analogia relationis* or analogy of relation between humanity and God. Just as God is relational, so is humanity relational; there is not just *being*, but "being-in-encounter." Just as God is essentially a relational being or being-in-relation, so too, is humanity seen as being-in-relation with others. This *analogia relationis* is unveiled in the humanity of Jesus Christ where God has bound himself to our humanity making every person a fellow-person of Jesus Christ. This is how Christ reveals the "real man" or "true person" as the complete or full-fledged covenant-partner with God. Barth writes: "The ontological determination of humanity is grounded in the fact that this one man among all others is the man Jesus. So long as we select any other starting point for our study, we shall reach only the phenomena of the human" (*CD* III/2: 132). Hence, it is our relation to Christ, as our representative head, which makes it possible to be in relations with other persons and to become free from the No of the powers. Without Christ's victory over the powers, we cannot be free from our insistent "self-reliance" to be free from others and God. Without Christ we are only left with the isolated monads of God and humanity, a deistic God, and a Nietzschean humanity. So, without Christ all that remains is power, ontological separateness, anomie, and atheistic nihilism. In Christ, however, humanity can, says Barth, "realize the togetherness of man grounded in human freedom" (*CD* III/2: 271).

Christian witness stands for an ethics of mutual togetherness as the basis for a public ethics of the common good. The "real man" of Jesus Christ, reveals humanity as really is, which then makes it possible for us to be and act in togetherness, freedom, and responsibility. In *CD* III/2 Barth argues that emerging from this Christological claim is our understanding of "being-in-encounter," which serves as the basis for I-Thou interpersonal relations, mutual perception, conversing, and assisting. First, being able to truly perceive the other face-to-face, as *Thou*, implies being open to the needs, desires, and hopes of the other. Truly being in fellowship and "mutual openness" rejects the impersonal relations so often found in bureaucratic structures and relations, which serves causes and ideologies rather than human dignity. "Bureaucracy is the form in which man participates with his fellows when this first step into mutual openness is not taken namely because of the intention of serving a cause, structure, or program rather than the true needs of the other" (*CD* III/2: 252). Second, this "mutual openness," this "I-thou relation," allows us to truly hear and speak with others. The stress here is put on active listening and then responding and not just talking; as he puts it, "[T]wo monologues do not constitute a dialogue" (*CD* III/2: 259). Conversation that is not mutually beneficial serves other personal or ideological interests, which prohibits the civil community from living out its mission for freedom, justice, and peace. Third, our mutual seeing and conversing also leads to mutual assistance, which makes justice possible. Unless we can truly see and converse with the other, we will not be able to truly help the other. Moreover, helping others without engaging and communicating with them face-to-face makes it a form of impersonal charity. So, being relates to action through our perception, conversing, and assisting others. Barth writes: "If I and Thou really see each other and speak with one another and listen to one another, inevitably they mutually summon each other to action" (*CD* III/2: 260–61). In seeing, speaking, and assisting others, we also allow others to see, speak, and assist us, and in this relational encounter, we learn more fully what it means to be *human*. It is being human, after all, which makes it possible for us to talk about an inclusive public ethics.

BARTH AND RADICAL ORTHODOXY: INCLUSIVISM OR ESOTERICISM?

As mentioned above, some of Barth's critics see Barth's legacy linked with the emerging theological movement known as Radical Orthodoxy, and in particular the theology of John Milbank. Without a doubt Radical Orthodoxy is one of the most important theological movements in recent years that seeks to begin from a strictly *theological* viewpoint. This overall sensibility they share with Barth. That is why we must expand our analysis of Barth's theology to compare him with others who remain more similar to his approach. In chapter 1, we saw how John Milbank and others have challenged the primacy of secularist frameworks in understanding modernity and postmodernity. Above all, they seek to purify Christian theology and ethics of its latent commitment to secular assumptions. On this point, Radical Orthodoxy has much in common with Barth's approach. Yet, one cannot draw a direct line between a theologian like Milbank and Barth; there are obvious differences. In the following section, we look at some of these differences, which help us further understand the dialectical complexity of Barth's ethics and with this a greater insight into Christian ethics as witness.

WHAT IS RADICAL ORTHODOXY?

John Milbank's theological task, at its core, is both deconstructive and constructive. First, it deconstructs the secular and seeks to find an alternative history of modernity, and then, second, it constructs an alternative Christian framework (*mythos*) that should govern Christian belief and practice. In the beginning of his most important work, *Theology and Social Theory*, Milbank emphatically proclaims: "Once, there was no secular."[21] Building upon this thesis, he creatively develops a genealogical study of secular social theory as an anti-Christian *mythos*, grounded in an ancient "ontology of violence." Milbank presumes that when secular social theory claims to be objective and neutral, the "governing assumptions of such theory are bound up with the modification or the rejection of orthodox Christian positions."[22] This deconstructionist method allows Milbank to argue that all secular discourse, at its core, is a form of Christian "heresy." Secular discourse, says Milbank, is "*constituted* in its secularity by 'heresy' in relation to orthodox Christianity, or else a rejection of Christianity that is more 'neo-pagan' than simply anti-religious."[23] Since it denies the Christian claim that God—in Christ—has established an "ontology of peace," the heretical *mythos* of secularism culminates in postmodern nihilism. Interestingly, Milbank also demonstrates the link between the nihilism of Frederich Nietzsche, as "ontology of violence," with its various precursors throughout history going back to the Ancient Greeks. This heretical ontology—as a form of Christian heresy—is simply posited to be true and real or natural, but it is no more real or natural than orthodox Christianity. Milbank and other Radical Orthodox thinkers like Philip Blond, therefore, presume a common post-secular viewpoint that seeks to deconstruct the secular as myth or heresy, while at the same time, providing a wide-ranging Christian *alternative* in belief and practice to secular modernity. As Blond writes: "To say we should now bring an end to the secular is to say that we should reverse the dreadful consequences of the liberal erasure of God and take myth back from out of the hands of the fascist where it has all too

21. Milbank, *Theology and Social Theory*, 9.
22. Ibid., 1.
23. Ibid., 3.

often fallen."[24] If Christians are to be truly *post*-modern, they must begin with an alternative theological story that begins prior to the triumph of secular, which unlike much postmodern thought predates modernity. This is why Radical Orthodox thinkers generally prefer Ancient and Medieval writers, like Augustine, and Aquinas, to Reformation or modern or postmodern ones like Luther, Calvin, or Barth. Their recovery of the "old" is, in their judgment, a truly catholic "old" and does not share in the post-Reformation dogmatic divisions within Christianity.

It is their particular blending of participatory ontology—as discussed earlier—and ecclesiology that guides Radical Orthodox thinkers away from a narrow interpretation of dogmatic theology, but toward the task of re-fashioning an entire worldview shaped by theology. Of all the communities that exist in the world, it is church, the *ecclesia*, which remains the only alternative to the postmodern nihilism of the modern *polis*, thus the only true and authentic *polis*. The Christian story is grounded in an alternative *polis*, the *ecclesia*, which stands in contrast to the *mythos* of "ontological violence" of the Greek *polis*. Regarding this, Milbank writes, the *ecclesia* begins with an "alternative *mythos*, equally unfounded, but nonetheless embodying an 'ontology of peace', which conceives differences as analogically related, rather than equivocally at variance."[25] Only in Christianity one finds the "precise opposite of nihilism—a creed which rigorously excludes all violence from its picture of the original, intended, and final state of the cosmos."[26] In Milbank's words, Christian social theory is "first and foremost an *ecclesiology*, and only an account of other human societies to the extent that the Church defines itself, in practice, as in continuity and discontinuity with these [other] societies."[27] The church stands against all secular influences, in thought and practice, on itself and society. Furthermore, this particular ecclesiology leads to a *radical* Christian account of philosophy and aesthetics, as well as social, cultural, political, and economic theory. As Milbank recently puts it, "I have always tried to suggest that participation can be extended also to language, history and culture: the whole realm of human making."[28] Since Radical Orthodoxy views the secular

24. Blond, "Introduction," 54.
25. Milbank, *Theology and Social Theory*, 279.
26. Ibid., 288.
27. Ibid., 380.
28. Milbank, *Being Reconciled*, ix.

disciplines as heretical positions within Christian discourse, there is no sufficient reason to allow them to remain independent or autonomous from Christian discourse. Doing this simply allows these secular frameworks to situate theology within their schemes of thought, rather than the other way around. Radical Orthodoxy desires to resituate theology in the academy as the "queen of the sciences." Theology should refuse to surrender its "claim to be a metadiscourse," and instead, position itself as "the queen of the sciences for the inhabitants of the *altera civitas*."[29] Yet, at this point we may raise the question: if theology is the only metadiscourse what does that do to the integrity of other so-called secular disciplines in the academy, and likewise, what does it do to theology? Obviously, the strategy of Radical Orthodoxy ought to be commended for its single-minded commitment to theology as a "counter-discourse" to the pervasive influence of secularism in the university, society, and even in the church. Yet, the question remains: does it go too far? Does it lose its dialectical balance?

Church and the Secular

It is just this dialectical tendency in Barth's thought, including his acceptance of the validity of the *secular* as a place where God may speak in parables, which raises problems for theologians like Milbank. Milbank worries that Barth's singular commitment to the dogmatic and exegetical task of theology presumes the "liberal" separation of theology from philosophy.[30] According to Milbank, Barth fails to be truly postmodern and Radically Orthodox because he fails to present a comprehensive theology that challenges the secularity and autonomy of other disciplines and in so doing ends up with a "secular theology."[31] Barth is too willing to accept the legitimacy of the secular in modern life by remaining tied to dogmatic and exegetical language. Interestingly, Milbank's problems with Barth are similar to critics like Gustafson or Lovin, namely Barth's apparent exclusivism keeps him from having a more comprehensive viewpoint. Milbank, of course, would emphatically reject the liberal approach to moral realism as secular reductionism, but he also fears that Barth has also given too much

---

29. Milbank, *Theology and Social Theory*, 380.

30. "For if philosophy determines what is to be and to know, then will it not predetermine how we know even Christ to be. Unless we allow that the structure of this event reorganizes also our ordinary sense of what is and what we can know, in such a way that the autonomy of philosophy is violated." Milbank, et al., *Radical Orthodoxy*, 21–22.

31. Ibid., 33.

away by dialectically accepting the secular voice as a legitimate "secular parable." In discussing Barth's thought on these points, we look further at his ecclesiology, something not discussed in detail so far in this book. Yet, his ecclesiology remains a vital piece of any ethics of Christian witness. It is also something that places him close to theologians like Milbank and Hauerwas, among the many others who have been influenced by their work. As we saw earlier in our comparison of Hauerwas and Barth, however, there are some important differences between these thinkers and this will also become further apparent with our comparison of Milbank and Barth.

Not unlike Milbank, Barth's discussion of the secular is invariably interconnected with his discussion of the church. In *CD* IV/2, Barth's sees the church as dialectically situated between the polarities of either a strict identification or separation with the secular world. The church seeks to avoid this tension by drifting toward either extreme position. These two poles, in truth, are but two sides of the same coin as the church, in both cases, remains preoccupied with its own "self-preservation." First, when the church seeks to identify with secular society it falls into the temptation of "alienation" or "secularization." The alienation of the church takes place when it "allows itself to be radically determined and established and engaged and committed and imprisoned" to a "particular philosophy or outlook as the norm of its understanding of the Word of God" (*CD* IV/2: 667). This view, which places the Word of God "side by side" with other speech and cognitive frameworks, whether ideologies, beliefs, or cultural practices. The church embraces these other frameworks because of its preoccupation with "self-preservation, in face of the all-powerful world" (*CD* IV/2: 667). It is this concern that lies at the heart of Barth's critique of the apologetic (synthesis) method of theology and ethics. Similar to Milbank, Barth resists giving voice to Christian convictions through the various academic languages of the sciences that comprise the secular academy. By committing this error, Christian ethics risks its own external deconstruction both internally and externally, that is, both undercutting the possibility of a truly theological ethics, while further marginalizing itself from the public realm.

Nevertheless, Barth is unwilling to stop his analysis with the temptation toward identifying the church with the world, which results in a kind of secular Christianity. Rather, the church can also be tempted to *separate* itself from the world, which leads to the temptation of "self-glorification" or "sacralisation" (*CD* IV/2: 668). Unlike the timidly of the alienated church, the "self-glorified" church seeks its "self-assertion" in the "particularity of its being and action in the world." It seeks to "represent itself as a world of its own within the world" (*CD* IV/2: 669). On this point, he further writes:

> It certainly knows the lordship and glory of Jesus Christ. And it discloses itself to be His body, the earthly-historical form of his existence, His ambassador to all other men, the representative of His right and claim to the world. It thus renounces any feelings of inferiority as compared with other societies and forms of life. It rejoices and boasts in is own vital and constructive power in its own being as the incomparable *communio*: the *communio* of the *sancti* in their relationship to the *sancta*; the *civitas Dei* on earth, which cannot be confused with any other society, but towers over them as once cathedrals did over the little towns clustering round about them. (*CD* IV/2: 669)

Ironically by attempting place itself "above" the world, says Barth, the church makes "pretentious claims for itself instead of soberly advocating the claim of God, it withdraws from the world" (*CD* IV/2: 669). By "slipping into sacralisation" the church separates itself "from its own origin and goal and loses its secret by trying to reveal it in itself, but also separates itself from its own pleasure from poor, sinful, erring humanity bleeding from a thousand wounds, trying to impose itself where its owes its witness, and denying and suppressing its witness by witnessing only to itself" (*CD* IV/2: 670). By seeking to remove itself from the world by isolating itself from the needs and voices of others it seeks its own "self-preservation." More dramatically, it even becomes resentful and antagonistic toward the secular *other*. In contrast, Christians "must listen to all other ethics in so far as it has to receive from them at every point the material for its own deliberations. To that extent its attitude to every other ethics is not negative but comprehensive" (*CD* II/2: 527). Christian ethics is not "negative but comprehensive" because it seeks to engage other forms of ethics in ways that elucidate Christian moral truth.

Subsequently when Christian moral discourse loses this "comprehensiveness" and becomes "negative" it becomes parochial and isolated and from other voices in the world at large. It risks becoming *esoteric*.[32] We recall that in both *Ethics* and *CD* II/2, Barth dialectically maneuvers between the approaches of synthesis and diastasis, of apologetics and isolation, and of reductionism and esotericism. "Can and should theology of all things be content to speak," asks Barth, "not with universal validity, but also eso-

---

32. Outka, "Particularist Turn," 108.

terically" (*CD* II/2: 526)? Are God's purposes in the world only limited to the witness from the church? Is the church the only place where there are witnesses to God's kingdom? If the only witnesses exist in the church, then it is possible for the world to never hear, in other languages, God's message of faith, hope, and love. We saw earlier how Barth understands secular language as being commandeered by the Word of God, which allows it to be used as witness to the gospel. Along these lines, Barth asks:"[W]hy should it not be possible for God to raise up witnesses from this world of tarnished untruth, so that true words are uttered and heard even where it might seem that at very best no more than crude or refined deception may be expected" (*CD* IV/3: 121)? When Christians prohibit listening to the Word in and through the voice of the *other* in "secular parables," they refuse to allow the Word of God to "illumine, accentuate, or explain the biblical witness in a particular time and situation" (*CD* IV/3: 115). By refusing to listen to the secular voice, Christians are rejecting, out of hand, the possibility that God may speak to them through the *other* voice in parabolic language. This becomes a risk in Milbank's theology and trends in Radical Orthodoxy. In saying this, however, I'm not claiming that Milbank or Radical Orthodoxy *are* esoteric. Instead I'm simply claiming that esotericism remains a risk for any form of ecclesial ethics or ecclesiologically-centered theology which disregards the voice of the other as a secular parable of truthful witness.

Secular and Secularism

In considering the divergences between Radical Orthodoxy and Barth, let us look further at an important distinction between *secularism* or secular reductionism and the *secular* or the secularizing trends (or process) of modernity itself. In Barth's view, unlike in Radical Orthodoxy, the secular or secularity is not anti-theological or heretical *per se* because it simply uses nontheological language in fashioning cognitive frameworks. This distinction is further elaborated upon in *CD* IV/3, where Barth makes a comparison between two types of "secularism." The first is its "absolute" form or the secularism of the "distant periphery" (*CD* IV/3: 118). This overt form, as in the case of atheism, most emphatically rejects God's reign and Word. In contrast, the second is a "mixed and relative" form of the "inner periphery" that proclaims belief in God, while indirectly rejecting the freedom of God's Word (*CD* IV/3: 118). Of these, it is not the antagonistic "absolute" form but the latter "relative" form of secularism, as particularly found in the church, which is more resistant to the Word simply because it seeks to control God's voice through its own misguided interpretations. This form chooses to silence God's Word from speaking to the church and the world by replacing God's Word with some other word. When the church seeks to control and dominate the Word of God, in various secular and ideological forms, it fails to be a faithful witness to what God has accomplished in Jesus Christ.

It follows that Barth argues that the secular is not to be feared as much as the overconfidence of the church's claim to speak *for* God through its own overt or hidden ideologies. Thus, what remains a risk for the Christian community is not the process of secularization *per se*, but the ideology of secular*ism*, or the reduction of all speech *to* the secular, particularly as its replaces or is placed "side by side" with the Word of God. Unlike the more contrastive position of Radical Orthodoxy, Barth's refuses to claim that the secular is always reduced to the ideology of secular*ism*, nor that it cannot stand on its own apart from the Word of God. Indeed, for all of its opposition to the religious, secularism, in both "near" and "distant" forms, stands under God's Word. In one of his memorable phrases, he writes: "No Prometheanism can be effectively maintained against Jesus Christ" (*CD* IV/3: 118). Therefore, even in the secular world, Jesus Christ is able to raise up witnesses from both the "closer" and "more distant" secular spheres. For the power of God's Word "neither the militant godlessness of the outer periphery of the community, nor the intricate heathenism of the inner, is an insurmountable barrier" (*CD* IV/3: 121). So affirming the secular or secularity assumes the validity of the nontheological and non-ideological voice of the *other*, and what is more important that God's Word may appear in secular parables.

There are theologians who have raised serious concerns about Milbank and Radical Orthodoxy. By seeking to restore the importance of theology, does it, as R. R. Reno aptly puts it, seek "to replace the presumptions of secularity with a Christian account of everything"?[33] On this point, Jeffrey Stout has written that Radical Orthodoxy has unintentionally become a kind of "new traditionalism." For all of its emphasis on the priority of theology, Stout argues that it presumes a hidden nontheological commitment to an "ideological expression of the enclave society."[34] He writes:

33. Reno, *Ruins of the Church*, 75.
34. Stout, *Democracy and Tradition*, 115.

Of course, radical orthodoxy does not officially prefer the enclave as a social form. It sometimes speaks—ever so briefly and abstractly—about the possibility of the Christian socialism. Otherwise, it wavers between nostalgia for Christendom's theocratic vision and a utopian dream of "eucharistic anarchism" that promises government without states. Milbank says the church has "misunderstood itself" when it draws boundaries around "the same" and excludes "the other." But radical orthodoxy's critique of the secular tends, under current circumstances, to reinforce the sort of boundary-drawing it officially opposes. It rejects the existing public sphere for failing to recognize the need for evangelical obedience to the rulership of Christ—that is, for failing to be the sort of political community that ceased to be possible when Christendom gave way to secularization. . . . From within radical orthodoxy's refuge of aggressive like-mindedness, prophetic denunciation of the secular "other" and the unmasking of liberal theological error ritually reinforce the enclave boundary, rather than healing the world.[35]

What makes the "new traditionalists" like Milbank—and MacIntyre and Hauerwas—problematic, says Stout, is not their particularism or single-mindedness commitment to a moral tradition like Christianity, but their *resentment* against the secular. It is no coincidence that Stout relies on Barth's theology, when he argues that the "secular world is not be feared or merely refused by anyone committed to charity and justice in dealing with others." "It is rather an arena in which a Christian can hope to proclaim God's word and observe the transfiguring effects of God's love on the lives of his creatures."[36] Although Stout's criticism of Radical Orthodoxy may be excessively harsh, he is correct to say that Barth's theology stands as an alternative to Radical Orthodoxy. Unlike Barth who gives space to the secular disciplines to speak through parables, Radical Orthodoxy argues that "every discipline must be framed by a theological framework."[37] No doubt both affirm a *diastasis* between a theological worldview and a secular one, but unlike Barth, Radical Orthodox thinkers often concentrate on forging a Christian (or theological) metadiscourse over and *against* the secular one. By absorbing all other viewpoints, this metanarrative privileges the

---

35. Ibid., 115.

36. Ibid., 109. Stout, in his brief discussion of Barth, relies principally on (*CD* IV/3) and on George Hunsinger's interpretation of Barth's theology in Hunsinger, *How to Read Karl Barth* and *Disruptive Grace*.

37. Milbank, et al., *Radical Orthodoxy*, 3.

church—as the only authentic *polis*—over all other forms of social community. This leads to overconfidence about the *poeisis* of theology and an overvaluing of the *ecclesia*, as counter-polis. Most importantly, it refuses to allow the Word of God to speak in secular parables, which invariably limits the freedom of God's Word.

Totus Christus and Christendom

The ecclesially-centered perspective of Radical Orthodoxy, in its own way, has *rightly* shifted Christian ethics from being driven by social-scientific to theological analysis and evaluation. This shares Barth's basic premise of beginning with a theological description of reality. The divergences between them surface in their respective accounts of the church/world relation. This spills over into their respective accounts of the relationship of Jesus Christ to the church. Radical Orthodoxy presumes that the whole Christ, *totus Christus*, is found within the visible *ecclesia*, the Body of Christ. The church is the *polis* in which Christ is present in the world. On this point, Barth would agree, but would be careful not to identify the church with Christ. "Salvation history is the history of the *totus Christus*, of the Head with the body and all its members. The *totus Christus* is *Christus victor*" (*CD* IV/3: 216). Christ the victor is also fully present in the church in his "historical form of his bodily-existence," but the church cannot claim to have victory over the powers, but only give witness to the fact that Christ, in his "prophetic witness" has victory over the powers. The church cannot claim eschatological perfection. Not unlike the individual Christian, the church is both a "worldly" community shaped by the realities of human sinful life *and* a reconciled community shaped by God's covenant of grace. The church is not a static, but an *emerging* community of witness, a pilgrim church, which freely responds to God's command of grace.

For Milbank what theology says about other societies or communities emerges from the particular *polis* of the church. Christian social theory, says Milbank, is "first and foremost an *ecclesiology*, and only an account of other human societies to the extent that the Church defines itself, in its practice as in continuity and discontinuity with these [other] societies." Indeed, he adds, "There can only be a distinguishable Christian social theory because there is also a distinguishable Christian mode of action, a definite practice."[38] In a similar manner, Hauerwas writes of, "the social significance of the

---

38. Milbank, *Theology and Social Theory*, 380.

church as a distinct society with integrity peculiar to itself." "The church," Hauerwas further says, "does not exist to provide an ethos for democracy or any other form of social organization, but stands as a political alterative to every nation, witnessing to the kind of social life possible for those that have been formed by the story of Christ."[39] With their attacks on individualism and political liberalism (particularly Hauerwas) and the secular world (particularly Milbank), Christian existence emerges principally from the *ecclesial* sphere, which remains the visible body of Christ on earth. This implies that their understanding of the church, although defined in relation to Christ, is also defined *apart* from the church's relationship to the other, as non-churched individuals or the world. So, it follows that the church remains not only an alternative *polis* to the communities of the world, but also the only authentic *polis* in the world. In contrast, although Barth maintains that Christians, as part of Christ's body on earth (the church), should also strive to maintain their particular identity in the world as witnesses to God's Word, this identity is dialectically linked with the other two spheres of personal and worldly existence, which stand under the authority of the Word. This point will be expanded upon in the next chapter.

Again, this discussion has a bearing on how the secular world is seen in relation to the church and has influence on how one sees the legacy of Christendom. In Barth's judgment, because the church bears witness to God's declarative Yes to the world, it refuses to stand against the secular world simply because of its secularity. Barth argues that the church does not mediate grace, but simply bears witness to the sacramental reality of Jesus Christ, the Word of God, which allows it to have a more positive understanding of the secular. Thus the secular world is not only something "out there" that stands against the church, but something "in here" that church encounters in its own movement between the extremes of "glorification" and "alienation." For all his uneasiness with modernity, Barth is more critical of a premodern unified Christendom than is Radical Orthodoxy, which remains more appreciative of the ethos where the church remained the preeminent cultural power. "It is a remarkable coincidence that at the very time and in the very situation when the secular world began to free itself from the Church," Barth writes, "the Church began, not to free itself from, but to be unmistakably free for the secular world, namely, free for the service of its own cause within the secular world which for so long it had

---

39. Hauerwas, *Community of Character*, 1.

for the most part neglected in pursuit of its own fantasies" (*CD* IV/3: 21). The diastasis of church and secular culture that led to end of Christendom was not a tragedy, because it both allows the church to rediscover its witness to the Word at the same time it leads to the "emancipation of the world from the church" (*CD* IV/3: 21). Although the world may deny God, God does not deny the world, or as Barth puts it, "we must not forget that while man may deny God, according to the Word of reconciliation God does not deny man" (*CD* IV/3: 118). Again, Barth insists that Christians recognize the priority of God's action in their response as witnesses to God's gracious command, and that one's moral responsibility consist of actions for the church, but also for others and the world.

Radical Orthodoxy's criticism of Barth, not unlike that of liberal theology, fails to understand the *dialectical* nature of his theology, which is rooted Christologically in the divinity-humanity of Jesus Christ. Rejecting both the divinization of culture, as found in liberalism, and the demonization of culture, as found in various dualistic Christian traditions (and in some Radical Orthodox thought), Barth argues that human culture, although secular, is nonetheless valued because of its *humanity*, which is revealed perfectly in Jesus Christ. The non-dialectical nature of Radical Orthodoxy—its absolute Yes to theology and No to the secular—risks falling into the trap of absolute *diastasis* between the Word of God and the world. No doubt this diastasis is similar to the themes developed in Barth's early writings, but even there, he remains committed toward developing a positive link, grounded in grace, between the Word of God and the world. So, although positively speaking Radical Orthodoxy exposes the hegemonic threat of secularism, it risks becoming non-dialectical and lacks self-criticism. We may recall that dialectical thinking, said Barth in 1922, must "correlate every position and negation one against the other, to clarify 'Yes' by 'no' and 'No' by 'yes' with persisting longer than a movement in a rigid Yes or No" (*WG*: 172). Radical Orthodoxy remains too firmly encamped in the No of its criticism of the "secular" and "secularity." This, as we shall see in a later chapter, becomes practically evident in their view of the economics and politics, which in the name of theology, becomes negatively prescriptive; the No appears louder than the Yes.

We may conclude this chapter by saying that if Christian social ethics is to engage the secular world as a form of Christian witness, it must avoid the risk of theological esotericism as well as secular reductionism (or secularism). Accordingly, it seeks to develop a dialectical position in between the risks of isolationism and diastasis as well as apologetics and cultural synthesis. Moving between these absolute positions, a Christian dialectical social ethics, grounded in Christian witness, emerges with the gracious freedom to correspond to God's command of grace, and further remains *free* to dialogue with important nontheological categories or secular parables, without reducing Christian thought to these categories. It must allow these discourses to simply speak as secular discourses, without *reducing* them to variant heretical Christian positions. Not all secular viewpoints are heretical simply because they are not Christian. This chapter has concluded that it is a false dilemma to argue that Christian ethics must be either exclusivistic, depending on particular Christian truth-claims, or inclusivistic, depending on some general abstract notion of creation, life, or natural law. Rather, Barth's dialectical approach points us in the direction of exclusive inclusiveness. This remains more exclusivistic than Lovin's unapologetic principle, and more inclusivistic of the secular *as* other, than Milbank's theological metadiscourse. Unlike the others, Barth dialectically weaves his way between the twin poles of synthesis and diastasis avoiding the risks of secular reductionism and theological esotericism.

PART FOUR

Christian Ethics as Witness
Political, Economic, and Environmental

CHAPTER TEN

Witness and Christian Responsibility

In this last section of the book, we carry through in practice what was developed in theory, namely that Christian ethics is "responsible witness of the Word of God" serving both "God and men" (*CD* IV/3: 609). In each movement, there is a corresponding dialectic of God's initiating action and human response. In chapters 7–8, we saw how the Yes of moral knowledge of the good, human agency, and moral judgment is followed by the No against the nothingness of sin, death, evil, and the powers. We are now able to discuss further how God's reconciling Yes provides the basis for a Christian ethics of responsible witness, or in ethical language, Christian moral responsibility. This completes the Yes-No-Yes pattern of Christian witness emerging from the divine-human covenant-partnership. This relational ethics of witness stands in contrast to many other traditions of social ethics today. It rejects the presumptions of the modern autonomous self, the postmodern antirealist self, and late-modern reflexive self. All of these are rejected because they view the human subject, apart from God, as the starting point for ethical reflection. Nevertheless, in this chapter we explore how Christian *responsibility* is described in *The Christian Life*, where Barth discusses the three relational spheres or "concentric circles" of Christian existence. These include the *personal* sphere or the relationship to others, the *ecclesial* sphere or relationship to the church, and the *social* sphere or one's relationship to the world. In response to God's gracious covenant,

Christians remain responsible to listen and give witness to the Word of God in these three relational spheres by first invoking God's action and presence within these spheres, and then seeking ways to be faithful witnesses within them. If the divine-human dialectic provides the theory for moral responsibility, then the individual-church-world dialectic provides the arena of action in which responsible behavior takes place. Christian moral responsibility engages in action for the *good* of the other, church, and world. At the end of the chapter, we look at how an ethics of responsible witness applies to the "liberation" of social ethics. This discussion corresponds to some of the material in earlier chapters and thus serves as a brief summary of earlier themes. It will also be avenue for opening up our more deliberative discussion of social ethics in chapters 11–13, where we discuss political, economic, and environmental witness.

MORAL RESPONSIBILITY AND CHRISTIAN WITNESS

As stated, Barth envisions Christian responsible witness as *ethics* occurring in three spheres or circles of Christian existence, namely the personal, ecclesial, and worldly (social). Here we look at each of these spheres and discuss how they relate to one another, and how this provides a theological framework for moral responsibility. Still, once we dig deeper into Barth's analysis, we also discover *dialectical* patterns both externally among the spheres and internally within the spheres themselves. Indeed, this back and forth movement allows these spheres to be living categories of social action and not static entities. Another way of putting it is that dialectical movement by itself brings freedom to the task of responsible judgment and action. This free movement is vitally important for any theory of Christian social ethics that wants to take seriously both human and divine freedom. In this book, I've used the category of "risk" to describe situations in which this freedom is endangered. Risk occurs when one position is not countered by another position, or when one polarity is not countered by an opposite dialectical viewpoint. Put negatively, a non-dialectical viewpoint creates risks for Christian ethics. Without moving back and forth, Christian ethics remains tied to one *absolute* perspective, which often makes it unable to encounter the freedom found in God's gracious command to be responsible witnesses to the Word of God. Instead, we must remember that Christian ethics, at its core, is rooted in Christian responsibility and witness, which seeks to give "the Word of God the precedence over all the other factors and motives that determine our lives" (*CL*: 181).

Moral Responsibility for the Other

We begin with the "narrowest circle," of Christian existence, namely the sphere of personal and interpersonal interaction. It is here where self-determination begins regarding personal and social action. This sphere cannot be completely separated or abstracted from its relation to the other spheres, or discarded as unimportant, while addressing the relevance of the other two spheres. "What he is and does here is important," says Barth, "not apart from, but precisely in relation to, what he does there, in the church and the world. It is precisely in that relationship that the question of what he is and does here in the narrowest circle acquires and has its relatively independent significance and commends itself for consideration before the other two questions" (*CL*: 183). Although Christian identity comprehensively belongs to the interrelationship of these three spheres, the study of this identity begins with a description of the *personal* (not ecclesial or social) existence. To deny the importance of this sphere would be to deny the importance of a theological analysis of the human person as shaped inevitably by the divine-human encounter in the history of Jesus Christ. In short, it would deny the humanity and personhood of Christ.

The dialectical analysis of the personal sphere avoids the two extremes of, on one hand, "ethical individualism," and on the other, ethical "collectivism" or, in other language, social enculturation.

> Human being is being with other humans. Apart from this relationship we become inhuman. We are human by being together, by seeing, hearing, speaking with, and standing by, one another as men, insofar, that is, as we do this gladly and thus do it freely. In Jesus Christ—the one who is for all the others—human existence is reflected in its vertical reality in the history of the relationship between God and man, and in its horizontal reality in the history that necessarily takes place between men. Here we stand before a question which, from the perspective of the Christian proclamation, stands over every individualistic and every collectivist humanism, old or new. It excludes neither individualism nor collectivism. It bears on the individual and also on society, but always on the concrete individual as distinct from other individuals, and always on the society founded on free reciprocal responsibility. It defends

discipline in the face of Nietzsche and freedom in the face of Marx.
. . . It is an exorable protest against any conception of man either
as master or as mass. It recognizes and acknowledges human dignity, duty, and rights only in the context of the realization that true
human existence means existence together with one's fellow man.
(*GHN*: 7–8)

The dialectic between individualism and collectivism is often used in various philosophical and sociological viewpoints, yet for Barth what makes this *true* is how it conforms to the "humanity of God" or "God's humanism." "It is when we look at Jesus Christ that we know decisively that God's deity does not exclude, but includes His *humanity*" (*HG*: 1). It is Christology, not anthropology or ideology, which drives Barth's view of the self as both individual and social, with neither side completely dominating the other. First, the error of individualism denies the reality of the *social* self, which is rooted in the denial of a common humanity as represented in the humanity of Jesus Christ; that is, Jesus Christ is the *one* representative of all humanity. Second, the error of collectivism denies the *individual* self, and with it, the *one* person of Jesus Christ, who lived, died, and was resurrected in first-century Palestine. In both cases, it is God's action *pro nobis*—and as consequence—*pro me* that sets the perimeters for the social and individual nature of the self. Barth rejects various modern philosophies that begin with an autonomous self or the collective self, or analogically, the self separate from or identified with God. The relationship between God and humanity remains a *personal*—not collective—one, in that God's command of grace is directed to all persons *pro nobis* in such a way that individuals know that Christ died *pro me*. Thus, when God addresses specific individuals it confirms the ongoing identity of that personal identity in such a way that the person discovers their true unique identity. It is through one's relationship with God that the individual becomes united with others, without collapsing individual identity into group consciousness or the interests of the other. "Man is bound to his fellow-man, but he cannot belong to him, i.e. he cannot be his property" (*CD* III/2: 270). It is misguided to assume that human relatedness presumes that a person's individuality is lost in the other, that is, a person becomes a "mere copy of the other" and so loses his or her individual "life, task, and responsibility" (*CD* III/2: 269). Moreover, it is also misguided for individuals to enslave and use the other for their own selfish purposes; the other does not belong to the self. Suffice it to say, both "blind alleys" of being a "slave" or a "tyrant" distort the moral ontology of Christian ethics because it fosters the polar risks of radical individualism or social enculturation. The true relationship between one person and another is "neither a slave nor tyrant, but both are companions, associates, comrades, fellows and helpmates" (*CD* III/2: 271).

At its core, Barth's interpersonal ethics is essentially an ethic of responsibility *for the other*. Just as God has chosen to be with and for humanity in Jesus Christ, so too, we choose to be with and for others. Just as God claims to be the *good* for humanity in Jesus Christ, so too, persons must claim to be the *good* for others. Moreover, when Barth speaks about our love for others, or "solidarity and fellowship" with others, then he is speaking about our openness to others. Responsible ethical action, implies "being in encounter is a being in the openness of the one to the other with the view to and on behalf of the other" (*CD* III/2: 250). Indeed, this implies the freedom of the other to such a degree, that both would be critical of imposing any moral law upon another's conscience. An ethic of responsibility *for* others, in other words, means not only loving and serving our neighbor, but also respecting the freedom of individual conscience. We recall that Barth's discussion of the freedom of the conscience belongs to his ethics of redemption and eschatology. Given the fact that he never completed this anticipated fifth volume of the *Church Dogmatics*, our only extensive discussion is in the *Ethics* lectures. "Violation of freedom of conscience, no matter how well intended, always means that the others upon whom I force myself with the claim of my conscience no longer hear their own" (*ET*: 194). Throughout his various ethical writings, Barth is consistent with the claim that the freedom of conscience depends upon the self's understanding of God's freedom to act and speak through the Word, which releases her from being preoccupied with her own moral consciousness as well as the consciences of others. Similar to the some versions of postmodern ethics mentioned earlier, Barth view of moral agency places the moral self before the social self. This means that the obligation for responsibility to be *with* and *for* the other exists prior to the socializing power of moral enculturation, as found in the church and society.

Being with and for others remains a difficult task because Christians continue to live in the dialectical "regime of vacillation and ambiguity," which is rooted in the reality of the person as *simul iustus et peccator*, both sinful and righteous (*CL*: 173ff.). As both a "sinner" and "saint," Christians neither live in complete darkness nor light, nor do they embody the realm of the "demonic or the angelic." The vacillation between these two "facts" comprises *how* persons encounter God's command to be responsible for the other. Indeed, since this "vacillation" remains the objective reality of the Christian life, the individual cannot act with supreme confidence that she always correctly comprehends God's command through the Word. Closer to Martin Luther than John Calvin on this point, Barth argued that the Christian's ability to do the good is often curtailed by the ambiguous condition of *simul iustus et peccator*.[1] This dialectic avoids the two extremes of absolutely denying God, which leads to the ignorance of the good (sinner), and the absolute certitude of God's will, which leads to confident knowledge of the good (saint). The first denies that God needs humanity, and the second that humanity needs God. It is within the tension of the dialectic between sinner and saint, which "God's Word reaches and touches and frees and claims" the person (*CL*: 185).

It is worth looking more deeply into Barth's discussion of *simul iustus et peccator* at this point, which reminds us that the sinner is always a saint and the saint is always a sinner. This will help us further clarify Barth's ethic of responsibility to be *with* and *for* the other. First, as sinner, Christians cannot act as if they are totally ignorant of God's command, or that it is simply irrelevant. Although persons may choose to disregard God's command to be with and for the other, they cannot alter the fact that they are essentially *related* to the other. The sinner can only fall so far, in that, "he cannot reverse his election and calling, which are not his own work but God's" (*CL*: 184). The sinner can never deny God's action with and for the other, because to do so denies God's covenant with humanity. Thus, although Christians are sinners and may choose to be responsible for others, they cannot do so without also being cognizant of their relationship to God, which unites them with others. The second claim is that Christians, as saints, cannot act as if they are totally cognizant of the "knowledge of God" or of God's command. There has never been a Christian who "has demonstrated and presented himself in a life that simply follows a consistent course from his election and calling, simply as a victorious fighter against sin, death, and the devil, simply in attestation of his knowledge of God, simply as figure of light" (*CL*: 185). "Indeed," he adds, "the most remarkable Christian personalities are as a rule the very ones whose image is marred by the heaviest shadows and deepest problems of character, habits, and decisions" (*CL*: 185). Christians can pray for God's sanctification, but

---

1. Hunsinger, *Disruptive Grace*, 279–304.

they cannot "make it their own task"; sanctification is wholly God's work. What this means is that the saint can never deny that God's action to be with and for the other, is *God's* work. Christians are saints only because of the covenant of grace, which establishes their relationship to God. It is this relationship that unites them with others, and declares their obligation to be with and for others. In both cases, therefore, the person, as sinner and saint, cannot deny her relationship to God or others because this would lead to a denial of herself.

One important result of this dialectical perspective is that ethics always remains an unfinished project. Hence emerging out of this knowledge of the persons as sinner and saint, the gap between human judgment and God's judgment, Christian social ethics remains *aporetic*, in that it is never satisfied with the standards it sets for itself, nor can it never hope completely to embody its own ideals. There is a genuine heterogeneity between what is and what ought to be. Timothy Gorringe writes: "A theology which is insufficiently 'aporetic' in this way will be marked by superficiality, and sometimes by dishonesty—the claim that Christianity has 'the answer for everything.'"[2] A Christian ethics, therefore, that remains insufficiently *aporetic* and non-dialectical, at its core, remains *overconfident* about the knowledge and action of the good. This positivist, indeed utopian mindset, Barth often deconstructed in his ethical writings for being too modern and not sufficiently theological. As stated before, there is always heterogeneity between the Word of God and our understanding and ability to enact it in our lives. This dialectic has important ramifications for Christian witness and discipleship. The devout Christian, in Barth's view, cannot move directly from the scriptural teachings and acts of Jesus to obligatory moral prescriptions. In *Ethics* he writes: "We are not Christ. We shall never be. Hence it is only with great caution and reserve that we can say that we are commanded to be Christ to our neighbor" (*ET*: 342). Unlike the content of many reductionistic versions, both liberal and conservative, as well as various versions of the *imitatio Christi* or programmatic discipleship, which begins with a prescriptive ethic of Jesus, Barth insists that the distance between Jesus Christ and us cannot be bridged by our virtuous actions. In the words of Gene Outka, we can follow Jesus, but "only at a distance."[3] Being witnesses to God's Word, means learning how to forgive, love, and

---

2. Gorringe, *Karl Barth*, 282.
3. Outka, "Following at a Distance," 144–60.

serve others only because we are "sinners saved by grace." Therefore, just as God's Word remains hidden, yet disclosed in history, so too, the normative task of the ethical life must remain both hidden and revealed. Ethics always remains an ambiguous task, not only because human beings are sinful and cannot live up to their own norms of love and justice, but because God is free at any moment to shatter our conceptualizations—or hegemonies—of these norms through the Word. Nonetheless, the *aporetic* nature of Christian ethics, should not lead to complacency and apathy, embodying a "variation of Stoic ethics" (*CL*: 186). Even though the Christian finds himself in a "midway place" there is:

> no resting, let alone settling down and making himself at home. In this midway place he can only be on the road as a pilgrim. . . . With purely provisional and relative, yet still with definite, steps, he will venture to contradict the contradiction in which he finds himself entangled to speak here and now and clear and impatient practical No to his own toleration of the contradiction, and to speak a No grounded in the great Yes of the gospel accepted by him, or, again positively, to set up against it a sign of the hope that lives within him. (*CL*: 187)

In the Christian's "zeal to honor God" and give "precedence to the Word," the disciple needs to decisively act "here and now." "The ground beneath his feet is on fire here. He can only hurry, move, and run. The unrest that the Word of God has brought into his life will never leave him so long as he has this life" (*CL*: 187). The vocative nature of ethical witness implies that Christians are to struggle and resist the evil that desecrates God's name, which invariably means not to "flow with the stream" but to "continually swim against it" (*CL*: 187). Christians cannot be modern utopians, nor can they passively wait for God's action to be finalized in history, rather God invites persons to act decisively, purposively, and confidently today against the "regime of vacillation," the "lordless powers" that distorts God's name in the world. In ethical action, the Christian should pray because prayer itself is perhaps the most important act a Christian can perform; prayer is ethics. This is why Barth's discussion of personal agency and correspondence emerges within an extended discussion of the Lord's Prayer. This prayer teaches Christians about the correspondence between divine and human agency (double agency), which provides the language for Christian ethics. By praying: "thy kingdom come, they will be done, on earth at it is in heaven," the believer acts by invoking the presence of God, and in so doing, invites God to act by empowering him to respond to God's Word. With prayer guiding the person's action, she must be "totally resolute yet totally modest, totally fearless yet totally without illusions, totally courageous yet totally humble" (*CL*: 185).

We may conclude this section by saying that similar to the risks of Barth's world, today's Christians must "swim against the stream" of both individualism and collectivism. Yet, in today's postmodern world, we are also more aware of how the "particularistic turn" raises new, and perhaps more serious, risks for Christians to resist, namely social enculturation, fragmentation, and tribalism. As stated earlier, social theorists, like Ulrich Beck, argue that social fragmentation fosters both individualization and tribalization, which perpetuate violence. Postmodern risk society is a threat to social solidarity and community, but also a threat to the dignity of the person, with greater emphasis on group and tribe consciousness. If sociality "goes all the way down," as Rorty reminds us, then persons are incapable of self-reflection, and incapable of developing or encountering moral norms that challenge their cultural morality. Without ideals, ethical thinking collapses into moral tribalism, ethical pluralism, and the loss of personal agency. In the end, both extremes presume a moral theory of antirealism, and reject the dialectical notion of persons-in-community. A theological view of agency presumes that human agency is intertwined with divine agency, which challenges the extremes of personal agency as completely self-determinative and autonomous or completely indeterminate and acculturated. Rather, agency is responsive and relational, to God and others. This is why both prayer and ethics are human actions that seek to continually respond to God as covenant-partner. In our age of risk and sullen resentment, Christian ethics must resist the powers that perpetuate the lies that God has not spoken clearly and definitively in the Word of God. The Christian witness resists the temptation that the No is stronger than the Yes, and that disbelief and cynicism are stronger than faith, despair is stronger than hope, and hate is stronger than love.

Moral Responsibly for the Church

The second sphere for Christian moral existence is the church or, as Barth prefers, the Christian community. Not unlike the dialectic of sinner and righteous in the personal sphere, Barth conceives a similar dialectic in the ecclesial sphere between the two extremes of "defect" and "excess" (*CL*: 136).

This distinction is similar to his discussion in *CD* IV/2 of the secular church of "alienation" and the sacral church of "glorification," as discussed in the last chapter. However, his focus in this section of the *CL* is the relationship of the church to that of the individual and the world, rather than a discussion pertaining to the church's identity. The point being that his discussion in the *CL* is more piercing and poignant. Again, a dialectical ethics of witness that *values* the identity of the church, as the body of Christ, must avoid these two extreme poles. The first pole, the "church in defect" chooses to be *ignorant* of the Word of God and risks becoming a secular church. This "harlot church," he says, "does not take itself seriously enough because it is only half sure of its cause;" indeed, it is "unfaithful to its determination vis-à-vis the world, which has been given to it with its establishing and upholding as the church of Jesus Christ" (*CL*: 137–38). Although this "church of Babylon" may proclaim the living God, it only "occasionally and not fundamentally speaks and acts 'as if' God has really acted decisively in Jesus Christ and the resurrection" (*CL*: 138). Nevertheless, as an "extroverted church," it remains anxious, burdened, and frightened concerning its relationship to the powers of politics, economics, and science. To avoid confrontation with these powers, this church seeks to align itself with the secular languages and authorities of the world. This church finds it necessary, therefore, to shape its message according to a secular language that appears to the "real world" as more comprehensive and conclusive; it remains a defensive and apologetic church that "for the sake of security wants to construct an ontology before beginning theology" (*CL*: 139). So, when the church fears being irrelevant to the secular despisers, and the extremes of esotericism, it inevitably moves toward the other risk of *secularism*. In doing this, it fails to "give precedence to the Word of God" and instead denies the Word's authority over church. It replaces the Word of God with some other secular word.

Since modernity, the most obvious risk for social ethics is to *deny* the importance of the church in both the task of personal and social ethics. When the ecclesial sphere of Christian ethics is denied, it inevitably distorts both individual and social existence, and with it, personal and social ethics. With the modern separation of ethics from theology, the Christian ethicist has often approached the topic of social ethics from only the two spheres of the individual and society (or the world), while avoiding the church altogether. Barth writes:

> The Christian is in the church. He is not just in it externally, accidentally, or incidentally. He is not in it merely in the sense that

he might first be a more or less good Christian by his personal choice and calling and on his own responsibility as a lonely hearer of God's Word, and only later, perhaps optionally and only at this own pleasure, he might take into account his membership in the church. If he were not in the church, he would not be in Christ. He is elected and called, not to the being and action of a private person with a Christian interest, but to be a living member of the living community of the living Lord Jesus Christ. It is by the Word which gathers and builds up this community and calls it to service that he is made personally responsible. The church's witness to the act of sanctifying his name which God has performed and will reveal is the witness with which he is most urgently commissioned. It is as one of this people, standing for all and for the cause of all in his own person, that he may and should pray, "Hallowed by thy name" ... (*CL*: 188)

When Christian ethics neglects the church's witness, it ceases being a *Christian* witness. This opens the door to another word as foundational, whether philosophical or scientific. Without the church's witness as its guiding mission, Christian ethics adopts other methodological strategies that propose a different moral ontology than the one revealed in the Word of God. This accommodationist (or apologetic) method, as we have seen, leads to the synthesis of theological and nontheological accounts of the self, world, and the moral life, which invariably leads to some form of secular reductionism. For example, once the framework of the social sciences is privileged, there remains little regard for the church as an important subject in ethical deliberation and reflection. Indeed, in many fine Christian ethics textbooks and compendiums, there is often very little about the church, or the relationship of ecclesiology and Christian ethics, or how theology shapes one's understanding of moral agency. In contrast, Barth reminds us that it is impossible to "give precedence to the Word" in social ethics, without "going through" the church. The Word of God empowers, through the Holy Spirit, the church with the task of being witnesses in the world. The Word of God is not principally heard in one's individual conscience (as an autonomous faculty of reason and experience), nor in the communities of the world (through social enculturation), but in the church, which remains the earthly community where the history of God's reconciliation of humanity, between the resurrection and the *parousia* is taking place. It follows that Christians cannot separate themselves from the Christian community in their task of being witnesses. They "will not take the form of a party or school—of—'ians.' But they will quietly and tenaciously take the position that the Word of God must be first heard in the church" (*CL*: 193). Simply put, for Barth, social ethics that does not include the church is not *Christian*. Even justifiable criticism of the church should not lead to a disassociation, or denial of responsibility, *for* the church. Whether one likes it or not, Barth says, the Christian "stands or falls with the cause of the church" (*CL*: 188).

At the other extreme, the "church in excess" remains supremely overconfident and *arrogant* of its knowledge of God. As a "holy church" it equates its own "form and action," its traditions and practices, with that of the Word of God. "*It* speaks his truth; *it* extends or denies his grace; *it* proclaims his law" (*CL*: 137). As an "introverted church" it is more preoccupied with *itself* than with the "Living Lord" that it serves; "it is primarily interested in itself, and in its Lord only for its own sake" (*CL*: 136). Moreover, as an "infallible church" it is supremely zealous to "be the church," but it often becomes misguided and confused of its own mission and purpose. In doing so, it obscures the Word of God and denies God's freedom to both reconcile and pronounce judgment on the church. "How can God be confessed," asks Barth, "when his Word is not free but bound" and when "the greater glory of God it is bound to the church?" (*CL*: 137). In short, the "church in excess" is a "presumptuous church which exalts and puffs itself up" (*CL*: 136). Similar to the first extreme, this church avoids listening and bearing witness to the Word by replacing it with some other word, but unlike the first, this overconfident church prioritizes itself and its "religion" over the world and the individual. It too fears the growing secularization of the world, but tries to overcome the tension between the church and world by triumphing *over* the world. In doing so, it rightly avoids secular*ism*, but it cannot avoid the other risk of theological esotericism. By obscuring the Word of God with "church-speak" it invariably distorts its relation to outsiders and the world, by denying that the World of God may speak there as well in its secular parables. It also ultimately fails to "give precedence to the Word" and instead replaces the Word of God with some churchly word.

The overconfident church privileges the church *over* the world, which leads to an undervaluing of the world. A church that remains preoccupied with its own "self-preservation" fails to adequately trust in the Word of God, and in doing so, begins to be resentful of the world, which limits its service and witness to the world. Consider Nicholas Healy's assessment:

Much contemporary ecclesiology and ecclesial ethics is geared towards thwarting what are seen as the detrimental affects upon the church of individualisms in it various forms, including theological constructivism, doctrinal and practical consumerism and the pervasive failure to obey church authorities. The concern to distinguish and separate, protect, and defend is widespread. It surfaces not only in Hauerwas and those he has influenced, but in Radical Orthodoxy, communion ecclesiology and in some forms of postliberalism, too. . . . For Barth, the fundamental problem is not that the church tries to appease modernity or preserve itself against it, though that is certainly part of it. Nor is the greatest threat today individualism, Constantinianism, constructivist theology, nominalism, or secularism. The greatest danger, I think Barth would say, is that the church will fail to be the church, that it will fail to be faithful and, above all, to hope and trust in God as it calls upon the Spirit in prayerful obedience to the Word. The church's faithfulness is displayed as it breaks down any and all theological barriers to our full acknowledgment, in all our thinking and practices, of the absolute necessity and sufficiency of the world of the Spirit and the Word, both in our midst and outside our churches' walls.[4]

Another way of putting the difference between ecclesial ethics and Barth is that the former group privileges the ecclesial sphere *over* the personal and social spheres, rather than keeping them in dialectical balance, as in Barth's case. By privileging the church over the other spheres, the church finds reasons to inevitably distort its view of these other spheres. This is how the church's worldview can become rather pessimistic, resentful, or cynical about the people and the world. This worldview, in *CD* IV/3, Barth calls the "anxious view" or view of the "uneasy conscience." Ironically, for all of its grandstanding about the church, it actually fails to understand itself as a witness to the work of Jesus Christ. Because it prioritizes itself, and not Christ, it ends taking "a tragic view of itself and its opponents, and might even make a bad situation worse" (CD IV/3: 239). It is the church, not Christ, who battles sin, death, and evil. *Christus victor* is replaced with *ecclesia victor*. When the church is seen as an end in itself, it reduces Jesus Christ, as *totus Christus*, to the visible *ecclesia*, the Body of Christ. It is true that Christ, in his historical bodily-existence is in the church, *totus Christus*. Yet, we have said, *totus Christus* is also *Christus victor*. Christ, not

---

4. Healy, "Karl Barth's Ecclesiology Reconsidered," 297–98.

the church, claims victory over the powers and achieves reconciliation; Jesus Christ, not the church, is Lord.

Moreover, failure to distinguish between Christ and the church not only undervalues Christ's headship, but it also overvalues the church's triumphant character, its institutional form, or its sociological function in shaping Christian character. John Webster warns that although focusing on the church—as a character-shaping community—might be a useful corrective to the decisionist trend in Christian ethics, there may be a hidden commitment to a theology of "social immanence," which reduces the "moral field" (or moral ontology) of Christian ethics to the social practices and beliefs of the community. "But worship—and, with it, ecclesiology—should not explain to occupy the whole moral field, and can only be kept within its proper limits when it is a function of language about God and God's acts in Christ and the Holy Spirit." Moreover, Webster adds, that "it runs the risk of not making sufficiently clear the distinction in kind between 'church' and 'sociality,' so that church comes to be a cultural and not a theological concept."[5] Both Webster and Christopher Insole have argued that what is needed, as a helpful corrective, to the emphasis on the visible church and its practices, is a stronger doctrine of the "invisible church" and "God's holiness."[6] With the focus on the visible community, the *invisible* nature of the church fades into the background, and with it, the mysterious action of the Spirit's divine agency. Does the church belong to us or to God? What does this say about the Spirit's freedom both inside and outside the church? Overall, these questions raise very serious problems about how the freedom of the trinitarian God relates to the church, its practices, and the world. Beginning with the freedom of God, we must say that Christian ethics, in its core, cannot originate *from* the church, but from the Word of God, who stands above the church as its head, savior, and judge. At the level of divine judgment, there must some *diastasis* between the Word of God and the church, just as there is between the church and the world. Unlike an ecclesial ethics or an ethics of the Christian community, Barth grounds the freedom of human subject in the freedom of the Word, which cannot be reduced to any social, historical, and cultural construction, including the church.

Generally speaking we see problems within the ecclesial sphere when the church moves too far in either direction of excess or defect. The crucial

5. Webster, *Word and Church*, 248–49.
6. Webster, *Confessing God*, 175–91; and Insole, *Politics of Human Frailty*, 125–57.

problem with these extremes of "defect" and "excess" is that they deny God's objective acts of reconciliation and redemption. The first denies the *activity* of the triune God, particularly the Holy Spirit, within the church, and the second, denies the activity of the triune God *in* the world. Both the human and divine *other* can potentially become marginalized and denied. This is because human and divine otherness is revealed in the *mystery* of the Word of God, and with it, the sacramental reality of Jesus Christ. An ethics of witness views the mission of the church as neither passive nor revolutionary. The object of the church's devotion is not to any "tradition or ancient custom or modern fashion, not to the dogma and confession of the fathers, not to the claims of any contemporary (philosophical or non-philosophical) movement, and certainty not to the wishes and demands that might be presented by political rulers or majorities" (*CL*: 193). It is not governed by a stoic ethic of complacency and acceptance of the status quo, but an ethic of resistance against all hegemonies that stand against the church, whether they are ideological, political, *or* ecclesial. It affirms both *totus Christus* and *Christus victor*. First, the church must give witness that *Christus victor* has defeated the powers. That is, it stands against the powers and resists its power of nothingness. Christians act in "resistance, not, of course, against the church but *for* the church, a countermovement that is to be initiated and executed within the church for the sake of the church" (*CL*: 192–93). Moreover, because Christ, as *totus Christus*, is present in the church, the church *is* a community of witness. It is a community of deliberation and conversation, which seeks to live under the authority of the Word of God, which always transcends any comprehensive human conceptualization. Hence, the ecclesial tradition must be respected and heard, but the Word may pass judgment upon past ethical pronouncements, just as it may upon past biblical moral prescriptions and rules.[7] With its central commitment to God's Word, as especially witnessed to in Scripture, the church seeks to halt, or at least slow down, the "pendulum swing" between excess and defect. In this slowed movement the church remains more aware of its mission and witness.

Moral Responsibility for the World

The last sphere of the Christian life is the world or the social spheres in which the individual and the church exist. Obviously, like the other two spheres, this one cannot be abstracted and isolated from the other two. The

---

7. See Biggar, *Hastening That Waits*, 97–145.

individual Christian belongs to the world as much as she does to herself and the church. The Christian does not *choose* to be in solidarity with the world, says Barth, but "is in solidarity with it from the very first" (*CL*: 194). Indeed, he adds: "He is not a Christian and a member of God's people for his own sake or for that of the church but in order to be a light in the world [Matt 5:14]" (*CL*: 195). As stated earlier, privileging the individual sphere leads to individualism and privileging the ecclesial sphere leads to a kind of ecclesial collectivism, both of which deny the worldliness of persons and the church. Admittedly, it remains a strong temptation for the pious Christian to "close the windows and doors against those outside, to withdraw into a Christianity of the individual or the church, and to be content with the problems that this in itself poses." Yet, he adds, the Christian is also a "child and citizen of the world—is outside as well as inside, in its worldly form it is his problem too" (*CL*: 196). Christians belong to the world as much as they belong to the church. Moreover, denying the world's value also rejects God's love for the world in the reconciliation of Jesus Christ. It is in this "outer sphere" where Christian ethics becomes public and practical. "It is here in this outermost circle," Barth says, that the Christian life "has its most practical scope or has none at all" (*CL*: 195).

Like the other spheres, there is dialectic between two extremes positions. These two extremes, lead to the following risks: 1) by stressing the *homogeneity* of the world to the church and the person, Christians inevitably endorse a kind of "Christian secularism" or secular Christianity; and 2) by stressing the *otherness* of the world, Christians create a false separation between themselves (and the church) and the world, which leads to the exclusion of the world. This first position of homogeneity between the world and the church finds its theological voice in liberal apologetics, which seeks to synthesize Christian beliefs with those of dominant culture or society or the cultured despisers of religion. This view, simply put, undervalues God's decisive action in the world, as both a judgment of No and Yes, against nothingness (and powers) and for reconciliation. Divine agency is often reduced to that of general providence or creator and worse yet, reduced to the co-creative power of the human will. The burden for transforming the world, therefore, falls entirely upon human shoulders to change the world. It often remains skeptical of Nicene trinitarianism or Chalecadonian Christology. In its attempt to make Christian belief relevant, it calls for a theology of *praxis*. In so doing, it overvalues the power of human action and undervalues the power of God's trinitarian action. Even though this position does not fear secularism, its temptation is always to strive for a "practical symbiosis" with the non-Christian way of life, so that the Christian way of life will not be seen as "alien" or unusual (*CL*: 198). It is committed to the apologetic task, as *poiesis*, of making theological discourse relevant to the modern age. There is no danger, therefore, for Christians to simply accommodate themselves to the process of secularization. To be sure, then, it *overvalues* the world's openness to the Word of God, and the Christian's ability to translate the Word into secular language and forms of life. Like the ecclesiology of defect, this view undervalues the church and overvalues the secular world, as a source of knowledge about God, humanity, and the world.

At the other extreme is the error that stresses the *otherness* of the world, in such a way that Christians stand against the world, while standing for the church. Again, this discussion is very similar to the church of excess, which overconfidently links the Word of God in its own practices, skills, and virtues. In this section, Barth is more concerned with the church's separation from the world. When the church rejects the world as "alien," it usually results in two kinds of Christian action, namely "principle monasticism" and "principle crusadism" (*CL*: 197–98). The first principle presumes that Christians ought to remain separate from the "tendencies, habits, and forms of life" of the world. That is, understanding himself as an "alien in an alien environment," the believer "wants to be as distant as he can so that in the language of the facts created by him in this distance and isolation he can stir the world to see a dimension alien to it, giving indirect visibility to the new and different thing that as a Christian he has to represent among it" (*CL*: 197). Even with the good intentions to give service and witness to God's kingdom, persons who choose this strategy err by linking their particular strategy with a general or systematic strategy of witness for all Christians. It becomes a "principle" instead of an individual calling. So, the church collectively denies God's freedom to engage individuals *as* individuals in Christian witness. By privileging the sociality (or ethos) of the church, the personal sphere, including the conscience, becomes reduced to the community, thus, ironically "collectivist." Moreover, by embellishing the difference from the world, the Christian fails to understand herself and the church as both righteous *and* sinful. This leads to the wrong understanding of the person (as saint but not sinner), the church (as excess but not defect), and the world (as fallen but not redeemed). The second position that stresses the *otherness* of the world is "principle crusadism." This view claims that the Christian way of life is "superior" to others, and therefore its task or witness is to "teach the world" or "call it to order." Instead of sectarian withdrawal, however, this position lead to a kind of activism, indeed even a militant activism, which unites the gospel with particular "intellectual, moral, and even political positions." Although its contempt for the world may not be as pronounced as in "principle monasticism," nevertheless, its "aim is to do injury to the worldliness of the world" (*CL*: 198). It fails to acknowledge that the world, in all its secularity, is also a place where the Word of God can be encountered; it fails to recognize that God's covenant of grace also extends to the world. Moreover, by absolutizing this strategy and making it universal (e.g., making it a "principle") for all Christians, it disregards the diversity of Christian witness and God's freedom to command such witness. In short, like the "monastic" view it misconstrues the personal and ecclesial spheres by non-dialectically taking one side of the polarity and ignoring the other.

A preferable interpretation of the church/world relationship is that it falls between homogeneity and otherness, that is, between complete identification and separation or assimilation and isolation. This is possible only when the church allows for the freedom and value of the secular to be other, without collapsing everything into the ideology of secularism. In so doing, the church can witness to the world without further collapsing into the myopia of its own self-preservation of defect (alienation) or excess (glorification). Christian social ethics, therefore, must avoid the false separation of the church from the world, the sacred from the secular, which affirms both a hegemonic triumph of the secular as well as a theological denial that God's covenant of grace remains excluded from the secular world. First, this entertains the possibility of thinking nontheologically about the potential hegemony of secularism. As Barth insists, "No Prometheanism can be effectively maintained against Jesus Christ" (*CD* IV/3: 118). Second, we may recall that God's Word can commandeer secular words, elevating them by grace, using them for God's own purposes. The secular realm is what it *is*, namely a non-churchly community that can potentially bring honor to God's name. However, this sanctifying of the secular remains God's work through the sanctifying power of the Word, and not something that Christians can accomplish through their own efforts of transformation of secular into the sacred. The church, like the individual and the world, cannot escape the "regime of vacillation," the eschatological tension of already and not yet that exists between the time of resurrection and the *parousia*.

Just as the church waits and hastens, praying for the fullness of God's kingdom, so too, does the world.

Nevertheless, the church's task is not to stand frozen in the dialectic between homogeneity and otherness with the world, but to be an active witness to the world that it too is reconciled as God's covenant-partner. Throughout Barth's political writings, he calls for Christian responsibility for the civil community. For this we can return to some of the important political essays discussed in chapter 3. In his 1938 Gifford Lectures, for example, he says Christians have no "universal valid duty" or "right" to "refuse the State our positive co-operation and our participation in its responsibility."[8] For Barth there is no such thing as a nonpolitical Christianity, and the church that ceases being political, ceases being a witness. In "Gospel and Law," he writes: "[T]he Church would not be the Church, if in her very existence . . . the Law of God, its commands, its questions, its admonitions and its accusations would not be visible and apprehensible also for the world, for the state and society" (*CSC*: 79). Moreover, in the 1946 essay, we saw how this intimate relationship of the ecclesial and civil communities, as inner and outer circles, both give witness to God's kingdom. The church's public witness, as inner circle, seeks to engage parabolic forms of witness within the secularity of the outer circle of civil community. That is, the church makes itself responsible for the shape and reality of the civil community by reminding the civil community of its own identity, self-limitations, and proper forms of political organization and action. This parabolic relation, as discussed in chapter 3, is worked out in twelve analogies between the church and civil community in the 1946 essay. Building on this several years later, Barth discusses six other analogies of "church law" that find correspondence in civil law. First, the church's law, in its pure form, simply provides a *service* to the other as its end, which simplifies and transcends the complex self-interested and reciprocal strategies of much secular law. Second, church law, in its witness to Christ, points beyond society to a divine law that provides *judgment* of the world and all human law. Third, church law demonstrates how law can be based on mutual *trust* not coercion. Fourth, church law demonstrates to the world, that law should place value on the community's *common good*, or as he puts it, the "total self-giving to all." Fifth, the church demonstrates how mutual *solidarity* and human *equality* can be practiced with a community of free persons, while rejecting society's emphasis on achievement,

---

8. Barth, *Knowledge of God and the Service of God*, 229.

materialism, and power. Lastly, the church demonstrates to society that the law is a free gift of God that remains *open-ended* and *dynamic*, or as he says, it is not a "frozen or static pond, but must be a living stream continuously flowing from worse to better" (*CD* IV/2: 724–25). Taken together, these six ecclesial laws (as a form of the gospel) can be a prototype or model of how the law of civil community ought to be established and practiced.

The two-way relationship of the Christian and civil communities also demonstrates how the secular community can be an "indirect witness" to the church and God's kingdom. In this section of *CD* IV/2, after discussing the six analogies that move from the church to world, he turns the argument around and places the church in learning role. In its relationship to the world, says Barth, it is possible that the "children of the world prove to be wiser than the children of light, so that in the question concerning its law the church has reason to learn from the world . . . receiving from it the witness which it ought to give" (*CD* IV/2: 725). Unlike some versions of ecclesial politics, Barth does not always assume that analogies always go in *one* direction, namely form the church to the world. The civil community can teach the church the practical embodiment of this law of the gospel in public life, because even as the "outer circle" it can speak in "secular parables of the kingdom" that bear witness to God's rule. The church, for example, can be inspired, even guided, toward serving others in the civil community and the larger world. Earlier in the 1946 essay, he argues that the "essence of Christian politics" is a "constant direction, a continuous line of discoveries on both sides of the boundary which separates the political from the spiritual spheres, a correlation between explications and applications" (*CSC*: 180). Where the "boundary" meets there can be overlap and mutual sharing. What this means is that Christian truth, whether expressed as church law or civil law, remain the form of the gospel, which is the basis for all law. Just as the civil community can learn from the church how to be itself, so too, the church can learn from secular parables of the civil community how to be the church. As a post-Christendom theologian, Barth assumes that modernity has led to both the church's freedom *from* the state and the state's freedom *from* the church. It was the legacy of Christendom, after all, that led the German Christians to support the Nazification of the state, and Hitler's genocidal policy, which led directly to the Holocaust. If the civil community is to be free it must be free from the power of the church, and if the church is to be free it must be free from the power of the state.

Lastly, the church's active witness to the civil community (and larger world) falls between the extreme monastic and crusading positions, which deny the church's relatedness to the secular world. These two extreme positions err because they *undervalue* the world and *overvalue* the Christian way of life. First, by adopting "a globally negative judgment on what the world seeks and does," Christians fail to acknowledge God's "objective" claim on the world through Jesus Christ (*CL*: 98). This view undervalues the importance of God's action and revelation for the good of the world, and instead stresses human action in either its ascetic or activist forms. Particular forms of witness are universalized and formalized, thus, further leading persons away from the Word of God as divine judgment as well as reconciliation. By undervaluing the world, Christians inevitably end up undervaluing the fact that God's Word stands *for* the world. In this view, God is apparently incapable of redeeming the world as it stands in its secularity. Second, they deny the import of God's action in the world by overvaluing their own competence and power to confront the world as teachers, judges, and conquerors. Christians cannot denounce the world as the "secular other" without elevating themselves above the world. Again, this leads to the errors of Christian perfectionism or individualism and ecclesial excess. In both cases, there is an "obscuring of the positive content of the witness which Christians owe to the world" (*CL*: 198). The Christian, he adds, "for the sake of his witness" may "from time to time have to make individual decisions of a monkish or crusading type" but he "should not try to be either a monk or a crusader." "Neither isolation from the world nor a militant approach to it can be a consistent law of his action in the world, for this must be the action of a witness" (*CL*: 198). Misunderstanding the task of Christian witness leads to the egregious belief that the monk and the crusader in principle become the Word of God in the world.

RESPONSIBLE SOCIAL WITNESS: THREE THEMES

So, what does it mean for Christians to be responsible witnesses among others, the church, and the world? How can we see ethical responsibility as a *form* of social witness? In chapter 7 we discussed how the "liberation" of individual moral judgment takes place, which leads to the freeing of moral agency, moral deliberation, appetites, desire, will, and conscience. Now we further this discussion about Christian liberation as it bears on responsible witness in society, or put differently, the liberation of social ethics *as* witness.

In approaching this question, we look further at Barth's "ethics of reconciliation" fragments in *The Christian Life*. These themes have been present in earlier chapters, thus, this section also serves as brief summary. First, social ethics is liberated as witness because, at its core, it remains positively *eschatological*. Beginning in his early writings, as discussed in chapter 2, Barth's eschatology provides the dialectical framework for his understanding of theological ethics. Christian witness *against* the powers and *for* the good of humanity is grounded in the eschatological reality of God's action. In knowing that one's provisional ethical actions remain a witness to the actual reality that God has initiated and completed, the Christian can remain confident and hopeful that their actions correspond to God's prior gracious actions of divine agency. Eschatology implies ethics just as ethics implies eschatology. What does it this mean to say that ethics is eschatological? In reflecting on Barth's thought, John Webster provides an excellent description of the eschatological nature of Christian ethics.

> Human moral action . . . is ordered towards the *telos* of history, which is the coming of Jesus Christ. That *telos* both relativizes and incites action. It relativizes action, because the end of history is the manifestation of Jesus Christ, the one who was and is and is to come; the end of history is not within the sphere of human competence or responsibility, and is hence a matter of prayer. But it incites action, because the Christian's prayer, *Maranatha!* is an active, not an inactive prayer, a prayer which invites, expects, indeed commands us to do in our sphere what is fitting in the light of the action of God to whom we pray. And so Christian eschatology is ethical, and Christian ethics are eschatological.[9]

The eschatological nature of ethics and Christian witness refuses to privilege the already over the not yet, nor the not yet over the already. Rather, the unveiling of the already occurs *within* the not yet and the not yet within already. This makes ethics dialectical. Barth consistently argues that divine action happens in *relation* to human action, which frees and empowers persons to engage in their limited efforts to foster peace, hope, and justice. Since only God's "perfect righteousness" can completely unveil the kingdom in its fullness, Christians are "forbidden to attempt the impossible" (*CL*: 265). This leads not to complacency and inactivity, but an *active* response to Christ's victory over the powers. It is misguided to place

9. Webster, *Word and Church*, 284–85.

the veiling of the not yet above the unveiling of the already or *visa versa*. God has decisively acted in Jesus Christ against the powers, and Christians can give witness to the reality of this fact in the world through their actions of faith, hope, and love. It follows that Christian eschatology rests in the objective fact that God has decisively acted, is acting, and will act in the future. As mentioned in chapter 2, this approach was first developed in *Ethics*, in which the freedom of the Christian conscience is eschatologically grounded in the dialectical reality of both waiting upon God's free action and responding by hastening toward the fulfillment of God's kingdom. As living witness of the Word in the world, Christians proclaim that the kingdom is both already and not yet. Rejecting this dialectical view, often leads Christians into either passive inactivity, or equating the kingdom of God with their own political, economic, or cultural strategies. Either way, they fully *separate* God's action from human action and place the emphasis on either divine *or* human action. In the first case, Christians place too much emphasis on divine action, which overshadows the human, and then puts too much emphasis on unveiling of the already within the not yet. What this view fails to see is the ambiguity of human action and the veiling of the not yet within the already. We might call this a *Docetic* eschatology, which often leads to the identification of God's agency with human political, social, or cultural transformational or revolutionary movements. The second error is *Ebionite* eschatology, which often leads to Christian asceticism, social inactivity, social sectarianism and separatism, and lack of social witness. This places too much emphasis human action, namely personal piety and holiness, which limits the divine agency in the world, and then puts too much emphasis on the veiling of the already within the unveiling of the not yet. What this view fails to see is that God is actively involved in the unveiling of the already within the not yet.

Second, an eschatologically directed form of social ethics as witness is liberated when it becomes *dialectical*. We've seen in previous chapters the importance of the dialectical nature of moral judgment and action. Ethics is dialectical because it is grounded in God's eschatological freedom to act past, present, and future. In other words, the freedom to move back and forth regarding particular courses of action is rooted in the fact that it is God, not humanity, which establishes human freedom. "Human freedom is the *gift* of God in the free outpouring of His grace. To call man free is to recognize that God has *given* him freedom" (*HG*: 75). The Christian is free to act dialectically in his moral decisions and courses of action because he does not have to be "afraid of taking sides for and against." Human fear about doing the right thing paralyzes into rigidity and ideological corruption. Dialectical freedom stands against the power of ideological reductionism. Since Christians are free from ideology, they are truly free to criticize and reject any particular moral strategy and absolute moral judgment of Yes and No, which in the end may threaten human freedom. All ideas, even moral ideas, pose a threat to human freedom and liberation, made possible by the gospel. Barth writes: "Their Yes and No in this sphere can always be only a relative Yes and No, supremely because if it were more they would be affirming and acknowledging the existence of those absolute or lordless powers, canonizing their deification, and instead of resisting the true and most dangerous enemies of man and his right, life, and work, offering them the most hazardous and fateful help" (*CL*: 268). Responsible judgment is not locked into an absolute Yes or No, nor does it seek to make absolute moral judgments binding for all people at all times. As Barth puts it, Christians have the freedom to "take a few steps or even to go a good way along either path as need requires" (*CL*: 201). Again, this does not imply that responsible moral deliberation and action is blind to particular courses of action. Between the absolute Yes and No there is a great deal of room to maneuver within the moral field. It first sets the perimeters of the debate by saying No to the powers and Yes to others, church, and the world. Thus, it both "revolts" *against* the dystopian nature of violence, despair, and oppression, and "struggles" *for* peace, hope, justice, and freedom. More binding than ethical ideals, principles, or values, therefore, is the "struggle for human righteousness" (*CL*: 205). This struggle involves the dialectical process of moving back and forth determining the "relative Yes and No" of practical moral judgment and action. This not only gives freedom to moral judgment and action, but as stated above, it prevents Christian ethics from being absorbed into any form of ideology or methodology that silences God's command of grace. Christians are confident in their actions of resistance against the powers only because *Christus victor* stands with and for the victimized. In knowing this, Christians can remain confident in their determination to engage in a specific course of action of "relative Yes and No" that fits the circumstances.

Lastly, social ethics as witness, shaped by eschatology, is liberated because it is *open-ended*. Christian ethics *is* Christian freedom when it emerges as the form of Christian witness, shaped by God's eschatological action. First, ethics emerges from the freedom to live in the "already," here and now, as disciples under the authority of God's Word. This is an open-ended process of correspondence, of listening and responding, of eschatologically waiting and hastening. It is a freedom to believe in the promise that the "God who has already created," is the same God who will continue to create "freedom, peace and joy for man" (*CL*: 270). It is this hope that empowers Christians to pray and believe that "thy kingdom [shall] come, thy will [shall] be done on earth as it is in heaven" (Matt 6:10). Living under God's free grace, allows Christians the *freedom* to pursue God's calling of discipleship in a responsible manner here and now. Related to this point, Kathryn Tanner writes: "One may sum up what Christianity stands for in the process of urging what one must do here and now. But since the Word of God is a free Word, the meaning of discipleship—what it really means to be a Christian—cannot be summed up in any neat formula that would allow one to know already what Christian discipleship will prove to include or exclude over the course of time."[10] Not only does Christian ethics exist in the already but also the not yet. Although we see through the glass darkly, this apparent limitation is actually a gift of freedom. It enables Christian moral responsibility to remain open-ended because, in the words of the *Barmen Declaration*, we live in a world "not yet redeemed." This enables ethics to remain a gift of freedom because its moral content does not rest on any particular Christian belief, norm, or practice, *per se*, but on God's freedom to encounter the world as it will be in its future redemption. This makes ethics as witness a journey that is open-ended and free from the burden of redeeming the world ourselves. No doubt we can alter our circumstances with our actions, but we act in "little steps" in our witness to the Word of God in the world (*CL*: 271). In giving witness to our world, Christians know their intentions and actions are always flawed by sins of individual and collective judgment and practice. Still, God *invites* Christians to act as witnesses, giving them *permission* to act decisively, purposively, and confidently today against powers that distorts God's name in the world, by seeking to "rise up and accept responsibility to the utmost of their power for the doing of a little righteousness" (*CL*: 265). In so doing, they are truly *free* from the powers, so they can freely respond to God's gracious command. Thus, they are liberated from complex task of determining moral actions and decisions on the veracity of "absolute principles." Christians remain cautious about making absolute judgments or determining absolute courses of action as Yes or No. Christians must decide

10. Tanner, *Theories of Culture*, 155.

what specific course of action they must take, but they do so in freedom and not as "prisoners" of any "sacrosanct consistency" (*CL*: 268). Rather, they are free to be open-ended in their judgments determining what could be "relative" or "partial" courses of action. This gift of open-ended freedom of choosing relative or partial courses of action is God's gift making ethics a way of freedom, not compulsion, power, or law. Instead, Christians can step forward in freedom, affirming the "relative Yes and No," which always means acting in responsible actions for the welfare of the other, the church, and the world. With this in mind, in the following three chapters we follow this dialectical pattern of "relative and partial Yes and No" in Christian social witness. In this, we also look for patterns of resistance and affirmation, finding ways to always "give precedence to the Word of God" in the world (*CL*: 168). Christian witness involves being for the individual, church, and the world, while resisting the lordless powers, including various forms of political, economic, and ideological absolutism.

CHAPTER ELEVEN

Political Witness: For Faith and Peace

In the next three chapters, we carry through in a practical way Christian responsible witness as social ethics in political, economic, and environmental practice. In the last chapter, we focused on responsible witness to the other, the church, and the world. In each case, there is a dialectical movement between synthesis and diastasis, between the homogeneity and heterogeneity of church and world. As demonstrated earlier, the church as the "inner circle" is a witness to the "outer circle" of the civil community demonstrating how it, as secular witness, can affirm social ethical practice that is free and open-ended as it dialectically moves between absolute positions of Yes and No. Barth reminds us that a Christian dialectical ethics moves in freedom between two uncompromising poles of thought of Yes and No, while moving forward in an open-ended process of "relative Yes and No" (*CL*: 268). This implies, in the end, that there is no one indefinite or fixed "Christian" position, nor is there some perfect middle point or synthesis, for in both cases this would jeopardize God's free command. Both absolute diastasis and synthesis remain problematic and potentially ideological or hegemonic. Social ethics begins with God's command leading to corresponding responsible human actions of witness. In so doing, it remains an ethics of openness and movement, and to forget this basic point, forgets the fact that ethics is responsible action in *relation* to God's command of grace, which always remains a *free* command, calling Christians to live out their witness in faith, hope, and love in responsible moral action, while standing with and for others, the church, and the world. In so doing, Christian ethics must be cautious about absolute moral judgments of Yes and No, and instead move freely within the practical task of making tentative judgments of "relative but still a definite Yes and No" (*CL*: 271). Ethics remains a free and open-ended discipline of witness, which moves like a circle from God's gracious action to our corresponding responsible and relative human actions.

CHRIST, POWERS, AND WITNESS

Since witness involves first encountering God's action, we must first return to God's prior reconciling initiative in Jesus Christ. For this we turn to the Yes-No-Yes pattern in *CD* IV/1–3, where the correlative action of God and humanity—made visible in Jesus Christ—extends by analogy to Christians in their responsible witness. In these volumes Barth works out, on a grand scale, the Chalcedonian Christology that shapes his theology as a whole, by linking it with numerous other issues in theology including soteriology, human sinfulness, ecclesiology, eschatology, and ethics. In each case the reconciler, Jesus Christ, in his threefold action as prophet, priest, and king, unveils and then defeats the power of human sin, enabling the Christian community to go forth into the world in witness. So, for example, in *CD* IV/1 Barth shows how God's turns toward humanity in Jesus Christ as truly God, in descending humiliation, justifies sinners in their opposition to God in sinful *pride* further revealing how the "gathering" of the Christian community can live and practice *faith* in responsive witness to God's gracious action. In *CD* IV/2 humanity responds to God in Jesus Christ as truly human, in ascending exhalation and fellowship, sanctifies sinners in their opposition to God in sinful *sloth* further revealing how the "upbuilding" of the Christian community can live and practice *love* in responsive witness to God's gracious action. Lastly, in *CD* IV/3 Jesus Christ, in the unity of his person, in his prophetic witness as *Christus victor*, says No to the powers and Yes to incorporating humanity as witnesses in his prophetic work, opposing the sin of *falsehood*, while further revealing how the "sending" of the Christian community can live and practice *hope* in responsive witness to God's gracious action. So in each case the actions of Jesus Christ provides grace by which Christians can act as responsible witnesses against the sins of pride, sloth, and falsehood and for the responsible practice of faith, love, and hope. Only in the *awareness* of the reconciling work of Jesus Christ comes the awareness of the sins of pride, sloth, and falsehood, which conceal or cloak the lived "objective" reality of faith, hope, and love that Christ makes possible in reconciliation. That is, in Jesus Christ's reconciling action *pro nobis,* he confronts and overcomes human sinfulness, thus making faith, love, and hope the true reality for those witnesses who follow him in discipleship and vocation. Christian responsible witness corresponds to God's gracious action in Jesus Christ in faith, love, and hope, while human sinfulness is the aggressive rejection, defiance, and opposition to that witness. "The sin of man is the human action which does not correspond to the divine action in Jesus Christ but contradicts it" (*CD* IV/1: 415). Standing against human sin, the practice of faith, hope, and love are possible only because of God's reconciliation, in which, the sinful powers of pride, sloth, and falsehood are acknowledged as defeated in Jesus Christ. This leads to the Christian liberation of responsible witness.

In mentioning these traditional "theological virtues" of faith, hope, and love we are not relying on a notion of virtue theory, narrative ethics, foundational ecclesial practices, or some form of ethical methodologism.[1] Rather, it is Jesus Christ—not the virtuous Christian—who is the "subject" of faith, hope, and love. These are not virtues nurtured through good works, practices, or habits but particular moral ways of responding in witness to the "One" who has acted *pro nobis* on humanity's behalf. In truth, human virtues can cloak the power of human sinfulness. "Evil always takes good care not to show itself as such. It always cloaks itself, hiding under the garment not only of innocence but of an exalted virtue" (*CD* IV/1: 434). Christian virtue is not acquired habit or quality of character that persons can achieve on their own, apart from the "One" who has acted in past, presently acts, and will act in the future. Jesus Christ is the same yesterday, today, and forever—the future hope for the world rests only on this fact, and this fact alone. Beginning here makes it possible for the Christian community to live as responsible witnesses of faith, hope, and love in the world. In *CD* IV/3, Barth writes:

> The case of hope is exactly the same as that of faith and love. It is not his Christian faith which justifies him, but the One in whom He may believe his righteousness. Nor is it his Christian love which sanctifies him, but the One whom he may love as his holiness. He hopes, indeed, on the basis and in the power and righteousness

---

1. Yoder, "Walk and Word," 82.

and holiness of the One in whom he may believe and whom he may love. He thus hopes in grateful awareness of his reconciliation to God perfectly accomplished in Him, of his membership of the divine covenant of grace and peace. (*CD* IV/3: 914–15)

Following Barth's logic, we can say that in dialectical fashion, Christian responsible witness stands *against* the powers but *for* faith, hope, and love in its resistance against the sins of pride, sloth, and falsehood. To be sure, these human sins all have an effect on the powers of leviathan, mammon, and ideology. Although Christ has defeated these powers they remain visible forces that seek to deprive humanity of faith, hope, and love, and consequently, human freedom, justice, and peace. So, in this and the following two chapters, we bring together, in dialectical fashion, the interplay of responsible witness and sin in the context of the powers of leviathan, mammon, and ideology. These powers will not prevail in the end, but they do nonetheless empower people to reject God's gracious covenant, and instead choose prideful power, slothful lethargy, and various forms of self-deception. The power of these forms of human sin becomes structured in the powers of leviathan, mammon, and ideology, which have power to create global political, economic, and environmental crises. Put differently, the risks of global violence, economic greed, and environmental destruction are the result of human sinfulness, and in particular, the sins of pride, sloth, and falsehood. Although these social risks are all affected by the sins of pride, sloth, and falsehood, our strategy narrows its focus by linking particular risks with particular sins and powers, and then showing how the witness of faith, hope, or love corresponds to these particular sins and powers. So, for example, although all sins affect the political power of leviathan, in this chapter, we focus in particular on the sin of pride and how it is resisted and overcome by the witness of faith, which is one important theme in *CD* IV/1. Moreover, in next two chapters we follow Barth's own logic of dialectically bringing into tension the sin of sloth with the witness of love (*CD* IV/2) and the sin of falsehood with the witness hope (*CD* IV/3). In each case, these dialectical encounters also correspond with the powers of mammon and ideology, so mammon is linked with sloth and ideology is linked with falsehood; these two are then resisted and overcome by the witness of love and hope. Overall, in all three chapters, the central argument is that our ethical actions for a better world are not grounded in the power of a Promethean ethics of human transformation, but in our corresponding *witness* to God's gracious action of reconciliation. God empowers our witness to stand *against* sin, evil, and the "lordless powers," at the same time God has further empowered us to stand *for* a "responsible witness of the Word of God" serving both "God and men" (*CD* IV/3: 609).

FAITH AND POLITICAL WITNESS
Christ against Pride

This chapter shows how the witness of faith overcomes the sin of pride (*CD* IV/1) and the power of leviathan, enabling Christians to give further witness, in words and action, for *peace* by supporting constitutional democracy under law, peacemaking, and global cooperation. As said above, the movement is Yes-No-Yes, namely the Yes of God's reconciliation, the No against human sin and the powers, and Yes of Christian responsible witness as ethics. In each movement Jesus Christ remains the central actor. To begin, let us look at *CD* IV/1, where Barth explores the Christological theme of Jesus Christ as Son of God, the great "high priest," who as mediator and judge justifies sinners through his atoning death on the cross. God does not seek equality with God, but humbly becomes the servant standing with humanity in Jesus Christ, the Son of God. In Jesus Christ, God acts *pro nobis*, thus, "renews and restores" the covenant that sinful humanity has "broken" (*CD* IV/1: 251). Jesus Christ, as the "authentic witness," is the "Mediator and pledge of the covenant. He is the Mediator of it in that He fulfils it—from God to man and from man to God" (*CD* IV/1: 136). Moreover, in this unveiling of the "Son of God's journey into the far country" and the "Judge that is judged in our place," we also see the unveiling of the sinfulness of human pride. The human sinful power of *pride* chooses to exalt the person above God, as his or her own judge and savior. "The whole world finds its supreme unity and determination against God in looking for justification from itself and not from God. Ironically, in its hostility to God, humanity "repeats the very sin of which it acquits itself" (*CD* IV/1: 220). That is, the sinfulness of pride is simply the rejection, disregard, and denial of God's free grace in forging a covenant-partnership with humanity and the world. Rather than allowing for this broken covenant relationship to dominate, God has acted *pro nobis* by seeking to exist "with man and as man in this fallen and perishing state" (*CD* IV/1: 215). In standing with us and *pro nobis* we see Christ's *faith* represented to us, so that we too can stand in faith with and for others. In their social witness, Christians are empowered to say No to pride and Yes to faith.

Nonetheless, the power of pride is both individual and communal, as it not only affects one's personal relationship with God but also the relationship of the civil community with God. In rejecting the "basis and guarantee" of human dignity in God's covenant-partnership, sinful pride demonstrates its power in disregarding the honor and dignity of the human person and the civil community. Pride causes people to seek their own self-aggrandizement, which ironically causes human dishonor and degradation (*CD* III/4: 665). The basis of true human dignity is replaced with conceit, unbridled power, and megalomania, which often remains cloaked or "concealed" within a language of personal or communal ethics or virtue or religion (*CD* IV/1: 447). Concealing pride enables persons to seek out various forms of self-improvement or "self-help" as a means for self-redemption and self-emancipation from God. Pride elevates one's self, gender, ethnicity, community, or nation over the dignity of the other by supporting various types of injustice, cruelty, discrimination, oppression, and violence, including the horrendous killing of innocent life through murder, war, and genocide. Furthermore, concealing pride within a veneer of "militant virtue" or "concealed religion" redefines good and evil according to the dominant ideology of power existing in society and then demands a "stringent sense of duty" upon all persons in society (*CD* IV/1: 450). Consequently, pride provides fertile soil for the power of leviathan to become operative in a civil community. Such a community denies its true identity as covenant-partner and secular witness to God's kingdom, and instead redefines itself according to its own particular emancipating ideology of power manifested in the visible authority of leviathan. In such a case, "demonism" in politics emerges in which the "state no longer serves man; man, both ruled and ruling, has to serve the state" (*CL*: 219).

Pride and Leviathan

The sin of pride becomes functionally and structurally operative in the power of leviathan or political absolutism. As discussed in chapter 8, leviathan promises security and protection through the "program and structure" of its government, but then uses its power to silence, threaten, and eventually annihilate all dissenting voices. Concealing itself in ideology, and even misguided virtue or religion, leviathan becomes a parody of the church, becoming an alternative religious institution of salvation. Barth saw National Socialism, for example, as an "anti-church" proclaiming a nationalistic myth that promised the Germans "everything necessary for body and soul, for life and death, for time and eternity."[2] Leviathan promises salvation through national identity, faith, and security. After the war, Barth saw Christian political witness standing "between East and West," between the American and Soviet empires, as a form of resistance against "empire," as a visible manifestation of leviathan, which "can be a monarchical, aristocratic, democratic, nationalist, or socialistic idea" (*CL*: 220). This is why, during the emerging Cold War, Barth claimed that both the United States and the Soviet Union, in their "world-political struggle for power" remained potential leviathans by cloaking their language of freedom and peace within the ideology of excessive fear and national security. "What they have in common is," says Barth, "finally, this: that they are both afraid of the other, because they both felt encircled and threatened by the other" (*AS*: 129). Driven by their particular "social and political-economic ordering of life" these two empires affirm two different ideologies, which affirm why the church must be willing to "walk between the two" (*AS*: 144). The witness of the confessing church must resist appeals to nationalism and national security as the basis for potential justification for war and nuclear annihilation.

Although the nuclear threat remains a serious risk, much has changed in our world since Barth's time. With his preference for constitutional democracy, Barth would have welcomed the collapse of the Soviet Union and the apparent ending of the Cold War in 1989, but would be disturbed by the continuing acceleration of violence around the world since then, whether in the Balkans, Africa, or the seemingly endless conflicts in Middle East. Rather than ushering in a more peaceful world, the end of the Cold War has led to new ethnic (tribal), religious, and ideological conflicts, including the rise of terrorism, the horrific events of 9/11, and the Wars in the Persian Gulf, Iraq, and Afghanistan. The demonic structure of leviathan remains a real threat during times when nation-states perceive immanent threats around every corner. Such was the policy of the Bush administration after the 9/11 attacks, which led to burgeoning surplus of books—as secular witness—critical of new "American Empire." The escalation of violence, in war, was further accentuated by break in military policy by authorizing torture of prisoners and terrorist suspects. Such "advanced interrogation techniques" were authorized by the Bush administration using the justification that they were necessary to make "America secure" against more terrorist attacks. Alternatively, with the election of Barack Obama in 2008 we have seen criticism of these torture techniques, and new American foreign policy

2. Barth, *Church and the Political Problem*, 41, 47.

directed toward more global cooperation. Yet, regardless of foreign policy strategy, the threat of empire remains a real possibility for any nation-state captured by the ideology of national security and nationalism. Furthermore, the power of leviathan is not reducible to the nation-state, as it emerges in other visible forms, like terrorist organizations such as Al Qaeda; it exists wherever its power is used to create violence and destruction of the human community. So, leviathan today wreaks havoc in the world through its various forms including, terrorism, tribalism, and nationalism. Although the tyrannical and totalitarian power of Hitler's Germany and Stalin's Soviet Union have faded into memory, there remains a new form of nationalism that seeks to undermine the church and civil community's witness to a more peaceful world. In *Hope in Troubled Times*, the authors write:

> The ideology of guaranteed freedom has let violence loose; it has set violence free to follow its own self-determined course in the illusion that, in exchange, violence will grant us freedom. But violence set free as an autonomous power is indifferent to truth, international law, and respect for life. If the West was spiritually unprepared for the Nazi onslaught of World War II, then how much more so are we spiritually unprepared to confront terrorism today! . . . The ideology of guaranteed freedom today bears all the traits of the alterative "religion" touted in Nietzsche's parable of the death of God. It is a belief system complete with its own prophets, oracles, articles of faith, history, orthodoxy, mythic rituals, and body of self evident truths. Most significantly, it possesses it own powerful incarnational drive: the activity of violence in all its manifestations. Violence is the ideology's word become flesh, *the* preeminent means recruited to achieve the end (goal) of guaranteed freedom.[3]

The ideology of "guaranteed national security" is driven by a wrong understanding of political freedom. This ideology assumes that freedom is achieved through *potentia* and not *potestas*. "*Potestas* is the power that follows and serves the law; *potentia* is the power that precedes the law, that masters and bends and breaks the law—it is the naked power which is directly evil" (*CSC*: 177). So, when a nation-state becomes consumed with its own national security, it risks turning its noble idea of freedom toward the evil of naked power and aggression. "Absolute freedom requires absolute force to accomplish, secure, and guarantee that freedom."[4] It is this rhetoric of

---

3. Goudzwaard, et. al., *Hope in Troubled Times*, 125.
4. Ibid., 120

freedom and security, in overcoming the possible threats to the nation-state, which justifies the continuing growth of the military industrial complex, the nuclear arms race during the Cold War, and the numerous conflicts throughout the globe since 1945 including the wars in Korea, Vietnam, and the Middle East. Today, the significant political threat is not from the nation-state as such, but from the random acts of violent terrorism. Worldwide terrorism has "far reaching consequences for law, the military, liberty, everyday life and the stability of the political system throughout the world, because it corrodes the security guarantees formerly provided by the basic institutions of the nation-state."[5] Driven by mysterious terrorist networks, these "murky terrorist agent networks are, as it were, 'violence NGOs.'"[6] Spreading fear and uncertainty, these networks hope to gain success, not by military assault, but by random acts of violence against innocent people.

Since the threat of terrorism remains an unknown threat, something that can occur at any time, it provides empowering support for the growth of the ideology of national security. Although terrorism remains a potential risk, so does the alarmist and predictable response to perceived terrorist threats, which remains guided by pride, fear, and the obsession with national security. Both responses are guided by manufactured risks that are created to justify our ideological perspectives. What is perceived to be truth is cloaked as a pseudo-gospel, a gospel of prideful power, which promises freedom through retributive violence. What is needed, therefore, is resistance not only against worldwide terrorism, but also against the prevalence of nationalist and retributive responses to political problems. What is needed is political forgiveness among belligerents, determining to find new ways to move beyond retribution toward mutuality and interdependence.[7] Yet, for true forgiveness to become *public* there must be some form of reconciliation and faith among past belligerents. This requires addressing the corrosive power of human pride, as a sinful rejection of being with and for others, and a turning toward God's healing covenant of grace as the source for truth and power to resist evil and affirm the good.

---

5. Beck, *World at Risk*, 39.
6. Ibid., 40.
7. There are many fine books on this the theme of political forgiveness; however, a good place to begin is the fine book: Shriver, *An Ethic for Enemies*. For a good collection of essays on this topic, see Biggar, *Burying the Past*.

Witness of Faith

The antithesis of sinful pride is the witness of faith. Faith is the public witness of power that *resists* the sinful force of pride manifested by the relative hegemonic power of leviathan. In *CD* IV/1, Barth places the sin of human pride—the source of leviathan's power—in dialectical tension with graciousness and goodness of faith. If pride emerges from the distrust of God and the promotion of self-redemption, then faith results from the trust established in God's gracious command and covenant-partnership with humanity and its public proclamation. In the narrative of *CD* IV/1, Barth's discussion of faith occurs after the doctrine of justification and the Holy Spirit's agency in the "gathering" of the church. In response to God's gracious act of justification, the faithful witness of the church corresponds to God's action by living its faith out in the world. The living faith of the church is not the "spirit of the individual Christian," the "spirit of the world," or even the "spirit of the community," but the "Spirit of God, God Himself, as He eternally proceeds from the Father and the Son" (*CD* IV/1: 656). Thus, "neither the Christian community nor the individual Christian can subjugate or possess or control Him, directing and overruling His work" (*CD* IV/1: 656). The Holy Spirit liberates humanity from the compulsion to trust false leviathans, ideologies, or other cultural hegemonies, by making possible the "acknowledgment, recognition, and confession" of faith (*CD* IV/1: 758). Faith corresponds to the Holy Spirit's power to gather the church together in being, time, and space. As the Spirit gathers the church, it empowers it to affirm, proclaim, confess, and embody its faith, in such a way, that it perceives the world differently than previously understood. "Faith is at once the most wonderful and the simplest of things. In it a man opens his eyes and sees and accepts everything as it—objectively, really and ontologically—is" (*CD* IV/1: 748).

> Faith is simply following, following its object. Faith is going a way marked out and prepared. Faith does not realize anything new. It does not invent anything. It simply finds that which is already there for the believer and also for the unbeliever. It is simply man's active decision for it, his acceptance of it, his active participation in it. This constitutes the Christian. . . . This distinguishes the Christian from the non-Christian. The object is like a circle enclosing all men and every individual man. In the case of the Christian this circle closes with fact that he believes. In the case of non-Christians it is still open at the point where he ought to believe but does not yet believe,

or no longer believes. The un-believer has not accepted the relationship to that which is in relationship to him. (*CD* IV/1, 742)

The difference between believers and nonbelievers is that the latter are not yet *aware* of their relationship to Jesus Christ, whose faith has set them free from the sin of pride. Christian *faith* is not feeling or experience, but an objective, living, and empowering form of relational knowledge and trust, which illuminates human reason and strengthens human will to fully respond to God's commands. The objective reality of faith is "like a circle enclosing every man" beginning with God's objective action in the Word of God leading to the human actions of freedom, obedience, and responsibility (*CD* IV/1: 742). In our encounter with Christ the "high priest," who as the Son of God and Lord, does not seek equality with God, but humbly becomes the servant standing with humanity, we clearly see the sinfulness of humanity's pride, which seeks to be exalted like God and become its own judge and savior. In Christ's overcoming of pride, we are liberated from pride's power. "I myself, the man of sin, who has not and will not overcome himself, am the one who finds that he is overcome in Him" (*CD* IV/1: 770). In our awareness that we are liberated by the "One" who stands *pro nobis*, we are liberated to stand in faith *for* others. Because of Christ's mediating role, human faith becomes "free act" of the person "grounded in the act of God, but not the act of God itself as such" (*CD* IV/1: 767). The witness of faith, says Barth, is "the most inward and central and decisive" act of Christian witness. Indeed, these acts of Christian witness are "expressions and confirmations of his Christian freedom, his Christian responsibility, his Christian obedience" (*CD* IV/1: 757–58). Faith enables the Christian to live freely in response to God's command for peace, justice, and freedom, which overcomes pride's power over individuals and communities.

Furthermore, faith is a public action that calls for free, obedient, and responsible witness against the political absolutisms of leviathan. Faith, by its very nature, is public witness. The "goal of faith as the free act of man is the act of his witness and therefore of his confession" (*CD* IV/1: 776). In confessing their public faith, Christians and the church are "eccentric," in that, "in faith man is no longer in control of his centre." *(CD* IV/1: 743). Public confession is the opposite of the prideful sin of concealment, in that it makes faith *public*, as inner witness, to the outer circle of the civil community that God's reconciliation has also liberated it to serve God, others, and the world. We recall that in the 1946 essay, Barth argues that the Christian community is the inner circle and the civil community is the outer circle of the visible kingdom of God. It follows that: "the existence of the State [is] an allegory, an analogue to the Kingdom of God which the Church preaches and believes in" (*CSC*: 169). The Christian community serves as a "model and prototype" of the civil community (*CSC*: 186). As members of the inner circle, Christians "are also automatically members of the wider circle. They cannot halt at the boundary where the inner and outer circles meet, though the work of faith, love and hope which they are under orders to perform will assume different forms on either side of the boundary" (*CSC*: 158–59). What Barth is saying is that the church declares to the civil community that it too can be a community of faith and peace. The civil community, in all its secularity, can be an "indirect witness" to God's kingdom by resisting the power of pride and leviathan that threatens to destroy the peace of the nation-state and global community.

So, one important question at this point is whether the church, in its public witness, should support a particular political position of the civil community. What does it mean for the church to be a political witness in its public faith? Although the church's public confession may lead to particular political positions and actions, for example, declaring that a particular war or particular course of economic action is unjust, the church must also be cautious about proclaiming *status confessionis* on any particular public issue. The Christian confession of faith leads to a public "confirmation, declaration, and impartation of what is known" (*CD* III/4: 73). Nevertheless, this public confession of faith must be cautious of declaring a specific public agenda by seeking an "attainment of ends even in the name of God" (*CD* III/4: 77). Again, there is a dialectical movement between absolute Yes and No. Barth warns that the church should not say No to anything it finds objectionable. Rather, like individual moral judgment, the church's public judgment should rely on its own "infallible tests" to determine whether a particular kind of confession ought to be a genuine *status confessionis*. These "infallible tests" include whether it is a clearly given witness in Scripture, whether it is an open-ended or closed strategy, and whether it emerges out the freedom of the church's witness or is coerced, pressured, and imposed by some ecclesiastical authority. Overall, the main point is that the church must be extremely cautious in its public proclamations over social or cultural issues, declaring them to be *status confessionis* of the church. When the church proclaims a *status confessionis* it is making a public declaration of faith. Even when the church speaks out against injustice this proclamation must be "distinguished from an arbitrary outburst of human resentment" (*CD* III/4: 82). When the church freely speaks it speaks not out of hate or resentment but out of love, faith, and hope. "Confession is decisively action," says Barth, "and not—or only incidentally—reaction" (*CD* III/4: 81). Witness leads to action, but it also "aims at no results and expects none" because it prioritizes God's action over human action, or put differently, places human action within the history of divine action. Christian confession, as action, always begins and ends with the fact that God is with us and for us in Jesus Christ, thus, the "same 'for' and 'with' will always include those whom it must first attack" (*CD* III/4, 82). This is why Christian witness never stands for causes or ideas, as such, but for how these positively addresses the welfare of persons and communities.

PEACE AND POLITICAL WITNESS

Christian political witness responds to God's command of grace by standing *against* potentially hegemonic ideologies, worldviews, or socially constructed paradigms that deprive humanity of its freedom, and *for* the dignity of other persons, communities, and the world. Accordingly, the church community serves the civil community by being a witness to its own law, in the form of the gospel, and its parabolic correspondence to civil law. So, for example, just as the equality of Christians is established in baptism, so too, the civil community ought to support, by law, the equality of its citizens. Further, just as a diversity of members is served by church community so too, the civil community is inclusive of differences and serves its citizens. Political moral judgment presumes that human power is corruptible through pride, sloth, and deception, and that the dignity of persons, communities, and the world suffer from excesses of power. Therefore, the political witness of the church and civil communities should be "counter-movements on behalf of humanity" that "call for the championing of the weak against every kind of encroachment on the part of the strong" (*CD* III/4: 544). Political moral judgment stands partially for the weak and against the strong, while at the same time, engaging in open-ended conversation and mutual cooperation. This leads to three important strategies, including standing for democracy and political freedom, for peacemaking, and for global cooperation.

For Democracy

First, let us determine whether the church as "model and prototype" gives witness to a particular type or structure of government. It's been pointed out that the integrity of the civil community is threatened by the power of leviathan, which rejects the *relation* between the church and the civil community, and instead forces these communities into of the polarities of synthesis or diastasis. These two-forms of extremism lead to the twin errors of Christian nationalism and anarchism. Just as the error of nationalism rests on a synthesis or *identification* of church and state as a visible manifestation of God's kingdom, so too, anarchism leads to the diastasis or *separation* of the church from the state, thus, separating civil community from God's reconciliation. At one extreme is Christian nationalism, which stands uncritically for the state, overvaluing its power, while undervaluing the church; this leads to various manifestations of Eusebianism or Constantinianism. In *CD* III/3 Barth develops a genealogy of the sin of nationalism and explains how these "masks of God" hide particular ideologies that promote the power of "demonism in politics," made visible in Nazism in Germany. When "peoplehood" becomes the determinative norm, Barth writes, it "inevitably introduces a foreign deity, a national god" (*CD* III/3: 305). This is why even the democratic states of Western Europe and the United States, are not "immune to the tendency to become at least a little Leviathan" (*CL*: 221). We saw earlier how nationalism is manifested in the ideology of "guaranteed" freedom and national security, and how this further leads to a potential escalation of violence. The problem, here, is ideological, but it is also ecclesiological, in that when the church fails to be an authentic witness of *faith*, the civil community is left without a witness thus opening the door to practice of politics that becomes potentially demonic.

At the other extreme is the second example of Christian anarchism, which overvalues the church, while it also undervalues the state. Self-proclaimed Christian anarchists, like Jacques Ellul and Vernard Eller, build their case for the anarchism by looking at the "crisis" theology of the early Barth.[8] Ellul argues that Christians ought to stand *against* the state's power by following in the footsteps of the protesting prophets and the nonviolent Jesus. Otherwise Christianity remains in danger of being "subverted" by the demonic powers of the state, and placing its hope in the "illusions" and "false idols" of worldly history and progress. Ellul writes: "Every modern state is totalitarian. It recognizes no limit either factual or legal." What this means, in theory, is that no "modern state is legitimate." "No present day authority can claim to be instituted by God, for all authority is set in

---

8. Eller, *Christian Anarchy*; and Ellul, *Anarchy and Christianity*.

the framework of a totalitarian state."⁹ Ellul argues that it is misguided to claim that some states, such as Western democracies, are legitimate while others, such as totalitarian regimes, are not. All states are illegitimate since they claim to have *absolute* authority over the communities in which they rule. This anarchistic position is more realistic about leviathan's power than the naiveté of the nationalistic view, but it also denies that God's reconciliation also applies to the civil community making it a secular witness, as outer circle, to God's kingdom. This error is also ecclesiological, in that, the church is more cognizant of its true political witness to God's kingdom, but denies the civil community its right to be a witness as well, which essentially prohibits the civil community from understanding and practicing true politics.

Unlike these two extreme positions, Barth points to a dialectical pattern of political witness that values both the church and civil community as the inner and outer circles of witness to God's kingdom. Both communities can resist leviathan, including its false ideologies of nationalism, guaranteed freedom and security, and terrorism, and can also positively witness to God's kingdom of freedom, peace, and justice. What kind of political community did Barth see as a political witness? Although he rejected viewing the civil community as an entirely "Christian" or "secular" state, he did say in 1946 "that the Christian line" following from the gospel moves in the direction of the "democratic state" (*CSC*: 181). "Democracy is not in the middle between anarchy and tyranny, but is above both, above this dichotomy."¹⁰ Both anarchy and tyranny are shaped by the power of *potentia* or "naked power" that "masters and bends and breaks the law," whereas democracy, as just state, attempts to rise above this struggle for power through *potestas* or the "power the serves the law" (*CSC*: 177).¹¹ A constitutional democracy is preferable because it seeks to balance the power of individual rights and responsibilities with community rights and responsibilities.

> The Christian concept of the righteous state which is endorsed now and always by the churches, undoubtedly has a distinct limitation and a distinct orientation. Since it aims at order, the righteous state

---

9. Ellul, *Ethics of Freedom*, 396.
10. Godsey, *Karl Barth's Table Talk*, 80–81.
11. Regarding this, Barth writes: "[B]ut the power of the good State differs from that of the bad State as *potestas* from *potentia*. *Potestas* is the power that follows and serves the law; *potentia* is the power that precedes the law, that masters and bends and breaks the law—it is the naked power which is directly evil" (*CSC*: 177).

contradicts and withstands all political, social, and economic tyranny and anarchy. And since it makes the rights of the community and personal responsibility the yardstick of order, *democracy* comes nearer to that ideal state than an aristocratic or monarchical dictatorship, *socialism* than an untrammeled capitalistic order with the social and business system based on it; a *federation of free states* (free also as such as possible from the principle of nationalism) than the rivalry of independent and uncontrollably competing national states.[12]

Although Barth did not sanction a particular form of government as sacrosanct, he argued the best so far is the form of constitutional democracy—a "just constitutional state" (*Rechtsstaat*) under the "rule of law."[13] This form of government serves as a parable of God's kingdom, giving witness to kind of government that embodies responsibility for the individual, church, and the world. "The church always stands for the constitutional State (*Rechtsstaat*), for the maximum validity and application of that twofold law (no exemption from and full protection by the law), and therefore it will always be against any degeneration of the constitutional State (*Rechtsstaat*) into tyranny or anarchy" (*CSC*: 172). First, a constitutional democracy, *establishes* human freedom in the governmental process and procedures, such as universal suffrage and human rights, which gives individual citizens and social groups, the opportunity to participate in the governance of the civil community. Second, it *limits* human freedom by placing persons and communities under the "rule of law," limiting the power of government, and providing safeguards against the abuse of these rights through emerging arbitrary power and authority of individuals or factions within the civil community. A "just" constitutional democracy (*Rechtsstaat*) grounds its authority, not in arbitrary judgments or whimsical power plays, but seeks to base its authority on principles of justice that transcend mere social convention. We recall earlier that Barth saw church law as parabolic or analogous to civil law by providing a model of moral *judgment*, of discerning right and wrong.[14]

12. Barth, *Church and the War*, p. 39.

13. The German term *Rechtsstaat* does not translate well into English—as it can mean "rule of law" or "constitutional state," or in combination, such as a "constitutional state under the rule of law." This word implies that the state's authority is grounded in "law" and not power or the will of the ruler, or even the "will of people." This law is not just arbitrary law, however, but a kind of law that embodies *justice*—a commitment to the common good. In theory, *Rechtsstaat* could apply to any state with a firm constitutional understanding of law, but it is often associated with the legacy of Western democracies.

14. No one has done more to bring this notion of *judgment* to the forefront of Christian political thought than Oliver O'Donovan. This concept is first given biblical and

In the 1946 essay, Barth claims that gospel proclamation, serves as an analogy for how the civil community *protects* the basic principles free speech, free assembly, and freedom from search and seizure. "With all its strength," says Barth, the church "will be on the side of those who refuse to have anything to do with the regimentation, controlling, and censoring of public opinion" (*CSC*: 177). Thus, gospel proclamation negatively critiques the state that seeks to *exempt* itself from this rule of law. The church and civil society should challenge any restrictions on free speech, practice of government-sponsored clandestine operations, including covert actions, secret police, and secret diplomacy. Moreover, in a *Rechtsstaat,* power must be balanced, so that will prohibit one particular ideology from dominating the entire society's politics; a non-ideological politics needs a balance of power. So, in another analogy, Barth uses the example of the diversity of spiritual gifts within the church to argue for a separation of powers within government, something that he discussed many years earlier in the *Ethics* lectures.[15] No one branch of government, or one group within society, can embody all powers of government, so this is why the constitutional state has legislative, executive, and judicial powers, which make, judge, and enforce the rule of law, through moral judgment, as the form of the gospel.

For Peacemaking

Furthermore, regarding the proper use of state-sponsored violence, the political witness of a *Rechtsstaat* dialectically moves between the absolutes of state-sponsored militarism (or crusadism) and absolute pacifism, and instead encourages an active *peacemaking* role for the state. In its open-ended witness to God's kingdom, the church and civil communities may move one direction or the other, but must remain firm in their witness for peace, justice, and order. Barth first formally develops this dialectical argument in his *Ethics*, where he writes: "There is no such thing as a 'good conscience'

---

theological grounding in his classic work, *The Desire of the Nations*. More recently he has applied it to the political practice of statecraft in *The Ways of Judgment*.

15. Because the *Ethics* lectures were given in three cycles from 1928–33, it is interesting to see how Barth made revisions in his lectures. Indeed, the changing political situation in Germany from 1929 to 1933, forced him to change his understanding of how democracy is structured. For example, in 1929, he said that leadership emerges as an "event" between the leaders and the persons in society, and that both leaders and citizens are "called by God's grace to do the work of the state," but later in 1933, added the negative statement that the leader "may be a usurper with great power and suggestion" and the forcefully democratic statement that the "state comes from the people" (*ET*: 448–49).

either in war or in peace" (*ET*: 471). The church that remains true to its confession will "keep itself free from militarism" as well as "with a friendly gesture rebuff the attentions of pacifism" (*ET*: 471). This dialectical movement occurs in Barth's own thought from 1914 through the Cold War; from being against war (World War I), to supporting it (World War II), to standing against it once again (Cold War). This open-ended movement often leads Barth's interpreters, on both sides of the debate, to be critical his dialectical position on war. On one side, John Howard Yoder, a pacifist, remains critical of Barth's arguments for supporting war, and claims that he didn't follow through on his pacifist leanings.[16] On the other side, Oliver O'Donovan, a just war theorist, remains critical of Barth's justification for war because, at the same time, he appears "reluctant to discuss the conditions for it, lest such a discussion serve to normalize the extraordinary."[17] Even though Barth's thought remains in constant movement, there is a consistent line that remains throughout which remains committed to the peacemaking function of the state, whilst allowing on rare and exceptional occasions for war. William Werpehowski sums up Barth's dialectical position by saying that Barth seeks to "connect evangelical politics and political realities by limiting war to is proper purpose, and extending political power's use short of war to effect forms of peace that meet more nearly the measure of creaturely humanity."[18] Barth's position is dialectical, open-ended, and remains contextually linked to God's command in specific circumstances.

Saying this, however, implies that both the church and state bear witness to God's kingdom by practice peacemaking, which implies that war remains the *opus alienum* of the state. Hence, in no way should war be seen as "a normal, fixed and in some sense necessary part of what on the Christian view constitutes the just state, or the political order demanded by God" (*CD* III/4: 456). Only in very unusual circumstances should the church and civil communities support war, such as in the case of self-defense, assisting a weaker neighbor, and as last resort to preserve one's community. By shifting the focus toward the active commitment of peacemaking, and suspending arguments for the state's use of force, the argument moves away from justifications for "just war" and toward practical strategies for

---

16. See especially, Yoder, *Karl Barth and the Problem of War*. Also see Clough, *Ethics in Crisis*, 89–98.

17. O'Donovan, *Just War Revisited*, 19. Also see O'Donovan, *Bonds of Imperfection*, 246–75.

18. Werpehowski, "Karl Barth and Politics," 240.

implementing justice and peace. Christian witness to peacemaking remains non-ideological and practical. Christians, says Barth, "cannot be pacifists in principle, only in practice" (*CD* IV/3: 550). So, what does it mean to be a practical pacifist, and how is this different from principled pacifist? For Barth, being a "practical pacifist," implies two things: 1) a "Christian concern for the fashioning of true peace among nations to keep war at bay"; and 2) a "Christian concern for peaceful measures and solutions among states to avert war" (*CD* III/4: 460). These two principles of "active peacemaking" and "averting war" provide a common vision for peacemaking for the church and civil community, and provide an alternative to the extremes of a "post-Constantinian theology of war" and the "absolutism of the pacifist thesis" (*CD* III/4: 460). The witness of peacemaking, therefore, can never be simply a synthesis between the just war and the pacifist positions, but remains much closer to the latter. All arguments in favor of war "are wrong if they do not start with the assumption that the inflexible negative of pacifism has almost infinite arguments in its favor and is almost overpoweringly strong" (*CD* III/4: 455). Hence, it actively engages in saying No to war by saying Yes to peacemaking. Peacemaking actively engages in the Yes of peacemaking by the No of unmasking or unveiling the false illusions of human pride that the nation-state uses in both going to war (*Jus ad bellum*) and moral conduct within war (*Jus in bello*).

Much of the debate over Barth's ethical position on war comes from his controversial discussion of war in *CD* III/4 in the section "The Protection of Life" (*CD* III/4: 379–470). In this section, Barth takes an "almost pacifist" position, in that he details the horrors of war demonstrating its immorality, only in the end to reverse his position and allow for war in unusual circumstances. This movement of No and Yes is not so much a contradiction in thought as a demonstration his dialectical logic at work. For most of this section he attempts to unmask the "myth of war" as a noble pastime and show how it is instead a horrendous tragedy of unnecessary killing of persons and destruction of communities. Barth assumes that the traditional arguments for just war are no longer valid because of modern technological warfare. First, in modern war the distinction between combatants and noncombatants has deteriorated, in that, all persons have, in effect, become combatants. Second, traditional arguments for *jus ad bellum* fail because modern wars are not fought for the noble reasons of honor and justice as much as "power," and in particular, economic power which seeks to "deploy power for the acquisition of more power" in its continuing quest for more of the earth's resources like "coal, potash, ore, oil, and rubber" (*CD* III/4: 451). Lastly, the traditional arguments for *jus in bello* are no longer relevant in modern war. The power of technology has made war an industry that focuses on "the increasing scientific objectivity of military killing," which has refined its "methods, instruments, and machines" for the sole act of killing people (*CD* III/4: 453). Consequently, although nations use the rhetoric of freedom, peace, and justice in waging war, the actual violent conflicts are driven, indeed "possessed" more by greed and economic power and the unethical acts of stealing, arson, lying and deception, and exploitation.

After this long litany of the fictions, illusions, and myths of war, Barth reverses his argument and supports war under the principle of the "exceptional" or "borderline" case (*Grenzfall*). His justification for using the *Grenzfall* principle is that "we cannot deny the possibility that God as the Lord of life may further its protection even in the strange form of its conclusion and termination rather than is preservation and advancement" (*CD* III/4: 398). Barth's justification in using this principle is rooted in his underlying commitment to Christian ethics as open-ended and dynamic and responsive to God's command. In this section, he uses this principle in his discussion of the ethical issues of suicide, abortion, euthanasia, capital punishment, self-defense, and tyrannicide, and war. In each case, except euthanasia, Barth finds exceptions to static rule of "thou shalt not kill." In each case, he uses a casuistic-like logic that first states the norm and then the exception; this norm/exception logic is not found in his other ethical writings. This becomes especially potentially problematic when he discusses the ethics of war. John Howard Yoder, for example, argues the problem is not Barth's openness and freedom regarding borderline situations, but that in the case of war, the exception itself becomes a kind of *normative* position, which is then used to defend a state's preparedness for war. So, Yoder says, "to say that the state should be constantly prepared for war is like saying that an honest man should always be prepared for lying or a faithful husband for divorce; it confuses an extreme eventuality with normality, thus demonstrating the inadequacy of the *Grenzfall* as a tool for straight thinking."[19] In the last analysis, says Yoder, "between Barth and an integral Christian pacifism the only differences lie at points where Bath did

---

19. Yoder, *Karl Barth and the Problem of War*, 107. Yoder further says that Barth, in 1962, admitted that "I spoke 99 per cent against war and the military," and then added that his discussion of war in *CD* III/4 was "not one the most felicitous passages in the *Church Dogmatics*." Ibid., 89.

not finish working out the implications of his originality."[20] Barth's thought was always in movement, says Yoder, and given enough time he would've taken a 100 percent position against war without exceptions, instead of his "99 percent position" against war.

So, what should we conclude about Yoder's criticism? On one side, Yoder rightly looks to Barth's methodological use of the *Grenzfall* in *CD* III/4 as a problem that cannot easily be reconciled with Barth's other ethical writings. Yet, on the other side, Yoder's strict commitment to pacifism "in principle" prohibits him from seeing the dialectical consistency of Barth's own position. First, Yoder is right to point to the *Grenzfall* as a problematic principle, especially as it applies to war. Barth does apply this casuistic norm/exception form of reasoning in an almost *ad hoc* fashion, which seems to contradict his more pervasive use of *dialectical* deliberation throughout his theological and ethical writings. Unlike other ethical writings, Barth departs from a back and forth reasoning to a more confident, determinative, even prescriptive, form of reasoning (*CD* III/4: 397–470). What is missing here in the "Protection of Life" section in *CD* III/4 is an extended discussion how Christian deliberation about these various ethical issues, like euthanasia and war, emerge within the context of the covenant-partnership as the "inner basis" of creation and the church's (and Christian's) witness to the civil community and the state. Nevertheless, this departure from dialectical reasoning doesn't necessary lead to the notion that his thought on war was unfinished or incoherent. He states clearly that the church *reminds* the civil community of active peacemaking, thus, stands against war. In the 1946 essay he states that the church's witness to "God of judgment and mercy" implies a place for reminding the state that it may, as an act of last resort, engage in violence as a way to maintain the peacemaking purpose of the state (*CSC*: 178). Therefore, the Christian No against war remains only a "relative No" because we still live, as the Barmen Declaration declares, in "partially redeemed" world. Being responsible for dignity of people, the church, and the community entails that the civil community must, on extremely rare occasions, use force when its "very existence and autonomy are menaced and attacked," and it is forced to "surrender its independence"(*CD* III/4: 461–62).

Even though Barth's use of the *Grenzfall* is troubling, his dialectical reasoning about the ethics of war remains consistent from his early to his

20. Ibid., 118.

late writings. The goal of peacemaking is never interrupted by the practice of preparing for war, but only seen as a "side effect" of the practical circumstances of a world not yet fully redeemed. This position is not logically undeveloped or inconsistent, but a further application of a dialectical "relative Yes and No" perspective, which allows *relative* rearmament during war and *relative* disarmament during peacetime. How can Barth be inconsistent by rejecting the extremes of massive military buildup in peacetime and radical disarmament during a time of war? Is it not responsibility of the *Rechtsstaat* to promote peace and limit military buildup, but not eradicate all weapons used to defend one's homeland against military threat? The movement back and forth between Barth's support and rejection of war is not as much a reversal of positions as a further clarification of the *range* of positions that Christians may have about war within the context of their witness against leviathan and for justice, freedom, and peace. Is it not possible that God's command to the democratic Western states, like Britain, France, the U.S., and others, was to actually *defend* its way of life against the "demonism" of National Socialism?

Barth's position on peacemaking and war is very similar to what is today called the "just peacemaking" tradition, which stands between the just war and pacifist traditions. Glen Stassen has argued there are three positions—not two—positions in Christian ethics, namely the just war and pacifist positions, but also the middle position of "just peacemaking."[21] Christians who support just peacemaking are more concerned with discussion about how to "prevent war" rather than whether war ought to be seen as just or unjust. However, when war actually starts, the peacemaking "middle position" is interrupted by the reality of war, which forces Christians to either to be for or against the current war. At that point, Christians can draw from both the just war and pacifist traditions in evaluating the current conflict, with the goal of ending the conflict and returning to their presumption for peacemaking. Along these lines, in their book *Faith and Force*, the just war thinker Brian Stiltner and the pacifist David Clough conclude by finding common ground in Barth's two aspects of "practical pacifism," the unmasking the false justifications for war while positively affirming the purpose of peacemaking and political forgiveness among belligerents. Stiltner and Clough demonstrate how to engage in a fruitful conversation about war and peace, and apply these discussions to the wars of recent memory including the Iraq and Afghanistan wars and terrorism. What is interesting

21. Stassen and Gushee, *Kingdom Ethics*, 174.

is they conclude that both positions of just war and pacifism are committed to unmasking the false justifications for war while positively affirming the purpose of peacemaking and political forgiveness among belligerents. Regarding this, they state: "we conclude this book with a brief proposal for Christians with pacifist and just war views that shows what they can do to shape the peacemaking vocation of the Church at the beginning of the twenty-first century."[22]

Barth's reflection on war remains important for conversations between just war and pacifist thinkers. In resisting the power of leviathan, the civil community may be forced to rely on the use of force, as a *free* response to very unusual circumstances when the state can only preserve this peacemaking role through the use of force. In our age of escalating global violence, the church's witness remains committed to peacemaking, but can it remain silent when innocent life is threatened by the risks of state-sponsored or terrorist violence? Since the most common risks today are terrorist violence, how should we think about the so-called "war on terrorism"? The risk of terrorism raises serious questions about military engagement that are not common to a nationalist perspective, in which nation-states stand in conflict with other nation-states. The primary risk for global society today, however, is not the power of that nation-state and nationalism, but ideological forms of terrorism promoted by intensified notions of ethnic or religious tribalism. This is not to say that it is impossible for one nation-state to wage war against another nation-state, such as happened in the Iraq War led by the Bush administration, but that incidence of worldwide terrorism remains a more common threat of violence than full-scale war among nation-states. In its witness to the civil community, the church stands against terrorism because it promotes peacemaking among the nations through global cooperation. "The only answer to global terror—but also to global financial risk, climate change and organized crime—is transnational cooperation."[23] The most serious risk to peacemaking today is not indiscriminate acts of terrorism, but the promotion of the ideology of *nationalism* against the common good of the international community of nations, ideologies that separate "us" from "them," that deny that the *other* is our covenant-partner. In standing for peacemaking, Christians reject any notion of a nationalist, tribal, or ethno-religious god. "The Father of Jesus Christ," says Barth, "who as such is the Creator, cannot be recognized in this national god." A

22. Clough and Stiltner, *Faith and Force*, 240.
23. Beck, *World at Risk*, 41.

"national god" is a "strange god" who calls for strange sacrifices on "alien alters" (*CD* III/4: 305). Whereas a strongly individualistic and egoistic (nationalistic) state would deny its international commitments, a responsible state or *Rechtsstaat* is energized and proactive in confronting the risks both within and outside its borders, moving always toward greater global cooperation.

For Global Cooperation

Christian political witness is committed to global cooperation. Just as the Christian community moves from "near to far," so too, the civil community moves from an inward preoccupation with itself toward a greater cooperation with outside communities. Christian ethics, says Barth, claims that "north and south and east and west are only relative concepts," thus, responsible commitment moves inevitably "from the narrower sphere to a wider, from our own people to other human peoples" (*CD* III/4: 293). Hence, this reverses the common understand of commitments to local and the global. The global becomes the local. One is a citizen of the world in the same way that one is a citizen of the local community. In the movement "from near to far," Christians must reject the false premise that national history is sacrosanct. Indeed, all national histories, in all their particularity and uniqueness, point to a common humanity, above all national differences. This unity of a common humanity, however, can never lead to a political unification within a global international state grounded in the ideology of internationalism. Rather, the unity of humanity's global covenant is revealed and made visible only in its election in Jesus Christ. "The history of His covenant with man, fulfilled and completed in the one Jesus Christ, is the centre of all history and the meaning and goal of all national history" (*CD* III/4: 297). In contrast to the story of Babel and the dispersion and fragmentation of humanity, is the miracle of Pentecost, which "shows us that this has nothing to do whatever to do with emancipation or an emergent internationalism." Rather it is God's action, through the Holy Spirit, that unites these diverse peoples, from diverse nations, into one people of God. Pentecost demonstrates that a new community, of diversity within unity, now exists only because of God's agency and this unity is the "goal and conclusion of the history of Israel and therefore of world history" (*CD* III/4: 323).

Saying this, however, does not imply that Christian ethics ought to "espouse an abstract internationalism and cosmopolitanism," but neither can it "espouse an abstract nationalism and particularism" (*CD* III/4: 312–13).

The dialectical movement between the local and the global, or national and international, is open-ended and fluid, moving from inner to the outer circle, and the outer to the inner circle. The twin errors remain the reductionisms of nationalism and internationalism, of the isolation of the nation-state from the international community, and the isolation of the global from the nation-state. "Nationalism and internationalism (and even supranationalism) may be dialectical concepts that balance one another" (*CD* III/4: 320). This dialectical balance, however, remains in movement between "relative Yes and No." In today's "world at risk" international conversation is crucial for a worldwide commitment to peacemaking, economic, and environmental cooperation. Ulrich Beck argues that an inclusive and global "cosmological moment" can only be reached if there is transformation of attitude and beliefs among individuals and communities, which drives them toward global cooperation and a sustainable future. "The 'cosmological moment' of world risk society means," says Beck, "first, the *conditio humana* of the irreversible non-excludability of those who are culturally different. We are all trapped in a shared global space of threats—without exit."[24] Rising above social and cultural differences, cosmopolitanism incorporates a diversity of nations, worldviews, religions, and value-systems. What unites people is the common *risks* that all persons face and the drive to seek solutions to such global problems. Although there is much to admire in cosmopolitism, it underestimates the discrepancy or distance between human knowledge and moral action. The crucial problem is not with our awareness of the risks, but with human action to resolve the toxic side-effects that the risks pose to human society. In addressing these risks, Christian political witness speaks to the nation-state and the international community—it moves outward from the nation to the global community, and returns from the global to the local. The relation of the local to global, of the relation to our "near and distant neighbors is a kind of circle in which we have constantly to remember the necessary loyalty on the one side and openness on the other" (*CD* III/4: 318). The church, in its ecumenical witness, proclaims to the civil community that it too is called to a new level of global responsibility, and in so doing, it can be an indirect witness to God's kingdom through the practice of peacemaking and cooperation among the nations.

---

24. Ibid., 56.

CHAPTER TWELVE

Economic Witness: For Love and Justice

This chapter follows the same pattern at the last chapter, but the focus shifts from political to economic witness. In so doing, we look at *CD* IV/2, where Jesus Christ embodies love and overcomes the sin of sloth, leading to "upbuilding" of the Christian community. Although the sins of pride and falsehood could equally apply to the power of mammon, this chapter correlates the sin of sloth with structural power of mammon. So, in dialectical fashion, sloth is juxtaposed with love, and mammon is juxtaposed with justice. Just as political witness leads to the practice of peace in the civil and global community, so too does *love* lead to the practice of justice in the civil and global community. More particularity, justice leads to strategies of social market economic reform, human practice of work, and global economic cooperation. Moreover, this leads us to ethical reflection that moves between absolute Yes and No, and strives for an ethics of openness and freedom. Christian economic ethics, like political ethics, must be cautious about incorporating foundationalist ideologies in forging economic policy decisions. We saw in earlier chapters, for example, how the rhetoric over economic globalization becomes a heated struggle between the ideologies of anti-globalism and pro-globalism. Christian economic ethics, if it is to remain a form of responsible witness, must seek to be non-ideological, while at the same time standing for the dignity of persons, communities, and the common good.

LOVE AND ECONOMIC WITNESS
Christ against Sloth

In *CD* IV/2, Barth explores the Christological theme of Jesus Christ as Son of Man, the man of Nazareth, who acts *pro nobis*, as our representative, in faithful obedience toward God as the "royal man" or the "exalted king." Whereas in the "Son of God" we see the "self-humbling in Jesus Christ the true God became and was and is also true man," but in the "Son of Man, the man Jesus of Nazareth" we see the "exaltation of man to fellowship with God" (*CD* IV/2: 155). He corresponds to God's covenant-partnership in perfect obedience, thus, further revealing what it means to give witness to God's kingdom in the world. In so doing, Jesus as the "royal man," as the "true human," does not "represent or defend or champion any programme— whether political, economic, moral, or religious, whether conservative or progressive." Thus, he is neither entirely revolutionary nor conservative, but presents a "radical antithesis" to positions by revealing, in the kingdom of God, the "limit and frontier" of all human positions (*CD* IV/2: 171ff.). All human political platforms, positions, and powers are challenged and overcome by God's kingdom. In giving witness to God's kingdom, Jesus Christ seeks "conformity with God Himself," which unveils the "relationship of God Himself to all the orders of life and value."(*CD* IV/2: 173). In Jesus' intense perseverance and dedication as "true witness" to God's kingdom and God's love, we also see the unveiling of the sin of sloth, which promotes inactivity, ignorance, and inhumanity. Just as the gracious faith of the Son of God stands committed to act against human pride, so too, the gracious love of the Son of Man, the royal man stands against human sloth. "It is grace, free grace, grace which is powerful against the powers which bind all creatures, that has overtaken them" (*CD* IV/2: 244). Indeed, in our sanctification we see Christ's *love* for God and for humanity, demonstrating that we too can love others, as we love God. In their social witness, Christians are empowered to say No to sloth and mammon and Yes to love.

What are the particular implications of the sin of sloth? The sin of sloth builds on pride, in that it both rejects one's justification and *sanctification*, thereby cutting off the possibility for true *liberating* personal transformation. Nevertheless, unlike pride the heroic sin of active defiance, the sin of sloth is a cowardly sin of inactivity, laziness, and pettiness. Whereas pride actively and publicly *distrusts* God, the sin of sloth passively and privately *mistrusts* God and humanity, while remaining satisfied with the "ordinary, trivial, and mediocre" (*CD* IV/2: 404). Sloth is evil, not because of action but of "inaction," not because of "rash arrogance" but because of "tardiness and failure which are equally forbidden and reprehensible" (*CD* IV/2: 403). Sloth causes us to "withdrawal into ourselves," and develops attitudes of resentment, apathy, and cynicism (*CD* IV/1: 407). Moreover, as a sin of passive idleness and weariness, sloth not only degrades the human person but also the civil community. Hence, it becomes the enemy of social ethics, as it blindly supports the *status quo*, remains comfortable with descriptive not normative ethics, and lacks imagination, vision, or hope. In its refusal to call for personal or social transformation, it also refuses to challenge or resist personal and social injustice, greed, or power. Accordingly, the subtleness of sloth makes it more of a risk to human freedom than does the overt sin pride, because in its "practical atheism" and "inhumanity" it rejects God's law, as the form of the gospel. In so doing, it remains powerless to challenge the tyrannical and ideological "establishment and defense of institutions, of law and order" (*CD* IV/2: 439).

Interestingly, sloth remains a particular temptation for postmodernity. That is, just as the sin of modernity is pride, the heroic affirmation of progress and revolution in defiance of tradition, the postmodern sin is sloth, the spineless indifference, and indeterminate indolence in skepticism toward the future. At its core, sloth is the "concealment" and denial of one's true nature, as discovered in the "real humanity" of Jesus Christ, but its double-mindedness extends into social and environmental inaction. "In our denial and concealment of that which we are and do we can and will only make it worse and really be and do it. Hypocrisy is the supreme repetition of what we seek to deny with its help" (*CD* IV/2: 437). Sloth promises pseudo-liberation but only brings isolation from others. It is the "I without the Thou," the withdrawn and isolated self who seeks to be emancipated from, and superior to other persons in the community (*CD* IV/2: 443). Sloth "begins with the omissions and actions of an indifferent association with one's neighbor to which there can be no juridical and hardly any moral objection. It then becomes the secret or blatant oppression and exploitation of one's fellow" (*CD* IV/2: 436). Sloth leads to oppressive forms of injustice and tyranny, in which persons become radically individualized and isolated from others, and incapable of challenging or resisting this impersonal force. Sloth allows oppressive power to emerge but lacks the intervening power to challenge its relative hegemony.

Sloth and Mammon

Just as pride empowers leviathan, so too, the sin of sloth empowers mammon. As stated, sloth is radically *individualistic*, in that it supports any belief or practice that preserves the isolation of one person from another. Radical individualism may be found in the "functions of the sacrosanct compulsory organization of the totalitarian or the no less sacrosanct free play of the forces of the democratic state" (*CD* IV/2: 439). Since sloth encourages individualism, it cannot resist the power of individualistic greed and materialistic achievement that empowers the love of mammon. In 1949, Barth wrote: "[A] law without gospel hopelessly places us in the service of both God and mammon."[1] The law, without the gospel, becomes absorbed into ideological framework or cultural practice. In a materialistic culture, then, the power of mammon becomes the *new law*—the law of success, achievement, and survival of the fittest. Although mammon is a power that belongs to all past and present societies and economic ideologies and practices, it becomes particularly acute in a capitalist society, where making money is esteemed and valued as ethically normative behavior. This does not imply that capitalism itself is demonic or embodies mammon. Mammon, says Barth, is not simply the accumulation of "material possessions, property, and resources" which provide "a secure livelihood," but the transformation of wealth into a powerful "idol" that has power over personal and communal identity and behavior (*CD* III/4: 222). Capitalism, or any economic system, becomes mammon when it seeks "emancipation from God," and offers the false "promise" that salvation occurs through material resources, economic power, or possessions (*CL*: 222). Mammon's power cannot be eradicated by any new economic order anymore than leviathan's power can be eradicated by better governments. "In the capitalist version," says Jon Gunneman, "economic growth expands the domain of individual liberty and choice; in the Marxist version, it ushers in the domain of socialist freedom, where human beings are the free creators of their own history."[2]

---

1. Quoted in Busch, *Great Passion*, 156.
2. Gunnemann, "Thinking Theologically about the Economic," 329. He further says: "This admixture of God and mammon, of the spiritual and the material, goes to the heart of the ambiguity of the economic. On the one side, economics is the study of the production of goods (and services) under conditions of finitude and modest scarcity; it deals with the material world. On the other side, it is the study of the allocation, exchange, and circulation of goods in society, all dependent on meaning or the spiritual world. Money represents the material; but it and its associated institution, the market, are primary in-

Mammon can be absorbed into any economic ideology, whether ancient, feudal, local, global, or modern capitalist, socialist, communist, or some combinations of systems.

Nevertheless, with greater individualization mammon becomes a threat not only to social solidarity and community, but personal relationships as developed in the workplace, friendships, marriage, and the family. Robert Nelson has explored the underlying theological and religious commitments of the main traditions of economics in the modern/postmodern era.[3] The most dominant neoliberal view of the last thirty years is the "Chicago School" of economics that presumes that persons are primarily driven by economic concerns, desires, and needs, and self-interested economic rationality is applied to non-market activities and exchanges including relationships of family and marriage, sex, health, education, politics, and the law.[4] Of course, behind the Chicago school, lies the economic free market tradition of Adam Smith and the later "Austrian school" (Ludwig von Mises and F. A. Hayek). Yet, it is the Chicago school, more than the Austrian school, which argues that with greater market control over people's lives also comes the "freeing of agency" through other personal choices. The market makes human freedom possible because it transforms human relations within civil society into monetary relations and practices. When the market becomes *the* accepted norm of economic analysis, it carries with it various other attached ideologies and logic which makes it a comprehensive theory. This theory, says Karl Polyani, is guilty of an "economistic fallacy" that abstracts the content and meaning of economics apart from its interdependence upon society, which leads to a fatal misunderstanding, and eventual reduction, of the understanding of economics itself.[5] Society

---

struments of exchange and allocation embedded in the realm of social meaning. Because money facilitates exchange and immensely extends the market's reach, the market in a modern economy is not simply a place where material goods are exchanged but becomes a principle of social organization and tranformative *power*." Ibid., 325.

3. Nelson, *Reaching for Heaven* and *Economics as Religion*. In the latter book, Nelson explores how secular faith commitments have developed from Paul Samuelson and the "Cambridge School" which dominated economics during the mid-late twentieth century, and others of the "Chicago School" and that have been influential for the past twenty-five years. Both schools claim to be neutral or value-free science, but more truthfully, like Marxism, are proponents of secular economic religion, driven to offer a new version of economic salvation through economic progress.

4. For a good discussion and evaluation of the "Chicago School," see Browning, "Egos without Selves," 127–46.

5. Polanyi, *Livelihood of Man*, 5–6.

becomes a market *ethos* and persons become redefined as *homo economicus*.[6] As the economic sphere expands into all areas of human life, including the moral practices of civil society and morality, it gradually shapes personal and communal behavior through espousing a highly individualized notion of human freedom, which "means market dependency in all dimensions of living."[7] This moral ontology "thins-out" the language of moral obligation, reducing moral actions to enlightened self-interest, utilitarian cost/benefit analysis, and the monetary value of commodity exchange.

Furthermore, when persons collapse market and personal needs together, they become victims of the power of sloth and mammon. Mammon assumes that anything short of lucrative success is entirely a *personal* failure, so economic misfortune is caused by personal actions, attitudes, and decisions. Despite its promise for freedom, mammon destroys the possibility of human freedom because it reduces free choices to the value of commodity exchange. Careers replace callings, and jobs replace careers; all that matters is the paycheck. Furthermore, mammon further eradicates freedom linking personal happiness, not with the activity of work, but with the leisurely activity of consumption. Although workers seek to have more leisure, more time to enjoy the rewards of labor, they continue to work more hours, finding less satisfaction with both their work and their personal lives. This leads to more consumerism and waste production, which contributes to the emerging environmental crisis of global climate change. Moreover, mammon, empowered by sloth, makes society comfortably apathetic about resisting social injustice, thus, incapable of resisting tyranny, warfare, or social fragmentation. It denies the humanity of others, which makes it a subtle and concealed power that inspires behavior that leads to inhumanity and injustice; it encourages people to look the other way when injustice is done. Sloth "seems irresistibly to awaken" people to engage in "mutual boasting or sinister collusion, of cold or hot warfare" (*CD* IV/2: 414). When sloth empowers mammon it seeks to control the ethos and law of civil community, which effectively undermines the possibility of political democracy and peacemaking. Mammon, says Barth, "can cause the market to rise and then to fall again. It can arrest this crisis and cause another. It can serve peace yet pursue cold war even in the midst of peace" (*CL*: 224). The civil community becomes incapable of giving witness to God's

---

6. For a further discussion of this subject, see my earlier article, "Religion and the Market," 483–504.

7. Beck, *Risk Society*, 132.

kingdom, but becomes leviathan, placing itself under the law of mammon rather than the law of God, and consequently becomes unwilling to make any real difference in the world.

Witness of Love

The antithesis of sinful sloth is the witness of love. In Barth's central discussions of love, in particular *CD* I/2 and *CD* IV/2, he rejects the notion that *agape* is a deontological moral principle, a universal norm that is dutifully obeyed, or a human virtue nurtured and perfected through repeated actions. Rather, *agape* is a specific kind of love made possible by Jesus Christ. "There can be no question of an extension in principle of the concept of Christian love for the neighbor into a universal love of humanity, unless we are radically to weaken and confuse it" (*CD* IV/2: 807). Just as there is no "natural faith" in God, so is there no "natural love" of God and neighbor; just as "Christian faith is the human response to God's justifying sentence, so Christian love is the human response to His direction" (*CD* IV/1: 102). The human act of *agape*, in other words, originates in the corresponding work of the Holy Spirit: "Only by the Holy Spirit do they become free for this action" (*CD* IV/2: 818). Therefore, in response to God's gracious action of sanctification, the Holy Spirit not only gathers the church in justification and faith (*CD* IV/1), but up-builds or *empowers* the church to be a visible witness in its proclamation, mission, and politics (*CD* IV/2).

> The goal in the direction of which the true church proceeds and moves is the revelation of the sanctification of all humanity and human life as it has already taken place *de iure* in Jesus Christ. In the exaltation of the one Jesus, who as the Son of God became a servant in order as such to become the Lord of all men, there has been accomplished already in powerful archetype, not only cancellation of the sins and therefore the justification but also the elevation and establishment of all humanity and human life and therefore its sanctification. That this is the case is the theme and content of the witness with which His community is charged. (*CD* IV/2: 620)

Although Christian love, corresponding to God's sanctifying power, first emerges within the love of the Christian community, it extends into the world through Christian witness and action. Christian love is always *widening* into relationships outside the church. This is possible because God's sanctifying power, made visible in the church, is a "witness to all others," in that it represents "the sanctification which has already come upon them too in Jesus Christ" (*CD* IV/2: 620). No doubt, this "representation is provisional" because both church and world exist "between the times" of the "already" and the "not yet," the resurrection and Christ's second coming. This is why, Barth adds, "the restriction of Christian love to the circle of brothers known to me cannot be theoretical and definitive, but only practice and provisional" (*CD* IV/2: 808). Christian love of the unbelieving neighbor is only truly possible, then, as a love for one who is eschatologically "in Christ." Loving an unbelieving neighbor as a future brother or sister in Christ is possible only because it "corresponds" to the prior divine promise of election within the divine-human covenant-partnership (*CD* I/2: 441).

Henceforth, just as the power of faith resists pride and leviathan, so too, the power of love resists sloth and mammon. The love command can never be reduced to a simply horizontal command to help others, but depends entirely on the vertical relationship between God and humanity. The vertical love of God makes it possible for the corrosive power of human sinfulness, like pride and sloth, to be destroyed and transformed into the *other* directed power of love. So, it is *agape*, which "breaks the dominion of the sinister forces to which the man alienated from God, the neighbor and himself is subject" (*CD* IV/2: 836). Indeed, by breaking the individualistic power of sloth and mammon, the witness and practice of love enables persons to develop solidarity and community, grounded in justice and the rule of law, in the form of the gospel. Since the law commands that we treat others with dignity and value, this "mutual love is the fulfilling of the law," which results in self-giving acts of neighbor-love for the good of the other (*CD* IV/2: 816). Again, principally this is an act of correspondence that "represents" the fact God loves, justifies, and sanctifies persons by acting *pro nobis* and restoring their covenant-partnership with God and others. Christians and the church can only point to this fact, or give witness to this fact, that God loves all people. "None of us can reveal to the other that God loves him and that he may love God in return" (*CD* IV/2: 815). Therefore, in their acts of correspondence, Christians both resist mammon (and sloth), and love God and neighbor as a *free* act, grounded in covenant of grace. Christians are never "channels" or "instruments" of divine action. Rather, in response to God's command of grace, persons "correspondingly" and "freely" act in Christian obedience and responsibility so that the "the covenant of grace, becomes two-sided instead of one-sided" (*CD* IV/2: 790).

This responsibility, furthermore, calls the Christian community and civil community to be a witness *for* economic justice, which seeks economic trust, solidarity, and concern for the common good. We recall that church law, as the form of the gospel, gives witness to the civil law through it practice of service, trust, concern for the common good, solidarity and equality, and open-ended moral judgment (*CD* IV/2: 724–25). First, the *I-Thou* relation, grounded in love, can truly remain open to the *needs* of the other, seeing them face-to-face, while the same time, rejecting powers, like mammon, which attempt to destroy human freedom and dignity. Second, it guides one to truly hear and speak with others in mutual *dialogue* that builds up persons and communities, rather than tears them down through oppression and injustice. Third, this leads to mutual *assistance* in social justice, rather succumbing to the power of mammon, greed, and economic exploitation. Being aware of human relatedness and love makes it possible for the church to be a witness to the civil community that Jesus came to "seek and save the lost," which explains why the church "will always choose the movement from which it can expect the greatest measure of social justice" (*CSC*: 173). "The poor, the socially and economically weak and threatened, will always be the object of its primary and particular concern, and it will always insist on the State's special responsibility for these weaker members in society." (*CSC*: 173). In standing economically with and for others, the church gives witness to God's love, demonstrating to the civil community that it too can challenge the radical individualism of mammon and seek economic solidarity and the common good.

JUSTICE AND ECONOMIC WITNESS

Christian economic ethics begins with the church's witness of love and justice, and then moves outward into society through parabolic language and action, choosing to stand with one's local and global community. This dialectical task says No to the powers of mammon and economic oppression, and Yes toward *relative* courses of action that seek to be responsible to the other, church, and world. In so doing, it must also avoid ideological pitfalls of extreme positions, while freely moving back and forth between these ideologies. Since the 1990s, Christian social ethics has rightly said No to an unregulated global free market (globalization) or the ideology of economic neoliberalism. Along with others in the "faculty club," Christian ethicists rightly point to the relative hegemonic systems of corporate power that do injustice to persons, communities, and the environment. In the past decade, numerous business scandals like Enron and the Wall Street meltdowns in recent years, demonstrate the power of mammon, and the resulting "demonic" corruption and greed of business. These scandals reveal the pervasive greed and corruption at work in the financial system, in which individual or group investors profit from engineering capital flows, while local communities, struggling businesses, and developing nations suffer economic losses. Since this crisis, however, we now see governments bailing out large investment firms, banks, insurance companies, and other business that remain vital to the worldwide capital markets. This has led to the reemergence of Neo-Keynesianism in the United States. Indeed, it is possible we may be moving toward a "global Keynesianism," which moves us further away from neoliberal model of free market globalism. This leads to more government regulation and oversight of financial and corporate institutions. Given these rapid changes in the economic system, what does it mean for the Christian ethics to give witness to God's love, standing against mammon, in a worldwide global economy? Christian witness stands *for* people and communities and not economic systems; it is neither utopian nor dystopian about global markets or economic theories. Rather, in its witness to God's love, it also gives witness to the civil community that it too can witness to God's kingdom by saying No to mammon but Yes to economic justice.

For Economic Justice

Christian economic witness begins with the church as the "inner circle" of witness to the "outer circle" of the civil community. Just as God stands with and for us in Jesus Christ, so should the church and civil community stand for the dignity and welfare of all persons. "Since God himself became man, man is the measure of all things" (*CL*: 172). Moreover, just as Christ came to the poor and lost, so too, the church should support civil governments that seek to address the needs of the "poor, the socially and economically weak and threatened" in society (*CSC*: 173). The economic support for the disenfranchised implies saying No to powers of mammon that corrupt the global economic system. It says No to the "unequivocally demonic process which consists in the amassing and multiplying of possessions expressed in financial calculations (or miscalculations)" of the "relatively few, who pull the strings," and use their power of "capital" to oppress the poor, while at the same time, promising "salvation" to the nations (*CD* III/4: 532). Where the power of global capitalism becomes potentially hegemonic and a risk to the welfare of persons, communities, and the environment, it must be challenged and resisted. Rejecting the abuses of economic neoliberalism, however, is directed against the ideology that shapes totalitarian systems and organizations and not people who remain victims of the destructive ideology.

This No against ideology and potentially hegemonic structures is matched by the proactive Yes to civil community's vocation as *guardian* of common good. As guardian, the civil community's law can draw from the church's law, which remains the form of the gospel. Civil law is parabolic of church law, thus, remains a secular parable of witness to God's kingdom. The church gives witness to the civil community that social ethics involves and ethics of "total self-giving," which means being committed to the welfare of the common good. In addition, the church's witness demonstrates why it is important to reject society's emphasis on achievement, materialism, and power, and instead seek to live in *solidarity* and human *equality* within the civil community of free persons under the rule of law under *Rechtsstaat* (*CD* IV/2: 724). Economic witness stands for people not economic systems. Thus, it remains critical of ideologies that promise a better future, including those that promise "social progress or even socialism," but at the same time, it "can and should espouse the cause of this or that branch of social progress or even socialism in the form most helpful at a specific time and place and a specific situation" (*CD* III/4: 545). Social ethics must be cautious of the extremes of ideological neoliberalism and socialism, or perhaps better "communism," while forging a middle way that seeks to reform the economy, making it a more humane "social market" or social economy. In this way, it must seriously engage the traditions of the "social market" economy, including Christian socialism, democratic socialism, or "social market" capitalism. Yet, in doing so, it must constantly return to the church's witness not some ideological form of economic practice.

Radical Orthodoxy has rightly shifted the discussion about economics from secular economic theory to the church's beliefs and practices. In doing this, however, the rhetoric often becomes contrastive in which a "divine economy" is posited *against* the heretical capitalist economy.[8] Saying this,

---

8. Milbank, *Theology and Social Theory*, 12–17. For a recent collection of Milbank's essays on political and economic thought, see Milbank, *Future of Love*. These essays include Milbank's most important essays of the last twenty-five years, including several on his ideas on Christian socialism. Also see Long, *Divine Economy* and Bell, Jr., *Liberation Theology*.

however, at times its language potentially becomes antagonistic rather than reforming. John Milbank, for example, longs for a pre-1848 Christian socialism that rejects modern economic assumptions about the private property and contractual exchange, and instead has proposed an economic ethics of "gift" grounded in God's gracious self-giving.[9] Milbank has consistently urged Christians to denounce the "secular reason" of both neoliberal capitalism and Marxism, and instead "insist that if the community resides in exchange, we must have a socialist market."[10] In a similar way, Stephen Long says that the "market as salvific institution is and must be heretical. All orthodox Christians should recognize its deceitful power and oppose it."[11] Beginning with the church's preaching and sacraments, especially the Eucharist, Christians must see the church as a "social institution" that must be "juxtaposed to other intuitions, such as the state, the military, the family, and the market."[12] In similar oppositional language, Daniel Bell argues that the church remains the only institution to resist a hegemonic transnational capitalism because, as an alternative *polis*, it offers an alternative understanding of the "technology of desire."[13] The capitalist *mythos* stands in contrast to an economy of "gift," which emerges from God's trinitarian relationship to the world, in which God unceasingly gives to the "other" without the need for reciprocation. God is never alienated in giving, nor expects something in return for a gift.[14]

Putting these ideas together, a "theological economics" begins with the notion of gift-exchange, as realized in the Eucharist, rather than commodity exchange, so evident in secular economics. Similar to Barth, Radical Orthodox thinkers begin their reflection on economics with the church's witness, but unlike Barth, these theologians further claim there is a "Christian" economics that begins with an alternative ecclesiology, as alternative *polis*, which creates a "socialist space." Barth too would reject the autonomous, utilitarian, and materialist understanding of the self and community, as found in modern neoliberalism, but would be more cautious of overvaluing specific ecclesiological practices as the "answer" to the

---

9. Milbank, *Theology and Social Theory*, 15.
10. Milbank, "Socialism of the Gift," 544.
11. Long, *Goodness of God*, 260.
12. Ibid., 26.
13. Bell, Jr., *Liberation Theology*, 71.
14. Milbank's theology of "gift" is fully developed in Milbank's book, *Being Reconciled*.

economic problem of injustice. Although the church can be a model for the secular economy, it cannot claim that it actually embodies a "divine economy" for that too closely identifies divine agency with the church itself. Consequently Christian ethics must be cautious about any absolutist "Christian" theory of "social market" economics (i.e., Christian socialism) or "theological economics." Economic witness does not isolate a Christian theory of economics from the real world economy, which leads to the distancing of the church from the civil community, but gives witness to a responsible form of economics *within* the civil community. Christian ethics must be cautious of any theology that makes the No consistently louder than the Yes.

Although the church bears witness to the secular economy, moreover, it remains too utopian to say that specific ecclesiological practice, like gift-exchange, will extend the "divine economy" into the secular world economy. Furthermore, if the intention is not to change the secular economy but only to reject it, while being a faithful witness the true "divine economy," then this risks separation and exclusion from secular society. When the secular economy is *separated* from a divine (or theological) one, this inevitably demonizes the global economy while overvaluing the theological economy. In her book *Economy of Grace*, Kathryn Tanner, for example, claims on theological grounds that there cannot be a direct line between God's gracious action, as pure gift, and human gift exchange. Hence, a theological economy, that grounds itself entirely on divine action or ecclesiological practice can easily become a "wild and unworkable ideal" that remains rather utopian, abstract, and unconnected with the real economy in which persons are engaged. Regarding, this point, she further writes:

> With nothing to gain from attention to the capitalist system it hopes to escape, theological economy might limit its purview to the Bible or to church practices, and model its self-reliant, small scale communities on, say, the subsistence agrarian economies of ancient Israel or on the desert monasteries of the early church, withdrawn from a world in which hope has been lost. Pretending to self-sufficiency, an alternative theological economy might in this way cut itself off from any sophisticated economic analysis of the realities of today's world—a sophisticated analysis of the real problems and potentials for change in the economic situation we now face, as the best academic disciplines of the day describe them.[15]

15. Tanner, *Economy of Grace*, 88.

Christian theologians and ethicists must seek to engage in a dialogical practice, which eventually provides an "opening for theological economy."[16] This opening for theological reflection, says Tanner, can lead to economic principles like mutual benefit and non-competitiveness, fostering greater cooperation and interdependence. These principles stand in contrast the rigid *laissez faire* principles of competition, enlightened self-interest, and profit maximization. Christian ethics can "eavesdrop" and even critically dialogue with economics, but it cannot, by itself, create a new theory or practice of economics. There is no Christian theory of economics like there is a theory of soteriology, ecclesiology, or the Trinity. This is not to say that Christian ethics is unable to make moral judgment, or provide "openings" for theology, to assess which economic theory is more consistent with Christian witness. In rejecting the neoliberal free market theory of the Austrian or Chicago schools, for example, theologians and ethicists can rightly prefer a "social market" theory that looks to more government oversight of the mixed economy. This latter theory rightly rejects, in the words of Karl Polanyi, the reductionistic "economistic fallacy," while calling for a greater interdependence of economics with other social forces. Polanyi insightfully claimed that this "double-movement" of society includes both market *expansion* and the enlarging capacity of society, through social institutions or associations, to *challenge* the values of the market. The "double movement," then, is personified in "two organizing principles in society," namely the "self-regulating market" of "economic liberalism" and the "social protection" of society, emerging in its social and cultural institutions and "protective legislation."[17] The formation of a social market democracy is possible because of the reflexive character of the organizations, beliefs, and practices of civil society, which invariably resists the self-interest of *laissez faire* capitalism. Since the problems of society are inherently *social* rather than political or economic, it is through a rediscovery of society (or community) that persons begin to engage, resist, and change the destructive features of the market's relative hegemony. Hence, Polanyi's "counter-movement," which rejects the ideologies of *laissez faire* neoliberalism and Marxism, is grounded in the inability of either the market or the state to control society, which relies on various social institutions and associations, like the church, that can speak out concerning individual and communal needs. In their witness to God's

---

16. Ibid., 89.
17. Polanyi, *Great Transformation*, 132.

kingdom, both the church and civil society can stand for economic justice and a humane social market that calls for social protection and democratic oversight of the economy.

For Economic Reform

Christian social witness engages in conversation "with" not "against" the "secular parables" of economics and other social sciences. Yet, how should such a dialogue continue? In 1988, the journal *Theology* carried an interesting debate between Robert Preston and John Milbank regarding the legacy and prospects of Christian socialism.[18] In his article "Christian Socialism Becalmed," Preston argues that many versions of Christian socialism, like Milbank's, invariably misunderstand the relationship between theology and economics, which leads to unrealistic or unworkable utopian economic strategies. Milbank responds by discrediting Preston's use—or better misuse—of theology, which overvalues economic science and undervalues the church as a real alternative to capitalism. Hence, the two issues of contention, are: 1) how should the dialogue between theology and economics be conceived? And 2) is there a real economic alternative to global capitalism? Preston, a trained economist and theologian, seeks to find creative ways to distinguish and relate the discourses in developing his *reformist* position for improving the ambiguities of capitalism toward a more just society. In contrast, Milbank's *radical* position rejects the secularist assumptions of the social sciences and seeks to develop a strictly theological economics, beginning with God's trinitarian gift-giving, and ending with human gift-exchange.

A dialectical economic ethics splits the difference between Preston and Milbank, while encouraging ongoing dialogue and critical engagement. In one way, Barth is closer to Milbank's radicalism by insisting upon the theological starting-point, yet in another, he is closer to someone like Preston, who distinguishes the two discourses, while reforming the economic system from within its current structures. We must recall that Barth consistently rejected extremes, whether Marxist socialism or free market capitalism, and instead saw theology move toward a practical "non-ideological politics, strictly orientated toward political issues themselves."[19] Economic witness, then, begins with a theological witness that invites secular descriptions of world processes, while at the same time offers a dialectical process of dis-

---

18. Preston, "Christian Socialism Becalmed," 412–16.
19. Jehle, *Ever Against the Stream*, 44.

cernment that avoids radical extremes of absolute Yes or No. Thus, it stands as an alternative to ideological positions of uncritically standing either for or against global capitalism. For these reasons, Barth's *reformist* view is closer to Preston, which led him to be generally supportive of—but not an apologist for—liberal constitutional democracy and a more left-leaning "social market" position of economic justice. Christians cannot equate the kingdom of God with their own economic strategies, nor can they base their thinking on utopian visions of a radically new worldwide economy. Since human action happens in correspondence to divine action, persons are free and empowered to engage in their limited efforts to reform *existing* economic systems. Christian eschatology rests in the objective fact that God has decisively acted, is acting, and will act in the future, not just for the church, but also for world and even the current global economy.

For Humane Work

Like Radical Orthodoxy, Barth, in *CD* III/4, places his discussion of economics and work within the context of the church. Economics and work is a practical example of how the church bears witness to God's kingdom. By placing human work within the context of the church, Barth sees the "active life" as a form of witness consisting of serving the church, but its "circumference" consisting of serving to the world, and fellow humanity, through daily work.

> What we now call the work of man corresponds to this providential rule. As God sees to His creature, and cares for it, in order that it may not cease as the object of His love, He requires of man the action corresponding to this care and providence. Addressing and claiming him as His covenant-partner, or, we may now say concretely, as a member of the Christian community, He also commands him—in order to makes this possible—to exist as His human creature, requiring that his active life should take this human form, and fulfill itself in this form. Work is this human form. (*CD* III/4: 517)

In corresponding to divine action in Christ, persons are empowered to freely engage in the "active life," a life of *freedom* to serve God and humanity through altering and shaping the structures of the human economy. As Barth writes, it is "only as a Christian, only as he is claimed for co-operation in the service of the Christian community and thus knows the meaning of work, that man finds himself summoned to it" (*CD* III/4: 523). All work can be corrupted by mammon or the "two-fold evil root" of individualization and materialism (*CD* III/4: 534). The first side of this dialectic denies the "social character of work," which shifts work from a cooperative and communal, activity to a competitive and individualistic "struggle for existence," and the second encourages an "empty and inordinate desire" for individual achievement, possessions, and power, which further isolates persons from each other and contributes for more injustice and exploitation (*CD* III/4: 534). There is reciprocal relationship between the communal nature of work and the prioritization of needs over wants or desires, just as there is between the individualization of work and the justification for greater struggle and competition for a modest scarcity of goods and resources. When a person seeks only her own advantage, she inevitably disadvantages the other, which leads to the "cost of the partial or even perhaps the total exclusion of the other form that which both desire" (*CD* III/4: 540). The corruption of work thereby drives people toward the exploitation, instrumentalization, and exclusion of the other.

In its witness to God's love, however, Christian witness affirms a humane understanding and practice of work. This does not imply that work should be principally viewed as an end in itself, nor as means to improve one's livelihood, family, society (or culture), or nation, but as a way to *serve* humanity's welfare, by promoting human freedom, dignity, solidarity, and the common good. Work is "objective" in that it purposefully serves the good of the individual and community. When persons misplace the cooperative nature of work for others, with a selfish and hostile struggle for human existence, they strip work of its freedom. Hence, by standing against the "two-fold evil" of individualization and materialism, Christian witness engages in a Word-centered "counter-movement," supporting the "weak" against the "strong," and affirming any movement, policy, or law that supports the "genuine and vital claims" of humanity's dignity and welfare (*CD* III/4, 538ff.). From the early *Romans* commentaries to *The Christian Life*, Barth dialectically argued, on one side, that the church should support and encourage democratic socialism while at the same time, the church's "decisive word cannot consist of the proclamation of social progress or socialism." Rather, he says, "it consists only in the proclamation of the revolution of God against 'all ungodliness and unrighteousness of man' (Rom 1:18), i.e., in the proclamation of his kingdom as it has already comes and comes" (*CD* III/4, 545). Writing in the early 1950s, Barth's criticism of the free market system is based, not on socialist ideology, but on ethical evaluations of justice as it pertains to the social practice of work. In saying this, however, he also argues that the historical critique of capitalism by Christian socialists and others no longer applies to the mixed market economies of the current era. There is, he says,

> no such thing as pure and undiluted capitalism, and that events have falsified, and in all probability will continue to falsify, more than one of the prophesies of doom pronounced over it, e.g., the increasing enrichment of fewer and fewer wealthy persons, the developing proletarianisation of even the middle classes, and the cumulative misery of the masses, especially of the proletariat who have nothing to lose but their chains. Nevertheless, of what avail are all these arguments in face of the simple fact that this system does permit in practice and demand in principle that man should make another man and his work a means to his own ends, and therefore a mere instrument, and that this is inhuman and therefore constitutes and injustice? (*CD* III/4: 543)

Barth's discussion of economic reform emerges out of the task of being a responsible Christian in the world. Rather than looking for simple solutions to the problems of competition and exploitation, like state-sponsored socialism, he offers a multilateral, practical, and non-ideological approach. Reform of economic governance should not be limited only to changes in nationalist, localist, or internationalist political authority, but can be drawn from all areas of civil society, including the private sector. Indeed, social "counter-movements" should encourage the reform of economic power structures that create injustice in worker contracts and greater inequality; and such counter-movements need not emerge only from the social movements of the church. The church is not the only witness to economic justice and reform. In a passing comment, for example, he praises the Swiss company the Zeiss group for their innovative co-management and cooperative practices, which demonstrates businesses' own capacity for moral reform (*CD* III/4: 543). As an "indirect witness" to God's kingdom, business organizations, like Zeiss, can challenge economic power arrangements, inhuman working conditions, and unjust economic practice through specific policy changes. When Christians act *for* the good of others, they also act *with* others toward the goals of social and economic justice, solidarity, and the welfare of the common good. In correspondence to God's love, Christians can actively work for economic interdependence that leads to greater mutual benefit and cooperation. In so doing, they can stand for equal and fair trade, eliminating debt, worker's rights and welfare provision, and since the 2008 crisis, seeking to regulate and curtail the problem of financial speculation within investment organizations. They must stand for the good of the real economy and its effect on persons, the church, and the world.

Giving witness to justice involves responsible involvement in social action groups, thereby leading to greater global cooperation. This multilateral global strategy seeks to practice international monitoring, and even regulation, of the global market and corporate activity by nation-states. This monitoring can occur through the empowerment of IGOs such as the UN, IMF, WTO, and the World Bank, as well as the impact of NGOs such as Amnesty International. The utopian goal of replacing the global economy with some form of a national, regional, or local economy will not address global risks and problems of disparity of wealth, poverty, and inhumane living conditions. Problems in the global economy require *global* cooperation from government and non-governmental organizations, including encouraging "globalization from below" through numerous social movements or networks calling for greater justice. These networks use communication networks, like the internet, media, or public action, to raise local and global awareness regarding particular problems affecting millions of people worldwide, which are often neglected by larger NGOs. One of the more well-known networks is the *International Campaign to Ban Landmines*, which won a Nobel Peace Prize. There are more than a hundred of these networks today; some seek to protect workers' and children's rights, or the environment, while others seek to expose corruption in governments and corporations. These are examples of what Barth called "social counter-movements," which effectively bypasses the bureaucratic movement from local to national to international agencies, and instead moves from individuals and small groups to collective action. Christians, as "Christian humanists," argues Barth, should participate in counter-movements, or what we call today "global policy networks," which often work with established NGOs and IGOs with the goal of making a real difference in the world. This contributes to greater global cooperation, through justice, in addressing the various economic risks that affect the "poor, the socially and economically weak and threatened" in society (*CSC*: 173).

Global Cooperation and Economy

With this in mind, it is better to say that Christian witness stands *ambiguously* "with," rather than absolutely for or against the global economy. Following Robert Preston, the term "ambiguity" refers less to the derogatory meaning of "uncertainty" or imprecision (although there are these elements in all theories) as to the dialectical "analysis of a phenomenon which has an important and valid aspect, but which at the same time has aspects, inseparable from what is valued, which are undesirable."[20] Social witness strives to work with and for persons, the church, and the world, which requires some form of economic production and wealth creation. A Christian ethics that concentrates solely on issues of distributive justice cannot account for the whys and hows of wealth creation and production, which leads to an incomplete theory of economics. Without economic production there is no possibility for justice. Because there is no perfect economic system, then Christian ethics is freed from the need to apologetically sanction a purely, sacred, divine, or Christian theory of economics. In *Christianity and the Market*, John Atherton echoes this strategy, when he writes:

> The result is that we can be liberated from the impulsive desire to produce the distinctively Christian, when addressing such matters as the contemporary economy. We can reject with confidence those pre-modern attempts to impose, however decisively or subtly, religious understandings on secular life. Whether they take the form of Roman Catholic social encyclicals, biblically based systems, liberation theology, the confessional theology of the World Council of Churches, or even the social principles of the mainstream liberal tradition, we are free to learn from them—and yet free to move beyond them.[21]

Atherton wisely argues that "social discipleship" in the "interim" period frees Christians to fully engage the market, valuing its positives and challenging it negatives, without reducing this viewpoint to ideology. This task of Christian social witness, says Atherton, implies three main characteristics. They are: 1) rejecting the idea there is only "one Christian tradition or response" that can adequately address our times, and rather Christians should "draw form a variety of responses because none can capture the complexity and plurality of the contemporary;" 2) this frees Christian social

20. Preston, *Religion and the Ambiguities of Capitalism*, 127.
21. Atherton, *Christianity and the Market*, 279.

though from obsession with the "distinctively Christian, the mythical holy grail of Christian social thought," which always seeks to "find answers that others have not seen," and instead it allows Christians to dialogue with others and address specific risks and challenges in our world; 3) addressing these risks should never force Christians to retreat from them into the apparent safety of "realpolitik and pietism."[22] Drawing false dualisms and equivocations, adds Atherton, forces Christians from the central task of speaking about the "interaction between market and challenges, and then with the provisional framework and dynamics related to it."[23] It remains non-dialectical to see the global market economy *only* as an irrevocably demonic, heretical, and hegemonic institution that poses a threat to persons and communities and stands against Christian witness. Rather, Christian witness stands with the global market, seeking to bring justice to the world through humanizing the economy. For this to occur, however, the emphasis needs to shift from notions of "free market" to "social market." The market cannot exist independently of humane social movements that seek to reform its capacity for economic justice. Obviously, the global economy can be corrupted through individual and corporate greed, power, and disregard for the dignity and integrity of persons and communities. Yet, an ethics of reconciliation affirms that even sinful persons, associations, and institutions can be transformed and become potential sources of blessing to the poor of the world. Christian witness, therefore, must continue to speak against the risks that endanger human life, while it stands for those elements that contribute to human freedom, peace, and security. It must say No but within the context of a greater Yes. Christian economic witness, in short, can seek a middle dialectical path standing with the global economy, which implies both *resisting* the evil it produces in our society while *affirming* its good.

22. Ibid., 272.
23. Ibid.

CHAPTER THIRTEEN

Environmental Witness: For Hope and Freedom

When Barth finally visited America, in 1962, he gave what would be his last set of public lectures, published together in the fine book, *Evangelical Theology*. In the introduction, he makes the cryptic remark that what is needed at this time, on both sides of the Atlantic, is not a return to the traditional orthodoxy of Thomism, Lutheranism, or Calvinism or the liberal theology of Harnack and Troeltsch, and most of all not "Barthianism," but what he calls a "theology of freedom."[1] A theology of freedom, says Barth, is: "marked by freedom from fear of communism, Russia, inevitable nuclear warfare and . . . all the aforementioned principalities and powers. Freedom *for* which you stand would be the freedom *for*—I like to say a single word—humanity. . . . It would be necessarily a theology of freedom, of that freedom to which the Son frees us, and which, as is his gift, is the one real human freedom."[2] In this quote, we are again reminded what "freedom" as "gift" means, and how this has bearing on Christian witness *as* ethics. We've seen how a Christian responsible witness emerges in the political and economic spheres, and how in each case this witness is possible only because it is grounded in the human *response* to God's freedom to act in the covenant of grace. Any other autonomous notion of human freedom or moral agency risks being shaped and controlled by the

1. Barth, *Evangelical Theology*, xii.
2. Barth, *How I Changed My Mind*, 79.

powers of leviathan, mammon, and ideology. This chapter takes this idea of freedom as the operative motif in environmental witness. In so doing, we look at *CD* IV/3, where Jesus Christ embodies hope and overcomes the sin of falsehood, leading to "sending" of the Christian community. Here we see how the sin of falsehood is juxtaposed against hope, and ideology is juxtaposed against freedom. It is in this struggle between ideology and hope where environmental witness takes place. We have seen how ideology is at work in both political and economic ethics, thus, of the three "spiritual powers" it is ideology that appears the most pervasive. Furthermore, ideology is strongly linked to the chthonic power of technology, particularity in various forms of utopianism. In summary, this chapter looks at *CD* IV/3, demonstrating how Christ's "prophetic witness" embodies hope and overcomes the sin of falsehood, empowering the church to live out its witness serving the world. In this context, the church's witness extends beyond the nation-state and economic system to that of the built and natural environment. In its environmental witness, Christians and the church declare hope to the world by affirming that the world does have the freedom to support global environmental reform and sustainability by affirming that God reconciling love is also for the world and non-human life.

HOPE AND ECOLOGICAL WITNESS
Christ against Falsehood

In *CD* IV/3, Barth explores the Christological theme of Jesus Christ as Prophet, the "true witness" as the "One" who brings together into unity of his person the two previous themes of *CD* IV/1–2. That is, in his prophetic office, Jesus Christ brings together the "high priest" and "royal man," God's "deity and humanity, of God's humiliation and man's exaltation, of the justification and sanctification of man, of faith and love" (*CD* IV/3: 4). As prophet, Jesus Christ acts *pro nobis* as "true witness" and "victor," in such a way that God's reconciliation is not only an "event fulfilled in him" but "in virtue of His revelation, it becomes the object, basis, and content of human knowledge" (*CD* IV/3: 217). In his prophetic witness, we see God's No against the powers and Yes for responsible witness most clearly revealed, and with this, the mission and witness of the church. The church is not only gathered by Christ the "high priest," nor built-up by Christ the true "king," but also given a task and mission by Christ the true "prophet." The church itself becomes a witness to God's Yes for the world. The church, as *totus Christus* or the "historical form of Christ's earthly existence" reveals to the world that "*totus Christus* is *Christus victor*" (*CD* IV/3: 216). Jesus Christ has acted, is acting, and will act in the future. In its witness to Christ's victory, the church remains confident that it correspondingly can act in victory in and through the Holy Spirit. "Our action is wholly ours, yet it is determined by His." That is, Jesus Christ "passes through our midst, striding through our time from His commencement to His goal" (*CD* IV/3: 363). In this way, Christians "are contemporaries of Jesus Christ and direct witness of His action, whether with closed or open or blinking eyes, whether actively or passively." Therefore, in the prophetic witness of Jesus Christ comes "the hope of us all in the promise of the Spirit addressed to all" (*CD* IV/3: 362–63). Nevertheless, this hope of Christ's actions *pro nobis*, further unveils the sin of humanity's self-deception and "falsehood," which rejects, denies, and replaces God's reconciliation in favor of their own self-deception. Still, Christ's hope for us, the world, and the cosmos, provides the basis for our acts of hope, knowing that God has acted, is acting, and will act in the future for everything that exists. In its social witness, Christians are empowered to say No to falsehood and ideology and Yes to hope.

What is the sin of falsehood and what are its implications for society? At its core, the sin of "falsehood" is more than telling lies or deceiving one's neighbor or the vices of deceit, dishonesty, or treachery. Rather, it is an "anti-spiritual phenomenon" that rejects God's true *promise* of reconciliation, which is revealed by the "true witness" of Jesus Christ. Living in the lies of falsehood "transforms truth into untruth and the true Witness into the untrue" (*CD* IV/3: 441). In contrast, living in the truth relies on the reconciling power of *Christus victor* to unmask the various disguises that people use to claim independence from God (*CD* IV/3: 165ff.). Affirming Christ as the "true witness" and "victor" exposes self-deception, whereas denying this reality provides greater opportunity for the sin of falsehood to claim its power over persons' view of themselves and the world. Still, not all forms of human disbelief, superstition, and error reach the dramatic stage of defiance against Jesus Christ. People can engage in all kinds of treachery, deceit, and malice, and yet self-deception does not assume that one must be a follower of the lies of tyrants like "Hitler, Mussolini, or Stalin" (*CD* IV/3: 438). Yet, adherence to dictators may be one particular outcome of falsehood, for when they deny Christ as "true witness" they inevitably choose to shape their lives according to alternative narratives of emancipation that promise freedom, success, or personal power. Only with "Sunday lies" comes the awareness of the practice of "everyday lies" (*CD* IV/3: 451). This is why only those aware of their reconciliation in Jesus Christ can begin to unmask the layers of self-deception, deceit, and falsehood that shape their lives. This is why the most dangerous lies are those that proclaim pseudo-Christian ideas or make reference to the importance of Jesus without recognizing him as the "truth" and "true witness." "Nothing is more dangerous than the falsehood in which he [a person] manages, or at least tries and thinks that he manages, to use the truth to silence the truth, or the true Witness, by finding for Him (Jesus Christ) a place, by championing Him, by making Him its Hero, Example and Symbol, yet all the time patronizing, interpreting, domesticating, acclimatising, accommodating, and gently but very defiantly and significantly correcting Him" (*CD* IV/3: 437, rev.).

There is a proclivity among thoughtful persons acquainted with Jesus Christ to transform him into something he is not, that is, a mystic or wisdom teacher, rebel or revolutionary, CEO or businessperson, citizen or solder, peasant or oppressed victim, psychologist or therapist, or educator or moral teacher. This may take the form of literature, philosophy, biblical studies, theology, or spirituality. Regardless, these fabrications of the historical Jesus deny that he is also the Christ, the Lord and Mediator. The most common deception follows in the footsteps of Arius, denying Christ's mediating and salvific mission for humanity's reconciliation, and then re-articulating the God-world relation in other correlative terms. "Lying is denial of free grace as the truly divine reality and possibility and repudiation of free gratitude as man's only possible response to it. Lying is the rash attempt to set up a situation between God and man in which Jesus Christ does not exist as mediator between them" (*CD* IV/3: 464). Without a mediator, the God-world relation, grounded in grace, becomes either more distant tending toward a separation (deism), or more closely linked tending toward an identification (pantheism or panentheism). Without the mediating work of Jesus Christ, people are forced to either adopt a position of a "god-less" or a "god-like" humanity. In either case, the specific role of the mediator is denied, which invariably closes off the open conversation between God and humanity as free agents, and makes one the consequent of, or contingent upon, the other. That is, either divine agency collapses into human agency or human agency collapses into divine agency; the first leads to grandiose claims of Prometheanism and the second to deterministic claims of fatalism. In either case, Christ as mediator and Lord becomes irrelevant.

Falsehood and Ideology

Just as the denial of justification leads to pride and loss of faith, the denial of sanctification leads to sloth and the loss of love, so too, the denial of vocation leads to falsehood, which inevitably leads to the formation of worldviews or ideologies. The formation of worldviews begins with the act of *evasion*—of avoiding the truth. "Evasion means trying to find another place where the truth can no longer reach or affect him, where he is secure from the invading hand of its knowledge, and from its implications" (*CD* IV/3: 435). Running away from the truth is also balanced by a seeking for alternative forms of truth, which together form a "real masterpiece and artistic triumph of falsehood" (*CD* IV/3: 436). People seek to find assurance, comfort, and sustaining satisfaction from the various sets of beliefs and practices that comprise their lives. These masterpieces of self-deception create a false sense of security and hope, which leads to a kind of "euphoria." Still, this emotion cannot be sustained indefinitely, for by denying God's reconciliation the person eventually places themselves under the judgment of others, of society, or some ideological authority. This is why persons often find themselves in "oscillation" in an "unceasing dialectic" between "euphoria" and "disillusionment" (*CD* IV/3: 470–71). Likewise this "tension or dialectic" between euphoria and disillusionment corresponds to two human experiences of "goodness" and "nothingness" in "relation to world history" (*CD* IV/3: 703). That is, we are aware of the meaningfulness and wonder of existence, at the same time, we are aware of its nihilism and tragedy. The person cannot live with this dichotomy, so he or she seeks to have "mastery over the problem" by constructing "world-pictures in an attempt to understand the cosmos and himself, or himself in the cosmos" (*CD* IV/3: 705).

Rather than leading to greater hope, however, the formation of worldviews more often lead to a greater confusion, cynicism, or pessimism emerging from the sin of falsehood and self-deception. Although this *weltanschauung* attempts to explain how existence can be both "glorious and yet also terrifying," it also creates a "state of *hominum confusione*," in which human freedom is constantly challenged by "demonized powers and forces," which appear both in and outside of human control (*CD* IV/3: 698). Therefore, it is the fundamental tension in *hominum confusione* that leads to the "inextricable intertwining or confusion of these two elements" resulting in the "relativising the one by the other" (*CD* IV/3: 696). So, these worldviews either tilt toward the utopian optimism of the goodness of existence, which limits nothingness, or tilt toward the ontological basis of nothingness, which diminishes a good creation. Although the utopian worldviews and ideologies of modernity continue to exert influence in the world, their power over the imagination is diminishing. Postmodernity is more realistic about the falsified hopes and illusions of modern utopianism or various "metanarratives of emancipation." This reinforces greater pessimism about such utopianism. The more humanity seeks to control the world and nature, says Barth, the more it "threatens him with even severer negation when he ventures to negate it" (*CD* IV/3: 700). Thus, the good creation itself appears to be a threat to human existence; nothingness seems to gain the upper hand. "The grace addressed to the creature of God now becomes judgment. The benefits objective and subjective assigned and displayed to man becomes plagues. As *corruptio optimi*, of the optimum of the opportunity afforded man, the confusion caused by him worked out as *corruptio pessima*" (*CD* IV/3: 700). When humanity seeks to *master* the cosmos through its own power, the powers become relatively hegemonic, and threaten humanity's freedom and liberation. This results in the triumph of nothingness and hopelessness of *corruptio pessima*. The experience of disillusionment and hopelessness reinforces the idea that we cannot trust our own ideas, narratives, principles, or experiences, which have tranquilizing effect over power and freedom in challenging the dominant ideology. In the modern age, the utopian scientific and materialistic worldviews, including human progress and other political or economic ideologies have led to postmodern denial, apathy, or despair. In either case, the power of ideology remains a potent force over human imagination, vision, and will.

As mention previously, ideology is a "lordless power" that seeks to deprive persons their own freedom as individuals and as members of a community that seeks justice, peace, and hope. Further, as stated, there are two central traditions of ideology, namely the "epistemological" (Marx) and "sociological" (Mannheim). Barth's notion of ideology remains in tension with these two viewpoints. First, similar to the broader sociological definition, Barth argues that there is a basic human proclivity for arranging "impressions and ideas in thoughts and groups of thoughts," and to use these ideas to form "solid presuppositions or preliminary sketches" used to justify perceptions and actions (*CL*: 224). However, the power of human sinfulness transforms these "relative" ideas into "absolute" ones, thereby changing them from "human" ideas to ones that are "quasi-divine" (*CL*: 225). Unlike Mannheim, Barth would claim there is no human "utopia" that emerges from a new ideology. Rather, human sin creates a "kingdom of human disorder" that persuades persons to seek to create and sustain ideologies in order to justify their own existence *apart* from God, leading to eventually the loss of hope. Second, similar to the Marxist "hermeneutics of suspicion" tradition, Barth argues that ideologies, like all powers, are "fictions" and "illusions" as well as "lying spirits" (*CL*: 233). Ideologies do become oppressive, depriving persons of their freedom and hope. Yet, Barth would obviously apply the same reasoning to Marxism and neo-Marxism. Like all ideologies, Marxism seeks to make converts while eliminating enemies who challenge its hegemony. All ideologies have the power to shape moral character through accepted "norms" and "dispositions" so that a person's "calculations, exertions, and efforts are now predestined by it" (*CL*: 225). All ideologies must be resisted by Christian social witness because they create the illusion that truth can be discovered in separation from the "true witness" and "true humanity" of Jesus Christ. This falsehood leads to self-deception and fabrications of the objective world, that is, a world of intimate relations between God, the world, and even the cosmos.

Moreover, as stated, ideologies can take the form of revolutionary (radical), nationalistic, materialistic, and protectionist worldviews. All of these ideologies are driven by positive action toward some goal or purpose, usually some form of utopian vision of a better world, and implemented by some form of political, instrumental, or technological power. This *teleological* dimension is important for both the descriptive and instrumental power of ideology. This dimension is developed by the father of ideological analysis—the Enlightenment French educator, Destutt de Tracy. De Tracy wanted to create a new foundational secular science for the study of ideas, what he called "ideology," which would reject traditional inherited ideas from religion or philosophy. We may summarize de Tracy's characterization of ideology as: 1) an "absolutized political or societal end (goal)"; 2) a "redefinition of currently held values, norms, and ideas" that "legitimize in advance the practical pursuit of the predetermined end"; and 3) a selection of the "means or instruments necessary for effectively achieving the all-important goal."[3] Given this, ideologies are more than just worldviews or illusions of oppression; they are, in fact, comprehensive schemes of power—or "cultural hegemonies"—shaped by a group of persons who have a shared commitment to particular ends or goals. They are, in short, teleologically driven, potential social or cultural hegemonies, with both the

3. Goudzwaard, et. al., *Hope in Troubled Times*, 33.

theoretical and instrumental means to achieve their particular goal. These include a set of ideas, but also forms of technological power to implement these ideologies through force. Interestingly, this teleological dimension can also be seen in *CD* IV/3, where Barth mentions a five-step progression of worldview (or ideological) formation and implementation. These are: 1) the "distancing" or separating of the worldview from the human person; 2) making the worldview impersonal or anti-relational by "escaping" from one's relationship to God and others; 3) the shift from the "particular" and "concrete" to the "general" and "abstract"; 4) it is then embodied in "practical ethics and perhaps politics" which is "set against others" who reject the worldview; and 5) it emboldens human power as "observer, constructor, and manager" and "sovereign master" over the environment (*CD* IV/3: 255–57). Taken together, this leads to a Prometheanism which absolutizes ideology as a teleological power to be used against other persons, the church, and the world. And yet, says Barth, "No Prometheanism can be effectively maintained against Jesus Christ" (*CD* IV/3: 118).

It is the teleological and instrumental dimensions of ideology that Barth has in mind when he discusses the "chthonic powers" of technology, entertainment, fashion, and sports. It is this pseudo-eschatological feature of ideologies, its power to shape human goals and purposes that gives it its teleological power. Of these, technology has the greatest influence on the way we live our lives, especially on the hyperactivity and addictions to work, speed, and military power. Like other chthonic powers, technology promises to take away the "little anxieties" of life, but in reality they "create new and bigger ones." "They seem to promise courage and a greater zest for life, but increased worry about life is the fulfillment of their promise" (*CL*: 228–29). In postmodernity the power of the visual image, in advertising and especially cinema, has become potentially hegemonic in its power to shape popular opinion, or perhaps worse yet, create an illusionary distraction preventing people from seeing what is truly important in the world. This negativity seems to govern the film industry, creating dreadful apocalyptic accounts of the future, in which humanity is destroyed by powerful forces outside human control, whether caused by global climate change or powerful forces of evil and destruction. We live in a constant state of fear and dread about the future. Ideologies of hope are being replaced by ideologies of despair, hopelessness, and anticipated catastrophe. People find distractions in being captivated by public sporting events like the Super Bowl or the Olympics or the latest cultural style, but hidden beneath these surface illusions lies an apocalyptic and dystopian view of the future. These "chthonic powers," of course, are not inherently evil, but become useful devices to embellish, especially in the power of advertising and entertainment, projected visions and illusions of the objective world.

Christian witness challenges any utopian or dystopian ideology that privileges naïve positivistic scientism, technological utopianism or evolutionary progress, or alternatively, fear, endless catastrophic scenarios, or earthly annihilation. In both cases, the only hope for humanity is a belief in a Promethean power of technological achievement. The power of utopian ideologies is less prevalent than a generation ago, although they still remain in our society, especially in the hope for medical breakthroughs in fatal illnesses or diseases. Besides medicine, which remains one of the last remaining technological hopes for humanity, is the hope for an environmentally sustainable or "green" economy. Nevertheless, in medicine and ecology, the fear and uncertainty of economic and environmental catastrophe remains a more pervasive force in shaping the contemporary worldviews of postmodern society. Postmodernity is where the risks associated with modernity have become reality, and with it, greater ambiguity and pessimism. James Lovelock, for example, who popularized the "Gaia hypothesis" in the 1970s has presented such a pessimistic scenario in his latest book, *The Revenge of Gaia*.[4] With the inevitability of catastrophe on the horizon, Lovelock calls for radical changes in energy production and limiting human population, for example, shifting toward nuclear, wind, and solar power, and cutting back human population to fewer than 1 billion. There are numerous books, such as Lovelock's, that are useful in diagnosing current risks, but these books are less helpful when they begin predicting the future, which often appears bleak unless there is radical human transformation. These books assume a Promethean view of human history and technological achievement, which cannot "be effectively maintained against Jesus Christ" (*CD* IV/3: 118). Such a language presumes that the only hope for humanity rests with humanity itself.

Witness of Hope

With this in mind, we now can see how Barth's discussion of hope in *CD* IV/3 corresponds to the powers of ideology and behind it the sin of falsehood. For there to be real hope, persons must be shaken from their self-

---

4. Lovelock, *Revenge of Gaia*.

deception. They must discover that truth confronts us and challenges our truth claims and experiences. The real nature of truth challenges a person's presupposed worldview, as it "unmasks man as it encounters him" (*CD* IV/3: 378). Awareness of reconciliation unmasks and reveals one's own form of self-deception, denial, or evasion. "To be free," says Barth, "he must be born again by God's Word and Spirit." "He must be born again to freedom and therefore to self-determination, i.e. to that which accrues to him as a responsible covenant-partner of the free and self-determining God, as His creature, as the one who is loved by Him" (*CD* IV/3: 447). Reconciliation makes hope possible because it provides a true *teleological* account of God's eschatological action. "As the divine Creator He cannot have created a remote and alien sphere abandoned to itself or to its own *teleology*" (*CD* III/1: 95, rev.). Christian hope cannot be separated from what God has done, is doing, and will do in the future, otherwise it leads to the sin of falsehood and the illusions of ideology, which not only deprives humanity of freedom but seeks to destroy humanity of its future. Christian hope is not about being optimistic about the future of human life as we know it, nor is it believing in a better place beyond death, nor is it an optimistic disposition or cheerful attitude about human hopes, dreams, and aspirations. Hope is not about the "American dream," or some other "fiction" or "illusion" of the "good life," nor is it the dreams of a more ecological society, a more democratic politics, or even a society free of discrimination and injustice. All these are important goals for human society and ethical action, and essential for an ethics of Christian witness. Yet, the "whence" and "wither" of this hope rests not in human action but *divine* action, as creator, reconciler, and redeemer. The person, says Barth, "does not guarantee his future by hoping any more than he justifies himself by believing or sanctifies himself by loving" (*CD* IV/3: 914).

Unlike the pseudo-eschatological wistfulness for a better world, Christian witness begins with God's promise that Jesus Christ is the same yesterday, today, and forever. The fact that God has acted, is acting, and will act in the future is the objective reality behind the Christian eschatological awareness of the already, the now, and the not yet. This "eschatological difference," is what separates Christian witness from other ideologies and worldviews, and Christian ethics from other ethical methods and systems. The witness of hope, therefore, is not just about the future, but remains linked with God's gracious past, present, and future actions. "If the Now cannot be separated from the Then in which it is grounded, nor the One Day from the Now, or the Then from the Now and the One Day or *vice versa*, each of these different forms of the one *parousia* of Jesus Christ maintains its individuality and is inseparably bound to the others in this individuality" (*CD* IV/3: 911). The three-forms of Christ's appearing, the incarnation, Pentecost, and consummation, remains "one event" interpreted three ways. The dialectical tension, then, between Christ's actual coming in the incarnation (already) and the future coming in the consummation (not yet), is understood as the "now" of the church, as the "earthly-form of his historical existence" (*CD* IV/3: 681ff.). Christian hope corresponds to the divine action of the Holy Spirit, as the "enlightening power of the living Lord Jesus Christ" revealing to the "whole world that the covenant between God and man concluded in Him [Jesus Christ] is the first and final meaning of its history, and that His future manifestation is already here and now its great, effective and living hope" (*CD* IV/3: 681). Although the "prophetic work" of Jesus Christ has "not yet reached its completion" with the third coming, the Christian witness of hope corresponds to the fact that God acts decisively in Jesus Christ for the benefit of humanity and all of creation. Therefore, between the already and the not yet, between Pentecost and consummation, Christ's coming remains an objective reality that makes faith, hope, and love a reality in the life of Christians, the church, and the world. Those who hope in Jesus Christ "cannot possibly droop or shake their heads; they can only lift them up" (*CD* IV/3: 922).

FREEDOM AND ECOLOGICAL WITNESS

Christian ecological ethics begins with the church's witness of hope and freedom, and then moves outward into society through parabolic language and direct action, choosing to stand "with" one's local and global community. This task stands against the powers of ecological domination, but stands for non-ideological relative courses of action that seek to be responsible to the other, church, and world. Perhaps the most important ideology that keeps people from acting responsibly in the face of environmental risks is TINA ("there is no alternative"). This worldview is agnostic about positive change pertaining to the natural and built environments; all that remains is the "world at risk." We recall Ulrich Beck saying that "When risk is perceived as omnipresent, three reactions are possible: *denial, apathy, or transformation.*"[5] Behind the worldview of TINA is the *denial* of the seri-

5. Beck, *World at Risk*, 48.

ousness of environmental risks and the *apathy* that anything can be done about them, and that *transformation* is not possible. Behind these attitudes, however, are the sins of sloth (apathy) and falsehood (denial), and even pride presumes human domination and power over nature. Against human sinfulness, which deprives humanity of its true freedom, is the church's witness that God stands in covenant relation with humanity and creation. In its witness to God's kingdom, it also calls upon the civil community, in its vocation as *guardian* of common good, to stand "with" and "for" the good of the natural and built environments. The church's witness points to a "wholly living law" that is "fluid and open" "with an equal responsibility both to the past and to the future." "By the established fact of its own law the Church can warn and encourage the world that even in the defective and provisional form of the present age true righteousness cannot be a frozen or static pond, but be a living stream continuously flowing from the worse to the better" (*CD* IV/2: 724). So, just as Christian witness points to the practice of political peacemaking and economic justice, it also points to open-ended and dynamic freedom to rise above the denial and apathy of TINA. It is possible to formulate policy and laws today that will benefit the future; it is possible to move toward greater sustainability and recognition that the rights of future generations are important. The shortsightedness of TINA is overcome by the public awareness that human societies have "responsibility to both the past and the future" (*CD* IV/2: 724).

For Creation's Covenant

An environmental ethics as witness begins with looking to divine action in Jesus Christ and then seeking responsible human action. Consequently, it bears witness to God's gift to the created cosmos. What is God's gift? God "did not merely gift a highest and best, a power of life and light which would help the cosmos, perhaps an endowment of the creation, perhaps a strengthening of the light of His covenant. No: He *gifted* to the cosmos His only Son and therefore nothing more or less than Himself" (*CD* IV/1: 71–72, rev). The gift that God gives to the cosmos is a victory of Jesus Christ's prophetic witness, which gives hope to the world. In God's self-giving, God has set humanity free, in the covenant of grace, to engage in an active life, a life of *freedom* to serve God and humanity through altering and shaping its relationship to the environment. Yet this does not make people entirely free *from* their relationship to the environment. In the person's "creaturely activity," the follower of Jesus "can take the form of correspondence to the divine activity" (*CD* III/4: 482). In her correspondence to God's action, the person is free to act upon the environment, but not in ways that challenge God's gracious purpose for the environment. God is sovereign over the environmental, just as God is sovereign over the political and the economic. Simply put, God has a covenant with creation, in which God remains sovereign. Yet, in modern liberal theology, this covenant understanding has led to a theology of co-creation or co-participation. Eberhard Busch writes:

> Knowledge of the goodness of creation, according to Barth, is threatened by the neo-protestant view that draws the creation into its own "preservation," in order to understand this process as "an ongoing creation" (*creatio continua*). As the source of its knowing, this view turns not to the faith in the biblically attested Creator, but to the general experience of becoming or a being caused. Its necessary content is the thought of a reciprocal relation between God and the world in which God becomes part of the world and is himself always in a process of becoming, while the human threatens to be divinized and to become the solemn co-creator. As such he is able to improve creation, but also to destroy it as well as to protect it against such misuse. The goodness of creation depends upon human cooperation.[6]

We recall, that Barth is very critical of any theology that establishes humanity as "a co-creator, co-savior or co-regent in God's activity" or a "co-God" (*CD* III/4: 482). God's "will and work" remains the prerogative of God alone and cannot, in any way, be persuaded by the co-participation of humanity. No person is a "second Jesus" but only a "witness of Jesus Christ and therefore of God's will and work" (*CD* III/4: 482). In chapter 7, we saw how the separation of human and divine agency leads to errors on both sides, thereby collapsing of the human into the divine or the divine into the human. In either case, the double agency of Jesus Christ is replaced with some other monistic or dualistic form of agency that jeopardizes God's covenant-partnership with humanity. The two basic implications of this distortion of agency are: 1) a theology that divinizes humanity and makes the person a "second Jesus"; and 2) and the naturalization of God which makes God contingent upon natural process and human decision-making. Both errors are common in much contemporary environmental or ecological theology, which changes how ethics ought to be understood.

6. Busch, *Great Passion*, 187.

We begin first with divinization of humanity which leads to a resurgence of Prometheanism, the grandiose claims that only humanity has the power to save and protect, as well as destroy and annihilate creation. Humanity, in fact, makes itself lord over creation and uses its power to dominate the built and natural environments. "The more he wants to compel and control, the more he himself is compelled and controlled" (*CD* IV/1: 433). Ironically, this Prometheanism place humanity under the power of ideology or technology, thus under the grasp of both the "spiritual powers" and "chthonic powers" (*CL*: 232). Although technology has benefited humanity, it also has destroyed the natural environment, thereby contributing to widespread deforestation and the loss of living habitats and extinction of species. By the late 1950s, for example, Barth wrote of how the automobile led to the "devastation of the countryside as freeways cut ruthlessly through arable land, pastures, and whole villages. We ask whether the speed that motorized man is allowed is not bought too dearly in view of its obvious hostility to life" (*CL*: 232). The power behind the human misuse of technology, like other powers, is the misuse of human freedom. That is, the problem is not with technology itself, but from the human "desire" to "use the power" as "technical mastery" or as a "technique of disorder," which is then used to comprehend human "meaning and purpose in itself." It is, says Barth, wrong for someone to "accuse technical skill of being 'souless'; he should accuse himself and his irrational will for power. He himself is the problem of modern technical skill" (*CD* III/4: 395). The "arrogance and illusion" of power justifies the destruction of human and non-human life as well as the natural and built environments (*CL*: 232). In choosing to stand apart from God's covenant-partnership, an ecological theology that makes humanity the sole power over creation, also chooses pride, sloth, and falsehood over faith, hope, and love, and with it, it succumbs to the destructive, rather than constructive, side of technology. Without God acting *pro nobis* in Jesus Christ, thereby becoming our Mediator, Savior, and Lord, then we ourselves become our own mediator, savior, and lord over the earth, endangering ourselves and non-human life.

In our secular society, we live in what Charles Taylor as aptly named the "immanent frame." In *A Secular Age*, Taylor discusses the various "cross-pressures," including eighteenth century "providential deism," naturalism, and materialism, all of which, shape today's "immanent frame." One of the best examples of our "secular age" is how immanentism has led to the general movement of language away from cosmos to that of the universe.

Unlike the cosmos, which "contains the sense of an ordered whole" including a divine transcendent reality (God) outside the self or nature, the *universe* "moves from an enchanted world, inhabited by spirits and forces, to a disenchanted one" that is meaningless but "vast, feels infinite, and is in the midst of an evolution spread over aeons."[7] It is here where our "limits touch nothing but absolute darkness," and we encounter our complete loneliness and "Godlessness."[8] At the same time, however, people are not comfortable affirming a purposeless, meaningless, and impersonal reality, and instead, remain attached to an idea of some form of all-inclusive order, a cosmos, that provides structure, meaning, and purpose for our lives. "There is a strong attraction to the idea that we are in an order of 'nature,' in which we are part of this greater whole, arise from it, and don't escape or transcend it, even though we arise above everything else in it."[9] Even within the "immanent frame" the emerging ecological consciousness places humanity within an orderly system of nature, but also ironically "above" it, calling us toward a hopeful sustainability. Yet, these ideas or "cross-pressures" are inherently self-contradictory, in that, materialistic, naturalistic, and immanentist frameworks are placed side-by-side with notions of the transcendental self arising above nature making ethics possible. On one hand, we live in a "Closed World System" (CWS) in which "nothing is demanded of us," or in which "we have no destiny we are called on to achieve."[10] On the other hand, persons also assume "the colossal success of modern natural science and the associated technology can lead us to feel that it unlocks all mysteries, that it will ultimately explain everything."[11]

For the Earth as Our Home

The materialism of the "immanent frame" can lead to either a kind of naturalistic determinism or a humanistic and Promethean power and control of nature. In either case, true human freedom is seriously jeopardized by naturalistic fate or "technical mastery" over nature. Indeed, even nature's freedom itself is jeopardized by its own naturalistic determinism or human power, which seems to thwart and stand against the power of nature itself. Without

7. Taylor, *Secular Age*, 323.
8. Ibid., 376.
9. Ibid., 547.
10. Ibid., 367.
11. Ibid., 548.

God's gracious covenant-partnership with humanity and creation, there is no hope for the freedom of transformation for either humanity or creation. Existence within the "immanent frame" cannot account for a meaningful reason for the world's own being *and* becoming—its past, present, *and* future existence. Being itself becomes fate. Barth writes: "[T]he world does not know itself. It does not know God, nor man, nor the relationship and covenant between God and man. Hence it does not know its own origin, state or goal" (*CD* IV/3: 769). In contrast to this Prometheanism, Christian witness declares that the reason Christians stand *for* the built and natural environment is too affirm that God has already made the judgment to stand with and for the creation and the cosmos in the reconciliation of the covenant-partnership. This makes it possible for Christians to work toward a constructive and wiser use of technology that benefits human and non-human life, both in the built and natural environments. "This building of a new world is in principle an unfinished task," says Timothy Gorringe, "a 'permanent revolution' to use a phrase of Karl Barth's. This revolution, we have seen, is guided by the criteria of sustainability, justice, empowerment, situatedness, and diversity."[12] Rather than separating or contrasting the natural and built environments, Gorringe seeks to integrate them calling for a "liberation theology of the environment" that "seeks to call the world 'home'."[13] An ecological ethics of witness seeks to find creative ways to integrate an environmentally sustainable economic system with new forms of technology so that the natural and built environments become more than living spaces, they become "home." Consequently, Christians should support technological innovation which limits the reliance and production of greenhouse gases by encouraging the use of geothermal, biomass, biofuels, hydroelectric, and perhaps most important, hydrogen fuel as alternatives to oil, coal, and other fossil fuels. Furthermore, Christians ought to encourage a renewed personal commitment to frugality, simplicity, energy conservation, and limiting of consumption and waste production. These practices are simply the next step in responding appropriately to the energy risks that societies face. These are practical, not ideological, decisions and actions. That is, Christians ought to be cautious about ideologically laden theories of absolute Yes and No, in which there is only one solution, one global fix, or one set of practices that will ensure human survival. This means being

---

12. Gorringe, *Theology of the Built Environment*, 250.
13. Ibid., 23.

critical of either/or scenarios, in which one path leads to life, hope, and survival, and the other path leads to death, destruction, and catastrophic consequences. In making such a claim, people are claiming power over life and death, which denies that they belong to God's covenant-partnership. This too is a misuse of freedom, which further keeps humanity under the control of the powers.

Moreover, affirming that the earth is our home is set within a broader set of *covenant* relations established by God. The covenant and creation are interrelated only because God has made this possible. In *CD* III/1, Barth's excurses on Genesis 1–2 provides the narrative for his larger discussion of how the creation is the "external basis of the covenant and covenant is the internal basis" of the creation. Just as the gospel gives content and form to the law, so too, the covenant gives content and form to the creation. Just as the creation narrative of Genesis 1 ends with covenantal promise of "Sabbath freedom, Sabbath rest and Sabbath joy" in which persons "participate," so too, the Genesis 2 narrative ends with covenant responsibility of co-humanity, as male and female, to engaged in the "work" of "inhabiting" and "cultivating" God's garden (*CD* III/1: 98; 249–50).

> The perfect earth is not a dry, barren or dead earth, but one which bears shrubs and vegetation and is inhabited. God will plant it. But to make that which has been planted thrive, God needs a farmer or gardener. This will be role of man. He thus appears as the being which must be able and ready to serve in order to give meaning and purpose to the planting of the earth. . . . He is not a new element planted by God like shrubs and vegetation. Seen even from this standpoint he has no independent position in the totality of creation. His nature is that of the earth on which lives and moves. . . . Thus the existence of man within the whole is indeed the existence of one who is commissioned to serve and work. He must give himself to till and keep the earth in order that it may have meaning when God will bring it to perfection. An in this function he fulfills the meaning of his own existence. (*CD* III/1: 235–37)

In Christian ecological ethics, one of the principle points of discussion is how the relationships between God, humanity, nature, and non-human life are understood. How are God and humanity related? How is God related to nature, humanity, and non-human life? How is humanity related to nature, non-human life, and God? For Barth, the created order, including nature and non-human life, must be understood from within the incarnational

God-human covenant-partnership, established in Jesus Christ. Thus, internal to creation is God's covenant-partnership to humanity, and by *analogy*, all non-human life. The earth is not only home to humans but to *all* non-human life. The covenant-partnership with God, therefore, serves as the basis for the human relationship to the non-human world, in which "as a living being in co-existence with non-human life, man has to think and act responsibly" (*CD* III/4: 350). Just as persons coexist and act with and for others, so too by analogy, they coexist and act with and for the non-human world. Personal responsibility to other persons and the non-human world are not univocal but neither are they equivocal; they are distinct but related responsibilities. So, just as persons care for others, they care for creation by "tilling" and "keeping" and "serving" creation. Moreover, just as persons sin against others, denying their essential coexistence with them, so too, persons sin again the non-human world, denying their coexistence with it as well. In a remarkable passage, Barth discusses responsibility toward caring for animals, encouraging the practice of "animal protection, care and friendship," while condemning unjust practices of brutal killing and mistreatment (*CD* III/4: 352–56). Therefore, human injustice against the non-human environment, like the human environment, is the result of sinfulness which denies the covenant as the "inner basis" of creation, and with it, the coexistence of one creature with another. It is a horrible misuse of freedom for humanity to remove itself from God's garden and make itself a "god" apart from all of creation. Having a covenant relationship with God also implies having a covenant relationship to nature and the non-human world.

Christian environmental witness, then, begins with a reaffirmation of creation as "good" because it is rooted in God's covenantal relationship, and not our positing of value to nature, through some form of biocentric theology. The covenant between God and creation, not nature, earth, or life, is the starting point for environmental ethics. "We must refuse to build either ethics as a whole or this particular part of ethics on the view and concept of a life which embraces man, beast and plant" (*CD* III/4: 349). Indeed, it is ironic that when persons give the earth or nature "value," apart from the covenant, they inevitably find alternative ideological justifications, other than exploitation, to continue to have power over it, that is, to manage and use it for our apparent goods. Even a noble environmentalist has a "desire" for "technical mastery" over the natural and built environments (*CD* III/4: 395). Prometheanism triumphs in ideas that we have the power to "save" the planet earth from annihilation or destruction. The truth is, of course, that despite our knowledge of the risks of global climate change, we also appear powerless to change our destructive practices. We cannot redeem ourselves from our own destructive practices, which are rooted in our desire for power and "technical mastery." Again, it is not technology itself, but people that create "the problem of modern technical skill" (CD III/4: 395). We are trapped in the natural world, driven by our desire for technological mastery, and incapable of harnessing this power for positive uses. We know the good what we must do, but we are unable to do it, because we cannot escape illusionary lure of human control and power. Yet, we continue to believe that we have Promethean power over nature, and with it, our power over God. In our control over nature, God appears powerless to act freely apart from human action because God's power is either absent or dependent on human power.

For the Cosmos

We are now able to discuss the second error resulting from a theology of co-creation, namely the fabrication of cosmologies that naturalize God. Earlier we saw how one of the consequences of the sin of falsehood is the drive to formulate ideologies and worldviews that deny God's covenant relationship with creation. In rejecting the covenant, theology looks for a reciprocal relationship that makes God part of the created order itself. Whereas Prometheanism elevates humanity to the status of God, the "immanent frame," including panentheism, naturalism, and materialism, reduces God to the status of humanity, nature, and the non-human world. Unlike political and economic ethics, however, there is a wider gap among ethicists about their fundamental cosmological convictions, including how they understand the various correlations and relations between God and nature, humanity, and non-human life. Yet, these differences, too, are rooted in the particular *cosmological* framework which gives shape to their view of ontological relatedness, of moral and spiritual standing, between God, nature, humanity, and non-human life. Therefore, the answers that one finds to these cosmological and ontological questions determine the particular way in which the background beliefs of environmental ethics are structured. Although there is much more agreement about what *ought* to be done, such as controlling pollution, limiting greenhouse gas production, and supporting a sustainable economy, there is more disagreement about what we ought to *believe* about the cosmos. The debate is not over global climate change and ozone depletion, but over what cosmology or worldview ought to shape the way humans think about themselves, nature, and non-human life. In forming worldviews, Barth writes:

> The world as seen and understood in any other way is not the world as it is; it is a mere picture of the world projected idealistically, positivistically, or existentially, scientifically or mythologically, with or without a moral purpose, pessimistically or lightheartedly, yet always within unhealthy naivety and one-sidedness. The world thinks that it knows itself when it draws and contemplates a book of such pictures, whereas in truth, or rather in the most radical untruth, it misses its own reality and is simply groping in the dark as it turns the various pages. (*CD* IV/3: 771)

Living within the "immanent frame" has led to various immanent worldviews or cosmologies that attempt to re-sacralize the created order. Indeed, this ideology of immanentism lies beneath or within the general strategy of much Christian environmental ethics. This strategy looks for a solution to the problems of nothingness and anomie, as evident in the disenchantment of nature, through the re-enchantment and re-sacralization of nature. So, rather than looking at God's covenant promise in Jesus Christ, they engage in the *poesis* of a reformulated doctrine of cosmology and nature as a way toward *praxis*. Turning from traditional church belief and practice, in particular, these ethicists turn toward a panentheistic *cosmology* that will supposedly inspire human hope about the possibility of a restored creation. It calls for the reenchantment of nature which has been disenchanted through modern technology. This results in a plethora of viewpoints including "deep ecology," ecofeminism, the Gaia hypothesis, biocentrism, theocentrism, environmental utilitarianism, environmental pragmatism, ecojustice, social ecology, socialist ecology, and ecological spirituality. This concentration on cosmology was largely shaped by critics of traditional Christian beliefs. It is generally agreed that Christian environmental ethics really emerged as a discipline in response to Lynn White's famous 1967 essay "The Historical Roots of Our Ecologic Crisis," in which he argues that Christian *cosmology* is largely to blame for the environmental crises.[14] Since, as Larry Rasmussen

---

14. White, "Historical Roots of Our Ecological Crisis," 1203–17. White argued that Christian beliefs about God and humanity's separation and domineering role over nature, led to destructive environmental practices, and that otherworldly conceptions of salvation have undermined personal responsibility for the environment. Since the argument was directed at the cosmological beliefs of Christianity, it remained crucial for theologians

puts it, "ethics and cosmology are inextricable, indissoluble" then it was necessary for a new cosmology to be affirmed that would integrate or synthesize God, nature, humanity, and non-human life.[15] Accordingly, it became necessary to affirm an integrationist or interdependent cosmology that grants sacred value to the earth, including nature and non-human life, and diminishes human "dominion" over nature. This led to a diversity of theologies, including liberation theology, ecological justice, feminist spirituality, and nature's integrity. In such theologies, what often wins is panentheism (or pantheism), nature (and the earth), the Spirit (or Wisdom/Sophia), and organic interdependence, while the causalities are a set of "traditional" or "classical" Christian beliefs such as traditional trinitarian theism, theocentrism, or even christocentrism.

To be sure, environmental ethics can be understood from within the frame of traditional Christian theism, derived from biblical and doctrinal sources, and responsible stewardship and care for creation models. Critics of this view claim, however, that these stewardship models remain largely anthropocentric, which leads to human control, management, and responsibility over nature and non-human life. Traditional theism needs to be replaced with ecologically friendly forms of panentheism, which immanently link God with nature and all life, empowering all of creation with sacredness, salvation, and meaning. One example of this trend is Sallie McFague, who seeks to go beyond the "classical" model in theology, economics, and ecology by developing a panenthestic cosmology or "model" of the earth as "God's body."[16] She insists that "God is incarnate *in the world*," and Jesus, as model and symbol, points to the fact that "each creature is a microcosm of divine incarnation; each of us is made in the image of God; and the destiny of all creation is to grow more fully into that reality."[17] Affirming both a "very high" and "very low" Christology, she sees the human Jesus as a *symbol* of how God is with humanity and the earth, which provides a

---

and ethicists to articulate an ecologically friendly Christian cosmology, which would foster moral responsibility for the environment.

15. Rasmussen, "Cosmology an Ethics," 178.

16. McFague, *Body of God*. The old model "presumes an individualistic and futuristic salvific model that ignores social economic, environmental problems," along with a misguided Christology of "Jesusoltry" that Jesus "does it all," and "God's unique incarnation, sacrifice, and resurrection, this takes place outside of and apart from us." McFague, *Life Abundant*, 159.

17. Ibid., 20.

new vision for ethical responsibility. Jesus' message is that God is "with" the world in God's body, which provides a mandate to continue God's purpose in our ecological sustainable moral practices. "If God is absent from the world, it is because we are; made in God's image, as agents of our own bodies, we are also God's auxiliary agents in and for the body of the world—our life work is to further the divine purpose of planetary prosperity."[18] When we act, God acts, and when God acts, we act. Yet, in either scenario, environmental ethics depends *entirely* on human action, for without these actions God cannot accomplish God's purposes. As McFague says, "unless we understand God as needing us, we will lack the will to take responsibility for the world."[19] In saying this, McFague collapses God's freedom into human freedom, and divine agency into human agency, while at the same time, making salvation dependent on human action rather than God's action. On this point, Paul Molnar writes:

> But for McFague, salvation means simply the survival of this world, while for Christians salvation means the beginning of a new creation, namely, our beginning to live the eternal life that is the gift of God and raising Jesus from the dead. Equating salvation with survival can only increase human anxiety and arouse a sense of self-reliance and ultimately hopelessness, while perceiving salvation as an act of God and his Word and Spirit will mean joy based on act of God that is full of promise because it is the promise of eternal life which is lived now by faith and hope in the coming of the Lord who alone can complete the salvation of the world in redeeming us and all creatures at his second coming.[20]

So, inasmuch as McFague attempts to reject anthropocentrism and defend panentheism, she cannot fully escape the lure of a co-management (or co-creatorship) theology and salvific Prometheanism. If the future existence of God's body depends entirely upon our ecological actions, then we have power both over God's purposes and God's existence itself in bodily form.[21]

    18. Ibid., 151. She further writes: "As the body of God, the world is a sacrament, the sacrament, the incarnation, of God so that while each thing is itself in all it marvelous particularity and uniqueness, it is at the same and in the through its own specialness, the presence of God. . . . We human beings are the hands and feet of God, a manifestation of God's loving presence." Ibid., 150–51.
    19. McFague, *Models of God*, 134.
    20. Molnar, *Incarnation and Resurrection*, 226–27.
    21. Although defending panentheistic theology, of God being with and in the world, Larry Rasmussen, more than McFague, remains cautious regarding the appar-

This is how panentheistic theology creates risks for much environmental ethics. Most basically, it elevates human agency at the expense of divine agency, which diminishes God's freedom to act *for* the eschatological promise of hope for all of creation. By denying that Jesus Christ is "true witness," mediator, and Lord, there is no way of really knowing whether God, as mediator, stands both "with" humanity "in" the world, but also "for" humanity, the world, or even the cosmos. What transforms the world is human consciousness and action, not divine consciousness and action. Yet, this creates a serious problem because people themselves are incapable of redeeming, healing, or solving the world's ecological problems. Prometheanism is double-edged, in that it gives us mastery over the earth but this mastery itself becomes destructively hegemonic. We become victims of our own power. Yet, this is not Christian witness, which emphatically insists that the powers have been defeated in Jesus Christ. It follows that Christian environmental witness resists human desire for mastery over the earth by proclaiming, once again, that "[N]o Prometheanism can be effectively maintained against Jesus Christ" (*CD* IV/3: 118).

In contrast to these works, Philip Jenkins rightly shifts the focus in environmental ethics away from cosmology toward soteriology, thus away from having the "correct" cosmological worldviews to God's salvific agency.[22] In doing so, he discusses the three main ethical models of ecojustice, stewardship, and ecological spirituality and the corresponding "ecologies of grace" of sanctification, redemption, and deification, by drawing on the theology of Thomas Aquinas, Karl Barth, and Sergei Bulgakov respectively. Moreover, by choosing Barth as the representative of the stewardship (and redemption) model, Jenkins positively brings Barth back into the conversation of environmental ethics, and in so doing, corrects the many misreadings and caricatures of Barth's theology. One such critic is Paul Santmire, who recounts how in a personal conversation with Barth, the younger theologian was discouraged from exploring nature as a subject

---

ent "Promethean" theology of "co-creatorship" and instead calls for "co-participants." See Rasmussen, *Earth Community, Earth Ethics*, 292. As co-participants persons can discover "a power throughout creation that serves justice throughout creation." This power, principally reveled in the cross and resurrection, makes a Christian environmental ethics "anything but Promethean in tone, or a substitution of ourselves for God." "It is," he adds, "instead, a humble power exercised in the sobering shadow of the cross and within full view of the considerable powers of destruction we have and wield." Ibid., 293.

22. Jenkins, *Ecologies of Grace*, 4.

of theology.[23] In his own writing, Santmire often criticizes Barth's theology as too anthropocentric and unable to extend his covenantal ethics to include nature and non-human life. The natural environment is *only* the stage where humanity is reconciled and elected in Jesus Christ. For Barth, nature is "a kind of stage to allow the eternally founded drama between God and humanity to run its course."[24] So, whereas humanity has a "dual status" as eternally elected and created "as such," nature has only the "single status" as created "as such." Since it has no "eternal determination" its reality becomes "purely instrumental" and separate from God's gracious covenant. Although Barth argues that creation is "very good," says Santmire, it has no "permanent meaning" like humanity, the civil community, or the church.[25] Challenging Santmire's interpretation of Barth, Jenkins demonstrates from careful analysis of various sections in *CD* III/4 that Barth shows "how redeeming grace leads back to earth in freedom, responsibility, and gratitude."[26] Jenkins argues that Barth shows the way forward for environmental ethics of stewardship, and that "earthcare bears comparable theological significance to practices like feeding the poor and preaching the good news."[27] Although Barth is helpful for the stewardship ethical strategy, Jenkins faults Barth for his view of the "orderliness" of creation as developed in *CD* III/4. Here, says Jenkins, Barth succumbs to "sexist, heterosexist, heirachrcalist, and absolutist" tendencies, as well as a "historicist" rather than "geographical" and "ecological" understanding of the reconciling covenant.[28] Regardless of Barth's "ambivalences, shortcomings, and inconsistencies," Jenkins' final analysis is that Barth's theology "bends in the other direction, as God claims human freedom within the environment of Jesus." "After Barth, the strategic logic of environmental stewardship can rely on the way of the Reconciler establishing habitat for humans to witness to God's will for a flourishing, exuberant earth."[29] In short, Barth provides a theological language and a framework for stewardship ethics.

23. Santmire, *Nature Reborn*, 117.
24. Santmire, *Travail of Nature*, 152. See ibid., 154.
25. Ibid., 154.
26. Jenkins, *Ecologies of Grace*, 187.
27. Ibid., 187.
28. Ibid., 178, 185.
29. Ibid., 186.

Although Jenkins provides a valuable corrective to Barth's critics, he neglects to fully draw out the implications of an eschatologically guided environmental ethics of witness. The teleological principles of ethics—Christian or otherwise—remains meaningless propositions about idealistic hopes without the better future actually *becoming* a reality. What is needed for real hope is an open-ended future guided by God's providential care for the created order, or more to the point, an open-ended future shaped by God's reconciliation and redemption of the created order. In an interesting passage in *CD* III/2, Barth says that if one were to explain the theological meaning of creation in philosophical language it would consist of a notion of "pure becoming" spreading benefit to humanity. "The philosophical equivalent for the theological idea of divine creation would have to be at least that of a pure and basic becoming underlying and therefore preceding all perception and being" (*CD* III/2: 340). A philosophy or worldview of "pure becoming" can only be true if it demonstrates that "this pure becoming is pure divine benefit preceding all knowledge and being and underlying all knowledge and being." (*CD* III/2: 342). The cosmos is not a meaningless materialistic void, but an open-ended meaningful and relational space created for the flourishing of life. "The cosmos surrounding man is not alien to God. It is not independent and sovereign in face of Him. It does not follow an intrinsic law, but the will and work of its Creator" (*CD* III/2: 16). There is a correspondence between the creation of the cosmos and the existence of human life, but one is not reducible to the existence of the other. The human person is not a microcosm of the cosmos, nor is the universe a macrocosm of the person. This presumption is one of the basic errors of the naturalism that underlies much ecological thought. Accordingly, even though both the cosmos and humanity are completely dependent upon their creator for their being and becoming, the mystery of this relationship is revealed not in the mystery of the cosmos itself, but in the *covenant* between God and humanity. In other words, the cosmos itself is "embraced by the same covenant" that exists between God and humanity (*CD* III/2: 19). God's covenant-partnership *with* the cosmos makes it a hospitable, meaningful, and beneficial place of becoming for human life and its relationship to the created environment. It is the covenant that makes ethics and hope possible, for without it, there is no reason to hope that ethics will make a difference in the world's future.

Whatever correlations there are between God and creation they are grounded in God alone and not in something else like nature, life, or earth.

Any form of ethics that places human beings side-by-side with God as co-creator, co-savior or co-regent remains dependent on the worldview of pantheism or panentheism. "In all its forms pantheism is a conception which does violence and injustice not only to God but also to the creature" (*CD* III/3: 86). Although some theologians, like McFague, see panentheism as better than pantheism, Barth argues that it is "actually worse" because it conceals it true commitment to a "higher synthesis" or "master-concept," in which "God must be mingled with something else" such as "naturalism, materialism, spiritualism, or idealism" (*CD* II/1: 312). Here, God only becomes what God truly is when God exists together *with* something other than God, like the earth or the cosmos. "God does not form a whole with any other being" (*CD* II/1: 312). This does not imply, however, that God is a transcendent, isolated, and self-contained monad completely separate and removed from what God has created. Indeed, God is "free to be immanent, free to achieve a uniquely inward and genuine immanence of His being in and with the being which is distinct from Himself" (*CD* II/1: 313). "It is just the absoluteness of God properly understood which can signify not only His freedom to transcend all that is other than Himself, but also His freedom to be immanent within it, and at such a depth of immanence as simply does not exist in the fellowship between other beings" (*CD* II/1: 313). This doctrine of "true immanence" is something that "pantheism or panenethism," in all of its "poetic fancy" cannot achieve, because it makes God's freedom contingent upon some other "master concept" outside of God (*CD* II/1: 313). In such a view, God is no longer free to establish a *personal* "bond between creation and covenant" but is reduced to some abstract and synthetic formula of God-world relations. That is, like puzzle pieces of a grand map of cosmology, God, humanity, non-human species, and nature are put together so they fit a particular worldview. This worldview is rooted in a panentheistic cosmology, which cannot use the language of an intimate I-Thou relationship between God and humanity, as expressed in God's covenant-partnership. It cannot do this, because it denies that this *personal* relation is made objectively real in Jesus Christ. In Jesus Christ, God also discloses what is objectively real for humanity, the world, and "the whole cosmos," namely that "the cosmos is shown to be embraced by the same covenant" (*CD* III/2: 18–19).

For Global Cooperation and Environment

For there to be real a transformation in environmental practice, therefore, people must have *hope* in an open-ended future in which persons can act for the good of the environment. It is God's action, not our ethical actions, which makes this hope possible. Hope leads to action. For there to be hope people must have faith that the future will be shaped by the redemptive power of good over evil. This eschatological promise rests on God's sovereign graciousness over creation and not in the reenchantment of nature or in human technological power. As we have seen, once an alternative panentheistic cosmology or worldview replaces the covenant as the "internal basis" of creation, then it becomes another example of the "immanent frame" and Prometheanism of our age. Hence, although Christians ought to encourage the movement toward a sustainable or "green economy," they also ought to be critical of the underlying cosmology or pseudo-eschatology present in these worldviews. The human promise rests not in our abilities to create a green economy, but in God's reconciliation with all that is, including the green economy. "So then (without having to create illusions about itself) the world is no longer a world without hope. As it stands under the verdict and direction of God, so too it stands under the promise of God" (*CD* IV/1: 115). What God has "*gifted* to the cosmos" is God's only Son and "therefore nothing more or less than Himself" (*CD* IV/1: 71–72). Since God has acted in pure love by giving God's self to creation, the creation remains an "object of God's love" (*CD* IV/1: 71). Christian environmental witness leads us to affirm the value of the environment because God loves creation. This enables Christians to choose to act in hope and freedom, as individuals and groups, locally, nationally, and globally, and as Christians or as human beings, who stand in covenant-partnership with God.

In the concluding sections of the last two chapters, we have discussed the importance of global cooperation as a public witness in peacemaking, economic reform, and now environmental reform. As stated previously, Christian ethics must resist the extreme positions of "abstract internationalism and cosmopolitanism," and "abstract nationalism and particularism" (*CD* III/4: 312–13). Christians must resist the false idea that persons are fundamentally either citizens of the nation-state or of the international community. What this means, in practice, is that Christian environmental witness moves in a circle from local to global and global to local. The church's affirmation of Pentecost teaches us that even in the church's globality (or catholicity) there is unity under the headship of Jesus Christ. In a similar way, even in global diversity so is there a unity of global cooperation among nations. To be sure, global cooperation in environmental reform is just as difficult as peacemaking and justice. Ideology always remains a powerful force that seeks to destroy human hope and freedom. Indeed, the ideological realties present in environmental reform present a unique set of challenges because of the relative hegemony of technological or "expert language" in ecological science. In earlier chapters, we saw how "expert language" itself becomes a risk to society's ability to openly address issues in environmental reform. For there to be a reformed democratic politics there needs to be a full incorporation of the "lay languages" of particular religious and cultural traditions, rooted in traditional beliefs and practices. In truth, environmental risks often remain hidden by technologically driven expert languages. "An initial insight is key, when it comes to hazards, no one is expert—especially not the experts."[30] Technological hegemony destroys the free initiative of people to take ownership over their environmental future and replaces it with the fate of the technological solution. That is, since technology itself is not good or evil, it remains an instrumental power of good or evil people. In either case, however, the power lies in the hands of the people who control the technology and not in the hands of those affected by its power. When people become powerless, there is neither hope for environmental reform nor political and economic reform. The worst part of this is that democratic politics itself becomes threatened by ideology and technology.

The pervasiveness of political cynicism and apathy toward government is rooted in our sense of powerlessness and hopelessness about the future. Ironically, with heroic Prometheanism comes a sense of defeat and fate. The dominance of the Promethean management model makes market-driven utilitarian logic relatively hegemonic. Max Oelschlager calls this logic the "dominant social matrix," which must be challenged if there is to be real environmental reform.[31] Substantial political change depends

30. Beck, *World at Risk*, 35.

31. Max Oelschlager says the "dominant social matrix" include: 1) nature has instrumental value only; 2) short-term economic interests override long-term issues like intergenerational equity; 3) current environmental risks or costs are often construed as 'non-market' concerns, thus, not applicable to economic analysis; 4) economic growth poses no danger to the environment; 5) the management of earth is feasible through technological solutions; and 6) interest-group politics is the best way to confront current and future environmental concern. These shortsighted perspectives avoid long-term

on a greater openness to incorporate the biblical narrative of "caring for creation" in public discourse. "There are no solutions for the systematic causes of ecocrisis, at least in democratic societies, apart from religious narrative."[32] Indeed, Oelschlager continues, "religious discourse, expressing itself in the democratic forum, offers the possibility of overcoming special interest politics—especially those which are narrowly economic—on environmental issues."[33] The biblical language of "caring for creation," is an inclusive language that provides for greater ecological sensitivity in bringing diverse people together, while encouraging the possibility for greater individual and communal responsible action. This does not imply that the biblical language itself become hegemonic, but works with scientific discourse so that both "might inform and reinforce each other in help to transform culture."[34] In a similar way, changes in environmental law, says Mark Sagoff, cannot be based "simply as personal wants or preferences; they are not interests to be 'priced' by market or by cost-benefit analysis, but are views or beliefs that may find their way, as public values, into legislation."[35] The public language for democratic social regulation emerges from "public values we choose collectively, and these may conflict with wants and interests we pursue individually."[36] Christian witness to God's covenant-partnership with humanity and creation is not only important for Christians but for all humanity. This is the basis for an environmental ethics of witness. Environmental politics cannot be defined by the endless battle between business and environmental activists, but as a collective affirmation or communal vision of the common good. Furthermore, the language of the common good, at its core, cannot be articulated as technological or utilitarian, but must draw on the biblical language of covenant, creation, and reconciliation.

The politics of environmental regulation seeks to build greater possibilities for sustainable development. Such regulation does not, as free-market supporters claim, interfere with the *telos* of business, but helps clearly define what business ought to be, namely economic institutions that

---

procedures for building a democratic society with a sustainable future that will support human civilization. Oelschlaeger, *Caring for Creation*, 54–55.

32. Ibid., 5.
33. Ibid., 57.
34. Ibid., 11.
35. Sagoff, *Economy of the Earth*, 28.
36. Ibid., 16–17.

serve the common good of society. "Businesses should literally compete to be more ecological," says Paul Hawken, "not only on moral or ethical grounds or because it is the 'right thing to do,' but because such behavior squarely aligns with the bottom line."[37] Such social regulation of destructive environmental practices may lead to the regulation of consumption and production limits, graduated tax penalties, emission fees, licenses and, more positively, incentives. Consequently, in the general movement toward global cooperation in the area of environmental reform there needs to be collaboration among local, regional, and national governments and international agencies and organizations. Governments obviously need policies that encourage social, ecological, and energy sustainability at the local, national, and international levels.[38] This may seem extremely difficult in the divided realities of American politics, which is dominated by Left/Right ideology. As stated above, however, just as environmental reform cannot result from technological expert language, so too it cannot emerge from the ideologies of right-wing or left-wing politics. Such ideologies, says Robert Paehlke, have nothing in common with the *tradition* of environmentalism, which historically understood cannot be captured by either conservatism or liberalism. Against conservatives, for example, environmental politics believes in increasing ecological regulation and enforcement, decreasing military spending, increasing long-term sustainable economic development, increasing expenditures in education, medical care, and provide criticism against the abuses of neoliberal globalization. However, against liberals, environmental politics also leads to social practices that encourage technological transformation away from unionized smoke stake industries, decreasing government deficits, increasing political decentralization, promoting small and medium-sized entrepreneurship, and encouraging biblical values and

---

37. Hawken, *Ecology of Commerce*, 167.

38. Such a policy could include, at the very least, six measures according to Christian economists Bob Goudzwaard and Harry de Lange. They are: 1) a prevention principle that punishes the polluter while rewarding pollution prevention; 2) enforcement of government established health standards for its citizens; 3) taxes on petrochemically-based, large-scale agricultural production while rewarding organic, small-scale farming; 4) promote intensive recycling and more ecological technologies; 5) seek improvements in urban housing, transportation, and community restoration; and 6) encourage environmental education at all levels. Unlike the current "postcare" economy, they say, a "precare economy includes rather than excludes people; it internalizes and takes responsibility for its effects rather than expels them to other sectors of society; and it practices restraint and replenishes rather than extracts." Goudzwaard and de Lange, *Beyond Poverty and Affluence*, 149.

language into the language of law and government.³⁹ The real effort for environmental reform can come from the practice of democratic politics in which the erosive power of special-interest politics is rejected, at the same time a diversity of conservative/liberal positions are voiced, not as ideology, but as the means toward supporting and enhancing the common good.

As environmental stewards, Christians can remain hopeful because their trust is not in human technological mastery over the environment, but in God's declarative Yes for the cosmos. Their environmental witness is grounded in the fact that God's gift of freedom and hope gives Christians the language of "caring for creation." In their witness, Christians declare to others that the created environment is more than nature, as it is the outer basis of the covenant that God has with humanity. In their witness, Christians can remain confident that God "is in the cosmos," because in this "disclosed relationship of God with man there is disclosed also His relationship with the universe" (*CD* III/2: 18). The created environment remains a place of hope because God has given the gift of hope to humanity, and by analogy, the created environment. All human hopes for a better future, therefore, rest in the "gift" of this one "great hope" (*CD* IV/1: 121). God has come to us in the created environment in Jesus Christ. This is the central point and cannot be forgotten, marginalized, or supplanted. The unique miracle and "gift" is not the created environment or nature itself, as this simply confuses God and nature. Rather, it is the gift of Jesus Christ who "takes place in the cosmos," thus, "takes place in reality" (*CD* IV/3: 226). We value the environment because Jesus Christ has made the environment his own; he has taken ownership over the created order. God coming to us in this way is the basis for Christian environmental witness. So, taken together, Christians, in their responsible witness, work toward environmental reform because creation remains an "object of God's love" (*CD* IV/1: 71). This means being a public witness to the covenant-partnership that God has established with humanity, and by analogy, the created environment. Nevertheless, the most important witness that Christian ethics can offer to the world is not technical solutions to environmental crises or global climate change but the objective fact that we can choose not to live in despair, apathy, or fear, and that the powers of global annihilation, catastrophe, and nothingness are defeated in the "strange battle" of Jesus Christ as "prophetic witness."

---

39. Paehlke, *Environmentalism*, 276–77.

CONCLUSION

In the last three chapters, we have seen how God's covenant-partnership with humanity calls people to become witnesses of faith, hope, and love, leading to the practice of peace, justice, and freedom. This, in turn, leads to the responsible affirmation of political, economic, and environmental witness, which leads to support for political, economic, and environmental reform leading to greater global cooperation. This is only possible because, in Jesus Christ, human moral agency is restored, healed, and allowed to live in free response to God's relational command of grace. "It is as He makes Himself responsible for man that God makes man, too, responsible" (*CD* II/2: 511). Christians correspond to God's action by saying *No* to the powers and *Yes* to responsible witness and action by standing *with* and *for* the dignity of the person, church, and world. The Christian is free because she does not *choose* to be in solidarity with the world, but "is in solidarity with it from the very first" (*CL*: 194). In response to God's gracious covenant, therefore, Christian ethics as witness makes its voice heard in public life. Yet in their political, economic, and environmental witness, Christians must not be utopian or ideological. However much they believe in their particular cause, they cannot identify their own "human strategies with the kingdom of God nor over 'against' it but 'along side' it, and in so doing, human righteous action will be 'kingdom-like'" (*CL*: 266). This frees Christian ethics "from wasting time and energy over the impassable limits of their sphere of action and thus missing the opportunities that present themselves in this sphere. (*CL*: 265). Barth's seeming un-heroic claim for humanity to do a "little righteous," and to do what is only "possible" seems out of step with the often heroic claims of some versions of Promethean social ethics that seeks to accomplish the impossible. In their discussions of "social transformation," many Christian ethicists need to be reminded of one important lesson, namely that there really is no theological basis to address the significant risks the world faces that does not involve the answer revealed in God's covenant of grace. In their acts of "little righteousness," Christians can do *something*, but they cannot expect to do what God does; for that they must be willing to wait and be patient, and most important, pray. Prayer, too, is Christian witness—*Lex orandi lex credendi*.

Bibliography

Andrews, Isolde. *Deconstructing Barth: A Study of the Complementary Methods in Karl Barth and Jacques Derrida.* Studies in the Intercultural History of Christianity 99. Franfurt: Lang, 1996.

Antonaccio, Maria and William Schweiker. *Iris Murdoch and the Search for Human Goodness.* Chicago: University of Chicago Press, 1996.

Atherton, John. *Christianity and the Market: Christian Thought for Our Times.* London: SPCK, 1992.

Balthasar, Hans Urs von. *The Theology of Karl Barth.* Translated by E. T. Oakes, SJ. San Francisco: Ignatius, 1992.

Banner, Michael. *Christian Ethics and Contemporary Moral Problems.* Cambridge: Cambridge University Press, 1999.

Barber, Benjamin R. *Jihad vs. McWorld.* New York: Times, 1995.

Barth, Karl. *Against the Stream: Shorter Post-War Writings 1946–52.* New York: Philosophical Library, 1954.

———. *The Call to Discipleship.* Translated by G. W. Bromiley. Edited by K. C. Hanson. Facets. Minneapolis: Fortress, 2003.

———. "Church and Culture." In *Theology and Church: Shorter Writings. 1920–28.* Translated by Louise Pettibone Smith. New York: Harper & Row, 1962.

———. *The Church and the War.* New York: Macmillan, 1944.

———. *The Church and the Political Problem of Our Day.* New York: Scribner, 1939.

———. *Church Dogmatics.* 4 vols. Translated and edited by G. W. Bromiley and T. F. Torrance. Edinburgh: T. & T. Clark, 1936–77.

———. *The Christian Life.* Translated by Geoffrey W. Bromiley. Grand Rapids: Eerdmans, 1981.

———. *Community, State, and Church: Three Essays.* With a New Introduction by David Haddorff. Eugene, OR: Wipf & Stock, 2005.

———. *The Epistle to the Romans.* 2nd ed. Oxford: Oxford University Press, 1933.

———. *Ethics.* Translated by Geoffrey W. Bromiley. New York: Seabury, 1981.

———. *Evangelical Theology: An Introduction.* Translated by Grover Foley. Grand Rapids: Eerdmans, 1985.

———. *God in Action.* Translated by E. G. Homrighausen and Karl J. Ernst. Manhasset, NY: Round Table, 1963.

———. *God Here and Now.* Translated By Paul M. Van Buren. With new introduction by George Hunsinger. London: Routledge, 2003.
———. *The Göttingen Dogmatics: Instruction in the Christian Religion. Volume I.* Edited by Hannelotte Reiffen. Translated by Geoffrey W. Bromiley. Grand Rapids: Eerdmans, 1991.
———. *How I Changed My Mind.* Richmond: John Knox, 1966.
———. *The Humanity of God.* Translated by J. N. Thomas. Richmond: John Knox, 1960.
———. *Karl Barth's Table Talk.* Edited by John Godsey. Richmond: John Knox, 1963.
———. *The Knowledge of God and the Service of God according to the Teaching of the Reformation: Recalling the Scottish Confession of 1560.* Translated by J. L. M. Haire and Ian Henderson. 1938. Reprint, Eugene, OR: Wipf & Stock, 2005.
———. *A Letter to Great Britain from Switzerland.* Translated by E. H. Gordon and George Hills. London: Sheldon, 1941.
———. *Protestant Theology in the Nineteenth Century: Its Background and History.* Translated by Brian Cozens and John Bowden. Introduction by Colin Gunton. Grand Rapids: Eerdmans, 2002.
———. *The Theology of John Calvin.* Translated by Geoffrey W. Bromiley. Grand Rapids: Eerdmans, 1995.
———. *The Theology of the Reformed Confessions.* Translated by Darrell L. Guder and Judith Guder. Louisville: Westminster John Knox, 2002.
———. *The Word of God and the Word of Man.* New York: Harper & Row, 1957.
Barth, Karl and Johannes Hamel. *How to Serve God in a Marxist Land.* Introductory Essay by Robert McAfee Brown. New York: Association, 1959.
Baudelaire, Charles. *Selected Writings on Art and Artists.* Translated by P. E. Charvet. Cambridge: Cambridge University Press, 1981.
Baudrillard, Jean. *Selected Writings.* Edited by M. Poster. Stanford: Stanford University Press, 1988.
Bauman, Zygmunt. *Globalization: The Human Consequences.* New York: Columbia University Press, 1998.
———. *Life in Fragments: Essays in Postmodern Morality.* Oxford: Blackwell, 1995.
———. *Postmodern Ethics.* Oxford: Blackwell, 1993.
Beck. Ulrich. *Risk Society: Towards a New Modernity.* Translated by M. Ritter. London: Sage, 1992.
———. *What Is Globalization?* Translated by Patrick Camiller. Cambridge: Polity, 2000.
———. *World at Risk.* Translated by Ciaran Cronin. Cambridge: Polity, 2009.
Beck, Ulrich, et al. *Reflexive Modernization: Politics, Tradition, and Aesthetics in the Modern Social Order.* Stanford: Stanford University Press, 1994.
Bell, Daniel. *The Coming of Post-Industrial Society.* New York: Basic, 1973.
———. *The Cultural Contradictions of Capitalism.* New York: Basic, 1976.
———. *The End of Ideology: On the Exhaustion of Political Ideas in the Fifties.* Glencoe: Free, 1960.
Bell, Daniel M., Jr. *Liberation Theology after the End of History: The Refusal to Cease Suffering.* London: Routledge, 2001.
Benhabib, Seyla. *Situating the Self: Gender, Community, and Postmodernism in Contemporary Ethics.* New York: Routledge, 1992.
Berger, Peter L., and Samuel P. Huntington. *Many Globalizations: Cultural Diversity in the Contemporary World.* Oxford: Oxford University Press, 2002.
Berkhof, Hendrik. *Christ and the Powers.* Translated by John H. Yoder. Scottdale, PA: Herald, 1977.

Bernstein, Richard J. *Habermas and Modernity.* Cambridge: Polity, 1985.
Best, Steven, and Douglas Kellner. *The Postmodern Turn.* New York: Guilford, 1997.
Biggar, Nigel. "Barth's Trinitarian Ethic." In *The Cambridge Companion to Karl Barth,* edited by John Webster, 212–27. Cambridge: Cambridge University Press, 2000.
———. *Burying the Past: Making Peace and Doing Justice after Civil Conflict.* Washington, DC: Georgetown University Press, 2003.
———. *The Hastening that Waits: Karl Barth's Ethics.* New York: Oxford University Press, 1993.
Blackburn, Simon. "How to be an Ethical Antirealist." *Midwest Studies in Philosophy* 12 (1988) 361–76.
Blond, Phillip. "Introduction: Theology before Philosophy." In *Post-secular Philosophy: Between Philosophy and Theology,* edited by Phillip Blond. New York: Routledge, 1998.
Bonhoeffer, Dietrich. *Ethics.* Translated by Neville Horton Smith. New York: Macmillan, 1955.
Borgmann, Albert. *Crossing the Postmodern Divide.* Chicago: University of Chicago Press, 1992.
Browning, Don S. "Egos without Selves: A Theological-Ethical Critique of the Family Theory of the Chicago School of Economics." In *The Annual of the Society of Christian Ethics,* edited by Harlen Beckley. Washington, DC: Georgetown University Press, 1994.
Brunner, Emil. *The Divine Imperative.* Philadelphia: Westminster, 1937.
Busch, Eberhard. *The Great Passion: An Introduction to Karl Barth's Theology.* Translated by Geoffrey W. Bromiley. Grand Rapids: Eerdmans, 2004.
Cahill, Lisa Sowle and James F. Childress. *Christian Ethics: Problems and Prospects.* Cleveland, OH: Pilgrim, 1996.
Card, Claudia. *Feminist Ethics.* Lawrence: University of Kansas Press, 1991.
Cavanaugh, William T. "The City: Beyond Secular Parodies." In *Radical Orthodoxy: A New Theology,* edited by John Milbank et. al., 182–200. London: Routledge, 1999.
Clifford, James. *The Predicament of Culture: Twentieth-Century Ethnography, Literature, and Art.* Cambridge: Harvard University Press, 1988.
Clough, David. *Ethics in Crisis: Interpreting Barth's Ethics.* Barth Studies. Hampshire, UK: Ashgate, 2005.
Clough, David and Brian Stiltner. *Faith and Force: A Christian Debate about War.* Washington, DC: Georgetown University Press, 2007.
Cochrane, Arthur. *The Church's Confession under Hitler.* Philadelphia: Westminster, 1962.
Cunningham, Conor. *Genealogy of Nihilism.* Radical Orthodoxy Series. London: Routledge, 2002.
Derrida, Jacques. *Specters of Marx.* Translated by Peggy Kamuf. New York: Routledge, 1994.
Donagan, Alan. "Common Morality and Kant's Enlightenment Project." In *Prospects for a Common Morality,* edited by Gene Outka and John Reeder, 53–72. Princeton: Princeton University Press, 1993.
Dreyfus, Hubert and Paul Rabinow. *Michel Foucault: Beyond Structuralism and Hermeneutics.* Chicago: University of Chicago Press, 1982.
Duchrow, Ulrich. *Global Economy: A Confessional Issue for the Churches.* Geneva: WCC, 1987.

Duchrow, Ulrich and Franz J. Hinkelammert. *Property for People, Not for Profit: Alternatives to the Global Tyranny of Capital.* Translated by Elaine Griffiths et al. London: Zed, 2004.
Eagleton, Terry. *Ideology: An Introduction.* London: Verso, 1991.
Eller, Vernard. *Christian Anarchy: Jesus' Primacy over the Powers.* Grand Rapids: Eerdmans, 1987.
Ellul, Jacques. *Anarchy and Christianity.* Translated by Geoffrey W. Bromiley. Grand Rapids: Eerdmans, 1991.
———. *The Ethics of Freedom.* Translated by Geoffrey W. Bromiley. Grand Rapids: Eerdmans, 1976.
Foucault, Michel. "The Ethic of the Care of the Self as a Practice of Freedom." In *The Final Foucault*, edited by James Bernauer and David Rasmussen, 1–20. Cambridge: MIT Press, 1988.
———. *The Order of Things: An Archaeology of the Human Sciences.* London: Tavistock, 1970.
———. *Power/Knowledge: Selected Interviews and Other Writings. 1972–1977.* Edited by C. Gordon. New York: Pantheon, 1980.
Frazer, Elizabeth and Nicola Lacey. *The Politics of Community: A Feminist Critique of the Liberal-Communitarian Debate.* Toronto: University of Toronto Press, 1993.
Fukuyama, Francis. *The End of History and the Last Man.* New York: Free, 1992.
———. "Second Thoughts: The Last Man in a Bottle." *National Affairs* 56 (1999) 16–44.
Geertz, Clifford. *The Interpretation of Cultures.* New York: Basic, 1973.
Giddens, Anthony. *The Consequence of Modernity.* Cambridge: Polity, 1990.
———. "Living in a Post-Traditional Society." In *Reflexive Modernization: Politics, Tradition, and Aesthetics in the Modern Social Order*, edited by Ulrich Beck, et al., 56–109. Stanford: Stanford University Press, 1994.
———. *Modernity and Self-Identity.* Cambridge: Polity, 1991.
———. *Runaway World: How Globalisation is Reshaping our Lives.* New York: Routledge, 2000.
Gill, Robin. *The Cambridge Companion to Christian Ethics.* Cambridge: Cambridge University Press, 2001.
Gilligan, Carol. *In a Different Voice: Psychological Theory and Women's Development.* Cambridge: Harvard University Press, 1982.
Gorringe, Timothy. *Karl Barth: Against Hegemony.* Oxford: Oxford University Press, 1999.
———. *A Theology of the Built Environment: Justice, Empowerment, Redemption.* Cambridge: Cambridge University Press, 2002.
Goudzwaard, Bob, and Harry de Lange. *Beyond Poverty and Affluence: Toward an Economy of Care.* Grand Rapids: Eerdmans, 1995.
Goudzwaard, Bob et al. *Hope in Troubled Times: A New Vision for Confronting Global Crises.* Grand Rapids: Baker, 2007.
Gramsci, Antonio. *Selections from Prison Notebooks.* New York: International, 1971.
Green, Clifford. *Karl Barth: Theologian of Freedom.* London: Collins, 1989.
Griffin, David Ray. *God and Religion in the Postmodern World.* Albany: State University of New York Press, 1989.
———. "Postmodern Theology and A/Theology: A Response to Mark C. Taylor." In *Varieties of Postmodern Theology*, edited by David Ray Griffin, et al., 29–61. Albany: State University of New York Press, 1989.
———, et al., editors. *Varieties of Postmodern Theology.* Albany: State University of New York Press, 1989.

Gunnemann, Jon P., "Thinking Theologically about the Economic." In *Christian Ethics: Problems and Prospects*, 315–33. Edited by Lisa Sowle Cahill and James F. Childress. Cleveland, OH: Pilgrim, 1996.
Gunton, Colin. *The Promise of Trinitarian Theology*. Edinburgh: T. & T. Clark, 1991.
Gustafson, James. *Ethics from a Theocentric Perspective: Volume Two, Ethics and Theology*. Chicago: University of Chicago Press, 1981.
Habermas, Jürgen. *The Philosophical Discourse of Modernity*. New York: Political, 1988.
Haddorff, David. "Karl Barth's Theological Politics." In *Community, State, and Church: Three Essays*. With a New Introduction by David Haddorff. 1–67. Eugene, OR: Wipf & Stock Publishers, 2005.
———. *Dependence and Freedom: The Moral Thought of Horace Bushnell*. Landham: University Press of America, 1994.
———. "The Postmodern Realism of Barth's Ethics." In *Scottish Journal of Theology* 57 (2004) 269–86.
———. "Religion and the Market: Opposition, Absorption, and Ambiguity." *Review of Social Economy* 58 (2000) 483–504.
Hart, Trevor. *Regarding Karl Barth: Toward a Reading of His Theology*. Eugene, OR: Wipf & Stock, 2005.
Harvey, David. *The Condition of Postmodernity: An Inquiry into the Origins of Cultural Change*. Oxford: Blackwell, 1989.
Hassan, Ihab. "The Culture of Postmodernism." *Theory, Culture, and Society* 3 (1985) 119–31.
Hauerwas, Stanley. "Agency: Going Forward and Looking Backward." In *Christian Ethics: Problems and Prospects*, edited by Lisa Sowle Cahill and James F. Childress, 185–95. Cleveland, OH: Pilgrim, 1996.
———. *A Community of Character*. Notre Dame: University of Notre Dame, 1981.
———. *The Hauerwas Reader*. Edited by John Berkman and Michael Cartwright. Durham: Duke University Press, 2000.
———. "On Doctrine and Ethics." In *The Cambridge Companion to Christian Doctrine*, edited by Colin Gunton, 21–40. Cambridge: Cambridge University Press, 1997.
———. "Mudochian Muddles: Can We Get Through Them If God Does Not Exist?" In *Wilderness Wanderings: Probing Twentieth-Century Theology and Philosophy*, 190–208. Westvew, CO: Boulder, 1999.
———. *The Peaceable Kingdom: A Primer in Christian Ethics*. Notre Dame: Notre Dame University Press, 1983.
———. *Performing the Faith: Bonhoeffer and the Practice of Nonviolence*. Grand Rapids: Brazos, 2004.
———. *Wilderness Wanderings: Probing Twentieth-Century Theology and Philosophy*. Westvew, CO: Boulder, 1999.
———. *With the Grain of the Universe*. Grand Rapids: Brazos, 2001.
Hauerwas, Stanley and Charles Pinches. *Christians among the Virtues: Theological Conversations with Ancient and Modern Ethics*. Notre Dame: University of Notre Dame University Press, 1997.
Hauerwas, Stanley, and Samuel Wells, editors. *The Blackwell Companion to Christian Ethics*. Oxford: Blackwell, 2004.
Hauerwas, Stanley, et al., editors. *Theology without Foundations: Religious Practice and the Future of Theological Truth*. Nashville: Abingdon, 1994.
Hawken, Paul. *The Ecology of Commerce: A Declaration of Sustainability*. New York: Harper Collins, 1994.

Healy, Nicholas M. "Karl Barth's Ecclesiology Reconsidered." *Scottish Journal of Theology* 57 (2004) 287–99.
Heckman, Susan. *Moral Voices, Moral Selves: Carol Gilligan and Feminist Moral Theory.* University Park: Pennsylvania State University Press, 1995.
Held, David et al. *Global Transformations: Politics, Economics, and Culture.* Stanford, CA: Stanford University Press, 1999.
Hemming, Laurence Paul. *Radical Orthodoxy? A Catholic Enquiry.* Burlington, VT: Ashgate, 2000.
Hunsinger, George. *Disruptive Grace: Studies in the Theology of Karl Barth.* Eerdmans: Grand Rapids, 2000.
———. *How to Read Karl Barth: The Shape of His Theology.* New York: Oxford University Press, 1991.
———. "Karl Barth's Christology: Its Basic Chalcedonian Character." In *The Cambridge Companion to Karl Barth*, edited by John Webster, 127–42. Cambridge: Cambridge University Press, 2000.
———. "Postliberal Theology." In *The Cambridge Companion to Postmodern Theology*, edited by Keven J. Vanhoozer, 42–57. Cambridge: Cambridge University Press, 2003.
Hütter, Reinhard. *Suffering Divine Things: Theology as Church Practice.* Grand Rapids: Eerdmans, 2000.
Insole, Christopher J. *The Politics of Human Frailty: A Theological Defense of Political Liberalism.* Notre Dame: University of Notre Dame Press, 2004.
Jameson, Frederic. *Postmodernism, or, the Cultural Logic of Late Capitalism.* London: Verso, 1992.
Jehle, Frank. *Ever Against the Stream: The Politics of Karl Barth. 1906–1968.* Translated by Richard and Martha Burnett. Grand Rapids: Eerdmans, 2002.
Jenkins, Willis. *Ecologies of Grace: Environmental Ethics and Christian Theology.* Oxford: Oxford University Press, 2008.
Johnson, William Stacey. *The Mystery of God: Karl Barth and the Postmodern Foundations of Theology.* Louisville: Westminster John Knox, 1997.
Jüngel, Eberhard. *Christ, Justice, and Peace: Toward a Theology of the State in Dialogue with the Barmen Declaration.* Translated by D. Bruce Hamill and Alan J. Torrance with Introduction by Alan J. Torrance. Edinburgh: T. & T. Clark, 1992.
Kant, Immanuel. *Foundations of the Metaphysics of Morals and What Is Enlightenment.* Translated with an introduction by Lewis White Beck. Indianapolis: Bobbs-Merrill, 1959.
Kaufman, Gordon. *In Face of Mystery.* Cambridge: Harvard University Press, 1993.
———. *The Theological Imagination: Constructing the Concept of God.* Philadelphia: Westminster, 1981.
Kumar, Krishan. *From Post-Industrial to Post-Modern Society: New Theories of the Contemporary World.* Oxford: Blackwell, 1995.
Lakeland, Paul. *Postmodernity: Christian Identity in a Fragmented Age.* Minneapolis: Fortress, 1997.
Lash, Scott. *Sociology of Postmodernism.* London: Routledge, 1990.
———. "Reflexivity and its Doubles: Structure, Aesthetics, Community." In *Reflexive Modernization: Politics, Tradition, and Aesthetics in the Modern Social Order*, edited by Ulrich Beck, et. al, 110–73. Stanford: Stanford University Press, 1994.
———. et al., editors. *Risk, Environment, and Modernity: Towards a New Ecology.* Theory, Culture & Society. London: Sage Publications, 1996.
Lash, Scott, and Jonathan Friedman. *Modernity and Identity.* Oxford: Blackwell, 1992.

Lindbeck, George. *The Nature of Doctrine: Religion and Theology in a Postliberal Age.* Philadelphia: Westminster, 1984.
Long, D. Stephen. *Divine Economy: Theology and the Market.* London: Routledge, 2000.
———. *The Goodness of God: Theology, the Church, and Social Order.* Grand Rapids: Brazos, 2001.
Loughlin, Gerard. "The Basis and Authority of Doctrine." In *The Cambridge Companion to Christian Doctrine*, edited by Colin Gunton, 41–64. Cambridge: Cambridge University Press, 1997.
Lovelock, James. *The Revenge of Gaia.* New York: Basic, 2006.
Lovin, Robin. *Christian Faith and Public Choices: The Social Ethics of Barth, Brunner, and Bonhoeffer.* Philadelphia: Fortress, 1984.
———. "Christian Realism: A Legacy and its Future." In *The Annual of the Society of Christian Ethics*, edited by John Kelsay and Sumner B. Twiss, 3–18. Washington, DC: Georgetown University Press, 2000.
———. *Christian Realism and the New Realities.* New York: Cambridge University Press, 2008.
———. *Reinhold Niebuhr and Christian Realism.* Cambridge: Cambridge University Press, 1995.
Lowe, Walter. *Theology and Difference: The Wound of Reason.* Bloomington: Indiana University Press, 1993.
Lyotard, Jean-Francois. *The Postmodern Condition: A Report on Knowledge.* Translated by Geoff Bennington and Brian Massumi. Minneapolis: University of Minnesota Press, 1984.
———. *The Differend: Phrases in Dispute.* Translated by George van den Abbeele. Theory and History of Literature 46. Minneapolis: University of Minnesota Press, 1988.
———. *Political Writings.* Translated by Bill Readings. Minneapolis: University of Minnesota Press, 1993.
MacIntyre, Alasdair. *After Virtue.* 2nd ed. Notre Dame: University of Notre Dame Press, 1984.
———. *Three Rival Versions of Moral Enquiry: Encyclopedia, Genealogy, and Tradition.* Notre Dame: University of Notre Dame Press, 1990.
———. *Whose Justice? Which Rationality?* Notre Dame: University of Notre Dame Press, 1988.
Mangina, Joseph L. *Karl Barth: Theologian of Christian Witness.* Louisville: Westminster John Knox, 2004.
Mannheim, Karl. *Ideology and Utopia: An Introduction to a Sociology of Knowledge.* London: Routledge & Kegan Paul, 1936.
Marx, Karl, and Frederick Engels. *The German Ideology.* London: Lawrence & Wishart, 1974.
McCormack, Bruce. *Karl Barth's Critically Realistic Dialectical Theology: Its Genesis and Development 1909–1936.* Oxford: Oxford University Press, 1995.
———. *Orthodox and Modern: Studies in the Theology of Karl Barth.* Grand Rapids: Baker, 2008.
McFague, Sallie. *The Body of God: An Ecological Theology.* Minneapolis: Fortress, 1993.
———. *Life Abundant: Rethinking Theology and Economy for a Planet in Peril.* Minneapolis: Fortress, 2001.
———. *Models of God: Theology for an Ecological, Nuclear Age.* Philadelphia: Fortress, 1987.

McKenny, Gerald. *Analogy of Grace: Karl Barth's Moral Theology*. Oxford: Oxford University Press, 2010.

———. "Heterogeneity and Ethical Deliberation." In *The Annual of the Society of Christian Ethics*, edited by John Kelsay and Sumner B. Twiss, 205–24. Washington, DC: Georgetown University Press, 2000.

Meeks, Wayne A. *The Moral World of the First Christians*. Library of Early Christianity 6. Philadelphia: Westminster, 1986.

Metzger, Paul Louis. *The Word of Christ and the World of Culture: Sacred and Secular through the Theology of Karl Barth*. Grand Rapids: Eerdmans, 2003.

Milbank, John. *Being Reconciled: Ontology and Pardon*. London: Routledge, 2003.

———. "The Gospel of Affinity." In *The Strange New Word of the Gospel: Re-Evangelizing in the Modern World*, edited by Carl E. Braaten and Robert W. Jenson, 1–20. Grand Rapids: Eerdmans, 2002.

———. *The Future of Love: Essays in Political Theology*. Eugene, OR: Cascade, 2009.

———. "The Programme of Radical Orthodoxy." In *Radical Orthodoxy? A Catholic Enquiry*, edited by Laurence Paul Hemming, 33–45. Burlington, VT: Ashgate, 2000.

———. "Reply to R. H. Preston." *Theology* 91 (1988) 412–16.

———. "Socialism of the Gift. Socialism by Grace." *New Black Friars* 77 (1996) 532–48.

———. *Theology and Social Theory: Beyond Secular Reason*. Oxford: Blackwell, 1990.

———. *The Word Made Strange: Theology, Language, and Culture*. Oxford: Blackwell, 1997.

———. et al., editors. *Radical Orthodoxy: A New Theology*. London: Routledge, 1999.

Moe-Lobeda, Cynthia. *Healing a Broken World: Globalization and God*. Minneapolis: Fortress, 2002.

Molnar, Paul. *Divine Freedom and the Doctrine of the Immanent Trinity: In Dialogue with Karl Barth and Contemporary Theology*. London: T. & T. Clark, 2002.

———. *Incarnation and Resurrection: Toward Contemporary Understanding*. Grand Rapids: Eerdmans, 2007.

Murdoch, Iris. *The Fire and the Sun*. Oxford: Clarendon, 1977.

———. *Metaphysics as a Guide to Morals*. New York: Penguin, 1993.

Murphy, Nancey. *Anglo-American Postmodernity: Philosophical Perspectives on Science, Religion, and Ethics*. Westvew, CO: Boulder, 1997.

Nelson, Robert. *Economics as Religion: From Samuelson to Chicago and Beyond*. University Park: Penn State University Press, 2001.

———. *Reaching for Heaven: The Theological Meaning of Economics*. Landham, MD: Rowman and Littlefield, 1991.

Niebuhr, H. Richard. *Christ and Culture*. New York: Harper and Row, 1951.

Nietzsche, Friedrich. "On Truth and Lie in the Extra-Moral Sense." In *The Portable Nietzsche*, edited by Walter Kaufmann, 42–46. New York: Viking, 1968.

———. *The Twilight of Idols*. Translated by Walter Kaufmann. New York: Viking, 1954.

———. *The Will to Power*. Translated by Walter Kaufmann. New York: Vintage, 1964.

Nimmo, Paul T. *Being in Action: The Theological Shape of Barth's Ethical Vision*. London: T. & T. Clark, 2007.

Noddings, Nel. *Caring: A Feminine Approach to Ethics and Moral Education*. Berkeley: University of California Press, 1984.

Nussbaum, Martha. "Virtue Revived" in *Times Literary Supplement* 4657 (July 3, 1992), 9.

Oelschlaeger, Max. *Caring for Creation: An Ecumenical Approach to the Environmental Crises*. New Haven: Yale University Press, 1994.

O'Donovan, Oliver. *The Desire of the Nations: Rediscovering the Roots of Political Theology.* Cambridge: Cambridge University Press, 1996.
———. *The Just War Revisited.* Cambridge: Cambridge University Press, 2003.
———. *The Ways of Judgment: The Bampton Lectures, 2003.* Grand Rapids: Eerdmans, 2005.
O'Donovan, Oliver, and Joan Lockwood O'Donovan. *Bonds of Imperfection: Christian Politics, Past and Present.* Grand Rapids: Eerdmans, 2004.
Ottati, Douglas. "The Reformed Tradition in Theological Ethics." In *Christian Ethics: Problems and Prospects*, edited by Lisa Sowle Cahill and James F. Childress, 45–59. Cleveland, OH: Pilgrim, 1996.
Outka, Gene. "Following at a Distance: Ethics and the Identity of Jesus." In *Scriptural Authority and Narrative Interpretation*, edited by Garrett Green, 144-60. Philadelphia: Fortress, 1987.
———. "The Particularist Turn." In *Christian Ethics: Problems and Prospects*, edited by Lisa Sowle Cahill and James F. Childress, 93–118. Cleveland, OH: Pilgrim, 1996.
———. "Following at a Distance: Ethics and the Identity of Jesus." In *Scriptural Authority and Narrative Interpretation*, edited by Garrett Green, 144–60. Philadelphia: Fortress, 1987.
Outka, Gene, and John Reeder. *Prospects for a Common Morality.* Princeton: Princeton University Press, 1993.
Paehlke, Robert C. *Environmentalism and the Future of Progressive Politics.* New Haven: Yale University Press, 1988.
Placher, William C. *The Domestication of Transcendence: How Modern Thinking about God Went Wrong.* Louisville: Westminster John Knox, 1996.
Polanyi, Karl. *The Great Transformation.* Boston: Beacon, 1957
———. *Livelihood of Man.* Edited by Harry W. Pearson. Studies in Social Discontinuity. New York: Academic, 1977.
Preston, Robert. "Christian Socialism Becalmed" *Theology* 91 (1988) 24–32.
———. *Religion and the Ambiguities of Capitalism.* Cleveland, OH: Pilgrim, 1991.
Putnam, Hilary. *The Many Faces of Realism.* LaSalle, IL: Open Court, 1987.
Rasmussen, Larry. *Earth Community, Earth Ethics.* Maryknoll, NY: Orbis, 1996.
———. "Cosmology and Ethics." In *Worldviews and Ecology: Religion, Philosophy, and the Environment*, edited by Mary Evelyn Tucker and John Grim, 173–80. Maryknoll, NY: Orbis, 1994.
Reno, R. R. *In the Ruins of the Church: Sustaining Faith in an Age of Diminished Christianity* Grand Rapids: Brazos, 2002.
Ricouer, Paul. *Oneself as Another.* Translated by Kathleen Blamey. Chicago: University of Chicago Press, 1992.
Roberts, Richard H. *A Theology on Its Way? Essays on Karl Barth.* Edinburgh: T. & T. Clark, 1991.
Robertson, Roland. "Globalization and the Future of Traditional Religion." In *God and Globalization Vol. I: Religion and the Powers of the Common Life*, edited by Max L. Stackhouse and Peter J. Paris, 53–68. Harrisburg, PA: Trinity, 2000.
———."Glocalization: Times-Space and Homogeneity-Heterogeneity." In *Global Modernities*, edited by Roland Robertson et al., 25–44. London: Sage. 1995.
———. et al. *Global Modernities.* London: Sage. 1995.
Rorty, Richard. *Contingency, Irony, and Solidarity.* Cambridge: Cambridge University Press, 1989.

———. "Cosmopolitanism with Emancipation: A Response to Lyotard." In *Modernity and Identity*, edited by Scott Lash and J. Friedman, 159–71. Oxford: Blackwell, 1992.
———. "Habermas and Lyotard on Postmodernity." In *Habermas and Modernity*, edited by Richard Bernstein, 161–75. Cambridge: Polity, 1985.
———. *Philosophy and Social Hope*. New York: Penguin, 2000
Rosaldo, Renalo. *Culture and Truth: The Remaking of Social Analysis*. Boston: Beacon, 1989.
Ruddick, Sara. *Maternal Thinking: Towards a Politics of Peace*. Boston: Beacon, 1989.
Sagoff, Mark. *The Economy of the Earth: Philosophy, Law, and the Environment*. New York: Cambridge University Press, 1988.
Santmire, H. Paul. *Nature Reborn: The Ecological and Cosmic Promise of Christian Theology*. Minneapolis: Fortress, 2000.
———. *The Travail of Nature: The Ambiguous Ecological Promise of Christian Theory*. Philadelphia: Fortress, 1985.
Schleiermacher, Friedrich. *The Christian Faith*. Edited by H. R. Mackintosh and J. S. Stewart, 1821–1822. Reprint. Edinburgh: T. & T. Clark, 1960.
———. *On Religion: Speeches to its Cultured Despises*. Cambridge: Cambridge University Press, 1988.
———. *Introduction to Christian Ethics*. Translated by John C. Shelley. Nashville: Abingdon, 1989.
Schweiker, William. *Power, Value, and Conviction: Theological Ethics in the Postmodern Age*. Cleveland, OH: Pilgrim, 1998.
———. *Responsibility and Christian Ethics*. Cambridge: Cambridge University Press, 1996.
———. *Theological Ethics and Global Dynamics: In the Time of Many Worlds*. Oxford: Blackwell, 2004.
———. "The Sovereignty of God's Goodness." In *Iris Murdoch and the Search for Human Goodness*, edited by Maria Antonaccio and William Schweiker, 209–35. Chicago: University of Chicago Press, 1996.
Shelley, John. "Translator's Introduction." In *Introduction to Christian Ethics*, Frederick Schleiermacher. Translated by John C. Shelley. Nashville: Abingdon, 1989.
Shriver, Donald W., Jr. *An Ethic for Enemies: Forgiveness in Politics*. Oxford: Oxford University Press, 1995.
Stackhouse, Max. "Christian Social Ethics in a Global Era: Reforming Protestant Views." In *Christian Social Ethics in a Global Era*, Max Stackhouse, 11–74. Nashville: Abingdon, 1995.
———. "General Introduction." In *God and Globalization Vol. I: Religion and the Powers of the Common Life*, edited by Max Stackhouse and Peter Paris, 1–52. Harrisburg, PA: Trinity, 2000.
———. *God and Globalization Vol. IV: Globalization and Grace*. Harrisburg, PA: Trinity, 2007.
Stackhouse, Max and Peter Paris. *God and Globalization Vol. I: Religion and the Powers of the Common Life*. Harrisburg, PA: Trinity, 2000.
Stackhouse, Max and Don Browning. *God and Globalization Vol. II: The Spirit and the Modern Authorities*. Harrisburg, PA: Trinity, 2001.
Stackhouse, Max and Diane B. Obenchain. *God and Globalization Vol. III: Christ and the Dominions of Civilization*. Harrisburg, PA: Trinity, 2002.
Stackhouse, Max, et al. *Christian Social Ethics in a Global Era*. Nashville: Abingdon, 1995.

Stassen, Glen and David Gushee. *Kingdom Ethics: Following Jesus in Contemporary Context.* Downers Grove, IL: InterVarsity, 2003.
Stout, Jeffrey. *Ethics after Babel: The Languages of Morals and Their Discontents.* Boston: Beacon, 1988.
———. *Democracy and Tradition.* New Forum Books. Princeton: Princeton University Press, 2004.
Tanner, Kathryn. *Economy of Grace.* Minneapolis: Fortress, 2005.
———. *Theories of Culture: A New Agenda for Theology.* Guides to Theological Inquiry. Minneapolis: Fortress, 1997.
Taylor, Charles. *The Ethics of Authenticity.* Cambridge: Harvard University Press, 1991.
———. "Foucault on Freedom and Truth." In *Foucault: A Critical Reader,* edited by David Couzens Hoy, 69–102. London: Blackwell, 1986.
———. *A Secular Age.* Cambridge: Harvard University Press, 2007.
———. *Sources of the Self: The Making of Modern Identity.* Cambridge: Harvard University Press, 1989.
Taylor, Mark C. *Erring: A Postmodern A/theology.* Chicago: University of Chicago Press, 1984.
Thiselton, Anthony. *Interpreting God and the Postmodern Self: On Meaning, Manipulation, and Promise.* Grand Rapids: Eerdmans, 1995.
Thompson, Geoffrey, and Christiaan Mostert. *Karl Barth: A Future for Postmodern Theology?* Adelaide: Openbook, 2000.
Todd Peters, Rebecca. *In Search of the Good Life: The Ethics of Globalization.* New York: Continuum, 2004.
Toynbee, Arnold. *A Study of History.* Vol. 9. London: Oxford University Press, 1954.
Tracy, David. "Public Theology, Hope, and the Mass Media: Can the Muses Still Inspire?" In *God and Globalization Vol. I: Religion and the Powers of the Common Life,* edited by Max L. Stackhouse and Peter J. Paris 231–54. Harrisburg, PA: Trinity, 2000.
———. "Theology and the Many Faces of Postmodernity." *Theology Today* 51 (1994) 104–14.
Vanhoozer, Keven J. *The Cambridge Companion to Postmodern Theology.* Cambridge: Cambridge University Press, 2003.
Vattimo, Gianni. *The End of Modernity: Nihilism and Hermeneutics in Post-Modern Culture.* Cambridge: Polity, 1991.
Ward, Graham. *Barth, Derrida and the Language of Theology.* New York: Cambridge University Press, 1995.
———. "Barth, Modernity, and Postmodernity." In *The Cambridge Companion to Karl Barth,* edited by John Webster, 274–95. Cambridge: Cambridge University Press, 2000.
———. "Introduction: Where We Stand." In *The Blackwell Companion to Postmodern Theology,* edited by Graham Ward, xii–xxvii. Oxford: Blackwell, 2001.
———, editor. *The Blackwell Companion to Postmodern Theology.* Oxford: Blackwell, 2001.
Webb, Stephen H. *Refiguring Theology: The Rhetoric of Karl Barth.* Albany: State University of New York Press, 1991.
Webster, John. *Barth's Ethics of Reconciliation.* Cambridge: Cambridge University Press, 1995.
———. "Barth, Modernity, and Postmodernity." In *Karl Barth: A Future for Postmodern Theology?* Edited by Geoff Thompson and Christiaan Mostert, 1–28. Adelaide: Openbook, 2000.

———. *Barth's Moral Theology: Human Action in Barth's Thought.* Grand Rapids: Eerdmans, 1998.

———. *The Cambridge Companion to Karl Barth.* Cambridge: Cambridge University Press, 2000.

———. Confessing *God: Essays in Christian Dogmatics II.* London: T. & T. Clark, 2005.

———. *Word and Church: Essays in Christian Dogmatics.* Edinburgh: T. & T. Clark, 2002.

Welch, Claude. *Protestant Thought in the Nineteenth Century. Volume I. 1799–1870.* New Haven: Yale University Press, 1972.

Welch, Sharon. *After Empire: The Art and Ethos of Enduring Peace.* Minneapolis: Fortress, 2004.

———. *A Feminist Ethic of Risk.* 2nd ed. Minneapolis: Fortress, 2000.

Werpehowski, William. "Ad Hoc Apologetics." *Journal of Religion* 66 (1986) 282–301.

———. "Karl Barth and Politics." In *The Cambridge Companion to Karl Barth*, edited by John Webster, 228–42. Cambridge: Cambridge University Press, 2000.

White, Lynn, Jr. "The Historical Roots of Our Ecological Crisis." *Science* 10 (1967) 1203–7.

Wink, Walter. *When the Powers Fall: Reconciliation in the Healing of the Nations.* Minneapolis: Fortress, 1998.

Wynne, Brian. "May the Sheep Safely Graze? A Reflexive View of Expert-Lay Knowledge Divide." In *Risk, Environment, and Modernity: Towards a New Ecology*, edited by Scott Lash et al., 44–83. London: Sage, 1996.

Yoder, John Howard. *Karl Barth and the Problem of War, and Other Essays on Barth.* Edited with foreword by Mark Thiessen Nation. Eugene, OR: Cascade, 2003.

———. *The Politics of Jesus: Vicit Agnus Noster.* 2nd ed. Grand Rapids: Eerdmans, 1994.

———. "Walk and Word: The Alternatives to Methodologism." In *Theology without Foundations*, edited by Nancey Murphy, et al., 77–90. Nashville: Abingdon, 1994.

Young, Iris. *Throwing Like a Girl and Other Essays in Feminist Philosophy and Social Theory.* Bloomington: Indiana University Press, 1990.

Index

absolutism, 280
abstraction, 29, 30
act-deontology, 206
action, freedom for, 240
actualism, 326
actualistic ontology, 214n14
advertising, 287
aesthetics, postmodernist approach to, 136–37
After Empire (Welch), 46
After Virtue (MacIntyre), 182
Against the Stream (Barth), 118
agape, 69, 400, 401
agency
    Christian witness and, 261–66
    distortion of, 427–28
    ethical methodology and, 258–61
    freeing of, 157, 177
    human and divine, 212–14, 436
    power and, 294–99
Althaus, Paul, 100, 101
analogia entis (analogy of being), 204–5
analogia fidei (analogy of faith), 204, 205
analogia relationis, 327
Analogy of Grace, The (McKenny), 252
anarchism, 382–83
anthropocentric error, 305
anti-globalism, 146, 148–49, 296, 298

antirealism, 166, 167, 168
anxiety, freedom from, 242
anxious view, 355
apathy, 425–26
apologetics, 78, 194, 319
Aquinas, Thomas. *See* Thomas Aquinas
Aristotle, 258n20, 259
atheism, 334
a/theology, 47
Atherton, John, 413–14
Augustine, 330
Austrian school, of economic, 398
avant garde, 35

Balthasar, Hans Urs von, 246
Banner, Michael, 259
baptism, 105, 224–25, 226
Barmen Declaration, 99–101, 115, 389
Barth, Karl
    accepting notion of general revelation, 205
    advocating for democracy, 383–85
    advocating a practical form of politics, 121–22
    on anthropocentric myth of modern thought, 191
    arguing against apologetics approach, 309

Barth, Karl (*continued*)
  arguing against equating God's kingdom with any social movement, 62, 63
  arguing against idealistic conceptions of ethics, 61
  attacking religious individualism, 61–62
  attracted to language of command, 207–8
  on basis for theological ethics, 27
  beginning to think about theological method, 64–65
  calling for Christian responsibility for the civil community, 361–62
  on central problem with modern Christian ethics, 70–71
  Chalcedonian pattern in, 211–14
  challenge of, 6
  challenging modernism and postmodernism, 57
  Christian humanism of, 122
  Christocentric view of moral agency, 215–17
  Christological shift in thinking of, 96
  Christological understanding of moral anthropology, 58
  Christology of, 247, 274–75
  committed to doing "only theology," 99, 103, 110–11
  committed to the Word of God, 57
  compared to Derrida, 129
  concentrating on Christology, 71–73
  consistent eschatology of, 90
  on covenant and creation, 322, 431
  on crisis in Christianity and culture, 70
  critical of the apologetic method of theology and ethics, 332
  critical of Swiss neutrality in World War II, 113–14
  critical of Western democracies, 109–10
  criticized for his divine command ethics, 205–7
  criticized for not attacking Soviet aggression, 118
  critiquing Kant's ethics, 70–71
  demands of, on a reader, 1
  denouncing Stalin, 122
  departing from anthropocentric foundations of modern theology, 57
  developing Christologically centered notion of the state, 111
  developing a consistent eschatology, 66
  developing more positive appreciation of culture, 72
  developing trinitarian concepts of ethics grounded in God's speech, 53
  dialectical consistency of thought in, 93
  dialectical ethics of, 55
  dialectical motif in writings of, 64–66, 212, 246–47, 249, 253–56, 331, 339–40
  dialectical view of culture, 73–74
  disaffection of, for extreme ideological causes, 117–18
  discovering doctrines of anhypostasis and enhypostasis, 247n3
  discussing economics and work in church context, 409–10
  distinguishing between analogy of being and analogy of faith, 204
  doctrine of creation, 321
  doing Christian ethics differently, 207
  early thought of, 54–55
  ecclesiology of, 262–63, 332–34
  on economic reform, 410–11
  emphasizing prayer as form of moral action, 86
  engaging in practical moral reasoning, 248–49
  environmental ethics of, 437–38
  ethics of, criticized, 313–21, 323, 324
  on ethics of creation, 86–87
  ethics grounded in one's relationship toward God and others, 55
  on ethics of reconciliation and redemption, 87–90

Index   461

ethics seeking positive Christian
   witness, 113
eudaemonistic view of his ethics,
   210–11
expelled from Germany, 106–7
on grace of God, 193–94. *See also*
   grace
Hauerwas compared to, on agency
   and witness, 256–66
hopeful about the Christian life, 3
importance of, for Christian social
   ethics, 2
integrating nontheological sources,
   128–29
inviting non-theological viewpoints
   into theological ethics, 317–18
lecturing on Reformed theology, 70
on main difference between Nazis
   and Soviet Communists, 122
moral realism of, inclusive of other
   viewpoints, 323–24
naming the powers, 280
nonfoundational ethics of, 93
open-ended vision of Christian ethics,
   121
opposed to linking Christian ethics
   with nationalism, 118–19
opposed to natural law theory, 109,
   323
outlining approaches to theological
   ethics, 78–81
on panentheism and pantheism, 440
placing ethics within dogmatics, 259
on placing gospel before law, 107
as polarizing figure, 205
postwar message of forgiveness and
   reconciliation with Germany, 114
on the powers, first extensive
   discussion of, 271
presenting a theology and ethics of
   witness, 2
on principalities and powers as
   destructive features of human
   life, 270
reassessing, 55–59
rejecting casuistry, 247–48, 255

rejecting methodological universalism
   of modern ethics, 93
rejecting modern view of the self, 54
rejecting natural theology, 101–2, 205
rejecting Schleiermacher's optimistic
   theology of culture, 72–73
relating ethics to theology, 8–9
relevance of, for postmodernity,
   58–59
remaining cautious about extreme
   positions of exclusion and inclusion, 74–75
responding to Hitler's rise, 98–99,
   101, 112–13
searching for divine trinitarian Other,
   54
seeing ethics in crisis, 67
seeking for alternative transcendental
   starting point for theology, 59–60
shifting focus toward God's revelation
   as trinitarian Other, 200
stance of, on nuclear weapons, 122
supporting Allied cause in World
   War II, 113
on tension between descriptive and
   normative ethics, 77–78
theological realism of, establishing
   his moral realism, 323
theology of the covenant, 87
theology of gospel and law, 215
transitioning thought of, in the 1930s,
   95–110
turning toward critical realism, 60
understanding God's gracious
   action, 7
on vertical nature of the covenant, 254
viewed as anti-modern thinker,
   55–56, 58, 76
viewed as modernist, 56
viewed as postmodern thinker,
   56–58, 92
on war, 387–92
warning about dangers of idolatry, 50
witnessing rise of Hitler, German
   Christian movement, and Confessing Church movement, 97–98

Barth, Karl (*continued*)
　on worldview formation, five-step progression of, 422
　Yes-No pattern in mature writings of, 229
Barth's Ethics of Reconciliation (Webster), 58
Baudelaire, Charles, 34, 36, 134
Bauman, Zygmunt, 5, 15, 38–39, 144, 178–80, 294
Beck, Ulrich, 15, 140, 141, 151, 153–56, 159, 178, 184–86, 300, 304, 351, 393, 425
being-in-action, implications of, for Christian ethics, 214–15
being-in-encounter, 327
Beiser, Frederick, 40
Bell, Daniel, 130, 405
beneficia Christi, 235
Berger, Peter, 146
Berkof, Hendrik, 275
Best, Steven, 131
Bible
　pointing to revelation, 74
　searching in, for God's otherness, 60
Biggar, Nigel, 56, 128, 210–11, 248–50, 303
Blackwell Companion to Christian Ethics, The (ed. Hauerwas and Wells), 261–62, 312
Blond, Philip, 329–30
Bonhoeffer, Dietrich, 207, 263n32, 320
Borgmann, Albert, 29, 30
boundaries, Christian distinctiveness formed at, 129
bracketing, 244
Brunner, Emil, 99n2, 101, 207, 320
Bulgakov, Sergei, 437
Bultmann, Rudolph, 99n2
Busch, Eberhard, 109, 272, 427
Bush administration, 375
Bushnell, Horace, 43

callings, 86–87
Calvin, John, 65n19, 315–16, 330

Cambridge Companion to Christian Ethics, The (ed. Gill), 310–12, 313
capitalism, global, 148
care, ethic of, 178, 180
Care of the Self (Foucault), 171–72
Cartesian self, characteristics of, 172
casuistry, 247–48, 251
categorical imperative, 37–38, 208–9
Catholic moral theology, relating moral philosophy and theology, 79
certainty, metanarrative of, 166
Chalcedonian Christology, 370
Chalcedonian pattern, in Barth's thought, 211–14
character ethics, community-based, 256–57
Chicago school, of economics, 398
Christ of Culture, 41
Christ and Empire (Rieger), 272–73n4
Christendom
　Barth's engagement in politics after age of, 123
　discipleship after, 230–34
　totus Christus and, 337–40
Christian Cartesianism, 97
Christian community
　analogies with civil community, 117
　as model for civil community, 114–17, 380
　political life of, 118
　political witness of, 381
　upbuilding of, 394
Christian doctrine, particularity of, 39–40
Christian ecological ethics, 431–32
Christian economic ethics, seeking to be non-ideological, 394
Christian environmental ethics, emergence of, 434–35
Christian environmental witness, 441–42
Christian ethicist, role of, 1–2
Christian ethics
　abstraction and separation of, from theological grounding, 30

Index   463

approach of, from general or particular stance, 310
becoming anthropocentric, 28
beginning with prior understanding of theological ethics, 7, 27
beginning with the Word of God, 201, 223
being general and inclusive, 323
concentrating on personal circumstances and action, 27
denying the ecclesial sphere of, 352–53
depending on witness of theological ethics, 13
dialoguing with other ethical discourses, 10–11
emancipated from grace, effects of, 109
embodied in Christians' lives, 41
engaging in theological ethics, 199
eschatological nature of, 89–90, 364–65
establishing the moral ontology for, 202
as ethics of witness to trinitarian command, 91
generalist perspective on, 24–25
grounding in Christian witness, 106
grounding in human activity, 217
heart of, gift of freedom within, 11
involving ethical reflection, 246
isolationist approach of, 312
as journey, 252
methodological task of, 208
as modern invention, 25n1
most important witness of, 445
moving beyond failures of modern liberal theology, 26
non-dialectical viewpoint creating risks for, 344
particularist perspective on, 24, 25
as pedagogical strategy, 254
as practical science, 24–25
practical side of, 227
reclaiming ethics from anthropocentric methodologies, 9

refusing to be a subcategory of ethics, 201, 202–3
related to particularity of Christian faith, 40–41
related to theology, 8–9
relation in, of human agency and divine action, 216–17
relevance of, for contemporary context, 26
remaining eschatological, 73
remaining theological, 26–27
as responsibility to bear witness to covenant relationship, 215
risking deconstruction of, 161–62, 332
rooted in responsibility and witness, 344–45
strategy of, 5–6
task of, 255–56
tradition's impact on, 182–84
two scenarios for, 86
understanding, in framework of dogmatic theology, 66
universalizing, 31–32
versions of, beginning with moral subject, 221
as witness to divine action, 201
Christian ethos, 234–36
Christian existence
  church-centered view of, 234–35
  concentric circles (spheres) of, 343–44, 345
Christian Faith, The (Schleiermacher), 39
Christian humanists, 412
Christianity
  intelligibility of, distinct from witness, 264
  as supreme example of religion, 40
Christianity and the Market (Atherton), 413
Christian liberation, 231–32, 237–43
Christian Life, The (Barth), 343
  discussing the lordless powers, 275
  dialectical reasoning in, 253
Christian moral discourse, risking becoming esoteric, 333

Index

Christian moral judgment, 243–56
    based in special ethics, 250
    dialectical, 253–56
    remaining cautious about courses of action, 279
Christian moral responsibility, 63–64, 93
Christian nationalism, 382
Christian naturalism, error of, 204–5
Christian perfectionism, 242, 363
Christian public ethics, 325–27
Christian Realism, 316
Christian responsibility, 17–18
Christian secularism, 358
Christian social action, as parable of heaven, 64
Christian social ethics
    aporetic nature of, 349, 350
    avoiding theological esotericism and secular reductionism, 339–40
    core problem for, 160–61
    eschatological nature of, 63
    listening to non-Christian concepts, 129
    and reflexive view of postmodernity, 142–43
    risk as element of, 153
Christian socialism, 405, 406, 408
Christian social theory, as ecclesiology, 330
Christian social witness
    leading to greater understanding of human freedom, 123–24
    not committed to ideology, 288
    resisting ideology, 421
    standing with the global market, 414
Christian witness
    agency and, 261–66
    arising in social and historical context, 127
    committed to global cooperation, 392–93
    eschatological difference of, 424–25
    growing out of God's freedom to act as self-witness, 103–4
    impossibility of, without freedom, 233
    linked to process of moral judgment, 243–44
    meaning of, 219–23
    not necessary to bring about God's divine action, 236
    patterned after biblical witnesses, 103–4
    rooted in vocation, 230
    after secularism, 122–24
    seeking non-ideological perspective, 298
    Yes-No-Yes pattern of, 269, 343, 370
Christians
    arrogance of, in making demands on God, 67–68
    fulfilling their political duty, 112–13
    identification of with Christ, error of, 71
    pious egocentricity of, 235
    relationship of, with Jesus Christ, 220–21
    staying free from ideologies, 288
Christology
    Barth's concentration on, 71–73, 211–12
    criticism of, 33
    focused on Jesus Christ as Prophet, 275
    focused on Son of God, 274–75
    focused on Son of Man, 275
christomonism, 222
Christ and the Powers (Berkof), 275
Christus victor, 17, 268, 269, 277, 305–7, 327, 337, 355–56, 357, 417
chthonic powers, 268, 280, 289–93, 422
Chung, Paul, 62
church
    active witness of, to the civil community, 363
    bearing witness to reality of the Word of God, 338
    being responsible in its freedom, 108
    being true to its witness, 124
    as culture, 234
    distinguishing, from Christ, 355–56
    egocentricity of, 235

Index   465

as emerging community of witness, 337
empowering of, to be a visible witness, 400
ethics of, related to witness, 6–7
in excess, 354
faithfulness of, 264–65
freedom of, to be itself, 231
freedom from the power of the state, 362
moral responsibility for, 351–57
moving toward secularism, 352
as only alternative to postmodern nihilism, 330
pacifist witness of, 257
as political witness, 380–81
recovering its own self, 6–7
relationship of, to the individual and the world, 352
responding to secularism, 105–6
standing with culture, 72–73
standing against powers, 270
witness of, as context for Christian ethics, 260–61
Church Dogmatics (Barth), 59
context for, 2
ethical discussions in, 198–99
first discussion of ethics in, 95
dialectical reasoning in, 253
responsibility, witness, and freedom as important threads in, 266
Yes-No pattern in, 229–30
church law, correspondence of, with civil law, 361–62
church and state
Barth addressing as Christian community and civil community, 116
belonging to Christ's kingdom, 270
related under God's divine act of justification, 111–12
church/world relationship, preferable interpretation of, 360–63
civil community
analogies with Christian community, 117

as guardian of the common good, 404, 426
as indirect witness to God's kingdom, 380
needing the church, 124
Clough, David, 390–91
Cold War, superpowers in, remaining potential leviathans, 375
collectivism, 345–46
error of, 346
resisting, 351
commands, 81–83, 86. *See also* divine command
contrasted with human choice, 96–97
drawing us toward God's Word, 91
commodity fetishism, 137, 146
community
forming identities, 180
impact of, on Christian ethics, 182
compulsion, freedom from, 240
concursus Dei, 224
Confessing Church movement, 98–100, 113
confession, public, 379–80
confusio hominum, 326
conscience
Christian view of, 88–91
liberation of, 241–42
constitutional democracy, 383–84
contemporary society, ambiguity of, 143
Contingency, Irony and Solidarity (Rorty), 175
control, 29, 32
correspondence
of divine and human action, related to witness, 222–23
invocation and, 225–28
setting framework for moral agency, 227
correspondence theory, 183–84
cosmology
naturalizing God, 433
panentheistic, 434
cosmopolitanism, 393
cosmopolitan moment, 159, 185

cosmos
  covenant-partnership with, 439
  differing beliefs about, 433–34
covenant, related to creation, 322
covenant-partnership, 97, 203
  with the cosmos, 439
  humanity's freedom within, 218–19
  meaning of, 231–32, 233
  with non-human nature, 432
  removal of, 217
  vertical relationship of, 249
creation
  caring for, 443
  ethics of, 86–87, 119–21, 250, 322
  God's covenant with, 427
  related to covenant, 322
creation-based ethics, 321
creeds, criticism of, 33
critical realism, Barth's turn toward, 60
critical reason, individual exercise of, 37
critical society, 141, 159, 184–85
cross-pressures, in postmodern age, 3–4
cultural analysis, 143
cultural contingency, 166
cultural fashion and taste, as chthonic powers, 290–91
cultural hegemony, 300, 301–2
cultural studies, 40
culture
  church standing with, 72–73
  as commodity, 137
  human, rejecting deification and demonization, 73
Cunningham, Conor, 52

Davos culture, 146–47, 149, 295
decision-making
  autonomous, freedom from, 239–40
  freedom of, 240–41
deconstructionist ethical theory, 164
deconstructionist ethics, 169–74, 176–77
deconstructionist postmodernism, 134–39
deconstructionist thought, 133–34
Deism, 44, 51

democracy, 383–85
  linking civil and Christian communities, 117–18
democratic socialism, 410–11
denial, 425–26
Derrida, Jacques, 15, 56, 57, 129, 135, 170, 171, 172, 173, 181
Descartes, Rene, 29, 30
desire, freedom from, 240
determinate messianism, 171
De Tracy, Destutt, 421
development, modern moral theories of, 180
diachronic justification, 183–84
dialectic, role of, in Barth's ethics, 246–47, 249, 253–56
dialectical thinking, vertical and horizontal, 65
diastasis
  between God and humanity, 60, 63, 65
  between humanity and the good, 68
différance, 170
difference, voices of, 46
discipleship, 16
  call to, 239–40
  after Christendom, 230–34
  impossibility of, without freedom, 233
  meaning for, of liberation, 238–43
  participating in divine agency and freedom, 232
  rooted in Christian witness, 230
Discourse on Method (Descartes), 29
disengagement, 39
disorder, kingdom of, 277–78
dissection, 29, 31
divine agency, priority of, 258
  as act, 207–11
  constancy and concreteness of, 251
  filling space between humans and God, 255
  as gift of freedom, 209
  grace of, 209–10
  intrinsic value of, 245
  not always understanding, 251

obedience to, 251–52
openness to, 250–51
as practical embodiment of the doctrine of election, 215
as series of correspondence between God and humanity, 208–9
theology of, 16
divine command ethics, 205–7
divine economy, 405–6
divine ethics, coming before human ethics, 10
divine-human covenant, rejection of, 237
Docetic eschatology, 365
dogmatics, relevance of, 58–59
dogmatic theology, 313
  related to ethics, 308–9
  understanding Christian ethics in framework of, 66
double agency, 213–14, 255
Duchrow, Ulrich, 297

Eagleton, Terry, 300–301n16
Ebionite eschatology, 365
ecclesial excess, 363
ecclesiology, importance of, for Christian ethics, 309
ecological risk, 154–55
ecological theology, 428
ecological witness, freedom and, 425–46
ecology, hope for, 423
economic cooperation, 296
economic ethics, 18–19
economic globalism, 295–96
economic interdependence, 411–12
economic justice, 402, 403–8
economic neoliberalism, 402–3
economic reform, 408–9
economic resources, as demonic power, 282–84
economic scandals, 403
economic systems, becoming mammon, 397–98
economic witness
  justice and, 402–14
  love and, 395–402
economistic fallacy, 407

Economy of Grace (Tanner), 406
Edwards, Jonathan, 315–16
election
  doctrine of, 215
  theological account of, 213–14
Elert, Werner, 100–101
Eller, Vernard, 382
Ellul, Jacques, 382–83
empire, threat of, 375–76
End of History and the Last of Man, The (Fukuyama), 295
End of Ideology, The (Bell), 294–95
Engels, Friedrich, 301
Enlightenment, 29
enlightenment error, 111
entertainment, as chthonic power, 291–92
environment
  global cooperation and, 441–45
  liberation theology of, 430
environmental ethics, 19
  beginnings of, 426–27
  shifting focus toward soteriology, 437
environmentalism, not linked with political ideologies, 444–45
environmental regulation, 443–44
environmental witness, 443, 445
Epistle to the Romans (Barth), 61
eschatology
  and the powers, 278–80
  role of, in ethics, 364–67
esotericism
  as risk for ethics, 333–34
  theological, 80
ethical action
  human, as parabolic of divine action, 69
  primary and secondary, 68–69
ethical discourse, social theory appealing to, 159
ethical individualism, 345
ethical instruction, 252
ethical life, normative task of, both hidden and revealed, 349–50
ethical methodology, agency and, 258–61
ethical particularism, 80

ethical perspectivism, 168, 169
ethical pluralism, 169
ethical reflection, 84–85, 245–46, 252
ethical relativism, 168–69
ethical theory, requiring synergism between God and man, 83
ethical thinking, requiring ideals, 351
ethical thought, postmodern, two types of, 164
ethic of care, 178, 180
ethic of responsibility, 347
ethic of risk, 46
ethics. *See also* Christian ethics; deconstructionist ethics; divine command ethics; economic ethics; environmental ethics; feminist ethics; general ethics; modern ethics; philosophical ethics; political ethics; special ethics; theological ethics
  annexation of, 9–10
  becoming possible by knowing and doing the good, 204
  as Christian witness, 252
  crisis of, 67
  demanding forgiveness and reconciliation, 12
  demanding responsibility, 12
  developing, without God, 191–92
  dogmatic theology related to, 308–9
  ecclesial approach to, 78–79
  effect on, of postmodernity, 138–39
  eschatological nature of, 278
  as gift of freedom, 367–68
  grounded in witness to God's action of reconciliation, 372–73
  growing role of, in global society, 160
  inclusiveness of, 12
  involving knowledge and practice, 12–13
  linked with dogmatics, 95
  modern, 22, 165
  moral framework for, 159
  moral responsibility in, 67
  nature of, confusion about, 5
  needing theology, 187–91, 192
  positive account of, 77
  postmodern, characteristics of, 165–66
  problem of, identical with problem of dogmatics, 68
  reduced to power, 190
  reflexive account of, 15
  related to power, 188
  related to theology, 24–28
  related to witness, 2–3, 6–7
  remaining in God's gracious judgment, 68
  separate from theology, 7–8
  separating metaphysics from, 191
  teleological principles of, 439
  tension between descriptive and normative, 77–78
  tradition-dependent, 166
  trinitarian conception of, 81
  as unfinished project, 349
Ethics (Barth), 59, 66, 77, 85, 119
  importance of, 75–76
  providing midway point in development of Barth's thought, 95–96
  showing shift toward vertically based deontological ethics, 97
ethics of creation, 250, 322
ethics of reconciliation, 198–99, 225, 237, 268
ethics of witness, 68, 199, 219–21, 357
ethnography, development of, 143–44
eudaemonism, 210–11
Europe, post-Christendom, setting the stage for, 15
Evangelical Theology (Barth), 415
evil, in context of creation and providence, 272
experts, language of, 157

faculty club culture, 146–48, 149, 295–96
faith
  accompanied by the proper understanding of God, 7
  based on knowledge of covenant-partnership with God, 203

objective reality of, 379
political witness and, 373–81
as response to God's grace, 204
witness of, 378–81
Faith and Force (Stiltner and Clough), 390–91
falsehood
ideology and, 419–23
juxtaposed against hope, 416–17
resulting from denial of vocation, 419
sin of, 417–18
fellowship, freedom for, 120
Feminist Ethic of Risk, A (Welch), 46
feminist ethics, 180
feminist theology, 296
fides quaerens intellectum, 7, 12–13
forgiveness
awareness of, 85–86
political, 377
Foucault, Michel, 15, 46, 57, 135, 171–73, 181
foundationalism, 32–33
Frazer, Elizabeth, 180
freedom
collapsing, God's and human, 436
corresponding to divine action, 222
ecological witness and, 425–46
ethics of, 108, 119–20
gift of, underlying Christian ethics, 11, 13
God's, establishing human freedom, 12
gracious permission to act in, 250
human, 209–10
human misuse of, 227
jeopardized, by technical mastery over nature, 429–30
relational nature of, 211
responsible, 218, 223
theology of, 415
trinitarian, 10, 11
two spheres of, 246
freeing of agency. *See* agency, freeing of
Freud, Sigmund, 180
Fukuyama, Francis, 295
functionalism, 31

fundamentalism, 158
future
ambiguity about, 4–5
fear of, 422–23
hope for, 4–5
hopelessness about, 442–43

Geertz, Clifford, 143
general ethics, 27
German Christian movement, 99, 100–101, 107, 109
German Evangelical Church, 98n1
German Ideology, The (Marx and Engels), 301
Giddens, Anthony, 29–30, 140–41, 150, 153, 159, 184, 300
gift exchange, 405
Gill, Robin, 310–11
Gilligan, Carol, 178, 180–82, 184
global capitalism, 295–96
global cooperation, 392–93
on economic issues, 412–14
environment and, 441–45
need for, 186
global free market, problems in, 296
globalism, 295–96, 403
distinguished from globalization, 151
neoliberal, 145
globalization, 138, 142, 143–44, 269, 402–3
age of, God's providential action in relation to, 161
contradictory features of, 150–51
development of ideologies about, 294–98
distinguished from globalism, 151
opposition to, 296–97
perspectives on, variety of, 144–49
postmodernity and, 145, 149–52
risks of, 155
varieties of, 151
global Keynesianism, 403
global policy networks, 412
Global Transformations (Held et al.), 144–45
glocalization, 151

goals, accomplishment of, losing confidence in, 4
God
  acting in conformity with, 223
  acting for the good of humanity, 218
  acting in a way to create witnesses, 103–4
  action of, 3, 81–82
  affirming humanity, 121
  agency of, as grounding for human action, 63
  classical understanding of, attacked, 48
  as constructed by modern theology, 50
  cooperating with humanity, 224
  correspondence of, to the Israelites, 10
  covenant with man, meaning of, 228
  as divine actor of reconciliation, 91
  existence of, 191–92
  forgiveness of, making ethics possible, 71
  freedom before, 120
  freedom from, 302
  freedom of, 66, 209, 231
  functions of, shifted away from 39
  grace of, responding to, 209
  humanity of, 346
  judgment of, as judgment of grace and election, 87
  knowledge of, mediated through sign or sacrament, 321
  making possible humanity's reconciliation with 274–75
  naturalizing of, 433
  obeying, for our own best good, 210–11
  as other, 51, 53, 54, 60–61
  owning the good and its embodiment in ethics, 10
  performance of, in Jesus Christ and the Spirit, 265
  relation of, to creation, 431–32
  relational view of, 14, 61
  sovereignty of, over the future, 4
  trinitarian action of, grounding theological ethics, 79–80
  as trinitarian commander, 81–83
  trinitarian freedom of, 10, 11, 321
God-consciousness, 39–40, 41
God and Globalization (Stackhouse), 160–61
Goebbels, Joseph, 287
Gogarten, Friedrich, 102n
good
  conception of, source for, 159
  discovery of, source for, 245
  God's demonstration of, 210–11
  human conceptions of, heterogeneity among, 81
  human knowledge of, detached from moral ontology, 52
  linking, to God, 192
  understanding, through the Word of God, 202
good will, 38
Gorringe, Timothy, 2, 270, 349, 430
gospel
  placing before law, 107–8
  truth of, found in God's faithfulness, character, and performance, 267
gospel and law. *See* law and gospel
Göttingen Dogmatics (Barth), 73–74
Goudzwaard, Bob, 444n38
grace
  actions of, as content of the moral law, 221
  as answer to ethical problem, 194
  answering problems of ethics and dogmatics, 68
  bridging human knowledge and God's revelation, 315
  coming before law, 221
  covenant of, 16, 214, 237, 252
  egocentric containment of, 235–36
  establishing structure for ethics, 204
  extending to powers of the state, 111
  freedom of, 89
  freeing humanity, 223
  God acting in and through the covenant of, 237

Index   471

law as form of, 108
liberation of, 240
limiting and liberating human freedom, 218–19
provided so Christians can act as responsible witnesses, 370–72
rejection of, 274
resulting in witness, 104–5
setting humanity free from the power, 271
shaping a believing person, 204
Gramsci, Antonio, 300, 301–2
grand narratives, of modernity, 135
Green, Clifford, 270
Grenzfall principle, 387–88
Griffin, David, 47
Gunneman, Jon, 397
Gunton, Colin, 50–51
Gustafson, James, 17, 30, 205, 313–16

Habermas, Jürgen, 140
Harnack, Adolph von, 43, 93
Harvey, David, 136–37
Hassan, Ihab, 136
Hauerwas, Stanley, 25, 204, 230, 256–66, 265, 311, 315, 332, 336–37
Hawken, Paul, 444
Hayek, F. A., 398
Healy, Nicholas, 354–55
Heckman, Susan, 182
Hegel, G. W. F., 41
hegemony
  not accounting for human alienation from God, 302
  powers and, 294, 300–307
Held, David, 144
hermeneutics of suspicion, 301
Hinkelammert, Franz, 297
history, postmodernist view of, 136
History of Sexuality (Foucault), 171–72
hominum confusione, 419–20
hope
  losing confidence in, 4
  message of, 3
  in a postmodern age, 3–5
  witness of, 423–25

Hope in Troubled Times (Goudzwaard et al.), 376
human, as parable of the divine, 64
human action
  grounded in God's agency, 63
  significance of, as corresponding to divine action, 224–28
human agency, priority of, 258
human beings, election of, in Jesus Christ, 213
human choice, role of, in ethical inquiry, 83–85
human dignity, 325
human-divine relation, beginning with Jesus Christ, 201–2
human freedom
  discovered in correspondence to God's freedom, 233
  distortion of, 238–39
  as state of being in covenant-partnership with God, 233
  theological view of, 236
human government, final form of, 295
humanism, worldwide interest in, 123
humanity
  creating its own reflexive powers, 302
  divinization of, 428
  hope for, 305
  liberated by God's grace, 223
  progress of, 41
human pleasure, as chthonic power, 291–92
human subject, as standard for knowledge of the good, 30
Hunsinger, George, 211–12, 213, 255
Huntington, Samuel, 146
Hütter, Reinhard, 43
hyperglobalists, 144, 145

ideological reductionism, dialectical freedom standing against, 366
ideology, 304
  altering and developing, 285–86
  becoming oppressive, 421
  central traditions of, 420
  creating enemies, 285

ideology (*continued*)
  as cultural hegemony, 421–22
  end of, 294–95
  freedom against, 118–22
  freedom from the power of, 304
  as lordless power, 420
  as most inclusive of the powers, 284–89
  promising freedom and solidarity, 287–88
  redefinition of, 301
  substance of, 286
  as *weltanschauung*, 301
Ideology and Utopia (Mannheim), 301
idolatry, dangers of, 50
imago Dei, 325–26
immanent frame, 428–30, 433
immanentism, 51–52
Immer, Karl, 107
In a Different Voice (Gilligan), 180
indecision, freedom from, 240
indeterminacy, 136
individual conscience, respecting the freedom of, 347
individualism, 36, 363, 397
  error of, 346
  resisting, 351
  temptation to, 238
Insole, Christopher, 356
intercession, 115
interdependence, resulting from cultural difference and otherness, 152
internalization, 177
internal realism, 182, 184
International Forum on Globalization, 147
interpersonal ethics, 347
invisible church, 356
invocation, correspondence and, 225–28
isms, 286
Israelites, annexing Canaan, as analogy relating to Christian ethics, 203, 205
I-thou relation, 327–28

Jameson, Frederic, 148, 150

Jehle, Frank, 121
Jenkins, Philip, 437, 438–39
Jesus Christ
  as basis for human-divine relation, 201–2
  becoming teacher of ethical maxims, 33–34
  call of, responding to, 239–40, 241
  distinguishing, from the church, 355–56
  double agency of, 255
  as entry point into discussion of human and divine agency, 212–14
  fabrications in the role of, 418
  faith of, represented to us, 373
  fellowship with, in context of Christian community, 11–12
  freedom and responsibility of, making possible human freedom and responsibility, 219
  gift of, taking place in the cosmos, 445
  giving witness to God's kingdom, 395
  God performing double action in, 214
  humanity of, 321
  humans' distance from, 349–50
  overcoming force of nothingness, 272–73
  as prophet, 275, 416
  reconciling work of, awareness of, 371
  relationship of, with the Christian, 220–21
  relationship with, as source of other relations, 327
  as representative of all humanity, 346
  as Son of Man, 395
  as source of human dignity, 327
  as subject of faith, hope, and love, 371
  three appearances of, 425
  victory over the power, denial of, 273
  witness of, 265, 274–75
Johnson, William Stacey, 56, 92
justice
  economic witness and, 402–14
  relating justification to, 111

justification
　denial of, 419
　relating justice to, 111
just peacemaking, 390
just war, 386–87

Kant, Immanuel, 37–39, 42, 70–71, 208–9
Kantianism, 31–32
Kaufman, Gordon, 47
Kellner, Douglas, 131
kingdom of God, 41
　civilizing power of, 42–43
　Jesus Christ giving witness to, 395
　organicist view of, 62
　standing above church and state, 100
Kirchliche Brudershaften, 122
Kohlberg, Lawrence, 180
Krisis, 66, 67
Kumar, Krishan, 32, 48, 149

Lacey, Nicola, 180
Lange, Harry de, 444n38
language, deconstructive view of, 170
Lash, Scott, 139–40
late-modernity, reflexive, 139–44
law
　as a form of the gospel, 108
　grace preceding, 221
　separated from grace, consequences of, 108–9
law and gospel
　Barth's theology of, 215
　at core of Lutheran-Reformed debate, 107
　debates over, 97, 100–102
　separation of, effects of, 109
lay language, 157–58
legalism, freedom from, 240–41
leviathan, 280–82, 304, 382
　power of, 18
　pride and, 374–77, 379
Levinas, Emmanuel, 178
liberal apologetics, 358
liberal ironist, 175–76

liberal theology
　apologetic/synthesis approach of, 312
　legacy of, 42–44
　modern, Schleiermacher as father of, 39
liberation
　affecting process of moral judgment, 243
　caveats relating to, 242–43
　Christian, 363–64
　distinguished from freedom, 237
　as framework for Christian responsibility and witness, 230
　governed by God's divine initiative, 242–43
　meaning of, for the Christian disciple, 238–43
liberation theology, 296–97
life, freedom for, 120
limitation, freedom in, 120–21
Lindbeck, George, 44
little narratives, 171
local narratives, 171
local resistance, 172
Long, Stephen, 405
Lord's Prayer, 226–27, 275, 350–51
Lord's Supper, remaining a witness through, 105
Loughlin, Gerald, 7
love
　economic witness and, 395–402
　healing relationships with God and with the human other, 69–70
　human action of, as parable to God's actions of love, 69
　leading to justice, 394
　resisting sloth and mammon, 401
　widening outside the church, 400–401
　witness of, 400–402
Lovelock, James, 423
Lovin, Robin, 17, 205, 316–17, 320, 324–25
Luther, Martin, 330, 348
Lyotard, Jean-Francois, 135, 148, 150, 170, 171, 172, 173

MacIntyre, Alasdair, 15, 166, 168, 178, 182–84, 188–89, 256, 259, 336
mammon, 282–84, 304
  linked with sloth, 394, 395, 397–400
  threat of, to personal relationships, 398–99
Mannheim, Karl, 300–301
Many Globalizations (ed. Huntington and Berger), 146
market, shaping human behavior, 398–99
Marx, Karl, 137, 300–301
McCormack, Bruce, 56, 60–61, 65, 66, 68, 247n3
McFague, Sallie, 435–36, 440
McKenny, Gerald, 250n9, 251–52
meaning, mystical, in nihilistic world, 48
messianic religion, recovery of, 132
metaethics, 188–89
metanarratives, of modernity, 135
metaphysics, separating, from ethics, 191
Metaphysics as a Guide to Morals (Murdoch), 191
methodological universalism, 29–34, 36, 131, 165
methodologism, 260
Milbank, John, 17, 25–26, 49, 133, 142–43, 189, 328–32, 334, 336–37, 405, 408
Mises, Ludwig von, 398
modern art, ambiguous nature of, 34
modern ethics
  characteristics of, 165
  legacy of, 14
modernism, 35–36
  characteristics of, 136n17
  favoring individualism, 36
modernity
  beginnings of, 28–29
  characteristics of, 29
  clashing ideological forces in, 35
  double-edged nature of, 29–30, 34
  fragmentation of knowledge in, 30
  grand narratives of, 135
  presuming humans' ontological independence, 30

relation of, to post, 131–32
  risks of, 140–41, 159
  self-assertive nature of, 174–75
  self-destructive aspect of, 34–35
modernization, 32, 35–36, 141–42, 184–86
modern subject, genealogy of, 172
modern theology
  God constructed by, 50
  sidetracking of, 48
modern thought
  anthropocentric myth of, 191
  drive of, toward secularism, 44
Moe-Lobeda, Cynthia, 296–97
Molnar, Paul, 205, 214, 436
money, power of, 283–84
moral action
  effect on, of ethical reflection, 245–46
  as responsive action of witness, 91
moral agency
  Barth's Christocentric view of, 215–17
  beginning with Christological question, 218
  redefining, 16
  rejecting divine agency, 299
moral character, as an event, 90
moral discernment, for the individual, 249–50
moral Esperanto, 31–32
moralism, freedom from, 240–41
moral judgment
  dialectical process of, 230
  ethical grounds for, lacking, 171
  liberation of, 269
  liberation's effect on, 243
  as positive process of deliberation, 243
  related to emotional experiences, 181
moral knowledge, 80, 167
moral law, universal, 38
moral ontology, 193–94
  problem of, in postmodernity, 189–90, 199
  traditions shaping, 200
  understanding, through the Word of God, 202

moral realism, 167–68
　based on theological realism, 205
　separating, from theological realism, 321–22
　theological account of, 319
　understanding, through the Word of God, 202
moral relativism, 239
moral responsibility, 178–80
moral theology, mediating position of, 79, 80–81
moral traditions, 183
Muller, Ludwig, 98
Munich Agreement, failure of, 109
Murdoch, Iris, 191
Murphy, Nancy, 150

nationalism, 391
　mixing church with, 118–19
　new forms of, 376
national security, ideology of, 376–77
National Socialism, as leviathan, 374–75
naturalism, basic error of, 439
natural law
　linked to ideology, 110
　reliance on, effects of, 109–10
natural theology, 100–101
　Barth's opposition to, 101–2, 205
　debates over, 97
nature, re-sacralization of, 434
Nature and Grace (Brunner), 101
Nelson, Robert, 398
neo-Keynesianism, 403
neoliberal globalism, 145
neoliberalism, 295–96
neo-protestantism, 42
new traditionalists, 336
Niebuhr, H. Richard, 41, 315–16
Niebuhr, Reinhold, 316, 317
Niemoller, Martin, 98
Nietzsche, Friedrich, 134, 172–73, 329
nihilism, 36, 329
　overcoming problem of, 193
　postmodern, 51–52
　qualified, 46
Nimmo, Paul, 223

normative ethics, 318
Notebooks (Nietzsche), 134
nothingness, 272–74, 277, 326
nuclear weapons, 122
Nussbaum, Martha, 164

Obama, Barack, 375–76
obedience, flowing from God's grace, 104
O'Donovan, Oliver, 384–85n14, 386
objective realism, 137
Oelschlager, Max, 442–43
openness, to God's command, 244–45
optimism, guardedness of, 4–5
other
　God as, 51, 53, 54, 60–61
　respecting the difference of, 132
　responsibility for, 70, 88, 178–80, 345–51
　as victim of social forces, 173
otherness
　importance of, 50–51
　responsibility to, 135–36
　voices of, 46
otherness of the other, 69, 173
Ottati, Douglas, 316
Outka, Gene, 166, 349

Paehlke, Robert, 444
panentheism, 51, 435–37, 440
pantheism, 51, 440
participatory ontology, 52, 330
particularism, cultural, 166–67
particularity, 39–40
Pastors Emergency League, 98
peace, political witness and, 381–93
Peaceable Kingdom, The (Hauerwas), 256–57
peacemaking, 385–92
personal interaction, 345
personalism, 326
personal resonance, 177
persons
　as co-creators, 217–18
　perception of, as having task to transform the world, 293–94

pessimism, stemming from human will, 4
Peters, Rebecca Todd, 296–97
philosophical ethics, 40
pietistic error, 111
Placher, William, 48
poiesis, commitment to, 43
Polanyi, Karl, 398, 407
political absolutism, 280–82
political agency, 305
political ethics, 18
political ideology, destructive potential of, 281–82
political organizations, 62
political thought, corruption of, by natural theology, 102
political witness
  faith and, 373–81
  peace and, 381–93
politics, engagement of, 99
possessions, anxiety surrounding, 282–83
post-Christendom world, church's and state's role in, 116
post-liberal viewpoint, 323–24
postmodern ethics
  characteristics of, 165–66
  deconstructionist, 169–74, 176–77
  forked rhetoric of, 176
  particularistic turn of, 166–67
  pragmatist, 169, 174–77
postmodernism
  characteristics of, 136n17
  common elements of, 45–46
  deconstructionist, 134–39
  distinct from postmodernity, 131
  origins of, 130
  reacting to global capitalism, 148
  rejecting ideology of modernization, 135
  restricting, to economic approach, 148–49
postmodernity
  ambiguity of, 36, 133
  Barth's relevance for, 58–59
  celebrating otherness, 135–36
  conditions of, 132–33
  crisis in, of human agency, 294
  debate in, about moral truth, 167–68
  distinct from postmodernism, 131
  as double-coded phenomenon, 48
  epistemological framework of, 190
  as eschatological term, 161
  ethical crisis of, 5
  globalization and, 145, 149–52
  liberating modernity's underside, 135–36
  moral realism as problem for, 110
  not allowing the other to speak, 52
  positive side of, leading to diversity of interpretation, 132
  postmodern turns within, 133
  relation of, to modernity, 131–32
  sloth as temptation for, 396
  theoretical perspective of, 150
  transition to, from modernity, 36, 164–66
  weak view of, 139
postmodern theology, ethics and, 44–53
post-structuralism, 170–74
potential, 376
potestas, 376
power
  agency and, 294–99
  as determinant of social change, 145
  dominating the language of ethics, 174
  ethics reduced to, 190
  for defining and evaluating risks, 157
  multiple faces of, 269
  overcoming problem of, 193
  preoccupation with, 187–88
  relation to, of ethics, 188
  value and goodness greater than, 188–89
power relations, 134
powers
  actions of, 271
  Barth's characterization of, 275–76
  Bible's portrayal of, 276
  Christian resistance to, source of, 278–79
  church standing against, 270

cooperating with, 274
eschatology and, 278–80
freedom from, 288–89
God's judgment against, 279
hegemony and, 294, 300–307
human protest against, 227
ignorance of, 278
limited and relative power of, 277
lordless, 275
naming, 280–93
real liberation from, possibility of, 270
replacing one with another, 279–80
saying no against, 16–17
spiritual forces and chthonic powers, 280
practical ethics, 250
practical pacifism, 390
practical reason, 37
pragmatism, 174–77
praxis
commitment to, 43
immanentist theology of, 46
theology of, 47
prayer, 226, 242, 446
as form of moral action, 86
as primary ethical activity of witness, 69
premodern theology, 48–49
Preston, Robert, 408, 413
pride
faith as the antithesis of, 378
leviathan and, 374–77, 379
linked with sloth, 395–96
overcome by witness of faith, 372
power of, 374
sin of, 373
as sin of modernity, 396
principalities and powers, renewed interest in, 269
principle crusadism, 359–60
principle monasticism, 359
private property, elimination of, 297–98
problems, global, 4
process theology, 47
pro-globalists, 145–46, 296

progress
becoming despair, 36
modern conception of, 33–34
Prometheanism, 428, 432–33, 437, 442
Promethean option, 51
propaganda, 286–87
Property for People, Not for Profit (Duchrow and Hinkelammert), 297
public ethics, 319, 320
pure becoming, 439
Putnam, Hilary, 182

quandary ethics, 256

Radical Orthodoxy, 49, 51–52, 316–17, 328–31, 334–39, 404–5
Rasmussen, Larry, 434–35
rationalistic reductionism, 247
Rauschenbusch, Walter, 43
realism
internal, 182, 184
theological, 57
reality, goodness of, 192
reason
growth of, linked with development of culture and the arts, 41
practical and critical, 37
reasoning, female vs. male, 181
Rechtfertigung und Recht (Barth), 111, 270
Rechtsstaat, 384–85
reconciliation, 91
ethics of, 82, 87–88, 198–99, 225, 237, 268
making hope possible, 424
as objective reality, 233–34
reconstruction, 29
redemption, ethics of, 82, 87, 88–90
reductionism, 31, 80
reflexive ethics, 164, 169, 177–86
beginning with encounter with the human other, 187
variety of thought in, 178
reflexive late-modernity, 139–44
reflexive modernization, 141–42, 184–86
Reflexive Modernization (Beck), 141

reflexive moral theory, modern in approach to theological ethics, 189–90
reflexive social theory, avoiding religion, 158
reflexive thought, 133–34
reflexivity, 139–40, 185
relationalism, 326
relational self, 180, 186, 187
relativism, hard and soft, 168–69
religion
  avoidance of, by reflexive social theory, 158
  as element of social ethics, 159–60
  growing role of, in global society, 160
  progressive voice of, 158
reminder, language of, 115
Reno, R. R., 335
repression, 172
resistance, 172, 296–97
responsibility, ethic of, 92, 108, 347
responsible witness, 221, 228
resurrection, God's freedom in acting in, 65–66
revelation
  absolute nature of, 74
  language of, 57
  witnesses to, 74
Revenge of Gaia, The (Lovelock), 423
Ricoeur, Paul, 187
righteousness, acts of, 446
risk, 143–44, 344
  analysis of, specific languages needed for, 300
  ecological, 154–55
  defining and evaluating, power related to, 157
  economic, 155–56
  epistemological, 186
  ethic of, 46
  experience and awareness of, 140–41, 157
  external, 153
  global, 152, 372
  increasing power of, 269
  manufactured, 153–54

  as means for encountering principalities and powers, 153
  not accounting for human alienation from God, 302
  omnipresence of, 425–26
  political, 156
  as secular parable, 268
  technological, 155
  winners and losers, 155
risk society, 185–86, 299–300, 351
Risk Society (Beck), 154, 185
Ritschel, Albrecht, 43, 93
Robertson, Roland, 151
Romans (Barth), 66–67, 90
Rorty, Richard, 15, 166, 174–76, 351
Rosaldo, Renato, 143

Sagoff, Mark, 443
salvation, "classic" view of, 235
sanctification, denial of, 419
Santmire, Paul, 437–38
Schleiermacher, Friedrich, 37, 39–42, 70, 72, 93, 205, 315
Schweiker, William, 169, 192, 205–6, 320
scientific reasoning, fascination with, 31
secular, resentment against, 336–37
Secular Age, A (Taylor), 44, 190, 428–29
secular community
  freedom from the power of the church, 362
  serving as witness to church and God's kingdom, 362–63
secular discourse, as form of Christian heresy, 329
secularism, 44–45
  Christian witness after, 122–24
  church's response to, 105–6
  distinct from the secular, 334–37
  implosion of, 138–39
secular reductionism, 302, 353
secular theology, 331
self
  continual remaking of, 170–71
  growing outward, toward society, 178

Index 479

modern, rejecting external moral
  order, 177
suspicious nature of, in postmodernity, 187–88
self-denial, 240
self-reliance, heresy of, 273
simul iustus et peccator, 347–49
sin, 89
  against another's dignity and intrinsic
    worth, 120–21
  awareness of, 85
  disorder of, 277, 421
  as rejection of Christian responsible
    witness, 371
skeptics, regarding globalization, 144,
  145
slogans, 286
sloth
  building on pride, 395–96
  as enemy of social ethics, 396
  linked with mammon, 394, 395,
    397–400
  as sin of postmodernity, 396
Smith, Adam, 398
social action groups, 412
social analysis, 143, 148–49
social counter-movements, 412
social enculturation, 345
social ethics
  eschatological nature of, 364–67
  liberation of, 364–67
  move toward, from social theory, 159
  risk for, 352–54
  without the church, 353–54
social fragmentation, 351
Social Gospel, 34, 43
social imminence, 356
sociality, evaluation of, 166–67
"social market" economy, 404, 406, 407
social organizations, 62
social sciences
  reliance on, 294
  shift toward, in balance of power,
    24–25

social theory
  distinguishing, from theological
    ethics, 299
  privileging, over theology, 161
social witness
  engagement in, 97
  three themes of, 363–68
society
  double movement in, 407
  postmodern, manufacturing risk
    production, 154
sociology, 40
solidarity, 47
soteriology, shifting environmental
  ethics toward, 437
Sources of the Self (Taylor), 177
Soviet aggression, Barth criticized for
  not attacking, 114, 118
special ethics, 27–28, 227, 250
Speeches (Schleiermacher), 39
speed, desire for, as chthonic power,
  292–93
spirits of the earth, 280
spiritual powers, 268
sports, as chthonic power, 291
Stackhouse, Max, 160–61
Stassen, Glen, 390
state, as part of the order of redemption,
  115
status confessionis, 380–81
stewardship models, anthropocentric, 435
Stiltner, Brian, 390–91
Stout, Jeffrey, 26, 167, 335–36
Study of History, A (Toynbee), 130
synchronic justification, 183, 184
systematic ethics, 92

Tambach lecture (Barth), 63–64
Tanner, Kathryn, 129, 367, 406–7
Taylor, Charles, 3–4, 39, 44–45, 173,
  177, 188, 189, 190, 428–29
Taylor, Mark C., 47–48
technology
  as chthonic power, 290, 293, 422
  misuse of, 428

terrorism
  risks of, 156
  threat of, 377
  war on, 391
texts, deconstructive view of, 170
the-anthropology, 214
theological economics, 405, 406–7
theological ethics, 7
  aim of, 202–3
  as basic framework for Christian ethics, 27–28
  beginning with God's revelation, 13, 57, 78, 81, 200–201
  divergent viewpoints in, bases for, 200
  eschatological nature of, 90
  modern ethics distanced from, 38
  needing new theology, 37
  primary interpretive task of, 209
  recovery of, in the modern period, 28
  rooted to God's trinitarian action, 79–80, 81, 129
  separating, from Christian ethics, 28
  task and theory of, relying on God's action, 90
  tieing in with social theory, 299–300
  trinitarian nature of, 210
theological realism, 57, 168, 202, 317
  providing basis for moral realism, 205
  separating moral realism from, 321–22
Theologishe Existenz heute (Barth), 99
theology
  changed into secular thought, 26
  dissection of, 31–32
  as dogmatics, 7
  modern, errors of, 25, 36–37, 48, 314–15
  panentheistic, 436–37
  polarization of, into transcendentalist and immanentist camps, 51
  political nature of, 270
  premodern, 33, 48–49
  related to ethics, 24–28
  separate from ethics, 7–8
  shaped by epistemic foundationalism and progress, 32–33
  task of, 43–44, 65
theology of freedom, 415
Theology and Social Theory (Milbank), 329
Thiselton, Anthony, 176
Thomas Aquinas, 258n20, 259, 330, 437
Three Rival Traditions of Moral Enquiry (MacIntyre), 182–83
Tillich, Paul, 99n2
TINA ("there is no alternative"), 19, 425–26
totality, war on, 171
totus Christus, 337–40, 355–56, 357, 417
Toynbee, Arnold, 130
Tracy, David, 45–46, 152
tradition, impact of, on Christian ethics, 182–84
tradition-dependency, 166
transcendence
  secular rejection of, 44
  theologies of, 51
transformation, choosing, over denial, apathy, or nihilism, 304–5
transformationalists, 144–45
transportation, as chthonic power, 292
trinitarian command ethics, 93, 110
Trinity
  criticism of, 33
  doctrine of, marginalizing, 51
  Word of God speaking through, 53
Troeltsch, Ernst, 43, 93
truth
  modern search for, 32
  openness to, preparing for, 244–45
two kingdoms theory, 100–102

unapologetic principle, 324–25
uneasy conscience, 355
universe, anthropocentric picture of, 33
Use of Pleasure (Foucault), 171–72
Utilitarianism, 31–32
utopian ideology, decreased influence of, 423
utopianism, pessimism toward, 420
utopian social movements, 299

Index 481

Vanhoozer, Kevin, 132
Vattimo, Gianni, 135
violence
  ontology of, 189
  state-sponsored, 385–86
virtue, as an event, 90
virtue ethics, 189
visual imagery, power of, 422–23
vocation, 16
  denial of, 419
  embodied in Christian witness and discipleship, 233
  prayer's role in, 242
vocation, rooted in relationship between persons and Jesus Christ, 220, 230

war. *See also* just war
  technology's effect on, 290
  on terrorism, 391
Ward, Graham, 49, 57, 131, 138–39
Weber, Max, 141
Webster, John, 58–59, 76–77, 110, 136, 161, 201, 202, 221, 323, 356, 364
Welch, Sharon, 46–48
Wells, Samuel, 261–62, 311
Werpehowski, William, 386
Western democracies, Barth's criticism of, 109–10
Which Justice? Which Rationality? (MacIntyre), 182–83
White, Lynn, 434
Wholly Other, God as, 60
Will to Power, The (Nietzsche), 172–73
With the Grain of the Universe (Hauerwas), 257
witness, 16
  becoming and remaining, 105
  as entry point into narrative of Barth's theology and ethics, 2
  ethics of, 68, 219–21, 357
  of faith, 378–81
  as flight, 105
  as language of the church's theology, 7
  patterned after biblical witnesses, 103–4
  relation of, to correspondence of divine and human action, 222–23
  standing for human dignity and value, 12
  theology and ethics of, 2
witness of hope, 423–25
Word of God, 53
  as basis for theological ethics, 200–201
  Christian ethics' relation to, 91–92
  coming to us in its otherness, 318
  denying the true revelation of, 102
  establishing general knowledge of ethics, 205
  given primacy in gospel and law, 107
  giving secular words their true meaning, 303
  as the Good overcoming problems of human power and postmodern nihilism, 193
  linking church and culture, 72
  making theology and ethics possible but not infallible, 65
  opening the opportunity for humans to know the good in our conscience, 88
  responding to, 84–85, 90–91
  revealing moral truth, 204–5
  revealing a relational view of God, 14, 55
  as source for ethics of witness, 219–20
  standing in judgment of all ideology, 99
  standing in judgment of ethical speech, 88
  threefold form of, 97
  underlying theological ethics, 57, 78
Word of God and the Word of Man, The (Barth), 59, 66
work
  discussing, in context of the church, 409
  humane understanding of, 410
world
  Christians standing against, 359–60

world (*continued*)
    homogeneity of, with the church, 358–59
    moral responsibility for, 357–63
world civilization, 32
World Council of Churches, 297
world at risk, 304
World Social Forum, 147
worldviews, formation of, 419–20, 434
worship
    empowering Christians to give witness, 262
    as primary ethical activity of witness, 69

Yoder, John Howard, 116, 257, 260–61, 386, 387–88
Young, Iris, 181

Zeiss group, 411
Zwingli, Ulrich, 74

www.ingramcontent.com/pod-product-compliance
Lightning Source LLC
Chambersburg PA
CBHW021230300426
44111CB00007B/494